Cognitive Technologies

For further volumes:
http://www.springer.com/series/5216

Cognitive Technologies

Managing Editors: D. M. Gabbay, J. Siekmann

Dov M. Gabbay · Odinaldo T. Rodrigues ·
Alessandra Russo

Revision, Acceptability and Context

Theoretical and Algorithmic Aspects

 Springer

Prof. Dr. Dov M. Gabbay
King's College London
Dept. Computer Science
London WC2R 2LS
United Kingdom
dov.gabbay@kcl.ac.uk

Dr. Odinaldo T. Rodrigues
King's College London
Dept. Computer Science
London WC2R 2LS
United Kingdom
odinaldo.rodrigues@kcl.ac.uk

Dr. Alessandra Russo
Imperial College London
Dept. Computing
180 Queen's Gate
London SW7 2BZ
United Kingdom
a.russo@imperial.ac.uk

Managing Editors
Prof. Dr. Dov M. Gabbay
Augustus De Morgan Professor of Logic
King's College London
Dept. Computer Science
London WC2R 2LS
United Kingdom

Prof. Dr. Jörg Siekmann
Forschungsbereich Deduktions- und
Multiagentensysteme, DFKI
Stuhlsatzenweg 3, Geb. 43
66123 Saarbrücken, Germany

Cognitive Technologies ISSN 1611-2482
ISBN 978-3-642-26430-6   ISBN 978-3-642-14159-1 (eBook)
DOI 10.1007/978-3-642-14159-1
Springer Heidelberg Dordrecht London New York

ACM Computing Classification (1998): I.2, F.4, H.2

Cover design: KünkelLopka GmbH, Heidelberg

Printed on acid-free paper

Springer is part of Springer Science+Business Media (www.springer.com)

Preface

We are happy to present our new book to the community. Although this is a book on revision theory, it uses general methodologies which are applied in other areas of logic. We would like to highlight these methodologies in this preface.

1. the idea of *logic by translation*

   Given a new logical system L, whose properties we want to investigate, we translate L into a well-known logic, usually classical logic C, modal logic or intuitionistic logic. We study the properties we want in the target logic and then translate back into L. Our approach of *revision by translation* (see Chapter 7) is an instance of that methodology. We can also do *interpolation by translation*. What is most well known in the community is semantics by translation and decidability and undecidability by translation. This is a common way of obtaining semantics or decidability results for logical systems.

2. meta-level/object-level movement

   Given a logic L, there may be some manipulations of L done in the meta-level. Such notions can be provability or consequence, e.g., $A \vdash B$ or deletion from a database. We may wish to bring these notions to the object level. This can be a complicated task. We all know about the problem of bringing the proof predicate into the object level. In this book we bring in the operation of deletion. Another lesser known result is the bringing in to the object level of a non-monotonic consequence relation $\vdash\!\!\sim$, and what we get when we do it correctly is a conditional in the object language.

3. context

   The use of context can determine how we use our logic. The context is a label in Labelled Deductive Systems and it is a very rich label in situation semantics. In revision theory, it affects the algorithms we use to revise, and in many cases it might tell us not to revise at all and instead to try to obtain more data or simply live with the inconsistency in a careful way.

Acknowledgements We would like to acknowledge feedback and collaborations with Krysia Broda, Fátima Cristina Canazaro Dargam, Artur d'Avila Garcez, Anthony Hunter, Luís Lamb, Jérôme Lang, David Makinson, Sanjay Modgil, Gabriella Pigozzi, Karl Schlechta and John Woods.
    This manuscript was written using LATEX. We used Paul Taylor's *commutative diagrams package* for some of the diagrams. Jane Spurr kindly helped in the solution of many formatting issues.

London,   *D. M. Gabbay*
September 2009   *O. T. Rodrigues*
                                                                                                            A. Russo

Contents

Chapter 1
Background and Overview

1.1 Introductory Discussion

Classical logic and intuitionistic logic take the view that anything follows from an inconsistency. Effectively, when inconsistency occurs in a database, it explodes. The semantics reinforces the nature of inconsistency — there is no classical or intuitionistic model for inconsistent data. In some systems, e.g., Labelled Deductive Systems [4], we can keep track of inconsistency and label exactly how contradictions are derived. This labelling allows us to execute different options for inconsistency. We show how this can be used for revision in Chapters 4, 5 and 6.

In fact, from a proof-theoretical perspective, inconsistency is a powerful theorem-proving technique for classical and intuitionistic logics — for any formula, if we show an inconsistency holds in the database, then the formula follows. Indeed, for classical logic it is even stronger — if we assume the negation of a formula, and show inconsistency follows, then the formula follows.

It is well known that for practical reasoning such proof-theoretical power is not compatible with human reasoning. The following will illustrate the point:

> The Americans are very much worried about computer information and technology falling into the wrong hands. As part of their security measures, they have instructed the CIA and the FBI to keep detailed files on computer scientists. The CIA and FBI cooperate in amalgamating their databases.

> In the case of Professor Nobody, an unfortunate discrepancy had occurred. The FBI had his address as Stanford University, and the CIA had his address as King's College. When the two databases were joined together, the union contained contradictory information. The computer using classical logic inferred that Professor Nobody was none other than Public Enemy No. 1.

There are several points of principle here. Firstly, classical and intuitionistic logics do not deal with contradictions correctly. Although, it is logically correct to infer from the above contradiction that Professor Nobody is Public Enemy No. 1, it is clearly an incorrect step in terms of human reasoning. More importantly, Professor Nobody's address is completely irrelevant to the question of whether he is Public Enemy No. 1 or not. We need to *control* what constitutes an inconsistency.

D. M. Gabbay et al., *Revision, Acceptability and Context*, Cognitive Technologies,
DOI 10.1007/978-3-642-14159-1_1, © Springer-Verlag Berlin Heidelberg 2010

Examples of this nature prompted the logic community to study logics such as relevant logics and paraconsistent logics, which do indeed isolate inconsistency by various means. But these logics do not offer strategies for dealing with inconsistency. There remains the question of what to do when we have two contradictory items of information in the database. Do we choose one of them? How do we make the choice? Do we leave them in and find a way "around" them? Other logics, such as certain non-monotonic logics, resolve some forms of inconsistency, but do not allow the representation of certain forms of inconsistent data, or give no answer when they are present. And of course there is the now vast field of belief revision.

A second point is more practical. The CIA agent may investigate Professor Nobody and find the charge the computer made to be ridiculous. They may suspect that there is a contradiction in the database but they may not know how to locate it. Generally, the contradiction may involve several steps of reasoning and may not be as blatant as in the case of Professor Nobody. We may have several simple and innocent-looking data items and some very reasonable rules which together give the wrong answers, but no single item is to blame. How do we debug our system in this case? Systems have been proposed that address aspects of these questions, such as the ones in Sections 4.4, 6.3 and 6.4 and in Chapter 5, as well as other truth maintenance systems.

From this second point, we can see that inconsistency is actually a spur to act on the basis of an undesirable state of affairs. If we are making a decision and we find an inconsistency in our reasoning, we seek to identify further information to resolve it. The following is an example (based on an example from [11]).

> Professor Nobody had purchased a tropical fish from the pet shop, together with a guide on tropical fish. The book stated that if the fish is an etropline, it comes from sea water, and if the fish is cichlid, it comes from fresh water. When he bought the fish he was told by the shop owner that the fish was a cichlid, but unfortunately, when he got home he realised that the bag containing the fish stated it was an etropline. Immediately, he rang the shop owner who clarified the situation by informing him that etroplines are a form of cichlid. Relieved, he put the fish in sea water.

This example also shows how strategies can be used to resolve inconsistency. In this case, it became apparent to Professor Nobody that since etroplines are a form of cichlid, the contradiction arising from the two types of water must be resolved by specialisation — etroplines are one exception to the general rule for cichlid. This is an example of a strategy based on using the more specialised rules when making decisions.

So far in our discussion, we have seen the need to isolate or handle inconsistencies in data in some way, or alternatively use them as a spur to acquire more information. Yet, for some kinds of reasoning, it seems desirable to maintain the inconsistency:

> Professor Nobody was 55 years old and wanted an early retirement. He could in fact retire with a full pension if he were ill. So Professor Nobody presented his Head of Department, Professor Somebody, with a letter certifying he had a heart condition. He was thus able to retire. His wife, Mrs Faith Nobody, however, heard of this letter and Professor Nobody told her that he was actually quite healthy and the letter was a trick to get an early retirement.

Mrs Nobody was relieved. Unfortunately, Professor Somebody overheard the conversation, and very angrily confronted Professor Nobody. Professor Nobody was undisturbed; he explained to Professor Somebody that he had to tell his wife what he had told her, in order to stop her worrying. This may have been the end of the story except that, unfortunately, Mrs Nobody overheard the conversation with Professor Somebody and was worried again. Professor Nobody assured his wife that he was quite healthy and that he had to tell Professor Somebody what he had told him in order not to get his pension revoked.

There is a basic inconsistency here, but there is no need to "restore" consistency. In fact, to restore consistency in this case is to cause disaster. If Professor Somebody meets Mrs Nobody in a party, he will pretend that her husband is healthy in order not to worry her, or least avoid the subject. Mrs Nobody will have to pretend that her husband is not healthy, so as not to cause trouble with the pension. Professor Nobody himself will pretend one way or the other depending on the occasion. The database as described *does not care* about the inconsistency. Everybody has a different perspective on what 'the truth' is and since they all agree on the course of action, there is no urgency to resolve the inconsistency. There are many situations where inconsistency can be used to best advantage in arguments. Take the following example (see [5]):

Professor Nobody was attending an ESPRIT project meeting in Brussels until Saturday. He had booked a Saturday afternoon flight back to London and had arranged for his wife to pick him up at the airport. However, on the Friday afternoon, he had a row with his project partners and decided to fly back to London that evening.

Without telling his wife of his altered travel plans, he returned home in the early hours of Saturday morning intending to give a pleasant surprise. He tiptoed to his bedroom intending to quietly slip into bed, but to his surprise, there was *another man* in his bed with his wife. Both were fast asleep. He was shocked and angry. But being a logician, he exercised self-restraint and paused to think. Then he left the house quietly, and went back to the airport. He caught a morning flight back to Brussels, and then returned to London on the flight his wife was expecting to see him on.

We know that Professor Nobody is a logician, but his behaviour does seem to be inconsistent. Most would have expected that perhaps he should have hit the other man, or perhaps he should have made a row. Indeed, we have inconsistencies at the object level and at the meta-level. The object-level inconsistencies include all expectations about his wife, Faith, being in the bed on her own, etc., and his new knowledge about his wife being unfaithful.

At the meta-level, if we view Professor Nobody as a classical database management system, we should expect, by comparison with the database system, that he resolve the conflict by adopting some strategy, such as confronting the other man (i.e., database deletion to maintain consistency), or alternatively that he should update the database by, say, leaving his wife. However, his action seems to be contrary to the rules of a classical database management system — he seems to be refusing to accept the new input. By going back to Brussels, and following his original plans, he is acting as if the new input had never been provided. The refusal of input is therefore inconsistent with the meta-level rules of a classical database management system.

However, instead of making a decision of what action to take when he saw his wife in bed with another man, he chose to pretend that he did not even know her. By not taking action at the time, he could choose to raise the issue with his wife when it suited him best. Essentially, he chose to adopt a strategy of "keeping his options open". Such a strategy therefore requires a more sophisticated formalisation of the meta-level rules of the "database management systems" which are defined for capturing aspects of human reasoning. Thus the database management system, which is more human-like, can delay or refuse input.

Indeed, the above example shows how argumentation is based on more sophisticated meta-level theories for using inconsistencies. To highlight this we show the same use in another example; see [5]:

> Professor Nobody had a research assistant called Dr. Lazy. One Monday Professor Nobody asked why Dr. Lazy had not come to work the previous week. Dr. Lazy said that he had been ill in bed all of the last week. Professor Nobody expressed sympathy at Dr. Lazy's ill health, but unfortunately for Dr. Lazy, Professor Nobody knew otherwise. For Professor Nobody had seen Dr. Lazy sunbathing in the Park every day last week. However, he did not tell Dr. Lazy what he knew. Over the course of the summer, this scenario was repeated four times. Upon the fifth occurrence, Professor Nobody sacked Dr. Lazy.

As in the previous example, Professor Nobody knew information to which he did not admit. Indeed, he acted as if he knew the contrary. For the above example, he talked with Dr. Lazy, as if he believed him, but he later expressed his lack of belief in him. In order to support such reasoning, he uses essentially inconsistent information in a way that benefits his overall argumentation strategies. Similarly in the earlier example, he pretended that he did not know his wife had been unfaithful, and then presented the contrary information to his advantage.

When reasoning with these examples, we are happy with the inconsistencies because we read them as signals to take action or signals which trigger some rules and deactivate other rules. We do not perceive ourselves as living in some platonic world contemplating for eternity which of two contradictory items to disregard. Rather, we constantly face inconsistencies in the real world, most of which we deal with without any problems.

We believe a solution for better handling of contradictions can be found by looking closely at the ways humans deal with them. In developing new frameworks, the following points need to be considered:

- We do not share the view that contradictions in a database are necessarily a bad thing, and that they should be avoided at all costs. Contradictory information seems to be part of our lives and sometimes we even prefer ambiguities and irreconcilable views. We must therefore seek logical principles that allow for contradictions in the same way that we humans allow for them, and even make them useful.
- Humans seem to intuitively grasp that some information is more relevant that other information. The notion of priority and preference for certain beliefs should be developed and used, probably through labelling (see Chapters 4, 5 and 6).
- There seems to be a hierarchy of rules involved in rationalising inconsistency. Rules of the form "When contradictory information is received about A, then

do B" seems to be used constantly. These are meta-rules, i.e., rules about rules, that in some cases would be more conveniently expressed at the object level. Full exploitation of these rules requires our database language to be able to talk about itself. See Chapter 8.

- There is a need to be careful about throwing things out of the database. Always keep an open mind that although A is rejected now (because of new information contradicting it), it may become useful again. Perhaps some uncertainty values may be attached to all data items. The frameworks presented in Chapters 4, 5 and 6 allow for the record of the history of updates and for the representation of relative confidence levels on information. Conflicts can in general be solved without actually removing the offending parts from the database.

- Learning is a process that is directed by inconsistency. For example, if we have a hypothesis to explain a system, we check our hypothesis by making a series of observations of the system: if the hypothesis predicts the observations, then we have increased confidence in the hypothesis, but if the hypothesis is the negation of the observation, then we have inconsistency. This inconsistency should initiate further learning about the system.

- Argumentation proceeds via inconsistency. If two people, say Jack and Joe, undertake a dialogue, the inconsistencies between Jack's and Joe's views constitute foci for the dialogue. If the objective of the dialogue is for one of the participants, say Jack, to exert a particular view upon Joe, then Jack will use inconsistencies in Joe's argument as support for Jack's point of view.

- Despite everything we do, although we may give various heuristic rules dealing with contradictory items of equal reliability and relevance, there will be no way of deciding which of the two items is the correct one. In this case, we can only wait and be suspicious of any computation involving them.

- In many cases, 'inconsistency' is too specific a concept. Even in classical logic, there may be theories that are consistent, but yet yield undesirable results. Furthermore, some logics do not have such a notion, and mechanisms to describe what is 'acceptable' need to be developed. We discuss this in more detail next.

1.2 Focusing on 'Acceptability' Rather than 'Inconsistency'

Without loss of generality, assume that our object of concern is some database Δ_t at time t based on some non-monotonic proof rules that give rise to a consistent theory (of all formulae that Δ_t can rationally prove). When a new piece of information β_a arrives, we move to a new time $s = t_a$ and a new consistent theory arising from Δ_s. A revision process may deliver Δ_s to us, by possibly throwing some elements of Δ_t out and bringing in some consequences of the (inconsistent) theory $\Delta_t^{\perp} = \Delta_t \cup \{\beta_a\}$.

In practice, however, humans may prefer to work with the inconsistent $\Delta_t^{\perp}$, reserving judgement on how to choose Δ_s (not only by using the revision process but also) by taking further 'test' actions that give some additional information that helps them choose a Δ_s. Thus, some actions get taken *because* of an existing inconsistency and in order to help with the revision process. This means that not only do we have a proof process which stretches over time but we also have a revision process that takes time and involves 'test' actions.

We claim there is a fundamental difference between the way humans handle inconsistency and the way it is currently handled in formal logical systems. The difference is on two fronts:

- Formal logical systems based on classical logic do not tolerate inconsistency, while humans can live with it.
- Humans may not tolerate certain theories (finding them unacceptable) even though these may be logically consistent. The human notion is more that of *acceptability* rather than consistency.

To a human, resolving inconsistencies or regaining acceptability is *not necessarily* done by immediately 'restoring' consistency and/or acceptability but by supplying rules telling one how to act when the inconsistency or unacceptability arises. For adequate commonsense modelling there is an urgent need to revise the view that inconsistency is a 'bad' thing, and to instead view it as mostly a 'good' thing. Inconsistencies can be read as signals to take external action, such as 'ask the user', or invoke a 'truth maintenance compromise revision system', or as signals for internal actions that activate some rules and deactivate other rules. In our view, inconsistency can be viewed according to context as a vital trigger for actions and for learning, and as an important source of direction in argumentation.

Unfortunately the consensus of opinion in the logic community is that inconsistency is undesirable, and there is no proper awareness that data may be consistent but yet unacceptable (although people do study integrity constraints). Many believe that databases should be completely free of inconsistency, and try to eradicate inconsistency from them by any means possible. Others address inconsistency by isolating it, and perhaps resolving it locally. All seem to agree, however, that data of the form q and $\neg q$, for any proposition q, cannot exist together, and that the conflict must be resolved somehow.

This view is too simplistic for capturing commonsense reasoning, and furthermore, fails to use the benefits of inconsistency in modelling cognition. Inconsistency in information is the norm, and we should feel happy to be able to formalize it. There are cases where q and $\neg q$ can be perfectly acceptable together and hence need not be resolved. In other cases, q and $\neg q$ serve as a welcome trigger for various logical actions. We see inconsistency as useful in directing reasoning, and instigating the natural processes of learning. We need to classify the various aspects of inconsistency and present logical systems which capture various strategies for reasoning with inconsistency and trigger a revision process when adequate.

1.3 Overview of This Book

Belief Revision is the process of rearranging an agent's set of beliefs in face of new (contradictory) information. From the philosophical point of view, the new belief is in conflict with some of the old beliefs. From the *mechanical* point of view, the theory representing the union of the old and new beliefs is inconsistent. It is well known that inconsistent classical logic theories prove everything and therefore an agent's inconsistent belief state is rendered useless for rational inferences. Consistency is therefore at the very core of the AGM revision process and *inconsistency* is the state which triggers the process. However, belief states where the inference mechanism is not based on classical logic or that do not possess a notion of consistency as such might still be considered *unacceptable* from a system's point of view.

As we mentioned in the previous section, we advocate instead for the concept of *acceptability* as the agent's state that triggers the revision process. The acceptability notion can be tailored to suit the application and might involve the notion of consistency as before, but can also be applied in contexts where inconsistency is tolerated or where the notion is not defined.

The idea of monitoring a system's state to trigger some action is not new and appears in many nuances in computer science and philosophy. It appears for instance as the triggers of database systems; in planning systems where the fact that a state does not satisfy a given goal triggers the search for a sequence of actions that move the system into a state that does; in software engineering during the requirements specification process when certain properties are not verified; as *integrity constraints*; and so on. However, we think that a unified view of the problem of change can help shed some light on the modelling of cognitive processes.

In summary, our view here is that when the *object* of concern, be it a belief state, a database or a theory, is deemed "unacceptable", action/change is required. The *nature* of the action/change varies and can be done

- at the object level

  - embedded mechanism for auto-repair

- depending on the context

  - various nuances and considerations, e.g., single step, iterated, etc.
    - algorithmic
      - compromise
      - controlled revision
      - resource-based
    - axiomatic
      - AGM
      - some translation techniques based on axiomatic definitions

- at the meta-level

  - the cause of unacceptability is identified and some actions may be taken which could change the context in which the object was considered unacceptable

Figure 1.1 illustrates the ideas presented above.

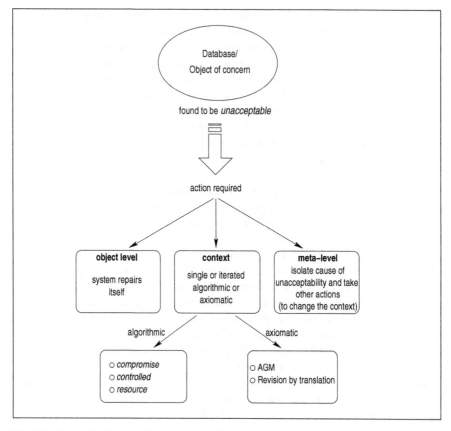

Fig. 1.1 Context in which revision is seen in this book

1.4 Notation Used in This Book

In this section, we assert some basic assumptions to be used throughout the book. $\mathbb{N}$ and $\mathbb{R}$ will denote the sets of natural and real numbers, respectively.

Definition 1.1. A *partial order* is a reflexive, transitive and antisymmetric relation on a set.

Definition 1.2. A *pre-order* is a reflexive and transitive relation on a set.

A binary relation $\leq$ on a set X is said to be *total* if it satisfies the following requirement: for every $x \in X$ and $y \in X$, either $x \leq y$ or $y \leq x$. As usual, $x < y$ abbreviates $x \leq y$ and $y \not\leq x$.

Definition 1.3. Let X be a set and $\leq$ be a (partial) pre-order on X and take an element x in X.

- x is *minimal* (mod $\leq$) if for no element y in X, $y < x$ holds.
- x is *minimum* if $x \leq y$ for all $y \in X$. If $\leq$ is also antisymmetric and such an x exists, it is unique and will be denoted by $\inf X$.
- x is *maximal* if for no element y in X, $x < y$ holds.
- x is *maximum* if $y \leq x$ for all $y \in X$. If $\leq$ is also antisymmetric and such an x exists, it is unique and will be denoted by $\sup X$.

Let us now define the language **L** of propositional logic:

Definition 1.4 (Language of propositional logic – L). The *language of propositional logic* is formed by the following:

- a finite set of *propositional variables* $\mathscr{P}^1$;
- the *propositional connectives* $\neg$, $\wedge$, $\vee$, $\rightarrow$ and $\leftrightarrow$;
- *well-formed formulae* of the language (wff), according to the following formation rules:

  - every propositional variable is a wff;
  - if φ and ψ are wff, then so are $\neg\varphi$, $\varphi \wedge \psi$, $\varphi \vee \psi$, $\varphi \rightarrow \psi$ and $\varphi \leftrightarrow \psi$;
  - nothing else is a wff.

In addition, we assume the following conventions: a *literal* is a propositional variable or the negation of a propositional variable. An *interpretation* is a function from $\mathscr{P}$ to $\{tt, ff\}$. That is, an interpretation maps each propositional variable to either *true* or *false*.

Definition 1.5. A *disjunct of propositional logic* is an expression of the form $l_1 \wedge l_2 \wedge \ldots \wedge l_n$, where each l_i is a literal.

In other words, a *disjunct* is a conjunction of literals.

We use $\mathscr{I}$ to denote the set of all interpretations of **L**. The satisfaction and derivability relations ($\Vdash$ and $\vdash$, respectively) for **L** are assumed to have their usual meanings (see [2], for instance). If an interpretation M satisfies a formula ψ, in symbols, $M \Vdash \psi$, we say that M is a *model of* ψ. $\mathrm{mod}\,(\psi)$ will denote the set of all models of ψ.

Suppose $\mathscr{P} = \{p, q, r\}$. We fix a linear ordering on the symbols of $\mathscr{P}$ and represent it as a list, say $[p, q, r]$. Moreover, we say that **L** is defined *over* $[p, q, r]$. This will allow us to refer to interpretations of **L** in the following way. We represent an interpretation I as a string of 0's and 1's, where the value 0 in a particular position in the string means that the propositional variable at the corresponding position in the list of symbols is assigned *ff* and the value 1 means that it is assigned *tt*. For example, if $I = 111$, then $I(p) = I(q) = I(r) = tt$. Similarly, if $I = 010$, then $I(p) = ff$, $I(q) = tt$ and $I(r) = ff$.

---

[1] The requirement of a finite set of symbols is made in [6] by Katsuno and Mendelzon, whose results we use.

The symbol $\equiv$ will be used in a rather ambiguous manner. In the context of propositional formulae, $\psi \equiv \varphi$ will denote $\psi \vdash \varphi$ and $\varphi \vdash \psi$. In the context of orderings and usually with a subscripted index, it will denote equivalence between elements of the set with respect to a given ordering. For instance, if the context is about ordering $\leq_\psi$, then $I \equiv_\psi I'$ will denote $I \leq_\psi I'$ and $I' \leq_\psi I$. In other circumstances where it may not be clear what $\equiv$ means, we will use the unabbreviated forms.

Notation 1 *Let $\leq$ be a pre-order on a set S, and M be a subset of S. The expression* $\min_\leq(M)$ *will denote the set of all elements in M which are minimal with respect to the ordering $\leq$.*

1.5 Basic Mathematical Notions

As mentioned in the previous sections, the interesting case in Belief Revision and Updates is when new information contradicts some of the information held by the agent, so that it has to decide what to keep from the previous theory in order to maintain consistency. The *informational economy* principle states that as much as possible of the informational content of the previous theory should be preserved. As a consequence, one expects to accommodate new information causing a *minimal change* to the previous belief state or representation of the world.

In order to determine what changes are minimal, some sort of measurement of the degree of change in information is necessary, and one possibility is to compare interpretations and/or classes of interpretations. In this section, we will present a brief introduction to some topology notions that will prove to be useful later.

Metric spaces were introduced as an abstraction of the properties of the Euclidean plane, but have been used in many other fields of science as a general framework to evaluate distance between elements of a given set.

Definition 1.6. A *metric space* is a tuple $\langle U, f \rangle$, where U is a set and $f : U \times U \longrightarrow \mathbb{R}$ is a function satisfying the following conditions:

(M1) $f(x,y) \geq 0$
(M2) $f(x,y) = 0$ iff $x = y$
(M3) $f(x,y) = f(y,x)$
(M4) $f(x,y) \leq f(x,z) + f(z,y)$

We say that f is a *metric* on U. Following [12], functions $g : U \times U \longrightarrow \mathbb{R}$ for which (M1)–(M4) is yet to be checked will be called *distance functions*. A metric f on U is *bounded* iff for some constant k, $f(x,y) \leq k$, for all $x,y \in U$.

Sometimes condition (M2) above is replaced by

(P)   If $x = y$, then $f(x,y) = 0$

where f is then called a *pseudometric*. Condition (M4) is known as the *triangle inequality property*.

In our case, we are interested in ways of evaluating distances between interpretations of the language. An introductory but very interesting overview of distances and metrics in epistemic contexts can be found in [10, Chapter 1]. Metric methods have also been used in logic programming as a means to study the semantics of logic programs [9, Chapter 6][3]. A more general account of the subject is given in [1, 7, 8].

Given a metric space $\langle U, f \rangle$, several interesting distance functions can be defined.

Definition 1.7. Let z be an element of U and X be a non-empty subset of U. The *point distance* $F(z,X)$ between z and X is defined as

$$F(z,X) = \inf \{f(z,x) \mid x \in X\}.$$

Let X and Y be two non-empty subsets of U. The *set distance* $F(X,Y)$ between X and Y is defined in an analogous way as

$$F(X,Y) = \inf \{f(x,y) \mid x \in X \text{ and } y \in Y\}.$$

Notice that the fact that a given pair $\langle U, f \rangle$ is a metric space does not imply that the pair $\langle 2^{\mathscr{U}} - \varnothing, F \rangle$ is also one, because it does not verify (M2) (take for instance any two distinct subsets of U with a non-empty intersection). The distance functions above are interesting because they provide means of evaluating the distance between a point and a set and between two sets, respectively. This will be useful to evaluate the distance between an interpretation and a class of models and between two classes of models.

Definition 1.8. An *r-neighbourhood of an element* $x \in U$ is an open ball $B_r(x)$.

Neighbourhoods define regions around a point x in a metric space whose elements are all under a maximum given distance (its radius). This notion will be used in the next chapter to define a centred system of spheres from a given distance function.

References

1. B. A. Davey and H. A. Priestley. *Introduction to Lattices and Order*. Cambridge Mathematical Textbooks. Cambridge University Press, Cambridge, 1990.
2. H. B. Enderton. *A Mathematical Introduction to Logic*. Academic Press, New York, 1972.
3. M. Fitting. Metric methods: three examples and a theorem. *The Journal of Logic Programming*, 21:113–127, 1994.
4. D. M. Gabbay. *Labelled Deductive Systems*. Oxford University Press, 1996.
5. D. M. Gabbay. *Elementary Logics: A Procedural Perspective*. Prentice-Hall, 1998.
6. H. Katsuno and A. O. Mendelzon. On the difference between updating a knowledge base and revising it. In P. Gärdenfors, editor, *Belief Revision*, pages 183–203. Cambridge University Press, 1992.
7. A. N. Kolmogorov and S. V. Fomin. *Elements of the Theory of Functions and Functional Analysis*, volume 1 — Metric and Normed Spaces. Graylock Press, 1957. Translated from the first (1954) Russian edition.

8. E. Kreyszig. *Introductory Functional Analysis with Applications*. John Wiley & Sons, 1989.

9. J. W. Lloyd. *Foundations of Logic Programming*. Springer–Verlag, second edition, 1987.

10. I. Niiniluoto. *Truthlikeness*. Kluwer Academic Publishers, 1989.

11. D. Nute. Defeasible reasoning and decision support systems. *Decision Support Systems*, 4:97–110, 1988.

12. Stephen Willard. *General Topology*. Addison-Wesley Publishing Company, 1970.

Chapter 2
Introducing Revision Theory

The investigation of how humans reach conclusions from given premises has long been the subject of research in the literature. It was the basis of the development of classical logic, for instance. The investigation of how humans change their minds in the face of new contradictory information is however somewhat more recent. Early accounts include the work of Ramsey [40, 41] in his insights into conditional statements, for instance, and subsequently the work on conditionals by Stalnaker [47] and by Lewis [32], among others. More recent work on the formalisation of *commonsense reasoning*, sometimes also called *non-monotonic reasoning* include [34, 5, 33, 42].

2.1 AGM Belief Revision

The now trademark term AGM is an acronym to the initials of the main proposers of this theory, namely, Carlos Alchourrón, Peter Gärdenfors and David Makinson. Carlos Alchourrón and David Makinson [3, 4] had done some work on theory change in the early 1980s, and, independently, Peter Gärdenfors had been working on belief change [21, 22] in the late 1970s and early 1980s. Together the three authors published the paper "On the Logic of Theory Change" in 1985 [2], which provided the basis for the theory of belief revision. Subsequently, Gärdenfors published a book entitled "Knowledge in Flux" [24], which is still one of the main references in this area.

Since then, the work on belief revision has flourished and followed several different approaches, although mainly based on two major paradigms: *coherentism* and *foundationalism*. Basically, the difference lies in the way the beliefs held by an agent are realised. According to the coherentist view, for a belief to be held by an agent, nothing is necessary apart from coherence of that belief with respect to the agent's inference system and the other beliefs she holds. All beliefs are equally supported as far as the agent is concerned. In the foundationalist view, however, a belief state can be seen as made up of two different components: the beliefs and their *justifications*.

D. M. Gabbay et al., *Revision, Acceptability and Context*, Cognitive Technologies,
DOI 10.1007/978-3-642-14159-1_2, © Springer-Verlag Berlin Heidelberg 2010

Beliefs are held only if they have a proper justification. Beliefs whose support is no longer accepted in the belief state are discarded. One simplified version of the foundationalist view records just a set of beliefs whose justification is not required, and the belief state is obtained by closing this set under the consequence relation. There is, hence, a clear distinction between *basic beliefs* (sometimes called *foundational* [28, page 31]) and *derived beliefs*. The set of basic beliefs is called the *belief base* and the revision process is usually called *base revision*. For a more detailed discussion, see the beginning of Chapter 4.

Other streams of the work on belief revision include the investigation of how to deal with priorities associated with the beliefs in the base and the study of properties of iterated revision. The former uses extra information available to help in the decision about what beliefs to retract when the new information is inconsistent with the current belief state. The reasoning about these priorities itself is quite complex, because in the general case, the agent has only partial information about the preferences for the beliefs in the base. This results in a number of possibilities requiring analysis over and above the problem of satisfiability. The investigation of iteration is, of course, of great importance to the area. More in-depth considerations started with [11, 15, 31] and other relevant work includes [16, 13].

We should make a remark here about the problems and complexity involved in the implementation of belief revision systems: the computational complexity of the problem of belief revision has been highlighted [25, page 98]. As we shall see, one of the desiderata for belief revision operations stipulates that the result of a revision is consistent provided that the revising information is consistent. Thus, even for the approaches that work with non-closed belief sets only, the revision operation is at least as hard as deciding the satisfiability of formulae. As a consequence of this, most of the formalisms for belief revision found in the literature which actually provide algorithms for computing the result of the process constrain themselves to a smaller fragment of first-order logic or, in most cases, to propositional logic [8, 10, 30]. The extra burden of reasoning about priorities only adds to the complexity of the problem.

Turning back to our brief introduction on the AGM theory of belief revision, we now proceed to present its main concepts and results.

From the reasoning point of view, it is useful to consider all consequences that follow from an agent's set of beliefs. Since the beliefs are represented in logic, this amounts to considering the closure of the set of beliefs under the logic's consequence relation. This closure is called the agent's *belief set*. As we said, some variations differentiate between a special corpus of beliefs (the *belief base*) and what can be inferred from it (the belief set). We will refer to these as *base revision* operations. Thus, if Cn is the consequence relation of a given logic and K is a belief set, then it is assumed that $K = \text{Cn}(K)$. For a belief A and a belief set K, $A \in K$, we say that A is *accepted* in K.

The basic framework of belief revision is governed by some desiderata of the operations on belief sets, called *the AGM postulates for belief revision*. The AGM theory lists three main types of belief change operations:

- *expansion*, when new information is simply included in the belief set, which is subsequently closed under the consequence relation. Expansions will be denoted using the symbol +.
- *contraction*, when the agent wants to retract some of the old beliefs. Notice that since the belief set is closed under the consequence relation, in order to retract a belief A, it may also be necessary to remove other beliefs that imply it. The contraction operator will be denoted by the symbol −.
- *revision*, which is the acceptance of a new belief in contradiction with the agent's current belief set. As opposed to a simple expansion, the idea is to guarantee consistency of the new belief set whenever possible.[1] This will require the removal of some of the old beliefs and hence contractions and revisions are closely interconnected. We shall look into novel techniques for contraction in Chapter 8.

Thus, the interesting cases are contractions and revisions. In fact, there are corresponding identities to translate between the two processes: the *Levi Identity* defines revisions in terms of contractions and the *Harper Identity* defines contractions in terms of revisions (see page 19). We will concentrate on the revision part here.

The general task of the revision process is to determine what is *rational* to support after the acceptance of a new belief which contradicts the existing belief set. As we mentioned before, some postulates describe in general terms desired properties of the operations. One of these properties is referred to as the *principle of informational economy* [24, page 49]:[2]

> ... when we change our beliefs, we want to retain as much as possible of our old beliefs – information is not in general gratuitous, and unnecessary losses of information are therefore to be avoided.

We now present the postulates for the revision operation as given in [24, pp. 54–56]. The following conventions are assumed: K is a set of formulae of the language representing the current belief set and A (B) is a formula representing the new belief triggering the belief change operation. We shall use the symbol ∘ to denote a "general" belief revision operation using subscripts as appropriate to denote a particular operation. In particular, the symbol $\circ_a$ will be used for a revision operation satisfying the AGM postulates. Thus, $K \circ_a A$ stands for the AGM revision of K by A. Note that since belief sets are closed under the consequence relation, there is only one inconsistent belief set. This special set is denoted by the symbol $K_\perp$ and will contain all wffs of the language.

AGM postulates for belief revision

($K^\circ 1$) $K \circ_a A$ is a belief set

This postulate requires that the result of the revision operation be also a belief set. One can perceive this as the requirement that the revised set also be closed under the consequence relation.

($K^\circ 2$) $A \in K \circ_a A$

---

[1] We shall see this is always possible unless the new belief itself is contradictory.

[2] This is one of the main references to the general theory of belief revision.

(K°2) is known as the *success postulate* and corresponds to the *insistent input policy* we will discuss later. It basically says that the revision process should be successful in the sense that the new belief is effectively accepted in the revised belief set.

(K°3) $K \circ_a A \subseteq \mathrm{Cn}(K \cup \{A\})$

(K°4)   If $\neg A \notin K$, then $\mathrm{Cn}(K \cup \{A\}) \subseteq K \circ_a A$

(K°5) $K \circ_a A = K_{\perp}$ only if A is contradictory

To understand what the above three postulates (K°3)–(K°5) say, we need to consider two cases. Let $K_1 = K \circ_a A$.

Case 1: $K \cup \{A\}$ is consistent in classical logic.

In this case, AGM says that we want $K_1 = K \circ_a A$ to be equal to the closure of $K \cup \{A\}$:

- postulate (K°3) says that $K \circ_a A \subseteq \mathrm{Cn}(K \cup \{A\})$.
- postulate (K°4) says that $\mathrm{Cn}(K \cup \{A\}) \subseteq K \circ_a A$.
- postulate (K°5) is not applicable, since $K \circ_a A$ is consistent.

Case 2: $K \cup \{A\}$ is inconsistent.

In this case, let us see what the postulates (K°3)–(K°5) say about K_1:

- postulate (K°3) says nothing about K_1. If $K \cup \{A\}$ is classically inconsistent, then any theory whatsoever is a subset of $\mathrm{Cn}(K \cup \{A\})$, because this theory is the set of all formulae, i.e., $K_{\perp}$.
- postulate (K°4) says nothing. Since $K \cup \{A\}$ is inconsistent in classical logic, we have $\neg A \in K$ (since K is a closed theory), so (K°4) is satisfied, because it is an implication whose antecedent is false.
- To understand what postulate (K°5) says in our case, we distinguish two subcases:

  (2.1) A is satisfiable.
  (2.2) A is contradictory.

  Postulate (K°5) says nothing about $K_1 = K \circ_a A$ in case (2.2) above; it however requires K_1 to be consistent whenever A is a satisfiable – case (2.1).

The above case analysis shows that the AGM postulates (K°3)–(K°5) have something to say only when $K \cup \{A\}$ is consistent, or if it is inconsistent then when A is satisfiable. The particular way of writing these postulates as quoted above makes use of technical properties of classical logic (the way inconsistent theories prove everything).

When we check the AGM postulates for logics other than classical, as we shall do in Chapter 7, we may have a different notion of consistency and so we are free to interpret what we want the revision to do in the cases where we think the new belief is in "conflict" with the current belief set. This needs to be done according to what is reasonable in the object (non-classical) logic. AGM for classical logic gives us no clue beyond (K°5) as to what to require when $(K \circ_a A) \cup \{B\}$ is inconsistent.

Summary of $(K°3)$–$(K°4)$

Postulates $(K°3)$ and $(K°4)$ effectively can be summarised by the following postulate:

$(K^{\circ}_{3,4})$ If A is consistent with K, then $K \circ_a A = Cn(K \cup \{A\})$

If K is finite, we can take it as a formula and $(K^{\circ}_{3,4})$ above corresponds to (R2) in Katsuno and Mendelzon's rephrasing of the AGM postulates for finite belief bases ([30, p. 187]; see also page 20): (R2) If $K \wedge A$ is satisfiable, then $K \circ_a A \leftrightarrow K \wedge A$.

$(K°6)$ If $A \equiv B$, then $K \circ_a A \equiv K \circ_a B$

$(K°6)$ specifies that the revision process should be independent of the syntactic form of the sentences involved. It is called the *principle of irrelevance of syntax* by many authors.

$(K°7)$ $K \circ_a (A \wedge B) \subseteq Cn((K \circ_a A) \cup \{B\})$
$(K°8)$ If $\neg B \notin K \circ_a A$, then $Cn(K \circ_a A \cup \{B\}) \subseteq K \circ_a (A \wedge B)$

To understand what postulates $(K°7)$–$(K°8)$ stipulate, we again have to make a case analysis. The postulates have to do with the relationship of inputting (A, B) as a sequence (first revising by A, then expanding by B), as compared with revising by $\{A, B\}$ at the same time (i.e, revising by $A \wedge B$). It is well known that AGM does not say enough about sequences of revisions and their properties.[3] The AGM postulates are the most general requirements.

We distinguish the following cases:

Case 1: A is consistent with K.
In this case, $K_1 = K \circ_a A$ is equal (by previous postulates) to $Cn(K \cup \{A\})$.

(1.1) B is consistent with K_1. In this case, the antecedent of $(K°8)$ holds and $(K°7)$ and $(K°8)$ together effectively say that $Cn((K \circ_a A) \cup \{B\}) = K \circ_a (A \wedge B)$.
We can use previous postulates to infer more of what is implicitly specified by the postulates, namely, that

$$(K \circ_a A) \circ_a B = Cn(K \circ_a A \cup \{B\}).$$

(1.2) B is inconsistent with $K_1 = K \circ_a A$, but B itself is satisfiable.
In this case, $Cn(K \circ_a A \cup \{B\})$ is $K_\perp$.

- $(K°7)$ holds because the right-hand side of the inclusion is the set of all wffs and any other set of formulae is included in this set.
- $(K°8)$ holds vacuously, since the antecedent of the implication is false.

(1.3) B is itself contradictory.

- $(K°7)$ requires that $K \circ_a (A \wedge B) \subset Cn((K \circ_a A) \cup \{B\})$ and
- $(K°8)$ holds vacuously.

---

[3] Iteration of the revision process is considered in Chapter 4.

The postulates say nothing new in this case, since the sets on either side of the inclusion in $(K°7)$ are equal to the set of all wffs of the language and $(K°8)$ is not applicable.

Case 2: A is not consistent with K, but A is itself satisfiable.

In this case, K_1 can be any consistent theory (by previous postulates), such that $A \in K_1$.

(2.1) B is consistent with K_1.
(2.2) B is inconsistent with K_1, but B itself is satisfiable.
(2.3) B is itself contradictory.

These three cases follow, respectively, the same reasoning of cases (1.1), (1.2) and (1.3) above.

Case 3: A is itself contradictory.

In this case, $K°_a A$ is the set of all wffs of the language. Whether or not B is consistent is irrelevant in the postulates in this case. $\text{Cn}(K°_a A \cup \{B\})$ is equal to $K_\perp$ and as for case (1.2) above

- $(K°7)$ holds because any set of wff is included in $K_\perp$.
- $(K°8)$ holds vacuously, since the antecedent of the implication is false.

Summary of $(K°7)$–$(K°8)$

Postulates $(K°7)$–$(K°8)$ do not tell us anything new (beyond what we can deduce from earlier postulates), except in the case where B is consistent with $K°_a A$ (case 1.1), when $(K°7)$ and $(K°8)$ together are equivalent to the postulate below:

$(K°_{7,8})$ $\text{Cn}((K°_a A) \cup \{B\}) = K°_a(A \wedge B)$, when B is consistent with $K°_a A$

$(K°7)$ and $(K°8)$ are the most interesting and controversial postulates. They capture in general terms the requirement that revisions be performed with a *minimal change* to the previous belief set. In order to understand them, recall that in a revision of K by A, one is interested in keeping as much as possible of the *informational content* of K and yet accepting A. It will prove useful to introduce some concepts at this stage. We say that a valuation (or interpretation) I is a *model* of a formula A if I satisfies A (i.e., $I(A)$ evaluates to *true*). This can be extended to sets of formulae in the usual way. We denote the set of all models of a formula A (or set of formulae Δ) by $\text{mod}(A)$ (or $\text{mod}(\Delta)$). Hence, in semantic terms $(K°7)$ and $(K°8)$ can be seen as a requirement on the models of the revised sets being somehow as similar as possible to models of K. The postulates do not constrain the operation well enough to give a precise meaning to the term "similar", and we agree that this is how it should be, since they represent only general *principles*.

$(K°7)$ says that if an interpretation I is among the models of A that are most similar to the models of K, and it happens that I is also among the models of B, then I should also be among the models of $A \wedge B$ that are most similar to models of K.

Similarly, to understand the intuitive meaning of $(K°8)$ consider the following situation: suppose that $(K °_a A) \wedge B$ is satisfiable. It follows that some models of A

that are closest to models of K are also models of B. These models are obviously in
$\text{mod}\,(A \wedge B)$, since by $(K°1)$, $\text{mod}\,(K \circ_a A) \subseteq \text{mod}\,(A)$. Now, every model in mod
$(A \wedge B)$ that is closest to models of K must also be a model of $(K \circ_a A) \wedge B$.

This situation is depicted in Figure 2.1, where interpretations are represented
around K according to their degree of similarity. The closer it is to $\text{mod}\,(K)$, the
more similar to K is an interpretation (the exact nature of this similarity notion is
irrelevant to the understanding of the postulates).[4]

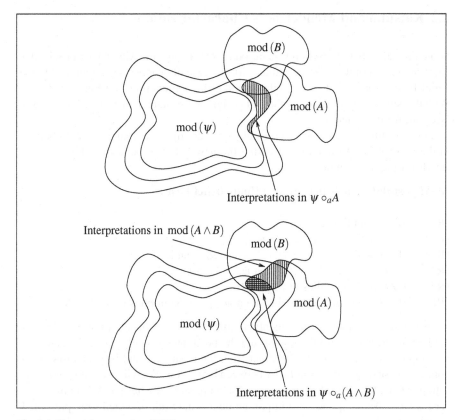

Fig. 2.1 Illustrating postulate $(K°8)$

As we mentioned before, revisions and contractions are intimately related. The
following two important equivalences are worth mentioning.

Levi Identity: $K \circ_a \varphi = (K - \neg\varphi)^+_\varphi$

Harper Identity: $K - \varphi = K \cap (K \circ_a \neg\varphi)$

---

[4] If we wish to extend the notion of AGM revision to logics which are not classical, we may have a
different notion of consistency (called *acceptability* in Section 2.12 below). In such a case we need
adopt only postulates $K°_1, K°_2, K°_{3,4}, K°_5$ and $K°_{7,8}$. This follows from our analysis of the postulates in
this section.

In [24], the following important result was shown.

Theorem 2.1. *If a contraction function verifies the AGM postulates for contraction and an expansion function verifies the AGM postulates for expansion and a revision function $\circ$ is defined in terms of both according to the Levi identity above, then $\circ$ verifies the AGM postulates for revision.*

2.2 Katsuno and Mendelzon's Characterisation

Some time after belief revision was introduced, Katsuno and Mendelzon provided a characterisation of the AGM postulates for the case of propositional logic and finite belief bases represented by a single formula (the conjunction of all basic beliefs). With this simplification in mind, the eight original postulates can be stated as follows (see [30] for more details).[5]

In the postulates below, ψ is a formula representing the conjunction of all beliefs in the base; A is a formula representing the new belief to be accepted and $\psi \circ_a A$ stands for the revision of ψ by A.

AGM postulates for belief revision (finite belief bases)

(R1) $\psi \circ_a A$ implies A
(R2)   If $\psi \wedge A$ is satisfiable, then $\psi \circ_a A \equiv \psi \wedge A$
(R3)   If A is satisfiable, then $\psi \circ_a A$ is also satisfiable
(R4)   If $\psi_1 \equiv \psi_2$ and $A_1 \equiv A_2$, then $\psi_1 \circ_a A_1 \equiv \psi_2 \circ_a A_2$
(R5) $(\psi \circ_a A) \wedge B$ implies $\psi \circ_a (A \wedge B)$
(R6)   If $(\psi \circ_a A) \wedge B$ is satisfiable, then $\psi \circ_a (A \wedge B)$ implies $(\psi \circ_a A) \wedge B$

In the same work [30], a semantical characterisation of all revision operators defined in terms of pre-orders satisfying the postulates was provided. This characterisation is useful as a tool to abstract from the postulates and instead allow us to concentrate on a notion of *similarity* between belief sets. We will use this characterisation in Chapter 3.1 to show that our revision operator satisfies the AGM postulates for revision. We recap the most important details here (all of which were presented initially in [30]).

The characterisation is semantical in nature. Therefore, it is based on a notion of similarity between valuations. For each formula ψ, it is assumed there is a pre-order $\leq_\psi$ satisfying minimum requirements. The intuitive meaning of $I \leq_\psi I'$ is that valuation I is at least as good at satisfying ψ as I' is.

Definition 2.1 (Faithful assignment for belief revision of formulae). A *faithful assignment for belief revision* is a function mapping each propositional formula ψ to a *pre-order* $\leq_\psi$ on $\mathscr{I}$, such that

---

[5] The simplification can be easily understood by following our analysis of the eight original postulates in the previous pages.

1. If $I, I' \in \text{mod}(\psi)$, then $I <_\psi I'$ does not hold.
2. If $I \in \text{mod}(\psi)$ and $I' \notin \text{mod}(\psi)$, then $I <_\psi I'$ holds.
3. If $\psi \leftrightarrow \varphi$, then $\leq_\psi = \leq_\varphi$.

That is, any two distinct models of a formula ψ are either incomparable or equivalent[6] with respect to $\leq_\psi$; any model of ψ is strictly better at satisfying ψ than any non-model of ψ, and orderings assigned to logically equivalent formulae are equivalent.

Notation 2 *Let $\leq$ be a pre-order on a set S, and M be a subset of S. The expression $\min_\leq(M)$ will denote the set of all elements in M which are minimal with respect to $\leq$.*

Theorem 2.2 ([30]). *A revision operator $\circ_a$ satisfies the AGM postulates for revision if and only if there exists a faithful assignment that maps each formula ψ to a total pre-order $\leq_\psi$, such that*

$$\text{mod}(\psi \circ_a A) = \min_{\leq_\psi}(\text{mod}(A)).$$

This characterisation is perhaps the best way to understand the general intuition behind the revision process. In the description above, A is the new belief to be accepted. Therefore, in order to verify (R1), the models of the revised belief set must be a subset of the models of A. Which ones? We expect these to be those which preserve as much as possible of the informational content of ψ. In order to do this, we need a means of comparing how well they fare with respect to ψ, which is what the ordering $\leq_\psi$ does. The minimum requirements $\leq_\psi$ must fulfil in order to verify the information preservation requirements expressed by (R1)–(R6) is specified by Definition 2.1. Therefore, the minimal elements in $\text{mod}(A)$ with respect to $\leq_\psi$ correspond exactly to the models of A which *best* preserve the informational content of ψ.

Now, if ψ is consistent with A, it is easy to see by Definition 2.1 that $\min_{\leq_\psi}(\text{mod}(A)) = \text{mod}(\psi) \cap \text{mod}(A)$. According to Theorem 2.2, these are the models of $\psi \circ_a A$, which is what (R2) requires. Also notice that the belief set is considered as a whole for comparison, since the ordering $\leq$ is indexed by ψ. This characterises the coherentist underpinnings of the basic AGM approach.

2.3 Counterfactual Statements and the Ramsey Test

There are references to the work on information change since the early 1930s [40] as well as in subsequent decades [7, 46, 48, 32]. There is in particular work on the so-called *counterfactual statements*. The best way to introduce the intuition behind a counterfactual statement is perhaps by presenting an example borrowed from Lewis' book on counterfactuals [32]:

---

[6] The pre-orders which result in operators verifying all the postulates are in fact total. Therefore, for this case, any two models of a formula have to be equivalent with respect to the ordering.

"If kangaroos had no tails, they would topple over."

Since the antecedent of the sentence is false, its evaluation as an implication in classical logic is trivially *true*. However, the *intended* meaning of such a sentence is more akin to something stated by Lewis in [32]:

"in any possible state of affairs in which kangaroos have no tails, and which resembles our actual state of affairs *as much as kangaroos having no tails permits it to*, kangaroos topple over"

The evaluation of conditional statements has always attracted interest in the literature [46, 1, 39, 36].

Speaking generically, a counterfactual is a sentence of the form

(CNT)   "If it were the case that φ, then it would also be the case that ψ"

We will borrow Lewis' notation here and represent the conditional in (CNT) by the expression $\varphi \square\!\!\rightarrow \psi$. It is natural to wonder how such sentences should be logically evaluated. The intended meaning described above suggests that one should accept the belief in φ, changing as little as possible one's current state of beliefs in order to maintain consistency, and then check whether ψ follows from the resulting belief state. This corresponds to the well-known *Ramsey Test*, inspired by one of Ramsey's philosophical papers [41, 40], and generalised to its present form by Stalnaker [47]. One could be easily misled to think that belief revision could be used as the belief change operation used in the Ramsey Test by taking $\varphi \square\!\!\rightarrow \psi$ as accepted in a belief set K whenever ψ is accepted in $K \circ \varphi$. In symbols,

(RT) $K \vdash \varphi \square\!\!\rightarrow \psi \overset{?}{\text{iff}} K \circ \varphi \vdash \psi$

However, it is well known that belief revision cannot be used to evaluate counterfactual statements as shown in [23] and [24, Section 7.4]. *Gärdenfors's impossibility theorem* showed us that whereas (RT) forces the belief change operation to be monotonic, belief revision is intrinsically non-monotonic. To see the first, assume (RT) is accepted, that $\circ$ is the belief change operation used to evaluate counterfactual statements and that for belief sets K_1 and K_2, it is the case that $K_1 \subseteq K_2$. We show that $K_1 \circ \varphi \subseteq K_2 \circ \varphi$. Take any ψ such that $\psi \in K_1 \circ \varphi$. By (RT), $\varphi \square\!\!\rightarrow \psi \in K_1$. Therefore, $\varphi \square\!\!\rightarrow \psi \in K_2$, and by (RT) again, $\psi \in K_2 \circ \varphi$. To see that belief revision is incompatible with monotonicity, recall the following postulates and consider Example 2.1.

($K^\circ 2$) $\varphi \in K \circ_a \varphi$

($K^\circ_{3,4}$)   If φ is consistent with K, then $K \circ_a \varphi = \text{Cn}(K \cup \{\varphi\})$

($K^\circ 5$) $K \circ_a \varphi = K_\perp$ only if φ is contradictory

Example 2.1. Consider three formulae φ, ψ and (non-contradictory) $\neg\varphi \vee \neg\psi$ and three belief sets K_1, K_2 and K_3, such that $K_1 = \text{Cn}(\{\varphi\})$, $K_2 = \text{Cn}(\{\psi\})$ and $K_3 = \text{Cn}(\{\varphi, \psi\})$. It can be easily seen that $K_1, K_2 \subseteq K_3$. By ($K^\circ_{3,4}$), $K_1 \circ_a (\neg\varphi \vee \neg\psi) = \text{Cn}(\{\varphi, \neg\varphi \vee \neg\psi\}) = \text{Cn}(\{\varphi, \neg\psi\})$; $K_2 \circ_a (\neg\varphi \vee \neg\psi) = \text{Cn}(\{\psi, \neg\varphi\})$; and since $\neg\varphi \vee \neg\psi$ is non-contradictory, $K_3 \circ_a (\neg\varphi \vee \neg\psi)$ is satisfiable. However,

i) $\varphi \in K_1 \circ_a(\neg \varphi \vee \neg \psi)$
ii) $\neg \varphi \in K_2 \circ_a(\neg \varphi \vee \neg \psi)$

and hence, either $K_1 \circ_a(\neg \varphi \vee \neg \psi) \not\subseteq K_3 \circ_a(\neg \varphi \vee \neg \psi)$ or $K_2 \circ_a(\neg \varphi \vee \neg \psi) \not\subseteq K_3 \circ_a(\neg \varphi \vee \neg \psi)$, since $\{\varphi, \neg \varphi\} \not\subseteq K_3 \circ_a(\neg \varphi \vee \neg \psi)$.

In semantical terms, the reason can be understood by recalling Lewis' formulation of satisfiability of counterfactuals via systems of spheres. Let us first introduce the notion of a *centred system of spheres* [32]:

Definition 2.2 (Centred system of spheres). Let $\mathscr{I}$ be a set of worlds. A centred system of spheres \$ is an assignment from $\mathscr{I}$ to a set of subsets of $\mathscr{I}$, $\$_I$, where for each $I \in \mathscr{I}$:

1. $\{I\} \in \$_I$ *(centring)*.
2. For all $S, T \in \$_I$, either $S \subseteq T$ or $T \subseteq S$ *(nesting)*.
3. $\$_I$ is closed under unions.
4. $\$_I$ is closed under non-empty intersections.

Systems of spheres are used to represent the degree of similarity between worlds. The smaller a sphere containing a world J in $\$_I$ is, the "closer" to world I world J is. The centring condition 1 can be interpreted as "there is no world more similar to world I than I itself". 1 can be replaced by

1'. For all $S \in \$_I, I \in S$.

This condition is often called *weak centring*.[7] If, in addition to conditions 1–4 above, we also have that for all I, $\bigcup \$_I = \mathscr{I}$, then we say that \$ is *universal*.

In terms of a system of spheres \$, a world I satisfies $\varphi \square\!\!\rightarrow \psi$, according to the following rules:

Definition 2.3 (Satisfiability of counterfactuals via a systems of spheres). Let $\mathscr{I}$ be a set of worlds, $I \in \mathscr{I}$ and \$ a centred system of spheres for $\mathscr{I}$:

$I \Vdash_\$ \varphi \square\!\!\rightarrow \psi$ iff

1. either $\forall S \in \$_I \ \mathrm{mod}\,(\varphi) \cap S = \varnothing$;
2. or $\exists S \in \$_I$ such that $\mathrm{mod}\,(\varphi) \cap S \neq \varnothing$, and $\forall I \in S, I \Vdash \varphi \rightarrow \psi$.

In case (1) above, we say that φ is not *entertainable* at I. That is, there is no sphere around I which intersects any worlds where φ is true. If \$ is universal, this happens only if $\mathrm{mod}\,(\varphi) = \varnothing$. The set of models of a counterfactual $\varphi \square\!\!\rightarrow \psi$ can be defined as $\mathrm{mod}\,(\varphi \square\!\!\rightarrow \psi) = \{I \in \mathscr{I} \,|\, \forall S \in \$_I \ (\mathrm{mod}\,(\varphi) \cap S \neq \varnothing$ implies $\forall J \in S \ J \Vdash \varphi \rightarrow \psi)\}$. As for case (2), since $\$_I$ is nested, it is sufficient to check whether $\varphi \rightarrow \psi$ is satisfied by every world in the innermost sphere S for which $S \cap \mathrm{mod}\,(\varphi)$ is non-empty. Intuitively, this intersection corresponds to the models of φ which are more similar (or closer) to I. Now, if we want to evaluate whether a counterfactual

---

[7] Update operations as semantically characterised by Katsuno and Mendelzon in [29] require strong centring (i.e., the innermost sphere in $\$_I$ contains just I itself).

$\varphi \square\!\rightarrow\! \psi$ is entailed by a belief set K, we have to check whether for each $I \in$ mod (K) condition (2) holds, i.e., whether the models of φ that are most similar to *each* of the models of K are also models of ψ.

It is not surprising that belief revision cannot be used to evaluate counterfactuals, since it fails to consider each model of K individually. The so-called *update operations* used to model the effects of execution of actions on the other hand do consider models of a theory individually [29]. Indeed, the relation between counterfactual statements and update operations was highlighted in [26, 43, 45].

It is also possible to abstract from centred systems of spheres and use instead a relation on the set of worlds to determine similarities with respect to a given world I. This is done via the definition of comparative similarity systems [32]:

Definition 2.4 (Comparative similarity system). A *comparative similarity system* is a function that assigns to each world I a tuple $\langle \leq_I, S_I \rangle$, where S_I is a set of worlds, representing the worlds that are accessible from I, and $\leq_I$ is a binary relation on worlds, representing the comparative similarity of worlds with respect to I, such that

1. $\leq_I$ is transitive
2. $\leq_I$ is strongly connected
3. $I \in S_I$
4. For any world $J, J \neq I$ implies $I <_I J$
5. $K \notin S_I$ implies K is $\leq_I$-maximal
6. For any $J, K, J \in S_I$ and $K \notin S_I$ implies $J <_I K$.

The intended meaning for $\leq_I$ is the following: if $J \leq_I K$, then world J is at least as similar to world I as world K is.

Lewis proved that there is a correspondence between the satisfiability of counterfactuals via systems of spheres and via comparative similarity systems. If we consider only *universal comparative similarity systems* (i.e., $S_I = \mathscr{I}$), the truth conditions for counterfactuals can be simplified as follows:

Definition 2.5 (Satisfiability of counterfactuals via comparative similarity systems). Let $\mathscr{I}$ be a set of worlds, $I \in \mathscr{I}$. Given a comparative similarity system as in Definition 2.4,

$$I \Vdash \varphi \square\!\rightarrow\! \psi \text{ iff}$$

1. either mod $(\varphi) = \varnothing$;
2. or $\exists M \in$ mod (φ) such that for any $N \in \mathscr{I} \ N \leq_I M$ implies $N \Vdash \varphi \rightarrow \psi$

These early results were very influential on the work of theory change carried out in the 1980s and later. We now turn to another very important semantical characterisation of belief change operations.

2.4 Grove's Systems of Spheres

In a very influential paper [27], Grove proposed a semantical characterisation of the AGM theory based on the so-called *systems of spheres*. The idea is similar to that of Lewis' own systems of spheres seen in the previous section (more details in [32]), except for a few differences. Firstly, the spheres in Lewis' systems contain *worlds*, whereas in Grove's formulation they contain *theories*. In addition, unlike in Lewis' systems where there is only one world in the centre, Grove's systems of spheres can contain a *collection* of theories in their centres.

Interestingly enough, Grove was one of the first to notice that Lewis' formulation was incompatible with belief revision [27]. The relationship between the types of systems of spheres proposed by Lewis and Grove on the one hand and formalisms for theory change on the other was explored in more detail in [29, 30, 43]. It turns out that strongly centred systems of spheres can be used in the modelling of the effects of the executions of actions, the so-called *update problem* [49, 30].

The starting point in Grove's formulation is the set $M_L^\top$ of all maximal consistent sets of the logic L. These in fact correspond to all (consistent) complete theories of L. Among these, some are of particular interest for a given (not necessarily complete) belief set K — the ones that *extend* it. The set of all such extensions is denoted by $|K|$ and formally defined as $\{m \in M_L^\top \mid K \subseteq m\}$. Notice that if K is $K_\perp$, then $|K|$ is simply $\varnothing$. Analogously, given a set S of maximal consistent sets of L, the set $t(S)$ is defined as $\bigcap\{S_i \in S\}$ or $K_\perp$ if $S = \varnothing$. It follows that $t(S)$ is also closed under logical consequence.[8]

In semantical terms, one can think of the set $\mathscr{I}$ of all valuations instead of $M_L^\top$. Analogously, $|K|$ would be directly associated with $\mathrm{mod}\,(K)$ and for a given set of valuations $S \subseteq \mathscr{I}$, $t(S) = \{\varphi \mid I \vDash \varphi \text{ for all } I \in S\}$. According to this view of the formulation, if K is $K_\perp$, then $|K| = \mathrm{mod}\,(K) = \varnothing$, and if $K = \mathrm{Cn}(\varnothing)$, then $|K| = \mathscr{I}$, as expected. However, viewing the revision process in terms of sets of formulae as done by Grove makes the relationship with the AGM postulates immediate, whereas viewing it semantically, i.e., in terms of valuations, gives us the interesting insight into the process summarised in Section 2.2.[9]

Definition 2.6 (Grove's systems of spheres). Let $\mathscr{S}$ be a collection of subsets of $M_L^\top$, and take $S \subseteq M_L^\top$. $\mathscr{S}$ is a called a *system of spheres centred on S* if it satisfies the following conditions:

(S1) $\mathscr{S}$ is totally ordered by $\subseteq$
(S2) S is the $\subseteq$-minimum of $\mathscr{S}$
(S3) $M_L^\top$ is the $\subseteq$-maximum of $\mathscr{S}$

---

[8] It is possible to construct a lattice by ordering theories of a logic L under set inclusion. In this case, $\mathrm{Cn}(\varnothing)$ will be the minimum and $K_\perp$ will be the maximum. The only inconsistent theory in the lattice is $K_\perp$ itself, with the elements of $M_L^\top$ sitting immediately below it. The only way to extend an element of $M_L^\top$ and retain closure under logical consequence is to jump to $K_\perp$.

[9] The semantical view is essentially the basis for the work by Katsuno and Mendelzon seen in Section 2.2 [29, 30].

(S4) For any wff φ, if $M_L^\top \cap |\varphi| \neq \varnothing$, then there is a smallest sphere in $\mathscr{S}$ intersecting $|\varphi|$.

Provided a formula φ is satisfiable, there is always a maximal consistent extension of $\mathrm{Cn}(\varphi)$. Since by (S3) the outermost layer in every system of spheres is $M_L^\top$ itself (i.e., *all* maximal theories of L), some maximal consistent extension of $\mathrm{Cn}(\varphi)$ will intersect $\mathscr{S}$ at some sphere. Condition (S4) only ensures that there are not infinitely many smaller spheres in $\mathscr{S}$ whose intersection with $|\varphi|$ is non-empty. We use S_φ to denote the *smallest* sphere around S in $\mathscr{S}$ whose intersection with $|\varphi|$ is non-empty if it exists, and if it does not, we define $S_\varphi = M_L^\top$. $f_S(\varphi)$ is used to denote the intersection itself, i.e., $|\varphi| \cap S_\varphi$. Notice that if φ is contradictory $f_S(\varphi) = \varnothing$. Intuitively, the function f_S selects the φ-worlds which are closest to S. This can be used to define a revision operation as follows [27]:

Definition 2.7 (Revision in terms of systems of spheres). Let $\mathscr{S}$ be a system of spheres centred on $|K|$.

$$K \circ_{\mathscr{S}} \varphi = t(f_K(\varphi))$$

Proposition 2.1. *If K and φ are consistent with each other, then $K \circ_{\mathscr{S}} \varphi = \mathrm{Cn}(K \cup \{\varphi\})$.*

Proof. Notice that if K and φ are consistent with each other, then $|K| \cap |\varphi|$ is non-empty, and hence $K_\varphi = |K|$. Therefore, $f_K(\varphi) = \{m \in M_L^\top \mid K \subseteq m \text{ and } \mathrm{Cn}(\varphi) \subseteq m\}$. It follows that $t(f_K(\varphi)) = \mathrm{Cn}(K \cup \{\varphi\})$. $\mathrm{Cn}(K \cup \{\varphi\}) \subseteq t(f_K(\varphi))$ comes directly from the definition of $f_K(\varphi)$. To see that $t(f_K(\varphi)) \subseteq \mathrm{Cn}(K \cup \{\varphi\})$, suppose $\gamma \in t(f_K(\varphi))$, but $\gamma \notin \mathrm{Cn}(K \cup \{\varphi\})$. γ is neither contradictory itself (for it belongs to $t(f_K(\varphi))$, by assumption), nor is it a tautology (for it does not belong to $\mathrm{Cn}(K \cup \{\varphi\})$, ditto); therefore it is possible to have two extensions m_1 and m_2 of $\mathrm{Cn}(K \cup \{\varphi\})$ in $f_K(\varphi)$ such that $\gamma \in m_1$ and $\neg\gamma \in m_2$. Since m_1 and m_2 are both consistent, $\gamma \notin m_2$, but this is a contradiction since $\gamma \in t(f_K(\varphi))$.*

The proof above establishes that $\circ_{\mathscr{S}}$ verifies $(K_{3,4}^\circ)$. In fact, $\circ_{\mathscr{S}}$ verifies all of the AGM postulates for revision. Grove has proved the following important results:

Theorem 2.3. *For any system of spheres $\mathscr{S}$ with centre on $|K|$, if $K \circ_{\mathscr{S}} \varphi$ is given as in Definition 2.7, then $\circ_{\mathscr{S}}$ verifies the AGM postulates for belief revision.*

Theorem 2.4. *If $\circ$ verifies the AGM postulates for belief revision, then for any belief set K, there is a system of spheres $\mathscr{S}$ with centre on $|K|$ such that $K \circ \varphi = t(f_s(\varphi))$.*

A depiction of a system of spheres around $|K|$ is given in Figure 2.2.

An alternative representation theorem is given in terms of total pre-orders $\leq_G$ on the set of wff of the language $\mathscr{L}$, satisfying the following conditions (we call such pre-orders *Grove relations*):

$(\leq_G 1)$ $\leq_G$ is total
$(\leq_G 2)$ $\leq_G$ is transitive

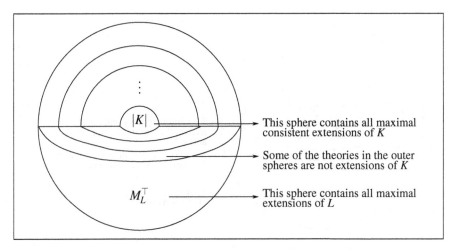

This sphere contains all maximal consistent extensions of K

Some of the theories in the outer spheres are not extensions of K

This sphere contains all maximal extensions of L

Fig. 2.2 A system of spheres around $|K|$

($\leq_G$ 3) If $\varphi \rightarrow (\psi \vee \gamma)$, then either $\psi \leq_G \varphi$ or $\gamma \leq_G \varphi$.
($\leq_G$ 4) φ is $\leq_G$ minimal if and only if $\neg\varphi \notin T$.
($\leq_G$ 5) φ is $\leq_G$ maximal if and only if $\neg\varphi$ is a tautology.

It is possible to define a revision operation in terms of a relation $\leq_G$ as follows (as usual, $<_G$ denotes the strict counterpart of $\leq_G$):

Definition 2.8 (Revision obtained from $\leq_G$).

$$T \circ_G \varphi = \{\psi \mid (\varphi \wedge \psi) <_G (\varphi \wedge \neg\psi)\}.$$

Grove has shown the following correspondences:

Theorem 2.5. *Let $\leq_G$ be any pre-order satisfying ($\leq_G$ 1)–($\leq_G$ 5). If a revision operation $\circ_G$ is defined according to Definition 2.8, then $\circ_G$ also satisfies* (K°1)–(K°8).

Theorem 2.6. *Any revision operator $\circ$ satisfying the AGM postulates can be defined in terms of some relation $\leq_G$ according to Definition 2.8.*

It is not surprising that $\leq_G$ can also be defined in terms of a system of spheres $\mathscr{S}$:

Definition 2.9 (Correspondence between a Grove relation and a system of spheres). Let $\mathscr{S}$ be a system of spheres with centre in $|S|$.

$\varphi \leq_G \psi$ if and only if $S_\varphi \subseteq S_\psi$.

Proposition 2.2. *If $\leq_G$ is given according to Definition 2.9, then it will also verify* ($\leq_G$ 1)–($\leq_G$ 5).

There is a relationship between Grove relations and the notion of *epistemic entrenchment*. This will be discussed in Section 2.5 below.

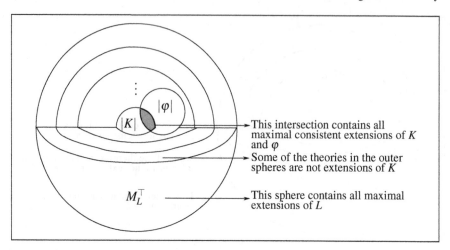

Fig. 2.3 A system of spheres when K and ϕ are consistent

2.5 Epistemic Entrenchment

One of the main criticisms against the AGM postulates is that although they define general properties of rational changes of belief, they do not actually provide
an explicit construction of the belief change operations themselves. The notion of
epistemic entrenchment helps to address this issue. Epistemic entrenchment can be
used to guide contraction operations. Since expansions can be trivially constructed,
and revisions can be defined from contractions and expansions via the Levi identity,
if one defines a contraction operation, then the three basic types of belief change
become available. Of course, it is also possible to start with revision as the basic
operation and obtain contraction via the Harper identity (see page 19 for the identities).

The idea behind epistemic entrenchment is to retain the more *informative* propositions during a contraction operation. This involves a comparison of the relative
strengths of propositions and is modelled by a so-called *epistemic entrenchment relation* $\leq_K$ for a given belief set K. Properties of such relations are given as postulates
presented below. In the following, φ, ψ and γ are formulae and $\varphi \leq_K \psi$ denotes "ψ
is at least as (epistemologically) entrenched as φ".

(EE1) $\varphi \leq_K \psi$ and $\psi \leq_K \gamma$ imply $\varphi \leq_K \gamma$
(EE2)   If $\varphi \vdash \psi$, then $\varphi \leq_K \psi$
(EE3)   Either $\varphi \leq_K \varphi \wedge \psi$ or $\psi \leq_K \varphi \wedge \psi$
(EE4)   If $K \neq K_\perp$, then $\varphi \notin K$ iff $\varphi \leq_K \psi$ for all ψ
(EE5)   If for all ψ, $\psi \leq_K \varphi$, then $\vdash \varphi$.

(EE1) simply stipulates that epistemic entrenchment relations should be transitive. (EE2) supports the principle of minimal change. Since belief sets are closed
under consequence relation, in the choice between giving up φ or ψ (given that

$\varphi \vdash \psi$), it makes more sense to give up φ first, since giving up ψ would ultimately require φ to be given up as well. Note that (EE2) implies reflexivity of $\leq_K$. (EE3) postulates that the loss of information incurred in giving up $\varphi \wedge \psi$ is equivalent to that of giving up either φ or ψ. This follows from the fact that (EE2) already constrains $\leq_K$ so that $\varphi \wedge \psi \leq_K \varphi$ and $\varphi \wedge \psi \leq_K \psi$. (EE1)–(EE3) jointly imply that $\leq_K$ is *total*. (EE4) expresses a minimality condition for $\leq_K$. It follows from (EE4) that all beliefs that are not in K are equivalent modulo $\leq_K$, since the ordering is total. Also notice that the proviso is necessary, because if $K = K_\perp$, then $\varphi \in K$ for all φ, in which case there would be an infinite descending chain of beliefs $\varphi >_K \psi_1 >_K \psi_2 > \ldots$ in K. (EE5) says that only the tautologies are maximal in $\leq_K$. The converse follows trivially from (EE2) and hence all tautologies are equivalent modulo $\leq_K$.

What is needed now is a way to define a revision function in terms of an epistemic entrenchment relation. This is done indirectly via a contraction function and the Levi identity as explained before.

Definition 2.10 (Contractions and epistemic entrenchment relations).

$\psi \leq_K \varphi$ iff $\psi \notin K-(\varphi \wedge \psi)$

In particular,

Theorem 2.7 (Correspondence between epistemic entrenchment relations and belief contraction). *Let $\leq_K$ and $-$ be defined according to Definition 2.10. It follows that $\leq_K$ satisfies (EE1)–(EE5) iff $-$ satisfies the AGM postulates for contraction.*[10]

These results are similar to the correspondences arising from revision operations defined in terms of Grove relations. This is not surprising. In fact, it is possible to define epistemic entrenchment relations and Grove relations in terms of each other.

Definition 2.11. For all formulae φ and ψ, $\varphi \leq_K \psi$ iff $\neg\varphi \leq_G \neg\psi$.

The properties of $\leq_G$ and $\leq_K$ are interconnected as given in the following theorem [24, page 96].[11]

Theorem 2.8. *A total pre-order $\leq_G$ satisfies ($\leq_G$ 1)–($\leq_G$ 5) iff $\leq_K$ as defined above satisfies (EE1)–(EE5).*

A number of revision formalisms using epistemic entrenchment were proposed. The reader is referred to [44, 50, 35] for more details.

---

[10] The postulates for contraction can be found in [24].

[11] This result appears as Lemmas 4.26 and 4.27 in that reference.

2.6 Discussion

We are now in a position to summarise the relationships between the several representations seen so far in this chapter, which are depicted in Figure 2.4. Roughly speaking, an arrow $\longrightarrow$ indicates that the object at its source has the properties stated by the object at its target; an arrow $\cdots$ indicates that there exists an object of the type of its target for each object of the type of its source; finally, a solid arrow indicates that the object at its target can be defined in terms of the object at its source. Thus, a relation verifying properties $(\leq_G 1)–(\leq_G 5)$ can be defined from a system of spheres $\mathscr{S}$ and vice versa via Definition 2.9. Theorem 2.8 establishes the correspondence between Grove relations and epistemic entrenchment relations defined according to Definition 2.11. An epistemic entrenchment relation $\leq_E E$ can be used to define a contraction function $-$. According to Theorem 2.7, $-$ will satisfy the AGM postulates for contraction. Via the Levi identity, it is possible to define a revision function $\circ_a$, which according to Theorem 2.1 will satisfy AGM postulates for revision. Theorem 2.2 establishes the correspondence between faithful assignments $\leq_{KM}$ (for a belief base KM), revision operators $\circ_{KM}$ defined in terms of these and the AGM postulates. The dashed arrow is to be interpreted as "given a revision operator $\circ_{KM}$ satisfying the AGM postulates for revision, there exists an associated faithful assignment $\leq_{KM}$." The rest of the diagram can be read in an analogous form.

2.7 Action Updates

It is worth mentioning briefly an area related to the problem of belief revision that has to do with the problem of updating a theory describing the state of the world following the execution of an action.

To avoid ambiguity with the term *update* used elsewhere in this book to refer to an input to a theory, belief set or database, we will reserve the term *action update* to describe the kind of information change used in the formalisation of the effects of the execution of actions.

The problem of an action update is then how to move from a description of the world defined in some formal language towards an updated description that reflects how the world changes when a given action is executed.

The similarity with belief revision is that if we assume that the *post-conditions* of an action α are represented by a formula A (i.e., properties observed in the real world after the execution of α), then one expects to "accept" A and yet keep as much as possible of the information about the state of the world before α was executed.

Since the description of the world is in general incomplete, it actually corresponds to a set of *possible states of the world*. Now, whereas in belief revision the belief set is considered as a whole when considering what formulae to keep or give up, in the case of action updates we need to give equal consideration to each of the possible states of the world. Therefore, we cannot consider the set of models of the belief set as a whole entity.

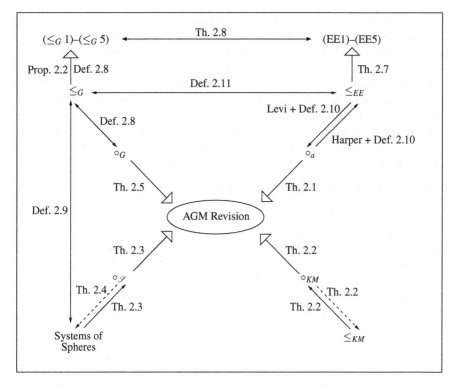

Fig. 2.4 Relationships between different revision formalisms

Another way to understand the intrinsic differences is to think of action updates and belief revision in the following way: in belief revision incompleteness of the theory corresponds to gaps in the knowledge about the world that can be filled when new information becomes available (since the world is considered *static*). In this sense, new information reduces the number of possibilities left open. The more one learns, the less the number of possible states of the world. In an action update, incompleteness of the theory means that the "true" state of the world is unknown and the agent must reason within a certain range of possibilities. When an action is executed, the world changes, and then each of these possibilities needs to be updated individually.

As for the case of belief revision, some postulates were proposed to capture general intuitions about the process. We will refer to these as the *postulates for action updates* and take them as general guidelines in the definition of our operators for actions in the next chapter. There are several reasons for this: firstly, because the postulates are intuitively simple and capture general principles about rational formalisation of the effects of actions. Moreover, they are flexible enough to support different interpretations of the meaning of actions. We will return to this point later in Section 3.1, and in Section 3.9.4 when talking about *ambiguous actions*.

The postulates for action updates were initially proposed by Katsuno and Mendelzon in [29], but in that work they were seen rather as alternative postulates for belief revision. In fact, they were supposed to model what was called *pointwise revisions*. Later on, the authors established the formal distinction between these two paradigms to *theory change* in [30], where a semantical characterisation of all operators defined in terms of partial orders (or pre-orders) satisfying the postulates for action updates was also given.

We recap the postulates below, where ψ is a formula of the language (the current representation of the world), A is a formula representing the post-conditions of the action to be executed and $\psi \diamond A$ stands for the action update of ψ by A.

Katsuno and Mendelzon's postulates for action updates

(U1) $\psi \diamond A$ implies A
(U2)   If ψ implies A, then $\psi \diamond A \equiv \psi$
(U3)   If both ψ and A are satisfiable, then $\psi \diamond A$ is also satisfiable
(U4)   If $\psi_1 \equiv \psi_2$ and $A_1 \equiv A_2$, then $\psi_1 \diamond A_1 \equiv \psi_2 \diamond A_2$
(U5) $(\psi \diamond A) \wedge B$ implies $\psi \diamond (A \wedge B)$
(U6)   If $\psi \diamond A$ implies B and $\psi \diamond B$ implies A, then $\psi \diamond A \equiv \psi \diamond B$
(U7)   If ψ is complete, then $(\psi \diamond A) \wedge (\psi \diamond B)$ implies $\psi \diamond (A \vee B)$
(U8) $(\psi_1 \vee \psi_2) \diamond A \equiv (\psi_1 \diamond A) \vee (\psi_2 \diamond A)$

Postulate (U1) is similar to (R1); that is, as for belief revision, the *principle of primacy of the update* is also required. (U2) and (U3) are weaker than (R2) and (R3). (U2) was called *laziness* in [6] (see Section 3.9). Notice that in (R3), the consistency of the revised theory depends solely on the consistency of the input sentence, whereas in (U3) it depends on both the input sentence and the previous belief state. This ultimately implies that consistency cannot be restored via an action update. (U4) and (U5) are equivalent to (R4) and (R5), respectively. (U6) says that if B is verified after the execution of an action with post-condition A in every possible world for ψ, and A is verified after the execution of an action with post-condition B in every possible world for ψ, then the results of both action updates are equivalent. The meaning of "complete" in (U7) is that ψ is associated with a unique possible world. (U8) is known as the *disjunction rule*. It ensures that all possible worlds are given equal consideration in the process.

As for belief revision, minimum requirements on the relation used to evaluate similarity must be imposed. The difference is that this time the relation is defined for each possible world, that is, for each valuation of the language. Thus, if $\leq_I$ expresses similarity with respect to world I, then $J \leq_I K$ means that world J is at least as similar to I as world K is. Again, $J <_I K$ is an abbreviation for $J \leq_I K$ and $K \not\leq_I J$. The following characterisation was presented in [30].

Definition 2.12 (Faithful assignment for action updates). A *faithful assignment for action updates* is a function mapping each valuation I to a partial pre-order $\leq_I$, such that

(2.1) For any $I, I' \in \mathscr{I}$, if $I \neq I'$, then $I <_I I'$.

We can see that the only strong requirement to be imposed on an ordering $\leq_I$ is that it be *centred* on I. In other words, I must be the minimum element in $\mathscr{I}$ with respect to $\leq_I$.

Theorem 2.9. *An action update operator* $\diamond$ *satisfies the postulates for action updates if there exists a faithful assignment that maps each valuation I to a partial pre-order* $\leq_I$, *such that*

$$\mathrm{mod}\,(\psi \diamond A) = \bigcup_{I \in \,\mathrm{mod}\,(\psi)} \mathrm{min}_{\leq_I}(\mathrm{mod}\,(A)).$$

We can now draw comments similar to those we made earlier for belief revision and emphasise the difference between the two processes. Since A is the formula to be accepted after the action update is performed, the models of the updated description must be a subset of the models of A (as in belief revision). But which ones? These must be those which preserve as much as possible of the informational content of *each one* of the models of ψ, since each model of ψ is the *possible 'real' world*. It is therefore not surprising that action updates were initially called *pointwise revisions* in [29]. Thus, this time the ordering $\leq$ must be indexed by valuations of the language, or *worlds*. For a given valuation I, $\leq_I$ must fulfil the requirements specified in Definition 2.12 in order to verify the information preservation requirements expressed by (U1)–(U8). Again, the minimal elements in $\mathrm{mod}\,(A)$ with respect to $\leq_I$ are the models of A which preserve most the informational content of I. If ψ implies A, then $\mathrm{mod}\,(\psi) \subseteq \mathrm{mod}\,(A)$. If $I \in \mathrm{mod}\,(A)$, it is easy to see that $\mathrm{min}_{\leq_I}(\mathrm{mod}\,(A)) = \{I\}$. Hence, $\cup_{I \in \,\mathrm{mod}\,(\psi)} \mathrm{min}_{\leq_I}(\mathrm{mod}\,(A)) = \mathrm{mod}\,(\psi)$, which is exactly (U2).

2.8 Generalising the Concept of Revision

So far, we have only discussed revision mechanisms that are directly related to the AGM formulation introduced in Section 2.1. In the next few sections, we will generalise the concept and introduce some extensions and alternatives to the original concept.

In order to illustrate some options for revision, we need to start by setting the scene for discussion. Consider an initial set of assumptions, say $\{X\}$. Using non-monotonic reasoning, assume we enlarge this set to the set $\Delta = \{X, M_j\}$, M_j being deduced from X using elimination rules. Suppose we now receive a belief or input A_1. We do not want to assume at this stage any properties about the nature and structure of Δ, except perhaps that it obeys certain logical principles, and therefore we will simply refer to it as a *database*.

The following can happen:

Case 1: A_1 is consistent with X but not with Δ.

In this case it is clear that the revised database $\Delta \circ A_1$ should be $\{X, A_1\}$ and possibly some of the M_j. Since M_j are only non-monotonic consequences of X, they need not be all retained. So we use some consistency maintenance process.

Case 2: $\{X, M_j, A_1\}$ is consistent.

In this case we might wish to retain M_j in the revised database and let $\Delta \circ A_1$ be $\{X, M_j, A_1\}$. On the one hand, we might reason that M_j follows non-monotonically from X but may not follow from the larger set $\{X, A_j\}$, so why keep it? On the other hand, we are dealing with E rules based on a coherent world picture, and if these rules yield M_j, and A_1 does not contradict it, why not accept it?

Case 3: A_1 is not consistent with X.

We have the two options. Either to proceed to reason from an inconsistent base or to maintain consistency in some manner.

Case 4: $\{X, A_1\}$ is consistent but can non-monotonically deduce some $\neg M_i$.

We clearly have to give $\neg M_i$ priority over M_i, as it can be proved from more data. This means that the proof system from $\{X, M_j, A_1\}$ should be a *defeasible* one; see [37, 38].

We thus need to study a mixture of controlled consistency maintenance algorithms and defeasible proof theory.

The rest of this section will deal with the machinery of compromise consistency maintenance. We are concerned with the following basic scenario. Let Δ be a finite consistent theory in some underlying logic L. Assume Δ has some internal structure. Let C be a consistent formula of L. We would like to input C into Δ at some specific point of its internal structure, to form a new theory, which we denote by $\Delta \circ C$. If $\Delta \cup \{C\}$ is *acceptable* to us according to some criteria,[12] then it is clear that $\Delta \circ C$ should be $\Delta \cup \{C\}$. The problem arises when $\Delta \cup \{C\}$ is not acceptable. In this case, we need to define what $\Delta \circ C$ is to be, by using some reasonable mechanisms.

Most of the traditional mechanisms for defining $\Delta \circ C$ that are intolerant of inconsistency try to restore consistency by adopting one of the following policies:

(a) The *non-insistent policy*, which rejects the input C and lets $\Delta \circ C = \Delta$.
(b) The *insistent policy*, which must accept the input C and restore consistency. For this purpose, the mechanisms identify a $\Delta_C \subseteq \Delta$ (to be rejected) such that $(\Delta - \Delta_C) \cup \{C\}$ is consistent. One then lets $\Delta \circ C$ be some consistent theory Δ' containing $(\Delta - \Delta_C) \cup \{C\}$. The details of how to identify Δ' and Δ_C depend on the particular approach of the particular system.
(c) A *discriminatory policy* that sometimes accepts the new input and sometimes rejects it, according to certain criteria.
(d) A *mixing policy* that accepts part but not all of the input and part but not all of the initial theory.

It is commonly accepted that any insistent revision process should satisfy some rationality postulates, and the family of revision operators governed by the AGM postulates seen in Section 2.1 is one of the main examples of processes in this category. We have also seen that the AGM postulates do not specify how to obtain $\Delta \circ C$.

---

[12] For classical logic, this is usually simply consistency, but see Chapter 7 for revision in logics that are not classical.

The underlying philosophy of the above approaches (independently of whether they want to accept or reject the input) is that inconsistency is bad and undesirable and consistency must be restored. So, to be able to input C into Δ when an inconsistency arises we crucially need to take steps to maintain consistency. Thus either C is rejected or if C is accepted then some part Δ_C of Δ must be thrown out so that consistency is maintained.[13]

In general terms, we support the view that inconsistency is not necessarily bad and in many cases it is even desirable [18, 19]. Inconsistency may be welcomed as a trigger for action and as long as the system knows what to do with it, it can be tolerated. Thus we may accept the input into the database even though it causes an inconsistency. In fact, the database may already be inconsistent to start with.

Following this approach, there are more options available for a system accepting an input and facing an inconsistency.

1. At one extreme it may proceed to maintain consistency in the traditional manner (*inconsistency-intolerant system*)
2. At the other extreme it may keep the inconsistent data but know, through some meta-level mechanisms, how to operate an inconsistent database, e.g., how to answer queries from the data without trivialising (*inconsistency-tolerant system*)

The mechanisms for giving answers from inconsistent data can vary, but they can in principle prove more than what can be obtained from a revised consistent version of the data. We give an example.

Consider the database

$$C \rightarrow B$$
$$C$$
$$\neg C$$

Most reasonable systems of reasoning with inconsistent data can afford to accept B as a conclusion, since B does not clash with $\neg C$, nor does it clash with C. Thus, no matter how we would maintain consistency, B can be accepted.

In the spirit of the above, we can offer an alternative mechanism for defining $\Delta \circ C$ as a consistent theory when $\Delta \cup \{C\}$ is inconsistent. We do not necessarily either reject C or throw out some $\Delta_C \subset \Delta$, but we can offer a *compromise*; we accept some of the logical consequences of C and some of the logical consequences of Δ_C and thus form the new consistent theory $\Delta \circ C$.

Thus, to summarise, in principle we allow for the following approaches:

1. In the inconsistency-intolerant approach:

   (a) the *non-insistent input policy*,[14]
   (b) the *insistent input policy*,
   (c) the *compromise input policy*

---

[13] Note that in the case of AGM, provided the input is satisfiable, consistency is restored *even* if the initial database is inconsistent. See (K°5) in Section 2.1.

[14] Some insist (see [9]), that the update must be put in even if it is itself contradictory.

2. In the inconsistency-tolerant approach:

Input C into Δ even if $\Delta \cup \{C\}$ is inconsistent and use mechanisms for reasoning from inconsistent databases. An example of such mechanism is *Labelled Deductive Systems* [17]. We also discuss this in Chapters 4 and 5.

We give more details about the idea of *compromise revision* in Section 2.10 with an example. The basic set up in the example is that we have a theory Δ which is consistent and an input C which is also consistent, and we want to look at $\Delta \cup \{C\}$, which is now unacceptable, and, more specifically, logically inconsistent. We know from everyday experience with a multitude of inconsistent data that one can still reason and get consequences from such theories. Thus $\Delta \cup \{C\}$, although inconsistent, can have a coherent set of consequences. Some of these consequences can be identified as consequences generated by C. Therefore, even if we insist on maintaining consistency and rejecting C, we can still compromise and take some of the consequences of $\Delta \cup \{C\}$. The particular example of Section 2.10 illustrates in context how the compromise process works.

We need, however, to hint at the mechanism involved in the general case. The problem is how to identify what consequences of $\Delta \cup \{C\}$ are reasonable. In classical logic, since $\Delta \cup \{C\}$ is inconsistent, it can prove anything! So, what consequences are 'generated' by C, i.e., what consequences do we take? Obviously we need to present Δ in a framework where 'control' over the consequences is possible. In order to do this, we need to tag the formulae in Δ with *labels* and give it and maintain some structure. This enables us to exercise full control over proofs and consequences. The simplest structure where control is possible is the list. We thus develop a labelled formulation and revision mechanisms for theories of the form

$$\Delta = (A_1, \ldots, A_n),$$

where Δ is a list of formulae. If we present Δ using labels it will have the form

$$\Delta = \{t_1 : A_1, \ldots, t_n : A_n\}, \ t_1 < \cdots < t_n,$$

where t_i's are atomic labels. In the sequel, we present Δ in either form, depending on the needs of the context.

There are many practical applications where such theories arise. For example, the list can be a temporal sequence of events, with $t_1 < \cdots < t_n$ representing moments of time or a linearly ordered list of information organised according to the reliability of their sources.

Our choice of theories as lists is in fact all we need in some contexts of revision. We observe that if we have a sequence of inputs, this also gives rise to a list, and so in the context of lists, we can easily consider databases which reflect inside them previous updates, and therefore we can define revision mechanisms which are sensitive to the history of past updates.[15] Thus, the labels can encode list structure of previous updates as well as priorities among data, while at the same time help us

---

[15] Iteration of the revision process is introduced in the next section.

maintain full control over proofs and consequences, and thus enabling us to implement our ideas of compromise and other forms of revision. The idea is developed further in Chapter 5, where labels are not necessarily linearly ordered.

We now continue our introduction with some extensions to traditional AGM revision.

2.9 Iterating the Revision Operation

As a process, belief revision can be seen as the refinement of a theory which represents how an agent perceives the world. As more and more information is gathered, the theory becomes more faithful to the real state of the world. It is only natural, thus, to consider what happens throughout successive applications of the revision operator. However, as discussed in Section 2.1, the AGM postulates have very little guidance to give about the iteration of the revision process. In what follows, we consider the simplified version of the postulates for finite belief bases introduced by Katsuno and Mendelzon. The only postulates related to iteration are (R5) and (R6), but they simply constrain the interaction between revisions and expansions:

(R5) $(\psi \circ_a A) \wedge B$ implies $\psi \circ_a (A \wedge B)$

(R6)   If $(\psi \circ_a A) \wedge B$ is satisfiable, then $\psi \circ_a (A \wedge B)$ implies $(\psi \circ_a A) \wedge B$

The constraint about interaction between successive *revisions* is limited to the case where a revision of K by A is followed by a revision by B and B is consistent with $K \circ_a A$. Since in this case B is consistent with $K \circ_a A$, (K°3) and (K°4) together imply $(K \circ_a A) \circ_a B = \mathrm{Cn}((K \circ_a A) \cup \{B\})$. (K°7) and (K°8) together imply that $K \circ_a (A \wedge B) = \mathrm{Cn}((K \circ_a A) \cup \{B\})$, and hence $(K \circ_a A) \circ_a B = K \circ_a (A \wedge B)$.

Subsequently, several attempts were made to capture the desirable behaviour of iterated revisions. Some of these include new postulates, such as (C1)–(C4), proposed by Darwiche and Pearl [11, 12, 13], whereas others are entirely new formulations based on the original AGM ideas [31].

We shall start firstly by analysing Darwiche and Pearl's approach. The account given here is quite brief and by no means complete. The reader should refer to the references given for a more comprehensive analysis.

2.9.1 Darwiche and Pearl's Postulates for Iterated Revisions

In [11], Darwiche and Pearl proposed some postulates to constrain the expected behaviour of iterated revisions. In that work, they point out that a distinction between belief and *epistemic* states is essential in the process, although a reformulation of the AGM postulates in order to reflect this only appeared later [12, 13]. The idea is to consider the epistemic state as the richer structure which results in a particular belief state. An immediate consequence of this is that the equivalence between epistemic states cannot be derived from the equivalence between belief sets. This approach is therefore consistent with the foundations paradigm and is supported by other authors [16, 31].

In the sense of Katsuno and Mendelzon's characterisation, belief states are represented by sets of sentences of propositional logic (finite belief sets). Since an epistemic state is an entity with richer structure, the simplified form of the AGM postulates put forward by Katsuno and Mendelzon needs to be rephrased. The reformulation in terms of epistemic states can be found below and was motivated by the observation that the original set of AGM postulates was incompatible with the new proposed postulates (C1)–(C4) (see [15] for a discussion).

In the following formulation, Ψ represents an epistemic state and $\mathrm{bel}(\Psi)$ represents the belief set associated with Ψ. However, we follow Darwiche and Pearl and use Ψ instead of $\mathrm{bel}(\Psi)$ in the context of propositional formulae. This lightens the notation. It should be clear then, for instance, that in (R*4) below, it is the epistemic states Ψ_1 and Ψ_2 that are meant in the first half of the postulate, and the belief sets $\mathrm{bel}(\Psi_1 \circ_a A_1)$ and $\mathrm{bel}(\Psi_2 \circ_a A_2)$ in the second one.

Darwiche and Pearl's postulates for revision of epistemic states

(R*1) $\Psi \circ_a A$ implies A

(R*2)   If $\Psi \wedge A$ is satisfiable, then $\Psi \circ_a A \equiv \Psi \wedge A$

(R*3)   If A is satisfiable, then $\Psi \circ_a A$ is also satisfiable

(R*4)   If $\Psi_1 = \Psi_2$ and $A_1 \equiv A_2$, then $\Psi_1 \circ_a A_1 \equiv \Psi_2 \circ_a A_2$

(R*5) $(\Psi \circ_a A) \wedge B$ implies $\Psi \circ_a (A \wedge B)$

(R*6)   If $(\Psi \circ_a A) \wedge B$ is satisfiable, then $\Psi \circ_a (A \wedge B)$ implies $(\Psi \circ_a A) \wedge B$

The above presentation is essentially the same as Katsuno and Mendelzon's, except for (R*4), which is strictly weaker than (R4). In (R*4), the condition is that the epistemic states are identical, instead of having the equivalence between belief sets required in (R4). This is reflected immediately in the semantical characterisation of revision operators satisfying (R*1)–(R*6).

Notation 3 *The models of an epistemic state Ψ will be denoted by* $\mathrm{Mod}(\Psi)$. *In other words,* $\mathrm{Mod}(\Psi) = \mathrm{mod}\,(\mathrm{bel}(\Psi))$.

The definitions and theorems contained in the rest of this section were presented in [13].

Definition 2.13 (Faithful assignment for revision of epistemic states). A *faithful assignment for belief revision of epistemic states* is a function mapping each epistemic state Ψ to a total pre-order $\preceq_\Psi$ on $\mathscr{I}$, such that

1. If $I, I' \in \mathrm{Mod}(\Psi)$, then $I \equiv_\Psi I'$.
2. If $I \in \mathrm{Mod}(\Psi)$ and $I' \notin \mathrm{Mod}(\Psi)$, then $I \prec_\Psi I'$ holds.
3. If $\Psi = \Delta$, then $\preceq_\Psi = \preceq_\Delta$.

Obviously, we say that $I \in \mathrm{Mod}(\Psi)$ if and only if $I \Vdash \mathrm{bel}(\Psi)$. Note that condition 3 above requires that the two epistemic states be *identical*. Darwiche and Pearl also proved the following theorem, which is the counterpart of Theorem 2.2 for epistemic states:

Theorem 2.10. *A revision operator* $\circ_a$ *satisfies postulates* $(R^*1)-(R^*6)$ *when there exists a faithful assignment that maps each epistemic state* Ψ *to a total pre-order* $\preceq_\Psi$, *such that*

$$\mathrm{Mod}(\Psi \circ_a A) = \min_{\preceq_\Psi}(\mathrm{mod}\,(A)).$$

Postulates $(R^*1)-(R^*6)$ can be augmented with the following postulates proposed by Darwiche and Pearl in order to model the actual iteration of the revision process.

(C1)   If $A \vDash B$, then $(\Psi \circ_a B) \circ_a A \equiv \Psi \circ_a A$
(C2)   If $A \vDash \neg B$, then $(\Psi \circ_a B) \circ_a A \equiv \Psi \circ_a A$
(C3)   If $\Psi \circ_a A \vDash B$, then $(\Psi \circ_a B) \circ_a A \vDash B$
(C4)   If $\Psi \circ_a A \nvDash \neg B$, then $(\Psi \circ_a B) \circ_a A \nvDash \neg B$

The meaning of the postulates above can be described as follows. (C1) says that revising an epistemic state Ψ by some information B and then revising it again by some *more specific* information A is the same as revising Ψ by A only. In [31], Lehmann showed that (C1) together with the AGM postulates implies (C3) and (C4). However, this is only the case when a distinction between the epistemic state and the belief state is ignored. The importance in this distinction was shown by Darwiche and Pearl in [13, Theorem 15], where they provided the reformulation of the AGM postulates in terms of the epistemic states seen above, i.e., $(R^*1)-(R^*6)$. We highlight once more the difference between this formulation and that of Katsuno and Mendelzon's: postulate (R^*4) is strictly weaker than (R4).

Notice the subtle difference between (C1) and (C2): in (C1), the new information is just a specialisation of some information learnt previously: A gives more detail about some information received previously (B). In (C2), however, the new information A *contradicts* something that was learnt before (B).

(C2) is one of the most controversial postulates of this series. It says that if an agent learns B first and then is given some information that contradicts this evidence (A), she should completely disregard any information conveyed by B. (C2) has been shown to be incompatible with the AGM postulates by Freund and Lehmann in [15]. However, if one considers the reformulation for epistemic states given by Darwiche and Pearl, they become indeed compatible. (C2) (and other similar versions of it) seems to undermine the principle of minimal change. It does not seem reasonable to discard completely the information conveyed by B simply because of the arrival of the contradictory information A.[16] We illustrate the difficulty with an example.

Suppose B is $p \wedge q$ and A is $\neg p \vee \neg q$. $\neg p \vee \neg q \vDash \neg(p \wedge q)$; therefore, (C2) applies, but the question is "should the agent completely discard the information conveyed

---

[16] This has some resonance with our earlier comments on compromise revision.

by $p \wedge q$ in the face of $\neg p \vee \neg q$?" After all, $p \leftrightarrow \neg q \models \neg p \vee \neg q$ and still keeps some of the informational content of $p \wedge q$. The acceptance of (C2) implies completely ignoring the fact that the agent ever believed in $p \wedge q$.

(C3) says that if after revising the epistemic state Ψ by A, the agent holds the belief in B, then this belief should also hold in the epistemic state obtained after revising Ψ by B and then by A.

(C4) is the negative counterpart of (C3). It says that if after revising Ψ by A the agent does not believe in $\neg B$, then she should not accept $\neg B$ after revising Ψ by B and then by A.

Postulates (C1)–(C4) deal explicitly with properties of iterated revisions. Darwiche and Pearl also provided a representation theorem reflecting how the faithful assignments for two consecutive epistemic states relate should the revision operator verify them. In other words, if Ψ is the current epistemic state and A is used to revise Ψ, then the ordering $\preceq_{\Psi}$ must relate to $\preceq_{\Psi \circ_a A}$ appropriately in order for (C1)–(C4) to hold. Thus,

Theorem 2.11. *If a given revision operator $\circ_a$ satisfies postulates* (R*1)–(R*6), *then $\circ_a$ satisfies* (C1)–(C4) *iff the operator and its corresponding faithful assignment satisfy:*

(CR1) *If $M,N \in$ mod(A), then $M \preceq_{\Psi} N$ iff $M \preceq_{\Psi \circ_a A} N$.*

(CR2) *If $M,N \in$ mod$(\neg A)$, then $M \preceq_{\Psi} N$ iff $M \preceq_{\Psi \circ_a A} N$.*

(CR3) *If $M \in$ mod(A) and $N \in$ mod$(\neg A)$, then $M \prec_{\Psi} N$ implies $M \prec_{\Psi \circ_a A} N$.*

(CR4) *If $M \in$ mod(A) and $N \in$ mod$(\neg A)$, then $M \preceq_{\Psi} N$ implies $M \preceq_{\Psi \circ_a A} N$.*

This ends our summary of Darwiche and Pearl's work on iterated revisions.

2.9.2 Lehmann's Approach: Belief Revision, Revised

In [31], D. Lehmann argues that the AGM postulates in their original belief set interpretation are incompatible with some desired properties of the iteration process (including postulate (C1) above) and advocates a revision of the complete framework. This led to the definition of the new postulates (I1)–(I7).

He considers belief states resulting from a finite sequence of revisions by consistent formulae. Epistemic states can thus be seen as simple lists of formulae and the corresponding belief states represented by [ ] and obtained by a particular revision procedure. For example, $[\alpha]$ represents the belief set obtained from the initial (empty) belief set revised by α. Subsequent revisions are represented by appending formulae to the end of the list: $[\alpha \cdot \beta]$ is the belief set obtained by revising $[\alpha]$ by β, and so forth. The postulates are listed below:

Lehmann's postulates for belief revision

(I1) $[\alpha]$ is a consistent theory

(I2) $\alpha \in [\sigma \cdot \alpha]$

(I3)   If $\beta \in [\sigma \cdot \alpha]$, then $\alpha \to \beta \in [\sigma]$
(I4)   If $\alpha \in [\sigma]$, then $[\sigma \cdot \gamma] = [\sigma \cdot \alpha \cdot \gamma]$
(I5)   If $\beta \vDash \alpha$, then $[\sigma \cdot \alpha \cdot \beta \cdot \gamma] = [\sigma \cdot \beta \cdot \gamma]$
(I6)   If $\neg\beta \notin [\sigma \cdot \alpha]$, then $[\sigma \cdot \alpha \cdot \beta \cdot \gamma] = [\sigma \cdot \alpha \cdot \alpha \wedge \beta \cdot \gamma]$
(I7) $[\sigma \cdot \neg\beta \cdot \beta] \subseteq Cn([\sigma], \beta)$

The only postulates that actually add new properties to the original AGM presentation are (I5) and (I7). The rest is a reformulation for the new framework. It is worth emphasising though that as in Darwiche and Pearl's formulation, the notion of an epistemic *state* plays a fundamental role in the process. For instance, the condition below, which is a consequence of (R4), does not follow from (I1)–(I7):

(IS)   If $[\sigma] = [\gamma]$, then $[\sigma \cdot \alpha] = [\gamma \cdot \alpha]$

Similarly, (I5) is related to (C1) above. It says that if α is a logical consequence of β, then revising by α and then revising by β is the same as revising by β only.

(I7) is a weaker version of (C2). It asserts that beliefs acquired from the revision by $\neg\beta$ should not be retained if the belief state is immediately revised by β. Notice that the precondition for (C2) is strictly weaker than that for (I7), whereas its postcondition is in turn at least as strong.

A negative result of this framework is that any revision procedure satisfying postulates (I1)–(I7) becomes trivial for an arbitrarily long sequence of revisions. The trivial revision procedure is the one which assigns $Cn(A)$ to $[\sigma \cdot A]$ whenever $\neg A \in [\sigma]$, and $Cn([\sigma] \cup \{A\})$ otherwise.

We have now concluded our introduction to the problem of iterating the revision process. We will discuss it in more detail in Chapter 4, where we propose a method for utilising an AGM revision operator in epistemic states represented in the spirit of Lehmann's sequences of revisions, and in Section 6.4, where we provide an entirely new algorithm to tackle the problem.

2.10 Compromise Revision

This section deals with an example which will illustrate the idea of the compromise approach briefly sketched previously.

Let the $\Delta = \{A, A \to B, A \wedge C \to D \wedge E, D \to \neg A\}$ be our base and the formula C be the input. Clearly, $\Delta \cup \{C\}$ is inconsistent. For instance, it can prove both A and $\neg A$. If we insist on maintaining consistency, we have several options for $\Delta \circ C$.

(a) Reject C (a non-insistent input policy),
(b) Accept C but reject some suitable Δ_C (an insistent input policy).

For case (b), depending on how we revise Δ, we may throw out any union of

$$\Delta_C^1 = \{A\},$$

$$\Delta_C^2 = \{A \wedge C \to D \wedge E\},$$

$$\Delta_C^3 = \{D \to \neg A\}.^{17}$$

Looking at this particular example and taking into consideration its meaning given below, it seems reasonable that we either end up with Δ (rejecting C) or with $\Delta_1 = \{C, A \to B, A \wedge C \to D \wedge E, D \to \neg A\}$ (rejecting Δ_C^1), i.e.,

$$\Delta_1 = (\Delta - \Delta_C^1) \cup \{C\}.$$

We now explain what our compromise approach would offer for this example. We consider the two options (a) rejecting C and (b) rejecting $\Delta_C^1 = \{A\}$:

(a) We observe that if C were admitted into the database, then $D \wedge E$ can be derived by modus ponens. Although D leads to inconsistency, E does not. So we can compromise and, although we reject C, we can still accept E.[18] Thus, the non-insistent, 'reject C' option would lead to the compromise database $\Delta \circ C = \Delta \cup \{E\}$.

(b) Similarly, throwing out $\Delta_C^1 = \{A\}$, would block the deduction of B and of $D \wedge E$. Since none of $\{B, D, E\}$ lead to any contradiction, we can compromise and take $\Delta \circ C = (\Delta - \Delta_C^1) \cup \{B, D, E\} \cup \{C\}$.

Note that the AGM postulates allow for a revision $\Delta \circ C$ to be of the form $\Delta' = (\Delta - \Delta_C) \cup \Delta'' \cup \{C\}$. Thus, from the AGM point of view, option (b) above, where we insist on accepting C but keep the consequences of $\Delta_C = \{A\}$, simply says that we want Δ'' to be the consequences of A, namely $\Delta'' = \{B, D, E\}$. We can therefore say that compromise revision for the insistent case (of accepting the input) is a particular way of choosing the AGM compatible revision $\Delta \circ C$ to contain exactly the consistent consequences of the minimally revised Δ (i.e., of what we throw out of Δ).

Of course, one can compromise by throwing out both C and Δ_C^1 and keeping in possibly more consequences of $\Delta \cup \{C\}$. This compromise would lead to, for example, $\Delta \circ C = \{A \to B, A \wedge C \to D \wedge E, B, D, E, D \to \neg A\}$. In the latter, we pushed both C and A out but accepted their consequences.

Consider the context where John is flying abroad on BA flight 945. He is booked to fly first class but when he shows up he discovers the first class was overbooked. Assume the following meaning to the symbols A, B, C, D, E of our example:

---

[17] Note that the AGM revision pursues an insistent input policy. It gives no details on how to compute $\Delta \circ C$. It only says that, provided C is satisfiable, $\Delta \circ C$ is a consistent theory satisfying the AGM postulates. Thus we can throw out, for example, both Δ_C^1 and Δ_C^2, and even add some new X, thus getting $\Delta \circ C = \Delta - \Delta_C^1 - \Delta_C^2 \cup \{X, C\}$. We want to take the view that $\Delta \circ C$ is to be obtained by throwing out a minimal part of Δ, that is, we throw out as little as possible so as to maintain consistency.

[18] We cannot accept D as this would lead to $\neg A$ and hence inconsistency.

$A =$ John is booked first class.

$B =$ John has double baggage allowance.

$C =$ First class cabin is full.

$D =$ John is seated in economy class.

$E =$ John gets a letter of apology from the airline.

The database Δ states (relative to flight BA 945) that John is booked first class, that such passengers get double baggage allowance and that if John is booked first class and the first class is full then John flies economy class, but gets a courtesy bonus. Further, the airline takes pride that no passenger booked first class ever travels economy. The update is that the first class is full.

We can be more specific about how we are modelling this airline booking example. Consider a many sorted predicate language $\mathscr{L}_1$ with the following predicates (the sorts are clear from the predicates' English translations).

- $S(x,y,b,t) =$ passenger x is assigned seat y on flight b date t.
- $V_1(y) = y$ is a first class seat.
- $V_2(y) = y$ is an economy class seat.
- $V_3(y) = y$ is not available.
- $A(x,b,t) = x$ is booked first class on flight b date t.
- $B(x,b,t) = x$ has a double baggage allowance on flight b date t.
- $C(b,t) =$ The first class cabin on flight b date t is full. (This predicate can be expressed using S and V_i.)
- $D(x,b,t) = x$ is seated in economy class on flight b date t.
- $E(x,b,t) = x$ gets a letter of apology from the flight b supervisor at date t.

The airline procedures are the following. Up to 60 minutes before the flight departure time booking can be accepted or cancelled according to certain rules. In the last 60 minutes before the flight, passengers with booking and valid tickets are assigned seats (boarding cards).

On the time of the flight, the official 'flight database' is closed. It includes a list of passenger names, their booking (economy or first class), their assigned seats (economy or first class) and their baggage allowance. There is also room for comments for each passenger name (apology, medical etc).

The closed database must satisfy the following:

- It must contain either $A(x,b,t_0)$ or $D(x,b,t_0)$ and not both for every passenger x with a boarding card.
- $\forall x \forall t (A \rightarrow B)$.
- $\forall x \forall t (A \wedge C \rightarrow D \wedge E)$.
- $\forall x \forall t (D \rightarrow \neg A)$.

- Some other obvious integrity constraints.

t_0 is the day of the flight. The 'input' $C(b,t_0)$ comes in on the day of the flight because, say, a seat is discovered damaged in the first-class cabin and so not all passengers booked first class can be assigned first class. Imagine that all other passengers with first-class booking have already been assigned seats in the first-class cabin. John is the last one and there are no seats to assign to him because the last seat has just been reported damaged. Thus John is assigned an economy seat. The consistency problem from the point of view of the flight supervisor is that if he or she leaves the recorded database as it is, then when it is officially closed it will not satisfy the constraints.

The supervisor is, however, in a position to do something. In logical terms, this is revision or consistency maintenance. In practical terms, the supervisor can do one of the following in the last minutes before the flight:

(a) Reject C. This can mean that the supervisor offers incentives (e.g., a 50% refund) to any passenger who will take the next flight, or that the supervisor quickly repairs the damaged seat.
(b) Take out A. This means that the supervisor changes John's first-class booking, (with John's consent, of course) and thus is able to officially record in the closed database an economy booking for John.

The first option makes sense. However, the second option requires some persuation and negotiation. The supervisor can let John enjoy the consequence of his booking (e.g., double baggage allowance) even though he is in economy. This is the compromise solution!

On the other hand, the compromise solution for the reject C option is a bit unsatisfactory! Had John flown economy (because the first-class cabin was full) he would have got a letter of apology. Now that the airline rejected C (i.e., repaired the seat or got some other people off the first class), John need not get a letter of apology.

We see nevertheless that there are circumstances where the compromise solution is most intuitive.

The temporal model we presented above has to do with databases which reflect reality. Certain formulae must be maintained in the database. We are free to take some actions in the real world resulting in formulae being placed in and taken out of the database, so that consistency is maintained. There is a period of time before the database is officially 'closed' when we take our actions with a view of affecting what the closed database will be.

There are many applications where the data in Δ is tied to programs initiating actions conditional on the data (payroll systems, students exams, etc.). Updates and inputs signify changes of rules or additional information. In such cases a later input has higher priority and may contradict earlier data. However, the consequences of earlier (now possibly rejected) data may have to remain in the database because they were the basis for actions already taken. Each application can decide according to its own needs which consequences to try and keep.[19]

We believe that any application involving a language for permission, where $\bigwedge x_i \rightarrow y$ means that we need to secure permission x_i in order to permit or make true y, would be an application where compromise is meaningful. The integrity constraints of the form $\bigwedge x_i \rightarrow \bot$ say that we cannot give too many permissions.

We must clarify the technical machinery used in our compromise procedure: we are given a consistent database Δ and an input X. We realise that $\Delta \cup \{X\}$ is inconsistent. We identify that if X is added to Δ then $Y_1, Y_2, Y_3 \ldots$ can be derived. We verify that say $\Delta \cup \{Y_3, Y_4 \ldots\}$ is indeed consistent and so we *compromise* and take the update $\Delta + X$ to be $\Delta \cup \{Y_3, Y_4, \ldots\}$.

These concepts need to be made precise. If $\Delta \cup \{X\}$ is inconsistent then (in many logics) it can prove everything; so how do we identify $Y_1, Y_2, \ldots$? Furthermore, what are the applications where such a mechanism is intuitive and makes sense? These issues will be dealt with in Section 6.3.

2.11 Controlled Revision

As we saw in Section 2.9, the AGM postulates have little to say about the iteration of the revision process. If we consider revision in general, i.e., not necessarily satisfying the AGM postulates, and in the case of non-monotonic logics, we already have some implicit notion of revision in the logic itself. The very idea of non-monotonicity implies that the theory gets automatically revised in view of new input.

In the case of inconsistency-tolerant logics, a satisfactory revision process needs to attend to the fact that unlike in the AGM approach, which can be seen as a

---

[19] Imagine each first day of the month the official data is a list of employees, ranks and salaries. Thus we may have the following official database in September 2009:

(Jan 2009, John, Lecturer, £1000)

⋮

(Sep 2009, John, Lecturer, £1000)

In October 2009 John was promoted retroactively from Jan 2009 to the rank of a Reader (Salary £1500). If we just update the database by merely recording our actions in October 2009, we may get the following database in October 2009.

(Jan 2009, John, Reader, £1000)

⋮

(Sep 2009, John, Reader, £1000).
(Oct 2009, John, Reader, £5500)

The database does not reflect what happened and seems to violate integrity constraints (a reader was underpaid for nine months before it was 'detected'). We need two-dimensional temporal logic to do this update properly. We need to record both event time and transaction time.

consistency-restoring approach, we already have mechanisms in the logic for getting intuitively acceptable consequences even from an inconsistent set of data.

If we think in terms of an algorithmic approach that supports iteration of the revision process, then we have two alternatives. The first one is to apply a revision operation in such a way that some desiderata for the iteration of the operation, like some of the ones seen in Sections 2.9.1 and 2.9.2, are verified. We propose such a mechanism in Chapter 4. The second option is to provide an entirely new algorithm that calculates consequences of the current epistemic state based on the history of inputs received by the agent. We provide such an algorithm, *controlled revision* [20], in Section 6.4, which we briefly introduce here.

Any algorithm for iterated revision requires some sort of memory mechanism that keeps track of the inputs the agent received or alternatively a history of what was removed from the database in previous revisions, since this information is relevant to the decision of what to accept and reject in the face of the current input. In general terms, this means that past effects of the revision process itself (sentences can be rejected and put in at different stages) may affect the non-monotonicty of the current theory.

The algorithm for controlled revision makes use of special labels attached to the formulae, providing a logical means for control and representation. The labels have multiple roles. One such role is to define the properties of our selected logic as distinguished from other logics, and another role is to annotate and control the iteration of the revision process.

The work has some resemblance to Doyle's *truth maintenance system* (TMS) [14], a problem solver subsystem whose task is to revise a database's *current* state by keeping records of logical consequences and checking changes caused by new data input. The advantage of this division of labour is that the problem solver can be implemented for any desired underlying logic (as long as it is clear in the logic what formulae support what other formulae). However, a TMS reserves no special theoretical role for an associated proof theory, being just a manipulator of a specific data structure. Basically, each state of a TMS consists of two elements: *nodes* and *justifications*. A node represents some information, whereas a justification indicates any *reasons* (i.e., formulae) supporting a particular belief. Each node can be marked 'in' or 'out', depending on whether or not it is part of the current belief set. There is no notion of the history of updates involved and a TMS only keeps track of the current state of beliefs.

The controlled revision algorithm seeks to address these issues by taking the notion of time into account. This allows us to trace back the justifications for actions taken in the past, and entitles us to reconsider prior states of the database in the light of new data or possibilities (as assumptions, suppositions, hypotheses, etc.). Controlled revision is presented in Section 6.4.

2.12 Revision by Translation

The idea of *revision by translation* differs significantly from the approaches discussed in this introduction. In all approches discussed so far, we were concerned with the problem of defining an operation for revision or at least of expressing principles governing one such operation.

The framework of revision by translation, on the other hand, asks a different question. Assuming we have an operator for the revision of belief sets represented in a particular logic, can we use it to revise belief sets of other logics? We shall see that, under certain circumstances, it is possible to "export" the machinery of the revision operation to other systems. The idea is to perform the revision of the target theory via its *translation* to first-order logic, perform the revision in the translation and then translate the results back. We outline the general schema below.

Let $\circ_a$ be a revision process in classical logic. Typically, given a classical logic theory Δ and an input formula ψ,[20] the operation $\circ_a$ gives us a new theory $\Gamma = \Delta \circ_a \psi$, corresponding to the result of the revision of Δ by ψ. Ideally, $\circ_a$ has some desirable properties, for instance, the AGM postulates introduced earlier.

We would like to *export* this machinery to other logics. For example, given a theory Δ of some logic $\mathbf{L}$ and an input $\mathbf{L}$-sentence ψ, can we define a revision operation $*_L$ such that $\Delta *_L \psi$ is a revised $\mathbf{L}$ theory and $*_L$ satisfies the AGM postulates? Can we make use of the revision operator of classical logic?

We can do this indirectly and under certain circumstances (the details are worked out in Chapter 7). We first need to translate the object logic $\mathbf{L}$ into classical logic; then we perform the revision there, and then we translate the results back. Now, suppose that τ denotes a translation function from $\mathbf{L}$ into classical logic and T^τ is a classical theory encoding the basic properties of $\mathbf{L}$. If the axiomatization given by T^τ is sound and complete, we have that for all Δ and α of the logic $\mathbf{L}$:

(2.2) $\Delta \vdash_{\mathbf{L}} \alpha$ iff $T^\tau \cup \Delta^\tau \vdash \alpha^\tau$

Therefore, we can define a revision operator $*_L$ in the logic $\mathbf{L}$ as follows:

Definition 2.14 (Belief revision in L). Let $\circ_a$ be a revision operator for classical logic, and let τ, T^τ be as above. We define

$$\Delta *_L \psi = \{\beta \mid \Delta^\tau \circ_a (\psi^\tau \wedge T^\tau) \vdash \beta^\tau\}$$

The motivation for this definition is as follows. Δ^τ is the translation of the original theory Δ in the logic $\mathbf{L}$. Δ is to be revised by ψ, which in classical logic is translated as ψ^τ. Since our revision operator works in classical logic, we revise instead Δ^τ by ψ^τ. However, we want the properties of the object logic (T^τ) to be preserved, since it describes how it works in classical logic. In fact, we want the

---

[20] There is no special need that the input is a single formula ψ. It can be a theory Ψ. The AGM postulates work for input theories as well.

resulting revised theory to satisfy T^τ. The only way to ensure this is to revise by $\psi^\tau \wedge T^{\tau}$.[21]

There are some difficulties which make the analysis rather interesting from the point of view of revision theory. One of them has to do with the notion of inconsistency in **L**. **L** may have theories Δ which are considered **L**-inconsistent whilst their translation Δ^τ is classically consistent.[22] Thus, we may have a situation in **L** where Δ is **L**-consistent, the input ψ is **L**-consistent, but $\Delta \cup \{\psi\}$ is **L**-inconsistent and requires **L**-revision. However, when we translate into classical logic we get $\Delta^\tau \cup \{\psi^\tau\} \cup T^\tau$, and this theory is classically consistent and so the revision will be equivalent to a simple expansion. We therefore need to move towards a more general notion than that of inconsistency. We call this notion *acceptability*. We can then write some additional axioms Acc that govern what theories in the object logic we deem acceptable, making the translation of unacceptable theories in the object logic *inconsistent* in classical logic. Having done this, we have that $\Delta^\tau \cup \{\psi^\tau\} \cup T^\tau \cup Acc$ is classically inconsistent whenever $\Delta \cup \{\psi\}$ is **L**-inconsistent, and thus a proper revision process can be triggered in classical logic.

There is a problem, however, with this approach. Classical revision of $\Delta^\tau \cup \{\psi^\tau\} \cup T^\tau \cup Acc$ may give us a theory Δ_c of classical logic such that the reverse translation $\Delta_\mathbf{L} = \{\alpha \mid \Delta_c \vdash \alpha^\tau\}$ is not a theory we are happy with in **L**. In other words, when we look at the relation between $\Delta \cup \{\psi\}$ and $\Delta_\mathbf{L}$ we are not happy in **L** to consider $\Delta_\mathbf{L}$ as the **L**-revision of $\Delta \cup \{\psi\}$. The reason that such a situation may arise has to do with the fact that the notion of inconsistency in classical logic is too strong. We now explain why: if K is a consistent theory in classical logic and $K \cup \{\psi\}$ is inconsistent in classical logic, then $\mathrm{Cn}(K \cup \{\psi\})$ is the set of all wffs. Our revision intuition wants to take a consistent subset K' of $\mathrm{Cn}(K \cup \{\psi\})$.

In the logic **L** with $K_\mathbf{L}$ and $\psi_\mathbf{L}$ and with a different notion of inconsistency, the theory $\mathrm{Cn}_\mathbf{L}(K_\mathbf{L} \cup \{\psi_\mathbf{L}\})$ may not be the set of all wffs of **L**. We still want to get a consistent subset $K'_\mathbf{L}$ of $\mathrm{Cn}_\mathbf{L}(K_\mathbf{L} \cup \{\psi_\mathbf{L}\})$ as the revision. Our strategy of revision by translation may give us a revised theory via translation which is not a subset of $\mathrm{Cn}_\mathbf{L}(K_\mathbf{L} \cup \{\psi_\mathbf{L}\})$ because in classical logic $\mathrm{Cn}(K_\mathbf{L}^\tau \cup \{\psi_\mathbf{L}^\tau\} \cup T^\tau \cup Acc)$ is too large (i.e., all wffs) and gives the revision process too much freedom. One way to address this difficulty is to tighten up the revision process in classical logic.

We consider three case studies. The first one is that of the propositional modal logic **K**. Because this logic shares a similar semantics with classical logic, the translation and revision process are relatively straightforward. We then proceed to analyse the case of Łukasiewicz' many-valued logic. Although this logic has semantics significantly different from that of classical logic, there are some similarities with respect to the notion of consistency. Finally, we analyse the case of Belnap's four-valued logic. This logic does not have a notion of inconsistency, and this directly

---

[21] Our method is restricted to logics **L** that have a translation τ that can be characterized by a classical theory T^τ. If the translation is, for example, semantically based, this means that the semantics of **L** can be expressed by a first-order theory T^τ, as is the case in many modal logics.

[22] In paraconsistent logics, for example, $p \wedge \neg p$ is considered inconsistent, but we do not have $p \wedge \neg p \vdash q$. Equation (2.2) of the translation still holds, i.e., for all α, $p \wedge \neg p \vdash \alpha$ iff $(p \wedge \neg p)^\tau \cup T^\tau \vdash \alpha^\tau$, but in classical logic $(p \wedge \neg p)^\tau \cup T^\tau$ is consistent!

affects the way we do revision on its translation to classical logic. We introduce the notion of *acceptability* for Belnap theories mapping unacceptable theories into inconsistent classical logic theories.

Revision by translation is presented in detail in Chapter 7.

2.13 A General Setting for Algorithmic Revision

We conclude this introduction by describing the general setting for revision as we see it. We present a theory of revision for arbitrary logics. Our proposed general methodology for revision enjoys the following properties:

1. The principles are based on proof theory. A theory Δ is presented as a (structured) collection of assumptions, and a deductive mechanism can derive all its consequences. Revision principles apply to Δ of this form.[23]
2. The principles apply to any logic and are not formulated just for (dependent on) classical logic.
3. They equally apply to monotonic and non-monotonic logics and theories.
4. They should involve the current theory Δ and input C and not past theories and past inputs, nor future inputs. (Note that in *Labelled Deductive Systems*, theories are structured, and so the theory structure may help recognise past inputs, but then the structure also contributes to inconsistency, and it is a whole different setup!)

We see the above principles as essential to any revision theory. Revision is syntactical; it should depend only on proof-theoretical considerations and not semantical considerations. There are applied logics, however, whose semantics come from applications. In such cases semantical considerations are acceptable.

To study revision, we need the following proof-theoretical notions:

1. A language for the declarative units and theories (databases).
2. The notion of a structured theory in the language. This can be any of the following.

---

[23] Note that AGM assumes Δ is deductively closed and that the logic is classical logic.

Logic	A theory is a ...
Classical or intuitionistic logic	Set of wffs.
Linear logic	Multisets of wffs.
Lambek calculus	Sequence of wff.
A Labelled Deductive System	Labelled theory (with structure induced by labels).

3. A notion of a controlled proof theory from structured databases which allows us to organise what is provable into priority levels.
4. A notion of a theory being *inconsistent* (or unacceptable, violating integrity constraints, etc.).
5. A notion of input of a formula A (or a declarative unit) into a theory.
   The following are examples of input notions:

Theory	Possible input notions
Set, multiset	Inclusion (one or more copies).
Sequence	Append at end (beginning) of sequence.
Labelled Theory	Include with a new label and information on how the new label relates to existing labels.

6. Some notion of priority among substructures of data.
7. An algorithm Π which takes a database and input and produces a new revised database. Π makes use of the priority notion.

   The above considerations show that, in general, principles of theory revision must be expressed in a metalanguage involving predicates over theory structure and inputs.
   Note that we need not distinguish between non-monotonic or monotonic logics. Rationality postulates can be given for the general case. These are expected to simplify and specialise for each particular logic. So, for example, one can justify and obtain the AGM postulates for the case of classical logic as a special case of general rationality principles, specialised to the particular properties of classical logic.

Let us now define a general input process for the case of databases which are sequences of data $(A_1, \ldots, A_n)$ with integrity constraints.

Definition 2.15. *Input functions*

1. Let $0, 1, 2, 3, \ldots$ be the finite ordinals, i.e.,

$$n + 1 = \{0, 1, \ldots, n\}.$$

Let I be a function giving for each ordinal n a value $I(n) \in n + 1$. I is called an input function. If n indicates the priority ordering of a database with

$$t_0 : A_0, \ldots, t_{n-1} : A_{n-1}, \; t_0 < t_2 < \cdots < t_{n-1}$$

and we want to input a new data item $a : C$, then $I(n) = k \in n + 1$ indicates the place in the priority of the input C. Namely, we will have the new database with priority

$$t_0 : A_0, \ldots, t_{k-1} : A_{k-1}, a : C, t_k : A_k, \ldots t_{n-1} : A_{n-1}.$$

Note that the labels $\{t_i\}$ only help with the calculations.
2. An input function is said to be *insistent* if $I(n) = n$, for all n.

It is said to be non-insistent if $I(n) = 0$, for all n.

Definition 2.16. *General input process*

1. Let I be an input function and let f be a sequence of formulae $f(i) = A_i$, $i = 1, 2, 3, \ldots$. Then (I, f) is called a general input process.
2. Let C be a set of integrity constraints. We can define two sequences of databases, using C and (I, f) as follows:

(1) Let $\Delta_0^+ = \Delta_0^* = C$.
(2) Assume Δ_k^+ and Δ_k^* are defined and are consistent and contain C as well as the data elements

$$t_1 : X_1, \ldots, t_{m_k} : X_{m_k}$$

with $t_1 < \cdots < t_{m_k}$. Let us input the element $a : A_k$ (where $A_k = f(k)$) into the $I(m_k)$ place to obtain the new databases $\Delta_{1,k}^+$ and $\Delta_{1,k}^*$, respectively. Let Δ_{k+1}^+ be the compromise database $(\Delta_{1,k}^+)_{\text{comp}}$ (as defined later in Definition 6.14) and let Δ_{k+1}^* be the database $(\Delta_{1,k}^*)_{\text{cons}}$ (as defined in Definition 6.13).
(3) Note that the database sequences are the result of inputting repeatedly A_i, $i = 1, 2, \ldots$, into C and maintaining consistency. For the case where I is an insistent input function and the Δ_k^* sequence, we get repeated AGM-style revision.

2.14 Outline of This Book

The rest of this book is structured as follows. In Chapter 3, we provide a gentle introduction to revision theory by presenting the fundamental concepts involved in it. We illustrate how the concept of minimal change can be applied and define basic operations for belief revision. We then propose an extension of the framework in Chapter 4 that supports the history of updates received by the agent, and in this context we analyse the problem of iteration of the revision process.

In Chapter 5, we consider a revision approach in which extralogical information in the form of preferences is available. More specifically, we consider belief bases augmented with (partial) preference orderings and provide a method for reasoning in this setting.

The context of the revision operation is considered in detail in Chapter 6, where we present three different methods: *abductive revision, compromise revision* and *controlled revision*. In addition, we analyse the revision of theories by input sets that are infinite.

In Chapter 7, we analyse properties of revision operations in theories whose logics are not classical through their translation into classical logic.

Chapter 8 concentrates on the analysis of how to effect belief change operations at the *object* level. This can be done by augmenting the language of a logic with special deletion operations.

We finalise with some discussions and conclusions in Chapter 9.

References

1. E. Adams. *The Logic of Conditionals.* D. Reidel, Dordrecht, Netherlands, 1975.
2. C. A. Alchourrón, P. Gärdenfors, and D. Makinson. On the logic of theory change: partial meet contraction and revision functions. *The Journal of Symbolic Logic*, 50:510–530, 1985.
3. C. A. Alchourrón and D. Makinson. On the logic of theory change: Contraction functions and their associated revision functions. *Theoria*, 48:14–37, 1982.
4. C. A. Alchourrón and D. Makinson. The logic of theory change: Safe contraction. *Studia Logica*, 44:405–422, 1985.
5. G. Brewka. *Nonmonotonic Reasoning — Logical Foundations of Commonsense*, volume 12 of *Cambridge Tracts in Theoretical Computer Science*. Cambridge University Press, October 1990.
6. G. Brewka and J. Hertzberg. How to do things with worlds: on formalizing actions and plans. *Journal of Logic and Computation*, 3(5):517–532, 1993.
7. R. Chisholm. The contrary-to-fact conditional. *Mind*, 55:289–307, 1946. Reprinted in *Readings in Philosophical Analysis*, edited by H. Feigl and W. Sellars, Appleton-Century-Crofts, New York, 1949, pp. 482–497.
8. M. Dalal. Investigations into a theory of knowledge base revision: Preliminary report. In Paul Rosenbloom and Peter Szolovits, editors, *Proceedings of the Seventh National Conference on Artificial Intelligence*, volume 2, pages 475–479, Menlo Park, California, 1988. AAAI Press.
9. M. Dalal. Investigations into a theory of knowledge base revision: Preliminary report. In *AAAI*, pages 475–479, 1988.
10. F. C. C. Dargam. *On Reconciling Conflicting Updates (A Compromise Revision Approach).* PhD thesis, Department of Computing, Imperial College, October 1996.

11. A. Darwiche and J. Pearl. On the logic of iterated belief revision. In Ronald Fagin, editor, *Proceedings of the 5th International Conference on Principles of Knowledge Representation and Reasoning*, pages 5–23. Morgan Kaufmann, Pacific Grove, CA, March 1994.

12. A. Darwiche and J. Pearl. On the logic of iterated belief revision. Technical Report R-202, Cognitive Science Laboratory, Computer Science Department, University of California, Los Angeles, CA 90024, November 1996.

13. A. Darwiche and J. Pearl. On the logic of iterated belief revision. *Artificial Intelligence*, 89:1–29, 1997.

14. J. Doyle. A truth maintenance system. *Artificial Intelligence*, 12:231–272, 1979.

15. M. Freund and D. Lehmann. Belief revision and rational inference. Technical Report TR 94-16, The Leibniz Center for Research in Computer Science, Institute of Computer Science, Hebrew University, July 1994.

16. N. Friedman and J. Y. Halpern. Belief revision: A critique. In *Proceedings of the 5th International Conference on Principles of Knowledge Representation and Reasoning*, pages 421–431, Cambridge, Massachusetts, 1996.

17. D. M. Gabbay. *Labelled Deductive Systems: Principles and Applications. Basic Principles*, volume 1. Oxford University Press, 1996.

18. D. M. Gabbay and A. Hunter. Making inconsistency respectable, part I. In Ph. Jorrand and J. Kelemen, editors, *In Proceedings of Fundamental of Artificial Intelligence Research (FAIR '91)*, volume 535 of *LNAI*, pages 19–32. Springer-Verlag, 1991.

19. D. M. Gabbay and A. Hunter. Making inconsistency respectable, part II. In R. Kruse M. Clarke and S. Moral, editors, *Proceedings of Euro Conference on Symbolic and Quantitive Approaches to Reasoning and Uncertainity*, volume 747 of *LNCS*, pages 129–136. Springer-Verlag, 1993.

20. D. M. Gabbay and G. Pigozzi. Controlled revision – an algorithmic approach for belief revision. *Journal of Logic and Computation*, 13(1):15–35, 2003. DOI: 10.1093/logcom/13.1.15.

21. P. Gärdenfors. Conditionals and changes of belief. *Acta Philosophica Fennica*, 30:381–404, 1978.

22. P. Gärdenfors. Rules for rational changes of belief. In T. Pauli, editor, *Philosophical Essays Dedicated to Lannart Aqvist on His Fiftieth Birthday*, volume 34 of *Philosophical Studies*, pages 88–101. Philosophical Society and the Department of Philosophy, Uppsala University, 1982.

23. P. Gärdenfors. Belief revision and the Ramsey test for conditionals. *The Philosophical Review*, 95:81–93, 1986.

24. P. Gärdenfors. *Knowledge in Flux: Modeling the Dynamics of Epistemic States*. A Bradford Book — The MIT Press, Cambridge, Massachusetts, and London, England, 1988.

25. P. Gärdenfors and H. Rott. Belief revision. In D. M. Gabbay, C. J. Hogger, and J. A. Robinson, editors, *Handbook of Logic in Artificial Intelligence and Logic Programming*, volume 4, pages 35–132. Oxford University Press, 1995.

26. G. Grahne. Updates and counterfactuals. In J. A. Allen, R. Fikes, and E. Sandewell, editors, *Principles of Knowledge Representation and Reasoning: Proceedings of the Second International Conference*, pages 269–276, San Mateo, California, 1991. Morgan Kaufmann.

27. A. Grove. Two modellings for theory change. *Journal of Philosophical Logic*, 17:157–170, 1988.

28. G. Harman. *Change in View: Principles of Reasoning*. MIT Press, Cambridge, Massachussetts, 1986.

29. H. Katsuno and A. O. Mendelzon. Propositional knowledge base revision and minimal change. *Artificial Intelligence*, 52(3):263–294, 1991.

30. H. Katsuno and A. O. Mendelzon. On the difference between updating a knowledge base and revising it. In P. Gärdenfors, editor, *Belief Revision*, pages 183–203. Cambridge University Press, 1992.

31. D. Lehmann. Belief revision, revised. In *Proceedings of the 14th International Joint Conference of Artificial Intelligence (IJCAI-95)*, pages 1534–1540, 1995.

32. D. K. Lewis. *Counterfactuals*. Harvard University Press, 1973.

33. W. Łukaszewicz. *Non-monotonic reasoning: formalization of commonsense reasoning.* Ellis Horwood, 1990.
34. J. McCarthy. Programs with common sense. In *Mechanisation of Thought Processes, Proceedings of the Symposium of the National Physics Laboratory*, pages 77–84, London, UK, 1958. Her Majesty's Stationary Office.
35. A. Nayak. Iterated belief change based on epistemic entrenchment. *Erkentnis*, 41:353–390, 1994.
36. D. Nute. Conditional logic. In D. M. Gabbay and F. Guenthner, editors, *Handbook of Philosophical Logic*, chapter Chapter II.8, pages 387–439. D. Reidel, Dordrecht, 1984.
37. D. Nute. Basic defeasible logic. *Intensional Logics for Logic Programming*, pages 125–154, 1992. Oxford University Press.
38. D. Nute. *Handbook of Logic and Artificial Intelligence*, volume 3, chapter Defeasible Logic, pages 353–395. Oxford University Press, 1994.
39. J. L. Pollock. A refined theory of counterfactuals. *Journal of Philosophical Logic*, 10:239–266, 1981.
40. F. P. Ramsey. Truth and probability. In R. B. Braithwaite, editor, *The Foundations of Probability and other Logical Essays*. Harcourt Brace, New York, 1931.
41. Frank Plumpton Ramsey. *Philosophical Papers*. Cambridge University Press, 1990. Edited by D. H. Mellor.
42. R. Reiter. A logic for default reasoning. *Artificial Intelligence*, 13:81–132, 1980.
43. O. Rodrigues, M. Ryan, and P.-Y. Schobbens. Counterfactuals and updates as inverse modalities. In Yoav Shoham, editor, *6th Conference on Theoretical Aspects of Rationality and Knowledge*, pages 163–174, 1996.
44. H. Rott. Preferential belief change using generalized epistemic entrenchment. *Journal of Logic, Language and Information*, 1:45–78, 1992.
45. M. D. Ryan and P.-Y. Schobbens. Intertranslating counterfactuals and updates. In W. Wahlster, editor, *12th European Conference on Artificial Intelligence (ECAI)*, pages 100–104. J. Wiley & Sons, Ltd., 1996.
46. R. Stalnaker. A theory of conditionals. *Studies in Logical Theory, American Philosophical Quarterly Monograph Series, No. 2*, 1968.
47. R. C. Stalnaker. *A Theory of Conditionals*, volume 2 of *American Philosophical Quarterly Monograph Series (Nicholas Rescher, ed.)*, pages 98–112. Blackwell, Oxford, 1968.
48. R. C. Stalnaker and Richmond H. Thomason. A semantic analysis of conditional logic. *Theoria*, 36:23–42, 1970.
49. M. Winslett. Reasoning about action using a possible models approach. In *Proc. National Conference on Artificial Intelligence (AAAI '88)*, pages 89–93, 1988.
50. W. Wobcke. On the use of epistemic entrenchment in nonmonotonic reasoning. In *10th European Conference on Artificial Intelligence (ECAI'92)*, pages 324–328, 1992.

Chapter 3
Stepwise Revision Operations

3.1 Introduction

In this chapter, we start our analysis of the problems of defining a revision operation in a classical logic setting. We will see that the most straightforward way of defining such an operator is to consider what happens when one single application of the operator takes place. This application is in a sense unaware of the agent's history of revision, and this has implications on the iteration of the revision process. For that reason, we call this type of revision operation *stepwise*. We will consider the iteration of the revision process in Chapter 4.

The starting point in the process is the introduction of the notion of information change between two belief states. It is possible to evaluate change either by providing a numerical value associated with the degree of change or by simply specifying how two states compare with other other in relative terms. Methods which are included in the first category provide a *quantitative measurement of change* and those in the latter provide a *qualitative evaluation*. We will now discuss them in more detail.

3.2 Quantitative Measurement of Change

For the case of propositional logic, one way of defining a distance function is by analysing the truth-values of propositional variables of valuations and considering the "distance" between two valuations as the number of propositional variables with different truth-values. In general, this distance notion is called the *Hamming distance*, after R. W. Hamming [10]. In the context of belief revision, it was first used in [4].

Recall that $\mathscr{I}$ is the set of all valuations.

Definition 3.1. Let M and N be two elements of $\mathscr{I}$. The *distance d between M and N* is the number of propositional variables p_i for which $M(p_i) \neq N(p_i)$.

D. M. Gabbay et al., *Revision, Acceptability and Context*, Cognitive Technologies,
DOI 10.1007/978-3-642-14159-1_3, © Springer-Verlag Berlin Heidelberg 2010

Proposition 3.1. *The function d is a metric on $\mathscr{I}$.*

Proof. Let M,N,O be elements of $\mathscr{I}$. We have to show that:

(M1) $d(M,N) \geq 0$
(M2) $d(M,N) = 0$ *if and only if* $M = N$
(M3) $d(M,N) = d(N,M)$
(M4) $d(M,O) \leq d(M,N) + d(N,O)$

(M1) and (M2). Clearly, $d(M,N)$ cannot be negative. If $d(M,N) = 0$, then $M(p_i) = N(p_i)$ for all $p_i \in \mathscr{P}$, and then $M = N$. If $M = N$, then they obviously agree with respect to every propositional variable, and hence $d(M,N) = 0$.

(M3) follows directly from Definition 3.1.

(M4) Let us identify valuations M,N,O with the sets M_l, N_l and O_l of (positive or negative) literals that they satisfy, respectively. We then define X to be $M_l - O_l$, that is, the set of literals l_i such that $l_i \in M_l$ and $l_i \notin O_l$, Y to be $M_l - N_l$ and Z to be $N_l - O_l$. It is easy to see that, for a given literal l_i and valuation M, if $l_i \notin M_l$, then $\neg l_i \in M_l$, and that there is a correspondence between the cardinalities of X, Y and Z and the distances $d(M,O)$, $d(M,N)$ and $d(N,O)$, respectively. We show that $|X| \leq |Y| + |Z|$ by proving that $X \subseteq Y \cup Z$.

Suppose $l_i \in X$, but $l_i \notin Y \cup Z$. If $l_i \in X$, then $l_i \in M_l$ and $\neg l_i \in O_l$. Either $l_i \in N_l$ or $\neg l_i \in N_l$. If $l_i \in N_l$, then $l_i \in Z$. On the other hand, if $\neg l_i \in N_l$, then $l_i \in Y$. In either case, $l_i \in Y \cup Z$, a contradiction.

3.2.1 Minimal Change and the Function d

The notion of *minimal change* is associated with the desire of minimising the loss of information incurred in accommodating new information consistently into a theory. More specifically, it relates to the "amount" of information from the old theory lost in the process. The idea is to preserve as much as possible of the old informational content. In the case of belief revision, the interesting case is when the new belief contradicts the information held in the previous belief set. In order to maintain consistency, some of the old beliefs have to be given up. There are usually many ways of doing this, and the more appealing ones are those which cause a minimal change to the old belief set.

What "change" means varies also depending on the kind of information change being performed. We have seen in Section 2.1 that belief revision evaluates change with respect to the agent's belief state as a whole. If one wants to minimise change, then the idea is to find the minimal distance between any two models of the belief state and the new belief. On the other hand, when reasoning about actions, as in the *update problem*, each model of this belief state actually represents a possible state of the world. If a change in the world occurs, e.g., when an action is performed, then each of the possible states/models needs to be considered individually. A minimal change is still the key idea. However, this time the focus is on each of the possible states/models and not on the theory as a whole.

As a more concrete example, consider the single formula $p \vee q$ and the new information $\neg p$. In the belief revision approach, the meaning of $p \vee q$ is that the agent holds the belief in $p \vee q$. She does not know which of p and q is true, but she believes that at least one of them is. When she is faced with $\neg p$, she has no reason to conclude that her old beliefs were incorrect, so she reasons that in fact q was true in the first place, and now she believes in $\neg p \wedge q$. Now, if one is considering the effects of the execution of actions, the information $p \vee q$ means that either property p or property q holds in the current state of the world. Suppose p is indeed true. The arrival of $\neg p$ certainly changes the agent's perception about p, since she now observes $\neg p$. However, the new input says nothing about q. Indeed, q might have been false all along. As a result, q cannot be concluded after the update is performed. It was this perception of change that motivated the inclusion of the *disjunction rule* in Katsuno and Mendelzon's postulates for updates [12].

The objective of this section is to analyse how the function d defined previously can be used to evaluate the degree of change caused by new information in both belief revision and updates.

3.2.1.1 Belief Revision

Since for belief revision we are interested in causing a minimal change to the old belief set considered as a whole, the idea is to evaluate distance between classes of valuations, namely the models of the current belief set and the models of the new belief.

We have seen in Definition 1.7 how to extend a distance function between elements of a set to a distance function between sets and between an element and a set. Here, we just need to cater to the special case of contradictory formulae, whose set of models is empty.

Definition 3.2. Let $\mathscr{M}$ and $\mathscr{N}$ be two classes of valuations of **L**. The *set distance D between $\mathscr{M}$ and $\mathscr{N}$*, $D(\mathscr{M}, \mathscr{N})$, is defined as

$$D(\mathscr{M}, \mathscr{N}) = \begin{cases} \inf\{d(M,N) \mid M \in \mathscr{M} \text{ and } N \in \mathscr{N}\} & \Rightarrow \text{if } \mathscr{M} \text{ and } \mathscr{N} \text{ are both non-empty} \\ \infty & \Rightarrow \text{otherwise} \end{cases}$$

Remark 3.1. If the class $\mathscr{M}$ is composed solely by a valuation I, that is, if $\mathscr{M} = \{I\}$, we shall call $D(\{I\}, \mathscr{N})$, the *point distance D between I and $\mathscr{N}$*, and for simplicity, we will drop the outer braces in $\{I\}$ and write $D(I, \mathscr{N})$ instead.

Proposition 3.2. *D is symmetric.*

Proof. This follows directly from Definition 3.2 and Proposition 3.1, since by (M3), d is symmetric.

Intuitively, the greater the distance between two formulae, the bigger the loss of information which occurs when combining them consistently. If the two formulae are consistent with each other, then they have a model M in common. By (M1), $d(M,M) = 0$ (see Proposition 3.10). On the other hand, if either formula is contradictory, then no useful information can be retrieved from it, and in this extreme case, the loss of information relative to it is maximum.

Now, the models of φ which preserve most the informational content of ψ according to distance d are those associated with minimum distance, i.e., those in the following set:

(3.1) $\{I \in \text{mod}(\varphi) \mid d(I, \text{mod}(\psi)) = D(\text{mod}(\psi), \text{mod}(\varphi))\}$

That is, we choose the elements in $\text{mod}(\varphi)$ whose distance to some element in $\text{mod}(\psi)$ is minimum. In general, we can define the following ordering of similarity with respect to ψ on the elements of $\mathscr{I}$:

Definition 3.3. For any $M,N \in \mathscr{I}$ and each formula ψ of propositional logic, $M \leq_\psi N$ if and only if

① $\text{mod}(\psi) = \varnothing$; or
② $\exists I \in \text{mod}(\psi)$ such that $\forall I' \in \text{mod}(\psi) \, d(M,I) \leq d(N,I')$

That is, M is at least as close to N with respect to ψ if there is some model I of ψ such that $d(M,I)$ is less than or equal to the distance between N and any model of ψ.

We can now show some properties of $\leq_\psi$ that we will need for our revision operation.

Proposition 3.3. *For each propositional formula ψ, $\leq_\psi$ is a pre-order.*

Proof. Reflexivity follows trivially when $\text{mod}(\psi) \neq \varnothing$ and condition ① ensures that it holds when $\text{mod}(\psi) = \varnothing$. For transitivity, the interesting case is as follows: suppose $M \leq_\psi N$, and $N \leq_\psi O$. If $M \leq_\psi N$, then $\exists I_1 \in \text{mod}(\psi)$, such that $\forall I' \in \text{mod}(\psi) \, d(M,I_1) \leq d(N,I')$. If $N \leq_\psi O$, then $\exists I_2 \in \text{mod}(\psi)$ such that $\forall I'' \in \text{mod}(\psi) \, d(N,I_2) \leq d(O,I'')$. $I_2 \in \text{mod}(\psi)$. Thus, in particular, $d(M,I_1) \leq d(N,I_2)$, and hence $M \leq_\psi O$.

Now consider the following function χ which assigns every propositional formula ψ to the pre-order $\leq_\psi$ on $\mathscr{I}$ defined above.

Definition 3.4. For each formula ψ of propositional logic

$\chi(\psi) = \{\leq_\psi, \mathscr{I}\}$

It should not surprise the reader that χ is in fact a faithful assignment for belief revision in Katsuno and Mendelzon's sense (see Section 2.2):

Proposition 3.4. *χ is a faithful assignment for belief revision.*

Proof. By Proposition 3.3, for each propositional formula ψ, $\leq_\psi$ is a pre-order. It can be seen easily that $\leq_\psi$ is also total. We are left to prove:

1. *If $M, N \in \mathrm{mod}\,(\psi)$, then $M <_\psi N$ does not hold.*
   If $M \in \mathrm{mod}(\psi)$, then $M \leq_\psi N$, because $\forall I' \in \mathrm{mod}(\psi)$, $d(M,M) \leq d(N,I')$.
   Also, $N \leq_\psi M$ for the same reason, since $N \in \mathrm{mod}\,(\psi)$, and hence $M \equiv_\psi N$.
2. *If $M \in \mathrm{mod}\,(\psi)$ and $N \notin \mathrm{mod}\,(\psi)$, then $M <_\psi N$.*
   Clearly, $M \leq_\psi N$ (see previous item). $N \not\leq_\psi M$, because since $N \notin \mathrm{mod}\,(\psi)$ and $d(M,M) = 0$, $\neg \exists I \in \mathrm{mod}\,(\psi)$ such that $d(N,I) \leq d(M,M)$.
3. *If $\psi \leftrightarrow \varphi$, then $\leq_\psi = \leq_\varphi$.*
   This follows directly, since d and $\leq_\psi$ are defined semantically.

In [11], Katsuno and Mendelzon used the same distance function d to define a faithful assignment for belief revision and prove that Dalal's revision operator [4] verifies the AGM postulates. The idea above is similar but corrects a few problems. They define a total pre-order $\leq_\psi$ on $\mathscr{I}$ as

$$I \leq_\psi J \text{ if and only if } \mathrm{dist}(\mathrm{mod}\,(\psi), I) \leq \mathrm{dist}(\mathrm{mod}\,(\psi), J)$$

where

$$\mathrm{dist}(\mathrm{mod}\,(\psi), I) = \min_{J \in \mathrm{mod}\,(\psi)} d(J, I).$$

This ordering is not well-defined in the general case, as ψ may be inconsistent and hence $\mathrm{mod}\,(\psi) = \varnothing$. As it turns out, a similar problem occurs with Dalal's revision operator when ψ is inconsistent (see discussions and comparisons with other work later in this chapter).

If $\mathrm{mod}\,(\psi)$ is non-empty, the ordering $\leq_\psi$ defines a system of spheres around $\mathrm{mod}\,(\psi)$. The innermost sphere contains the models of ψ, the next sphere contains these and the valuations which differ from these by the truth-value of one propositional variable, and so forth (see Figure 3.1).

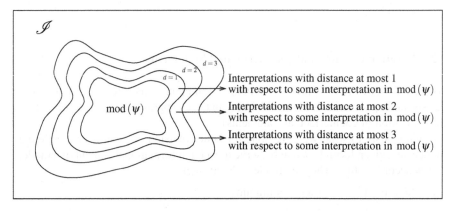

Fig. 3.1 A system of spheres around $\mathrm{mod}\,(\psi)$ based on $\leq_\psi$

The valuations which are closer to the centre preserve more of the informational content of ψ (according to d). When $d = 0$, all of the informational content of ψ

is kept, since we are still within the boundaries of $\text{mod}(\psi)$. The farther away we are from the centre, the bigger the loss of information, because other valuations which do not satisfy ψ are included as well, for instance, those which differ with respect to the value of one propositional variable, and so forth. In the extreme case, all information is lost and we are left with the whole of $\mathscr{I}$ (which essentially means that the agent only "knows" the tautologies). For a concrete example, consider $p \wedge q$. In the centre we have $\text{mod}(p \wedge q)$, and then the valuations that differ from these with respect to to at most the truth-value of either p or q and then those valuations which differ with respect to at most the truth-values of both. This can be seen in Figure 3.2. To grasp the intuitive meaning of this, we reason as follow: if you believe in $p \wedge q$ and you are told that it is not the case that both p and q are true, then the next best thing is to think that at least one of them is still true; hence, $(p \vee q) \wedge \neg(p \wedge q)$. Subsequently, if that is still not the case, nothing about p or q can be said.[1]

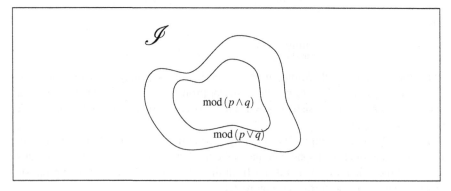

Fig. 3.2 A system of spheres around $\text{mod}(p \wedge q)$ based on $\leq_{p \wedge q}$

3.2.1.2 Action Updates and Counterfactual Statements

As we mentioned in the previous section, action updates require a *pointwise* comparison among the models of the old theory in the evaluation of change (and so does the evaluation of counterfactual statements).

Analogously to what we have done for belief revision, we can characterise the models of a given formula φ that preserve most the informational content of a model I of ψ according to d. They are in the following set:

(3.2) $\{J \in \text{mod}(\varphi) \mid d(I, J) \text{ is minimum}\}$

For the general case, it is interesting to compare the elements of $\mathscr{I}$ with respect to similarity to a given world I. Again, we need an auxiliary ordering:

---

[1] The only thing the agent will then believe are the properties of the logic itself, i.e., its tautologies. AGM does not allow these to be revised since the resulting revised belief set is still within the logic. See Chapter 7 for an interesting discussion about this.

Definition 3.5 (Closeness of valuations via function d).

$M \leq_I N$ if and only if $d(M,I) \leq d(N,I)$

That is, a valuation M is at least as close to valuation I as valuation N if and only if its distance to I is not greater than the distance between N and I.

Proposition 3.5. *For each $I \in \mathscr{I}$, $\leq_I$ is a pre-order.*

Proof. Straightforward.

We can also define the following function ξ_d:

Definition 3.6. For each $I \in \mathscr{I}$,

$$\xi_d(I) = \{\leq_I, \mathscr{I}\}$$

Proposition 3.6. ξ_d *is a faithful assignment for updates.*

Proof. We have already shown that for each I, $\leq_I$ is a pre-order. Now, notice that if $N \neq I$, then $d(N,I) > 0$. On the other hand, $d(I,I) = 0$, and hence $I <_I N$, for any $N \in \mathscr{I}$, such that $N \neq I$.

Each ordering $\leq_I$ induces a series of r-neighbourhoods with centre I. For $r = 1$, we have $B_1(I) = \{J \in \mathscr{I} \mid d(I,J) < 1\} = \{I\}$ (centring). For $r = 2$, we have $J \in B_2(I)$ if and only if $d(I,J) < 2$, that is, all valuations that differ from I in *at most* one propositional variable, and so forth. This is a special case of Lewis' comparative similarity systems, and is illustrated in Figure 3.3.

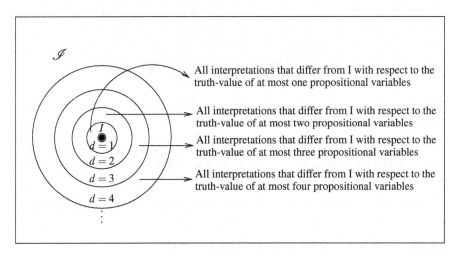

Fig. 3.3 A system of spheres around I based on $\leq_I$

More formally,

Definition 3.7. Take the metric space $\langle \mathscr{I}, d \rangle$ and consider the following function $\odot : \mathscr{I} \longrightarrow 2^{\mathscr{I}}$, such that $\odot(I) = \{B_k(I) \mid k \in \mathbb{N}\}$. That is, $\odot$ assigns open balls of radius $k = 0, 1, 2, \ldots$ to elements of $\mathscr{I}$.

Proposition 3.7. $\odot$ *is a centred system of spheres.*

Proof. (centring) Take $k = 1$. $B_1(I) = \{J \in \mathscr{I} \mid d(I, J) < 1\} = \{I\}$. Thus, $\{I\} \in \odot(I)$.
(nesting)   Suppose $S, T \in \odot(I)$. It follows that $S = B_{k_s}$ and $T = B_{k_t}$ for some $k_s, k_t \in$
* $\mathbb{N}$. If $k_s = k_t$, then $S = T$. Suppose $k_s < k_t$. If $M \in S$, then $d(I, M) < k_s$ and*
*   hence $d(I, M) < k_t$. Therefore, $M \in T$ (and similarly for $k_t < k_s$).*
(closure)   Closure under unions and non-empty intersections is satisfied trivially,
*   since $\mathscr{I}$ is finite.*

The proposition above shows that the same similarity notion used for updates can be used to evaluate counterfactuals. In fact, it has been shown that updates and counterfactuals are related [13, 9]. It is possible to translate between axioms for updates (postulates) and axioms for counterfactuals. This can be found in detail in [15].

The idea is that to evaluate a counterfactual in a given belief set, first accommodate its antecedent in each one of the models of the belief set causing a minimal change (that is, *update* it), and then evaluate whether the consequent holds in the updated belief state.

We finalise this section by considering a variation of the function d that can also take causality into account. Causal changes are changes in the truth-values of propositions that are triggered by changes in the values of other propositions.

One important issue in considering the distance between valuations in this context is how to evaluate what changes are in fact *primitive changes*. Let us define that a change in the value of a propositional variable of a valuation is primitive if it does not depend on the change of value of any other propositional variable.

Obviously, we have to refine the above definition in order to say explicitly what *dependence* means. We need to assume that the information representing causality is given somehow. This can be done in the following way.

Definition 3.8. A *causal rule* is an expression of the form $\varphi \Rightarrow D$, where φ is a formula of propositional logic and D is a disjunct.

Notice that we have intentionally used a new connective above. This is to avoid confusion with the connective $\rightarrow$ of our logic. The intuitive reading of a rule $\varphi \Rightarrow D$ is that

"changes leading to the satisfaction of D are triggered by changes leading to the satisfaction of φ"

Definition 3.9. A *causal rule set* is a set of causal rules.

Definition 3.10 (Satisfiability of causal rules). A valuation I satisfies a causal rule $R = \varphi \Rightarrow D$, in symbols, $I \Vdash R$, if and only if $I \Vdash \varphi \wedge D$. $\vdash$ is defined similarly: $\psi \vdash \varphi \Rightarrow D$ if and only if $\psi \vdash \varphi \wedge D$.

The reason why we require that I satisfy φ *and D* above can be justified as follows: if I does not satisfy φ, then I does not activate the triggering condition of R; therefore, the changes reported by D should not be taken into account anyway. On the other hand, if I does satisfy φ, then we expect to reevaluate the change occurred only if D is also satisfied by I. Therefore, the worlds for which we should reevaluate change with respect to R are exactly those which satisfy φ and D.

Now suppose J is a model of R and we want to evaluate the distance between J and I. The change between I and J measured by d has to be adjusted by exactly the number of propositional variables in D that are assigned different truth-values by I.

Therefore, we can define the following distance function, which takes into account a set of causal rules $\mathcal{R}$.

Definition 3.11. Let $\mathcal{R}$ be a set of causal rules and let I and J be two valuations. The *relativised distance between J and I with respect to the set* $\mathcal{R}$, in symbols, $d_{\mathcal{R}}(I,J)$, is calculated as follows:
$d_{\mathcal{R}}(I,J) =$

$$\begin{cases} d(I,J), \text{ if } J \not\Vdash R \text{ for any } R \in \mathcal{R} \text{ or} \\ d(I,J) - \sup\{d(I',I) \mid \varphi \Rightarrow D \in \mathcal{R} \text{ and } I' \in \text{mod}(D)\} \text{ otherwise} \end{cases}$$

Notice that, unlike d, $d_{\mathcal{R}}$ is not symmetric.
We now consider a slightly different approach to the evaluation of change.

3.3 Qualitative Measurements of Change

In the previous section we considered a distance function whose value provides a quantitative measure of the degree of similarity between valuations and classes of valuations. One advantage of this is that it makes possible a direct definition of a total ordering on $\mathcal{I}$.

Even though the distance d provides an indication of the magnitude of the difference between two valuations, it has little to say about the qualitative value of the change in information itself.

In this section, we consider another way of comparing valuations by analysing the sets of propositional variables which differ with respect to the truth-values assigned by these valuations. The function presented here was initially proposed by Borgida [2].

Definition 3.12. Let M and N be two elements of $\mathcal{I}$. The *difference set between M and N*, in symbols, diff(M,N), is the set of propositional variables p_i for which $M(p_i) \neq N(p_i)$.

It is easy to see that diff is a symmetric function. That is, diff$(M,N) =$ diff(N,M). diff is not a metric in the sense of Definition 1.6, even though it is possible to generate one from it. For instance, notice that for any valuations M and N, $|\text{diff}(M,N)| = d(M,N)$.

The function diff was used in a number of formalisms both for belief revision and updates, including Borgida's revision operator, extended in [5], Winslett's *possible models approach* [19], Weber's revision operator [18] and, in a sense, in Satoh's formalism as well [16].

Similarly to what was done to the function d, we can define closeness with respect to a given valuation I via the function diff presented above, in symbols, $\sqsubseteq_I$, in the following way:

Definition 3.13 (Closeness of valuations using the function diff).

$M \sqsubseteq_I N$ if and only if $\text{diff}(M,I) \subseteq \text{diff}(N,I)$

Proposition 3.8. $\sqsubseteq_I$ *is a pre-order.*

Proof. It is straightforward to see that $\sqsubseteq_I$ is reflexive. For transitivity, suppose that $M \sqsubseteq_I N$. It follows that $\text{diff}(M,I) \subseteq \text{diff}(N,I)$. Similarly, if $N \sqsubseteq_I O$, then $\text{diff}(N,I) \subseteq \text{diff}(O,I)$. It follows that $\text{diff}(M,I) \subseteq \text{diff}(O,I)$, and hence $M \sqsubseteq_I O$.

The reader might want to check that $\sqsubseteq_I$ is also antisymmetric. However, unlike $\leq_I$, $\sqsubseteq_I$ is not a total ordering on $\mathscr{I}$:

Example 3.1. Consider three valuations I, M and N, such that $I(p) = M(p) = tt$, $I(q) = N(q) = tt$ and $M(q) = N(p) = ff$. I, M and N agree in the truth values of all other propositional variables.

It follows that $\text{diff}(M,I) = \{q\}$ and $\text{diff}(N,I) = \{p\}$. Neither $\text{diff}(M,I) \subseteq \text{diff}(N,I)$, nor $\text{diff}(N,I) \subseteq \text{diff}(M,I)$, and therefore M and N are incomparable with respect to $\sqsubseteq_I$.

Using function diff directly to evaluate similarity between valuations according to Definition 3.13 has some implications for belief revision. The example above demonstrates that $\sqsubseteq_I$ defines a partial order on $\mathscr{I}$. In [11, Theorem 5.2], Katsuno and Mendelzon showed that partial pre-orders on $\mathscr{I}$ can be associated with revision operators which only verify a weaker version of the AGM postulates. The weakening applies basically to postulate (R6), which is dropped in favour of the rules below:

(R6′)   If $\psi \circ_a A \rightarrow B$ and $\psi \circ_a B \rightarrow A$, then $\psi \circ_a A \leftrightarrow \psi \circ_a B$
(R6″) $(\psi \circ_a A) \wedge (\psi \circ_a B) \rightarrow \psi \circ_a (A \vee B)$

Note the similarities between (R6′) above and (U6) and between (R6″) and (U7):

(U6)   If $\psi \diamond A \rightarrow B$ and $\psi \diamond B \rightarrow A$, then $\psi \diamond A \leftrightarrow \psi \diamond B$
(U7)   If ψ is complete, then $(\psi \diamond A) \wedge (\psi \diamond B) \rightarrow \psi \diamond (A \vee B)$

(R6′) and (U6) are identical. In (U7), the requirement that ψ is complete is to make sure that there is just one valuation satisfying it, if any. In fact, it is because of the formulation of (U7) that Katsuno and Mendelzon require that the language be defined over a *finite* set of propositional variables.

Not surprisingly, all the revision operators defined via this function [2, 16, 18] fail to verify (R6), even though they are shown to verify weaker versions of it. It must be pointed out that at that time, there was still some confusion about the differences between belief revision and updates and about what they could be applied to. Thus, some of the *revision* postulates cited above in fact could be seen as *update* postulates. The situation was clarified by Katsuno and Mendelzon in [12] in a follow-up to their paper in [11].

However, diff can be used as a distance function for updates, since the orderings required for that operation need not be total. In fact, we have shown in [8] that $\sqsubseteq_I$ can be used in the definition of a faithful assignment for updates.

Since we now have some distance functions formally defined, it is now possible to use them specifically for belief revision and in the reasoning about actions. First, let us consider some representation issues.

3.4 Representation Issues

As we have seen previously, belief revision can be perceived as a selection of some of the models of the new input to the old theory. This selection is based on similarity to the models of the old theory. Thus, if we had some way of manipulating these models syntactically, a simplification of the method could be achieved. One alternative is to represent the formulae in an appropriate normal form. Disjunctive normal form is especially suitable for reasoning about models.

Definition 3.14. A formula is said to be in *disjunctive normal form* (DNF) if it is a disjunction of conjunctions of literals.

In other words, a formula φ is in disjunctive normal form if it is in the form of $D_1 \vee D_2 \vee \ldots \vee D_k$, where each D_i is a disjunct (i.e., a conjunction of literals).

Remark 3.2. We will use capital letters from the middle of the alphabet, P, Q, ... to denote disjuncts of propositional logic.

Even though there is the extra cost of converting the formulae to DNF, the conversion itself does not reduce the expressive power of the language, since for any formula φ of classical propositional logic there exists a tautologically equivalent formula φ' in DNF [6, Corollary 15C]. Some people may argue that DNF is not a suitable representation for formulae, because it undermines the perception of the formula by a human, but normal forms greatly simplify syntactical manipulations and have been widely used in theorem-proving techniques, e.g., resolution, and many theorem provers, e.g., [7]. Perhaps the most common example is the language of horn clauses, which constitutes a special case of formulae in *conjunctive normal form* (CNF) [17]. These formulae are constituted by a conjunction of disjunctions of literals. It is well known that there are algorithms to convert between CNF and DNF. The cost of the conversion is linear in the size of the formula if a conversion algorithm such as the *matrix method* is used. This method can be found in [1]. It is worth pointing out, however, that even though a set of clauses can be seen as a formula in CNF, that is, the conjunction of all clauses in the set, each clause itself is a special case of a formula in DNF: each disjunct is constituted by a single literal and each clause has exactly one positive literal (and zero or more negative literals).

Example 3.2 (Formulae in disjunctive normal form).

formula	equivalent formula in DNF
$p \vee q$	$p \vee q$
$q \rightarrow \neg r$	$\neg q \vee \neg r$
$p \leftrightarrow q$	$(p \wedge q) \vee (\neg p \wedge \neg q)$

In our case, the advantage of working with DNF is that we can see each of the disjuncts of a formula ψ in DNF as a representation of a class of its models. Moreover, we will see that it is also easier to calculate distances between models in this way.

Our operators, to be presented next will be based on the composition of disjuncts and the function d. Therefore, it is useful to specialise this function for this particular case. We have already extended d to classes of valuations in the previous chapter. Let us generalise the notion, so we can speak of distance between formulae as well. As expected, the distance between formulae can be introduced as the distance between their sets of models.

Definition 3.15. Let φ and ψ be formulae of propositional logic. The *semantical distance between φ and ψ, $dist_{\mathscr{I}}(\varphi, \psi)$,* is defined as $D(\text{mod}(\varphi), \text{mod}(\psi))$.

Example 3.3. According to Definition 3.15, $dist_{\mathscr{I}}(p \rightarrow q, p \wedge q) < dist_{\mathscr{I}}(p \rightarrow q, p \wedge \neg q)$, because we can take $M \in \text{mod}(p \rightarrow q)$, such that $M \Vdash p \wedge q$. It follows that $D(\text{mod}(p \rightarrow q), \text{mod}(p \wedge q)) = 0$. On the other hand, it is easy to check that $\inf\{d(M,N) | M \in \text{mod}(p \rightarrow q), N \in \text{mod}(p \wedge \neg q)\} = 1$.

Definition 3.16. Let ψ be a formula of propositional logic. The expression $\text{var}(\psi)$ will denote the set of propositional variables occurring in ψ.

Since we are considering finite sets of propositional variables, the metric d is in fact bounded. In the language **L**, d is bounded by $|\mathscr{P}|$. In particular,

Proposition 3.9. *Let φ and ψ be two satisfiable formulae of propositional logic.*

$$dist_{\mathscr{I}}(\varphi, \psi) \leq |\text{var}(\psi) \cup \text{var}(\varphi)|$$

Proof. $dist_{\mathscr{I}}$ is defined as the minimum distance between any two elements of mod (ψ) and mod (φ), or ∞ if any of them is empty (which is not the case here). For the propositional symbols that do not occur in one of the formulae, we can always pick a truth-value assignment that agrees with respect to the truth-value of the symbol in the other assignment.

Proposition 3.10. *Let φ and ψ be two formulae of propositional logic.*

$dist_\mathscr{I}(\varphi, \psi) = 0$ *if and only if* $\mathrm{mod}\,(\varphi) \cap \mathrm{mod}\,(\psi) \neq \varnothing$

Proof. ($\Leftarrow$) *If* $\mathrm{mod}\,(\varphi) \cap \mathrm{mod}\,(\psi) \neq \varnothing$, *then* $\exists M \in \mathscr{I}$ *such that* $M \Vdash \varphi$ *and* $M \Vdash \psi$. *By Definition 3.1,* $d(M, M) = 0$; *by Definition 3.2,* $D(\mathrm{mod}\,(\varphi), \mathrm{mod}\,(\psi)) = 0$, *and then* $dist_\mathscr{I}(\varphi, \psi) = 0$.
($\Rightarrow$) *If* $dist_\mathscr{I}(\varphi, \psi) = 0$, *then* $\exists M \in \mathrm{mod}\,(\varphi)$ *and* $\exists N \in \mathrm{mod}\,(\psi)$, *such that* $d(M, N) = 0$. *By Proposition 3.1,* $M = N$, *and hence* $\mathrm{mod}\,(\varphi) \cap \mathrm{mod}\,(\psi) \neq \varnothing$.

There are two advantages to using DNF. The first one is the calculation of the distance between disjuncts, which we show next. The second one is that revision can be made by simple superimposition of literals. This will be shown in the next section.

Definition 3.17. Let P and Q be disjuncts of propositional logic. The *syntactical distance between P and Q, $dist(P, Q)$,* is defined as

$dist(P, Q) =$

$$\begin{cases} \infty, \textit{ if either } P \textit{ or } Q \textit{ is contradictory (or both); or} \\ \text{the number of distinct pairs of opposite literals in } P \text{ and } Q \text{ otherwise} \end{cases}$$

where by *opposite literals* we mean literals of the same propositional variable that have different truth-value assignments.

Proposition 3.11. *Let P and Q be disjuncts of propositional logic.*

$dist(P, Q) = dist_\mathscr{I}(P, Q)$.

Proof. This follows directly from the definitions.

Example 3.4.
$dist(p \wedge q, \neg q) = dist_\mathscr{I}(p \wedge q, \neg q) = D(\mathrm{mod}\,(p \wedge q), \mathrm{mod}\,(\neg q)) = 1$.
$dist(p \wedge q, r) = dist_\mathscr{I}(p \wedge q, r) = D(\mathrm{mod}\,(p \wedge q), \mathrm{mod}\,(r)) = 0$.

3.5 Revision of Formulae

All of the operators in this chapter will be defined for formulae in DNF through manipulation of their disjuncts. However, in order to model the different changes in information, this combination has to reflect the particular requirements of each kind of information change. For example, as we saw, provided the new belief is not itself contradictory, the revision operation results in a consistent belief set even if the original belief set was previously inconsistent. This property is not shared by the update operation.

We provide two basic forms of combining formulae in DNF, or rather, their disjuncts, namely, *prioritised revision of disjuncts* and *prioritised update of disjuncts*.

They will be used to model belief revision and updates, respectively. The term "prioritised" is used because the disjunct which revises (or updates) is assumed to have priority over the revised (updated) one. This is done in order to verify the *principle of primacy of the update*.

Definition 3.18 (Prioritised revision of disjuncts). Let $P = \bigwedge_i l_i$ and Q be disjuncts of propositional logic.

The *prioritised revision of P by Q, denoted $P \overset{\frown}{Q}^*$*, is a new disjunct R, such that

$$R = \begin{cases} Q, \text{ if } P \text{ is contradictory} \\ Q \wedge \{l_i \mid \text{neither } l_i \text{ nor its opposite literal occur in } Q\} \text{ otherwise} \end{cases}$$

The first condition in Definition 3.18 ensures that the disjunct to be revised will be ignored in case it is contradictory. This condition is the only consistency check necessary to achieve (consistent) revisions and can be easily performed, since it amounts to checking whether a disjunct has both positive and negative occurrences of the same propositional variable. The second condition selects the literals that can be included in the revised disjunct. Literals l_i occurring in P whose negation occurs in Q should not be included in the revised disjunct to avoid contradiction. On the other hand, if l_i itself occurs in Q, then there is no need to include it either, as the revised disjunct always contains Q and therefore l_i as well.

Note that a disjunct P is associated with a class of models. Another way of visualising this is to see it as a syntactical representation of a *partial valuation*, that is, a valuation in which the truth-values of some propositional variables are undefined, namely those which do not occur in P. When P is to be revised by another disjunct Q, they may share some propositional variables. Whenever the truth-values of these propositional variables do not agree, the one associated with Q overrides the one associated with P — this is the *corrective* part of the revision. Undefined values in either of the valuations are defined in terms of the available values in the other — this is the *consistent* part of the revision. Combining disjuncts in this way is a sort of *prioritised zipping* (see Figure 3.7). This is not to say that every zipped pair of disjuncts fares equally with respect to minimal change. Obviously, some combinations are more compatible (i.e., have minimum distance). These will be the ones we will keep as the result of the revision.

We now establish some important properties of this method.

Proposition 3.12. $P \overset{\frown}{Q}^* \vdash Q$.

Proof. This follows immediately from Definition 3.18, since all the literals in Q are always preserved.

Proposition 3.13. $P \overset{\frown}{Q}^*$ *is contradictory if and only if Q is contradictory.*

Proof. According to Definition 3.18, if P is contradictory then it is ignored in the process.

Propositions 3.12 and 3.13 will ultimately ensure that (R1) and (R3) are verified, respectively.

So far we have defined how to 'resolve' or 'revise' the disjuncts of a formula in DNF, but this is not enough to achieve revisions of the formulae as a whole. What still remains to be done is to define which combinations are to be kept after a revision operation.

In order to simplify matters and lighten the notation, the following convention will be assumed:

Remark 3.3. The formulae involved in the operations to be defined next are assumed to be in DNF. Moreover, if ψ is in DNF, we say that $P \in \psi$ whenever P is a disjunct occurring in ψ.

Definition 3.19 (Revision of formulae). Let ψ and φ be formulae in DNF. The *revision of ψ by φ, $\psi \circ_r \varphi$*, is a new formula γ in DNF such that:

$$\gamma \leftrightarrow \bigvee \{\widehat{PQ}^* \mid P \in \psi, Q \in \varphi, \text{ and } dist(P, Q) \text{ is minimum}\}$$

That is, to compute the revision of ψ by φ, consider the *Cartesian product* of the disjuncts in ψ and φ, then choose those pairs with minimum distance according to *dist*, and finally take the disjunction of the revision of disjuncts in all such pairs. Strictly speaking, there will be a number of such formulae γ, since one can pick the revised disjuncts in any order. Obviously, they will be all equivalent modulo $\vdash$.

The operator $\circ_r$ takes advantage of the good properties of formulae in DNF: disjuncts are effectively syntactical representations of classes of models. Moreover, superimposing a disjunct Q over a disjunct P is the same as selecting the models of Q that are closest to models of P with respect to distance d. The whole revision process becomes much simpler, because it amounts to selecting the combinations with minimum disagreement and then applying the simple superimposition procedure.

Example 3.5 ($p \wedge q$ revised by $\neg q$).

Here there is just one combination to consider. Therefore, we just superimpose $\neg q$ over $p \wedge q$. This results in $p \wedge \neg q$. Semantically, this means that the models of $\neg q$ that are most similar to models of $p \wedge q$ are exactly those which satisfy p.

The revision operator just defined also demonstrates that contraction is not necessarily more primitive than revision, as suggested by the *Levi Identity*, mentioned in Chapter 2, page 19.

We now analyse properties of the revision operator just defined.

3.6 Properties of the Revision Operator $\circ_r$

One of the things we want to ensure is the success of the revision operation. This is required by (R1) (see page 20).

Proposition 3.14. $\mathrm{mod}\,(\psi \circ_r \varphi) \subseteq \mathrm{mod}\,(\varphi)$.

Proof. By Definition 3.19, $\psi \circ_r \varphi$ will be constituted by disjuncts of the form $\widehat{PQ}^*$, where $Q \in \varphi$. By Proposition 3.12, $\widehat{PQ}^* \vdash Q$, and then $\mathrm{mod}\,(\widehat{PQ}^*) \subseteq \mathrm{mod}\,(Q)$. If $M \in \mathrm{mod}\,(\psi \circ_r \varphi)$, then $M \Vdash R$ for some $R \in \psi \circ_r \varphi$, and hence $M \Vdash Q$ for some $Q \in \mathrm{mod}\,(\varphi)$. It follows that $M \in \mathrm{mod}\,(\varphi)$.

Proposition 3.15. $\mathrm{mod}\,(\psi \circ_r \varphi) = \varnothing$ *if and only if* $\mathrm{mod}\,(\varphi) = \varnothing$.

Proof. By Definition 3.19, $\psi \circ_r \varphi$ will be constituted of disjuncts of the form $\widehat{PQ}^*$, where $P \in \psi$ and $Q \in \varphi$. By Proposition 3.13, $\widehat{PQ}^*$ is unsatisfiable if and only if Q is unsatisfiable. ($\Leftarrow$) If $\mathrm{mod}\,(\varphi) = \varnothing$, then there is no disjunct $Q \in \varphi$ such that Q is satisfiable, and then there is no disjunct $\widehat{PQ}^* \in \psi \circ_r \varphi$ such that $\widehat{PQ}^*$ is satisfiable. Hence, $\mathrm{mod}\,(\psi \circ_r \varphi) = \varnothing$. ($\Rightarrow$) If $\mathrm{mod}\,(\psi \circ_r \varphi) = \varnothing$, then there is no disjunct $\widehat{PQ}^* \in \psi \circ_r \varphi$ such that $\widehat{PQ}^*$ is satisfiable, and then there is no disjunct $Q \in \varphi$ such that Q is satisfiable.

Propositions 3.14 and 3.15 are the counterparts for formulae of propositions 3.12 and 3.13.

From the definition of revision of formulae and the properties of d, we can also characterise the models of $\psi \circ_r \varphi$:

Proposition 3.16. *Suppose* $M \in \mathrm{mod}\,(\varphi)$. $M \in \mathrm{mod}\,(\psi \circ_r \varphi)$ *if and only if* $\forall N \in \mathrm{mod}\,(\varphi)$, $\forall I' \in \mathrm{mod}\,(\psi)$, $\exists I \in \mathrm{mod}\,(\psi)$ *such that* $d(M,I) \leq d(N,I')$.

Proof. ($\Leftarrow$) Suppose that $\forall N \in \mathrm{mod}\,(\varphi)$, $\forall I' \in \mathrm{mod}\,(\psi)$, $\exists I \in \mathrm{mod}\,(\psi)$ such that

(3.3) $d(M,I) \leq d(N,I')$

but $M \notin \mathrm{mod}\,(\psi \circ_r \varphi)$.

By Proposition 3.15, $\mathrm{mod}\,(\psi \circ_r \varphi) \neq \varnothing$, and then $\exists O \Vdash \widehat{PQ}^*$ for some $P \in \psi$, $Q \in \varphi$. It follows that $dist(P,Q) < dist(P',Q')$ for all $P' \in \psi$, $Q' \in \varphi$, such that $M \Vdash \widehat{P'Q}$. Therefore, $\exists J \in \mathrm{mod}\,(P)$ such that for all $I'' \in \mathrm{mod}\,(\psi)$

(3.4) $d(O,J) < d(M,I'')$

But this is a contradiction, since $O \Vdash \varphi$, $J \Vdash \psi$ and then by (3.3), $d(M,I) \leq d(O,J)$ (take $I'' = I$ in (3.4)).

($\Rightarrow$) If $M \in \mathrm{mod}\,(\psi \circ_r \varphi)$, then $M \Vdash \widehat{PQ}^*$ for some $P \in \psi$, $Q \in \varphi$, such that $dist(P,Q)$ is minimum. Now, suppose $\exists N \in \mathrm{mod}\,(\varphi)$ and $\exists I' \in \mathrm{mod}\,(\psi)$ such that $\forall I \in \mathrm{mod}\,(\psi)$, $d(N,I') < d(M,I)$. $N \Vdash P'$ and $I' \Vdash Q'$ for some $P' \in \varphi$ and $Q' \in \psi$. It follows that $dist(P',Q') < dist(P,Q'')$ for all $Q'' \in \psi$, a contradiction, since we assumed that $dist(P,Q)$ was minimum.

Corollary 3.1. *Suppose* $M \in \mathrm{mod}\,(\varphi)$. *If* $M \notin \mathrm{mod}\,(\psi \circ_r \varphi)$, *then* $\exists N \in \mathrm{mod}\,(\varphi)$, $\exists I' \in \mathrm{mod}\,(\psi)$, *such that* $\forall I \in \mathrm{mod}\,(\psi)$, $d(N, I') < d(M, I)$.

In the limiting case, when $\mathrm{mod}\,(\psi) = \varnothing$, we have $\mathrm{mod}\,(\psi \circ_r \varphi) = \mathrm{mod}\,(\varphi)$.[2] In the revision of ψ by φ, we are interested in the least conflicting combination of models of ψ and φ. If $\mathrm{mod}\,(\psi) \neq \varnothing$ and a model M of φ is not among the models of the revision of ψ by φ, then it is because there is a model N of φ whose distance from a particular model of ψ is strictly less than the distance between M and *any* model of ψ.

Figure 3.4 shows the trivial situation in belief revision, that is, when a revision in the proper sense is not necessary (remember that expansions are a special case of revisions): both formulae are consistent and have some models in common. New information is used only to refine the information already available in the previous belief state. This corresponds to the verification of (R2).

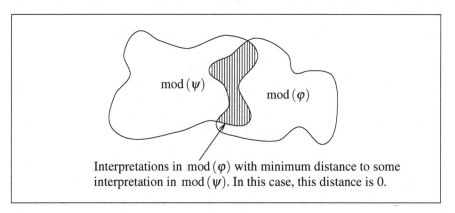

Interpretations in $\mathrm{mod}\,(\varphi)$ with minimum distance to some interpretation in $\mathrm{mod}\,(\psi)$. In this case, this distance is 0.

Fig. 3.4 Valuations in $\mathrm{mod}\,(\psi \circ_r \varphi)$, when $\mathrm{mod}\,(\psi) \cap \mathrm{mod}\,(\varphi) \neq \varnothing$

Figure 3.5 shows the situation when the new formula φ is inconsistent with the previous belief set ψ. The *principle of the primacy of the update* requires higher priority for the new belief. Therefore, it is the previous belief state that has to change and accommodate the new information. In the picture, each contour line around $\mathrm{mod}\,(\psi)$ contains the valuations with one unit of change with respect to some valuation in the level within. In other words, valuations in one layer differ from valuations in the layer immediately inside with respect to the truth-value of some proposition. As we move outwards, one of the contour lines will eventually intersect $\mathrm{mod}\,(\varphi)$, since it is non-empty. The models of the revised belief set are exactly those in the innermost non-empty intersection.

Figure 3.6 represents the situation when the formula representing the previous belief set is contradictory. Nothing of its informational content is used, and the models of the revised belief state are exactly the models of the new formula (if any).

---

[2] See Proposition 3.18.

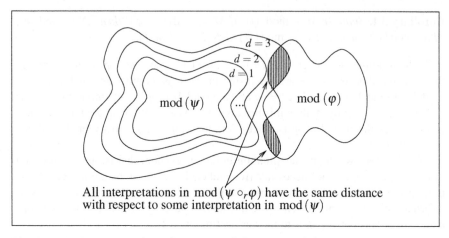

All interpretations in $\mathrm{mod}\,(\psi \circ_r \varphi)$ have the same distance
with respect to some interpretation in $\mathrm{mod}\,(\psi)$

Fig. 3.5 Valuations in $\mathrm{mod}(\psi \circ_r \varphi)$ when $\mathrm{mod}(\psi) \neq \varnothing$, $\mathrm{mod}(\varphi) \neq \varnothing$ and $\mathrm{mod}(\psi) \cap \mathrm{mod}(\varphi) = \varnothing$.

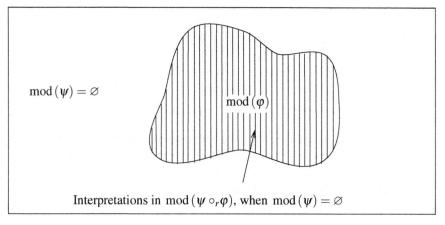

Interpretations in $\mathrm{mod}\,(\psi \circ_r \varphi)$, when $\mathrm{mod}\,(\psi) = \varnothing$

Fig. 3.6 Valuations in $\mathrm{mod}\,(\psi \circ_r \varphi)$, when $\mathrm{mod}\,(\psi) = \varnothing$

We now proceed to prove that $\circ_r$ verifies the AGM postulates for belief revision. From Proposition 3.4, we know that function χ is a faithful assignment for belief revision. According to Theorem 2.2, we only have to show that $\mathrm{mod}(\psi \circ_r \varphi) = \min_{\leq_\psi}(\mathrm{mod}(\varphi))$.

Theorem 3.1. *The revision operation defined by* $\circ_r$ *verifies the AGM postulates for belief revision.*

Proof. ($\subseteq$) i) *If* $\mathrm{mod}\,(\psi) = \varnothing$, *then all disjuncts in* ψ *are contradictory, and hence* $\mathrm{mod}\,(\psi \circ_r \varphi) = \mathrm{mod}\,(\varphi)$. *But if* $\mathrm{mod}\,(\psi) = \varnothing$, *then all valuations are equivalent with respect to* $\leq_\psi$, *and therefore* $\min_{\leq_\psi}(\mathrm{mod}\,(\varphi)) = \mathrm{mod}\,(\varphi)$.

ii) *Suppose* $\mathrm{mod}(\psi) \neq \varnothing$ *and that* $M \in \mathrm{mod}(\psi \circ_r \varphi)$, *but* $M \notin \mathrm{min}_{\leq_\psi}(\mathrm{mod}$ $(\varphi))$. *By proposition 3.14,* $M \in \mathrm{mod}(\varphi)$. *By Proposition 3.16,* $\forall N \in \mathrm{mod}(\varphi)$, $\forall I' \in \mathrm{mod}(\psi)$, $\exists I \in \mathrm{mod}(\psi)$, *such that*

(3.5) $d(M,I) \leq d(N,I')$

$M \notin \mathrm{min}_{\leq_\psi}(\mathrm{mod}(\varphi))$ *and* $\mathrm{mod}(\varphi) \neq \varnothing$; *therefore* $\exists O \in \mathrm{mod}(\varphi)$, *such that* $O <_\psi$ M. *Therefore,* $\exists J \in \mathrm{mod}(\psi)$ *such that* $\forall J' \in \mathrm{mod}(\psi)$

(3.6) $d(O,J) < d(M,J')$

In particular, (3.6) holds for $J' = I$ *of (3.5):* $d(O,J) < d(M,I)$, *and then* $M \notin \mathrm{mod}$ $(\psi \circ_r \varphi)$ *(letting* $N = O$ *and* $I' = J$ *in (3.5)), a contradiction.*

($\supseteq$) *If* $M \in \mathrm{min}_{\leq_\psi}(\mathrm{mod}(\varphi))$, *then* $\neg \exists N \in \mathrm{mod}(\varphi)$, *such that* $N <_\psi M$ *holds.* *That is,* $\neg \exists N \in \mathrm{mod}(\varphi)$, $\exists I \in \mathrm{mod}(\psi)$ *such that* $\forall I' \in \mathrm{mod}(\psi)$, $d(N,I) <_\psi$ $d(M,I')$. *Therefore,* $\forall N \in \mathrm{mod}(\varphi)$, $\forall I \in \mathrm{mod}(\psi)$, $\exists I' \in \mathrm{mod}(\psi)$, *such that* $d(M,I') \leq_\psi d(N,I)$. *By Proposition 3.16,* $M \in \mathrm{mod}(\psi \circ_r \varphi)$.

Proposition 3.17. $\mathrm{mod}(\varphi \circ_r \varphi) = \mathrm{mod}(\varphi)$.

Proof. If $\mathrm{mod}(\varphi) = \varnothing$, then by (R1), $\mathrm{mod}(\varphi \circ_r \varphi) = \varnothing$. By (R3), if $\mathrm{mod}(\varphi \circ_r \varphi) = \varnothing$, then $\mathrm{mod}(\varphi) = \varnothing$. If $\mathrm{mod}(\varphi)$ *is non-empty, then by* (R2), $\mathrm{mod}(\varphi \circ_r \varphi) = \mathrm{mod}(\varphi \wedge \varphi) = \mathrm{mod}(\varphi)$.

Proposition 3.18. *If* $\mathrm{mod}(\psi) = \varnothing$, *then* $\mathrm{mod}(\psi \circ_r \varphi) = \mathrm{mod}(\varphi)$.

Proof. If $\mathrm{mod}(\psi) = \varnothing$, then all disjuncts in ψ are contradictory. By Definition 3.18, $\widehat{PQ}^* = Q$ for all $P \in \psi$, $Q \in \varphi$. It follows that $\vdash \psi \circ_r \varphi \leftrightarrow \varphi$.

It could be argued that the revision operator is then too restrictive in the cases where the previous belief set ψ is inconsistent, but we believe that without extra structural information about ψ, no information can be reasonably "recovered" from it. This situation can be at least partly rectified if the belief base is provided as a set of formulae with some additional information to help in the decision process, either as list, as suggested by Lehmann (see Section 2.9.2), or in a similar way to that proposed by [14]. We will consider these alternatives in the next two chapters.

Corollary 3.2. *If* $\mathrm{mod}(\psi) \cap \mathrm{mod}(\varphi) \neq \varnothing$, *then* $\mathrm{mod}(\psi \circ_r \varphi) = \mathrm{mod}(\varphi \circ_r \psi)$.

Proof. If $\mathrm{mod}(\psi) \cap \mathrm{mod}(\varphi) \neq \varnothing$, then $\psi \wedge \varphi$ is satisfiable. From (R2), it follows that $\mathrm{mod}(\psi \circ_r \varphi) = \mathrm{mod}(\varphi \circ_r \psi) = \mathrm{mod}(\psi) \cap \mathrm{mod}(\varphi)$.

That is, the order in which the revision operator is applied is irrelevant when the formulae involved are consistent with each other.

Proposition 3.19. *Suppose* $\mathrm{mod}(\psi)$ *and* $\mathrm{mod}(\varphi)$ *are both non-empty. If* $\mathrm{mod}(\psi \circ_r \varphi) = \mathrm{mod}(\varphi \circ_r \psi)$, *then* $\mathrm{mod}(\psi) \cap \mathrm{mod}(\varphi) \neq \varnothing$.

Proof. If $\mathrm{mod}(\psi) \neq \varnothing$, then by (R3), $\exists M \in \mathrm{mod}(\varphi \circ_r \psi)$. By (R1), $M \in \mathrm{mod}(\psi)$. By assumption, $M \in \mathrm{mod}(\psi \circ_r \varphi)$. By (R1) again, $M \in \mathrm{mod}(\varphi)$.

The two previous results establish the cases when $\circ_r$ is commutative. It is not associative, though:

Proposition 3.20. $\circ_r$ *is not associative.*

Proof. We give a simple counterexample as a proof.

$$\begin{pmatrix} p \\ \circ_r \\ r \wedge \neg r \end{pmatrix} = \begin{matrix} r \wedge \neg r \wedge p \\ \circ_r \\ q \end{matrix} = q \qquad\qquad \begin{matrix} p \\ \circ_r \\ p \end{matrix} \qquad\qquad \begin{matrix} p \\ \circ_r \\ \begin{pmatrix} r \wedge \neg r \\ \circ_r \\ q \end{pmatrix} \end{matrix} = \begin{matrix} p \\ \circ_r \\ q \end{matrix} = q \wedge p$$

The example above uses a rather trivial case to prove the proposition. However, even if each formula involved in the revision process is itself satisfiable (considered individually), there are cases when $\circ_r$ is not associative (see the discussion in Example 4.1, page 110, in Chapter 4).

We have other reasons to believe that a revision operator *should not be* associative. Consider, for instance, the two sequences of revisions $(\psi \circ_r \varphi) \circ_r \gamma$ and $\psi \circ_r (\varphi \circ_r \gamma)$. For belief revision, there is an implicit notion of priority of the formula that revises. In the first sequence, only the information conveyed by φ is available to the mechanism of revision to compute what information conveyed by ψ shall be preserved in $\psi \circ_r \varphi$. Following [5], we can call this information the *knowledge of ψ retained by $\psi \circ_r \varphi$*. On the other hand, in $\psi \circ_r (\varphi \circ_r \gamma)$, this decision is based on the information conveyed by γ as well. This might affect what is reasonable to continue to believe from formula ψ. Moreover, the information conveyed by φ used to compute the knowledge of ψ retained by $\psi \circ_r (\varphi \circ_r \gamma)$ is not necessarily the same as that used in the decision for $\psi \circ_r \varphi$, since some of it may have not been retained by $\varphi \circ_r \gamma$. A deeper investigation into the plausibility of associativity for belief revision is provided in Chapter 4.

We now turn to a series of examples illustrating the revision operator presented in this chapter.

Example 3.6 (Revisions of Formulae).

1. When the formulae are consistent with each other, the order of the revision is irrelevant (see Corollary 3.2).

   Revision of p by $p \rightarrow (q \wedge r)$ and revision of $p \rightarrow (q \wedge r)$ by p (in DNF p and $\neg p \vee (q \wedge r)$):

   a. $p \circ_r (\neg p \vee (q \wedge r))$

b. $(\neg p \vee (q \wedge r)) \circ_r p$

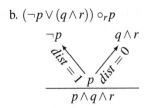

The revision of the disjuncts in the two formulae of this example can be seen in Figure 3.7.

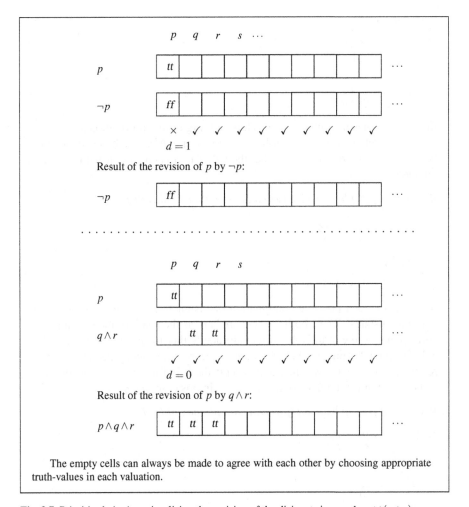

Fig. 3.7 Prioritised *zipping*: visualising the revision of the disjuncts in p and $\neg p \vee (q \wedge r)$

2. If the formulae are inconsistent with each other, then the formula which revises has priority over the revised one.

Revision of $\neg p$ by $p \wedge q$ and revision of $p \wedge q$ by $\neg p$ (formulae are already in DNF):

a. $\neg p \circ_r (p \wedge q)$

$$
\begin{array}{c}
\neg p \\
dist = 1 \Big\uparrow \\
\underline{p \wedge q} \\
p \wedge q
\end{array}
$$

b. $(p \wedge q) \circ_r \neg p$

$$
\begin{array}{c}
p \wedge q \\
dist = 1 \Big\uparrow \\
\underline{\neg p} \\
\neg p \wedge q
\end{array}
$$

In (a.), $p \wedge q$ has priority over $\neg p$. Thus, nothing of the informational content of $\neg p$ can be retained. In (b.), $\neg p$ has priority over $p \wedge q$. The belief in p cannot be kept, since it contradicts $\neg p$, but the belief in q is consistent with $\neg p$ and is retained.

3. *Revision of $p \wedge q$ by $\neg p \vee \neg q$ (formulae are already in DNF):*

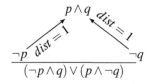

In this case, each possible combination of disjuncts of the two formulae have the same distance. Thus, both of them are kept as the result of the revision. This corresponds to the intuitively correct attitude: either to accept $\neg p$, rejecting the belief in p but keeping the belief in q, or to accept $\neg q$, keeping the belief in p and retracting the belief in q. The agent accepts the belief in $\neg p \vee \neg q$, but still keeps some of the informational content of $p \wedge q$. In this case, $p \vee q$.

4. *Revision of $p \wedge \neg p$ by $p \vee q$ (formulae are already in DNF):*

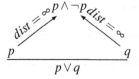

Now we have a contradictory formula to be revised. All disjuncts in the formula are contradictory and are ignored. The result is just the disjunction of the disjuncts in $p \vee q$, which is obviously equivalent modulo $\vdash$ to $p \vee q$.

5. *Revision of $p \vee q$ by $p \vee q$ (formulae are already in DNF):*

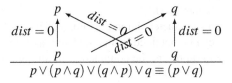

$$p \vee (p \wedge q) \vee (q \wedge p) \vee q \equiv (p \vee q)$$

In this example, consider the revision of a formula by itself. We intuitively do not expect to have any changes, since no knowledge will be added or retracted. Indeed, this is a consequence of postulates (R1), (R2) and (R3) (see Proposition 3.17).

3.7 Other Belief Change Operators

In this section we discuss other operators for belief revision. One such operation is *contraction*. Contraction results in some loss of beliefs previously held by an agent without acquisition of any new information. We have seen that revision can be defined in terms of contractions and expansions.

We also present another operation that can be used in an epistemic context. This operation is called *consolidation* here. The idea is as follows: given two formulae K and φ, where $K \wedge \varphi$ is possibly contradictory, find a formula K' such that $K \vdash K'$ and $K' \wedge \varphi$ is not contradictory, provided φ is itself not contradictory.

3.7.1 Belief Contraction

We have mentioned that revisions and contractions are closely related. Indeed, it is possible to define one of the operations in terms of the other, even though there is no common agreement as to which one should be taken as primitive. According to Levi, we should take contraction as the primitive operation and then define revision as follows, where $K - A$ and K_A^+ denote the contraction and expansion of K by A, respectively. For the case of finite bases represented by a single formula, K_A^+ is simply $K \wedge A$.

$$K \circ_a A = (K - \neg A)_A^+$$

That is, the revision of a belief set K by a formula A is obtained by first contracting K by $\neg A$ (and hence eliminating possible inconsistencies with the new formula to be incorporated), and then adding A. We have seen that the identity above is known as the *Levi Identity*.

Notice that our revision operation was defined without mention to any contraction operation. We have also seen that it is possible to define contractions in terms of revisions in the following way:

$$K - A = (K \circ_a \neg A) \cap A$$

The above identity is known as the *Harper Identity*.

Following Katsuno and Mendelzon's characterisation for finite belief bases used so far [12], a contraction operator $-$ can be obtained from a revision operator $\circ_a$ in the following way. Again, we use ψ to represent the conjunction of all beliefs in a finite belief base K.

Definition 3.20 (Contractions in terms of revisions). Let $\circ_a$ be a revision operator. The contraction of ψ by A, $\psi - A$, is the formula

$$\psi \vee (\psi \circ_a \neg A)$$

where $\psi \circ_a \neg A$ is the revision of ψ by $\neg A$.

In terms of the semantical characterisation for a revision operator presented in Section 2.1 of Chapter 2, this corresponds to

$$\mathrm{mod}\,(\psi - A) = \mathrm{mod}\,(\psi) \cup \min_{\leq_\psi}(\mathrm{mod}\,(\neg A))$$

We recall the AGM postulates for contractions rephrased for finite knowledge bases given in [12] next.

AGM postulates for belief contraction

(C1) ψ implies $\psi - A$
(C2)   If ψ does not imply A, then $\psi - A \leftrightarrow \psi$
(C3)   If A is not a tautology, $\psi - A$ does not imply A
(C4)   If $\psi_1 \leftrightarrow \psi_2$ and $A_1 \leftrightarrow A_2$, then $\psi_1 - A_1 \leftrightarrow \psi_2 - A_2$
(C5) $(\psi - A) \wedge A \rightarrow \psi$

It is possible to state the following theorem:

Theorem 3.2. *If a revision operator $\circ_a$ verifies the AGM postulates for belief revision, then the contraction operator $-$, defined in terms of $\circ_a$ verifies the AGM postulates for contractions.*

Proof.

(C1) *We prove that* $\mathrm{mod}\,(\psi) \subseteq \mathrm{mod}\,(\psi - A)$. *Suppose* $M \in \mathrm{mod}\,(\psi)$, *but* $M \notin \mathrm{mod}\,(\psi - A)$. *Therefore,* $M \notin \mathrm{mod}\,(\psi \vee (\psi \circ_a \neg A))$. *Therefore,* $M \notin \mathrm{mod}\,(\psi) \cup \mathrm{mod}\,(\psi \circ_a \neg A)$, *a contradiction.*

(C2) *We prove that if ψ does not imply A, then* $\mathrm{mod}\,(\psi - A) \subseteq \mathrm{mod}\,(\psi)$. *(The other half follows from (C1).) Suppose* $\exists M \in \mathrm{mod}\,(\psi - A)$, *such that* $M \notin \mathrm{mod}\,(\psi)$. *If* $M \in \mathrm{mod}\,(\psi - A)$, *then* $M \in \mathrm{mod}\,(\psi) \cup \mathrm{mod}\,(\psi \circ_a \neg A)$. *It follows that* i) *either* $M \in \mathrm{mod}\,(\psi)$, *a contradiction; or* ii) $M \in \mathrm{mod}\,(\psi \circ_a \neg A)$. *Since* ψ *does not imply A, $\psi \wedge \neg A$ is satisfiable, and then by (R2),* $\mathrm{mod}\,(\psi \circ_a \neg A) = \mathrm{mod}\,(\psi) \cap \mathrm{mod}\,(\neg A)$. *Therefore,* $M \in \mathrm{mod}\,(\psi)$, *again a contradiction.*

(C3) *We prove that* $\exists M \in \mathrm{mod}(\psi{-}A)$, *such that* $M \notin \mathrm{mod}(A)$. *Since* A *is not a tautology,* $\neg A$ *is satisfiable. By* (R3), $\psi \circ_a \neg A$ *is also satisfiable. By* (R1), $\psi \circ_a \neg A$ *implies* $\neg A$, *and hence* $\psi \circ_a \neg A$ *does not imply* A. *Therefore,* $\exists M \in \mathrm{mod}(\psi \circ_a \neg A)$, *such that* $M \notin \mathrm{mod}(A)$. *Since,* $\mathrm{mod}(\psi{-}A) = \mathrm{mod}(\psi) \cup \mathrm{mod}(\psi \circ_a \neg A)$, $M \in \mathrm{mod}(\psi{-}A)$.

(C4) *This follows directly from* (R4).

(C5) *Suppose* $\exists M \in \mathrm{mod}((\psi{-}A) \wedge A)$, *such that* $M \notin \mathrm{mod}(\psi)$. *If* $M \in \mathrm{mod}((\psi{-}A) \wedge A)$, *then* $M \in \mathrm{mod}(\psi{-}A)$ *and* $M \in \mathrm{mod}(A)$. *If* $M \in \mathrm{mod}(\psi{-}A)$, *then* $M \in \mathrm{mod}(\psi) \cup \mathrm{mod}(\psi \circ_a \neg A)$. *Either* i) $M \in \mathrm{mod}(\psi)$, *a contradiction; or* ii) $M \in \mathrm{mod}(\psi \circ_a \neg A)$; *but then by* (R1), $M \in \mathrm{mod}(\neg A)$. *But again this is a contradiction, since* $M \in \mathrm{mod}(A)$.

As expected, we can define an operator $-_r$ in terms of our operator $\circ_r$ defined in the previous section. In what follows, we assume that given a formula A of propositional logic, there is an algorithm to compute a formula $\neg A'$, such that $\neg A'$ is in DNF and $\vdash A \leftrightarrow A'$.

Definition 3.21. Let ψ and A be two formulae of propositional logic where ψ is in DNF. The contraction of ψ by A, $\psi -_r A$, is the formula

$$\psi -_r A = \psi \vee (\psi \circ_r \neg A).$$

Proposition 3.21. $-_r$ *verifies the AGM postulates for contractions.*

Proof. It follows trivially, since

$$\mathrm{mod}(\psi -_r A) = \mathrm{mod}(\psi) \cup \mathrm{mod}(\psi \circ_r \neg A).$$

The mechanism of the contraction operation may be better understood in semantical terms. Suppose ψ is to be contracted by A, resulting in formula ψ'. If $\psi \nvdash A$, then ψ' is just ψ. On the other hand, if $\psi \vdash A$, then $\mathrm{mod}(\psi) \subseteq \mathrm{mod}(A)$. The goal is to find a formula ψ', such that $\mathrm{mod}(\psi') \subseteq \mathrm{mod}(A)$ does not hold, and yet $\mathrm{mod}(\psi')$ has some resemblance to $\mathrm{mod}(\psi)$. One way of achieving this is to add some valuations from $\mathscr{I} - \mathrm{mod}(A)$ to the class of models of ψ. These valuations, according to Definition 3.20, are those which satisfy the revision of ψ by $\neg A$. That is, valuations which keep as much as possible of the informational content of ψ, and yet satisfy $\neg A$.

Example 3.7 (Belief contraction via Levi Identity).

1. If ψ does not imply A, then $\mathrm{mod}(\psi -_r A) = \mathrm{mod}(\psi)$.

   Contraction of $p \wedge q$ by r: $(p \wedge q) \vee ((p \wedge q) \circ_r \neg r)$

   Revision of $p \wedge q$ by $\neg r$:

Final result:

$$(p \wedge q) \vee (p \wedge q \wedge \neg r) \equiv p \wedge q$$

2. In a contraction of $p \wedge q$ by q, we are interested in "losing" the information about q only. This is different from revising by $\neg q$, because in that case $\neg q$ is accepted after the revision is performed. In other words, when contracting $p \wedge q$ by q, we expect to retain the belief in p, but stay agnostic about q.

Contraction of $p \wedge q$ by q: $(p \wedge q) \vee ((p \wedge q) \circ_r \neg q)$

Revision of $p \wedge q$ by $\neg q$

Final result:

$$(p \wedge q) \vee (p \wedge \neg q) \equiv p$$

3. What should be expected from the contraction of ψ by ψ ?

Contraction of $p \wedge q$ by $p \wedge q$: $(p \wedge q) \vee ((p \wedge q) \circ_r (\neg (p \wedge q)))$

$\neg (p \wedge q) \equiv (\neg p \vee \neg q)$

Revision of $p \wedge q$ by $\neg p \vee \neg q$:

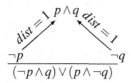

Final result:

$$(p \wedge q) \vee (\neg p \wedge q) \vee (p \wedge \neg q)$$

The result is equivalent to $p \vee q$, since $\mathrm{mod}((p \wedge q) \vee (\neg p \wedge q) \vee (p \wedge \neg q)) = \mathrm{mod}(p \vee q)$. This happens because $p \vee q$ is the formula which conveys most of the informational content of $p \wedge q$, without deriving it. That is, it is not necessary to give up both beliefs in p and q in order to give up the belief in $p \wedge q$.

4. Iteration of contractions
   If $p \wedge q$ is contracted by both p and q in any given order, the result is a complete loss of information, as expected.

Contraction of $p \wedge q$ by p and then by q

4.1: Contraction of $p \wedge q$ by p

Revision of $p \wedge q$ by $\neg p$:

$$p \wedge q$$

$$\underline{\neg p}$$
$$\neg p \wedge q$$

Result of the first contraction:

$$(p \wedge q) \vee (\neg p \wedge q) \equiv q$$

4.2: Contraction of $(p \wedge q) \vee (\neg p \wedge q)$ by q:

Revision of $(p \wedge q) \vee (\neg p \wedge q)$ by $\neg q$:

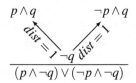

$$\underline{\qquad\qquad\qquad\qquad}$$
$$(p \wedge \neg q) \vee (\neg p \wedge \neg q)$$

Result of the second contraction:

$$(p \wedge q) \vee (\neg p \wedge q) \vee (p \wedge \neg q) \vee (\neg p \wedge \neg q)$$

It is easy to see that $\text{mod}\,((p \wedge q) \vee (\neg p \wedge q) \vee (p \wedge \neg q) \vee (\neg p \wedge \neg q)) = \mathcal{I}$.

5. *Contraction of $p \wedge q$ by $p \vee q$*

$$\neg(p \vee q) \equiv (\neg p \wedge \neg q)$$

Revision of $p \wedge q$ by $\neg p \wedge \neg q$

$$p \wedge q$$

$$\underline{\neg p \wedge \neg q}$$
$$\neg p \wedge \neg q$$

Final result:

$$(p \wedge q) \vee (\neg p \wedge \neg q)$$

It could be argued that the result should be $\neg p \wedge \neg q$, instead of the obtained result $p \leftrightarrow q$. But, notice that a contraction of ψ by A should derive neither A, because of (C2), the success postulate, nor $\neg A$, since otherwise it would be sufficient to define $\psi - A$ as $\psi \circ_a \neg A$. In fact, $\neg p \wedge \neg q \vdash \neg(p \vee q)$, whereas $p \leftrightarrow q \nvdash \neg(p \vee q)$.

3.7.2 Consolidating Information on the Belief Base

Another interesting possibility is to define an operator which, given two formulae ψ and A, returns another formula, say ψ', representing the maximum non-contradictory information from ψ which can be consistently accepted in the presence of A. In other words, if the formula $\psi' \wedge A$ is contradictory, then it is *not* because of ψ' (A must be the culprit). Let us call such an operation *consolidation* and represent the consolidation of ψ by A by the expression $\psi \ominus A$. The motivation for a consolidation is to obtain a consistent belief base from a possibly inconsistent one in the face of new non-contradictory information.

Notice that a consolidation is quite different from a revision. From (R3), we already know that $\psi \circ_r A$ is consistent whenever A is consistent. What we want is to find a mechanism to provide us with the following equivalence:

(3.7) $\psi \circ_r A \equiv (\psi \ominus A) \wedge A$

The idea is to make it possible to replace ψ by $\psi \ominus A$ in the belief base in order to restore its consistency and use ordinary methods of theorem-proving to make deductions.

We need to make a small remark first. The operators are all based on formulae in DNF. Contradiction can be represented by a disjunct, for instance, $p \wedge \neg p$. However, *truth* cannot. We therefore need to represent it somehow. We choose the symbol $\top$. Some minor modifications need to be made in the definition of revision of disjuncts to take this into account. That is, the revised disjunct is just Q when P is $\top$. We avoid redefining them formally. We also use $\bot$ to represent a contradictory disjunct and lighten the notation. The other necessary modifications are in the computation of the distance between disjuncts:

Definition 3.22. Let P and Q be disjuncts of propositional logic.

$dist(P,Q) =$
$$\begin{cases} \infty, & \text{if either } P \text{ or } Q \text{ is contradictory (or both); or} \\ 0, & \text{if either } P \text{ or } Q \text{ is } \top; \text{ or} \\ \text{the number of distinct pairs of opposite literals occurring in } P \text{ and } Q, \\ \quad \text{otherwise} \end{cases}$$

This modification is justified, since $dist(P,Q) = dist_{\mathscr{I}}(P,Q) = D(\mathrm{mod}\,(P), \mathrm{mod}\,(Q))$. Given that neither P nor Q is contradictory, if either of them is $\top$, say P, it follows that $dist(\top,Q) = D(\mathrm{mod}\,(\top), \mathrm{mod}\,(Q))$. Since $\mathrm{mod}\,(\top) = \mathscr{I}$, we have that $dist(\top,Q) = 0$ for any non-contradictory Q, because $D(\mathscr{I},I) = 0$ for any I.

There are a number of cases to be considered in the consolidation of ψ by A, which are summarised in Table 3.1.

In cases (1) and (3) of that table, nothing of the informational content of ψ can be obtained. Thus, we expect to obtain *truth* only. Notice that in (1) we could have chosen to return ψ, because if A is contradictory, then $A \wedge \psi$ would be equivalent to $\psi \circ_r A$ anyway. However, we want to always return a "clean" residual of ψ in the presence of A. If A is contradictory but ψ is not (2), then $\psi \ominus A$ should return ψ

	$\psi \equiv \perp$	$\psi \not\equiv \perp$
$A \equiv \perp$	(1)	(2)
$A \not\equiv \perp$	(3)	(4)

Table 3.1 Cases to consider in the consolidation of ψ by A

itself (or a formula tautologically equivalent to it), since ψ cannot be blamed for the contradiction obtained in the revision of ψ by A. There is also an implicit extreme case embedded in situation (4) above, which is when ψ and A are consistent with each other. In this case we expect $\ominus$ to keep all of the informational content of ψ, and not only the information that together with the revising formula is equivalent to revision itself. There is a subtle difference. For instance, consider the revision of $p \vee q$ by $\neg p$. If we were to follow the requirements stated by equivalence (3.7) only, we could say that $(p \vee q) \ominus \neg p$ is just q, since $(q \wedge \neg p) \equiv (p \vee q) \circ_r \neg p$. This case will be treated separately by the algorithm.

As expected, we first show how to consolidate disjuncts.

Definition 3.23 (Prioritised consolidation of disjuncts). Let $P = \bigwedge_i l_i$ and Q be disjuncts of propositional logic.

The *prioritised consolidation of P by Q*, denoted $\widehat{PQ}$, is a new disjunct R, such that

$R =$
$$\begin{cases} \top, \text{ if } P \text{ is contradictory;} \\ \text{otherwise:} \\ \quad \begin{cases} P, \text{ if } Q \text{ is contradictory} \\ \bigwedge \{l_i \,|\, \text{the literal opposite in sign to } l_i \text{ does not occur in } Q\}, \\ \qquad \text{if } Q \text{ is not contradictory and this set is non-empty} \\ \top, \text{ otherwise} \end{cases} \end{cases}$$

The conditions in Definition 3.23 correspond to the requirements mentioned previously. If P is the disjunct to be consolidated by Q, we replace it by $\top$ if it is contradictory. If the consolidating disjunct Q is contradictory, then we preserve P. Otherwise, we keep only the literals in P that can be consistently accepted by Q or replace P by $\top$ if none of the literals occurring in P can be preserved.

We can now obtain $\ominus$ directly from Definition 3.23 as follows:

Definition 3.24 (Consolidation of formulae). Let ψ and A be formulae of propositional logic in DNF. The *consolidation of ψ by A*, $\psi \ominus A$, is a new formula γ in DNF such that:

$$\gamma = \begin{cases} \psi, \text{ if } \exists P \in \psi \text{ and } \exists Q \in A \text{ such that } dist(P, Q) = 0 \\ \bigvee \{\widehat{PQ} \,|\, P \in \psi, Q \in A, \text{ and } dist(P, Q) \text{ is minimum}\} \\ \text{otherwise} \end{cases}$$

Notice that we have used an implicit consistency check in the first condition of Definition 3.24, as we check whether there are combinations of disjuncts with distance 0. If there is such a combination then it is because the formulae are consistent with each other, in which case we wish to preserve all of ψ. The other requirements are met by the interaction between Definitions 3.24 and 3.23.

We are now able to prove equivalence (3.7):

Theorem 3.3. $\psi \circ_r A \equiv (\psi \diamond A) \wedge A$

Proof. Case 1: Suppose ψ is contradictory. It follows that all disjuncts in ψ are contradictory and hence $\forall P \in \psi$ and $\forall Q \in A$, $\widehat{PQ} = \top$. Therefore, $\psi \diamond A = \bigvee \top \equiv \top$. By Proposition 3.18, $\mod(\psi \circ_r A) = \mod(A) = \mod((\psi \diamond A) \wedge A)$.
Case 2: ψ is not contradictory. There are two subcases: i) A is contradictory. In this case, all disjuncts in ψ will be selected, since all combinations of disjuncts from the two formulae will have distance ∞. By Definition 3.23, $\forall P \in \psi$ and $\forall Q \in A$, $\widehat{PQ} = P$, and hence $\psi \diamond A \equiv \psi$. Also notice that, in this case, $\mod(\psi \circ_r A) = \varnothing = \mod(\psi \wedge A)$. ii) A is not contradictory. If ψ and A are consistent with each other, then for some $P \in \psi$ and $Q \in A$, $dist(P,Q) = 0$, and hence $\psi \diamond A = \psi$. This follows from Definitions 3.10 and 3.11 and Definition 3.24. By (R2), $\psi \circ_r A \leftrightarrow \psi \wedge A$. The other case is when a non-trivial revision of ψ by A is required. That is, ψ and A are both non-contradictory but not consistent with each other. To simplify, consider only the non-contradictory disjuncts in ψ and A. They can be eliminated without loss of generality. In both processes the disjuncts chosen will be the same, namely, those with minimum distance. The disjuncts in $\psi \circ_r A$ will be of the form $\widehat{PQ}^*$, where $P \in \psi$ and $Q \in A$, and $\widehat{PQ}^* = Q \wedge \{l_i \mid l_i(\text{or the literal opposite in sign to } l_i) \text{ does not occur in } Q\}$. Notice that $\bigwedge \{l_i \mid l_i(\text{or the literal opposite in sign to } l_i) \text{ does not occur in } Q\}$ is almost exactly $\widehat{PQ}^*$, except that it does not include literals l_i that already occur in Q, so that $Q \wedge \{l_i \mid l_i(\text{or the literal opposite in sign to } l_i) \text{ does not occur in } Q\} \leftrightarrow Q \wedge \widehat{PQ}^*$. Thus, if $P_1, \ldots, P_j$ and $Q_1, \ldots, Q_k$ are the disjuncts chosen from ψ and A, respectively, in the revision we have

$$\bigvee_{m=1}^{k} \left(\bigvee_{n=1}^{j} Q_m \wedge \widehat{P_n Q_m} \right)$$

and we need to show that this is equivalent to

$$\left(\bigvee_{m=1}^{k} Q_m \right) \wedge \left(\bigvee_{m=1}^{k} \bigvee_{n=1}^{j} \widehat{P_n Q_m} \right).$$

But this can be proved by ordinary manipulations using De Morgan's laws.

We reexamine the examples used for the revision operator:

Example 3.8 (Extracting consistent information).

1. p consolidated by $p \to (q \land r)$:

   $p \to (q \land r)$ is equivalent to $\neg p \lor (q \land r)$ in DNF.
   According to Definition 3.24, this is just p, since $dist(p, q \land r) = 0$.

2. $\neg p$ consolidated by $p \land q$:

   Nothing of the informational content of $\neg p$ can be preserved in face of $p \land q$. The result is then $\top$. However, $p \land q$ consolidated by $\neg p$ gives us q.

3. $p \land q$ consolidated by $\neg p \lor \neg q$:

   We have seen that the best combinations of disjuncts in this case are

   (3.8) $\langle p \land q, \neg p \rangle$ and   (3.9) $\langle p \land q, \neg q \rangle$

   From (3.8) we obtain q and from (3.9) we obtain p. The result is therefore $p \lor q$. Notice that $(p \lor q) \land (\neg p \lor \neg q)$ is equivalent to $(p \land \neg q) \lor (q \land \neg p)$ (which is exactly $(p \land q) \circ_r (\neg p \lor \neg q)$).

4. $p \land \neg p$ consolidated by $p \lor q$

   Now we have a contradictory formula to be analysed. All disjuncts in that formula are contradictory and are ignored by $\ominus$. The result is $\top$.

5. $p \lor q$ consolidated by $p \lor q$ gives us $p \lor q$ again, since it is consistent with itself.

3.8 Comparison with Other Belief Change Operators

Most of the early revision operators proposed in the literature were actually *update* operators. The confusion arose because at the time they were presented, the work in belief revision was still emerging. There was some expectation that work initially done to model updates in databases could fit within the belief revision perspective, and vice versa. Later on, it was made clear that, in spite of many similarities, the two kinds of theory change have some fundamentally distinct characteristics. Under the belief revision approach, the world is a static entity about which an agent constantly refines his own perceptions and beliefs. On the other hand, actions cause a direct change to the world and the update operation must take this into account and try to minimise changes to each possible state of the world (in the interesting case, the agent only has partial information about the world).

Accordingly, we cannot place Borgida's "revision" operation [2, 5] into the belief revision category, since it was first devised to model the handling of exceptions in database systems. The same remark applies equally to Weber's revision operator [18]. Therefore, in this section, we will restrict ourselves to Dalal's revision operator, which indeed performs belief revision in the AGM sense. The presentation of the operator is quite brief. A full description of the formalism can be found in [4, 5].

We first explain briefly how Dalal revisions are defined and then compare the results with our own operator.

The ideas are very similar. We start by defining a system of spheres around each valuation of the language. To our knowledge, the connections with Lewis' systems of spheres have not been investigated previously. The next two definitions appeared in [4]; the following two in [5].

Definition 3.25. Let I be a valuation

$$g(I) = \{J \in \mathscr{I} \mid J \text{ and } I \text{ differ in the truth-value of at most one propositional symbol}\}$$

Definition 3.25 is now extended to classes of valuations:

Definition 3.26. Let $\mathscr{M}$ be a class of valuations

$$g(\mathscr{M}) = \bigcup_{I \in \mathscr{M}} g(I)$$

For a formula ψ, $G(\psi)$ is defined in terms of its models as

$$\mathrm{mod}\,(G(\psi)) = g(\,\mathrm{mod}\,(\psi))$$

Definition 3.27. Let $G^k(\psi)$ $(k \geq 0)$ be defined recursively as follows:

$$G^0(\psi) = \psi$$
$$G^k(\psi) = G(G^{k-1}(\psi))$$

The revision operator is then defined (semantically) as

Definition 3.28. If A is an 'update' to the theory ψ of a database, then the updated theory of the database, in symbols, $\psi \circ_d A$, is defined as:

$$\mathrm{mod}\,(\psi \circ_d A) = \mathrm{mod}\,(G^k(\psi)) \cap \mathrm{mod}\,(A)$$

where k is the least value for which $\mathrm{mod}\,(G^k(\psi)) \cap \mathrm{mod}\,(A) \neq \varnothing$.

By using some results obtained in [18], Dalal also provides a way to compute $\psi \circ_d A$ *syntactically* (the following Lemma is given is [18]):

Lemma 3.1. *Let ψ be a formula and p a propositional symbol. There exist formulae ψ_p^+ and ψ_p^- such that*

- ψ_p^+ *and* ψ_p^- *do not contain p; and*
- $\psi \equiv (p \wedge \psi_p^+) \vee (\neg p \wedge \psi_p^-)$

According to Weber, ψ_p^+ and ψ_p^- can be obtained by replacing each p in ψ by $\top$ and $\bot$ respectively. These constants can then be eliminated through standard simplifications of classical logic. What Lemma 3.1 actually does is to 'isolate' the symbol p from the formula ψ. This is then used to calculate a *resolvent of a formula* with respect to a propositional symbol [18].

Definition 3.29. Let ψ be a formula which may contain a symbol p. If ψ_p^+ and ψ_p^- are formulae obtained in accordance with the previous lemma, then

$$res_p(\psi) = \psi_p^+ \vee \psi_p^-$$

is called the *resolvent of ψ with respect to p*.

Intuitively, ψ and $res_p(\psi)$ admit change with respect to to the truth-value of p only. That is, the models of $res_p(\psi)$ are the models of ψ plus the valuations which differ from them with respect to at most the truth-value of p.

The definition of *res* is then extended to a set of symbols [18]:

Definition 3.30. If $\{p_1, p_2, \ldots, p_k\}$ is a set of symbols and ψ is a propositional formula, then

$$res_\varnothing(\psi) = \psi$$
$$res_{\{p_1,p_2,\ldots,p_k\}}(\psi) = res_{\{p_2,\ldots,p_k\}}(res_{p_1}(\psi))$$

Weber also proved that the order of the symbols chosen in the definition above is not important. Now let us use the symbol $\text{var}(\psi)$ to denote the propositional symbols appearing in ψ.

Theorem 3.4 ([5, Theorem 5.5]). *Let ψ be a formula and* $\text{var}(\psi) = \{p_1, p_2, \ldots, p_k\}$.

$$G(\psi) = res_{p_1}(\psi) \vee \ldots \vee res_{p_k}(\psi)$$

We are now in a position to define the revision of ψ by A, in symbols, $\psi \circ_d A$, according to Dalal [4].

Definition 3.31. Let ψ and A be two formulae of propositional logic. The update of ψ by A, $\psi \circ_d A$, is defined as:

$$\psi \circ_d A = G^k(\psi) \wedge A$$

where k is the least value of i for which $\text{mod}\,(G^i(\psi)) \cap \text{mod}\,(A) \neq \varnothing$.

In order to show the similarities between the two formalisms we first have to make some remarks.

Proposition 3.22. *If ψ is unsatisfiable, then so is $G^k(\psi)$ for any k.*

Proof. First notice that $g^k(\varnothing) = \varnothing$ for any k (by Definition 3.26). If ψ is unsatisfiable, then $\text{mod}\,(\psi) = \varnothing$. By Definitions 3.26 and 3.27, $\text{mod}\,(G^k(\psi)) = g^k(\text{mod}\,(\psi)) = \varnothing$.

As a result, $\circ_d$ cannot always verify the following postulate:

(R3)   If A is satisfiable, then $\psi \circ_a A$ is also satisfiable

Consider for instance the revision of ψ by A, for any satisfiable A and any contradictory ψ. This is just a technicality and presented here more for historical reasons. Apart from this extreme case, Dalal's revision operator $\circ_d$ and our $\circ_r$ are equivalent:

Theorem 3.5. *If ψ is satisfiable, then*

$$\text{mod}\,(\psi \circ_d A) = \text{mod}\,(\psi \circ_r A).$$

Proof. We just have to see that

$$\text{mod}\,(G^k(\psi)) = \{M \in \mathscr{I} \mid \exists I \in \text{mod}\,(\psi) \text{ such that } d(M,I) \leq k\}$$

but $\psi \circ_d A = G^k(\psi) \wedge A$, where k is the least value of i, for which the above conjunction is consistent.

($\subseteq$) *If $M \in \text{mod}\,(\psi \circ_d A)$, then $\exists I \in \text{mod}\,(\psi)$ such that $d(M,I)$ is minimum. It follows that*

$$\forall N \in \text{mod}\,(A)\ \forall I' \in \text{mod}\,(\psi)\ \exists I \in \text{mod}\,(\psi) \text{ such that } d(M,I) \leq d(N,I').$$

By Proposition 3.16, $M \in \text{mod}\,(\psi \circ_r A)$.

($\supseteq$) *If $M \in \text{mod}\,(\psi \circ_r A)$, then by Proposition 3.16,*

$$\forall N \in \text{mod}\,(A)\ \forall I' \in \text{mod}\,(\psi)\ \exists I \in \text{mod}\,(\psi) \text{ such that } d(M,I) \leq d(N,I').$$

Suppose $M \notin \text{mod}\,(\psi \circ_d A)$. Since $M \in \text{mod}\,(A)$ and ψ is satisfiable, $\exists N \in \text{mod}\,(G^j(\psi)) \cap \text{mod}\,(\psi)$ such that $j < k$. If $N \in \text{mod}\,(G^j(\psi)) \cap \text{mod}\,(\psi)$, then $\exists I' \in \text{mod}\,(\psi)$, such that $d(N,I') \leq j$; but then $d(N,I') < d(M,I)$ for all $I \in \text{mod}\,(\psi)$, a contradiction.

We can easily see that Dalal's method involves several more computation steps than our own. Consider, for instance, the revision of ψ by A. Firstly, there is the computation of $res_p(\psi)$ for each $p \in \text{var}(\psi)$, which in its turn needs several symbol manipulation and simplification steps: to replace p by $\top$ and $\bot$ and then simplify the resulting formulae. This is followed by a consistency check in every step of the computation, until a satisfiable conjunction with the new formula is obtained.

On the other hand, our procedure is based on a straightforward mechanism, namely the *prioritised resolution algorithm*, with a single and simplified consistency check of disjuncts. The drawback is the extra cost of converting the formulae to DNF in case they are not initially expressed in that way. As we mentioned before, if it is a Horn clause, then it is already in DNF. If it is in CNF in general, this can be done in time which is linear in the size of the formulae involved.

3.9 Operators for Reasoning About the Effects of Actions

In this section we present some operators that can be used in reasoning about the effects of the execution of actions. We discuss some of the problems involved and show how they can be solved using our methodology. Furthermore, we show that faithful assignments for updates are a particular case of Lewis' comparative similarity systems, and therefore that our update operation can also be used to evaluate counterfactual statements.

3.9.1 Updates of Sentences via Distance d

The basic difference between the combination of disjuncts described in Section 3.5 and the one we now present is that the former ignores the disjunct with the lower priority when it is contradictory, whereas the latter ignores the one with the higher priority. This is to reflect one property of action updates described by the postulate below:

(U2)   If K implies A, then $K \diamond A$ is equivalent to K

(U2) is based on the assumption that if the description of the world is inconsistent, then there is no point in "guessing" what the world looks like after the execution of an action. If consistency is to be restored, this should be achieved via revisions, not via updates, as pointed out in [12].

Definition 3.32 (Prioritised action update of disjuncts). Let $P = \bigwedge_i l_i$ and Q be disjuncts of propositional logic.

The *prioritised update of P by Q, denoted $P\overset{\frown}{Q}$*, is a new disjunct R, such that

$$R = \begin{cases} P, & \Rightarrow \text{if } P \text{ is contradictory} \\ Q \wedge \{l_i \mid l_i (\text{or the literal opposite in sign} \\ \qquad \text{to } l_i) \text{ does not occur in } Q\} & \Rightarrow \text{otherwise} \end{cases}$$

That is, the general case is treated exactly as for belief revision; we add to the updating disjunct only the literals that do not occur in it. If the disjunct to be updated is contradictory, we maintain the inconsistency so that the whole process can verify (U2).

Proposition 3.23. $P\overset{\frown}{Q} \vdash Q$.

Proof. If P is non-contradictory, then all of the literals in Q are preserved in $P\overset{\frown}{Q}$, and then $P\overset{\frown}{Q} \vdash Q$. If P is contradictory, then so is $P\overset{\frown}{Q}$, and hence $P\overset{\frown}{Q} \vdash Q$, trivially.

The definition of revision of sentences could be done straightforwardly in the previous chapter, because when doing revision one is concerned with minimising the distance between *any* models of the two formulae representing the current belief set and the new input. However, in an action update of ψ by φ, every single model of ψ represents a possible state of the world that needs to be taken into account in the process. This assumption was captured in postulate (U8), called the *disjunction rule* (see Section 2.7). It is not possible to verify this rule syntactically without first finding a suitable representation of the relevant models of ψ.

Notation 4 *From now on, we will represent valuations as strings of 0's and 1's according to a pre-defined enumeration of the propositional symbols, say, p, q, r, ..., and where 0 in a position stands for* false *for the symbol at that position and 1 stands for* true. *For example, 10..., stands for the valuation that assigns tt to p and ff to q.*

Now, consider the following example.

Example 3.9 (Performing an action update).

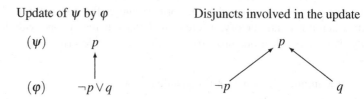

In the action update of ψ by φ shown above, we cannot simply consider the distance between a disjunct in ψ and the disjuncts in φ, because each disjunct in ψ possibly represents many models of ψ. Suppose our language $\mathscr{L}$ is defined over the symbols $[p,q]$ only. The disjunct p in ψ actually represents two models of ψ, one that satisfies $p \wedge q$ and the other that satisfies $p \wedge \neg q$, namely 11 and 10, respectively. The only model of $\neg p \vee q$ with minimum distance with respect to 11 is 11 itself. However, the models of $\neg p \vee q$ with minimum distance with respect to 10 are 00 and 11. The result of the action update should then be the union of all such models. That is, $\{00, 11\}$. If we would just combine the disjuncts in φ with each of the disjuncts in ψ, such that the resulting combination had minimum distance, the result would be $p \wedge q$, since $dist(p,q) = 0$. But then we would be neglecting the model 10, implicitly represented by the disjunct p.

In order to perform this operation syntactically, we need to represent explicitly some classes of models of each of the disjuncts in ψ which are relevant in the computation of the action update by φ. This can be accomplished by "augmenting" ψ with the missing propositional variables occurring in φ. Therefore, we will refer to this operation as augmentation of ψ with respect to φ. First, let us show how to augment a disjunct with respect to a sentence.

Definition 3.33 (Augmentation of a disjunct with respect to a sentence). Let P be a disjunct, φ a sentence in DNF, and $\mathscr{Q} = [q_1, \ldots, q_k]$ an enumeration for the set $var(\varphi) - var(P)$. We define

$$\mathbb{P}_0^\varphi = \{P\}$$
$$\mathbb{P}_i^\varphi = \{P' \wedge q_i, P' \wedge \neg q_i\}, \text{ such that } P' \in \mathbb{P}_{i-1}^\varphi$$

The augmentation of P with respect to φ and enumeration $\mathscr{Q}$, $\mathsf{C}_\varphi^\mathscr{Q}(P)$, is the disjunction

$$\bigvee Q \in \mathbb{P}_k^\varphi.$$

If $var(\varphi) - var(P) = \varnothing$, then $k = 0$ and $\mathsf{C}_\varphi^\mathscr{Q}(P)$ is P itself.

Example 3.10. Let P be p, $\varphi = \neg p \vee (q \wedge r)$ and $\mathscr{Q} = [q, r]$. $\mathsf{C}_\varphi^\mathscr{Q}(P) = (p \wedge q \wedge r) \vee (p \wedge q \wedge \neg r) \vee (p \wedge \neg q \wedge r) \vee (p \wedge \neg q \wedge \neg r)$. It is easy to see that $M \Vdash P$ iff $M \Vdash P'$ for some $P' \in \mathsf{C}_\varphi^\mathscr{Q}(P)$.

Augmentation as presented in Definition 3.33 does not alter the class of models of the disjunct involved in the process:

Proposition 3.24. *Let P be a disjunct and φ be a formula of propositional logic, and $\mathbf{C}_\varphi^{\mathcal{Q}}(P)$ the augmentation of P with respect to φ and some enumeration $\mathcal{Q} = \{q_1, \ldots, q_k\}$ of the propositional variables occurring in φ but not in P:*

$$\mathrm{mod}\,(\mathbf{C}_\varphi^{\mathcal{Q}}(P)) = \mathrm{mod}\,(P).$$

Proof. If $\mathcal{Q}$ is empty, then it follows trivially. Thus, suppose $\mathrm{var}(\varphi) - \mathrm{var}(P) \neq \varnothing$.

- *($\mathrm{mod}\,(\mathbf{C}_\varphi^{\mathcal{Q}}(P)) \subseteq \mathrm{mod}\,(P)$). If $M \in \mathrm{mod}\,(\mathbf{C}_\varphi^{\mathcal{Q}}(P))$, then $M \Vdash P \wedge l_1 \wedge \ldots \wedge l_k$ for some literals l_i built from $\mathcal{Q}$, and then $M \Vdash P$.*
- *($\mathrm{mod}\,(P) \subseteq \mathrm{mod}\,(\mathbf{C}_\varphi^{\mathcal{Q}}(P))$). Suppose $M \Vdash P$. Either $M \Vdash q_1$, in which case $M \Vdash P \wedge q_1$, or $M \Vdash \neg q_1$, and then $M \Vdash P \wedge \neg q_1$. Thus $M \Vdash P'$ for some $P' \in \mathbb{P}_1$. Suppose $M \Vdash P'$ for some $P' \in \mathbb{P}_{k-1}$. Either $M \Vdash P' \wedge q_k$ or $M \Vdash P' \wedge \neg q_k$ for some $P' \in \mathbb{P}_{k-1}$, and hence $M \in \mathrm{mod}\,(\mathbf{C}_\varphi^{\mathcal{Q}}(P))$.*

Remark 3.4. Since the particular enumeration $\mathcal{Q}$ chosen to compute the augmentation of a disjunct with respect to a sentence is irrelevant to the properties we are interested in, we assume there exists such a suitable enumeration, and the reference to it will be dropped in the remainder of this chapter.

Definition 3.34 (Augmentation of a sentence with respect to another sentence). Let ψ and φ be two sentences of propositional logic in DNF. The augmentation of φ with respect to ψ is the sentence

$$\mathbf{C}_\psi(\varphi) = \bigvee_{P \in \varphi} \mathbf{C}_\psi(P)$$

where each $\mathbf{C}_\psi(P)$ is the augmentation of disjunct P in φ with respect to ψ.

Proposition 3.25. $\mathrm{mod}\,(\mathbf{C}_\psi(\varphi)) = \mathrm{mod}\,(\varphi)$.

Proof. It follows trivially from Proposition 3.24.

It is worth emphasising that the augmentation process described above provides all the literals relevant to compute the distance between valuations of the language, even though each augmented disjunct might still be associated with a class of valuations. For example, suppose $\mathbf{L}$ over $[p, q, r]$ and consider the following augmentation of p with respect to $p \vee q$: $(p \wedge q) \vee p \wedge \neg q$. In an action update of p by $p \vee q$ we are interested in every model of p individually. Therefore, the augmented disjunct is not usually "complete" with respect to the language (which is possible only when the alphabet of the language is finite anyway). For instance, $p \wedge q$ is not complete, since it does not say anything about r. Strictly speaking, the augmentation should be extended to all symbols of the language, but this is not necessary, because when computing the distances, the non-added literals do not occur in the sentence for which the augmentation was made. In other words, they cannot increase the distance, because for each non-added propositional variable p_i there will always be a valuation satisfying both the disjunct and the updating sentence, which agrees with respect to the truth-value of p_i.

In the example above we would have the following situation:

Example 3.11. The initial action update of p by $p \vee q$ below

is expanded to the following action update after the augmentation of literals is performed:

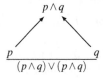 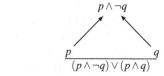

For simplicity, we will show the left-hand side of the action update above only. The result obtained is equivalent to $p \wedge q$. We show below how the process would be performed had we augmented the disjunct in the left-hand side of the diagrams above with respect to propositional variable r as well:

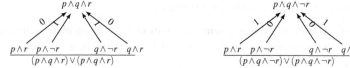 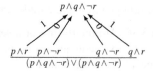

We can see that the final result when we take the disjuncts obtained in the action update of the augmented pairs together, omitting duplicate disjuncts, is the sentence $(p \wedge q \wedge r) \vee (p \wedge q \wedge \neg r)$, which is equivalent to $p \wedge q$ itself.

Now we can define how to action update formulae using d as the evaluating distance function:

Definition 3.35 (Action update of formulae via d). Let ψ and φ be two formulae of propositional logic in DNF. The *action update of ψ by φ*, $\psi \diamond_r \varphi$, is a formula γ such that:

$$\gamma = \bigvee_{P \in \mathcal{C}_\varphi(\psi)} \{ \widehat{PQ} \mid Q \in \varphi \text{ and } dist(P,Q) \text{ is minimum} \}$$

There might be duplicate disjuncts after an action update is performed. They can be generated either in the augmentation process (originating from different disjuncts) or by the superimposition algorithm itself. This obviously does not alter the results. An improvement in efficiency may be obtained if the implementation takes this into account and provides a mechanism to eliminate redundancies.

3.9.2 Properties of the Action Update Operator

Our objective in this section is to prove some properties of the action update operator. We start by characterising the models of $\psi \diamond_r \varphi$.

Proposition 3.26. *Suppose* $M \in \text{mod}(\varphi)$. $M \in \text{mod}(\psi \diamond_r \varphi)$ *iff* $\exists I \in \text{mod}(P)$ *for some* $P \in C_\varphi(\psi)$, *such that* $\forall I' \in \text{mod}(\varphi)$, $\forall I'' \in \text{mod}(P)$, $d(M,I) \leq d(I',I'')$.

Proof. $(\Leftarrow)$ *If* $M \in \text{mod}(\varphi)$, $M \Vdash Q$ *for some* $Q \in \varphi$. *Let* I *be such that* $I \Vdash P$ *for some* $P \in C_\varphi(\psi)$, *and* $\forall I' \in \text{mod}(\varphi)$, $\forall I'' \in \text{mod}(P)$, $d(M,I) \leq d(I',I'')$; *it follows that* $dist(P,Q) \leq dist(P,Q')$ *for all* $Q' \in \varphi$. *Thus,* $\overset{\circ}{P\overset{\frown}{Q}} \in \psi \diamond_r \varphi$, *and hence* $M \in \text{mod}(\psi \diamond_r \varphi)$.

$(\Rightarrow)$ *If* $M \in \text{mod}(\psi \diamond_r \varphi)$, *then*

$$M \Vdash \overset{\circ}{P\overset{\frown}{Q}}, \text{ for some } P \in C_\varphi(\psi), \, Q \in \varphi$$

such that $dist(P,Q)$ *is minimum. This* Q *is such that it provides the combination with that particular* P *with minimum distance between models of* P *and models of all* $Q \in \varphi$, *and hence of models of* P *and* φ. $M \Vdash Q$. *Thus,* $\exists I \in \text{mod}(P)$ *such that* $\forall I' \in \text{mod}(\varphi)$ *and* $\forall I'' \in \text{mod}(P)$, $dist(M,I) \leq dist(I',I'')$.

Corollary 3.3. *Suppose* $\text{mod}(\psi \diamond_r \varphi) \neq \varnothing$ *and that* $M \in \text{mod}(\varphi)$. *If* $M \notin \text{mod}(\psi \diamond_r \varphi)$, *then* $\forall P \in C_\varphi(\psi)$, $\exists I \in \text{mod}(P)$ *and* $\exists N \in \text{mod}(\varphi)$, *such that* $\forall I' \in \text{mod}(P)$, $d(N,I) < d(M,I')$.

That is, if the action update of ψ by φ has some models, and a given valuation M is not among them, then it is because among the models of φ, there is a model N whose distance with respect to some model of ψ is less than the distance between M and any model of each disjunct P in $C_\varphi(\psi)$ considered individually.

We now proceed to prove that $\diamond_r$ verifies the postulates for action updates proposed by Katsuno and Mendelzon.

First we need a faithful assignment for action updates based on our distance function d. We can use the ordering $\leq_I$ from Definition 3.5 for this:

Theorem 3.6. *The action update operation defined by* $\diamond_r$ *verifies the postulates for action updates presented in Section 2.7.*

Proof. We are left to show that

$$\text{mod}(\psi \diamond_r \varphi) = \bigcup_{I \in \text{mod}(\psi)} \min_{\leq_I}(\text{mod}(\varphi)).$$

$(\subseteq)$ *This part is easy. If* $M \in \text{mod}(\psi \diamond_r \varphi)$, *then* $\exists P \in C_\varphi(P)$ *and* $\exists I \in \text{mod}(P)$, *such that* $\forall N \in \text{mod}(\varphi)$ *and* $\forall I' \in \text{mod}(P) \, d(M,I) \leq d(N,I')$. *In particular,* $\forall N \in \text{mod}(\varphi)$, $d(M,I) \leq d(N,I)$, *and thus* $M \in \min_{\leq_I}(\text{mod}(\varphi))$.

$(\supseteq)$ *Suppose that*

$$M \in \bigcup_{I \in \text{mod}(\psi)} \min_{\leq_I}(\text{mod}(\varphi))$$

but $M \notin \text{mod}(\psi \diamond_r \varphi)$. It follows that $M \in \text{min}_{\leq_I}(\text{mod}(\varphi))$ for some $I \in \text{mod}(\psi)$, and then $I \Vdash P$ for some $P \in C_\varphi(\psi)$. $M \in \text{mod}(\varphi)$. By Definition 3.6, $\forall N \in \text{mod}(\varphi)$

(3.10) $d(M,I) \leq d(N,I)$

Since $M \notin \text{mod}(\psi \diamond_r \varphi)$, $\forall Q \in C_\varphi(\psi)$, $\exists J \in \text{mod}(Q)$ and $\exists N \in \text{mod}(\varphi)$, such that $\forall J' \in \text{mod}(Q)$

(3.11) $d(N,J) < d(M,J')$

Since $Q \in C_\varphi(\psi)$ and $J, J' \in \text{mod}(Q)$, then J and J' agree in every truth-value of the atoms in Q, and hence with respect to the atoms in φ as well. Notice that (3.11) also holds for the particular P of (3.11). Thus, we know that $\exists J \in \text{mod}(P)$, and $\exists N \in \text{mod}(\varphi)$, such that

(3.12) $d(N,J) < d(M,I)$

But $P \in C_\varphi(P)$; since both $J, I \in \text{mod}(P)$, they agree in every truth-value of the atoms in P, and hence with respect to the atoms in φ as well. From (3.12), we can conclude that N and J agree in more truth-values of atoms not in P or φ than M and I do. But this is a contradiction, since from (3.10), M and I must agree in every truth-value of the atoms not in P or φ.

Figure 3.8 illustrates the action update of ψ by φ when they are together inconsistent. In an analogy to the revision process described before, it is possible to perceive it as a revision of each one of the models of ψ by φ (a *pointwise revision* of ψ by φ, so to speak). The contour lines around each model of ψ represent units of change with respect to that valuation (possible world). When one of these contour lines *reaches* $\text{mod}(\varphi)$, the intersection is taken. The final result is the union of all such intersections. Strictly speaking, this is not necessarily the case for revisions and action updates in general, as revisions require total orderings in their faithful assignments, whereas partial orderings are sufficient for action updates.

Figure 3.9 illustrates the action update of ψ by φ when they have some models in common. There is little difference with respect to the action update described previously. The models in the intersection play no special role. However, as a result of their being in the intersection, they can be counted as being among the models of the updated theory, since they have minimum distance with respect to themselves. If there are models of ψ not in the intersection (that is, when (U2) is satisfied trivially), they may require that models of φ outside the intersection of the models of the two sentences be also included. As an example, see valuation I' in Figure 3.9. If $\text{mod}(\psi) \subseteq \text{mod}(\varphi)$, then the models of the updated theory are exactly those in the intersection (that is, $\text{mod}(\psi)$). This corresponds to (U2).

Example 3.12 (Action updates of sentences via d).

1. We start with an example from Winslett's scenario in [19]. Suppose we have a room with exactly two objects: a magazine and a newspaper. All we know is that either the magazine or the newspaper is on the floor. We then send a robot to the room and ask it to pick up the magazine from the floor.

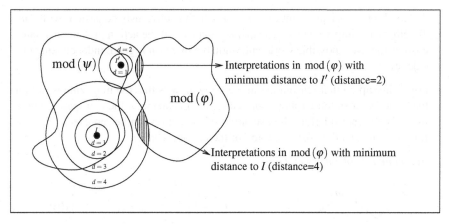

Fig. 3.8 Valuations in $\mathrm{mod}(\psi\diamond_r\varphi)$, when $\mathrm{mod}(\psi) \neq \varnothing$, $\mathrm{mod}(\varphi) \neq \varnothing$ and $\mathrm{mod}(\psi) \cap \mathrm{mod}(\varphi) = \varnothing$

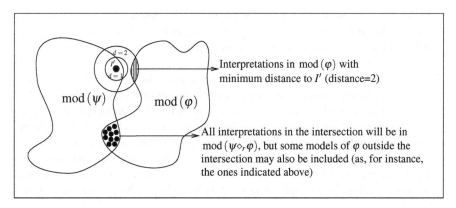

Fig. 3.9 Valuations in $\mathrm{mod}(\psi\diamond_r\varphi)$, when $\mathrm{mod}(\psi) \cap \mathrm{mod}(\varphi) \neq \varnothing$

We use m to represent the fact that the magazine is on the floor and n to represent the fact that the newspaper is on the floor. The scenario before the execution of the action can then be represented by the sentence $m \vee n$ and the post-condition of the action by $\neg m$.

Action update of $m \vee n$ by $\neg m$:

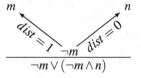

All we are supposed to know after the execution of the action is that the magazine is not on the floor; the newspaper may or may not be. Notice that had we used revisions, the result would have been $\neg m \wedge n$. The reason can be easily understood: $m \vee n$ is equivalent to $\neg m \rightarrow n$, which is obviously consistent with $\neg m$. Together they imply $\neg m \wedge n$. The *disjunction rule* of the action update postulates ensures that each possible world entertainable by $m \vee n$ is given independent consideration.

2. Following up on that reasoning, all we know now is that the magazine is not on the floor. We then tell a robot to put either the magazine or the newspaper on the floor. The scenario before the execution of the action can be represented by the formula $\neg m$, and the post-condition of the action by $m \vee n$.

Action update of $\neg m$ by $m \vee n$:

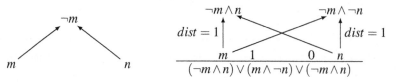

In this case, we need to augment the formula to be updated. The results can be seen on the right-hand side of the figure above. In both worlds, the magazine is not on the floor. However, in one of them the newspaper is on the floor ($\neg m \wedge n$), whereas in the other one it is not ($\neg m \wedge \neg n$).

In the first world, nothing has to be done, since the post-conditions of the action are already satisfied (as the newspaper was already on the floor anyway). This is required by (U2) and corresponds to what Brewka and Hertzberg defined as *laziness* in [3] (see discussion in Section 3.9.4 in this chapter). It has been pointed out in the same work that sometimes laziness may not be adequate.

The second alternative represents the world in which neither the magazine nor the newspaper are on the floor and either of them is then put on the floor (but not both, as this would imply distance 2 with respect to the current state of the world).

As a result, we cannot conclude any longer that the magazine is not on the floor. This is what is expected, since the robot's choice might have been to put it on the floor all along.

3.9.3 Action Updates of Sentences via Distance diff

The remarks about augmentation made for the action update operator we have defined via function d also apply to the operator we will define in this section. The difference here is in the way the distances are evaluated. We now consider a qualitative measurement of change, namely the function diff.

We have already mentioned that diff has been widely used as a distance function for action update operations in the literature. Perhaps the most well known framework using this distance function is Winslett's *possible models approach* (PMA). The same methodology used for the operators we have defined can be used to obtain a variation of the action update operator, which provides an implementation for the propositional version of PMA.

The definition is roughly straightforward and follows Definition 3.35. The only difference is that now the check for the best combination of disjuncts is more elaborate because we have to check for set inclusion instead. Formally,

Definition 3.36 (Action update of formulae via diff). Let ψ and φ be two formulae of propositional logic in DNF. The *action update of ψ by φ via* diff, $\psi \otimes_r \varphi$, is a formula γ such that:

$$\gamma \leftrightarrow \bigvee_{P \in \mathcal{C}_\varphi(\psi)} \{\widehat{PQ} \mid Q \in \varphi \text{ and } \mathrm{diff}(P,Q) \text{ is minimal with respect to } \subseteq\}$$

Notice that we are talking about *minimal elements* instead of *minimum elements* as in Definition 3.35. This is natural since diff induces a natural (non-total) set inclusion ordering on $2^{\mathscr{P}}$. It does not interfere with the satisfaction of the action update postulates, because faithful assignments for action updates, unlike their revision counterparts, are not required to be associated with total pre-orders.

In particular, we can use the following faithful assignment for action updates based on the ordering $\sqsubseteq_I$ defined previously in Section 3.3.

Definition 3.37. For each $I \in \mathscr{I}$,

$$\xi_{\mathrm{diff}}(I) = \{\sqsubseteq_I, \mathscr{I}\}$$

Proposition 3.27. ξ_{diff} *is a faithful assignment for action updates.*

Proof. We have already shown that for each I, $\sqsubseteq_I$ is a pre-order. Now, notice that if $N \neq I$, then $\mathrm{diff}(N,I) \neq \varnothing$. On the other hand, $\mathrm{diff}(I,I) = \varnothing$, and hence $I \sqsubset_I N$ for any $N \in \mathscr{I}$, such that $N \neq I$.

Example 3.13 (Action updates of formulae via diff).

1. We reexamine Example 3.12 with the new operator based on diff. Recall that in the first situation, we have a room with exactly two objects, namely a magazine and a newspaper, and that all we know is that either the magazine or the newspaper is on the floor. The goal is to pick up the magazine from the floor. Again, we use m to represent the fact that the magazine is on the floor and n to represent the fact that the newspaper is on the floor. Thus, initially we have $m \vee n$ and we want to action update this by $\neg m$:

Action update of $m \vee n$ by $\neg m$ (via diff):

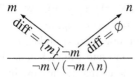

The results coincide with the previous example. All we are supposed to know after the execution of the action is that the magazine is not on the floor; the newspaper may or may not be.

2. Following up on that reasoning, all we know now is that the magazine is not on the floor. We then tell the robot to put either the magazine or the newspaper on the floor. The scenario before the execution of the action can be represented by formula $\neg m$, and the post-condition of the action by $m \lor n$.

Action update of $\neg m$ by $m \lor n$ via diff:

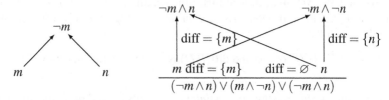

In this case, we need to augment the formula to be updated. The results can be seen on the right-hand side of the figure above. In both worlds, the magazine is not on the floor. However, in one of them the newspaper is on the floor ($\neg m \land n$), whereas in the other one it is not ($\neg m \land \neg n$).

As before, nothing has to be done in the first world, since the post-conditions of the action are already satisfied. The second one represents the world in which neither the magazine nor the newspaper are on the floor; either of them is then put on the floor (but not both, as this would imply distance 2 with respect to the current state of the world).

3.9.4 Ambiguous Action Updates

In [3], Brewka and Hertzberg pointed out that action update operations such as PMA cannot be used to model the effects of execution of the so-called *ambiguous actions*. An ambiguous action is an action whose post-conditions represent a number of non-deterministic states of the world. The classical example for this kind of action is that of tossing a coin. All we know is that we will get heads or tails, but we will not know which until the action is actually executed.

Suppose that in the current state, the agent has a coin with the head facing up (represented by the formula h) and that t is used to represent the fact that the tail is facing up. Thus, the current state of the world can be represented by the formula $h \land \neg t$. Now suppose the agent flips the coin. How can we model this? After the action is executed, all we are expected to know is $(h \land \neg t) \lor (t \land \neg h)$.[3] We will call this kind of information change operation an *ambiguous action update*.

It is not possible to model the results of an ambiguous action update by an ordinary action update operation in the sense of Katsuno and Mendelzon's characterisation. One of the postulates for action updates states that if the new informa-

---

[3] We have to consider the action update of $(h \land \neg t)$ by $(h \land \neg t) \lor (t \land \neg h)$ in order to express explicitly that $h \land t$ is not possible. This can be avoided by using integrity constraints.

tion is already implied by the belief state, then it should be left unchanged. Since $h \wedge \neg t \vdash (h \wedge \neg t) \vee (t \wedge \neg h)$, $(h \wedge \neg t) \diamond_r ((h \wedge \neg t) \vee (t \wedge \neg h)) \equiv h \wedge \neg t$.

Postulate (U2) pressuposes exactly the *awareness* and *laziness* assumptions highlighted by Brewka and Hertzberg in [3], which we quote below:

(U2)   If K implies A, then $K \diamond A$ is equivalent to K

- **Awareness:** The planner knows whether some of the alternative post-conditions already hold before the action.
- **Laziness:** If the planner knows that one of the alternative post-conditions already holds, then it does not bring about any of the other post-conditions.

We can see that *awareness* corresponds exactly to the *if* part of (U2), and that *laziness* corresponds exactly to its *then* part. As pointed out by the aforementioned authors, ambiguous actions require a different treatment, in which laziness cannot be assumed. A semantical characterisation of ambiguous action updates in the sense of those of Sections 2.2 and 2.7 is not available, but it is quite a simple matter to provide an operation to model this kind of information change syntactically using the current methodology. We will refer to this operation as an *ambiguous action update of formulae.*

Definition 3.38 (Ambiguous action update of formulae). Let ψ and $\varphi = P_1 \vee P_2 \vee \ldots \vee P_k$ be two formulae of propositional logic in DNF, where each P_i represents a possible effect of the action described by φ. The *ambiguous action update of ψ by φ*, in symbols, $\psi \odot \varphi$, is a formula γ such that:

$$\gamma \leftrightarrow \bigvee_{i=1}^{k} \psi \diamond_r P_i$$

Postulate (U8) already ensures that each possible model of the current state ψ is taken into account. Since the operator $\diamond_r$ verifies the postulates for action updates, the ambiguous action update operator also takes each possible model of the current state into account individually. What Definition 3.38 does is to ensure that each of the possible outcomes of the action is considered individually as well. Note that in practice each possible outcome of the action could be represented as a formula in DNF on its own. In that case, the operator would take a formula ψ in DNF and a set of formulae $\Gamma = \{\varphi_1, \ldots, \varphi_k\}$ in DNF and return another formula in DNF which would be equivalent to the disjunction of the action update of ψ by each φ_i.

A semantical characterisation of an ambiguous action update of ψ by $\{\varphi_1, \varphi_2, \ldots, \varphi_k\}$ would consist in choosing among the models of φ_1 those that are closest from each of the models of ψ, and then adding these to the models of φ_2 that are closest to each of the models of ψ, and so forth. The $\varphi_{i's}$ would be used to state *where* the ambiguity lies.

We can see that the belief base is treated in the same way as that of ordinary action updates. The new information is interpreted slightly differently, but minimality still plays a central role in the process. The following examples show ambiguous action updates being performed and emphasise the importance of background knowledge when reasoning about actions.

Example 3.14 (Ambiguous action updates). Let us now reconsider the coin example, but this time by using ambiguous action updates:

$$
\left(
\begin{array}{c}
h \wedge \neg t \\
\odot \\
(h \wedge \neg t) \vee (t \wedge \neg h)
\end{array}
\right)
\Rightarrow
\left(
\begin{array}{c}
h \wedge \neg t \\
\diamond_r \\
h \wedge \neg t
\end{array}
\right)
\vee
\left(
\begin{array}{c}
h \wedge \neg t \\
\diamond_r \\
t \wedge \neg h
\end{array}
\right)
$$

$$
\frac{(h \wedge \neg t) \qquad \vee \qquad (t \wedge \neg h)}{(h \wedge \neg t) \vee (t \wedge \neg h)}
$$

The possible outcomes of the action have to be stated explicitly in each of the disjuncts. Notice that we have also explicitly stated that the state in which we obtain both heads and tails $(h \wedge t)$ is not possible. This can be avoided by using formulae to describe the general behaviour of the world. The result of the action update reflects the ambiguity of the action. After it is performed it is no longer possible to derive $h \wedge \neg t$, that is, that we have *heads* in the new state. An ordinary action update would simply result in $h \wedge \neg t$, which already held in the previous belief state. This is a direct consequence of (U2). Each of the disjuncts in the updating formula performs an independent action update of the previous belief state. Notice that other information in the previous belief state consistent with the new information would also be kept.

It is useful to have a separate set of formulae where general information about the behaviour of the world can be represented (e.g., the information about the behaviour of flipping a coin considered previously). It makes the description of the current scenario and of the post-conditions of the actions simpler. For instance, in [3], the information $h \leftrightarrow \neg t$ can be stated separately and is called *background knowledge*. It is possible to do something similar with the operators defined here by considering extra information in the process. This will be partly done in the next section, and related ideas will also be discussed in the following chapters, where more structure will be available for the update operations.

3.9.5 Taking Causality into Account

In Section 3.2 we have shown how to modify the distance d to take causality into account. Given a set of causal rules $\mathscr{R}$, the derived distance function with respect to $\mathscr{R}$ was denoted by $d_{\mathscr{R}}$. We can use this function to define a variation of the action update operator. But before that, we first need to show how $d_{\mathscr{R}}$ can be calculated for disjuncts.

Definition 3.39. Let P and Q be disjuncts and take a set $\mathscr{R}$ of causal rules. The distance between P and Q relative to $\mathscr{R}$, in symbols, $dist_{\mathscr{R}}(P,Q)$, can be calculated as follows

$$dist_{\mathscr{R}}(P,Q) =$$
$$\begin{cases} dist(P,Q) & \Rightarrow \text{ if } Q \not\Vdash R \text{ for any } R \in \mathscr{R} \text{ or} \\ dist(P,Q) - \sup\{dist(D,P) \mid \varphi \Rightarrow D \in \mathscr{R}\} & \Rightarrow \text{ otherwise} \end{cases}$$

What the definition above essentially does is to compensate for the increase in the overall distance motivated by causal changes.

In order to define the new action update operation, all we have to do is to change Definition 3.35 accordingly:

Definition 3.40 (Action update of formulae via $d_{\mathscr{R}}$). Let ψ and φ be two formulae of propositional logic in DNF and $\mathscr{R}$ be a set of causal rules. The *action update of ψ by φ with respect to $\mathscr{R}$, $\psi \circledcirc_r \varphi$*, is a formula γ such that:

$$\gamma = \bigvee_{P \in C_{\varphi}(\psi)} \{\widehat{PQ} \mid Q \in \varphi \text{ and } dist_{\mathscr{R}}(P,Q) \text{ is minimum}\}$$

It is useful to illustrate the use of this operation.

Example 3.15. We consider an example used by Brewka and Hertzberg in [3].

The current scenario is composed by a room in which there are two switches that control one lamp. We represent the fact that switch 1 is on by sw_1 and that it is off by $\neg sw_1$, and similarly for switch 2 (sw_2 and $\neg sw_2$, respectively). Also, we represent the fact that the lamp is on by *on* and that it is on if and only if both switches are on. In the present situation, switch 1 is off, switch 2 is on and, consequently, the lamp is off ($\neg on$). We can consider the causal rule $R = sw_1 \wedge sw_2 \Rightarrow on$ to represent the fact that a change in the truth-values of sw_1 and sw_2 to *tt* causes the change of the truth-value of *on* to *tt*.

This scenario can be represented in the following way: $IC = sw_1 \wedge sw_2 \leftrightarrow on$ (the integrity constraints); $\mathscr{R} = \{sw_1 \wedge sw_2 \Rightarrow on\}$ (there is only one causal rule) and $\psi = \neg sw_1 \wedge sw_2 \wedge \neg on$ (the current state of the world).

Suppose we want to action update ψ by sw_1. That is, what happens when switch 1 is turned on? To deal with the integrity constraints in this simplified scenario, we first revise sw_1 by IC prior to the action update to ψ (this will be discussed in more detail in Section 4.8, Example 4.7):

The reader can check that an acceptable translation of IC to DNF is $(\neg sw_1 \wedge \neg on) \vee (\neg sw_2 \wedge \neg on) \vee (sw_1 \wedge sw_2 \wedge on)$. It is also easy to check that the revision of sw_1 by this formula yields $(sw_1 \wedge \neg sw_2 \wedge \neg on) \vee (sw_1 \wedge sw_2 \wedge on)$.

We are left with the following action update:

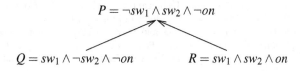

$$P = \neg sw_1 \wedge sw_2 \wedge \neg on$$

$$Q = sw_1 \wedge \neg sw_2 \wedge \neg on \qquad R = sw_1 \wedge sw_2 \wedge on$$

No augmentation of literals is necessary here. If we were to use our ordinary action update operator $\diamond_r$, we would be left with

$$\varphi = (sw_1 \wedge \neg sw_2 \wedge \neg on) \vee (sw_1 \wedge sw_2 \wedge on)$$

because both Q and R have distance 2 with respect to P. Notice that $\varphi \vdash IC$, so the action update is sound with respect to the integrity constraints. However, the distance between R and P is intuitively smaller than the distance between Q and P, because the change in the truth-value of on in R with respect to the value it had in P was caused by the required action update of P by sw_1 in the first place, and therefore this change should have been disregarded in the calculation of the distance.

This is exactly what the new distance function does. Remember that we have defined the satisfiability of a causal rule $\varphi \Rightarrow D$ as the same as the formula $\varphi \wedge D$ (see page 62).

$$dist_{\mathscr{R}}(P,Q) = dist(P,Q) = 2 \text{ (since } Q \not\vdash sw_1 \wedge sw_2 \Rightarrow on)$$
$$dist_{\mathscr{R}}(P,R) = dist(P,R) - \sup\{dist(on,P)\} = 2 - 1 = 1 \text{ (since } R \vdash sw_1 \wedge sw_2 \Rightarrow on)$$

The result of the action update is then simply $\overset{\curvearrowright\circ}{PR} = sw_1 \wedge sw_2 \wedge on$.

This concludes our introduction to the problem of reasoning about the effects of the execution of actions.

Unfortunately, the simple operations defined in this chapter cannot account for practical applications of belief change. In particular, there is the problem of iteration. Moreover, they give no scope for distinguishing between formulae in the current database which may play different roles or have different associated priorities. We will investigate these issues in the next two chapters.

References

1. K. H. Bläsius and H.-J. Bürckert. *Deduction Systems in Artificial Intelligence*. Ellis Horwood Limited, 1989.
2. A. Borgida. Language features for flexible handling of exceptions in information systems. *ACM Transactions on Database Systems*, 10:563–603, 1985.
3. G. Brewka and J. Hertzberg. How to do things with worlds: on formalizing actions and plans. *Journal of Logic and Computation*, 3(5):517–532, 1993.
4. M. Dalal. Investigations into a theory of knowledge base revision: Preliminary report. In Paul Rosenbloom and Peter Szolovits, editors, *Proceedings of the Seventh National Conference on Artificial Intelligence*, volume 2, pages 475–479, Menlo Park, California, 1988. AAAI Press.
5. M. Dalal. Updates in propositional databases. Technical report, Department of Computer Science, Rutgers University, February 1988. Technical Report DCS-TR-222.
6. H. B. Enderton. *A Mathematical Introduction to Logic*. Academic Press, New York, 1972.
7. D. M. Gabbay and F. Kriwackzeck. A goal directed theorem prover for intuitionistic logic based on conjunction and implication. Technical report, Department of Computing, Imperial College of Science and Technology — University of London, 1986.
8. D. M. Gabbay and O. Rodrigues. A methodology for iterated theory change. In D. M. Gabbay and Hans Jürgen Ohlbach, editors, *Practical Reasoning — First International Conference on Formal and Applied Practical Reasoning, FAPR'96*, Lecture Notes in Artificial Intelligence. Springer Verlag, 1996.
9. G. Grahne. Updates and counterfactuals. In J. A. Allen, R. Fikes, and E. Sandewell, editors, *Principles of Knowledge Representation and Reasoning: Proceedings of the Second International Conference*, pages 269–276, San Mateo, California, 1991. Morgan Kaufmann.

10. R. W. Hamming. Error detecting and error correcting codes. *Bell System Technical Journal*, 26(2):147–160, 1950.

11. H. Katsuno and A. O. Mendelzon. Propositional knowledge base revision and minimal change. *Artificial Intelligence*, 52(3):263–294, 1991.

12. H. Katsuno and A. O. Mendelzon. On the difference between updating a knowledge base and revising it. In P. Gärdenfors, editor, *Belief Revision*, pages 183–203. Cambridge University Press, 1992.

13. O. Rodrigues, M. Ryan, and P.-Y. Schobbens. Counterfactuals and updates as inverse modalities. In Yoav Shoham, editor, *6th Conference on Theoretical Aspects of Rationality and Knowledge*, pages 163–174, 1996.

14. M. D. Ryan. *Ordered Presentation of Theories — Default Reasoning and Belief Revision*. PhD thesis, Department of Computing, Imperial College, U.K., 1992.

15. M. D. Ryan and P.-Y. Schobbens. Intertranslating counterfactuals and updates. In W. Wahlster, editor, *12th European Conference on Artificial Intelligence (ECAI)*, pages 100–104. J. Wiley & Sons, Ltd., 1996.

16. K. Satoh. Non-monotonic reasoning by minimal belief revision. In *Proceedings of the International Conference on 5th Generation Computer Systems*, pages 455–462, Tokyo, 1988.

17. L. S. Sterling and E. Y. Shapiro. *The Art of Prolog*. MIT Press, 1986.

18. A. Weber. Updating propositional formulas. In L. Kerschberg, editor, *Proceedings of the First Conference on Expert Database Systems*, pages 487–500. The Benjamin Cummings, 1987.

19. M. Winslett. Reasoning about action using a possible models approach. In *Proceedings of AAAI-88*, pages 89–93, San Mateo, CA, Saint Paul, MN, 1988. Morgan Kaufmann.

Chapter 4
Iterating Revision

4.1 Introduction

In the previous chapter we presented some operators that could be used to perform
revision in the AGM sense and action updates complying with Katsuno and Mendelzon's semantical characterisation of these operations.

It is well known that even though the postulates capture the intuitions behind *rational changes of belief* and the expected properties of the execution of actions, they
are severely limited by the lack of extra information supporting the representation
of the current state of affairs or beliefs. Some of these limitations were discussed in
Chapter 2 in the sections related to the iteration of the revision process. In particular,
the realisation of the initial *corpus of beliefs* (or the description of the world in the
case of action updates) into a unit with little structure (a formula in the finite case or
a theory, otherwise) brings several difficulties to reasoning about more sophisticated
scenarios.

In the case of belief revision, *derived beliefs* and *basic ones* become indistinguishable, not to mention other issues related to priorities, entrenchment and the
history of updates. In the case of action updates, it is also unrealistic to work with a
single formula representing the description of the world, because in general there is
a complex and rich network of relationships and interdependencies between world
properties, for instance, *integrity constraints*, causality rules, etc.

The lack of structure is one of the main criticisms against the *standard* AGM
approach to belief revision, although to be fair, it was not not originally ever envis-
aged to consider such aspects. Regarding the distinction between the initial corpus
of beliefs and all beliefs that can be derived from it, AGM supports the coherentist
view which considers all beliefs equally worthy of consideration, partly because it
represents an idealised view of the process.

In [12, Chapter 4], Harman highlights the differences between the *coherence* and
foundational paradigms. The former claims that the beliefs in a belief state do not
need any support other than *coherence* with respect to the inference system in order
to be accepted by the agent, whereas the latter insists that for a belief to be held by an

D. M. Gabbay et al., *Revision, Acceptability and Context*, Cognitive Technologies,
DOI 10.1007/978-3-642-14159-1_4, © Springer-Verlag Berlin Heidelberg 2010

agent it needs a proper *justification*. Thus beliefs whose justifications are no longer accepted are discarded. A justification for a belief could be, for instance, that it follow from other beliefs which have independent justifications. Such fundamental beliefs that do not depend on any other beliefs in the belief state are sometimes called *foundational beliefs*. In order to distinguish the basic beliefs from the derived ones, a *base* for the belief set must be assumed and the belief set itself is the result of closing the *belief base* under the consequence relation. As a result, beliefs in the belief set can only be retracted via contraction of beliefs in the base. We have seen that this approach is often called *base revision*.

The supporters of the coherence theory claim that it is too expensive to keep track of all justifications for the beliefs. However, for computer science applications, having a finite base for the belief set seems to be the only feasible alternative, and hence base revisions have been supported by many authors [13, 10, 16]. Keeping track of the justifications can be simplified if we assume that the beliefs in the base are basic and do not need extra justification, whereas beliefs in the belief state are justified by the beliefs in the base which imply them. We will henceforth endorse the following assumption:

(J1)   The beliefs in a belief base are self-justified

following [12]. Notice that beliefs that are not basic, may become so by our simply adding them to the base. We will not make any assumptions at this stage as to how the base itself is going to be presented.

Independently of the paradigm chosen, there is still the problem of deciding what beliefs to retract when a contraction or revision by a conflicting belief needs to be performed. This decision cannot be made based on logical grounds only. We have seen that one of the alternatives to help in this choice is to use an ordering on the beliefs called epistemic entrenchment [8, 21]. The idea is to retract formulae less entrenched in the ordering first whenever necessary. Under the coherence view, all formulae in the belief set must be ordered, since they all have the same status. However, a further complication is that whenever a belief change operation is performed a new ordering for the new (revised) belief set needs to be generated if revision is to be performed again.

The base revision approach has less of a problem in this sense and several authors suggest it as an alternative solution to the choice problem [4, 18, 22]. All we need to do is to provide belief bases with an ordering on their formulae. The ordering essentially specifies priorities between the formulae and is used to solve conflicts when they arise. Formulae with higher priority are preferred to those with lower priority when a contraction/revision has to be made and one of the formulae must be given up. One of the first examples of such an approach was Ryan's *ordered theory presentations* (OTPs). For the case of belief revision, Ryan considered OTPs whose ordering was linear. Thus, the belief base can be seen as a list of formulae, where formulae appearing later in the list are assumed to have higher priority than the ones appearing earlier. A revision is performed by appending a formula to the previous base and thus giving it highest priority. The ordering ultimately results in an ordering on interpretations of the language, from where the preferred models of the theory are taken. This provides a semantical approach to the problem. The idea of considering bases as lists of formulae is both simple and elegant and lists can be used to represent the history of updates as well.

OTPs can be seen as being part of a general class of base revision operations which use priorities to solve conflicts. We will refer to these operations as *prioritised base revision*, a term coined by Nebel in [18].

In this chapter, we present *structured databases* (SDBs), which offer a syntactical approach to belief revision, by using ideas similar to those used in prioritised base revision. We perceive the belief base as a set of components provided with additional information about the *priorities* or preferences assigned to them. We allow the components of the base to be nested structured bases as well, so that more complex inference patterns can be represented. The idea is to use the simple revision operations defined in the previous chapter, and hence formulae are expressed in disjunctive normal form (DNF).

This chapter assumes linearity of the ordering of the formulae in the base as a stepping stone to more sophisticated revision operations to be defined later and because it allows us to analyse properties of the iteration of the revision process more naturally.

4.2 Motivating the Importance of Structure for Belief Revision Operations

In the previous section we mentioned briefly the differences between the coherence and foundations paradigms for belief revision. In this section we analyse a simple example to discuss the importance of having a richer structure representing an agent's belief state in the design of operations for rational changes of belief.

To start, assume our agent initially believes that tweety is a penguin, and assume that this represented by the formula

(4.1) pt

and also that she believes that penguins cannot fly. When this rule is applied to the individual 'tweety', we get the following particular instance of this rule that is relevant to our discussion, i.e., if tweety is a penguin, it does not fly, which can be represented as

(4.2) $pt \rightarrow \neg ft$

Using modus ponens, we get that tweety does not fly and hence our agent concludes that both tweety is a penguin and that it does not fly, i.e., the conjunction $pt \wedge \neg ft$:

$$\frac{pt \quad \wedge \quad pt \rightarrow \neg ft}{pt \wedge \neg ft}$$

Now suppose our agent sees tweety flying. She is now forced to accept the belief that tweety can indeed fly and hence needs to revise her belief set with the formula

ft. This can only be accepted consistently by giving up some of the old beliefs. Intuitively, there are only two rational ways of doing this.

1. either by rejecting pt, that is, since penguins cannot fly, tweety must not be a penguin;
2. or by rejecting the fact that penguins cannot fly altogether (since tweety is a penguin that does fly, some penguins *can* indeed fly).

However, our agent's belief system is coherentist and in her belief set she has a multitude of beliefs, all carrying equal standing, including pt, $pt \rightarrow \neg ft$, $\neg ft$, $pt \wedge \neg ft$, ... The previous beliefs are all there, but unfortunately, our agent does not have the ability to distinguish between, for instance, the beliefs pt and $\neg ft$. Now assume that we use AGM and we choose the finite representation of belief sets suggested by Katsuno and Mendelzon (see Section 2.2). Our agent's belief state will be simplified to the formula $pt \wedge \neg ft$.[1] With the arrival of ft, now we can only rely on the similarity between worlds to calculate what models of ft are most similar to models of $pt \wedge \neg ft$. If the Hamming distance is used, this will be $pt \wedge ft$ (the other model will have distance 2), and as a result our agent will keep the belief in pt and reject the belief in $\neg ft$. Most formalisms for belief revision based on a direct application of AGM would give similar results (including the revision operator $\circ_r$ presented in the previous section) [22, 5, 1].

Intuitively, we would expect to give more importance to the beliefs (4.1) and (4.2) and consider $\neg ft$ merely as a belief *derived* from the two other more fundamental ones. This can be achieved by differentiating the belief base from the belief set. Our agent's belief base will be the set $\{pt, pt \rightarrow \neg ft\}$ and her belief set will contain $Cn(\{pt, pt \rightarrow \neg ft\})$, as expected. Revision can now operate on the base and hence we do not have to worry about the fact that $\neg ft$ is only a consequence of 4.1 and 4.2. However, our agent will still have to choose between 1 and 2.

When we have to change our beliefs in light of new contradictory information, we make this choice based on implicit degrees of confidence we associate with the beliefs. We may, for instance, trust some sources of information more than others, and hence assign different priorities to the information we accept. In any case, this extra information does not represent the beliefs in question themselves, but rather it provides information *about* them. One interesting possibility may be to consider this extra information about beliefs as beliefs as well (and revise them!). However, we will restrict ourselves to using extra information to guide the revision process only. We now revisit the problem of iteration, which is also related.

4.3 Iteration of the Revision Operation

We saw in Section 2.9 that one of the main shortcomings of the AGM framework is that it gives us little guidance with respect to how future belief changes will interact

---

[1] It is easy to see that $Cn(\{pt, pt \rightarrow \neg ft\}) = Cn(\{pt \wedge \neg ft\})$.

with the imminent one. Moreover, it gives no indication whatsoever with respect to any of the past revisions. The minute a belief is accepted, it becomes indistinguishable from any other (this is the basis of coherence). Postulates (R5) and (R6) give some guidelines about revisions followed by expansions, but say nothing about revisions followed by revisions. Even worse, many formalisms proposed for belief revision make it impossible to iterate the process. In general this happens because part of the burden of choosing what beliefs to keep is transferred to extraneous mechanisms that are important as philosophical exercises but do not yield algorithms through which the new belief state can be obtained effectively. Examples of such mechanisms are the selection functions used in partial meet revisions and partial meet contractions.

Let us recap briefly some of the notions involved. A more complete account can be found in [7] (the following definition can be found on page 76 of that reference).

Definition 4.1 (Maximal subset that fails to imply a formula). A set K' is a maximal subset of K that fails to imply φ iff the following conditions are met:

- $K' \subseteq K$
- $\varphi \notin \mathrm{Cn}(K')$
- $\forall K'', K' \subset K'' \subseteq K$ implies $\varphi \in \mathrm{Cn}(K'')$

In other words, if K' is a maximal subset of K that fails to imply a formula φ, then any larger subset of K would result in the derivation of φ. It is useful to define the collection of all such subsets.

Notation 5 *The symbol $K \perp \varphi$ will be used to denote the set of all subsets of K that do not imply φ.*

The set $K \perp \varphi$ plays a very important role in the definition of contraction and revision operators. Different operations can be defined simply in terms of appropriate subsets of $K \perp \varphi$.

Definition 4.2 (Selection function for contraction). Let S be a selection function which selects a non-empty subset of $K \perp \varphi$ if $K \perp \varphi$ itself is non-empty, or K otherwise.

Definition 4.3 (Partial meet contractions). The *partial meet contraction* of K by φ according to selection function S is the set $\bigcap S(K \perp \varphi)$.

S is used to determine which among the maximal subsets of K that do not imply φ are more plausible. There are two limiting cases for such a selection function. If it selects *all* of $K \perp \varphi$, then the resulting contraction operation is called a *full meet contraction*. On the other hand, if it selects a singleton, i.e., a single element of $K \perp \varphi$, then the resulting contraction function is called a *maxichoice contraction*.[2] Anything inbetween is simply called a partial meet contraction.

---

[2] A full meet contraction is known to be too drastic an operation, whereas a maxichoice contraction on the other hand is too 'conservative' — see [11, page 74] for more details.

The above types of contractions can be used together with the Levi Identity to define the corresponding operations of *full meet*, *maxichoice*, and *partial meet* revisions.

The point we are trying to make here is that in practice the choice problem is not in fact solved, since little is said about the construction of such selection functions. Of course, the characterisations provide good insights into the problem of belief change, but when it comes to actually constructing an algorithm to perform the change operations they are of little help.

Let us give a *temporal perspective* to the problem of belief revision. Under this perspective, novelty of information is associated with the priority the associated belief had within the belief base. This makes sense in the light of the AGM postulates. Now, consider the revision of K by φ followed by the revision by ψ. It does not seem reasonable that a piece of information which played a major role in the revision process of K, that is, φ, suddenly be left with no special status at all among the beliefs in K retained in the process when the subsequent revision by ψ is performed. We could therefore argue for the serialisation of the revision process and consider belief bases as sequences of revisions, in a similar fashion to those of OTPs [22], Nebel's *prioritised base revision*, and Lehmann's characterisation [15], and in a sense similar to that of Fagin et al. as well [4].

The revision operator would then be used on the formulae in the base according to the priorities assigned to them. However, we are left with the problem of how to interpret the sequence of revisions obtained, because, as shown previously, our revision operator $\circ_r$ is not associative. Let us explore this point a bit further.

Example 4.1 (Non-associativity of $\circ_r$).

1. $(p \circ_r (p \rightarrow q)) \circ_r \neg q$

2. $p \circ_r ((p \rightarrow q) \circ_r \neg q)$

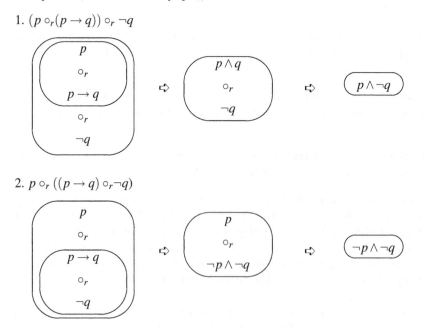

In case (1) above, the agent initially believes in p and $p \rightarrow q$, which results in a belief state in which he believes in both propositions p and q. When the new belief $\neg q$ arrives, he gives up the belief in q, but keeps the belief in p. On the other hand, in (2) above, the agent reasons backwards. His priority is to believe in $\neg q$, and subject to this, in $p \rightarrow q$. He then is led to believe in $\neg p$ (if he believed in p, he would have to believe in q, which he does not). As he proceeds in his reasoning, he realises that he cannot keep the belief in p, because it contradicts the other two beliefs.

In both cases, the two initial revision results are compulsory for any revision operator verifying the AGM postulates, since the formulae are consistent with each other. That is, $p \circ_r (p \rightarrow q)$ and $(p \rightarrow q) \circ_r \neg q$ must be $p \wedge q$ and $\neg p \wedge \neg q$, respectively, if $\circ_r$ is to verify the postulates. Also for the same reason, $p \circ_r (\neg p \wedge \neg q)$ must be $\neg p \wedge \neg q$. On the other hand, the postulates do not constrain $(p \wedge q) \circ_r \neg q$ well enough to guarantee that $p \wedge \neg q$ is the only possible outcome of the revision process. However, it does not seem rational that the agent should also give up the belief in p, especially if the postulates support the coherentist view. That is, as far as the postulates are concerned, $\{p,q\}$ and $\{p \wedge q\}$ represent exactly the same belief state. One argument would be the syntactical difference between the formula $p \wedge q$ and the formulae p and q given independently, but belief revision is supposed to be independent of the syntax anyway (see $(K^\circ 6)$ and the discussion on page 17). Even so, the reasonable thing to do would be to question the acceptance of p instead of going for the acceptance of $\neg p$. A deeper investigation into this matter still remains to be done.

In the next section we will advocate for the right-associative use of the revision operator in spite of the fact that every revision will require a complete recomputation of the sequence of revisions performed so far. This interpretation of the sequence of operations leads to a reflection of the agent's own beliefs and provides intuitive results for belief revision. However, this is not the case for action updates. The action update operation seems to be intrinsically left-associative. We expect states of the world to be updated in line with flow of time, not the other way around.

4.4 Prioritised Databases

In the generalised version of the linear framework presented at the end of this chapter, we will allow points in the structure to be nested structures themselves. However, it is easier to start with a simpler linear structure in which points are associated with formulae only. We called this type of representation of an epistemic state a *prioritised database* (PDB) in [6, 20].

PDBs remember the history of updates by simply appending successive revisions to the end of the list. However, they aim to uphold the following principles during the belief change operations

• conservativity

- prioritisation
- consistency

Conservativity is the application of the principle of minimal change to PDBs; it states that whenever a belief is found to be inconsistent with other higher priority beliefs, as much as possible of its informational content should be kept according to some fixed criteria (as opposed to simply disregarding the belief as a whole). Prioritisation requires that beliefs with higher priority have precedence over those with lower priority; and finally, consistency requires that some mechanism is provided to ensure that the belief state associated with a PDB is consistent whenever possible.[3] Our algorithm for superimposition of literals provides an efficient way to preserve consistency and ensure conservativity at the formula level, and as we said, the priorities among the beliefs are determined simply by the order in which they appear in the list (this is the same order in which they are given as inputs to the agent).

Definition 4.4 (Prioritised database). A *prioritised database (PDB)* is a list of formulae $\Delta = [\varphi_1, \ldots, \varphi_k]$.

As mentioned before, formulae appearing later in the list have priority over those appearing earlier. The list itself can be seen as the record of the evolution of the information received by the agent. You can see it as providing a *temporal perspective* to the problem of belief revision. This perspective will be used to fine-tune the choice of beliefs to keep during successive belief changes.

The simplest way of using the order of beliefs in a PDB is to consider different possibilities for the application of the revision operator to them. We can treat the list as a sequence of revisions to be applied. However, as we have seen, the operator $\circ_r$ is not associative. Therefore, there are two immediate interpretations for the sequence of revisions of a PDB Δ: either we consider $\circ_r$ as a left-associative operation (the usual practise) or we treat it as a right-associative one.

In order to discuss these possibilities in more detail, let us introduce some notation at this stage. For a given PDB Δ, we define operators *() and ()* that return to us the result of revising the formulae in Δ under the left- and right-associative interpretations, respectively.

We thus obtain *Δ, read *left Delta*, and Δ*, read *right Delta*. The symbol ε will be used to denote the empty sequence of formulae. Formally,

Definition 4.5. Let $\Delta = [\varphi_1, \varphi_2, \ldots, \varphi_k]$ be a PDB, with $k \geq 0$.

$$^*\Delta = \begin{cases} \top & \Rightarrow \text{if } \Delta = \varepsilon \\ \varphi_k & \Rightarrow \text{if } k = 1 \\ ((\varphi_1 \circ_r \varphi_2) \circ_r \ldots) \circ_r \varphi_k & \Rightarrow \text{if } k > 1 \end{cases}$$

$$\Delta^* = \begin{cases} \top & \Rightarrow \text{if } \Delta = \varepsilon \\ \varphi_k & \Rightarrow \text{if } k = 1 \\ \varphi_1 \circ_r (\ldots \circ_r (\varphi_{k-1} \circ_r \varphi_k)) & \Rightarrow \text{if } k > 1 \end{cases}$$

---

[3] This is not possible if the belief with highest priority is itself contradictory.

Since the formula with the highest priority plays an important role, we want to have it accepted in the new belief state. As we can see, under either interpretation, the last formula in a PDB is always accepted:

Proposition 4.1. *Let* $\Delta = [\varphi_1, \varphi_2, \ldots, \varphi_k]$ *be a PDB.* $^*\Delta \vdash \varphi_k$ *and* $\Delta^* \vdash \varphi_k$.

Proof. By (R1), $\varphi \circ_r \psi \vdash \psi$. *Thus,* $^*\Delta = ((\varphi_1 \circ_r \varphi_2) \circ_r \ldots) \circ_r \varphi_k \vdash \varphi_k$. *On the other hand,* $\vdash$ *is transitive. Remember that* $\varphi_{k-1} \circ_r \varphi_k \vdash \varphi_k$, *and* $\varphi_1 \circ_r (\ldots \circ_r (\varphi_{k-1} \circ_r \varphi_k)) \vdash$ $(\ldots \circ_r (\varphi_{k-1} \circ_r \varphi_k))$

Thus, in order to *accept* new information in a PDB Γ all we have to do is to append it to Γ. Formally,

Definition 4.6. Let $\Delta = [\varphi_1, \ldots, \varphi_k]$ be a PDB and ψ a formula. The *acceptance of* ψ *by* Δ is obtained by appending ψ to Δ.

We will now assume the *right*-associative interpretation of the revision operator when we talk about PDBs. The reasons will be explained later. First, we need to characterise the models of a PDB.

Definition 4.7. Let Δ be a PDB. The models of Δ, in symbols, $\text{Mod}(\Delta)$, are the valuations in the set $\text{mod}(\Delta^*)$.

Notice that the symbol Mod has been used previously to denote the set of models of an epistemic state. This should cause no confusion. In fact, we can regard Δ as the epistemic state and Δ^* the associated belief state.

Let us present some examples to illustrate the use of prioritised databases:

Example 4.2 (Applications of prioritised databases).

1. We start with an example from Nebel's prioritised base revision [19, page 57]:
   "During the investigation of a crime, detective Holmes decides to interrogate a suspect. The suspect tells him that at the time the crime was commited he was swimming at the beach":

   swimming at the beach ⟼ b

   "Thinking about the case, Mr Holmes recollects that on that particular day the sun was shining, because when he left for work it was too bright and he had to come back to fetch his sunglasses."

   sun is shining ⟼ s

   "He also knows that if the sun is shining and one goes to the beach for a swim they get a sun tan (t)."

   swimming at the beach when the
   sun is shining results in a sun tan ⟼ $(b \wedge s) \to t \equiv \neg b \vee \neg s \vee t$

Mr Holmes gives higher priority to the information he is certain about. This results in the following PDB:

$$[b, s, \neg b \vee \neg s \vee t]$$

From this information, Mr Holmes observes that the suspect should have a sun tan (t), which he does not.

He then adds this information ($\neg t$) to the PDB to revise his beliefs about the whole case.

$$[b, s, \neg b \vee \neg s \vee t, \neg t]$$

As a result, Mr Holmes concludes that the suspect must have lied about his having been to the beach that day for a swim: $\neg b$.

2. The opening example of Gardenförs' book [7, page 1]:

"Oscar used to believe that he had given his wife a gold ring at their wedding. He bought it in a jeweller's shop in Casablanca. At the time, he thought it was a real bargain. Thus, before buying it, in order to certify that it was made of 24 carat gold, he decided that he should go and have it checked at the jeweller next door. If the jeweller told him that it was gold, then it would be fine:

      if another jeweller tells me it is made of gold, then it is ➠ $t \rightarrow g$
      made of gold

In fact, the other jeweller certified to him that the ring was made of 24 carat gold (t), so he was certain that his ring was made of gold:

$$(t \rightarrow g) \circ_r t \equiv t \wedge g$$

However, one day Oscar was cleaning his boat and some sulphuric acid hit the ring. He noticed that it was stained (s). Oscar then remembered from his knowledge of chemistry that the only acid that could stain gold was aqua regia. So if the ring was stained by sulphuric acid, then it was probably not made of gold: $s \rightarrow \neg g$."

So far, the story amounts to the following PDB:

$$[\neg t \vee g, t, s, \neg s \vee \neg g]$$

From this information, Oscar concludes that his belief in the next door jeweller's certification of the ring was wrong:

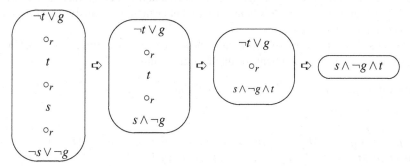

Item 1 of the above example can be formalised as a prioritised base revision (see section on related work later in this chapter). We will see that PDBs in general preserve more of the informational content than linear prioritised belief bases (Example 4.6).

We now analyse properties of the revision of PDBs in more detail.

4.4.1 Properties of the Revisions of PDBs

In this section we discuss some properties of the iterated revisions achieved by PDBs. In order to do this, we analyse a slightly more general setting.

We have seen that a PDB is a sequence of formulae of the form $[\varphi_1, \varphi_2, \ldots, \varphi_k]$, and that a PDB is interpreted as the sequence of revisions $\varphi_1 \circ_r (\ldots \circ_r (\varphi_{k-1} \circ_r \varphi_k) \ldots)$. What we want to provide here is a semantical characterisation of the revision operator with respect to the PDB itself, that is, how valuations of the language compare with each other with respect to the information in the PDB.

In a what follows, for a list of formulae $[\varphi_1, \ldots, \varphi_k]$, we consider the sequence of revisions $\varphi_1 \circ_a (\ldots \circ_a (\varphi_{k-1} \circ_a \varphi_k))$, where $\circ_a$ is *any* revision operator satisfying the AGM postulates (we then get the results for PDBs as a corollary).

The following ordering can be used to describe the general behaviour of the right-associative interpretation of a sequence of AGM revisions of the form $\varphi_1 \circ_a (\ldots \circ_a (\varphi_{k-1} \circ_a \varphi_k))$ (the following definitions and results first appeared in [20]). $M \leq_x N$ and $M \preceq_x N$ means that valuation M is at least as good at satisfying x as valuation N is.

Definition 4.8. Let $\Gamma = [\varphi_1, \varphi_2, \ldots, \varphi_k]$ be a sequence of formulae to be revised from right to left by a revision operator satisfying the AGM postulates, $\leq_{\varphi_i}$ be the faithful assignment for belief revision for each formula φ_i in Γ, as in Definition 3.3, and $i, j \in \{1, \ldots, k\}$.

$M \preceq_\Gamma N$ iff for all i, $N <_{\varphi_i} M$ implies $\exists j > i$ such that $M <_{\varphi_j} N$

Note that if Γ is ε, that is, an empty sequence, then $M \equiv_\Gamma N$ for all $M, N \in \mathscr{I}$, vacuously. The greater the index of the formula, the more recent the information it represents. Thus, what the definition above says is that the failure of a valuation M to be at least as good at satisfying a formula received at time i as another valuation N can only be compensated by $M's$ being strictly better than N at satisfying a formula received at some later time.

Of course, if there is just one formula in the sequence Γ, we expect $\preceq_\Gamma$ to behave exactly as the faithful assignment for that formula. Thus,

Proposition 4.2. *Suppose $\Gamma = [\gamma]$ for some formula γ.*

$M \preceq_\Gamma N$ iff $M \leq_\gamma N$

Proof. ($\Rightarrow$) Suppose $M \preceq_\Gamma N$. By Definition 4.8, for all i, $N <_{\varphi_i} M$ implies $\exists j > i$ such that $M <_{\varphi_j} N$. There is just one formula in Γ. Thus, $\neg \exists j > 1$. Therefore, $N \not<_\gamma M$. Since $\leq_\gamma$ is total, $M \leq_\gamma N$.
($\Leftarrow$) Suppose $M \leq_\gamma N$, but $M \not\preceq_\Gamma N$. By Definition 4.8, if $M \not\preceq_\Gamma N$, then $\exists i$ such that $N <_{\varphi_i} M$ and $\neg \exists j > i$ such that $M <_{\varphi_j} N$. Well, there is just one formula in Γ; therefore, $i = 1$ and $\varphi_1 = \gamma$. If $N <_\gamma M$, then $M \not\leq_\gamma N$, a contradiction.

Also, since the sequence is finite, there must be a point in time which settles any ties between two valuations (in the worst case this is time k — remember that $\leq_\varphi$ is total). Actually, the sequence does not have to be necessarily finite, as long as it has an end point in time (revisions are done backwards).

Proposition 4.3. $M \preceq_\Gamma N$ iff for all i, $N <_{\varphi_i} M$ implies $\exists j > i$ such that $M <_{\varphi_j} N$ and $\forall k \geq j$, $M \leq_{\varphi_k} N$.

Proof. ($\Leftarrow$) Straightforward. ($\Rightarrow$) Suppose $M \preceq_\Gamma N$ and that $N <_{\varphi_i} M$ for some i. Take the maximum j such that $j > i$ and $M <_{\varphi_j} N$ holds. The existence of such j is guaranteed by Definition 4.8 and by the fact that we are considering finite lists of formulae.[4] For any $k \geq j$, it is not the case that $N <_{\varphi_k} M$, because then it would be the case that $M \not\preceq_\Gamma N$. Since the orderings $\leq_{\varphi_{i's}}$ are all total, it follows that $M \leq_{\varphi_k} N$ for all $k \geq j$.

We also expect $\preceq_\Gamma$ to have some desirable properties.

Proposition 4.4. $\preceq_\Gamma$ is a pre-order.

---

[4] Or orderings with a maximum.

Proof. Reflexivity follows directly from reflexivity of each $\leq_{\varphi_i}$. As for transitivity, suppose $M \preceq_\Gamma N$ and $N \preceq_\Gamma O$. We shall show that $M \preceq_\Gamma O$.

Suppose $M \not\leq_{\varphi_i} O$ for some i; we have to show that $\exists j > i$ such that $M <_{\varphi_j} O$.

i) *If $M \leq_{\varphi_i} N$, then either $N \leq_{\varphi_i} O$ or $O <_{\varphi_i} N$ (since $\leq_{\varphi_i}$ is total). In the first case, $M \leq_{\varphi_i} O$ because $\leq_{\varphi_i}$ is transitive, a contradiction. If $O <_{\varphi_i} N$, then from $N \preceq_\Gamma O$, $\exists x > i$ such that $N <_{\varphi_x} O$. If $M \leq_{\varphi_x} N$, then we are done, because $M <_{\varphi_x} O$; so we just take $j = x$. Otherwise, $N <_{\varphi_x} M$, and then $\exists y > x$ such that $M <_{\varphi_y} N$. But $y > x > i$, and hence $N \leq_{\varphi_y} O$, and then $M <_{\varphi_y} O$. Set $j = y$ in this case.*

ii) *If $M \not\leq_{\varphi_i} N$, then $N <_{\varphi_i} M$. Since $M \preceq_\Gamma N$, take $x > i$ such that $M <_{\varphi_x} N$ and for all $k \geq x$, $M \leq_{\varphi_k} N$ (such x exists by Proposition 4.3). If $N \leq_{\varphi_x} O$, then $M <_{\varphi_x} O$, and thus we just need to set $j = x$. Otherwise, $O <_{\varphi_x} N$, and since $N \preceq_\Gamma O$, $\exists y > x$ such that $N <_{\varphi_y} O$. But $y > x > i$. Thus, $M \leq_{\varphi_y} N$, and hence $M <_{\varphi_y} O$. We just set $j = y$ in this case and the proof is finished.*

Proposition 4.5. $\preceq_\Gamma$ *is total.*

Proof. This is easy to show. For suppose $M \not\preceq_\Gamma N$. By Definition 4.8, $\exists x$ such that $N <_{\varphi_x} M$ and $\forall y > x$, it is not the case that $M <_{\varphi_y} N$. Since all $\leq_{\varphi_y}$ are total, it follows that $N \leq_{\varphi_y} M$. This implies that $N \preceq_\Gamma M$, by Proposition 4.3. Clearly, $\neg \exists i \geq x$ such that $M <_{\varphi_i} N$, and if $\exists i < x$ such that $M <_{\varphi_i} N$, then all we have to do is set $j = y$.

Definition 4.9. Let $\varkappa$ be a function such that, for each sequence of formulae Γ

$$\varkappa(\Gamma) = \{\preceq_\Gamma, \mathscr{I}\}.$$

Theorem 4.1. $\varkappa$ *is a faithful assignment for revision of epistemic states.*

Proof. We have to prove that $\varkappa$ satisfies the conditions stated in Definition 2.13. By Proposition 4.4, for each epistemic state Γ, $\preceq_\Gamma$ is a pre-order. By Proposition 4.5, $\preceq_\Gamma$ is also total. If Γ is empty or $\Gamma = [\gamma]$, for some formula γ, then the three conditions follow immediately from Definitions 2.1 and 4.2. Thus, suppose $\Gamma = [\varphi_1, \ldots, \varphi_k]$ for some $k > 1$. As we have done for PDBs, we use the expression $\mathrm{Mod}(\Gamma)$ to represent the set of models of the belief state resulting from the epistemic state Γ. Since we consider the right-associative interpretation of the operator $\circ_a$, this amounts to considering $\mathrm{Mod}(\Gamma) = \mathrm{mod}\,(\varphi_1 \circ_a (\ldots \circ_a (\varphi_{k-1} \circ_a \varphi_k) \ldots))$. The three conditions and the respective proofs are listed below.

1. *$M, N \in \mathrm{Mod}(\Gamma)$ implies $M \equiv_\Gamma N$.*

   Suppose $M \in \mathrm{Mod}(\Gamma)$, $N \in \mathrm{Mod}(\Gamma)$, but $M \prec_\Gamma N$. If $M \in \mathrm{Mod}(\Gamma)$, then $M \in \min_{\leq_{\varphi_1}} (\min_{\leq_{\varphi_2}} (\ldots \mathrm{mod}\,(\varphi_k) \ldots))$. On the other hand, if $M \prec_\Gamma N$, then $\exists i$ such that $N <_{\varphi_i} M$ and $\neg \exists j > i$ such that $M <_{\varphi_j} N$. If $i = k$, then by Definition 2.1, $M \notin \mathrm{mod}\,(\varphi_k)$ and hence $M \notin \mathrm{Mod}(\Gamma)$, a contradiction. If $i < k$, then from $N \in \mathrm{Mod}(\Gamma)$, it follows that $M \notin \min_{\leq_{\varphi_i}} (\ldots (\mathrm{mod}\,(\varphi_k)) \ldots)$ and thus $M \notin \mathrm{Mod}(\Gamma)$, again a contradiction.

2. $M \in \mathrm{Mod}(\Gamma)$ and $N \notin \mathrm{Mod}(\Gamma)$ implies $M \prec_\Gamma N$.

Suppose $M \in \mathrm{Mod}(\Gamma)$, $N \notin \mathrm{Mod}(\Gamma)$, but $N \preceq_\Gamma M$. If $N \notin \mathrm{Mod}(\Gamma)$, then $N \notin \min_{\leq_{\varphi_1}}(\min_{\leq_{\varphi_2}}(\dots \mathrm{mod}\,(\varphi_k)\dots))$. If $N \notin \mathrm{mod}\,(\varphi_k)$, then $M <_{\varphi_k} N$, and thus $N \npreceq_\Gamma M$, a contradiction. Therefore, take the greatest index i such that $N \notin \min_{\leq_{\varphi_i}}(\min_{\leq_{\varphi_{i+1}}}(\dots \mathrm{mod}\,(\varphi_k)\dots))$, but $N \in \min_{\leq_{\varphi_{i+1}}}(\dots \mathrm{mod}\,(\varphi_k)\dots)$ (if $i = k-1$, then $N \in \mathrm{mod}\,(\varphi_k)$). Obviously, $M \in \min_{\leq_{\varphi_{i+1}}}(\dots \mathrm{mod}\,(\varphi_k)\dots)$. It follows that $M <_{\varphi_i} N$, and $\neg \exists j > i$ such that $N <_{\varphi_j} M$, and hence $N \npreceq_\Gamma M$, a contradiction.

3. $\Gamma = \Delta$ implies $\preceq_\Gamma = \preceq_\Delta$.

Immediate.

Theorem 4.2. Let $[\varphi_1, \dots, \varphi_k]$ be a sequence of formulae representing the epistemic state Γ. Consider Γ^*, where the revision operators are AGM-compliant, and let the revision of Γ by β be obtained by appending β to it and computing $(\Gamma : \beta)^*$.

It follows that this revision scheme satisfies postulates (R^*1)–(R^*6).

Proof. All we have to show is that for any sequence Γ, $\mathrm{Mod}(\Gamma \circ_a \beta) = \min_{\preceq_\Gamma}(\mathrm{mod}\,(\beta))$.

We start with the limiting cases. The new epistemic state is obtained by simply appending β to Γ. Thus, if $\Gamma = \varepsilon$, $\Gamma \circ_a \beta = [\beta]$, and then $\mathrm{Mod}([\beta]) = \mathrm{mod}\,(\beta)$. It is easy to see that $\min_{\preceq_\varepsilon}(\mathrm{mod}\,(\beta)) = \mathrm{mod}\,(\beta)$. It is also straightforward to prove that the theorem holds when $\mathrm{mod}\,(\beta)$ is empty.

Let $\Gamma = [\varphi_1, \dots, \varphi_k]$ be a sequence of formulae. It follows that $\mathrm{Mod}(\Gamma \circ_a \beta) = \mathrm{mod}\,(\varphi_1 \circ_a (\dots (\varphi_k \circ_a \beta)))$.

($\subseteq$) Suppose $I \in \mathrm{Mod}(\Gamma \circ_a \beta)$, but $I \notin \min_{\preceq_\Gamma}(\mathrm{mod}\,(\beta))$. If $I \in \mathrm{mod}\,(\Gamma \circ_a \beta)$, then $I \in \mathrm{mod}\,(\beta)$. It follows that $\exists J \in \mathrm{mod}\,(\beta)$ such that $J \prec_\Gamma I$. By Proposition 4.3, $\exists x$ such that $J <_{\varphi_x} I$ and $\forall y > x$, $J \leq_{\varphi_y} I$. On the other hand, if $I \in \mathrm{Mod}(\Gamma \circ_a \beta)$, then

$$I \in \min_{\leq_{\varphi_1}}(\dots(\min_{\leq_{\varphi_x}}(\min_{\leq_{\varphi_{x+1}}}(\dots \min_{\leq_{\varphi_k}}(\mathrm{mod}\,(\beta))))))$$

We know that $J <_{\varphi_x} I$. Notice that if $I \in \min_{\leq_{\varphi_{x+1}}}(\dots(\min_{\leq_{\varphi_k}}(\mathrm{mod}\,(\beta))))$, so does J. This is guaranteed by the fact that $\forall y > x$, $J \leq_{\varphi_y} I$. But this is a contradiction, because $J <_{\varphi_x} I$ and therefore $I \notin \min_{\varphi_x}(\min_{\varphi_{x+1}}(\dots \min_{\varphi_k}(\mathrm{mod}\,(\beta))))$.

($\supseteq$) Suppose $I \in \min_{\preceq_\Gamma}(\mathrm{mod}\,(\beta))$, but $I \notin \mathrm{Mod}(\Gamma \circ_a \beta)$. If $I \notin \mathrm{Mod}(\Gamma \circ_a \beta)$, then

$$I \notin \min_{\leq_{\varphi_1}}(\dots(\min_{\leq_{\varphi_x}}(\min_{\leq_{\varphi_{x+1}}}(\dots \min_{\leq_{\varphi_k}}(\mathrm{mod}\,(\beta))))))$$

Obviously, $I \in \mathrm{mod}\,(\beta)$, so let x be the greatest index for which

$$I \notin \min_{\leq_{\varphi_x}}(\min_{\leq_{\varphi_{x+1}}}(\dots(\min_{\leq_{\varphi_k}}(\mathrm{mod}\,(\beta)))))$$

It follows that $\exists J \in \min_{\leq_{\varphi_{x+1}}}(\dots(\min_{\leq_{\varphi_k}}(\mathrm{mod}\,(\beta))))$ such that $J <_{\varphi_x} I$ (if $x = k$, then the expression on the right-hand side of $\in$ is just $\mathrm{mod}\,(\beta)$). But $I \in \min_{\preceq_\Gamma}(\mathrm{mod}\,(\beta))$; therefore, by Definition 4.8 $\exists y > x$ such that $I <_{\varphi_y} J$. If $x = k$, this is a contradiction. If $x < k$, then this contradicts $J \in \min_{\leq_{\varphi_{x+1}}}(\dots(\min_{\leq_{\varphi_k}}(\mathrm{mod}\,(\beta))))$.

As a consequence of this theorem, and because $\circ_r$ complies with the AGM postulates, the revision procedure achieved by PDBs also verifies postulates (R^*1)–(R^*6).

Corollary 4.1. The revision scheme achieved by PDBs verifies postulates (R^*1)–(R^*6).

4.4.2 Discussion about Iteration of Revision

We now discuss more specifically how the ordering $\preceq$ evolves as new formulae are added to a PDB. Note that, in general, this applies to any scheme that uses AGM operators in the right-associative interpretation. Of course, different faithful assignment orderings will result in different results, but the principles are exactly the same. In fact, one does not even need to assume that the same operator is used in all stages, as long as the right assignment is used in the analysis at the appropriate time.

Since we are considering the specific operator $\circ_r$, we must also consider the faithful assignment that characterises it. Suppose our initial PDB is composed solely of formula p. The ordering in this case is just $\leq_p$, shown below. For simplicity, we consider $\mathscr{L}$ over $[p, q, r]$ only.

$$000, 001, 010, 011$$
$$\uparrow$$
$$100, 101, 110, 111$$

There is not much information in the PDB at this initial stage and the ordering above reflects that; it only makes a distinction between the valuations that satisfy p and those which do not.[5] The models of p are obviously the minimal elements in the ordering.

By adding the formula $p \to q$ to the PDB above, the ordering changes to reflect the new priorities:

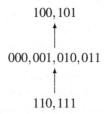

$$100, 101$$
$$\uparrow$$
$$000, 001, 010, 011$$
$$\uparrow$$
$$110, 111$$

Now we have three classes of valuations: in the most important one we have 110 and 111, which are exactly the only two models of the two formulae. The best alternatives to these valuations are the valuations $000, 001, 010, 011$. These are exactly the valuations that although failing to satisfy p, at least satisfy the most important formula in the PDB: $p \to q$. The next level contains the valuations that do not satisfy $p \to q$, but satisfy p.

The addition of r to the PDB results in the following rearrangement of the ordering:

---

[5] These are exactly what conditions 1 and 2 of Definition 2.1 require (see page 20).

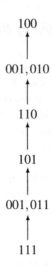

The minimal elements of this ordering are exactly the models of the three formulae. The next class contains the valuations that satisfy the two more important formulae of the PDB, followed by the class with the valuations that satisfy the more important formulae and the least important one.

The other four classes of the ordering follow a similar reasoning, except that they contain the valuations that fail to satisfy r. If that is not possible, the next best thing is to satisfy the other two formulae. This is represented by valuation 110. The next two valuations satisfy the second formula and the least preferred valuation satisfies only the least important formula.

Perhaps a little more interesting is to see how the ordering above is obtained. First, one needs to order the valuations according to the more important formula: r. Since $\leq_x$ is total, it will generate a number of equivalence classes. Each of these classes need to be in turn ordered according to the next formula in the PDB, which in this case is $p \to q$. Finally, one has to order the resulting classes according to the last formula p (see Figure 4.1).

This interleaving of faithful assignments is only possible because a PDB uses its list representation as a record of the history of updates. Thus, in a sense the computation of a PDB's consequences (i.e., its associated belief state) 'remembers' past updates. A PDB can hence be considered a special case of a *revision operator with memory*, as subsequently defined by Konieczny and Pérez in [14].

More formally, we can show the relation between the ordering of a given PDB Γ and the ordering of Γ revised by a formula β in the following way:

Proposition 4.6. *Let* $\Gamma = [\varphi_1, \ldots, \varphi_k]$ *be a PDB,* β *be a formula,* $\preceq_\Gamma$ *be the faithful assignment for epistemic states for* Γ *and* $\leq_\beta$ *be the faithful assignment for formulae for* β.

$M \preceq_{\Gamma \circ_r \beta} N$ *iff* $N \leq_\beta M$ *implies* $M \leq_\beta N$ *and* $M \preceq_\Gamma N$

where $\preceq_{\Gamma \circ_r \beta}$ *is the faithful assignment for the PDB* $[\varphi_1, \ldots, \varphi_k, \beta]$.

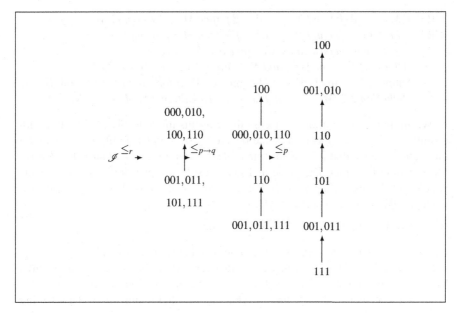

Fig. 4.1 Embedding orderings in PDBs.

Proof. ($\Rightarrow$) *Suppose* $M \preceq_{\Gamma \circ_r \beta} N$ *and* $N \leq_\beta M$. *By Definition 4.8, for* $0 \leq i \leq k+1$, $N <_{\varphi_i} M$ *implies* $\exists j, i > j \leq k+1$ *such that* $M <_{\varphi_j} N$. *Clearly,* $M \not<_{\varphi_{k+1}} N$, *since* $N \leq_\beta M$. *Therefore,* $M \leq_\beta N$ *and if* $N <_{\varphi_i} M$ *for* $0 \leq i \leq k$, *then* $\exists j, i < j \leq k$ *such that* $M <_{\varphi_j} N$. *By Definition 4.8 again,* $M \preceq_\Gamma N$.
($\Leftarrow$) *Suppose* $N \leq_\beta M$, *but* $M \not\preceq_{\Gamma \circ_r \beta} N$. *If* $M \not\preceq_{\Gamma \circ_r \beta} N$, *then* $\exists i, 0 \leq i \leq k+1$ *such that* $N <_{\varphi_i} M$ *and* $\neg \exists j > i$ *such that* $M <_{\varphi_j} N$. *This is a contradiction, for if* $i = k+1$, *then* $M \not\leq_\beta N$, *and if* $i \leq k$, *then* $M \not\preceq_\Gamma N$. *On the other hand, if* $N \not\leq_\beta M$, *then* $M <_\beta N$, *and* $M \preceq_{\Gamma \circ_r \beta} N$ *follows trivially.*

With the above characterisation we can prove the following result.

Theorem 4.3. *The revision method achieved by PDBs satisfies postulates* (C1), (C3) *and* (C4).

Proof. The proof is obtained via Darwiche and Pearl's semantic characterisation of postulates (C1), (C3) *and* (C4), *namely conditions* (CR1), (CR3) *and* (CR4), *and Proposition 4.6 above.*

(CR1) *If* $M, N \in \mod(\beta)$, *then* $M \preceq_\Gamma N$ *iff* $M \preceq_{\Gamma \circ_a \beta} N$.
    Suppose $M, N \in \mod(\beta)$. *By Definition 2.1,* $M, N \in \mod(\beta)$ *implies* $M \leq_\beta N$ *and* $N \leq_\beta M$.
    ($\Rightarrow$) *Suppose* $M \preceq_\Gamma N$. *By Proposition 4.6, from* $N \leq_\beta B$, $M \leq_\beta N$ *and* $M \preceq_\Gamma N$; *then* $M \preceq_{\Gamma \circ_a \beta} N$.
    ($\Leftarrow$) *Suppose* $M \preceq_{\Gamma \circ_a \beta} N$. *By Proposition 4.6, since* $N \leq_\beta M$, $M \leq_\beta N$ *and* $M \preceq_\Gamma N$.

(CR3) *If $M \in \text{mod}(\beta)$ and $N \in \text{mod}(\neg\beta)$, then $M \prec_\Gamma N$ implies $M \prec_{\Gamma \circ_a \beta} N$.*
(CR4) *If $M \in \text{mod}(\beta)$ and $N \in \text{mod}(\neg\beta)$, then $M \preceq_\Gamma N$ implies $M \preceq_{\Gamma \circ_a \beta} N$.*
   For these two constraints, we prove a stronger result:
   (CR⋆) *If $M \in \text{mod}(\beta)$ and $N \in \text{mod}(\neg\beta)$, then $M \prec_{\Gamma \circ_a \beta} N$.*
   Suppose $M \in \text{mod}(\beta)$ and $N \in \text{mod}(\neg\beta)$. It follows that $N \notin \text{mod}(\beta)$. By Definition 2.1, $M <_\beta N$, and hence by Definition 4.8, $M \prec_{\Gamma \circ_a \beta} N$.

We are now in a position to discuss these results more deeply. Let us start with postulate (C2). There has been some debate about the plausibility of (C2) in the literature. It seems that (C2) is incompatible with the *principle of minimal change*. The example by which Darwiche and Pearl justify the plausibility of (C2) is arguable (see details in [3, page 12]). We reproduce it below, so that we can discuss it at length. We also recap postulate (C2).

(C2)   If $A \vDash \neg B$, then $(\Psi \circ_a B) \circ_a A \equiv \Psi \circ_a A$

Example 4.3. Our agent starts with the belief that lady X is smart and that she is also rich (*smart* $\wedge$ *rich*). This epistemic state is then revised by $\neg smart$ and, subsequently, by *smart*. Since *smart* $\wedge$ *rich* is followed by some information that contradicts this observation, namely, $\neg smart$, the postulate applies and requires that the resulting epistemic state be equivalent to the initial state revised by the second observation only. In other words, the intermediate observation should be disregarded:

$$\begin{pmatrix} smart \wedge rich \\ \uparrow \\ \neg smart \\ \uparrow \\ smart \end{pmatrix} \equiv \begin{pmatrix} smart \wedge rich \\ \uparrow \\ smart \end{pmatrix}$$

The point we would like to raise here is that the reason why (C2) seems reasonable in this example is because nothing of the informational content of the first revising formula can be kept when facing the second revision. After all, what could be consistently kept from $\neg smart$ in the face of *smart*?

However, consider the following modified scenario: we start with an initially empty epistemic state which is to be revised by *smart* $\wedge$ *rich* and then by $\neg smart$.

$$\begin{pmatrix} \varnothing \\ \uparrow \\ smart \wedge rich \\ \uparrow \\ \neg smart \end{pmatrix} \stackrel{?}{\equiv} \begin{pmatrix} \varnothing \\ \uparrow \\ \neg smart \end{pmatrix}$$

The postulate applies here too, because $\neg smart \vdash \neg(smart \wedge rich)$. If we adopt the principle of minimal change, it seems counterintuitive to give up the belief in *rich* in the face of ¬*smart* only. It might have been the case that our observation with respect to lady X's being smart was wrong, but this does not necessarily mean that our belief in her being rich was inaccurate too. The acceptance of the postulate requires this though.

Re-analysing (CR2), we can see this in another way:

(CR2)   If $M, N \in \text{mod}(\neg A)$, then $M \preceq_\Psi N$ iff $M \preceq_{\Psi \circ_a A} N$.

The fact that both M and N do not satisfy A is not sufficient to consider them equally good at satisfying A. Therefore, the ordering $\leq_A$ might change the way M and N relate in $\preceq_{\Psi \circ_a A}$ with respect to the way they used to relate in $\preceq_\Psi$.

Regarding (C3) and (C4), we have shown that the following condition holds:

(CR⋆)   If $M \in \text{mod}(\beta)$ and $N \in \text{mod}(\neg\beta)$, then $M \prec_{\Gamma \circ_a \beta} N$.

(CR⋆) is stronger than each of the corresponding conditions on the faithful assignment orderings (CR3) and (CR4):

(CR3)   If $M \in \text{mod}(\beta)$ and $N \in \text{mod}(\neg\beta)$, then $M \prec_\Gamma N$ implies $M \prec_{\Gamma \circ_a \beta} N$.
(CR4)   If $M \in \text{mod}(\beta)$ and $N \in \text{mod}(\neg\beta)$, then $M \preceq_\Gamma N$ implies $M \preceq_{\Gamma \circ_a \beta} N$.

The motivation for (CR⋆) comes from the following observation: when Γ is revised by β, the new top priority is to satisfy β (if possible at all). If M satisfies β, but N does not, it should not matter how M and N related before with respect to $\preceq_\Gamma$. In the new ordering $\preceq_{\Gamma \circ_a \beta}$, M should be preferred to N.

Within the family of revision operators with memory [14], only the so-called *basic memory revision operator* satisfies (C2). The basic memory revision operator partitions the set of all valuations into at most two equivalence classes, one with the models of the new belief φ (if any) and the other with the valuations that do not satisfy φ, preferring the first class to the second if it is non-empty. Therefore, it is only able to distinguish models of the new belief from valuations that fail to satisfy it. All other revision operators with memory fail to satisfy (C2). For a further discussion, the reader is referred to [14].

We now continue our discussion on iteration by considering how PDBs relate to Lehmann's postulates [15] (see Section 2.9.2) and we also put forward some questions.

One of the negative results of Lehmann's approach is that for any long enough sequence of revisions, the revision procedure becomes trivial. In Lehmann's terminology, a trivial revision procedure does the following job

$$[\sigma \cdot \alpha] = \begin{cases} \text{Cn}(\alpha), & \text{if } \neg\alpha \in [\sigma] \\ \text{Cn}([\sigma], \alpha), & \text{otherwise} \end{cases}$$

This is obviously against the principle of minimal change. Lehmann suggests that because postulates (I1)–(I7) are closely related to the AGM's original postulates, no reasonable revision satisfying these postulates can comply with the principle of minimal change. It seems to us that the problem lies in postulate (I7) below.

(I7) $[\sigma \cdot \neg\beta \cdot \beta] \subseteq \text{Cn}([\sigma], \beta)$

(I7) is a weaker version of Darwiche and Pearl's (C2), which we have also argued to be counterintuitive with respect to minimal change. The revision procedure defined by PDBs, even though not complying with (I1)–(I7), does comply with the original AGM postulates and the widely accepted (C1), (C3) and (C4). More importantly, the longer the sequence of revisions, the more structured the ordering for the PDB and the less trivial the whole revision process.

As suggested by the rounded boxes in Example 4.1, PDBs can be easily extended to allow for more complex structures of revisions at a given point. This has two advantages: firstly, it frees the formalism from a fixed interpretation of the application of the revision operation (the left-associative interpretation can be obtained with an appropriate grouping); secondly, it allows for the representation of different classes of priorities among the beliefs in a base. This is the main motivation for the definition of *structured databases*.

4.5 Structured Databases

In order to enrich the structure in a prioritised database, all we have to do is to extend Definition 4.4 accordingly:

Definition 4.10 (Structured databases). A *structured database (SDB)* is a list of objects $\Delta = [\delta_1, \ldots, \delta_k]$, each of which is a formula of propositional logic or another SDB.

What the definition above tells us is that PDBs can be seen as a special case of SDBs, where the objects in the lists are simply formulae of propositional logic.

We need some auxiliary definitions. The one below evaluates how deeply nested a given SDB is. For this we formalise the notion of the *level of an SDB*.

Definition 4.11 (Level of an SDB). The level of any formula of propositional logic is 0. Let $\Delta = [\delta_1, \ldots, \delta_k]$ be an SDB. The level of Δ, in symbols, level(Δ), is defined recursively as follows:

$$\mathrm{level}(\Delta) = \sup_{1 \leq i \leq k} \{\mathrm{level}(\delta_i)\} + 1$$

Thus, an SDB of level 1 is just a PDB as defined previously, as expected. SDBs can also be perceived as structures associated with a family of orderings. In this way, it is possible to concentrate on a given level and to abstract ourselves from the embedded orderings by referring to all the formulae associated with a given node by the node name itself. This is useful when we want to talk specifically about properties of an SDB of a particular level, for instance. Figure 4.2 illustrates the idea. We could refer to the structure associated with label x as x itself, and say that Γ is simply $[w, x, y, z]$, instead of the more precise but perhaps too-detailed description $[w, [[d, e, f], b, c], y, z]$.

In Figure 4.3, if we ignore the orderings of the embedded SDBs of Γ, we will be left with some equivalence classes under the ordering of Γ. That is, the formulae

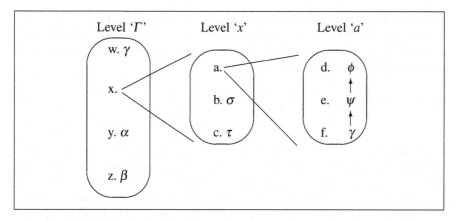

Fig. 4.2 Another way of visualising an SDB

in the embedded SDBs $x = [a, b, [d, e]]$ and $a = [[\phi, \psi, \gamma], \sigma, [\tau, \rho]]$ are all equivalent with respect to the ordering of Γ. The embedded orderings are used to solve conflicts within each of the classes. This makes it possible to represent clusters of structured formulae. In Example 4.5, we will show how to represent default and integrity constraints in this way.

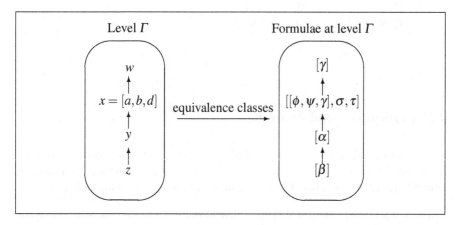

Fig. 4.3 Visualising the top-level classes of SDB Γ

Naturally, an interpretation has to be given about the way the information in an SDB is perceived. Any SDB of level greater than 0, for instance, could be assigned either the left or right interpretations mentioned earlier. However, since now we allow multiple levels of nesting, we can assume one interpretation from which the other can also be obtained. As before, we will consider the right-associative interpretation.

Definition 4.12 (Perceiving the information in an SDB). Let $\Delta = [\delta_1, \delta_2, \ldots, \delta_k]$ be an SDB. The interpretation of the information in Δ is a formula in DNF and denoted val(Δ) . We define val(δ) for δ a formula as δ itself. For SDBs, val is defined recursively in the following way:

$$\text{val}(\Delta) = \begin{cases} \top, & \text{if } \Delta = \varepsilon \\ \text{val}(\delta_k), & \text{if } k = 1 \\ \text{val}(\delta_1) \circ_r (\ldots \circ_r (\text{val}(\delta_{k-1}) \circ_r \text{val}(\delta_k))), & \text{otherwise} \end{cases}$$

The idea is to successively reduce each non-terminal element in the SDB until it evaluates to a formula in DNF, thus reducing it to a prioritised database, to which the revision operator can be applied under the right-associative interpretation. Since substructures are allowed, it is also possible to obtain the left-associative interpretation of the revision operation via appropriate groupings. In fact, mixed types of association can be obtained, since we now have the means of implicitly 'parenthesising' the sequence of revisions. This makes it possible to control where the coherentist view is applied.[6]

Example 4.4 (Obtaining the left-associative interpretation). Let $\Delta = [\varphi_1, \ldots, \varphi_k]$ be a PDB. The SDB $\Gamma = [[[[\varphi_1, \varphi_2], \ldots], \varphi_{k-1}], \varphi_k]$ evaluates to $^*\Delta$:

$$\text{val}(\Gamma) =$$
$$\text{val}([[[\varphi_1, \varphi_2], \ldots], \varphi_{k-1}]) \circ_r \text{val}(\varphi_k) =$$
$$(\text{val}([[\varphi_1, \varphi_2], \ldots])) \circ_r \text{val}(\varphi_{k-1})) \circ_r \varphi_k =$$
$$((\text{val}([\varphi_1, \varphi_2]) \circ_r \ldots) \circ_r \varphi_{k-1}) \circ_r \varphi_k =$$
$$\vdots$$
$$= (((\varphi_1 \circ_r \varphi_2) \circ_r \ldots) \circ_r \varphi_{k-1}) \circ_r \varphi_k = {}^*\Delta$$

4.6 Applications and Examples

The extra structure available in an SDB allows for the definition of different classes of priorities among its substructures. This is very useful to represent components with different status in a belief base, as can be seen in the following examples.

Example 4.5 (Using additional information in belief revision). Suppose our agent has a number of beliefs represented as an SDB Δ, where the formulae in Δ are partitioned into three classes: *Default*, *KB* and *PF*. The class *Default* represents information about which the agent is not very certain, and hence gives it the lowest priority in Δ; *KB* represents general beliefs held by the agent and *PF* contains special beliefs which the agent holds very firmly (these are expected never to be given up).

1. Initially, *Default* $= \{bt \rightarrow ft\}$, representing the belief that "if tweety is a bird, then it flies"; *KB* $= \{bt\}$ contains the belief "tweety is a bird"; and *PF* $= \{pt \rightarrow$

---

[6] Once a given node is 'resolved', all beliefs gain equal standing.

$\neg ft\}$ contains the belief "if tweety is a penguin, then it definitely does not fly". This *integrity constraint* is given the highest priority and the default information the lowest one.

The interpretation of this SDB is that the information in *KB* is to be subjected to the protected formulae *PF* and the result then superimposed on the default information. This is to be understood as extracting from the defaults only the information compatible with the rest of the knowledge base plus protected formulae. Obviously, only the information in *KB* consistent with the protected beliefs *PF* is to be extracted. Δ can be seen as the SDB

$$[[bt \rightarrow ft], [[bt], [pt \rightarrow \neg ft]]]$$

shown below.

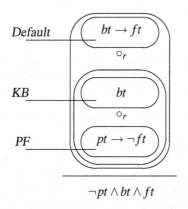

$$\neg pt \wedge bt \wedge ft$$

Note that $bt \circ_r (pt \rightarrow \neg ft)$ results in $bt \wedge (pt \rightarrow \neg ft)$, which is consistent with $bt \rightarrow ft$. No information about pt is available. Since it is not known whether or not tweety is a penguin, the agent assumes that it is not, in order to accept the information represented in the defaults.

The result of this SDB is then equivalent to $\neg pt \wedge bt \wedge ft$. In other words,

"tweety is a bird, it is not a penguin and it can fly"

It can be verified that this result is equivalent to the conjunction of all of the three formulae in Δ (they are all consistent, so revisions as expected amount to simple expansions).

2. Now, suppose that later on the agent finds out that tweety is in fact a penguin. He can add this information to the knowledge base by appending it to the list (*KB*). This guarantees that it will be accepted in *KB*, but not necessarily in the SDB, as *KB* itself is subject to *PF*. The resulting SDB is therefore

$$[[bt \rightarrow ft], [[bt, pt], [pt \rightarrow \neg ft]]]$$

This can be depcited as follows. Note that the new belief will be completely rejected if it is found to be inconsistent with the protected formulae. In this case, it is not a matter of verifying the *principle of primacy of the update*, but rather of limiting the situations when the agent is prepared to accept new inputs (in this case, as long as it does not contradict *PF*).

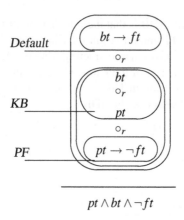

Note that $bt \circ_r pt$ gives us $pt \wedge bt$, and $(pt \wedge bt) \circ_r (pt \rightarrow \neg ft)$ gives us $pt \wedge bt \wedge \neg ft$. In this case, nothing of the informational content of *Default* can be retained. The agent finally concludes that

"tweety is a bird, it is a penguin and it cannot fly"

In the example above, even if the defaults are inconsistent with the rest of the belief state, whatever information conveyed by them that is consistent with it would still be incorporated. It is possible to avoid this, by adopting an all-or-nothing approach. This can be accomplished by requiring that the revision of the defaults by the rest of the belief base be declined when the defaults are inconsistent with it. For the propositional case and under our methodology, it is easy to check for consistency, as two formulae ψ and φ in DNF are consistent with each other if and only if there are disjuncts $P \in \psi$ and $Q \in \varphi$ such that $dist(P, Q) = 0$.

4.7 Related Work

PDBs can be considered as a special type of base revision called *prioritised base revision*, a term coined by Nebel in [17]. In this section, we make some comparisons between ours and other formalisms. We start with Nebel's prioritised base revision.

4.7.1 Prioritised Base Revision

A *prioritised belief base* is a pair $\Gamma = \langle K, \sqsubseteq \rangle$, where K is a belief base and $\sqsubseteq$ is a total pre-order on K. $\sqsubseteq$ represents priorities in K, where $x \sqsubseteq y$ denotes that y has at least the same priority as x. If $\sqsubseteq$ is also antisymmetric, Γ is called a *linear prioritised belief base*. It is also assumed that $\sqsubseteq$ always has maximal elements. The relation $\sqsubseteq$ is called an *epistemic relevance ordering* by Nebel.

K can be partitioned into a set of equivalence classes induced by $\sqsubseteq$. That is, a family of subsets of K whose elements are at the same priority level mod $\sqsubseteq$. Let us call such a partitioning $\overline{K}$. If K is finite, Γ can be represented as a list $\Gamma = [K_1, \ldots, K_n]$ where the K_i's are the partitions of K generated by the equivalence relation induced by $\sqsubseteq$. Moreover, if Γ is linear, then each K_i is just a singleton.

In order to obtain a revision of H by φ, in symbols, $H * \varphi$, a Levi Identity approach is used. H is first contracted by $\neg\varphi$ and then expanded by φ. The contraction of H by $\neg\varphi$ uses the epistemic relevance ordering and is called *prioritised removal of $\neg\varphi$ from H*, in symbols, $H \Downarrow \neg\varphi$. It is a *family* of subsets of K of the form

$$X = \bigcup_{K_i \in \overline{K}} \{H_i\}$$

where each H_i is a subset of K_i. Furthermore, $X \in \Gamma \Downarrow \neg\varphi$ iff $\forall X' \subseteq K$ and $\forall i$:

$$X \cap (K_i \cup \ldots \cup K_n) \subset X' \cap (K_i \cup \ldots \cup K_n) \text{ implies } \neg\varphi \in Cn(X')$$

where K_n is the class containing the maximal elements in K with respect to $\sqsubseteq$. That is, starting from the most prioritised equivalence class, we consider maximal subsets of each class that together with the set being constructed do not imply $\neg\varphi$. There will possibly be a number of such X's, as there are possibly many combinations of subsets of each class that do not imply $\neg\varphi$. Therefore, to obtain the belief state in the prioritised removal of $\neg\varphi$ from Γ it is necessary to take the set $\bigcap \{Cn(X) \mid X \in \Gamma \Downarrow \neg\varphi\}$.

The prioritised base revision of Γ by φ then amounts to the following equivalence:

$$\Gamma * \varphi =^{def} Cn(\bigcap \{Cn(X) \mid X \in \Gamma \Downarrow \neg\varphi\} \cup \{\varphi\})$$

Thus, as for PDBs and SDBs, iteration requires a recomputation of the revision process. If K is finite, then $\Gamma * \varphi$ can be finitely represented and the result is simply

$$Cn(\bigvee (\Gamma \Downarrow \neg\varphi) \wedge \varphi)$$

Finite prioritised belief bases and the PDBs presented in this chapter have much in common. If the prioritised belief base is not linear, but is finite, it is possible to represent it as a PDB by taking the list of conjunctions of the formulae in each priority class. Unlike with the removal of formulae that occur in the prioritised base revision, the amount of information of each class preserved will depend on the distance function used. This is, of course, subject to the same criticisms about representing knowledge bases as the conjunction of their formulae. On the other hand, if there are many formulae in each class, the number of subsets in $\Gamma \Downarrow \neg\varphi$ could be considerably large.

Finite linear prioritised belief bases do not suffer from such a drawback. As the classes in $\Gamma \Downarrow \neg\varphi$ are simply singletons, they provide a unique result. However, it has been pointed out that linearity can be quite a strong restriction [9, page 94]. PDBs and prioritised belief bases are very similar, because the singletons can be directly translated to formulae in the PDB. The main difference is that linear prioritised belief bases operate on an all-or-nothing basis at each level. That is, whenever a formula ψ from a class K_i is inconsistent with the accumulated result from the higher priority classes, it is simply ignored and the formula in the next priority level is considered, and so forth. In a PDB, such a formula ψ would be *revised* instead by the result of the revision so far accumulated. Consequently, it can be argued that PDBs preserve more of the informational content of the beliefs in each class than prioritised linear base revisions, as can be seen in the example below.

Example 4.6. Consider the following linear prioritised belief base

$$K = [\{p \wedge q\}, \{p \rightarrow r\}],$$

and suppose we want to revise it by $\neg q$. We first need to construct $K \Downarrow q$. We have to take elements from K starting at the highest priority level and make sure that they do not imply q. Thus, the result is just $\{p \rightarrow r\}$, since the inclusion of $p \wedge q$ would imply q. The prioritised revision of K by $\neg q$ is then

$$Cn(\{p \rightarrow r\} \cup \{\neg q\}).$$

However, if we had $\{p, q\}$ instead of $\{p \wedge q\}$ the result would be different, as the belief in p would be maintained.[7]

With PDBs, the required revision would be obtained by simply appending $\neg q$ to the PDB $[p \wedge q, p \rightarrow r]$, and computing the sequence of revisions (we write the formulae in DNF in the diagrams below):

Remember that revisions in a PDB are right-associative. In the final result, the belief in p can be retained, and since $p \rightarrow r$ is also supported, the agent also holds the belief in r. In a prioritised base revision not only would the belief $p \wedge q$ be retracted (and consequently the belief in p), but also the formerly held belief r. This example also shows that PDBs and SBBs are not as sensitive to syntax as an ordinary base revision. When each cluster in an SBB is resolved into a formula, the revision is accomplished by the operator which complies with the AGM postulates. At that stage, the syntax becomes irrelevant, because in the revision process what is actually being taken into account are the sets of models of the formulae involved.

SBBs provide a more flexible mechanism for the specification of priorities. Consequently, more complex structures can be expressed. It also has the advantage of

---

[7] Prioritised belief bases are therefore more sensitive to syntax too.

always providing a unique result and making it possible to iterate revisions very straightforwardly. In the next chapter we analyse how the requirement on linearity of the ordering of a PDB could be relaxed to enhance expressivity.

4.7.2 Ordered Theory Presentations

Ordered theory presentation (OTP) [22] is a formalism that can be used in reasoning about epistemic changes. The main idea is to have a belief base provided with an associated *partial* order. The ordering can be used to solve conflicts between formulae in the base when they arise. For belief revision, the ordering is required to be total and the base finite [22, Section 4.4]. Thus, OTPs for the special case of belief revision, can be included among the formalisms for linear prioritised base revision.

The main differences between OTPs and other formalisms for prioritised base revision are in the ways conflicts are solved. In particular, the *extension* of an OTP is determined semantically, whereas SDBs offer a syntactical approach to the problem. The consequences that can be obtained from an OTP are defined in terms of preferred models of the theory, whereas in SDBs they are obtained via successive and (possibly) recursive applications of the revision operator.

Another important difference is in the way change is evaluated. In OTPs, this is done via a notion called *natural consequence*, whereas in SDBs it is based on a distance function. The idea behind natural consequences is to restrict the classical consequences of a formula that are to be used in the evaluation of change. Analogously to the distance function diff analysed previously, natural consequence gives rise to a partial order on the set of valuations with respect to formulae. As an example, we can consider the ordering on valuations obtained in the two formalisms.

Consider the language $\mathscr{L}$ over $[p,q]$. Again, we represent valuations as in Notation 4 (see page 89). In what follows, valuations appearing lower in the diagrams are preferred to those above them (see Figure 4.4).

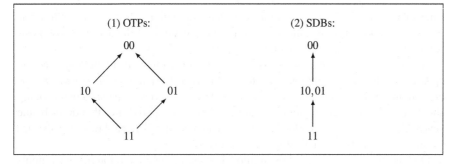

Fig. 4.4 Comparative change for $p \wedge q$ in OTPs and SDBs

In (1), 10 and 01 are incomparable because they satisfy different natural consequences of $p \wedge q$, namely p and q, respectively. In (2), they are considered equivalent,
because they have the same distance with respect to the models of $p \wedge q$, that is, to
11 ($dist = 1$). In this sense, OTPs offer a *qualitative* evaluation of change, whereas
SDBs offer a more *quantitative* one. The distance function in SDBs results in a total
ordering on the set of valuations, which ultimately leads to the satisfaction of the
postulates at each point where the revision operator is applied.

In both cases, the relative ordering on components (formulae) is required to be
linear, which means that it is not possible to specify beliefs with the same relative
priorities or beliefs with incomparable levels of priority. If they are consistent, then
we can simply take their conjunction. However, if they are not, another mechanism
to extract only the consistent information from them needs to be provided.

Another difference is that we have allowed for the definition of embedded structured bases in any given point of the SDB, which makes it possible to represent
more complex patterns of inference.

4.8 Using Additional Information for Action Updates

We briefly mentioned that the right-associative interpretation of the sequence of
formulae in a PDB is not intuitively suited for the representation of belief states
in the reasoning about action. However, by using SDBs, we are free to choose any
interpretation and represent a more complex hierarchy between the formulae in the
base. In this section, we will analyse some examples of the use of SDBs for more
complex problems in reasoning about the effects of actions.

The first obvious example is to see the sequence of formulae of a PDB (or an
SDB) as the record of the sequence of updates to a given database. For instance, the
sequence of updates seen in Examples 3.12.1 and 3.12.2, could be directly represented as the SDB:

$$[[m \vee n, \neg m], m \vee n]$$

where the embedded structure represents that the action whose post-condition is
$m \vee n$ was executed in the state reached by the execution of the action whose post-
condition is $\neg m$ in the state where the property $m \vee n$ holds.

Another example of the use of extralogical information in the modelling of action
updates is in the representation of protected formulae [23] or *integrity constraints*, as
they are more commonly known in the area. Any framework to be used in reasoning
about the effects of actions should be able to handle properly rules that describe the
general behaviour of the world. These rules can describe physical laws or properties
intended to be satisfied in all states of a given system.

One question that arises is how to model properly the interaction between inputs
to the knowledge base and the protected formulae. Both characterisations for belief
revision and updates include the so-called *success postulate*:

(R1) $K \circ_a A$ implies A
(U1) $K \diamond A$ implies A

That is, the new formula is always accepted in the new belief state. If the protected formulae are encoded as part of the old knowledge base, they can be overridden by new incoming information. Intuitively, this is not a desirable result. In [13], Katsuno and Mendelzon proposed a modified version of the revision operator $\circ_a$, denoted by $\circ_a^{IC}$, which takes into account a formula IC representing the protected formulae. $\circ_a^{IC}$ is defined as

$$\psi \circ_a^{IC} \varphi \equiv \psi \circ (\varphi \wedge IC)$$

It is straightforward to see that if $\circ_a$ verifies (R1) above, then the protected formulae are always satisfied. On the other hand, as pointed out in [13], if the new information is inconsistent with the integrity constraints, then the new revised belief set is also inconsistent. This is rather undesirable. An alternative option would be to weaken (R1) (and/or (U1)) so that the revised (updated) belief set implies the new formula only if it does not contradict the protected formulae. That is, using the terminology of Chapter 3.1, where K represents the belief set and A the new formula to be incorporated:

(R1′) If $IC \wedge A$ is consistent, then $K \circ_a A$ implies A

This obviously contradicts the *principle of primacy of the update*. A different perspective is to adopt some control at the meta-level. That is, one still supports new information being accepted in the revised belief state, but declines the *revision process* completely if the new information is inconsistent with the integrity constraints. In other words, the revision process is always successful, but the agent may decide to decline it.

Another alternative is to include in K only the consequences of A that are consistent with IC. This is against the *principle of primacy of the update*, but at least ensures consistency of the new belief set and verification of the integrity constraints at all times. It must be pointed out that such an approach is not adequate for all applications. If the update actually represents a change in the world, that is, in Winslett's terminology [24] if it is a *change-recording update*, then it should not be used. Change-recording updates represent information about how the world now *is*. They cannot be questioned. If the integrity constraints were violated, then something is wrong and appropriate measures should be taken.

However, in certain situations, the inclusion of only some of the consequences of the new formula seems appropriate. As pointed out by Dargam [2], sometimes the agent is concerned about how to reconcile conflicting interests, and a compromise is sought, where consequences of the update which are consistent with the integrity constraints are still allowed to be included. In this sense, the update is not reflecting a change that has occurred, but rather suggesting what change is more satisfactory to solve the conflict. We called this compromise revision and will discuss it further in Section 6.3.

Compromise revision has a more complex reasoning pattern, but under the SDB perspective we could define the revision of K by A respecting IC as

$K \circ_r (A \circ_r IC)$.

That is, we first revise A by the protected formulae and then revise K by the result obtained. If we proceed in this way we can ensure that the integrity constraints are verified whilst we still allow consequences of A that are consistent with them to be also included.

Similarly, we could also define the action update of K by A respecting IC, the compromised action update of K by A under IC, as

$K \diamond_r (A \circ_r IC)$.

Notice that in both cases we have considered the *revision* of the new formula by the integrity constraints (instead of *updating* it). This is justified since in an update of A by IC, each model of A would be considered individually. This would be conceptually incorrect, since the models of A are not considered individually in the process of updating K by A.

Again, we could define the ambiguous action update of a formula ψ by a formula $\varphi = P_1 \vee P_2 \vee \ldots \vee P_k$, verifying IC in the following way (calling this operation a *committed ambiguous action update*):

Definition 4.13 (Committed ambiguous action updates). Let ψ, IC and $\varphi = P_1 \vee P_2 \vee \ldots \vee P_k$ be formulae of propositional logic in DNF, where IC represents integrity constraints and each P_i represents a possible effect of the action described by φ. The *committed ambiguous update* of ψ by φ, in symbols, $\psi \odot^{IC} \varphi$, is the formula

$$\bigvee_{i=1}^{k} \psi \diamond_r (P_i \circ_r IC)$$

Committed ambiguous updates can also be used to make sure that information about the domain is taken into account during the update process. In the previous chapter we showed the example of tossing a coin. In that example, we had to specify explicitly as post-condition of the action that the only possibility is either heads or tails, but not both. We could have instead represented this as an integrity constraint of the form $(h \wedge \neg t) \vee (t \wedge \neg h)$. The following example shows how the operator for committed ambiguous action updates can be used to model ambiguous action updates that use such extralogical information about the domain. Notice that in this case, the integrity constraints are used solely to prune out the possibilities of the post-conditions of the action, as $(h \wedge \neg t) \vee (t \wedge \neg h)$ is obviously consistent with $h \vee t$.

Example 4.7 (Using priorities to represent integrity constraints in action updates).

Let us reconsider the example of the previous chapter. Remember that in the initial state, the coin had *heads* up, and this was represented by the formula h. Say, the agent also had some other unrelated information stating that it was cold today, represented by the formula c. This is not relevant to the update in question, but we want to illustrate that the update operation preserves this kind of unrelated information. The initial state can then be represented by the formula $h \wedge c$.

The protected formula states that in every state either heads or tails is possible, but never both of them simultaneously. This can be represented by the formula $h \leftrightarrow \neg t$, which is equivalent to $(h \wedge \neg t) \vee (t \wedge \neg h)$ in disjunctive normal form.

The information above, as well as the evolution of the update process, can be seen in Figure 4.5.

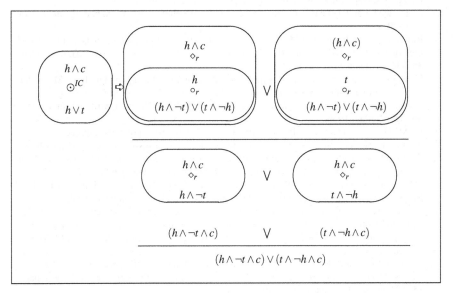

Fig. 4.5 Illustrating the use of extralogical information to describe specific information about the domain

Since we want to perform a committed ambiguous action update, each disjunct of the formula representing the post-conditions of the action is revised by the protected formulae first. As a result, the disjunct which represents the situation in which heads is obtained, h, when revised by the protected formula, results in the intended valid situation for the scenario. That is, if by flipping the coin 'heads' is obtained, then 'tails' is not: $\neg t$. The same occurs for the other disjunct t. In this sense, the protected formula *refines* the meaning of the post-conditions of the action with respect to the agent's background knowledge about the world.

The resulting revised disjuncts then proceed to update the previous belief state individually (second layer of the figure). The result is what we intuitively expect. Notice that the independent piece of information c was preserved during the whole process.

In the next chapter, we will consider how to drop the requirement of linearity associated with the priorities of a belief base.

References

1. M. Dalal. Investigations into a theory of knowledge base revision: Preliminary report. In Paul Rosenbloom and Peter Szolovits, editors, *Proceedings of the Seventh National Conference on Artificial Intelligence*, volume 2, pages 475–479, Menlo Park, California, 1988. AAAI Press.
2. F. C. C. Dargam. *On Reconciling Conflicting Updates (A Compromise Revision Approach)*. PhD thesis, Department of Computing, Imperial College, October 1996.
3. A. Darwiche and J. Pearl. On the logic of iterated belief revision. *Artificial Intelligence*, 89:1–29, 1997.
4. R. Fagin, J. D. Ullman, and M. Vardi. On the semantics of updates in databases. In *Proceedings of the ACM SIGACT-SIGMOD Symposium on Principles of Database Systems*, pages 352–365, Atlanta, GA, 1983. ACM.
5. D. M. Gabbay and O. Rodrigues. A methodology for iterated theory change. In D. M. Gabbay and Hans Jürgen Ohlbach, editors, *Practical Reasoning — First International Conference on Formal and Applied Practical Reasoning, FAPR'96*, Lecture Notes in Artificial Intelligence. Springer Verlag, 1996.
6. D. M. Gabbay and O. Rodrigues. Structured belief bases: a practical approach to prioritised base revision. In D. M. Gabbay, Rudolf Kruse, Andreas Nonnengart, and Hans Jürgen Ohlbach, editors, *Proceedings of First Internation Joint Conference on Qualitative and Quantitative Practical Reasoning*, pages 267–281. Springer-Verlag, June 1997.
7. P. Gärdenfors. *Knowledge in Flux: Modeling the Dynamics of Epistemic States*. A Bradford Book — The MIT Press, Cambridge, Massachusetts, and London, England, 1988.
8. P. Gärdenfors and D. Makinson. Revisions of knowledge systems using epistemic entrenchment. In Moshe Y. Vardi, editor, *Proceedings of the Second Conference on Theoretical Aspects of Reasoning About Knowledge*, pages 83–95, Monterey, California, March 1988. Morgan Kaufmann.
9. P. Gärdenfors and H. Rott. Belief revision. In D. M. Gabbay, C. J. Hogger, and J. A. Robinson, editors, *Handbook of Logic in Artificial Intelligence and Logic Programming*, volume 4, pages 35–132. Oxford University Press, 1995.
10. S. O. Hansson. A dyadic representation of belief. *Belief Revision*, pages 89–121, 1992.
11. S. O. Hansson. *A Textbook of Belief Dynamics: Theory Change and Database Updating*. Kluwer Academic Publishers, The Netherlands, 1999.
12. G. Harman. *Change in View: Principles of Reasoning*. MIT Press, Cambridge, Massachusetts, 1986.
13. H. Katsuno and A. O. Mendelzon. Propositional knowledge base revision and minimal change. *Artificial Intelligence*, 52(3):263–294, 1991.
14. S. Konieczny and R. P. Pérez. A framework for iterated revision, 2000.
15. D. Lehmann. Belief revision, revised. In *Proceedings of the 14th International Joint Conference of Artificial Intelligence (IJCAI-95)*, pages 1534–1540, 1995.
16. D. Makinson. How to give it up: a survey of some recent work on formal aspects of the logic of theory change. *Synthese*, 62:347–363, 1985.
17. B. Nebel. A knowledge level analysis of belief revision. In Ron J. Brachman, Hector J. Levesque, and R. Reiter, editors, *Proceedings of the first International Conference on Principles of Knowledge Representation and Reasoning*, pages 301–311. Morgan Kaufmann, Toronto, Ontario, 1989.
18. B. Nebel. Belief revision and default reasoning: Syntax-based approaches. In J. Allen, R. Fikes, and E. Sandewall, editors, *Proceedings of the Second International Conference on Principles of Knowledge Representation and Reasoning*, pages 417–428. Morgan Kaufmann, 1991.
19. B. Nebel. Syntax-based approaches to belief revision. In P. Gärdenfors, editor, *Belief Revision*, number 29 in Cambridge Tracts in Theoretical Computer Science, pages 52–88. Cambridge University Press, 1992.
20. O. Rodrigues. *A methodology for iterated information change*. PhD thesis, Department of Computing, Imperial College, 1998.

21. H. Rott. Preferential belief change using generalized epistemic entrenchment. *Journal of Logic, Language and Information*, 1:45–78, 1992.
22. M. D. Ryan. *Ordered Presentation of Theories — Default Reasoning and Belief Revision*. PhD thesis, Department of Computing, Imperial College, U.K., 1992.
23. M. Winslett. Reasoning about action using a possible models approach. In *Proceedings of AAAI-88*, pages 89–93, San Mateo, CA, Saint Paul, MN, 1988. Morgan Kaufmann.
24. M. Winslett. Epistemic aspects of databases. In C. J. Hogger D. M. Gabbay and J. A. Robinson, editors, *Handbook of Logic in Artificial Intelligence and Logic Programming*, volume 4, pages 133–174. Oxford University Press, 1995.

Chapter 5
Structured Revision: Non-linear Methods for Information Change

In the previous chapter we proposed a framework in which belief bases were represented as a structured set of components. These components were related according to a linear ordering expressing the relative priorities of each one of them. Linear PDBs and SDBs are conceptually simpler because they allow a direct application of the operators defined in earlier chapters. Each non-terminal component of the base can just be recursively reduced by means of the operators into a sentence representing the belief state of the agent.

It has been pointed out, however, that linearity can be quite a strong assumption. It is not always the case that the agent can determine the priorities among all components of the base. At the other extreme, there are a number of proposals in the literature that study how to revise a belief base with no priority information at all, among which are the ones based on partial meet and maxichoice revision functions.

In this chapter we extend the ideas presented in Chapters 3 and 4 by considering how to "revise" and reason about the information conveyed by a belief base provided with a *partial* order among its components.

5.1 Identifying Inconsistency

Let us start by analysing how the logical consequences of a consistent set of sentences in DNF can be computed. Consider, for example, the set $K' = \{p, p \rightarrow q, q \rightarrow r\}$. This set is consistent and its set of models is the same as the set of models of the sentence $p \wedge q \wedge r$. We know from the work on disjuncts that disjuncts can be associated with classes of models and that these classes can be ranked according to compatibility by using a distance function. That is, a disjunct P may be considered 'closer' to some disjuncts than others. What is more important for the topic of this section is the fact that if two sentences φ and ψ are consistent with each other, then there is also a consistent combination of disjuncts $P \wedge Q$ for some P taken from φ and some Q taken from ψ.

D. M. Gabbay et al., *Revision, Acceptability and Context*, Cognitive Technologies,
DOI 10.1007/978-3-642-14159-1_5, © Springer-Verlag Berlin Heidelberg 2010

At this point, we need to fix some notation and introduce some graphical depiction of the ideas described here.

Definition 5.1. Let $K = \{\varphi_1, \ldots, \varphi_k\}$ be a set of sentences. A *matrix representation of K* is obtained by listing a logically equivalent form in DNF of each sentence in K in an (arbitrary) given order. The rows of the matrix are filled by sentences of K, and the columns by the disjuncts of the DNF of each sentence (again in some arbitrary order).

Notation 6 *We will use the symbol $\mathcal{M}_K$ to denote a chosen matrix representation of K.*

Strictly speaking, $\mathcal{M}_K$ may not be in fact a matrix, for some sentences might have less disjuncts than others, but this is irrelevant, as we could always fill in the missing columns with $\top$ without affecting satisfiability. The representation above is merely a tool for the development of the ideas presented here.

The matrix representation presented here is not entirely new. Numerous variations of this method are known as the *matrix method* or as the *connection method* [2, 3], and these ideas date back to the 1960s [17, 9, 1]. However, the modifications we propose provide an elegant way to reason about inconsistency in an integrated environment where priorities can also be taken into account. There are well known connections between the matrix method and other methods for automated deduction, such as tableaux and resolution. It is out of the scope of this work to explore them here, but it is worth pointing out the relationship, as it opens the perspective for the optimisation of our particular procedure. A good source of information can also be found in [4].

Definition 5.2. Let K be a set of sentences and $\mathcal{M}_K$ a matrix representation of K. A *path in $\mathcal{M}_K$* is a set $\wp$ of disjuncts, each one taken from a corresponding row in $\mathcal{M}_K$. We denote the set of all paths in $\mathcal{M}_K$ by paths$(\mathcal{M}_K)$.

The important point in the definition above is that a given path contains exactly one *representative* of each sentence in the belief base. A matrix representation of K' can be seen in Figure 5.1.

Notation 7 *Let $\wp$ be a path. The conjunction of all disjuncts visited in path $\wp$ will be denoted by $\sigma(\wp)$. If $\wp$ is empty, $\sigma(\wp)$ is simply $\top$.*

In a consistent set of sentences, the intersection of the sets of models of all sentences is non-empty. For a given set K, the consistency of K guarantees the existence of a path in $\mathcal{M}_K$ whose disjuncts can be consistently combined (see Proposition 5.1).

Proposition 5.1. *Let $K = \{\varphi_1, \ldots, \varphi_k\}$ be a set of sentences and $\mathcal{M}_K$ a matrix representation of K. Given $I \in \mathscr{I}$,*

$$I \Vdash K \text{ iff } I \Vdash \sigma(\wp_i) \text{ for some path } \wp_i \in \text{paths}(\mathcal{M}_K)$$

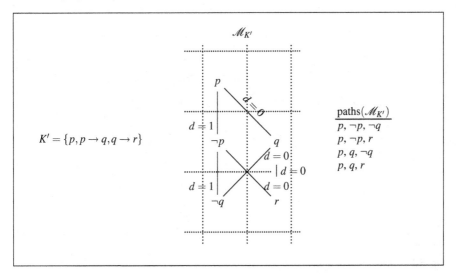

Fig. 5.1 Paths in a matrix representation

Proof. (⇐) *Suppose that* $I \Vdash \sigma(\wp_i)$ *for some path* $\wp_i$; *then* I *satisfies all of the disjuncts in path* $\wp_i$. *Therefore,* $I \Vdash \varphi_i$ *for* $1 \leq i \leq k$, *and hence* $I \Vdash K$.

(⇒) $I \Vdash K$. *Therefore,* $I \Vdash \varphi_i$ *for* $1 \leq i \leq k$. *For each i, let* P_{φ_i} *be a disjunct in* φ_i *such that* $I \Vdash P_{\varphi_i}$. *The existence of such a disjunct is guaranteed by the fact that each* φ_i *is satisfiable by* I. *It follows that* $I \Vdash \bigwedge_{i=1}^{k} P_{\varphi_i}$. *Let* $\wp_i$ *be a path that goes through all such* $P_{\varphi_i}s$. *By construction of the matrix, such a paths exists. Since* $I \Vdash \bigwedge_{i=1}^{k} P_{\varphi_i}$, *it follows that* $I \Vdash \sigma(\wp_i)$.

If there is a clash in the truth-values of propositional variables in *all* possible paths in the matrix representation, then the corresponding set is unsatisfiable. Consider, for instance, the set $K = \{p, p \rightarrow q, q \rightarrow r, \neg r\}$ and one of its possible representations as a matrix of disjuncts given in Figure 5.2. There is no possible combination of disjuncts, taking one from each sentence in K, such that all propositional variables in the combination agree with respect to their truth-values. The paths in the matrix of Figure 5.2 can be seen in Figure 5.3.

This form of visualising the sentences can be applied to the techniques described in the previous chapters. However, the problem considered then was simpler, because, as only two sentences were involved, the paths always had length 2. Moreover, one of the levels in the path had priority over the other one. In order to obtain the revision of one sentence by the other, all we had to do was choose the paths with minimal conflict of disjuncts (measured by *dist* or *d*) and then superimpose the disjuncts of the revising sentence in order to ensure consistency.

Let us consider the revision of the set $K' = \{p, p \rightarrow q, q \rightarrow r\}$ by $\neg r$. This revision is non-trivial because $K' \cup \{\neg r\} = K$ is inconsistent. If $\neg r$ is in fact to be accepted and the consistency of K restored, some of the sentences in K have to be retracted. The possibilities that would keep as many sentences of K as possible are:

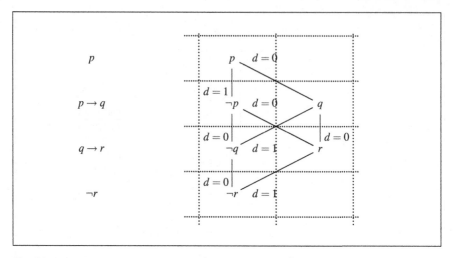

Fig. 5.2 A matrix representation of the set $\{p, p \rightarrow q, q \rightarrow r, \neg r\}$

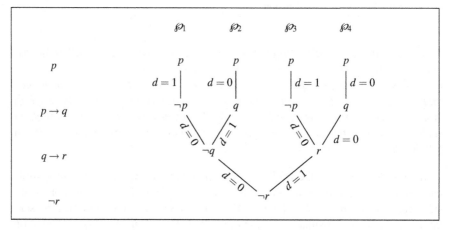

Fig. 5.3 Paths going through the matrix representation shown in Figure 5.2

1. to accept p and $p \rightarrow q$ and reject $q \rightarrow r$;
2. or to accept p and $q \rightarrow r$ and reject $p \rightarrow q$;
3. or to accept $p \rightarrow q$ and $q \rightarrow r$ and reject p

A choice between (1), (2) and (3) cannot be made, because the priorities between the sentences in K' are not determined. The possibilities above correspond exactly to the maximal subsets of K' that fail to imply r, in symbols, $K'_{\perp} r$.

Now let us think in terms of $\mathcal{M}_K$, a matrix representation of K, again. If it is not the case that all sentences in K are contradictory, then, for each path in paths$(\mathcal{M}_K)$, there is an associated sub-path which is consistent. This is easy to see, because each path contains a disjunct of each sentence. For instance, consider path $\mathcal{P}_3$ in Figure 5.3. In order to restore its consistency we could leave out either p or $\neg p$, *and* either r or $\neg r$. Whenever a disjunct is left out, its associated sentence is left without a representative in the path. For instance, leaving p and r out would make the sentences p and $q \rightarrow r$ lose a representative in the matrix. There is a correspondence between the consistent sub-paths in the matrix and the consistent subsets of the associated set of sentences. If we further analyse the labels, we can distinguish those combinations that are associated with a maximal number of sentences from the base. For instance, the sub-path of $\wp_3$ without both p and r, i.e., $\neg p$ and $\neg r$, would correspond to the consistent subset of the base $\{p \rightarrow q, r\}$, which is not maximal — we shall see that this subset would eventually be subsumed by other larger subsets of the base represented by sub-paths of other paths.

For the time being, we assume that each sentence of a set K is associated with a unique label. The full formalism will be presented later. We can redefine paths$(\mathcal{M}_K)$ so that each disjunct includes the label of the sentence from which it is taken.

Definition 5.3. Let K be a set of sentences and $\mathcal{M}_K$ a matrix representation of K. A *labelled path in* $\mathcal{M}_K$ is a set $\wp$ of expressions of the form $\alpha : P$, where P is a disjunct taken from each row in $\mathcal{M}_K$ and α is the label of the sentence represented by that row.

We have chosen to use the same symbol to denote the set of all labelled paths in $\mathcal{M}_K$ that we have used for the non-labelled counterpart: paths$(\mathcal{M}_K)$. This should cause no confusion, as from now on we will refer to sets of labelled sentences only.

Definition 5.4 (Label set of a path). Let $\wp$ be a path. The *label set of* $\wp$ is the set $\mathrm{ls}(\wp)$:

$$\mathrm{ls}(\wp) = \{\alpha \mid \alpha : P \in \wp\}$$

Definition 5.5 (Label abstraction of a set of paths). Let Λ be a set of paths. The *label abstraction of* Λ is the set $\mathrm{La}(\Lambda)$:

$$\mathrm{La}(\Lambda) = \{\mathrm{ls}(\wp) \mid \wp \in \Lambda\}$$

Notice that the set above is naturally ordered by set inclusion. More interesting to us is the set of all sub-paths in paths$(\mathcal{M}_K)$ which yield consistent combinations of disjuncts.

Definition 5.6 (Consistent sub-paths). Let K be a set of sentences, $\mathcal{M}_K$ a matrix representation of K and paths$(\mathcal{M}_K)$ the set of all paths in $\mathcal{M}_K$. The set of *consistent sub-paths of* $\mathcal{M}_K$ is defined as follows:
paths$^\top(\mathcal{M}_K) =$
   $\{\xi \mid \exists \wp \in$ paths$(\mathcal{M}_K)$ such that $\xi \subseteq \wp$ and $\sigma(\xi)$ is not contradictory $\}$

The idea now is to find which consistent sub-paths correspond to the maximal consistent subsets of a set of sentences. The set of all labelled disjuncts of a set K of sentences in DNF is also naturally ordered by set inclusion. We could restrict this ordering to the elements of paths$^\top(\mathcal{M}_K)$ and take the maximal elements. However, this would not give us the maximal consistent subsets of K, because a sentence can be satisfied in possibly several ways depending on the chosen disjuncts. That is why we need to abstract ourselves from the disjuncts and think in terms of the sentences that are being "represented" in each consistent sub-path. By extracting the label part of each sub-path, we will be left with a set of sets of labels, which, as we said, is ordered by set inclusion. The maximal elements of this set can be used to recompose the sub-paths and obtain the maximal consistent subsets of K.

Definition 5.7 (Maximal consistent sub-paths of a matrix). Let $\mathscr{M}_K$ be a matrix representation of a set K. The *maximal consistent sub-paths of* $\mathscr{M}_K$, mcs($\mathscr{M}_K$), are the elements of the set below:

mcs($\mathscr{M}_K$) =
$\quad \{\wp \in \text{paths}^\top(\mathscr{M}_K) \mid \text{ls}(\wp) \text{ is } \subseteq\text{-maximal in } \text{La}(\text{paths}^\top(\mathscr{M}_K))\}$

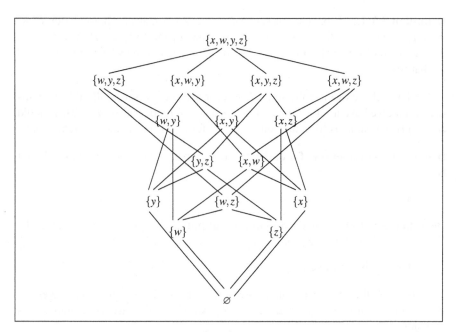

Fig. 5.4 Set inclusion ordering on the set $2^{\{x,w,y,z\}}$

Let us give an example to help fix the definitions and clarify the ideas presented.

Example 5.1. Let $K = \{x : \neg r, w : q \rightarrow r, y : p \rightarrow q, z : p\}$ be a set of labelled sentences and $\mathscr{M}_K$ a matrix representation for K as in Figure 5.2.

$\wp \in \text{paths}(\mathcal{M}_K)$	$\xi \subseteq \wp$ is a maximal consistent sub-path	$\text{ls}(\xi)$
$\{x:\neg r, w:\neg q, y:\neg p, z:p\}$	$\{x:\neg r, w:\neg q, y:\neg p\}$	$\{x,w,y\}$
	$\{x:\neg r, w:\neg q, z:p\}$	$\{x,w,z\}$
$\{x:\neg r, w:\neg q, y:q, z:p\}$	$\{x:\neg r, w:\neg q, z:p\}$	$\{x,w,z\}$
	$\{x:\neg r, y:q, z:p\}$	$\{x,y,z\}$
$\{x:\neg r, w:r, y:\neg p, z:p\}$	$\{x:\neg r, y:\neg p\}$	$\{x,y\}$
	$\{x:\neg r, z:p\}$	$\{x,z\}$
	$\{w:r, y:\neg p\}$	$\{w,y\}$
	$\{w:r, z:p\}$	$\{w,z\}$
$\{x:\neg r, w:r, y:q, z:p\}$	$\{x:\neg r, y:q, z:p\}$	$\{x,y,z\}$
	$\{w:r, y:q, z:p\}$	$\{w,y,z\}$

$\text{paths}^\top(\mathcal{M}_K)$ contains all consistent combinations of disjuncts from different sentences in K. For $\xi \in \text{paths}^\top(\mathcal{M}_K)$, $\text{ls}(\xi)$ tells us which sentences these correspond to. The set of all such possibilities is therefore $\text{La}(\text{paths}^\top(\mathcal{M}_K))$.

We now proceed in two stages. First, we need to identify what are the consistent subsets of the base. These will be naturally ordered under set inclusion. However, we cannot simply take the maximal consistent subsets, because they may not correspond to sets that verify the priorities expressed with the base. In a subsequent phase, we isolate those consistent subsets which do verify the priorities, and then we take the maximal ones.

Stage 1: Minimising inconsistency

The power set of the set of labels in K is ordered by set inclusion. This can be seen in Figure 5.4, where an arc between two sets indicates that the set underneath is contained in the set above. If we restrict this ordering to $\text{La}(\text{paths}^\top(\mathcal{M}_K))$ we will get what is shown in Figure 5.5. The set which is not in a grey box does not correspond to a consistent combination of sentences. The maximal elements of this restricted ordering correspond to the maximal consistent combinations of sentences in K.

$\subseteq$-maximal elements in $\text{La}(\text{paths}^\top(\mathcal{M}_K)) =$

$$\{\{w,y,z\},\{x,w,y\},\{x,y,z\},\{x,w,z\}\}$$

$\text{mcs}(\mathcal{M}_K) =$
$$\{\{w:r, y:q, z:p\},\{x:\neg r, w:\neg q, y:\neg p\},\{x:\neg r, y:q, z:p\},$$
$$\{x:\neg r, w:\neg q, z:p\}\}.$$

The reader can check that

$$\bigcup_{K'\in K_\perp\perp} \text{mod}(K') = \text{mod}(\bigvee_{\xi\in\text{mcs}(\mathcal{M}_K)} \sigma(\xi))$$

($K_\perp\perp$ is given in Definition 4.1).

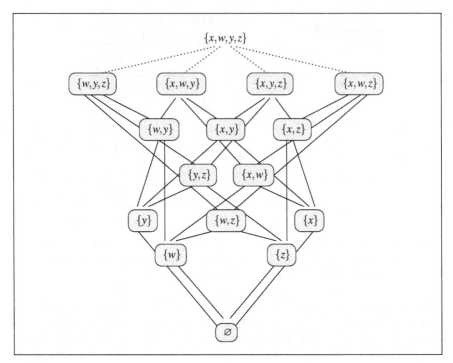

Fig. 5.5 Ordering of the Figure 5.4 restricted to the set of labels appearing in paths$^\top (\mathcal{M}_K)$ (chosen elements appear in the boxes)

Stage 2: Prioritising

If we want a sentence to be satisfied, say $\neg r$, we need to ensure that we pick only consistent sub-paths that contain a representative of it, in this case, sub-paths containing label x. This can be seen in Figure 5.6. The maximal elements now correspond to the maximal consistent subsets of K that derive $\neg r$:
$\subseteq$-maximal elements in La(paths$^\top (\mathcal{M}_K)$) containing $x =$

$$\{\{x,w,y\},\{x,y,z\},\{x,w,z\}\}$$

which correspond to the following sub-paths in paths$^\top (\mathcal{M}_K)$:

$$\{\{x:\neg r, w:\neg q, y:\neg p\}, \{x:\neg r, y:q, z:p\}, \{x:\neg r, w:\neg q, z:p\}\}$$

It is easy to check that $\bigcup_{K'\in K_\perp r}\ \ \mod (K'\cup\{\neg r\}) =$
$\qquad \mod ((\neg r\wedge\neg q\wedge\neg p)\vee(\neg r\wedge q\wedge p)\vee(\neg r\wedge\neg q\wedge p))$

Assuming that not all sentences in K are contradictory, we can prove the following correspondence:

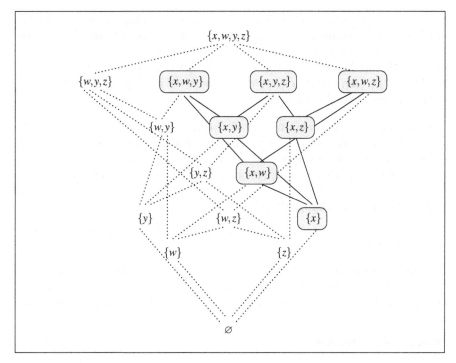

Fig. 5.6 Ordering of the Figure 5.5 restricted to the consistent sub-paths that contain x (shown in the boxes)

Theorem 5.1. *Let K be a finite set of sentences and $\mathcal{M}_K$ a matrix representation for K.*

$$\bigcup_{K' \in K_\perp \perp} \mathrm{mod}\,(K') = \mathrm{mod}\,\Big(\bigvee_{\xi \in \mathrm{mcs}(\mathcal{M}_K)} \sigma(\xi)\Big)$$

Proof. ($\subseteq$) Suppose $I \in \bigcup_{K' \in K_\perp \perp} \mathrm{mod}(K')$ for some $K' = \{\alpha_1 : K'_1, \ldots, \alpha_j : K'_j\}$. Consider a matrix representation $\mathcal{M}_{K'}$ for K'. By Proposition 5.1, $\exists \wp_i \in \mathrm{paths}(\mathcal{M}_{K'})$ such that $I \Vdash \sigma(\wp_i)$. Since $K' \subseteq K$, there exists a labelled path $\wp$ in $\mathcal{M}_K$ such that $\wp_i \subseteq \wp$. Moreover, $\sigma(\wp_i)$ is not contradictory, and hence $\wp_i \in \mathrm{paths}^\top(\mathcal{M}_K)$. From the definition of $K_\perp \perp$, $\forall K''$, $K' \subset K'' \subseteq K$ implies $K'' \vdash \perp$. Suppose there exists a sentence $\beta : \psi \in K - K'$. It follows that $\forall P \in \psi$, $\sigma(\wp_i) \wedge P \vdash \perp$. As a result, for any $P \in \psi$, $\wp_i \cup \{\beta : P\} \notin \mathrm{paths}^\top(\mathcal{M}_K)$. Therefore, $\mathrm{ls}(\wp_i)$ is $\subseteq$-maximal in $\mathrm{La}(\mathrm{paths}^\top(\mathcal{M}_K))$, and hence $\wp_i \in \mathrm{mcs}(\mathcal{M}_K)$, and hence $\wp_i \in \mathrm{mcs}(\mathcal{M}_K)$. It follows that $I \in \mathrm{mod}\,(\bigvee_{\xi \in \mathrm{mcs}(\mathcal{M}_K)} \sigma(\xi))$.

($\supseteq$) Suppose that $I \in \mathrm{mod}\,(\bigvee_{\xi \in \mathrm{mcs}(\mathcal{M}_K)} \sigma(\xi))$. It follows that $I \Vdash \sigma(\xi)$ for some $\xi \in \mathrm{mcs}(\mathcal{M}_K)$. If $\xi \in \mathrm{mcs}(\mathcal{M}_K)$, then $\mathrm{ls}(\xi)$ is $\subseteq$-maximal in $\mathrm{La}(\mathrm{paths}^\top(\mathcal{M}_K))$. Let

$$K' = \{\varphi \mid \varphi \text{ is the sentence assigned by some label in } \mathrm{ls}(\xi)\}.$$

Since $I \Vdash \sigma(\xi)$, $I \Vdash K'$, because then I satisfies at least one disjunct of every sentence in K'. Also, K' is maximal, for suppose there exists a satisfiable set K'' such that $K \subset K'' \subseteq K$. Take a sentence $\alpha : \psi \in K'' - K'$. Since K'' is satisfiable, so is $\sigma(\xi) \wedge P$, for some disjunct P in ψ. Therefore, the path $\xi \cup \{\alpha : P\} \in \text{paths}^\top(\mathcal{M}_K)$ and hence $\text{ls}(\xi) \subset \text{ls}(\xi) \cup \{\alpha\}$, and then $\text{ls}(\xi)$ is not $\subseteq$-maximal in $\text{La}(\text{paths}^\top(\mathcal{M}_K))$. This is a contradiction, since $\xi \in \text{mcs}(\mathcal{M}_K)$.

Example 5.1 also illustrates the use of two principles widely used in Belief Revision. In Stage 1, the objective is to minimise change, in the sense that we want to retract as few sentences as possible in order to achieve consistency. This is the *principle of minimal change*, which in our specific case amounts to the following:

Principle of minimal change (PMC)

"choose the sub-paths in the matrix that result in the maximal consistent combinations of the sentences involved".

(PMC) is sometimes in conflict with another principle, usually called the *principle of primacy of the update* [7]. We prefer to use a more general principle, the *principle of prioritisation*, as this allows us to give priority to the updating information only when we see fit.

Principle of prioritisation (PP)

"no sentence with lower priority can block the acceptance of another sentence with higher priority."

(PP) is used in Stage 2 of the example by giving the highest priority to the sentence $\neg r$ to ensure that the revision process is successful. In the example, the combination $\{w : r, y : q, z : p\}$ violates this principle because the sentences associated with w, y and z all had lower priority than the sentence associated with x, and they blocked the inclusion of x in the set. So, if one sentence had to be left out to perform the revision, it certainly should not be the one labelled with x.

With this in mind, we can now develop further our ideas about priorities.

5.2 Reasoning with Partial Priorities

In this section we consider a more general setting in which more information about priorities on sentences can be expressed. In the previous examples, we had just two levels of priorities: the highest one, associated with the revising sentence; and the lowest one, associated with the other sentences in the base. We want to be able to express partial priorities among the sentences in the initial base as well. The objective is to determine what conclusions are reasonable to derive from such a setting.

We have to start by discussing what the available information about priorities means. These priorities can have a number of different plausible interpretations, some interpretations more appropriate to some applications than others. For instance, in some contexts, the priorities may assert information about specificity of the sentences, whereas in others they might be related to the confidence the agent holds in each sentence. We call these interpretations *policies of prioritisation*. We explore one of such policies and show how it can be implemented by using the methodology presented here.

We need first to formalise our informal notion of labelled sets of sentences.

Definition 5.8 (Labelled belief base). A *labelled belief base* is a tuple $\mathsf{B} = \langle \mathscr{J}, \leq, f \rangle$, where $\mathscr{J}$ is a set of labels, $\leq$ is a (partial) pre-order on $\mathscr{J}$ and f is a function assigning elements of $\mathscr{J}$ to sentences of **L**.

Notation 8 *For convenience, we will sometimes refer to a labelled belief base* $\mathsf{B} = \langle \mathscr{J}, \leq, f \rangle$ *by means of the set of labelled sentences* $K_\mathsf{B} = \{x : \varphi \mid x \in \mathscr{J} \text{ and } f(x) = \varphi\}$, *assuming the ordering* $\leq$ *on* $\mathscr{J}$ *implicitly.*

Since $\leq$ is a *pre-order*, a labelled belief base may include sentences with the same level of priority.

5.2.1 Degree of Confidence/Reliability of the Source

As mentioned above, the ordering $\leq$ might have different interpretations. For some applications, the ordering on the sentences of the belief base can be realised as the *degree of confidence* the agent has about each sentence. This degree might be associated with the reliability of the source from which the epistemic input was obtained. It is not our objective here to provide information of the kind "the agent believes in φ with degree γ of confidence", but merely to use the information about reliability to solve conflicts when they arise, giving preference to the more reliable sentences. Remember that sentences here are not associated with any numerical values. They are simply *related* according to $\leq$.

In this specific policy, $x \leq y$ means that x is at least as reliable as y. $x < y$ ($x \leq y$ and $y \not\leq x$) means that x is more reliable than y.

Consider the labelled belief base $\mathsf{B}' = \langle \mathscr{J}', \leq', f' \rangle$, where $\mathscr{J}' = \{w, y, z\}$ and $\leq'$ and f' are as illustrated in the picture below.

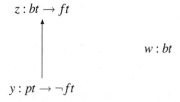

That is, all the agent knows is that he is more confident about the rule $pt \rightarrow \neg ft$ than about the rule $bt \rightarrow ft$. This can be interpreted as the agent believing that the rule if tweety is a penguin, then it does not fly ($pt \to \neg ft$) is more reliable than the rule if tweety is a bird, then it flies ($bt \to ft$). The agent also believes that tweety is a bird (bt), even though he does not know anything about the reliability of this information with respect to the two other sentences.

There is no conflict in B' and, therefore, the agent can accept the three sentences without analysing his confidence in them. He concludes $bt \wedge ft \wedge \neg pt$. The conclusion $\neg pt$ comes from the fact that, by accepting bt and $bt \to ft$ he has to accept ft and then by accepting $pt \to \neg ft$ he concludes $\neg pt$.

Now, suppose the agent is given the information pt and this information is to be given the highest priority in B'. This results in a new labelled belief base $B = \langle \mathscr{J}, \leq, f \rangle$, where $\mathscr{J} = \{x, w, y, z\}$ and $\leq$ and f can be seen in the diagram shown in Example 5.2.

Example 5.2 (Adding contradictory information).

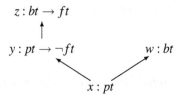

In order to accommodate pt consistently, the agent must give up at least one of the three sentences he accepted previously. The retractions of each of these sentences corresponds to each of the maximal subsets of K' that fails to imply $\neg pt$. These possibilities are listed in Figure 5.7.

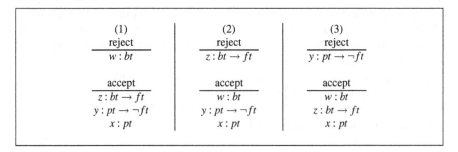

(1) reject	(2) reject	(3) reject
$w : bt$	$z : bt \to ft$	$y : pt \to \neg ft$
accept	accept	accept
$z : bt \to ft$	$w : bt$	$w : bt$
$y : pt \to \neg ft$	$y : pt \to \neg ft$	$z : bt \to ft$
$x : pt$	$x : pt$	$x : pt$

Fig. 5.7 Possibilities of restoring consistency in Example 5.2

From those possibilities, we only want to rule out case (3). The justification for this is the following: one out of the three sentences has to be retracted. In case (1), we decided to reject bt. This is plausible, because it might be in fact the case that the information conveyed by bt was inaccurate in the first place. In situation (2), $bt \to ft$ is rejected. Again this is plausible, because we do not know the relative priorities between $bt \to ft$ and bt, and $bt \to ft$ has lower priority than $pt \to \neg ft$.

However, in situation (3), we are violating the asserted preference for $pt \rightarrow \neg ft$ by rejecting it when faced with $bt \rightarrow ft$.

Situation (3) is an example of the violation of (PP) within the given interpretation of the preference ordering. Had we asserted that the explicit priority of $pt \rightarrow \neg ft$ over $bt \rightarrow ft$ expressed information about, say, specificity, things would be different. The reasoning would evolve from more specific sentences towards less specific ones.

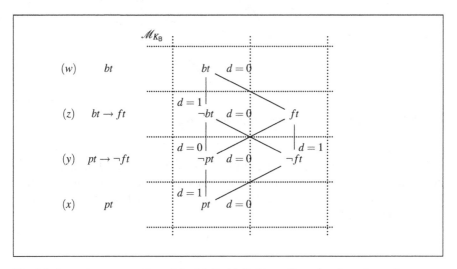

Fig. 5.8 A matrix representation of the labelled belief base $K_B = \{w : bt, z : bt \rightarrow ft, y : pt \rightarrow \neg ft, x : pt\}$

One can analyse this example with the tools presented in the previous section. Let us consider the matrix representation $\mathcal{M}_{K_B}$ for K_B given in Figure 5.8. The paths associated with this particular matrix representation can be seen in Figure 5.9. Table 5.1 shows the paths associated with $\mathcal{M}_{K_B}$, their maximal consistent sub-paths and the corresponding label sets of these sub-paths.

Obviously, the best possibility would be the inclusion of all four sentences, but we have seen that this leads to inconsistency. This is indicated by the absence of a path in $\text{paths}^\top(\mathcal{M}_{K_B})$ with all four labels. The ordering of set inclusion on the power set of $\mathcal{J}$ is obviously constant for all belief bases with the same number of sentences. What changes is its restriction to the labels appearing in $\text{paths}^\top(\mathcal{M}_{K_B})$ for each K_B. In this case, it is the same as the one presented in the previous section and can be seen in Figure 5.5.

By (PMC) alone, we could choose any of the maximal elements in the restricted ordering,

$$\{x, w, z\}, \qquad \{y, w, z\}, \qquad \{x, y, w\} \quad \text{and} \quad \{x, y, z\},$$

but now we have more priorities to take into account, so only some of these actually verify (PP). We have previously argued that $\{x, w, z\}$ should be ruled out because it

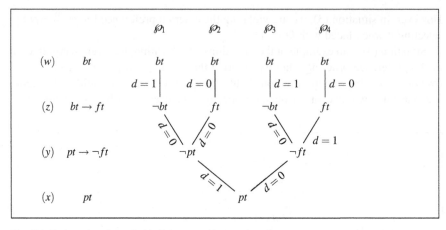

Fig. 5.9 Paths going through the disjuncts of the matrix $\mathcal{M}_{K_B}$

contains z but does not contain y even though $y < z$. It should be clear that $\{y, w, z\}$ should also be ruled out, since it does not contain x, which is the minimum element (mod $\le$) in the set of labels. We are then left with the two sets below, which correspond to possibilities (1) and (2) in Figure 5.7:

$$\{x, y, w\} \text{ and } \{x, y, z\}$$

$\wp \in \mathrm{paths}(\mathcal{M}_{K_B})$	$\xi \subseteq \wp$ is a maximal consistent sub-path	$\mathrm{ls}(\xi)$
$\{x : pt, y : \neg pt, z : \neg bt, w : bt\}$	$\{x : pt, z : \neg bt\}$	$\{x, z\}$
	$\{x : pt, w : bt\}$	$\{x, w\}$
	$\{y : \neg pt, z : \neg bt\}$	$\{y, z\}$
	$\{y : \neg pt, w : bt\}$	$\{y, w\}$
$\{x : pt, y : \neg pt, z : ft, w : bt\}$	$\{x : pt, z : ft, w : bt\}$	$\{x, w, z\}$
	$\{y : \neg pt, z : ft, w : bt\}$	$\{w, y, z\}$
$\{x : pt, y : \neg ft, z : \neg bt, w : bt\}$	$\{x : pt, y : \neg ft, z : \neg bt\}$	$\{x, y, z\}$
	$\{x : pt, y : \neg ft, w : bt\}$	$\{x, y, w\}$
$\{x : pt, y : \neg ft, z : ft, w : bt\}$	$\{x : pt, y : \neg ft, w : bt\}$	$\{x, y, w\}$
	$\{x : ft, z : ft, w : bt\}$	$\{x, w, z\}$

Table 5.1 Paths, consistent sub-paths and associated label sets of the matrix $\mathcal{M}_{K_B}$ (see Example 5.2)

Notice that one can abstract from paths, disjuncts and satisfiability and think only in terms of the partial ordering provided. This separates the problem into two parts: one reasoning about satisfiability (which we have seen in the matrix representations) and the other reasoning about what would be reasonable to give up, considering the priorities given.

The second part of the problem can be summarised as follows: given a pre-order $\leq$ on $\mathcal{J}$, where $\leq$ expresses confidence of the agent on the reliability of the elements in $\mathcal{J}$, and two subsets X and Y of $\mathcal{J}$, find out whether X should be preferred to Y, or Y should be preferred to X, or neither, according to $\leq$. This means defining an ordering $\preceq$ on $2^{\mathcal{J}}$. Let us fix the interpretation of $\preceq$ as follows: $X \preceq Y$ means that the overall satisfiability of sentences of X is at least as plausible as Y's. As usual, we use $X \prec Y$ to denote $X \preceq Y$ and $Y \not\preceq X$.

The ordering $\preceq$ is similar in idea to the ordering of words in a dictionary. However, in a dictionary the "alphabet" is linearly ordered and the comparisons are done with respect to the positions occupied by the letters in each word. That is, we compare the first letter of the two words and if there is a tie, we compare the second one, and so on. The first difficulty we face is that our "alphabet" is not linearly ordered. We have assumed that $\leq$ is only a partial pre-order. The second difficulty is that, unlike words, the entities we are trying to compare are not sequences of elements of this alphabet, they are *sets*. Moreover, in a dictionary initial segments of words come before larger segments. In our case, it seems intuitively clear that if $X \subset Y$, we would like to prefer Y to X. After all, ultimately we want to maximise satisfiability. If there is no dispute with respect to prioritisation, the larger the set, the better. Therefore, $\preceq$ should verify

(1) $Y \subseteq X$ implies $X \preceq Y$

We have to find a mechanism to capture our intuitions. That is, we want $\preceq$ to somehow encompass the priorities expressed by $\leq$, according to the confidence policy. How shall we make the comparisons? In order to help us elucidate this question, let us consider again the already familiar Example 5.2 of the last section.

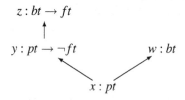

In one of the last stages of our reasoning we had the following sets of labels corresponding to consistent combinations of sentences in the set:

$\{x,w,z\}$ $\{y,w,z\}$ $\{x,y,w\}$ $\{x,y,z\}$;

and we argued that, among these, $\{y,w,z\}$ was clearly not preferred. The reason was that x, which is associated with the most preferred sentence in the set, is in all other sets but not in $\{y,w,z\}$. In our analogy with a dictionary, $\{x,w,z\}$, $\{x,y,w\}$ and $\{x,y,z\}$ all "start" with x, which comes before all other letters. And thus, we were left with

$\{x,w,z\}$ $\{x,y,w\}$ $\{x,y,z\}$.

From these, we argued that $\{x,w,z\}$ was not so reasonable. We would rather keep $\{x,w,y\}$, because, given the chance to choose between y and z, we would opt for y, which is preferred to z.

A solution can be found by comparing what each set contributes to the satisfiability of the original base as a whole. We could be tempted to define $\preceq$ as follows:

Attempt 1 $X \preceq Y$ if $\forall y \in Y.\exists x \in X$ such that $x \leq y$.

This would make $\{y,w,z\}$ less preferred than the other sets, but fails, in certain cases, to capture the very primitive notion expressed in (1) above. For instance, suppose that $x \in X$ is the minimum with respect to $\leq$. It would follow that $\forall Y$, $x \in Y \subseteq X$ implies $Y \equiv X$ (mod $\preceq$).

Example 5.3. According to Attempt 1, $\{x\} \preceq \{x,w,y,z\}$ and $\{x,w,y,z\} \preceq \{x\}$.

Clearly, $\{x,w,y,z\}$ should be preferred to $\{x\}$, since it satisfies all the sentences that $\{x\}$ does, and some sentences that $\{x\}$ does not. So perhaps we should analyse the sentences that one of the sets satisfies but the other one does not. Again, we might be tempted to use the following definition:

Attempt 2 $X \preceq Y$ iff $\forall y \in Y - X.\exists x \in X - Y$ such that $x \leq y$.

In other words, X is at least as good as Y if for every element y which is in Y but not in X, there is an element x in X but not in Y that is at least as important as y. Intuitive as it might seem, this definition has a serious drawback.

Proposition 5.2. $\preceq$ *according to Attempt 2 is not a transitive relation.*

Proof. We give a counterexample: suppose $\mathscr{I} = \{x,y,z\}$, $\leq$ is as depicted in the diagram below and $X = \{x\}$, $Y = \{y\}$ and $Z = \{x,z\}$.

$$(5.1) \qquad \begin{array}{c} z \\ \uparrow \\ x,y \end{array}$$

It follows that $X \preceq Y$, $Y \preceq Z$, but $X \not\preceq Z$, because $\neg\exists x \in X - Z$ such that $x \leq z$.

In the example above, we expect *both* $X \preceq Z$ and $Y \preceq Z$ not to hold. The justification for this is as follows: x and y are equivalent with respect to $\leq$. Therefore, as far as $\leq$ is concerned, whether to pick x or y is a matter of no concern.[1] $Z \prec Y$ should hold because x "defeats" y, but no other element in Y is left to beat $z \in Z$.

Let us formalise these notions more precisely.

Definition 5.9. $X \preceq Y$ iff

- $Y = \varnothing$;

---

[1] Imagine a hypothetical alphabet, exactly like the English one, except that we have two first letters: a_1 and a_2. "$a_1$pple" should come before "$a_2$rt", since a_1 and a_2, although distinct, have the same precedence, but "p" comes before "r".

- or $\exists x \in X, \exists y \in Y$, such that $x \le y$ and $X - \{x\} \preceq Y - \{y\}$;
- or $\exists x \in X, \exists Y' \subseteq Y$, such that $Y' \neq \varnothing$ and $\forall y \in Y'.x < y$ and $X - \{x\} \preceq Y - Y'$

That is, $X \preceq Y$ if Y is empty or if it is possible to match elements of Y with elements in X in the following fashion: an element x in X may be matched with any number of strictly weaker elements from Y or with at most one element y from Y which is as strong as x. X is at least as plausible as Y overall if all elements in Y can be matched in this fashion.

It can be checked that Definition 5.9 corrects the problems identified in Proposition 5.2. The ordering on $2^{\mathscr{J}}$ for the partially ordered set $\langle \mathscr{J}, \le \rangle$ considered in that proposition can be seen in Figure 5.10.

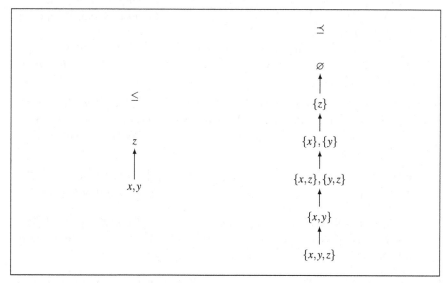

Fig. 5.10 $\preceq$ ordering on the set $2^{\{x,y,z\}}$ with respect to $\le$

We now prove a number of results about $\preceq$.

Proposition 5.3. $X \preceq Y$, $x \notin X$, $y \notin Y$ and $x \le y$ imply $X \cup \{x\} \preceq Y \cup \{y\}$.

Proof. This follows directly from Definition 5.9. $X \cup \{x\} \preceq Y \cup \{y\}$ if $\exists x' \in X \cup \{x\}$, $\exists y' \in Y \cup \{y\}$, such that $x \le y$ and $(X \cup \{x\}) - \{x'\} \preceq (Y \cup \{y\}) - \{y'\}$. Take $x' = x$ and $y' = y$. Since $x \notin X$ and $y \notin Y$, $(X \cup \{x\}) - \{x'\} = X$ and $(Y \cup \{y\}) - \{y'\} = Y$.

Proposition 5.4. $X \preceq Y$, $x \notin X$, $Y' \cap Y = \varnothing$ and $\forall y \in Y'.x < y$ imply $X \cup \{x\} \preceq Y \cup Y'$.

Proof. This is similar to the previous proposition and follows directly from Definition 5.9. $X \cup \{x\} \preceq Y \cup Y'$ if $\exists x' \in X \cup \{x\}$, $\exists Y'' \subseteq Y \cup Y'$, such that $\forall y' \in Y''.x < y'$ and $(X \cup \{x\}) - \{x'\} \preceq (Y \cup Y') - Y''$. Take $x' = x$ and $Y'' = Y'$. Since $x \notin X$ and $Y' \cap Y = \varnothing$, $(X \cup \{x\}) - \{x'\} = X$ and $(Y \cup Y') - Y'' = Y$.

Proposition 5.5. $X \preceq Y$ implies $\forall y \in Y. \exists x \in X$ such that

- either $x \leq y$ and $X - \{x\} \preceq Y - \{y\}$;
- or $\exists Y' \subseteq Y$ such that $y \in Y'$, $\forall y' \in Y'.x < y'$ and $X - \{x\} \preceq Y - Y'$.

Proof. Proof by induction on $|Y|$. The proposition holds vacuously when $|Y| = 0$. Assume that it holds for all Y such that $|Y| < k$.

Now, suppose $|Y| = k > 0$, $X \preceq Y$ and $y \in Y$.

- *either $\exists x' \in X. \exists y' \in Y$ such that $x' \leq y'$ and $X - \{x'\} \preceq Y - \{y'\}$. In this case, if $y = y'$, then we just take $x = x'$ and the proof is finished. Otherwise, $y \in Y - \{y'\}$. Since $|Y - \{y'\}| < k$, by the inductive hypothesis $\exists x'' \in X - \{x'\}$ such that*

  - *either $x'' \leq y$ and $X - \{x'\} - \{x''\} \preceq Y - \{y'\} - \{y\}$. In this case, notice that $x' \notin X - \{x'\} - \{x''\}$ and $y' \notin Y - \{y'\} - \{y\}$. By Proposition 5.3, $X - \{x''\} \preceq Y - \{y\}$. Just take $x = x''$.*
  - *or $\exists Y'' \subseteq Y - \{y'\}$ such that $y \in Y''$ and $\forall y'' \in Y''.x' < y''$ and $X - \{x'\} - \{x''\} \preceq Y - \{y'\} - Y''$. $x' \notin X - \{x'\} - \{x''\}$ and $y' \notin Y - \{y'\} - Y''$. By Proposition 5.3, $X - \{x''\} \preceq Y - Y''$. Take $x = x''$ and $Y' = Y''$.*

- *or $\exists x' \in X$ and $\exists Y'' \subseteq Y$ such that $Y'' \neq \varnothing$ and $\forall y'' \in Y''.x' < y''$ and $X - \{x'\} \preceq Y - Y''$. If $y \in Y''$, we just take $Y' = Y''$ and $x = x'$. Otherwise, $y \in Y - Y''$. Since $Y'' \neq \varnothing$, $|Y - Y''| < k$, and we can apply the inductive hypothesis. That is, $\exists x'' \in X - \{x'\}$ such that*

  - *either $x'' \leq y$ and $X - \{x'\} - \{x''\} \preceq Y - Y'' - \{y\}$. In this case, notice that $x' \notin X - \{x'\} - \{x''\}$ and $Y'' \cap (Y - Y'' - \{y\}) = \varnothing$. By Proposition 5.4, $X - \{x''\} \preceq Y - \{y\}$. Just take $x = x''$.*
  - *or $\exists Y_1 \subseteq Y - Y''$ such that $y \in Y_1$ and $\forall y'' \in Y_1.x'' < y''$ and $X - \{x'\} - \{x''\} \preceq Y - Y'' - Y_1$. $x' \notin X - \{x'\} - \{x''\}$ and $Y'' \cap (Y - Y'' - Y_1) = \varnothing$. By Proposition 5.4, $X - \{x''\} \preceq Y - Y_1$. Take $x = x''$ and $Y' = Y_1$.*

Lemma 5.1. $X \preceq Y$ and $X' \subseteq X$ implies $\exists Y' \subseteq Y$ such that $\forall y_1 \in Y'. \exists x_1 \in X'$ such that $x_1 \leq y_1$ and $X - X' \preceq Y - Y'$.

Proof. Proof by induction on $|X|$. If $|X| = 0$, then $X = \varnothing$. Since $X \preceq Y$, $Y = \varnothing$. $X' \subseteq X$ implies $X' = \varnothing$. Take $Y' = \varnothing$. The proposition follows vacuously.

Assume that the proposition holds for $|X| < k$ and suppose $|X| = k$. Take $X' \subseteq X$. Since $X \preceq Y$:

- *$Y = \varnothing$. In this case take $Y' = \varnothing$. It follows that $X - X' \preceq Y - Y'$.*
- *or $\exists x \in X$ and $\exists y \in Y$ such that $x \leq y$ and $X - \{x\} \preceq Y - \{y\}$. Since $|X - \{x\}| < k$, it follows by the inductive hypothesis that $\forall X'' \subseteq X - \{x\}$, $\exists Y'' \subseteq Y - \{y\}$ such that $\forall y' \in Y''. \exists x' \in X''$ such that $x' \leq y'$ and $X - \{x\} - X'' \preceq Y - \{y\} - Y''$.*

  - *either $x \in X'$. Take $X'' = X' - \{x\}$ and $Y' = Y'' \cup \{y\}$. $X - X' = X - \{x\} - X''$ and $Y - Y' = Y - \{y\} - Y''$. $x \leq y$; therefore, $\forall y_1 \in Y'. \exists x_1 \in X'$ such that $x_1 \leq y_1$ and $X - X' \preceq Y - Y'$.*

- or $x \notin X'$. Take $X'' = X'$ and $Y' = Y''$. $x \notin X - \{x\} - X''$ and $y \notin Y - \{y\} - Y''$. By Proposition 5.3, $(X - \{x\} - X'') \cup \{x\} \preceq (Y - \{y\} - Y'') \cup \{y\}$. Therefore, $X - X' \preceq Y - Y'$.

- or $\exists x \in X$, $\exists Y'' \subseteq Y$ such that $Y'' \neq \varnothing$ and $\forall y \in Y''.x < y$ and $X - \{x\} \preceq Y - Y''$.

  - either $x \in X'$. Take $X'' = X' - \{x\}$. Since $X'' \subseteq X - \{x\}$ and $|X - \{x\}| < k$, by the inductive hypothesis, $\exists Z \subseteq Y - Y''$ such that $\forall z \in Z.\exists x' \in X''$ such that $x' \leq z$ and $X - \{x\} - X'' \preceq Y - Y'' - Z$. Take $Y' = Y'' \cup Z$. It follows that $X - X' \preceq Y - Y'$.
  - or $x \notin X'$. $X' \subseteq X - \{x\}$. Since $X - \{x\} \preceq Y - Y''$, it follows by the inductive hypothesis that $\exists Z \subseteq Y - Y''$ such that $\forall z \in Z.\exists x' \in X'.x' \leq z$ and $X - \{x\} - X' \preceq Y - Y'' - Z$. Take $x_1 = x'$ and $Y' = Z$. $x \notin (X - \{x\} - X')$ and $Y'' \cap (Y - Y'' - Z) = \varnothing$. By Proposition 5.4, $X - X' \preceq Y - Y'$.

Proposition 5.6. $\preceq$ *is a pre-order.*

Proof. Reflexivity is obvious. The proof of transitivity is done by induction on $|Z|$. If $|Z| = 0$, then $Z = \varnothing$ and hence $X \preceq Z$ follows trivially. Assume that whenever $|Z| < k$, $X \preceq Y$ and $Y \preceq Z$ imply $X \preceq Z$, and suppose $|Z| = k > 0$, $X \preceq Y$ and $Y \preceq Z$. We show that $X \preceq Z$.
From $Y \preceq Z$,

- *either $\exists y \in Y.\exists z \in Z$ such that $y \leq z$ and $Y - \{y\} \preceq Z - \{z\}$.*
  From $X \preceq Y$ and Proposition 5.5, $\exists x \in X$ such that $x \leq y$ and

  - *either $X - \{x\} \preceq Y - \{y\}$. Since $|Z - \{z\}| < k$, the inductive hypothesis applies and therefore $X - \{x\} \preceq Z - \{z\}$. $\leq$ is transitive; therefore, $x \leq z$. From Proposition 5.3, $X \preceq Z$.*
  - *or $\exists Y' \subseteq Y$ such that $y \in Y'$, $\forall y' \in Y'.x < y'$ and $X - \{x\} \preceq Y - Y'$. Take $Y'' = Y' - \{y\}$. $Y'' \subseteq Y - \{y\}$. Since $Y - \{y\} \preceq Z - \{z\}$, by Lemma 5.1 it follows that $\exists Z' \subseteq Z - \{z\}$ such that $\forall z' \in Z'.\exists y'' \in Y''$ such that $Y - \{y\} - Y'' \preceq Z - \{z\} - Z'$. Notice that $Y - \{y\} - Y'' = Y - Y'$, because $Y'' = Y' - \{y\}$. Since $|Z - \{z\} - Z'| < k$, it follows from the inductive hypothesis that $X - \{x\} \preceq |Z - \{z\} - Z'|$. Since $x \notin X - \{x\}$, $(\{z\} \cup Z') \cap (Z - \{z\} - Z') = \varnothing$, and $\forall z'' \in \{z\} \cup Z'.x < z''$, by Proposition 5.4, $X \preceq Z$.*

- *or $\exists y \in Y$, $\exists Z' \subseteq Z$ such that $Z' \neq \varnothing$ and $\forall z \in Z'.y < z$ and $Y - \{y\} \preceq Z - Z'$.*
  From $X \preceq Y$ and Proposition 5.5, $\exists x \in X$, such that $x \leq y$ and

  - *either $X - \{x\} \preceq Y - \{y\}$. Since $Z' \neq \varnothing$, it follows that $|Z - Z'| < k$. By the inductive hypothesis, $X - \{x\} \preceq Z - Z'$. Also, notice that since $y < z$ for all $z \in Z'$, $x < z$ for all $z \in Z'$. $x \notin X - \{x\}$ and $(Z - Z') \cap Z' = \varnothing$. By Proposition 5.4, $X \preceq Z$.*
  - *or $\exists Y' \subseteq Y$, $y \in Y'$ and $\forall y' \in Y'.x < y'$ and $X - \{x\} \preceq Y - Y'$. Now take $Y'' = Y' - \{y\}$. $Y'' \subseteq Y - \{y\}$. By Lemma 5.1, $\exists Z'' \subseteq Z - Z'$ such that $\forall z' \in Z''.\exists y'' \in Y''$ such that $y'' \leq z'$ and $Y - \{y\} - Y'' \preceq Z - Z' - Z''$. Since $Y - \{y\} - Y'' = Y - Y'$, and $|Z - Z' - Z''| < k$, it follows by the inductive hypothesis that $X -$*

$\{x\} \preceq Z - Z' - Z''$. *Notice that $x < z''$, for all $z'' \in Z' \cup Z''$. Also, $(Z - Z' - Z'') \cap (Z' \cup Z'') = \emptyset$. By Proposition 5.4, $X \preceq Z$.*

Definition 5.9 subsumes the converse of the set inclusion ordering, and hence ensures that our intuitions about set inclusion are also verified.

Proposition 5.7. $Y \subseteq X$ *implies* $X \preceq Y$.

Proof. Proof by induction on $|Y|$. If $|Y| = 0$, then $Y = \emptyset$, and then the proposition holds trivially. Assume that it holds for $|Y| = k$ and suppose $|Y| = k+1$. Take $x \in Y$. Since $Y \subseteq X$, $x \in X$. Therefore, $\exists x' \in X$ and $\exists y' \in Y$ such that $x' \leq y'$. For this we just set $x' = y' = x$. $|Y - \{y'\}| = k$ and $Y - \{y'\} \subseteq X - \{x'\}$, and hence, by the inductive hypothesis, $X - \{x'\} \preceq Y - \{y'\}$. By Definition 5.9, $X \preceq Y$.

However, the converse is not true. It might be the case that $X \preceq Y$, but $Y \subseteq X$ does not hold. An appropriate mapping between elements of X and Y is sufficient for $X \preceq Y$ to hold.

Proposition 5.8. *Let $\langle \mathscr{J}, \leq \rangle$ be a partial pre-order. $\mathscr{J}$ is the minimum on $\langle 2^{\mathscr{J}}, \preceq \rangle$, and $\emptyset$ the maximum.*

Proof. It is easy to see that $\mathscr{J}$ is the minimum: for any $X \in 2^{\mathscr{J}}$, $X \subseteq \mathscr{J}$. Therefore, by Proposition 5.7, $\mathscr{J} \preceq X$ for all $X \in 2^{\mathscr{J}}$. Similarly, $X \preceq \mathscr{J}$ only if $X = \mathscr{J}$. That $\emptyset$ is the maximum follows directly from Definition 5.9.

We are now in a position to define the consequences of a labelled belief base under the confidence approach.

Definition 5.10 (Maximal plausible sub-paths of a matrix). Let $\mathscr{M}_K$ be a matrix representation of a set K. The *maximal plausible sub-paths of $\mathscr{M}_K$*, mps($\mathscr{M}_K$), are the elements of the set:

$$\text{mps}(\mathscr{M}_K) = \{\wp \in \text{paths}^\top(\mathscr{M}_K) \mid \text{ls}(\wp) \text{ is } \preceq\text{-minimal in La}(\text{paths}^\top(\mathscr{M}_K))\}$$

Notice the similarity between Definitions 5.10 and 5.7.

Definition 5.11 (Flattening a labelled belief base). Let $B = \langle \mathscr{J}, \leq, f \rangle$ be a labelled belief base and $\mathscr{M}_{K_B}$ a matrix representation for K_B. The result of flattening out B, in symbols FLATTEN_BASE(B), is the sentence $\bigvee_{\xi \in \text{mps}(\mathscr{M}_{K_B})} \sigma(\xi)$.

The definition above takes advantage of the fact that as we recombine the disjuncts, we obtain again a sentence in DNF. This allows us to express complex priority relationships by embedding structured belief bases in others. The overall result can be computed by recursively computing the result of each node that is not a sentence.

Definition 5.12 (Consequences of a labelled belief base under the confidence approach). Let $B = \langle \mathscr{J}, \leq, f \rangle$ be a labelled belief base and $\mathscr{M}_{K_B}$ a matrix representation for K_B. The set of *logical consequences of B* is the set:

$$\text{Cn}(B) = \text{Cn}(\{ \bigvee_{\xi \in \text{mps}(\mathscr{M}_{K_B})} \sigma(\xi)\})$$

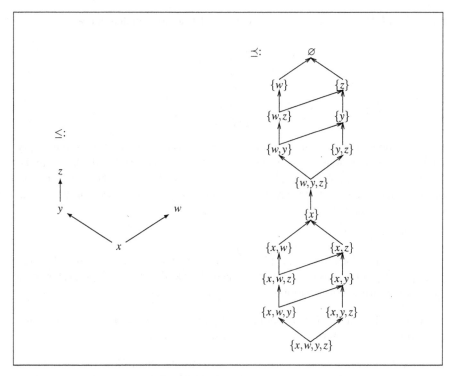

Fig. 5.11 $\preceq$ ordering on the set $2^{\{x,w,y,z\}}$ with respect to $\leq$

Now let us reexamine Example 5.2. The maximal consistent sub-paths are represented by the label sets

$$\{x,w,z\}, \qquad \{y,w,z\}, \qquad \{x,y,w\} \qquad \text{and} \qquad \{x,y,z\}.$$

These can be found in Table 5.1. The derived ordering $\preceq$ on $2^{\{x,w,y,z\}}$ for $\leq$ of this example can be seen in Figure 5.11. Therefore, the $\preceq$-minimal elements of $2^{\{x,w,y,z\}}$ are the sets $\{x,w,y\}$ and $\{x,y,z\}$. The consistent sub-paths in the matrix corresponding to these sets are

$$\{x: pt, y: \neg ft, z: \neg bt\} \qquad \text{and} \qquad \{x: pt, y: \neg ft, w: bt\}.$$

These are the maximal plausible sub-paths of the matrix, according to Definition 5.10.

The set of logical consequences of the labelled belief base are then

$$\text{Cn}(\{((pt \wedge \neg ft \wedge \neg bt) \vee (pt \wedge \neg ft \wedge bt)\}$$

These correspond to the two possibilities in Figure 5.7 that we argued were the most plausible, namely (1) and (2).

It is interesting to notice the relation between the principle of prioritisation and the principle of minimal change. Consider another example:

Example 5.4. $\mathsf{B} = \langle \{x,y,z\}, \leq, f \rangle$, where $\leq$ and f are as depicted below.

The combination of the three sentences is inconsistent. There are four non-empty consistent combinations of sentences, namely the ones assigned to the labels in the sets in $C = \{\{x,z\},\{x\},\{y\},\{z\}\}$. The ordering $\preceq$ on $2^{\{x,y,z\}}$ can be seen in Example 5.5.1 (left-hand side). If we restrict that ordering to the set C, we can see that the only minimal element in C is $\{x,z\}$. Therefore,

$$\mathsf{Cn}(\mathsf{B}) = \mathsf{Cn}(\{b \wedge c \wedge a\}).$$

Notice that z does not block the acceptance of y in this case, and therefore the principle of prioritisation is verified. Indeed, $\{x,y\}$ would have been preferred to $\{x,z\}$ if the former combination were consistent.

We now show a number of examples of partial pre-orders on sets of labels and the corresponding ordering $\preceq$ on the power set of these sets.

Example 5.5 (Some sample orderings). In the examples that follow, the set of labels is $\mathscr{J} = \{x,y,z\}$. For each pre-order $\leq$ on $\mathscr{J}$ shown on the left-hand side, we show the resulting ordering $\preceq$ on $2^{\mathscr{J}}$.

Notice that $\mathscr{J}$ itself is always the minimum element on $\langle 2^{\mathscr{J}}, \preceq \rangle$ and $\varnothing$ is always the maximum. In each of the following examples, the ordering $\leq$ on $\mathscr{J}$ is shown on the left-hand side of the figures and the corresponding $\preceq$ on $2^{\mathscr{J}}$ on the right-hand side.

1. Chains and antichains:

   If the original priority ordering is a chain (left-hand side of the figure below), the four first classes in the ordering on the powerset of labels are those which contain the minimum element: x. If all elements can be accepted, so much the better. Otherwise, we try to include y first and that failing, we try to include z. If neither is possible, we try to accept x by itself. The other possibilities are similar, but exclude x. Notice that if x by itself could not be accepted, it is because it is associated with a contradictory sentence.

   On the other hand, if the original priority ordering is an antichain (right-hand side of the figure below), then the plausible subsets with two elements are all subsets with two elements, and they are all incomparable with respect to $\preceq$. The subsets with one element are also incomparable among themselves, but are strictly worse than the supersets containing them.

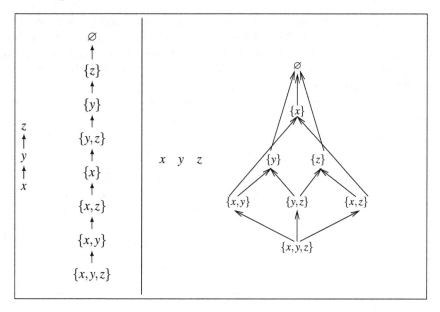

2. For the priority ordering on the left-hand side of the figure below, among the subsets in the powerset of labels with two elements, the one that contains the minimal elements in $\langle \mathscr{J}, \leq \rangle$ is preferred to all other combinations with two elements, which are themselves incomparable (as they satisfy different incomparable elements). The singleton $\{z\}$, which contains the maximum on $\langle \mathscr{J}, \leq \rangle$, is preferred to $\varnothing$ only.

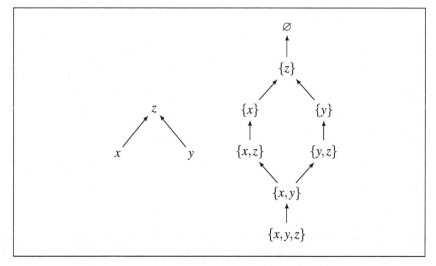

3. The ordering in the figure below branches out whenever a decision needs to be made between y and z. This reflects the incomparability of y and z in the original ordering (on the left-hand side of the figure below). Had y been specified as equivalent to z mod $\leq$, the result would have been an equivalence between $\{x,y\}$ and $\{x,z\}$, and between $\{y\}$ and $\{z\}$ (mod $\preceq$).

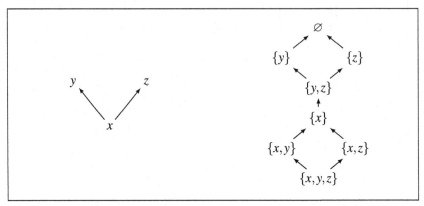

4. The figure below contains a more interesting example, which motivates our principle of prioritisation. Given the chance to choose among $\{x,y\}$, $\{x,z\}$ and $\{y,z\}$, the most plausible subsets are $\{x,y\}$ and $\{x,z\}$. Even though $\{x,y\}$ cannot be compared to $\{y,z\}$, $\{x,z\}$ is strictly better than $\{y,z\}$, and, by taking the minimal elements of $\{\{x,y\},\{y,z\},\{x,z\}\}$ with respect to $\preceq$, the acceptance of $\{y,z\}$ is blocked. $\{x,z\}$ is preferred to $\{y,z\}$, because they both satisfy z, but $\{x,z\}$ also satisfies x, which is preferred to y and is not satisfied by $\{y,z\}$.

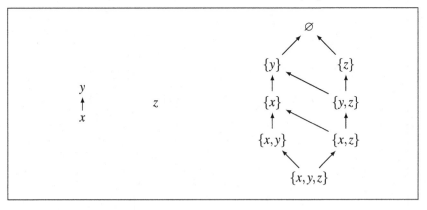

5. A more detailed example can be found below. We will restrain ourselves to comments on some interesting pairs of subsets only. For instance, $\{w,y,x\}$ and $\{w,y,z\}$ are incomparable, because x and z cannot be compared. Similarly, $\{w,x,z\}$ is incomparable to $\{y\}$, because there is no element in $\{w,x,z\}$ which is at least as good as y. On the other hand, $\{w,y,x\}$ is better than both. It should be

obvious why that combination is better than $\{y\}$. It is also better than $\{w,x,z\}$, because y is strictly better than z and the remaining elements in the two sets can be cancelled out with each other.

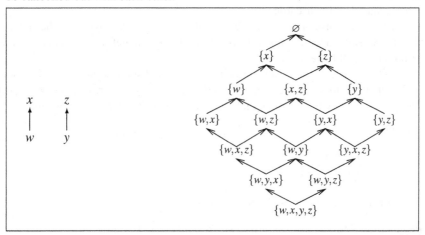

Summary of the method:

It is useful to briefly recap the method we have presented in this chapter:

1. choose any matrix representation of the set of sentences
2. consider the consistent sub-paths of the paths in this matrix
3. consider the ordering $\preceq$ on the set of labels of the sentences
4. restrict the elements of this ordering to the labels associated with consistent sub-paths
5. take the minimal elements of this restricted ordering
6. these elements are associated with sentences of the matrix representation, and each of them has at least one consistent sub-path obtained in item 2. Take the conjunction of each of these consistent sub-paths
7. and finally, take the disjunction of the conjunctions obtained in the previous step.

5.2.1.1 Computational Issues

In the previous section, we have presented a policy for the treatment of priorities in partially ordered belief bases. One interesting feature of the method is the separation of the satisfiability problem from the problem of determining plausible conclusions according to the partial order available.

An ordering $\preceq$ on the power set of the set of labels associated with the sentences in the base was defined to determine the most plausible conclusions. In this section, we illustrate some ways by which the comparisons done with respect to $\preceq$ may be optimised, by exploiting specific aspects of the ordering. We also show that in certain cases, most of the computation used to calculate this ordering may be reused when the base is augmented by a new sentence.

We have seen that $Y \subseteq X$ implies that $X \preceq Y$. Checking for set inclusion is quite a simple operation and should always be used before $\preceq$ is computed. Since we are interested in the minimal elements mod $\preceq$, whenever a superset is found, all of its subsets may then be discarded.

Let us now consider the case when a labelled belief base receives the input of a sentence to be given the highest priority in the new belief base. This is the most common case of belief revision.

Let $\mathsf{B}' = \langle \mathscr{J}', \leq', f' \rangle$ be a labelled belief base and suppose $\alpha : \varphi$ is to be added to B' (where α does not occur in $\mathscr{J}'$) and given the highest priority on $\mathscr{J}' \cup \{\alpha\}$. This is obtained by the following labelled belief base $\mathsf{B} = \langle \mathscr{J}, \leq, f \rangle$, where

$$\mathscr{J} = \mathscr{J}' \cup \{\alpha\} \qquad \leq = \leq' \cup \{(\alpha, \beta) \mid \beta \in \mathscr{J} \cup \{\alpha\}\}$$

$$f(x) = \begin{cases} f'(x), & \text{if } x \in \mathscr{J}' \\ \varphi & \text{otherwise} \end{cases}$$

Now consider the orderings $\preceq'$ on $2^{\mathscr{J}'}$ and $\preceq$ on $2^{\mathscr{J}}$.

Proposition 5.9. *The following statements hold for $X, Y \in 2^{\mathscr{J}}$.*

1. *If $\alpha \in X$ and $\alpha \notin Y$, then $X \prec Y$.*
2. *If $\alpha \notin X$ and $\alpha \notin Y$, then $X \preceq' Y$ implies $X \preceq Y$.*
3. *If $\alpha \in X$ and $\alpha \in Y$, then $X - \{\alpha\} \preceq' Y - \{\alpha\}$ implies $X \preceq Y$.*

Proof.

1. i) $(X \preceq Y)$. If $Y = \varnothing$, then the proposition holds trivially. Otherwise, take $Y' = Y$. It follows that $\forall y \in Y'.a < y$. $Y - Y' = \varnothing$, and hence $X - \{\alpha\} \preceq Y - Y'$. By Definition 5.9, $X \preceq Y$.
   ii) $(Y \npreceq X)$. Suppose $Y \preceq X$. It follows from Proposition 5.5 that $\forall x \in X, \exists y \in Y$ such that $y \leq x$. Take $x = \alpha$. Since α is the minimum and $\alpha \notin Y$, $\neg \exists y \in Y$ such that $y \leq x$, a contradiction.

2. *Proof by induction on $|Y|$. If $|Y| = 0$, then $X \preceq Y$, trivially. Assume that the proposition holds whenever $|Y| < k$. We show that it holds for $|Y| = k$. Suppose that $X \preceq' Y$, then*

   - *either $\exists x \in X. \exists y \in Y$ such that $x \leq' y$ and $X - \{x\} \preceq' Y - \{y\}$. $|Y - \{y\}| < k$. Since $\alpha \notin X - \{x\}$ and $\alpha \notin Y - \{y\}$, by the inductive hypothesis $X - \{x\} \preceq Y - \{y\}$. $\leq' \subseteq \leq$, and then $x \leq y$. By Proposition 5.3, $X \preceq Y$.*
   - *or $\exists x \in X. \exists Y' \subseteq Y$ such that $Y' \neq \varnothing$ and $\forall y \in Y'.x <' y$ and $X - \{x\} \preceq' Y - Y'$. This item is similar. Since $\leq' \subseteq \leq$, $\forall y \in Y'.x < y$. $|Y'| > 0$ and hence $|Y - Y'| < k$. By the inductive hypothesis, $X - \{x\} \preceq Y - Y'$. By Proposition 5.4, $X \preceq Y$.*

3. $\alpha \notin X - \{\alpha\}$ and $\alpha \notin Y - \{\alpha\}$. By item (2), $X - \{\alpha\} \preceq Y - \{\alpha\}$. Since $\alpha \leq \alpha$, by Proposition 5.3, $X \preceq Y$.

What the proposition above says is: (1) combinations with the newly accepted sentence are strictly better than the ones without it; (2) combinations without the new sentence are related to each other exactly in the same way they were before the inclusion of the new sentence; (3) two combinations with the new sentence are related exactly as they used to be without the new sentence.

Obviously, if the sentence with highest priority is itself contradictory, its label will not be in any set in $\text{paths}^\top(\mathcal{M}_{K_B})$, and then the relevant part of the new ordering $\preceq$ will behave as the old one $\preceq'$, as shown in item (2).

It is believed that other improvements in the overall complexity of the method might also be achieved by analysing the interaction between the procedure for finding the maximal consistent sub-paths and the behaviour of $\preceq$. This is left as future work.

5.2.2 Linearisations

An alternative solution to the problem of reasoning with partial information about priorities is proposed in [5, page 74], in the formalism known as preferred subtheories. We present it here for discussion.

Definition 5.13. Let $<$ be a strict partial ordering on a finite set of premises T. S is a *preferred subtheory of T* iff there exists a strict total ordering $(t_1, \ldots, t_n)$ of T respecting $<$ (i.e., $t_j < t_k$ implies $j < k$) such that $S = S_n$ with

$$S_0 = \varnothing,$$
$$S_i = \begin{cases} S_{i-1} \cup \{t_i\}, & \text{if } S_{i-1} \cup \{t_i\} \text{ is consistent} \\ S_{i-1} & \text{otherwise} \end{cases} \quad (0 < i \leq n)$$

The approach of linearisation of the (partial) ordering $<$ can be implemented in our methodology in two ways. In order to simplify the method, we now consider the case where $\leq$ is in fact a partial order – that is, we require antisymmetry of $\leq$. First consider the PDBs that can be associated with each one of the linearisations obtained. These PDBs can be constructed by considering the inverse order of the given linearisation. That is, the most important sentence in the linearisation occupies the last position in the list, and so on. For each such PDB Δ we then compute Δ^*. The comparison about the results obtained in this fashion and those obtained by the preferred subtheories formalism are similar to the comparisons we made to linear prioritised base revision (see Section 4.7.1). Each preferred subtheory resulting from one such linearisation is equivalent to the corresponding linear prioritised base revision.

The second way is to simulate the behaviour of the computation of the preferred subtheories by using our matrix representation. Since now we have a linear ordering, we can lay down the matrix exactly according to this ordering. We consider lists of sentences resulting from each linearisation, such that the most important sentence in the linearisation corresponds to the first sentence in the list, the second-most important sentence corresponds to the second sentence in the list, and so on.

Definition 5.14. Let $\Delta = [\varphi_1, \ldots, \varphi_k]$ be a list of sentences. A *prioritised matrix representation of K* is obtained by listing a logically equivalent form in DNF of each sentence in K such that the first row of the matrix corresponds to the first sentence in the list, and so on. The rows of the matrix are filled by sentences of K, and the columns by the disjuncts of the DNF of each sentence.

Notation 9 *We will use the symbol $\mathcal{M}_K^\Delta$ to denote the matrix representation of K according to Δ.*

Definition 5.15 (Preferred consistent sub-paths). Let $\Delta = [\varphi_1, \ldots, \varphi_k]$ be a list of sentences and $\mathcal{M}_K^\Delta$ a prioritised matrix representation of K. The *preferred consistent sub-paths of $\mathcal{M}_K^\Delta$* are contained in the set ξ_k constructed in the following way:

$$\xi_0 = \varnothing$$
$$\xi_i = \begin{cases} \{ \wp \wedge P \mid \wp \in \xi_{i-1},\ P \in \text{ row } i \text{ and } \wp \wedge P \text{ is consistent} \}, & \text{if this is non-empty} \\ \xi_{i-1} & \text{otherwise} \end{cases}$$

where $0 < i \leq k$.

That is, we start with the empty set and most prioritised row in the matrix for which there exists a consistent disjunct. We then proceed until we reach row k. For each path $\wp_{i-1}$ obtained in row $i-1$, $\wp_{i-1}$ is expanded into n paths $\wp_{i-1} \wedge P_1, \ldots, \wp_{i-1} \wedge P_n$ where each P_i is a disjunct in row i which is consistent with $\wp_{i-1}$. If n is 0, then the path $\wp_{i-1}$ cannot be expanded in this step and we consider another path obtained in row $i-1$. If all such paths cannot be expanded, we consider the next row. It is important to emphasise that if at least one path is consistent with at least one disjunct of the current row, then it blocks the inclusion of all paths from the previous row which could not find *any* consistent combination with a disjunct of the current row. When no paths from the previous row can be consistently combined with any disjunct of the current row, then the sentence associated with the current row cannot be accepted in the present linearisation.

If we take the disjunction of all preferred consistent sub-paths of $\mathcal{M}_K^\Delta$, we get a sentence which is tautologically equivalent to the set of logical consequences of the linearisation associated with Δ.

For its structure, the idea is similar to the computation of a disjunctive normal form of a sentence in conjunctive normal form via the matrix method. However, we have sentences in DNF in the rows and as the output of the method, and a check for consistency in each row, which makes it also resemble a little the resolution method with priorities added.

5.3 Clustering

The idea for clustering takes advantage of the fact that a structured belief base can be flattened out into a single sentence. The result of a complex cluster can be computed by recursively flattening out any complex sub-clusters until only sentences are left, when we can use the procedure described in Section 5.2. This allows for the representation of very complex ordering structures.

These complex ordering structures may be used, for instance, in situations where one wants to specify preferences within a group of sentences with a similar role, and yet needs the groups of sentences to be themselves ranked within a containing super-structure. One example for the application of this idea is in the representation of requirements in software specification. Systems' properties can usually be divided into a number of distinct categories, e.g., safety requirements, factual information, economy requirements, etc. During the development process, inconsistencies may arise in the specification. Being able to reason rationally with these inconsistencies represents an advantage of the refinement process. In this context, one could prefer to give priority to safety requirements over, say, economy requirements. Similarly, within each group of formulae in a given category, some properties may be more important than others and a second level of prioritisation may be useful. The clustering method allows for the representation of these complex priorities without trivialising the results of an evolving specification. By analysing the relationship between the consequences obtained in the structured base and the consequences of each cluster in the base, one can reason about inconsistency and refine the specification accordingly.

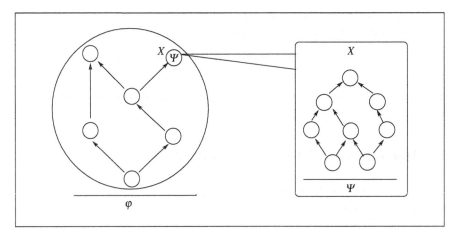

Fig. 5.12 Example of a complex structuring of sentences

Another possible use of clusters is in the resolution of conflicts in a group of agents, where clusters could represent the information of individual agents, which can then be put together to represent the information of the group. This seems very appealing since each agent would then be allowed to represent his own belief priorities in a uniform way. An illustration of these ideas can be found in Figure 5.12.

Complex ordering structures over belief bases can be captured by extending Definition 5.8 in the following way:

Definition 5.16 (Structured cluster). A *structured cluster* is a tuple $\Xi = \langle \mathscr{C}, \sqsubseteq$ $, g \rangle$ where $\mathscr{C}$ is a set of labels, $\sqsubseteq$ is a (partial) pre-order on $\mathscr{C}$ and g is a function assigning elements of $\mathscr{C}$ to either a sentence of **L** or a labelled belief base.

It is useful to evaluate how nested a given cluster is. For this we formalise the notion of "level of a cluster" in the following way.

Definition 5.17 (Level of a cluster). The level of a formula of propositional logic is 0. Let $\Xi = \langle \mathscr{C}, \sqsubseteq, g \rangle$ be a structured cluster. The level of Ξ, in symbols, level(Ξ), is defined recursively as follows:

$$\mathrm{level}(\Xi) = \max_{i \in \mathscr{C}} \{\mathrm{level}(g(i))\} + 1$$

Thus, a cluster of level 1 is just a labelled belief base as defined previously. We can flatten out a labelled belief base via Definition 5.11. Hence, we can also flatten out a cluster of higher order by recursively flattening out all embedded sub-clusters as follows (this is simply an extension to Definition 5.11).

Definition 5.18 (Flattening a structured cluster). Let $\Xi = \langle \mathscr{C}, \sqsubseteq, g \rangle$ be a structured cluster. The result of flattening out Ξ, in symbols, FLATTEN_CLUSTER(Ξ), is the sentence in DNF obtained in the following way:

FLATTEN_CLUSTER(Ξ) =
$$\begin{cases} \text{FLATTEN\_BASE}(\Xi) & \Rrightarrow \text{ if level}(\Xi) = 1 \\ \text{FLATTEN\_CLUSTER}(\Xi') & \Rrightarrow \text{ otherwise} \end{cases}$$

where Ξ' is the cluster obtained from Ξ by replacing the function g by the function g', such that $g'(i) = $ FLATTEN_CLUSTER($g(i)$) for all $i \in \mathscr{C}$.

It is easy to see that the FLATTEN_CLUSTER(Ξ) returns a sentence in DNF.

5.4 Applications in Software Engineering

We now present an application of clustered belief revision in the specification of requirements of software systems.

5.4.1 Requirements Specification

Conflicting viewpoints inevitably arise in the process of requirements elicitation. Conflict resolution, however, may not necessarily happen until later in the development process. This highlights the need for requirements engineering tools that support the management of inconsistencies [16, 19].

Many formal methods of analysis and elicitation rely on classical logic as the underlying formalism. Model checking, for example, typically uses temporal operators on top of classical logic reasoning [14]. This facilitates the use of well-behaved and established theorems and proof procedures. On the other hand, classical logic does not accept inconsistency, in the sense that one can derive anything from an inconsistent theory. For example, one can derive any proposition B from propositions A and $\neg A$. This is known as *theory trivialisation*, and is clearly undesirable in the context of requirements engineering, where inconsistency often arises [13, 11].

Paraconsistent Logics [6] attempt to ameliorate the problem of theory trivialisation by weakening some of the axioms of classical logic, often at the expense of reasoning power. For instance, Belnap's four-valued logic (see Section 7.6) allows for non-trivial logical representations where propositions can be both true and false, but does not verify basic inference rules such as *modus ponens*. While appropriate for concise modelling, logics of this kind are too weak to support practical reasoning and the analysis of inconsistent specifications.

The clustered belief revision technique presented earlier in this chapter takes a different view and uses theory prioritisation to obtain plausible (i.e., not trivial) conclusions from an inconsistent theory while exploiting the full power of classical logic reasoning. This allows the requirements engineer to analyse the results of different possible prioritisations by reasoning classically, and to evolve specifications that contain conflicting viewpoints in a principled way. The analysis of user-driven cluster prioritisations can also give stakeholders a better understanding of the impact of certain changes in the specification.

In this section, we show how clustered belief revision can support requirements elicitation and evolution. We illustrate the idea through a simplified version of the light control case study [12], assuming the existence of a tool that translates requirements given in the form of "if then else" rules into the (more efficient) disjunctive normal form (DNF) for classical logic reasoning and cluster prioritisation.

5.4.2 An Example with the Light Control System

In what follows, we adapt and simplify the light control case study (LCS) [10] in order to illustrate the relevant aspects of our revision approach. The LCS case study describes the behaviour of light settings in an office building. We consider two possible light scenes: a *default* light scene and a *chosen* light scene. Office lights are set to a default level upon the entry of a user, who can then override this setting to a chosen light scene. If an office is left unoccupied for more than T_1 minutes, the system turns the lights off. When an unoccupied office is reoccupied within T_2 minutes, the light scene is reestablished according to its immediately previous setting. The value of T_1 is set by the facilities' manager whereas the value of T_2 is set by the office user [12].

A dictionary of the symbols used in the LCS case study is given in Table 5.2. Literals without prime denote properties of the current state of the system, and primed literals denote properties of the next state (e.g., *occupied* denotes that a user is in the office at time t, and *occupied'* denotes that a user is in the office at time $t + 1$).

proposition	meaning
occupied	a user is in the office
user_in	a user enters an unoccupied office
user_out	a user leaves an office unoccupied
temp_unocc	the office is unoccupied for less than T_2 minutes
unoccupied	the office is unoccupied for T_1 minutes or more
elapsed_T_i	T_i minutes have elapsed
chosen_lights	office lights are as set by the user
default_lights	office lights are in the default setting
alarm	the alarm is activated
gte_lux$_1$	day light level is greater or equal to the light level required by the chosen or default light scene (lux_1)
gte_lux$_2$	day light level is greater or equal to the maximum luminosity achievable by the office lights (lux_2)
no_lights	office lights are off

Table 5.2 Dictionary of symbols used in the specification

A partial specification of the LCS is given below:

Behaviour rules

$r_1 : user\_in \rightarrow occupied'$
$r_2 : occupied \land user\_out \land \neg elapsed\_T_2 \rightarrow temp\_unocc'$
$r_3 : temp\_unocc \land elapsed\_T_1 \rightarrow unoccupied'$
$r_4 : temp\_unocc \land user\_in \rightarrow occupied'$
$r_5 : unoccupied \rightarrow no\_lights'$
$r_6 : temp\_unocc \land user\_in \rightarrow chosen\_lights'$
$r_7 : user\_in \rightarrow default\_lights'$

Rules r_5 to r_7 specify the intended behaviour of the office lights: *no_lights* indicates that the office lights are off; *chosen_lights* indicates that the office lights are as set by the user; and *default_lights* indicates that the office lights are in the default setting. We assume that the initial chosen light scene is set to the default one.

In our study, we require that the light control system satisfy two types of properties: *safety* properties and *economy* properties. The safety properties include *i)* the lights are not off in the default light scene; *ii)* if the fire alarm (*alarm*) is triggered, the default light scene must be established in all offices; and *iii)* T_3 minutes after the alarm is triggered, the lights must all be turned off (i.e., only emergency lights must be on). The value of T_3 is set by the facilities manager. The above requirements are represented by rules s_1 to s_4:

Safety rules

$s_1 : alarm \land \neg elapsed\_T_3 \rightarrow default\_lights'$
$s_2 : alarm \land elapsed\_T_3 \rightarrow no\_lights'$
$s_3 : default\_lights \leftrightarrow \neg no\_lights$
$s_4 : default\_lights' \leftrightarrow \neg no\_lights'$

Economy properties include the fact that, to the extent to which it is feasible, the system ought to use natural light to achieve the light levels required by the office light scenes. Sensors can check *i)* whether the luminosity coming from outside is enough to surpass the luminosity required by the current light scene; and *ii)* whether the luminosity coming from outside is greater than the maximum luminosity achievable by the office lights. The latter is useful because it can be applied independently of the current light scene in an office. Let lux_1 denote the luminosity required by the current light scene, and lux_2 the maximum luminosity achievable by the office lights. The above can be summarised as follows: *i)* if the natural light is at least lux_1 (gte_lux_1) and the office is in the chosen or default light scene, then the lights must be turned off; and *ii)* if the natural light is at least lux_2 (gte_lux_2), then the lights must be turned off. The above properties are represented as follows:

Economy rules

$e_1 : gte\_lux_1 \land (chosen\_lights \lor default\_lights) \rightarrow no\_lights'$
$e_2 : gte\_lux_2 \rightarrow no\_lights'$

Now, consider the following scenario. On a bright summer's day, John is working in his office when suddenly the fire alarm goes off. He leaves the office immediately. Once outside the building, he realises that he left his briefcase behind and decides to go back to fetch it. By the time he enters his office, the alarm has been going off for more than T_3 minutes. This situation can be formalised as follows:

i_1: John enters the office (*user_in*)
i_2: The alarm is sounding (*alarm*)
i_3: T_3 minutes or more have elapsed since the alarm went off (*elapsed_T_3*)
i_4: day light provides luminosity enough to dispense with artificial lighting
    (gte_lux_2)

We get inconsistency in two different ways:

1. Because John walks in the office (i_1), the default light setting is chosen (r_7). By s_4, the lights must be on in this setting. This is a contradiction to safety rule s_2, which states that lights should be turned off T_3 minutes after the alarm goes off.

    $user\_in$ (i_1), $alarm$ (i_2), $elapsed\_T_3$ (i_3)
    $default\_lights' \rightarrow \neg no\_lights'$ (s_4)
    $user\_in \rightarrow default\_lights'$ (r_7)
    $alarm \land elapsed\_T_3 \rightarrow no\_lights'$ (s_2)

2. Similarly, when John walks in the office (i_1), the default light scene is set (r_7). This effectively forces the lights to be turned on (s_4). However, by e_2, this is not necessary since the amount of luminosity coming from outside is higher then the maximum luminosity achievable by the office lights (gte_lux_2).

    $user\_in$ (i_1), gte_lux_2 (i_4)
    $default\_lights' \rightarrow \neg no\_lights'$ (s_4)
    $user\_in \rightarrow default\_lights'$ (r_7)
    $gte\_lux_2 \rightarrow no\_lights'$ (e_2)

We are, therefore, in a situation where inconsistency in the light scenes occurs due to a safety property violation and an economy property violation. We need, therefore, to reason about the courses of action necessary to deal with this problem. Using clustered belief revision, we can arrange the several components of the specification in different priority settings by grouping rules in clusters, e.g., safety cluster, economy cluster, etc. The organisation of the information in each cluster can be done independently but the overall prioritisation of the clusters at the highest level requires input from all stakeholders. Once the specification has been refined with priorities over clusters, the framework should be able to cope with potential inconsistencies without trivialising the results. The formalism can allow for arbitrary orderings *inside* the clusters as well, but this is not considered here for reasons of space and simplicity.

Let us now illustrate the approach. In the scenario described previously, we might wish to prioritise safety rules over the other rules of the specification, but not have yet enough information from the stakeholders to decide on the relative strength of economy rules. In this case, we would ensure that the specification satisfies the safety rules but not necessarily the economy ones.

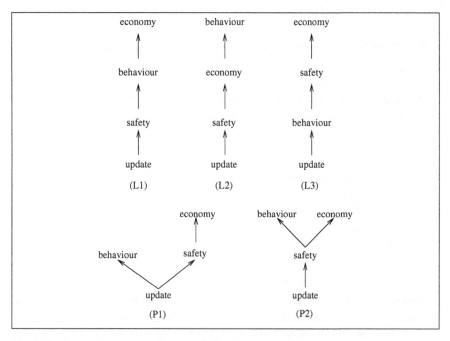

Fig. 5.13 Linearly (L1, L2 and L3) and partially (P1 and P2) ordered clusters

Let us assume that sensor and factual information is correct and therefore not subject to revision. We combine this information in a cluster called "update" and give it the highest priority. In addition, we assume that safety rules must have priority over economy rules. At this point, no information on the relative priority of behaviour rules is available. With this in mind, it is possible to arrange the clusters with the update, safety, behaviour and economy rules as depicted in Figure 5.13.[2] Prioritisations L1, L2 and L3 represent all possible linear arrangements of these clusters with the assumptions mentioned above, whereas prioritisations P1 and P2 represent the corresponding partial ones. As already mentioned, each of the components economy, behaviour, safety and update could be associated with its own partial priority order as well, allowing for the expression of more complex relationships between individual properties.

The overall result of the clustered revision will be consistent as long as the cluster with the highest priority (factual and sensor information) is not itself inconsistent. When the union of the sentences in all the clusters is indeed inconsistent, in order to restore consistency, some rules may have to be withdrawn. The result will be such that rules will be kept as long as their inclusion does not cause inconsistency with other rules in a cluster with higher priority.

For example, take prioritisation L1. The sentences in the safety cluster are consistent with those in the update cluster; together, they conflict with behaviour rule r_7 (see Figure 5.14).

---

update + safety include (in DNF):
$user\_in \wedge alarm \wedge elapsed\_T_3 \wedge gte\_lux_2 \wedge no\_lights' \wedge \neg default\_lights'$

behaviour includes (in DNF):
$\neg user\_in \vee default\_lights'$

result 1: $user\_in \wedge alarm \wedge elapsed\_T_3 \wedge gte\_lux_2 \wedge no\_lights' \wedge \neg default\_lights'$

Fig. 5.14 Conflict with behaviour rule r_7

Since r_7 is given lower priority in L1, it cannot be consistently kept and it is withdrawn from the intermediate result. The final step is to incorporate what can be consistently accepted from the economy cluster, for example, e_2.[3] Notice, however, that r_7 could have been kept given a different arrangement of the priorities.

The refinement process occurs by allowing one to reason about these different orderings and the impact of rules in the current specification without trivialising the results. Eventually, a final specification that is consistent regardless of the priorities between the clusters, i.e., in the classical logic sense, may be reached, although this is not essential in our framework.

Prioritisations L2 and P2 give the same results as L1, i.e., withdrawal of r_7 is recommended. On the other hand, in prioritisation L3, the sentence in the behaviour cluster is consistent with those in the update cluster; together, they conflict with safety rule s_4 (see Figure 5.15). Since the safety cluster is given lower priority in

---

[2] Recall that a connecting arrow between clusters indicates priority of the source cluster over the target one.

[3] e_1 is also implicitly incorporated since we can neither prove the antecedent nor the negation of the consequent.

---

update + behaviour include (in DNF):
$user\_in \land alarm \land elapsed\_T_3 \land gte\_lux_2 \land default\_lights'$

safety includes (in DNF):
$((\neg default\_lights' \land no\_lights') \lor (\neg default\_lights' \land \neg alarm) \lor (\neg no\_lights' \land \neg alarm) \lor$
$(\neg default\_lights' \land \neg elapsed\_T_3) \lor (\neg no\_lights' \land \neg elapsed\_T_3))$

---

result 2: $user\_in \land alarm \land elapsed\_T_3 \land gte\_lux_2 \land default\_lights' \land no\_lights'$

Fig. 5.15 Conflict with safety rule s_4

L3, both sentences s_2 and s_4 cannot be consistently kept. One has to give up either s_2 or s_4. However, if s_4 were to be kept, then e_2 would be required to be withdrawn. The only way to cause minimal change to the specification is to keep s_2 instead, since it allows the inclusion of e_2.

Finally, prioritisation P1 offers a choice between the sets of clusters {update, safety, economy} and {update, behaviour, economy}. The former corresponds to withdrawing r_7 reasoning in the same way as for L1, L2 and P2, while the latter corresponds to withdrawing s_4 as in the case of L3. It is not possible to make a choice based on the available priority information, and hence the disjunction of results 1 and 2 above is taken.

In summary, from the five different cluster prioritisations analysed, a recommendation can be made to withdraw a behaviour rule in three of them, to withdraw a safety rule in one of them and to withdraw either a behaviour or a safety rule in one of them. From these results and the LCS context, the withdrawal of behaviour rule r_7 seems more plausible. In more complicated cases, a decision support system could be used to help in the choice of recommendations made by the clustered revision framework.

Clustered belief revision could then be used to analyse the results of different specification prioritisations, reasoning classically, and to evolve specifications that contain conflicting viewpoints in a principled way. Other logic-based approaches could also be used to tackle the problem of handling inconsistency and evolving requirements specifications. For instance, a belief revision approach for default theories [21] could be adopted, whereby specifications can be formalised as default theories in terms of defeasible and non-defeasible requirements. Inconsistencies introduced by an evolutionary change can be resolved by performing a revision operation over the entire specification, and changes in the specification, for resolving inconsistency, can be handled by a belief revision operator that changes the status of information from defeasible to non-defeasible, and vice versa. Trivialisation during the reasoning process can be avoided by not taking into consideration non-defeasible requirements, in the same way as, in a clustered belief revision, requirements with lower priority that are inconsistent with requirements with higher priority are not considered in the computation of the revised specification. The cluster approach would, however, provide the engineer with means (i.e., different levels of priorities) for better fine-tuning the specification and reasoning with different levels of defeasibility. Similarly, a cluster-based approach would provide additional dimensions and therefore a more refined reasoning process about inconsistencies than approaches with a single *preference ordering relation* (e.g., [18]).

Our application of clustered belief revision to requirements engineering provides not only a technique for revising requirements specifications using priorities, but also a methodology for handling evolving requirements. As the emphasis is on the use of priorities for reasoning about potentially inconsistent specifications, the approach can also be used to check the consequences of a given specification and to reason about "what if" questions that arise during evolutionary changes. A possible venue for further research is the use of machine learning techniques [15] to support automated revision of requirements specifications [8, 20]. Consider, for instance, the LCS example. Assume that a person in a particular office needs to have a light scene that violates the economy properties of the specification. This is a *scenario* which, in terms of machine learning, can be seen as an example to be learnt. This example, when trained, may evolve the specification into a consistent new specification as new concepts (or rules) may be added to the specification, according to the scenarios available for training. However, contrary to belief revision approaches, not all machine learning techniques guarantee consistency of the new specification, nor do they all satisfy the principle of minimal change. A detailed, formal comparative analysis of these two methods of theory revision in the context of requirements evolution would be highly desirable, but is outside the scope of this book.

References

1. P. B. Andrews. Refutations by matings. *IEEE Transactions on Computers*, 25:801–807, 1976.
2. W. Bibel. On matrices with connections. *Journal of the Association for Computing Machinery*, 28:633–645, 1981.
3. W. Bibel. *Automated Theorem Proving*. Vieweg Verlag, Braunschweig, 2nd revised edition, 1987.
4. K. H. Bläsius and H.-J. Bürckert. *Deduction Systems in Artificial Intelligence*. Ellis Horwood Limited, 1989.
5. G. Brewka. *Nonmonotonic Reasoning — Logical Foundations of Commonsense*, volume 12 of *Cambridge Tracts in Theoretical Computer Science*. Cambridge University Press, October 1990.
6. N. C. A. da Costa. On the theory of inconsistent formal systems. *Notre Dame Journal of Formal Logic*, 15(4):497–510, 1974.
7. M. Dalal. Investigations into a theory of knowledge base revision: Preliminary report. In Paul Rosenbloom and Peter Szolovits, editors, *Proceedings of the Seventh National Conference on Artificial Intelligence*, volume 2, pages 475–479, Menlo Park, California, 1988. AAAI Press.
8. A. S. d'Avila Garcez, A. Russo, B. Nuseibeh, and J. Kramer. Combining abductive reasoning and inductive learning to evolve requirements specifications. In *IEE Proceedings — Software*, volume 150, pages 25–38, 2003.
9. M. Davis. Eliminating the irrelevant from mechanical proofs. In *Proceedings of the Symposium on Applied Mathematics XV*, pages 15–30, American Mathematical Society, Providence, RI, 1963.

10. S. Queins et al. The light control case study: problem description. *Journal of Universal Computer Science*, 6(7), 2000. Special Issue on Requirements Engineering: the Light Control Case Study.

11. D. Gabbay and A. Hunter. Making inconsistency respectable 1: A logical framework for inconsistency in reasoning. In Ph. Jorrand and J. Kelemen, editors, *Foundations of Artificial Intelligence Research*, LNCS 535, pages 19–32. Springer, 1991.

12. C. Heitmeyer and R. Bharadwaj. Applying the SCR requirements method to the light control case study. *Journal of Universal Computer Science*, 6(7), 2000. Special Issue on Requirements Engineering: the Light Control Case Study.

13. A. Hunter and B. Nuseibeh. Managing inconsistent specifications: Reasoning, analysis and action. *Transactions on Software Engineering and Methodology*, October 1998.

14. M. R. Huth and M. D. Ryan. *Logic in Computer Science: Modelling and Reasoning about Systems*. Cambridge University Press, 2000.

15. T. Mitchell. *Machine Learning*. McGraw Hill, 1997.

16. B. Nuseibeh, J. Kramer, and A. Finkelstein. A framework for expressing the relationships between multiple views in requirements specification. *IEEE Transactions on Software Engineering*, 20(10):760–773, October 1994.

17. D. Prawitz. An improved proof procedure. *Theoria*, 26:102–139, 1960.

18. M. D. Ryan. Defaults in specification. In *IEEE Proceedings of International Symposium on Requirements Engineering (RE93)*, pages 266–272, January 1993. San Diego, California.

19. G. Spanoudakis and A. Zisman. Inconsistency management in software engineering: Survey and open research issues. In S. K. Chang, editor, *Handbook of Software Engineering and Knowledge Engineering*, pages 329–380. World Scientific, 2001.

20. A. van Lamsweerde and L. Willemet. Inferring declarative requirements specifications from operational scenarios. *IEEE Transactions on Software Engineering*, 1998. Special Issue on Scenario Management.

21. D. Zowghi and R. Offen. A logical framework for modeling and reasoning about the evolution of requirements. In *Proc. 3rd IEEE International Symposium on Requirements Engineering RE'97*, Annapolis, USA, January 1997.

Chapter 6
Algorithmic Context Revision

6.1 Introduction

In Chapter 3, we provided a number of operations for belief change. The revision operator was then used to analyse the process of iteration in Chapter 4, making use of the fact that consecutive inputs to a database (belief base) naturally give rise to a linear order on the beliefs in that database. We dropped the linearity restriction in Chapter 5 and considered alternatives for dealing with the extra structure available in the database. However, in all of the above, we have not looked into (or attempted to modify) the particular characteristics of the logic L used for the reasoning, apart from the obvious considerations on consistency of the database itself.

In this and the next chapters, we start looking into the logic, by providing alternative proof procedures or by considering the interaction between the belief change operations and the underlying proof procedure more closely. The formalisms in this chapter all offer an algorithmic proof procedure that takes the context of the proofs into account in the definition of the belief change operations.

6.2 Abductive Revision

As we saw in Chapter 2, *expansion* is one of the three basic types of belief change operations. An expansion is simply the addition of a new belief into an agent's belief set, and in the case of classical logic, it can be defined simply as $Cn(\Delta \cup \{Q\})$, where Δ is the current belief set, Q is the new belief and Cn is the consequence relation of the logic.

An *abduction* is fundamentally different from an expansion in that an agent seeks out an *explanation* that together with the current belief set Δ allows her to conclude Q. So, for example, if Δ is $Cn(\{p \Rightarrow q\})$, an expansion by q will result in $\Delta' = Cn(\{q, p \Rightarrow q\})$, whereas an abductive process for a logic L formulated with a goal-directed proof procedure would result in $\Delta'' = Cn(\{p, p \Rightarrow q\})$. In general, the

D. M. Gabbay et al., *Revision, Acceptability and Context*, Cognitive Technologies,
DOI 10.1007/978-3-642-14159-1_6, © Springer-Verlag Berlin Heidelberg 2010

abductive process needs to take many considerations into account, including that of the proof procedure Π_L for the logic L and possibly some other constraints θ.

Notice that since the concept of abduction is intrinsically connected with the notion of proof, we may use it not only to make proofs succeed (by adding the missing components), but also to make them *fail* (by removing components necessary to complete a given proof). Thus, in our previous example, if we want to make the proof of q fail from Δ'', the procedure may suggest the contraction of p. So, in general, we can think of a metafunction $Abduce(\Delta, Q, constraints, x)$ for a database Δ and input Q satisfying *constraints*, where $x = 0$ if we want the query Q to fail from Δ, and 1 if we want it to succeed.

The purpose of this section is to introduce a general methodology of abduction in logical systems and demonstrate it through the application of abduction in a labelled deductive system (*LDS*) with implication.

Given a logical system L (L may be a monotonic or non-monotonic logic[1]), a theory Δ in L and a wff Q, there are several possible interactions to consider between L, Δ and Q.

1. *Consequence*
   We can ask whether $\Delta \vdash_L Q$
2. *Contraction/deletion*
   If $\Delta \vdash_L Q$ holds, we can ask how we revise Δ to a theory Δ' (if L is a monotonic logic, we require that $\Delta' \subseteq \Delta$) such that $\Delta' \nvdash_L Q$.
3. *Consistency*
   If $\Delta \nvdash_L Q$, we can ask whether $\Delta \cup \{Q\}$ is consistent in L.
4. *Revision*
   If $\Delta \cup \{Q\}$ is not consistent, we can ask how we revise $\Delta \cup \{Q\}$ to a Δ' preferably satisfying $\Delta' \subseteq \Delta \cup \{Q\}$, such that $\Delta' \vdash_L Q$ and Δ' is consistent.
5. *Abduction*
   If $\Delta \nvdash_L Q$, we can ask what X we can add to Δ to get $\Delta' = \Delta \cup \{X\}$ such that $\Delta \cup \{X\} \vdash_L Q$ (if L is non-monotonic we may delete X from Δ to get a Δ' such that $\Delta' \vdash Q$). We would, of course, like X to be as logically weak as possible.

A possible answer to (1) is a proof theory system for L. Such a system would be an algorithm Π_L which, for a given Δ and Q, if it terminates, may give an answer yes, denoted $\Pi_L(\Delta, Q) = 1$, or an answer no, denoted $\Pi_L(\Delta, Q) = 0$. The answer to (2) may be through a contraction mechanism which tells us what to take out to make Q unprovable (see Section 3.7.1 and Chapter 8 for mechanisms for contraction). The third question requires, instead, a semantical interpretation or model-building

---

[1] The consequence relation $\vdash_L$ of a monotonic logic satisfies

1. *Reflexivity*: $\Delta \vdash_L A$ if $A \in \Delta$
2. *Monotonicity*: $\Delta \vdash_L A$ implies $\Delta, \Delta' \vdash_L A$
3. *Cut*: $\Delta, A \vdash_L B$ and $\Delta' \vdash_L A$ imply $\Delta, \Delta' \vdash_L B$.

For a non-monotonic logic (2) is replaced by the weaker

2'. *Restricted monotonicity*: $\Delta \vdash_L A$ and $\Delta \vdash_L B$ imply $\Delta, A \vdash_L B$.

process, whereas the fourth question can be addressed by means of a revision mechanism which tells us how to revise a theory in order to accept as input Q (there are many examples of these mechanisms throughout this book.[2] Finally, question (5) can be addressed by an abduction mechanism, which is the concern of this section.

The above considerations use the concepts of "logic", which includes notions of "consistency" and "consequence", "theory" and "formula". To answer any of the above questions in a general setting, we need to have general settings for these notions. As motivated in Chapter 1 of [3], a logic L is generally defined in terms of both its consequence relation (what proves what in L), and a specific proof procedure Π_L. Classical logic with a tableaux proof theory is therefore not the same as classical logic with a resolution proof theory. In a general setting, a theory (or database) can be seen as a structured family of wffs (data items or declarative units). The structure of the data can be sets, multisets, sequences, or even a general algebraic structure. Depending on the structure, both a formula and its negation may coexist by residing in different locations within the structure. Thus, a general notion of "consistency" for theory (or structured database) is needed, and in this book we have put forward the view that it should be given in terms of the notion of *acceptability*. So, some databases are acceptable and some are not.[3]

Furthermore, in the case of a database theory, the notion of a theory has also to include definitions of how the database receives new input, and because of the underlying structure, also where the new input has to be placed.[4] Similarly, notions of how a formula can be removed from the database and what the new database would look like are needed. Other required notions are how to join together two databases and how to decompose a database into several databases.

A unifying formal setting for general notions of logic and theories is that of a *labelled deductive system* (*LDS*). In an *LDS*, data is provided as a *declarative unit* of the form $t : A$, where t is a label from an algebra and A is a wff from a given logic L. Within the *LDS* methodology, a general notion of abduction can also be formulated. An abductive mechanism can, in general, be defined so to reflect the following characteristics:

- *meta-level property*
  Abduction is a meta-level notion and should be understood in the context of object-level/meta-level interaction.

- *dependence on proof theory*
  Abduction for a logic L_1 depends on the proof procedure Π_{L_1} for L_1. Different proof procedures may give rise to different abductive mechanisms.

---

[2] Note that the cases (2) and (4) can be quite complex in the case of non-monotonic theories.

[3] In traditional logics, a theory Δ is acceptable if and only if it is consistent, i.e., $\Delta \nvdash \perp$. However, a more general notion of acceptability may be employed for traditional logics as well. We may find some theories unacceptable even though they are consistent.

[4] In traditional logics, where theories are sets of formulae, the addition of new input is formalised simply by set union.

- *relationship with the data*
  Abductive principles can be part of the data. In other words, a declarative item of data can be either a (labelled) formula or a principle of abduction.

- *influence on the logic*
  Abductive principles can be a new principle of proof. In other words, new rules can be abduced, allowing the abductive mechanism for L_1 to modify Π_{L_1} itself. The effect of such modification can enrich the logic L.

- *a second background logic*
  Given a logic L_1 with a proof theory Π_{L_1} for it, two independent components are needed in order to define an abductive mechanism for L_1: a procedure for the abduction (which will make use of the proof theory of L_1, and can be thought of as the *explanation component* of the logic), and an additional, possibly completely different, logic L_2, which can be thought of as the *plausibility component*. The abductive procedure determines, using the logic L_1 and its proof theory, possible candidate formulae that can be abduced. The logic L_2 can be used to decide which candidates it is plausible to choose as the abductive answer.[5]

Given a logic L and proof procedure Π_L, an abductive process can be seen as a recursive metafunction *Abduce* that follows the computation steps of a meta-predicate *Success* defined over a given proof procedure Π_L, and that yields modifications to the database at every step where the *Success* meta-predicate seems to fail in the proof task. The suggested modifications are designed to help *Success* achieve its aim.

In order to discuss the ideas involved in the definition of *Abduce*, we first need to present an *LDS* goal-directed system for $\Rightarrow$, which will be later used in the definition of the abduction algorithm given in Section 6.2.4.

6.2.1 Introducing LDS for $\Rightarrow$

We have proposed that the best way of describing the abduction mechanism in its general form is to present it within the framework of a *labelled deductive system* [3]). This framework is general enough to contain as special cases most, if not all, well-known logics, whether classical, non-classical, monotonic or non-monotonic.

We now introduce a typical *LDS* formulation for implication $\Rightarrow$, within which we discuss the principles of abduction.

To present an *LDS* for implication $\Rightarrow$ we require an algebra $\mathscr{A}$ of labels of the form $(\mathbb{A}, f, \varphi)$, where $\mathbb{A}$ is a set of labels, f is a binary operation on $\mathbb{A}$ and φ is a binary compatibility relation on $\mathbb{A}$. This is not the most general definition, but it is sufficient for having a general system in which abduction principles are explained.

---

[5] In the a very general setting, the logic L_2 itself may involve also its own abduction process, and so on.

f, φ are necessary predicates in any *LDS*. Different logics may have additional relations and functions on $\mathbb{A}$, besides the compulsory f and φ. The most common additions are an ordering $<$ and the constant d. φ is in the language with $f, <$ and d.

Our notion of a *well-formed declarative unit* is defined as a pair $\alpha : B$, where α is a label, i.e., $\alpha \in \mathbb{A}$, and B is a traditional wff in the propositional language with $\Rightarrow$ and with atomic propositional variables $\{q_1, q_2, q_3, \ldots\}$.

Using the above algebra we can present the implication elimination rule $(f, \varphi) \Rightarrow E$ as follows:

- $(f, \varphi) \Rightarrow E$ rule:

$$\frac{\alpha : A; \beta : A \Rightarrow B; \varphi(\beta, \alpha)}{f(\beta, \alpha) : B}$$

We need to assume that $\varphi(\beta, \alpha)$ is a decidable predicate over $\mathbb{A}$ and that f is a total recursive function on A. This makes the rule effective. This rule is a *general labelled modus ponens* rule. We shall see later in Definition 6.1 how to use it.

We need one more notion. Let $t(x)$ be a term of the algebra built up using the function symbol f and the variable x ranging over $\mathbb{A}$. The function $\lambda x t(x)$ is a unary function over $\mathbb{A}$ which may or may not be definable in $\mathscr{A}$.

We say that $\lambda x t(x)$ is φ-*realisable* by an element $\alpha \in \mathbb{A}$ if and only if the following holds

$$\forall x [\varphi(\alpha, x) \Rightarrow f(\alpha, x) = t(x)]$$

We denote this α, if it exists, by $(\eta x) t(x)$.

We must assume that our algebra is such that it is decidable to check whether $(\eta x) t(x)$ exists, and if it does exist we have algorithms available to effectively produce it.

Given an $(f, \varphi) \Rightarrow E$ rule, we can define the implication introduction rule $(f, \varphi) \Rightarrow I$ as follows:

- To show $\gamma : A \Rightarrow B$, assume $x : A$ and $\varphi(\gamma, x)$ and prove $f(\gamma, x) : B$,[6] where x is a new atomic variable.

The traditional way of writing this rule is as follows.

Show $\gamma : A \Rightarrow B$ from a subcomputation:

show $f(\gamma, x) : B$
$x : A; \varphi(\gamma, x)$ assumptions
$\vdots$
$f(\gamma, x) : B$

Exit with $\gamma : A \Rightarrow B$

We are now ready to define the notion of a database in *LDS* more formally.

---

[6] In practice, one proves $t(x) : B$ for some term $t(x)$, and then shows that $\gamma = (\eta x) t(x)$.

Definition 6.1 (Labelled database).

A *labelled database* Δ is a set of declarative sentences (labelled formulae) together with a set of compatibility relations of the form $\varphi(\alpha_i, \beta_i)$ on the labels of Δ.

Part of the notion of a database is the notion of where to place additional inputs. Thus, if we want to add the declarative unit $x : B$ to the database Δ to get a new database Δ', we need an insertion operation. We can assume that with a labelled database there is a meta-predicate $\Psi_+(\Delta, \Delta', x : B)$ stating that Δ' is the result of inserting $x : B$ into Δ. We also need the notion of deleting $x : B$ from Δ. We can use the meta-predicate $\Psi_-(\Delta, \Delta', x : B)$. Of course Ψ_- and Ψ_+ satisfy some obvious properties. These predicates need not be definable in the algebra $\mathscr{A}$, but could be of a higher order. We can write $\Delta' = \Delta + (x : B)$ for insertion and $\Delta' = \Delta - (x : B)$ for deletion, provided we understand $+$ and $-$ as referring to Ψ_+ and Ψ_-. Ψ_+ and Ψ_- must be computable. In practice we can express Ψ_- and Ψ_+ in the algebra.[7]

Definition 6.2 (Derivability in a labelled database). We define the notion $\Delta \vdash \alpha : A$ by induction on the number of nested uses of the $\Rightarrow I$ rule.

1. $\Delta \vdash_0 \alpha : A$ if and only if there exists a sequence of labelled wffs $\alpha_1 : A_1, \ldots, \alpha_k : A_k$ such that each $\alpha_i : A_i$ is either an item of data in Δ or is obtained from the previous two elements

   $$\alpha_m : A_m, \alpha_n : A_n, m, n < i$$

   via the $(f, \varphi) \Rightarrow$-elimination rule. This means that $\varphi(\alpha_n, \alpha_m)$ can be proved from $\Delta, A_n = A_m \Rightarrow A_i$ and $\alpha_i = f(\alpha_n, \alpha_m)$. We also have $\alpha_k : A_k$ is $\alpha : A$.

2. We say $\Delta \vdash_{n+1} \alpha : B \Rightarrow C$ if and only if $\Delta + \{x : B; \varphi(\alpha, x)\} \vdash_m f(\alpha, x) : C$, where x is a new variable and $m \leq n$.

   We write $\Delta \vdash_\infty \alpha : A$ if for some $n, \Delta \vdash_n \alpha : A$.
   Let Ψ be a decidable meta-predicate on pairs of the form (S, α) where S is a data structure of labels and α is a label.[8] Given a database Δ let $S_\Delta = \{\alpha \in \mathbb{A} \mid$ for some formula $B, \alpha : B \in \Delta\}$.
   We write $\Delta \vdash_\Psi B$ if for some $\alpha, \Delta \vdash_\infty \alpha : B$ and $\Psi(S_\Delta, \alpha)$ holds.[9]

   We say B is a theorem of the logic if $\varnothing \vdash_\Psi B$.

---

[7] We let $\Delta' = \Delta \cup \{x : B\}$, but by definition we also add some formulae about x, relating x to the labels y of Δ. For example, the labels in Δ may be linearly ordered by $<$. We may agree that all inputs $x : B$ receive the highest priority in the ordering, in which case the formula to add is $\forall y(y \leq x)$. We write $\Psi_+(\Delta, \Delta', x : B)$ to say Δ' is the result of proper input of $x : B$ into Δ.

[8] Although Ψ is a predicate on the algebra it need not be first-order. It need only be recursive. S is usually a sequence of labels.

[9] Note that the logic $\vdash_\Psi$ can turn out to be either monotonic or non-monotonic. It depends on Ψ and the properties of the input function.

6.2.2 Goal-Directed Algorithm for $\Rightarrow$

One of our general abduction principles for general logics is that abductive procedures do not depend only on the consequence relation (i.e., on $\Delta \vdash A$ alone), but
depend also on the proof procedure given for finding whether $\Delta \vdash A$ or not. In other
words, we abduce something in the context of our algorithmic search. To make this
concrete, we offer in this section a general goal-directed proof procedure for our
LDS for $\Rightarrow$. We will then show how abduction can hinge upon it.

In fact, we will show how abduction can be dependent on any general type of
proof-theoretical procedure, since our goal-directed algorithm is a typical reduction
algorithm. It makes good sense to illustrate abduction using a goal-directed system
because the very idea of abduction is goal-directed. We have $\Delta \nvdash A$ and we are
looking for ways to prove A. A is our goal!

The goal-directed computation seeks to find for a given Δ and B whether $\Delta \vdash_\psi B$,
namely, whether there exist any labels β such that $\Delta \vdash_\infty \beta : B$ and $\Psi(S_\Delta, \beta)$ hold.

We begin by observing that each declarative formula in the database has the form
$\alpha : A_1 \Rightarrow (A_2 \Rightarrow (\cdots \Rightarrow (A_n \Rightarrow q)\ldots))$ where q is atomic. q is called the *head of the
unit* and $(A_1, \ldots, A_n)$ is called its *body* (sequence). Consider the question of whether
$\Delta \vdash_k \delta : A$. A can have one of two forms:

1. A can be an atom q
2. A can have the form $A = (B \Rightarrow C)$ for some B, C.

Also recall from the previous section that

3. $\Delta \vdash_\psi A$ if for some $\delta, k, \Delta \vdash_k \delta : A$ and $\Psi(S_\Delta, \delta)$ holds.

In the first case, if $\Delta \vdash_k \delta : q$, then there must exist an $\alpha : A_1 \Rightarrow (A_2 \Rightarrow \cdots (A_n \Rightarrow
q)\ldots)$ in Δ and labels $\alpha_1 \ldots, \alpha_n$ such that $\Delta \vdash_k \alpha_i : A_i$, and labels $\delta_1, \ldots, \delta_n = \delta$ such
that the following all hold:

$$\delta_1 = f(\alpha, \alpha_1); \varphi(\alpha, \alpha_1)$$
$$\delta_2 = f(\delta_1, \alpha_2); \varphi(\delta_1, \alpha_2)$$
$$\vdots$$
$$\delta = \delta_n = f(\delta_{n-1}, \alpha_n); \varphi(\delta_{n-1}, \alpha_n)$$

Let us abbreviate the above as

$$\delta = f[\alpha, (\delta_1, \ldots, \delta_n)]$$

and

$$\varphi[\alpha, (\delta_1, \ldots, \delta_n)].$$

Of course it may be the case that there is no item of data in the database with
head q. In this case we are stuck and the computation clearly cannot continue. We
say that we have *immediate failure* at this point.

Another possibility of immediate failure is that although a clause does exist, φ
cannot be satisfied. Again we cannot go on.

In the second case, if $\Delta \vdash_k \delta : B \Rightarrow C$ holds, then if we add $x : B$ to Δ for a new variable x, we must have that

$$\Delta + \{x : B\} \vdash_m f(\delta, x) : C$$

for some $m \leq k - 1$.

Given the above, we can write a constraints logic programming program (the algebra of constraints is our algebra $\mathscr{A} = (\mathbb{A}, f, \varphi)$) for the meta-predicate

$$Success(\Delta, \delta : A, \text{constraints}, \theta) = 0 \text{ or } 1$$

where Δ is a labelled database (with labels containing variables), $\delta : A$ is the current goal, *constraints* is a set of constraints on the labels and θ is a possibly partial substitution for the label variables.

Success $= 1$ means the computation succeeds, and
Success $= 0$ means the computation finitely fails.

Of course the computation can loop or just continue forever for whatever reason. So the two options are not exhaustive. The consequence relation meaning of *Success* $= 1$ means that $\Delta \theta \vdash \delta \theta : A$ and $\mathscr{A} \vdash \text{constraints} \, \theta$.

We now give a recursive definition. The definition is formulated using meta-predicates $\Psi_\in, \Psi_+, \Psi_-, \Psi_d$ and Ψ. This way we can change the computation for different logics by varying the Ψs (see [5] for details). In general, the Ψs need to satisfy some desirable conditions. Their meaning is as follows. $\Psi_\in$ tells us when an atomic query can succeed or fail from a database in *one step* (*immediate success* or *failure*). Ψ_+ is an insertion predicate, Ψ_- is a deletion predicate and Ψ_d is a decomposition predicate: given a database Δ and databases $\Delta'_1, \ldots, \Delta'_n$, it may be that Δ'_i are a decomposition of Δ in some way. We write $\Psi_d(\Delta, \Delta'_1, \ldots, \Delta'_n)$ to express this relation. Note that n may vary and that the decomposition may not be disjoint. Ψ tells us when a proof is acceptable.

The choice of Ψs proposed below is for the simple resource logic's case.

Definition 6.3. We define the meta-predicate (immediate) $Success(\Delta, \delta : A, \text{constraint}, \theta) = 1$ or 0, where θ is a substitution to label variables, as follows:

1. *immediate success case:*
   (Immediate) $Success(\Delta, \delta : q, \text{constraints}, \theta) = 1$ if q is atomic and $\delta \theta = \alpha \theta$ for some label α such that $\Psi_\in(\Delta \theta, \delta \theta : q)$ holds and the constraints are provable in the algebra $\mathscr{A}$.

   In the case of resource logics, $\Psi_\in(\Delta, \delta : q)$ can be, for example, $\alpha : q \in \Delta$.

2. *implication case:*
   $Success(\Delta, \delta : B \Rightarrow C, \text{constraints}, \theta) = x$ if for $\Delta' = \Delta + (a : B)$ (i.e., Δ' such that $\Psi_+(\Delta, \Delta', a : B)$) we have $Success(\Delta', f(\delta, a) : C, \text{constraints}, \theta) = x$ for a new atomic constant a. Recall that Ψ_+ says that Δ' is the (usually unique) result of inserting $a : B$ into Δ.

   In the case of resource logics, $\Psi_+(\Delta, \Delta', a : B)$ is $\Delta' = \Delta \cup \{a : B\}$.

3. *immediate failure case:*
   (Immediate) $Success(\Delta, \delta : q, constraints, \theta) = 0$ for q atomic if either the constraints are not provable under the substitution θ or there is no clause in the database Δ with head q such that $\Psi_{\in}(\Delta\theta, \delta\theta : q)$ holds.

4. *cut reduction case:*
   $Success(\Delta, \delta : q, constraints, \theta) = 1$ (respectively, 0) if for some (respectively, any) $E = (\alpha : A_1 \Rightarrow (A_2 \Rightarrow \ldots (A_n \Rightarrow q)\ldots))$ in Δ and for some (respectively, any) new variables $\delta_1, \ldots, \delta_n$ and some (respectively, all) choices of $\Delta'_1, \ldots, \Delta'_n$ and $\Delta'_0 = \{\alpha : A_1 \Rightarrow (A_2 \Rightarrow \ldots (A_n \Rightarrow q)\ldots)\}$ such that $\Psi_d(\Delta, \Delta'_0, \ldots, \Delta'_n)$ holds and substitution θ' extends θ to $\delta_1, \ldots, \delta_n$, we have for each $1 \leq i \leq n$ (respectively, for some i) $Success(\Delta'_i, \delta_i : A_i, constraints', \theta') = 1$ (respectively, 0), where $constraints' = constraints \cup \{\delta\theta' = f[\alpha\theta', (\delta_1\theta', \ldots, \delta_n\theta')]\} \cup \{\varphi[\alpha\theta', (\delta_1\theta', \ldots, \delta_n\theta')]\}.$[10]

5. *consequence:*
   We have $\Delta \vdash A$ if for some variable δ and some substitution θ for δ we have $Success(\Delta, \delta : A, \{\Psi(S_\Delta, \delta)\}, \theta) = 1$.

Note that the computation may not be decidable unless we assume we have recursive algorithms for all the conditions and meta-predicates mentioned in it and all ranges of choice are computably finite.

The computation may loop, so a historical loop checker may be needed.

The above algorithm is a typical reduction algorithm. We start with an initial state involving $(\Delta, A, parameters)$ and rewrite or reduce it to other states. Some states (Γ, B, P) are reduced to *Success* and some states may be such that no reduction rules apply, in which case we can say they are reduced to *(immediate) failure*.

The typical abduction principle will consider the history of the reduction up to a point of failure and tell us what to do at that stage.

Of course the process may loop, but in the propositional case a historical loop checker can take care of that, and so we may assume that the parameters include a device that eliminates looping.

Example 6.1. In any logic, consider $q \Rightarrow q \vdash ?q$.
   $Success(q \Rightarrow q, q, no\ constraints) = x$ simply loops.

Example 6.2. Consider the following example for linear logic. The labels are multisets. Note that the computation is displayed as "Data $\vdash$? Goal; constraints".

1. $\varnothing \vdash ?\delta : (A \Rightarrow (A \Rightarrow B)) \Rightarrow (A \Rightarrow B); \delta = \varnothing$
2. $\{a_1\} : A \Rightarrow (A \Rightarrow B) \vdash ?\delta \cup \{a_1\} : A \Rightarrow B; \delta = \varnothing$
3. $\{a_1\} : A \Rightarrow (A \Rightarrow B), \{a_2\} : A \vdash ?\delta \cup \{a_1, a_2\} : B; \delta = \varnothing$
4. We split here into two parallel computations, listed below as (5a) and (5b). Using the clause $\{a_1\} : A \Rightarrow (A \Rightarrow B)$.
5. a. $\{a_1\} : A \Rightarrow (A \Rightarrow B), \{a_2\} : A \vdash ?x_1 : A$

---

[10] Δ_0 appears in Ψ_d as a parameter containing the formula we are using in this rule.

b. $\{a_1\} : A \Rightarrow (A \Rightarrow B), \{a_2\} : A \vdash ?x_2 : A$

The constraints for both 5a and 5b (done in parallel) are

$$\{a_1\} \cup \{x_1\} \cup \{x_2\} = \delta \cup \{a_1, a_2\} \text{ and } \delta = \varnothing$$

5a can succeed by substituting $\theta(x_1) = a_2$, and similarly 5b can succeed by substituting $\theta(x_2) = a_2$. Thus, we get the constraints to be $\{a_1, a_2, a_2\} = \{a_1, a_2\}$.

Since for linear logic we are dealing with multisets, this computation fails, because the constraints cannot be satisfied and there are no other options for the computation. In the case of relevance logic, the labels are sets. Therefore, the constraints are satisfied and the computation succeeds.

The above computation can be made more efficient. Our first optimisation move is to throw out of the database any clause 'used' by rule 3. This saves us time because we are allowed to use each clause at most once.

So, condition 4 of the definition of the *Success* predicate can be modified by changing Ψ_d and requiring it to say that $\Delta_i' \subseteq \Delta \dot{-} \{\alpha : (A_1 \Rightarrow \ldots \Rightarrow (A_n = q) \ldots)\}$ for all i.

Since also all the clauses in the database must be used, we can further modify Ψ_d to be the conjunction of the two following conditions:

- $\bigcup_{i=1}^{n} \Delta_i' = \Delta \dot{-} \{\alpha : (A_1 \Rightarrow \ldots \Rightarrow (A_n \Rightarrow q) \ldots)\}$
- $\Delta_i' \cap \Delta_j' = \varnothing$ for $i \neq j$.

We will need to change clause 1 of the algorithm to be

- $Success(\Delta, \delta : q, constraints, \theta) = 1$ if $\{\alpha : q\} = \Delta$ and $\alpha\theta = \delta\theta$, i.e., change $\Psi_\in$ to the condition $\{\alpha : q\} = \Delta$.

The computation of our example will now be short and quick as follows (we do not even need to use the labels):

$$\varnothing \vdash ?(A \Rightarrow (A \Rightarrow B)) \Rightarrow (A \Rightarrow B)$$

if

$$A \Rightarrow (A \Rightarrow B) \vdash ?A \Rightarrow B$$

if

$$A; A \Rightarrow (A \Rightarrow B) \vdash ?B$$

if

$$A \vdash ?A \text{ and } \varnothing \vdash ?A$$

if

success and *failure.*

We take this opportunity to indicate options for abduction. Our purpose is to succeed. The simplest option in the case of linear logic is to *duplicate A* (as we are missing one copy of A).

This would normally be done at the stage where $\{a_2\} : A$ was put into the database. At that stage $A \Rightarrow (A \Rightarrow B)$ was already in the database, so we need to add to the database the wff $(A \Rightarrow (A \Rightarrow B)) \Rightarrow A$ (rather than adding just A).

So, in order for $(A \Rightarrow (A \Rightarrow B)) \Rightarrow (A \Rightarrow B)$ to succeed from the empty database, we need to abduce $(A \Rightarrow (A \Rightarrow B)) \Rightarrow A$ into the database. This will not help in our case, where the logic is linear logic, because to get A we need another copy of $A \Rightarrow (A \Rightarrow B)$. So we are better off putting A in the database. This can be more readily seen in the case of the more optimised computation where failure results from $\varnothing \vdash ?A$.

Another option for abduction is to regard the constraints as satisfied if they hold for the labels when regarded as sets. This means changing the proof procedures to those of relevance logic. [5] shows how to formulate many logics in a goal-directed way.

6.2.3 Discussion on the Abduction Procedure

Let our starting point be Definition 6.3. This definition gives the recursive rules for the meta-predicate

$Success(\Delta, \delta : A, constraints, \theta) = x.$

For $x = 1$ we want the computation to succeed, and for $x = 0$ we want it to fail. We now examine what kind of difficulties we encounter in defining the abduction algorithm using Definition 6.3 as a basis:

Case of immediate success or failure:
We need to examine what can happen in the case of clauses 1 and 3 of Definition 6.3.

Case $x = 1$.
Clause 1 says that $Success(\Delta, \delta : q, constraints, \theta) = 1$ (i.e., $\Delta\theta \vdash_{constraints} \delta\theta : q$) if two conditions hold:

(a) The constraints mentioned in *constraints* are all provable in $\mathscr{A}$ for the substitution θ.
(b) $\Psi_{\in}(\Delta\theta, \delta\theta : q)$ holds.

If either (a) or (b) cannot be shown to hold, then *success* cannot do its job and our abduction process can be activated to help.

If (a) cannot be shown to hold, we may choose to add axioms to our algebra $\mathscr{A}$ so that the new algebra $\mathscr{A}'$ can prove the constraints. This amounts to a change of the logic. Our abduction policy is not to change the logic (at least not in this manner). Thus, in this case our abduction will not help. So, let us consider the case where the constraints can be proved but where (b) fails, that is, $\Psi_{\in}(\Delta\theta, \delta\theta : q)$ does not hold. We can look for a Δ' such that $\Psi_{\in}(\Delta'\theta, \delta\theta : q)$ does hold.

Whether we can find such a reasonable Δ' depends on $\Psi_{\in}$. For example, for the case of resource logics and the $\Psi_{\in}$ suggested in Definition 6.3, namely the $\Psi_{\in}$ saying that $\delta\theta : q \in \Delta\theta$, we can always find a Δ': we simply add (input) $\delta : q$ into Δ, i.e., let $\Delta' = \Delta + (\delta : q)$. In other words, using the predicate Ψ_+, we find the Δ' such that $\Psi_+(\Delta, \Delta', \delta : q)$ holds.

For a general $\Psi_\in$, we do not know whether a Δ' can be found. We are going to have to stipulate some properties of $\Psi_\in$:

- $\Psi_\in$ *abduction axiom*:
  For every finite Δ and any $\delta : q$ and any $x \in \{0,1\}$ such that $\Psi_\in(\Delta, \delta : q) = x$ ($\Psi_\in = 1$ means $\Psi_\in$ holds, $\Psi_\in = 0$ means $\Psi_\in$ does not hold), there is an effective procedure to produce a finite set (which may be empty) of databases $\{\Gamma_1, \Gamma_2, \ldots, \Gamma_k\}$ such that $\Psi_\in(\Gamma_i, \delta : q) = 1 - x$. We denote this set by $\mathbf{Ab}_1(\Delta, \delta : q, 1 - x)$.

Let us see what this algorithm can be for some of the examples we know. Note that the nature of the abduction depends on the application area in which it is being used. In the application area all of these algorithms have a meaning, and the choice of algorithm for $\Psi_\in$ and indeed for any other Ψ will be dictated by the needs of the application.

- For $\Psi_\in(\Delta, \delta : q) = (\delta : q \in \Delta)$ the algorithm is to let Γ be $\Delta + (\delta : q)$, as already mentioned.
- For the condition $\Psi_\in(\Delta, \delta : q) = (\{\delta : q\} = \Delta)$, let the algorithm be to delete all other data from Δ except $\delta : q$ if $\delta : q \in \Delta$, and if $\delta : q \notin \Delta$ let the algorithm give us nothing. (We do not want to add $\delta : q$ to Δ for reasons having to do with the application area.)

Now to the other case.
Case $x = 0$.
This case is the opposite of the case $x = 1$: *we want the computation to fail*. So if the computation succeeds, this means that the *constraints* can be proved as well as that $\Psi_\in$ holds. We will not fiddle with the logic and make the constraints unprovable. We will concentrate on $\Psi_\in$. We have that $\Psi_\in(\Delta\theta, \delta\theta : q)$ holds and we want to make it not hold. Again, we need to stipulate an algorithm that yields for each Δ and $\delta : q$ such that $\Psi_\in(\Delta, \delta : q)$ holds a set (possibly empty) of $\{\Gamma_1, \ldots, \Gamma_k\}$ options such that $\Psi_\in(\Gamma_i, \delta : q)$ fails to hold. We use $\mathbf{Ab}_1(\Delta, \delta : q, 0)$ to produce the set.

For example, we can adopt the algorithm that takes $\delta : q$ out of Δ (i.e., let $\Gamma = \Delta - \{\delta : q\}$), i.e., we solve $\Psi_-(\Delta, \Gamma, \delta : q)$.

Let us now consider the case of $\Rightarrow$.

Case of $\Rightarrow$:
In order to deal with abduction for a goal of the form $\delta : B \Rightarrow C$, we are going to need some additional machinery. We know that $Success(\Delta, \delta : B \Rightarrow C, constraints, \theta) = x$ if and only if $success(\Delta + (a : B), f(\delta, a) : C, constraints, \theta) = x$, where a is a new atomic label and $+$ is the insertion operation. The abduction process should replace Δ by a new Γ which will facilitate the success/failure of the computation. Suppose now that using abduction Γ_a replaces $\Delta + (a : B)$ in giving the desired success/failure value x to the goal $?f(\delta, a) : C$. We now ask ourselves, what is the appropriate

replacement Γ of Δ? We want a theory Γ such that upon adding $a : B$ to it (i.e., forming $\Gamma + (a : B)$) we get Γ_a. So we want (using the meta-operator '*the x such that $F(x)$ holds*'):

'*the Γ such that $(\Gamma + (a : b) = \Gamma_a)$*'

Let $\mathbf{Ab}_\Rightarrow(\Gamma_1, a : B)$ be a metafunction giving *the Γ such that* $(\Gamma + (a : B) = \Gamma_1)$ when it exists, and $\varnothing$ otherwise.

Let us get a rough idea what this Γ can be.

If we ignore the labels for a moment, we really want the database $\Gamma = (B \Rightarrow \Gamma_1)$, because when we add B to Γ we can get Γ_1.

Thus (ignoring labels), we get

$$\mathbf{Ab}_\Rightarrow(\Gamma_1, B) = \{B \Rightarrow X \mid X \in \Gamma_1\}.$$

Since Γ_1 is supposed to be $Abduce(\Delta + B, C)$, we get the 'rough' equation:

- $Abduce(\Delta, \delta : B \Rightarrow C) = (a : B) \Rightarrow Abduce\ (\Delta + (a, B), f(\delta, a) : C)$

where a is a new constant and the operation $(a : B) \Rightarrow \Gamma_a$ has some meaning for theories Γ_a and units $a : B$. We are not defining this operation but are using it intuitively to explain the kind of operation we need to do abduction in the case of $\Rightarrow$.

If we do not have labels, as in, e.g., intuitionistic logic, let us see what we get.

Assume the abduction problem is $Abduce(\{A \Rightarrow (B \Rightarrow q)\}, B \Rightarrow q)$.

This reduces to

$$B \Rightarrow Abduce(\{B, A \Rightarrow (B \Rightarrow q)\}, q)$$

$Abduce(\{B, A \Rightarrow (B \Rightarrow q)\}, q)$ reduces to $Abduce(\{B, A \Rightarrow (B \Rightarrow q)\}, A)$ and $Abduce\{B, A \Rightarrow (B \Rightarrow q)\}, B\}$.

The second computation, $Success(\{B, A \Rightarrow (B \Rightarrow q)\}, B) = 1$ is successful and so *Abduce* does not change the database, but the first one recommends that we add A to the database. So it is intuitively clear that

$$Abduce(\{B, A \Rightarrow (B \Rightarrow q)\}, q) = \{\{B, A \Rightarrow (B \Rightarrow q), A\}\}$$

Therefore our new theory is:

$$Abduce(\{A \Rightarrow (B \Rightarrow q)\}, B \Rightarrow q) =$$
$$\{\{B \Rightarrow B, B \Rightarrow (A \Rightarrow (B \Rightarrow q)), B \Rightarrow A\} =$$
$$\{\{B \Rightarrow A, B \Rightarrow q\}\} = \{\Delta'\}.$$

Let us take another point of view of abduction. Since intuitionistic logic is monotonic, let us look at $Abduce(\Delta, A)$ as telling us *what to add* to Δ to obtain a Δ' which makes A succeed. In this case, $Abduce(\{A \Rightarrow (B \Rightarrow q)\}, B \Rightarrow q) = B \Rightarrow Abduce(\{A \Rightarrow (B \Rightarrow q), B\}, q) = B \Rightarrow A$.

So $B \Rightarrow A$ needs to be added to Δ to get Δ'. Thus,

$$\Delta' = \{A \Rightarrow (B \Rightarrow q), B \Rightarrow A\}$$
$$= \{B = q, B \Rightarrow A\}.$$

We are getting the same result!

Let us see if we can be more specific about the operation $(a : B) \Rightarrow \Gamma$.

Consider the database $\Gamma_1 = \{\alpha : A\}$. We want to turn it into $\Gamma = \{\beta : B \Rightarrow A\}$ such that $\Gamma + (a : B)$ is 'equivalent' to $\alpha : A$.

Let us try the modus ponens:

$$\frac{\beta : B \Rightarrow A; a : B}{f(\beta, a) : A}$$

Thus, we have to solve '*the β such that* $(f(\beta, a) = \alpha)$', and let

$$(a : B) \Rightarrow \{\alpha : A\} = \{\beta : B \Rightarrow A\}.$$

Thus $\mathbf{Ab}_{\Rightarrow}(\{\alpha : A\}, a : B) = \{\{\beta : B \Rightarrow A\}\}$.

Of course, in a general *LDS* database the $\mathbf{Ab}_{\Rightarrow}$ function can be more complex to define.

Case of database decomposition:

We now consider the case where an atomic query $\delta : q$ unifies with a head of a clause in the database. This is rule 4 of Definition 6.3.

This case decomposes the database into several databases using the Ψ_d predicate. This decomposition forces us to consider the question of what to do with the replacement databases proposed by *Abduce* after the decomposition. We will get output for the abduction metafunction at the points of difficulty of the *Success* predicate but these replace databases deep into some iterated decomposition. How do we propagate the replacements upwards?

Let us illustrate the problem by being more specific. The abductive algorithm for the $\Psi_{\in}$ case, for both $x = 0$ and $x = 1$ replaces Δ with a new Γ. This Γ is proposed in the middle of an overall computation. We need to examine the 'replacement' operation and how it interacts with decomposition. A simple example will illustrate our problem (we will ignore the constraints). Suppose we have a clause $E = (q_1 \Rightarrow (q_2 \Rightarrow a)) \in \Delta$. We ask $Success(\Delta, \delta : a, constraints, \theta) = 1$. Rule 4 of Definition 6.3 tells us to look at partitions databases Δ_1' and Δ_2' such that $\Psi_d(\Delta, \{E\}, \Delta_1', \Delta_2')$ holds and labels δ_1, δ_2 such that $Success(\Delta_i', \delta_i : q_i, constraints', \theta_i) = 1$ for $i = 1, 2$ hold. E appears in Ψ_+ as a parameter. It may be that to make these succeed we abduce Γ_1, Γ_2 for the two subcomputations.

Our question is, how does the replacement of Δ_i' by Γ_i yield a replacement of Δ by Γ? What is Γ? How do we construct it?

Recall that the idea of abduction is to ask for the initial database Δ and a goal $\delta : A$ the predicate $Success(\Delta, \delta : A, constraints, \theta) = x$, and we expect our abduction metafunction to answer: $Abduce(\Delta, \delta : A, constraints, \theta, x) = \{\Gamma\}$. Thus Γ is the result of abduction, and then we are supposed to be assured that $Success(\Gamma, \delta : A, constraints, \theta) = x$ succeeds!

Let us present our problem clearly. We have $\Delta_1', \Delta_2', \Gamma_1, \Gamma_2$ and Δ and we are looking for a Γ. What we know is the following:

- $\Psi_d(\Delta, \{E\}, \Delta_1', \Delta_2')$
- Γ_1 is abduced to replace Δ_1'
- Γ_2 is abduced to replace Δ_2'

- Ψ_+ holds for Γ_i and $\delta_i : q_i$.

We need to know a corresponding Γ to replace Δ such that $\Psi_d(\Gamma, \{E\}, \Gamma_1, \Gamma_2)$ holds.
   To find the Γ we need to know more about the Ψs.
   We need some basic axioms relating the properties of the Ψs. We perhaps need to stipulate inverse functions that allow one to retrieve Δ from any $\Delta_1, \ldots, \Delta_n$, i.e., we need

- $\forall n \forall \Delta_1, \ldots, \Delta_n \exists! \Delta \Psi_d(\Delta, \Delta_1, \ldots, \Delta_n)$.
   Let us introduce a new function $\mathbf{Ab}_+$ with $\mathbf{Ab}_+(\Delta_1, \ldots, \Delta_n) = \Delta$.

- $\bigwedge_{j=1}^{n} \Psi_d(\Delta_n, \Delta_n^1, \ldots, \Delta_n^{k(n)}) \wedge \Psi_d(\Delta, \Delta_1, \ldots, \Delta_n) \Rightarrow \Psi_d(\Delta, \Delta_1^1, \ldots, \Delta_1^{k(1)}, \ldots, \Delta_n^1, \ldots, \Delta_n^{k(n)})$.

- $\forall \Delta \forall n \exists \Delta_1, \ldots, \Delta_n \Psi_d(\Delta, \Delta_1, \ldots, \Delta_n)$ (note that the decomposition need not be disjoint and Δ_i can be empty).

- $\Psi_+(\Delta, \Delta', a : B) \Rightarrow \Psi_-(\Delta', \Delta, a : B)$

We also want some compatibility of Ψ_d with Ψ_+ and Ψ_-. If we regard Ψ_d as a decomposition of Δ into $\Delta_1, \ldots, \Delta_n$ and regard $\Psi_+(\Delta, \Delta', a : B)$ as an insertion of $a : B$ into Δ to form Δ', then do we expect $\Psi_d(\Delta', \Delta, \{a : B\})$ to hold?
   We can have an even stronger condition, namely that Δ can be generated by successive inputs of its own elements:

- $\forall \Delta \exists n \exists (\alpha_1 : A_1, \ldots, \alpha_n : A_n) \exists \Delta_1, \ldots, \Delta_{n-1} \bigwedge_{i=1}^{n-1} \Psi_+(\Delta_{i+1}, \Delta_i, \alpha_{i+1} : A_{i+1}) \wedge \Psi_+(\varnothing, \Delta_1, \alpha_1 : A_1)$.

The problem of soundness

   This is not all that is needed. We started from a decomposition Δ_1', Δ_2' of Δ. We abduced and got Γ_1, Γ_2 and formed Γ. Now we must assume the original clause $E = (q_1 \Rightarrow (q_2 \Rightarrow a))$ is in Γ. In such a case, it is obvious that we can use the clause to decompose Γ back into Γ_1, Γ_2, and ensure that the computation from Γ succeeds.[11]
   What happens if we want to fail? In this case, for every clause, say $q_1 \Rightarrow (q_2 \Rightarrow a)$, and every decomposition, say Δ_1', Δ_2', the *Abduce* predicate will choose some replacement, say Γ_1 for Δ_1', for which the computation $\Gamma_1 ? q_1$ fails. Thus, when we form Γ to replace Δ, we do not care if $q_1 \Rightarrow (q_2 \Rightarrow a) \in \Gamma$. If it is in Γ, however, we must worry about whether it gives rise to *new* decompositions Γ_1', Γ_2' such that $\Gamma_i' ? q_i$ succeed. In fact, we must worry about new clauses in Γ with heads q for which there are successful decompositions. This is again the problem of ensuring soundness.
   There are two ways for going around this difficulty. The first is to make some strong assumptions on the decomposition and $\mathbf{Ab}_+$ predicates. One such possible assumption is that Γ has the same clauses with head q as Δ, and the changes are only in the addition or deletion of atoms. Such an assumption may not be enough,

---

[11] This means that the function $\mathbf{Ab}_+(\Delta_0, \Delta_1, \ldots, \Delta_n) = \Delta$ must satisfy $\Delta_0 \subseteq \Delta$. Δ_0 is the parameter $\{E\}$ in our case.

however; without knowing the specific properties of Ψ_d we may not be able to formulate additional assumptions.

The second method may be in principle more general. We compose $\Gamma = \mathbf{Ab}_+(\Gamma_1, \Gamma_2)$ to replace Δ but we are not assured (by any strong assumptions) that $\Gamma ?q$ fails. We compute $Success(\Gamma, q)$. If it fails, then fine; we take this Γ as the result of the abduction. If it succeeds, then we either say that the abduction process produces nothing or we apply abduction again to $\Gamma ?q$. This will produce a Γ_1, and now we iterate the process. To ensure that this process does not loop forever, we could introduce some complexity assumptions either on the number of iterations or on Ψ_d and $\mathbf{Ab}_+$, which will tell us that abduction involves adding or deleting wffs from a finite set of wffs constructed from the initial database and query. This assumption is enough to allow for a loop checker based on the history of the proofs to work.

6.2.4 Abduction Algorithm for $\Rightarrow$

Following our discussion, we are now ready to write the abduction algorithm

Definition 6.4 (Abduce metafunction).

1. $Abduce(\Delta, \delta : q, constraints, \theta, 1) = \{\Delta\}$ if $Success(\Delta, \delta : q, constraints, \theta) = 1$.

2. $Abduce(\Delta, \delta : q, constraints, \theta, 1) = \varnothing$ if $\mathscr{A} \nvdash constraints\ \theta$

3. $Abduce(\Delta, \delta : q, constraints, \theta, 1) = \{\Gamma_1, \dots, \Gamma_k\}$ if $\mathscr{A} \vdash constraints\ \theta$; $\Psi_\in(\Delta\theta, \delta\theta : q)$ does not hold, and $\mathbf{Ab}_1(\Delta\theta, \delta\theta : q, 1) = \{\Gamma_1, \dots, \Gamma_k\}$.
   Note that each $\Gamma \in \mathbf{Ab}_1$ satisfies $\Psi_\in(\Gamma\theta, \delta\theta : q)$. $\mathbf{Ab}_1$ may yield $\varnothing$ if the abduction is not possible.

4. $Abduce(\Delta, \delta : q, constraints, \theta, 0) = \{\Delta\}$ if $Success(\Delta, \delta : q, constraints, \theta) = 0$.

5. $Abduce(\Delta, \delta : q, constraints, \theta, 0) = \{\Gamma_1, \dots, \Gamma_k\}$ if $\mathscr{A} \vdash constraints\ \theta$; $\Psi_\in(\Delta\theta, \delta\theta : q)$ does hold, and $\mathbf{Ab}_1(\Delta\theta, \delta\theta : q, 0) = \{\Gamma_1, \dots, \Gamma_k\}$.
   Note that for each $\Gamma \in \mathbf{Ab}_1$ we have that $\psi_1(\Gamma\theta, \delta\theta : q)$ does not hold. $\mathbf{Ab}_1$ may give $\varnothing$ if the abduction is not possible.

6. $Abduce(\Delta, \delta : B \Rightarrow C, constraints\ \theta, x) = \{\Gamma_1, \dots, \Gamma_k\}$, where for each Γ_i there exists a Γ_i' such that $\Gamma_i' \in Abduce(\Delta + (a : B), f(\delta, a) : C, \theta, x)$ and $\Gamma_i = \mathbf{Ab}_\Rightarrow(\Gamma_i', (a : B))$.

We now consider the case of decomposition. We need some notation first. Let Δ be a database and $\delta : q$ be a goal. By a decomposition $D(\Delta, \delta : q)$ we mean a choice of a clause E of the form $\alpha : A_1 \Rightarrow (\dots \Rightarrow (A_n \Rightarrow q) \dots)$ in Δ, called the clause of D, and of databases $\Delta_1', \dots, \Delta_n'$ such that $\Psi_d(\Delta, \{E\}, \Delta_1', \dots, \Delta_n')$ holds. n is referred to as the length of the decomposition and depends on E. To introduce the rules for $Abduce$, recall that by rule 4 of Definition 6.3, $Success(\Delta, \delta : q, constraints, \theta) = 1$ (respectively, 0) if for some D (respectively, all D) and some $\delta_1, \dots, \delta_n$, we have for all i (respectively, some i) $Success(\Delta_i', \delta_i : A_i, constraints', \theta') = 1$ (respectively, 0).

7. $Abduce(\Delta, \delta : q, constraints, \theta, 1)$ wants to make success out of failure, so it will give all options for success. So, for each D, it will give a set of $\Gamma_{e_1}^D, \Gamma_{e_2}^D, \ldots$ that will make this choice of D succeed. For the choice of D to succeed we need all $Success(\Delta_i', \delta_i : A_i, constraints', \theta') = 1$.

Let $Abduce(\Delta_i', \delta_i : A_i, constraints', \theta', 1) = \{\Gamma_{i,1}^D, \Gamma_{i,2}^D \ldots \Gamma_{i,k(i)}^D\}$, i.e., the set of options for replacing Δ_i' and succeeding.

The replacement for Δ will be all possible choices $\Gamma_e^D = \{\mathbf{Ab}_+(\{E\}, \Gamma_{1,e(1)}^D, \ldots, \Gamma_{n,e(n)}^D) \mid e$ a function giving each $1 \leq i \leq n$ a value $1 \leq e(i) \leq k(i)\}$. We therefore define: $Abduce(\Delta, \delta : q, constraints, \theta, 1) = \{\Gamma_e^D \mid$ D, e as above, and such that the clause of D is in Γ_eD$\}$.

8. Consider now $Success(\Delta, \delta : q, constraints, \theta) = 0$. This fails if for some D we have for all $i = 1, \ldots, n, Success(\Delta_i', \delta_i : A_i, constraints'\theta') = 1$.
So for every D we choose an index $1 \leq \mathbf{c}(D) \leq n$ and replace $\Delta_{\mathbf{c}(D)}'$ by $\Gamma_{\mathbf{c}(D)}'$ from the set $Abduce(\Delta_{\mathbf{c}(D)}', \delta_{\mathbf{c}(D)} : A_{\mathbf{c}(D)}, constraints', \theta', 0)$.

Let $\Gamma_{\mathbf{c}}^D = \mathbf{Ab}_+(\{E\}, \Delta_1', \ldots, \Delta_{\mathbf{c}(D)-1}', \Gamma_{\mathbf{c}(D)}', \Delta_{\mathbf{c}(D)+1}', \ldots, \Delta_n')$.

Let $Abduce(\Delta, \delta : q, constraints, \theta, 0) = \{\Gamma_{\mathbf{c}}^D \mid$ D and c as above and $Success(\Gamma_{\mathbf{c}}^D, \delta : q, constraints, \theta) = 1\}$.

9. In case there are no strong assumptions on $\mathbf{Ab}_+$ and Ψ_d ensuring that the $\Gamma_{\mathbf{c}}^D$ produced in the preceding item 8 above are sound, we iterate the *Abduce* computation for each candidate $\Gamma_{\mathbf{c}}^D$ until we either find such candidates or give up and produce $\varnothing$.

Theorem 6.1 (Soundness of abduction). *If* $\Gamma \in Abduce(\Delta, \delta : A, constraints, \theta, x)$, *then* $Success(\Gamma, \delta : A, constraints, \theta) = x$. *Of course*, $Abduce(\Delta, \delta : A, constraints, \theta, x)$ *may be empty.*

Proof. By induction on the definition of Abduce.
We follow the clauses of Definition 6.4.

1. *Clear*
2. *Nothing to prove*
3. *By definition,* $\mathbf{Ab}_1(\Delta\theta, \delta\theta : q, 1)$ *produces* Γ_i *which satisfy* Ψ_+, *and so* Success = 1 *holds.*
4. *Clear*
5. *By definition,* $\mathbf{Ab}_1(\Delta\theta, \delta\theta : q, 0)$ *produces* Γ_i *for which there is failure of* $\Psi_\in$, *and so* Success = 0 *holds.*
6. *Clear from the definitions.*
7. *The abduction replaces* Δ *by* Γ. *To check the success predicate for* Γ *we had to assume that* Success$(\Gamma, \delta : q, constraints, \theta) = 1$.
8–9. *Again, measures were introduced in this clause to ensure that the choices of* Γ *produced by the* Abduce *function do the job.*

6.2.5 *Abduction for Intuitionistic Logic*

Intuitionistic logic is monotonic and requires no labels and therefore no constraints. Doing abduction for it becomes simple. In Definition 6.3, $\Psi_\in(\Delta, q)$ becomes $q \in \Delta$. The decomposition $\Psi_d(\Delta, \{E\}, \Delta_1, \ldots, \Delta_n)$ does not need the parameter Δ_0 and can be taken as $\bigwedge_{i=1}^n \Delta_i = \Delta$. $\Psi_+(\Delta, \Delta', A)$ is $\Delta' = \Delta \cup \{A\}$, and $\Psi_-(\Delta, \Delta', A)$ is $\Delta' = \Delta - \{A\}$.

The computation rules for $Success(\Delta, A) = x$, $x \in \{0, 1\}$ become the following:

Definition 6.5 (*Success* for intuitionistic logic).

1. *immediate success case*
   $Success(\Delta, q) = 1$ for q atomic if $q \in \Delta$.

2. *implication case*
   $Success(\Delta, B \Rightarrow C) = x$ if $Success(\Delta \cup \{B\}, C) = x$.

3. *immediate failure case*
   $Success(\Delta, q) = 0, q$ atomic, if q is not the head of any clause in Δ.

4. *cut reduction case*
   $Success(\Delta, q) = 1$ (respectively, $Success(\Delta, q) = 0$) for q atomic if for some (respectively, all) clauses of the form $A_1 \Rightarrow (A_2 \Rightarrow \ldots \Rightarrow (A_n \Rightarrow q) \ldots) \in \Delta$ we have that for all i (respectively, for some i) $Success(\Delta, A_i) = 1$ (respectively, $Success(\Delta, A_i) = 0$).

5. *consequence*
   We have $\Delta \vdash A$ if and only if $Success(\Delta, A) = 1$.

We can therefore see $Abduce(\Delta, A, x)$ as yielding a set of wffs to add (for $x = 1$) or delete (for $x = 0$) from Δ to make A succeed or fail, respectively.

We can therefore expect the following:

- $\Delta + Abduce(\Delta, A, 1) \vdash A$
- $\Delta - Abduce(\Delta, A, 0) \nvdash A$

We can simplify our notation and write $\Delta ? Q = x$ for $Success(\Delta, Q, constraints, \theta) = x$ and $Abduce^\pm(\Delta, Q) = \{\Gamma_1, \ldots, \Gamma_k\}$, where Γ_i are all alternative sets of wffs to be added or taken out of Δ to yield the desired results.

We therefore have the following connection between the old and new notations:

$$Abduce(\Delta, Q, constraints, \theta, 1) = \{\Delta + \Gamma \mid \Gamma \in Abduce^+(\Delta, Q)\}$$
$$Abduce(\Delta, Q, constraints, \theta, 0) = \{\Delta - \Gamma \mid \Gamma \in Abduce^-(\Delta, Q)\}$$

Definition 6.6 (Abduce for intuitionistic logic).

1. $Abduce^+(\Delta, Q) = \{\varnothing\}$ if $\Delta ? Q = 1$
2. $Abduce^-(\Delta, Q) = \{\varnothing\}$ if $\Delta ? Q = 0$
3. $Abduce^+(\Delta, q) = \{q\}$ if q is atomic and is not the head of any clause in Δ
4. $Abduce^-(\Delta, q) = \{q\}$ if $q \in \Delta$, q atomic

5. $Abduce^+(\Delta, A_1 \Rightarrow (A_2 \Rightarrow \ldots (A_n \Rightarrow q) \ldots)) = \{A_1 \Rightarrow (A_2 \Rightarrow \ldots (A_n \Rightarrow X) \ldots) \mid$
   $X \in Abduce^+(\Delta \cup \{A_1, \ldots, A_n\}, q)\}$
6. $Abduce^-(\Delta, A_1 \Rightarrow (A_2 \Rightarrow \ldots (A_n \Rightarrow q) \ldots)) = \{A_1 \Rightarrow (A_2 \Rightarrow \ldots (A_n \Rightarrow X) \ldots) \mid$
   $X \in Abduce^-(\Delta \cup \{A_1, \ldots, A_n\}, q)\}$

For clauses (7) and (8) below, we need to assume that

$$B^j = (B_1^j \Rightarrow \ldots \Rightarrow (B_{n(j)}^j \Rightarrow q) \ldots), \, j = 1, \ldots, m,$$

lists all clauses of heads q in Δ.

We also need the notion of a choice function $\mathbf{c}$. For each $1 \leq j \leq m$, $\mathbf{c}(j)$ is a theory $\Gamma = \mathbf{c}(j)$ such that for some $1 \leq i \leq n(j)$, $\Gamma \in Abduce^-(\Delta, B^j)$.

7. $Abduce^+(\Delta, q) = \{\{Abduce^+(\Delta, B_i^j) \mid i = 1, \ldots, n(j)\} \mid j = 1, \ldots, m\}$.
8. $Abduce^-(\Delta, q) = \{\Gamma_{\mathbf{c}} \mid \mathbf{c}$ is a choice function as explained above and $\Gamma_{\mathbf{c}} = \bigcup_{j=1}^m \Gamma_{\mathbf{c}(j)}\}$.

The explanation for clause (8) is the following: for each clause B^j as above, we want to choose an $1 \leq i \leq n(j)$ such that $\Delta ? B_i^j = 0$ to ensure that we look to $Abduce^-(\Delta, B_i^j)$.

Our choice functions are functions $\mathbf{c}$ choosing for each $j = 1, \ldots, m$ an $1 \leq i \leq j$ and a theory $\mathbf{c}(j) \in Abduce^-(\Delta, B_i^j)$.

Let $\Gamma_{\mathbf{c}} = \bigcup_{j=1}^m \Gamma_{\mathbf{c}(j)}$.

Remark 6.1.

1. Note that $Abduce^+$ and $Abduce^-$ are defined independently of each other.
2. Note that in the previous definition if $B^j = q$, then clause 4 of the definition of $Abduce^-$ gets activated.

Example 6.3.

1. Consider $\Delta = \{a\}?q$.
   The $Abduce^+$ wff is q.
   The new abduced theory for success is $\{a, q\}$.

2. Consider $\Delta = \{a \Rightarrow (b \Rightarrow q), a, c \Rightarrow (d \Rightarrow q)\}?q$.
   The $Abduce^+$ candidates are $\{\{b\}, \{c \Rightarrow d\}\}$. There are two new abduced theories for success, $\Delta \cup \{b\}$ and $\Delta \cup \{c \Rightarrow d\}$.

3. Consider $\Delta = \{q, a \Rightarrow q\}?q$. The $Abduce^-$ candidate is $\{q\}$. The new abduced theory for failure is $\Delta - \{q\} = \{a \Rightarrow q\}$.

Theorem 6.2. $\Delta \cup \Gamma \vdash Q$ for any $\Gamma \in Abduce^+(\Delta, Q)$.

Proof. The proof is by induction on the definition of the Abduce predicate.

1. *If the set* $Abduce(\Delta, Q)$ *contains* $\varnothing$, *then this means* $\Delta \vdash Q$.
2. *Assume that* $Q = q$ *is atomic and that it is not the head of any clause. Then the abduced formula is* q, *and clearly,* $\Delta, q \vdash q$.

3. Assume Q has the form

$$Q = A_1 \Rightarrow (\ldots \Rightarrow (A_n \Rightarrow q)\ldots).$$

Then the abduced set is

$$A_1 \Rightarrow \ldots \Rightarrow (A_n \Rightarrow \text{Abduce}^+(\Delta \cup (A_1,\ldots,A_n),q),\ldots).$$

where $A_1 \Rightarrow (\ldots(A_n \Rightarrow \{\Gamma_1,\ldots,\Gamma_k\})\ldots)$ denotes the set of all theories of the form $\Gamma_i^{\Rightarrow}$

$$\Gamma_i^{\Rightarrow} = \{A_1 \Rightarrow (A_2 \ldots \Rightarrow (A_n \Rightarrow X)\ldots) \mid X \in \Gamma_i\}.$$

We need to show $\Delta \cup \Gamma_i^{\Rightarrow} \vdash Q$ for any $\Gamma_i^{\Rightarrow} \in A_1 \Rightarrow (\ldots \Rightarrow (A_n \Rightarrow \text{Abduce}^+(\Delta \cup \{A_1 \ldots, A_n\}, q)\ldots))$.
By the induction hypothesis

$$\Delta \cup \{A_1,\ldots,A_n\} \cup \Gamma_i \vdash q \text{ for any } \Gamma_i \in \text{Abduce}^+(\Delta \cup (A_1,\ldots,A_n),q);$$

hence,

$$\Delta \cup \{A_1,\ldots,A_n\} \cup \Gamma_i^{\Rightarrow} \vdash q;$$

hence,

$$\Delta \cup \Gamma_i \vdash Q$$

4. Assume $Q = q$ is atomic and let $B^j = B_1^j \Rightarrow (\ldots \Rightarrow (B_{n(j)}^j \Rightarrow q)\ldots), j = 1,\ldots,m$, be all the clauses in Δ with head q.

Then we need to show

$$\Delta \cup \Gamma \vdash q \text{ for } \Gamma \in \text{Abduce}^+(\Delta,q)$$

where $\text{Abduce}^+(\Delta,q) = \{\Gamma_1^j \cup \ldots \cup \Gamma_{n(j)}^j \mid \Gamma_i^j \in \text{Abduce}^+(\Delta,B_i^j), j = 1,\ldots,m\}$.

By the induction hypothesis for j fixed, we have

$$\Delta \cup \Gamma_i^j \vdash B_i^j$$

for $i = 1,\ldots,n(j)$.
Hence for each j, since B^j is in Δ, we have:

$$\Delta \cup \bigcup_{i=1}^{n(j)} \Gamma_i^j \vdash q.$$

This concludes our discussion on the abductive process. Since our language does not contain negation, all databases are consistent. It would be possible to introduce a new atom $\perp$ in the language to represent falsity, and hence have $q \Rightarrow \perp$ as $\neg q$. However, this would work more like an acceptability constraint, since we would not have a database with $\{q, q \Rightarrow \perp\}$ prove everything. In order to make the proof procedure behave classically, the notion of derivability would need to be adjusted, and, consequently, so would the corresponding abduction algorithm.

6.3 Compromise Revision

This section presents the approach of *compromise revision* within the context of a *labelled deductive system LDS* [1, 4]. This formulation allows us to show how the labels and the labelling mechanism of an *LDS* can be used to support a *compromise mechanism* for revision. For simplicity of the presentation, we will consider only the case of a propositional language with $\Rightarrow$. No specific assumption is made on the underlying logic as the connective $\Rightarrow$ can be seen as the implicational fragment of a variety of non-classical logics, including linear logic, intuitionistic logic and classical logic.

We start introducing the language used in the formalism, followed by the definition of a proof.

6.3.1 Introducing Compromise Revision for $\Rightarrow$

Definition 6.7 (Language for the formalism). Let Q be a set of atoms and let $\perp$ be a special atom, possibly not in Q.[12] Let S be a set of atomic labels.

- a wff is a formula built up using Q and $\Rightarrow$.
- an integrity constraint is a wff of the form $(A_1, \ldots, A_n) \Rightarrow \perp$, where A_i are formulae.
- a database $\Delta = (t_i : A_i, \mathsf{C})$ is a set of *declarative units* of the form $t_1 : A_1, \ldots, t_k : A_k$, where t_i are all atomic and pairwise different labels from S and the A_i's are wffs; and C is an integrity constraint.
- we use $t_1 < t_2$ to denote that the formula A_1 associated with t_1 has lower priority than the formula A_2 associated with t_2. An input A into a database is inserted as a new declarative unit $a : A$, where a is a new label with the highest priority with respect to those already existing in the database.[13] Thus,

$$\Delta + \{a : A\} = (t_i : A_i, a : A, \mathsf{C}) \text{ with } t_i < a \text{ for all } t_i \text{ such that } t_i : A_i \in \Delta.$$

The idea is to retract the declarative units with the lowest priority if necessary to maintain consistency during a revision operation. The reader may ask, where does the ordering on Δ come from? The simplest way of looking at it is to assume that the database was built in stages, by first inputting A_1 into the empty database and

---

[12] $\perp$ does not mean *falsity*. We merely use it to write integrity constraints of the form $(A \wedge B) \Rightarrow \perp$, meaning we do not want both A and B to be derivable. Stronger logics will have more properties for $\perp$, for example, that $\perp$ proves anything, and these additional properties will turn $\perp$ into *falsity* and $A \Rightarrow \perp$ into $\neg A$ for any wff A. We leave the option open on whether to use $\perp$ just as a marker for integrity constraints ($\perp$ not in Q) or allow it to be an atom of the language which has only some of the aspects of *falsity*.

[13] This is to ensure the *principle of primacy of the update*, but as you shall see, we can adopt different policies for insertion.

then continuing with a sequence of inputs. This would give a natural linear ordering on the database, assuming consistency maintenance is done by throwing out some of the old inputs.

Definition 6.8. We define the notion of $\Delta \vdash_{\alpha,m,n} A$, for A a wff or $\bot$; α a sequence of labels; m the number of nested uses of $\Rightarrow$ introduction; and n the total number of uses of $\Rightarrow$ elimination, as follows.

1. $\Delta \vdash_{\alpha,0,0} A$ if $\alpha : A \in \Delta$.
2. $\Delta \vdash_{\gamma,m,r} A$ if for some $C, C \Rightarrow A$, we have that $\Delta \vdash_{\alpha,m_1,s_1} C$ and $\Delta \vdash_{\beta,m_2,s_2} C \Rightarrow A$, and $\gamma = (\beta\alpha)$ and $r = 1+s_1+s_2$ and $m = \max(m_1,m_2)$.
   This is our modus ponens. We may wish to restrict its application by requiring that a meta-level condition $\varphi(\beta,\alpha)$ be satisfied first (see Remark 6.2).
3. $\Delta \vdash_{\alpha,m+1,n} A \Rightarrow B$ if $\Delta \cup \{x : A\} \vdash_{\beta,m,n} B$ for some n and where x is a new atom labelling A: $\alpha = \beta - x$.
4. $\Delta \vdash_{\alpha,m,n} \bot$ if and only if for some $(A_1,\ldots,A_n) \Rightarrow \bot \in \Delta$, $\Delta \vdash_{\alpha_i,m_i,n_i} A_i$, and m is $\max\{m_i, 1 \le i \le n\}$, $n = 1+\Sigma n_i$ and $\alpha = \alpha_1 \ldots \alpha_n$.

Note that there may be more than one triple (α,m,n) such that $\Delta \vdash_{\alpha,m,n} A$.

Remark 6.2. The reader should note that the above definitions actually formulate a *labelled deductive system* (LDS), as discussed in the previous section (see also [3], for more details). The LDS rule for modus ponens is

$$\frac{\alpha : A; \; \beta : A \Rightarrow B, \; \varphi(\beta,\alpha)}{f(\beta,\alpha) : B}$$

where α is the label for A; β the label for $A \Rightarrow B$; φ is a (compatibility) licensing meta-predicate in the language of labels and f is a function giving the new label.

In our particular case, the labels are *resource labels*, tracing the history of the proof. For a sequence of labels α, let $\langle\alpha\rangle$ be the set of labels in the sequence, which we call the *support set* associated with a wff. Thus, we may choose to specify the condition $\varphi(\beta,\alpha)$ above as follows:

$$\frac{\alpha : A; \; \beta : A \Rightarrow B, \; \langle\alpha\rangle \cap \langle\beta\rangle = \varnothing}{\beta\alpha : B}$$

The condition $\varphi(\beta,\alpha)$ above, i.e., $\langle\alpha\rangle \cap \langle\beta\rangle = \varnothing$, ensures that (as in linear logic) each assumption is used at most once! But, of course, different conditions can be defined to capture different logics.

To define a consequence relation $\vdash$, we need to say when

$$A_1,\ldots,A_n \vdash B$$

We may choose to define, for example,

$$A_1,\ldots,A_n \vdash B$$

if and only if for arbitrary pairwise different atomic labels $t_1, \ldots, t_n$ we have

$$\{t_1 : A_1, \ldots, t_k : A_k\} \vdash_{\alpha,m,n} B$$

such that

$$\langle \alpha \rangle = \{t_1, \ldots, t_n\}.$$

The notion of $\Delta \vdash_{\alpha,m,n} A$ would have to be modified a bit by adding in item (2) of the definition the meta-predicate $\varphi(\beta, \alpha)$ as a necessary license. The logic $\vdash$ just defined is linear logic with implication.

The following definition shows how to generate from a given set of ordered labels an ordering over the sets of labels.

Definition 6.9 (Priority ordering). Let $(T, <)$ be a finite linearly ordered set. Assume

$$T = \{t_1, \ldots, t_n\}$$

and that

$$t_1 < t_2 < \cdots < t_n.$$

A *compromise priority ordering* on 2^T is the ordering relation defined as follows. Assume

$$T_i = \{t_1^i, \ldots, t_{m_i}^i\}, \quad i = 1, 2$$

and assume that

$$t_1^i < t_2^i < \cdots < t_{m_i}^i.$$

We write $m_i = 0$ to mean $T_i = \varnothing$. We define

$T_1 < T_2$ if $m_1 = 0$ and $m_2 \neq 0$

or $m_1, m_2 \neq 0$ and $t_{m_1}^1 < t_{m_2}^2$

or $m_1, m_2 \neq 0$ and $t_{m_1}^1 = t_{m_2}^2$ and

$$\{t_1^1, \ldots, t_{m_1-1}^1\} < \{t_1^2, \ldots, t_{m_2-1}^2\}.$$

Lemma 6.1. *Let $T = \{t_1, \ldots, t_n\}$ be a totally linearly ordered set of labels. The following two properties hold for the ordering $<$ on finite subsets of T given in Definition 6.9:*

1. The ordering $<$ is totally linear.
2. For any subsets T_1 and T_2 of T, if $T_1 \subseteq T_2$ then $T_1 \leq T_2$.

Proof.

1. The proof is by induction. Consider two subsets $T_1 = \{t_1^1 < \cdots < t_{m_1}^1\}$ and $T_2 = \{t_1^2 < \cdots < t_{m_2}^2\}$. The base case is when at least one of m_1 and m_2 is $= 0$. Then, by definition of $<$, $T_1 < T_2$. Assume $m_1 > 0$ and $m_2 > 0$, such that $t_{m_1}^1 < t_{m_2}^2$. Then *by Definition 6.9, $T_1 < T_2$. Similarly if $t_{m_2}^2 < t_{m_1}^1$. Assume now that $t_{m_1}^1 = t_{m_2}^2$. By inductive hypothesis, $\{t_1^1, \ldots, t_{m_1-1}^1\} < \{t_1^2, \ldots, t_{m_2-1}^2\}$. Hence, $T_1 < T_2$.*

2. Similar to the previous case.

The ordering of Definition 6.9 can be generated numerically. Let τ be a function associating a number $\tau(t)$ with each label t. For any $S \subseteq T$ let

$$\tau(S) = \{\tau(t) \mid t \in S\}.$$

$\tau(S)$ is a set of numbers ordered according to magnitude, with the following properties:

- $\tau(t_1) < \cdots < \tau(t_n)$,
- for each $m \leq n$ we have $\tau(t_m) = 2(\tau(t_1) + \cdots + \tau(t_{m-1}))$.

Let

$$T_i = \{t_1^i, \ldots, t_{m_i}^i\}, \quad i = 1, 2$$

be two subsets of T. Let

$$\tau_i = \tau(t_1^i) + \cdots + \tau(t_{m_i}^i)$$

(if $m_i = 0$, then $\tau_i = 0$).
We claim the following.

Lemma 6.2. $T_1 \leq T_2$ *as in Definition 6.9 if and only if $\tau_1 \leq \tau_2$.*

Proof. By induction.

1. *We assume $T_1 \leq T_2$, and show $\tau_1 \leq \tau_2$. We distinguish several cases:*

   (a) *If $m_1 = m_2 = 0$ then $T_1 = T_2 = \varnothing$ and $\tau_1 = \tau_2 = 0$.*
   (b) *If $m_1 = 0$ then $\tau_1 = 0$ and $\tau_1 \leq \tau_2$.*
   (c) *If $m_1, m_2 \neq 0$ and $t_{m_1}^1 < t_{m_2}^2$, assume $t_{m_1}^1 = t_j$, the jth element of T. Then $t_{m_2}^2 = t_k$, with $j < k$; then, we have*

   $$\tau_1 = \tau(t_1^1) + \cdots + \tau(t_{m_1}^1) \leq \tau(t_1) + \cdots + \tau(t_j) < \tau(t_{i+1}) \leq \tau(t_k) \leq \tau_2.$$

   (d) *Assume $m_1, m_2 \neq 0$ and further assume $t_{m_1}^1 = t_{m_2}^2$.*

   Since $T_1 \leq T_2$, this implies that $T_1 - \{t_{m_1}^1\} \leq T_2 - \{t_{m_2}^2\}$. We can assume by induction that

   $$\tau_1 - \tau(t_{m_1}^1) \leq \tau_2 - \tau(t_{m_2}^2)$$

   and hence $\tau_1 \leq \tau_2$.

2. *Assume $\tau_1 \leq \tau_2$ and show $T_1 \leq T_2$.*

   (a) *If $\tau_1 = 0$ then $T_1 = \varnothing$, and so $T_1 \leq T_2$.*

(b) If $\tau_1, \tau_2 \neq 0$, then $m_1, m_2 \neq 0$. We claim we cannot have $t^2_{m_2} < t^1_{m_1}$ because that would imply $\tau_2 < \tau_1$ as in case (1c) above. Hence $t^1_{m_1} \leq t^2_{m_2}$. If $t^1_{m_1} < t^2_{m_2}$, we get $T_1 < T_2$. If $t^1_{m_1} = t^2_{m_2}$, we get that $\tau_1 - \tau(t^1_{m_1}) \leq \tau_2 - \tau(t^2_{m_2})$, and hence by the inductive hypothesis

$$T_1 - \{t^1_{m_1}\} \leq T_2 - \{t^2_{m_2}\}$$

and therefore $T_1 \leq T_2$.

This completes the proof of the lemma.

It may be helpful to think of $\tau(t_i)$ as the value of the statement A_i. Thus \$100:A_i means the information which A_i expresses is worth \$100. The database is ordered according to value. When we use modus ponens, say

$$\$10: A$$
$$\frac{\$20: A \Rightarrow B}{(\$10, \$20): B}$$

The value of B increases since it is derived from a broader base. We shall define later what value we give to B.[14]

When we want to throw out some data in order to maintain consistency, we throw out the lesser-valued assumptions, so that less money is wasted. The longer the proof of a formula, the more valued it is because we invest effort in proving it.

Example 6.4. To understand the meaning of the ordering, assume we can get a contradiction from a labelled database $\{t_1 : A_1, \ldots, t_4 : A_4\}$ in two ways: one by using $\{t_1 : A_1, \ t_3 : A_3\}$ and the integrity constraints to prove $\bot$, and the other by using $\{t_2 : A_2, \ t_3 : A_3\}$ and the integrity constraints. We want to know which set of assumptions to throw out, $\{A_1, A_2\}$ or $\{A_3\}$, in order to maintain consistency. We assume that $t_1 < t_2 < t_3 < t_4$. To decide, we compare

$$T_1 = \{t_1, t_2\} \quad \text{and} \quad T_2 = \{t_3\}.$$

---

[14] We can give numerical ordering to infinite sets as well. Consider a sequence of data of the form $A_0, A_1, A_2, \ldots$ ordered by $A_i < A_j$ if and only if $j < i$. Let $\tau(n) = \frac{1}{2^n}$. Then

$$\sum_{m \geq n+1} \tau(A_m) = \sum_{m \geq n+1} \frac{1}{2^m} = \frac{1}{2^{n+1}} \sum_{m \geq 0} \frac{1}{2^m} = \frac{1}{2^{n+1}} \cdot 2 = \frac{1}{2^n} = \tau(A_n).$$

Thus, we set

$$\tau(Y) = \sum_{X < Y} \tau(X).$$

We can thus define ordering between sets of wffs

$$T_1 \leq T_2 \text{ if and only if } \sum_{X \in T_1} \tau(X) \leq \sum_{X \in T_2} \tau(X).$$

According to the definition of $<$ as extended to sets, we first compare the sets by the highest label. Since $t_2 < t_3$, we throw out A_1 and A_2.

Note that there are other ways of maintaining consistency. The simple-minded way is to take out the first n wffs of the lowest priority which restore consistency. This policy applied to our example would again take out $\{A_1, A_2\}$.

Let Δ be a database and let $<$ be a linear ordering of the labels in Δ. We want to extend the ordering $<$ to all labels of the form (α, m, n). We use the $\$$ value of the labels as guidance. Suppose $\Delta \vdash_{\alpha, m, n} A$. This means that to prove A we have used the support set $\langle \alpha \rangle$ (and therefore the wffs associated with it). Note that α itself records the order in which the formulae were used in the proof. Suppose we want to charge for the information 'A'. First, we charge the value $\tau(\langle \alpha \rangle)$. Then we want to charge for the effort of proving A from the data. This means we want to put a price $\tau((m, n))$ associated with the length of the proof. We can assume that for long proofs the additional cost of one more proof step is marginal. Thus, we give a lower value to proofs of direct modus ponens ($m = 0$) and a higher value to proofs which use $\Rightarrow$-introduction more heavily. A lexicographic ordering can then be defined as follows.

Definition 6.10. Let Δ be a database and let $<$ be a linear ordering of the labels in Δ. The ordering $<$ can be extended to all labels of the form (α, m, n) in the following way:

$$(\alpha_1, m_1, n_1) < (\alpha_2, m_2, n_2) \text{ if and only if}$$

(a) $\langle \alpha_1 \rangle \subset \langle \alpha_2 \rangle$

or (b) $\langle \alpha_1 \rangle = \langle \alpha_2 \rangle$ and $m_1 < m_2$

or (c) $\langle \alpha_1 \rangle = \langle \alpha_2 \rangle$ and $m_1 = m_2$ and $n_1 < n_2$

or (d) $\langle \alpha_1 \rangle = \langle \alpha_2 \rangle$ and $m_1 = m_2$ and $n_1 = n_2$ and α_2 is a longer sequence than α_1

or (e) $\langle \alpha_1 \rangle = \langle \alpha_2 \rangle$ and $m_1 = m_2$ and $n_1 = n_2$ and α_1 and α_2 are of the same length, and $\alpha_1 < \alpha_2$ as sequences in the lexicographic ordering, meaning that α_2 is the first to use a data item of higher value.

Remark 6.3.

1. Since for $t : A \in \Delta$ we have $\Delta \vdash_{t,0,0} A$, the linear ordering defined in Definition 6.10 is compatible with the linear ordering on the labels of Δ (through the identification of 't' with '$(t, 0, 0)$').
2. The linear ordering is well ordered: every set of labels $\{(\alpha, m, n)\}$ has a first element. Hence, for every A provable from Δ there exists a minimal label $\mu_{\Delta, <}(A)$ such that $\Delta \vdash_{\mu_{\Delta, <}(A)} A$.

Definition 6.11 (Inconsistent databases). A database Δ is said to be *inconsistent* if for some α, m, n, $\Delta \vdash_{\alpha,m,n} \bot$. The symbol $\mu_{\Delta,<}(\bot)$ denotes the degree of inconsistency of Δ.

Let Δ be a database with data $t_1 : A_1, \ldots, t_n : A_n$, $t_1 < \ldots < t_n$. An input $a : C$ can be inserted anywhere in the sequence, i.e.,

$$t_1 < \cdots < t_i < a < t_{i+1} \cdots < t_n.$$

We identify in particular two cases:

(1) *insistent input $t_n < a$*
(2) *non-insistent input $a < t_1$*

It may be that C is already provable from Δ, in which case the input has just the effect of giving C an additional label. Thus, we may have

$$t_1 : C, \ t_2 : A_2, \ldots t_n : A_n, \ a : C.$$

As in the general theory of *LDS* one can talk about aggregation of labels, in the above case the label for C can be $t_1 \uplus a$, so making the input increase the priority of C.

The example below is related to our introductory example in Section 2.10. Note that we represent a formula $(X \wedge Y) \Rightarrow (U \wedge Z)\}$ as $\{X \Rightarrow (Y \Rightarrow U), X \Rightarrow (Y \Rightarrow Z)\}$ and $\neg X$ as $\{X_1, (X, X_1) \Rightarrow \bot\})$. Thus, if we want $D \Rightarrow \neg A$ in the database (as below), we state that $D \Rightarrow A_1$ and then specify $(A, A_1) \Rightarrow \bot$ as an integrity constraint.

Example 6.5. Let our database Δ contain the following formulae.

$t_1 : A$
$t_2 : A \Rightarrow B$
$t_3 : A \Rightarrow (C \Rightarrow D)$
$t_4 : A \Rightarrow (C \Rightarrow E)$
$t_5 : D \Rightarrow A_1$

(C) $(A, A_1) \Rightarrow \bot$.

We have

$$\Delta \vdash_{t_2 t_1, 0, 1} B$$

$$\Delta \vdash_{t_3 t_1, 0, 1} C \Rightarrow D$$

$$\Delta \vdash_{t_4 t_1, 0, 1} C \Rightarrow E$$

$$\Delta \cup \{x : C\} \vdash_{t_3 t_1 x, 0, 2} D$$

$$\Delta \cup \{x : C\} \vdash_{t_4 t_1 x, 0, 2} E$$

$$\Delta \cup \{x : C\} \vdash_{t_1 t_5 t_3 t_1 x, 0, 3} \bot.$$

Thus, although $\Delta \cup \{x : C\}$ is not consistent, it can prove E with $y_1 = (t_4 t_1 x, 0, 2)$ and prove D with $y_2 = (t_3 t_1 x, 0, 2)$, and $\Delta \cup \{y_1 : E, y_2 : D\}$ is consistent. Also, $\Delta \cup \{x : C\} \vdash_{t_2 t_1, 0, 1} B$ and $(\Delta - \{t_1 : A\}) \cup \{x : C\}$ are consistent with B and D.

Let Δ be a database and assume that the data in Δ has the form $t_1 : A_1, \ldots, t_n : A_n$ with $t_1 < \cdots < t_n$. Assume also that Δ is inconsistent. Our purpose is to use the ordering $<$ to decide which subset of Δ to throw out in order to maintain consistency. We must identify a lowest priority (w.r.t. $<$) set such that if it is taken out, *all* of the proofs of $\bot$ will fail. The definitions below lead to this set.

Definition 6.12 (Priority consistency maintenance). A subset $S \subseteq \{t_1, \ldots, t_n\}$ is said to be inconsistent if for some α, m, n such that $\langle \alpha \rangle = S$ we have $\Delta \vdash_{\alpha, m, n} \bot$. A set S' is said to be *critical* for $\bot$ if every inconsistent set S intersects it and no proper subset S'' of S' has this property. Critical sets exist. A set $S^\bot$ is said to be minimally critical for $\bot$ if it is critical for $\bot$ and for every other critical set S' we have $S^\bot \subseteq S'$. By Lemma 6.1, $S^\bot$ exists uniquely. So, let $S^\bot$ be the minimal critical set for Δ and let $\Delta^\bot$ be

$$\Delta^\bot = \{t_i : A_i \mid t_i \in S^\bot\}.$$

Then $\Delta - \Delta^\bot$ is consistent. We let Δ_{cons} be this set and refer to it as our *priority consistency maintenance*. Note that this set may be empty if every member of Δ is contradictory.

Definition 6.13 (∗-revision). Let Δ be a consistent database with data $t_1 : A_1, \ldots, t_n : A_n$ with $t_1 < \cdots < t_n$. Let $a : C$ be a consistent[15] and insistent input into Δ and let Δ_1 be the database $\Delta \cup \{a : C\}$ with $t_n < a$. Define $\Delta * (a : C)$ as follows:

- If Δ_1 is consistent, let $\Delta * (a : C) = \Delta_1$.

---

[15] When we say that $a : C$ is a consistent input into Δ, we mean that $a : C$ is consistent relative to the integrity constraints of Δ. We have to take this view because we are not allowed to revise our integrity constraints, only our data. So, for example, if $\Delta = (\varnothing, C \Rightarrow \bot)$, the input C is inconsistent relative to the integrity constraints of Δ, and hence we will not insist on accepting it. If we ignore the integrity constraints of Δ, then the input is consistent, but Δ is unacceptable with respect to C and we have no way of maintaining consistency.

- If Δ_1 is not consistent, let $\Delta * (a : C)$ be $(\Delta_1)_{\text{cons}}$, as defined in Definition 6.12.

Note that since $a : C$ is itself consistent and it has the highest priority in Δ_1, it will remain in $(\Delta_1)_{\text{cons}}$, and therefore our $*$-revision does not necessarily contradict the AGM postulates. This will be further examined in Section 6.3.2. The above notion of revision can also be defined for

$$\Delta * (a_1 : C_1, \ldots, a_m : C_m),$$

for a sequence $a_1 < \cdots < a_m$ in the same manner. We shall see later that if $a_2 : C_2$ is consistent with $\Delta * (a_1 : C_1)$ then

$$(\Delta * (a_1 : C_1)) * (a_2 : C_2) = \Delta * (a_1 : C_1, a_2 : C_2).$$

Since we can regard the labels as just indicating the order of priority of the assumptions, we can present the data in Δ as $(A_1, \ldots, A_n)$, in which case $\Delta * (a : C)$ can be presented as $\Delta * C$, or also as $(A_1, \ldots, A_n) * C$, ignoring the integrity constraints of Δ (assumed to be fixed).

Let Δ and Δ_1 be as in Definition 6.13 and let us assume Δ_1 to be inconsistent. Rather than settle for the revised theory $\Delta * C$, which just throws out some of the data in Δ_1, we would like to rescue some of the consequences of Δ_1 by compromising. The rest of this section presents the compromised revision approach.

We say $S^{\perp}$ is *critical* for a wff X if for every α, m, n such that $\Delta_1 \vdash_{\alpha,m,n} X$ we have $\langle \alpha \rangle \cap S^{\perp} \neq \varnothing$. This means that $\Delta_1 \vdash X$ but $\Delta_1 - \Delta_1^{\perp} \nvdash X$. Let $s_X = (\alpha_0, m_0, n_0)$ be the *minimal* (α, m, n) such that $\Delta_1 \vdash_{(\alpha,m,n)} X$. Since these labels are lexicographically and linearly ordered, we get a linear ordering of all X such that $S^{\perp}$ is critical for X. First (i.e., with lowest priority) in the ordering come the X's, which can be proved from $\Delta_1^{\perp}$ alone, and then come the rest. The compromise revision algorithm allows us to add to $\Delta_1 - \Delta_1^{\perp}$ as many of these X's as possible. Note that for each $s : A \in \Delta_1$, the label "s" can be seen as "$(s, 0, 0)$", since $\Delta_1 \vdash_{s,0,0} A$. With this identification, the priority label $(s, 0, 0)$ can be compared with the label $s_{X'}$ of any X' in the sequence, and we can certainly input $s_{X'} : X'$ into the theory $\Delta_1 - \Delta_1^{\perp}$, since the labels in this theory are $<$-comparable with $s_{X'}$.

We must be careful here because we may have in our system axioms of the form

$$(X \Rightarrow Y) \Rightarrow (X \Rightarrow (X \Rightarrow Y)),$$

which generates an infinite number of formulae of the form $X \Rightarrow (X \Rightarrow \ldots \Rightarrow (X \Rightarrow Y) \ldots)$. To avoid it, we can limit the formulae we consider to subformulae of the formulae in the database or possibly to a certain length of proof. We can thus assume that we are considering some reasonably chosen set of consequences that we wish to include (i.e., compromise on). We order the X's as $X_1, X_2, X_3, \ldots$, where X_i has higher priority than X_j for $i > j$.[16] We are now ready to define compromise revision more formally.

---

[16] Note that we put into Δ_{comp} X's of higher priority first. This means that if it takes longer to prove X, then it is more likely that X is consistent with the data!

Definition 6.14 (Compromise revision). Let Δ and Δ_1 be as in Definition 6.13 and assume that Δ_1 is inconsistent. The revised database

$$\Delta_{\text{comp}} \supseteq \Delta_1 - \Delta_1^{\perp}$$

is defined by induction as follows.

1. Let $\Delta_{\text{comp}}^0 = \Delta_1 - \Delta_1^{\perp}$ (with labels $(t_i, 0, 0)$).
2. Assume Δ_{comp}^m has been defined for $m \geq 0$ and is consistent. Let

$$\Delta_{\text{comp}}^{m+1} = \Delta_{\text{comp}}^m \cup \{s_{X_i} : X_i\}, \quad \text{if this is consistent}$$
$$= \Delta_{\text{comp}}^m, \qquad\qquad\qquad \text{otherwise}$$

Let $\Delta_{\text{comp}} = \bigcup_m \Delta_{\text{comp}}^m$.

We denote Δ_{comp} as $\Delta + C$.

Example 6.6. Let us reconsider the Example 6.5 for the application of our compromise algorithm. We rewrite it as

$(t_1, 0, 0): \quad A$ (data in Δ)

$(t_2, 0, 0): \quad A \Rightarrow B$ (data in Δ)

$(t_3, 0, 0): \quad A \Rightarrow (C \Rightarrow D)$ (data in Δ)

$(t_4, 0, 0): \quad A \Rightarrow (C \Rightarrow E)$ (data in Δ)

$(t_5, 0, 0): \quad D \Rightarrow A_1$ (data in Δ)

$(a, 0, 0): \quad C$ (input)

$(A, A_1) \Rightarrow \perp$ (integrity constraint)

We are giving the input $a : C$ the highest priority, i.e., $t_1 < \cdots < t_5 < a$. This is therefore the case of an *insistent input policy*. Let us proceed to compute $\Delta + C$. The set Δ_1 is inconsistent. We have

$$\Delta_1 \vdash_{t_1 t_5 t_3 t_1 a, 0, 3} \perp.$$

The critical subsets of labels for $\perp$ are

$$T_1 = \{(t_1, 0, 0)\}, \quad T_3 = \{(t_3, 0, 0)\}, \quad T_5 = \{(t_5, 0, 0)\} \text{ and } T_6 = \{(a, 0, 0)\}.$$

The minimally critical set for $\perp$ is T_1. Therefore

$$\Delta_{\text{comp}}^0 = \Delta_1 - \{(t_1, 0, 0) : A\}.$$

The sequence of $X's$ for which T_1 is also critical is

$$(t_2t_1,0,1):B$$

$$(t_3t_1a,0,2):D$$

$$(t_4t_1a,0,2):E$$

The priority order from higher to lower is

$$X_1=E,\ \ X_2=D,\ \ X_3=B.$$

We add them in stages. D causes inconsistency and is not added, and so the compromise theory $\Delta+\{a:C\}$ is the following, in order of their labels:

$(t_2,0,0):\quad A\Rightarrow B$

$(t_2t_1,0,1):\quad B$

$(t_3,0,0):\quad A\Rightarrow(C\Rightarrow D)$

$(t_4,0,0):\quad A\Rightarrow(C\Rightarrow E)$

$(t_5,0,0):\quad D\Rightarrow A_1$

$(a,0,0):\quad C$

$(t_4t_1a,0,2):\quad E$

$(A,A_1)\Rightarrow\bot.$

Notice that the compromise solution does not have the input C at highest priority. E has highest priority.

Let us now check what happens if we follow a *non-insistent input policy* This means we give $a:C$ the lowest priority. Thus, the labels are now ordered $a<t_1<\cdots<t_5$. The critical subsets are the same but the minimal critical subset now is $T_6=\{(a,0,0)\}$. Therefore, in this case the initial compromise set is $\Delta_1-\{(a,0,0):C\}$ i.e., it is Δ. The sequence of X's for which T_6 is also critical now depends on the logic of the labels. Assuming the axiom of commutativity,

$$X\Rightarrow(Y\Rightarrow Z)\equiv Y\Rightarrow(X\Rightarrow Z).$$

We get

$$\Delta_1 \vdash_{t3a,1,2} A \Rightarrow D$$

$$\Delta_1 \vdash_{t4a,1,2} A \Rightarrow E.$$

The one with higher priority is the second one. We cannot add $A \Rightarrow D$ as a compromise because it leads to inconsistency, but we can add

$$(t_4a, 1, 2) : A \Rightarrow E.$$

The final compromise database for the case of the non-insistent input policy is

$$\Delta \cup \{(t_4a, 1, 2) : A \Rightarrow E\}.$$

$A \Rightarrow E$ comes in priority after $A \Rightarrow (C \Rightarrow E)$ but before $D \Rightarrow A_1$.

Thus the non-insistent compromise policy does not just reject C but allows for its consequence $A \Rightarrow E$ to be accepted with an appropriate place in the ordering.

We now proceed with some simplifying theorems for our revision process.

Definition 6.15 ($\star$-revision). Let Δ be a database of the form

$$\Delta = ((A_1, \ldots, A_n), C),$$

where $A_1, \ldots, A_n$ are the data and C are the integrity constraints. Let N be an additional list $(C_1, \ldots, C_m)$ of inputs. Assume that Δ is consistent and N is consistent relative to the integrity constraints of Δ. We define $\star$-revision by induction as follows:

(1) Let $\Delta_{n+1}^\star = (N, C)$.
(2) Assume $\Delta_i^\star$ has been defined for all $i > m$. Define $\Delta_m^\star$ to be $\Delta_{m+1}^\star$ if $\Delta_{m+1}^\star$ is inconsistent with A_m. Otherwise, let

$$\Delta_m^\star = (A_m, \Delta_{m+1}^\star).$$

(3) Let $\Delta \star N = \Delta_1^\star$.

The idea of $\star$-revision is to look at $(A_1, \ldots, A_n, N, C)$ and go through the list top to bottom, i.e., go through $(A_n, A_{n-1}, \ldots)$, and accept A_i into the revised theory if it is consistent to add it, otherwise skip A_i and consider A_{i-1}, for $i = n, n-1, \ldots, 1$.

We now prove that $\star$-revision and $\ast$-revision provide the same results.

Theorem 6.3 (Equivalence of revisions $\ast$ and $\star$). *Let Δ and N be as in Definition 6.15. Then*

$$\Delta \ast N = \Delta \star N.$$

Proof. The proof is done by induction on the length of the data sequence in Δ.

For data as a one-point sequence the equivalence is clear. Assume the equivalence holds for $\Delta = (A_1, \ldots, A_k, C)$. Consider

$$\Delta_0 = (A_1, \ldots, A_{k+1}, \mathsf{N}, \mathsf{C})$$

and assume that

$$\Delta_0^{\perp} = (A_{i_1}, \ldots, A_{i_r}) \; 1 \le i_1 < i_2 < \cdots < i_r < k+1.$$

This means that $\Delta * \mathsf{N} = \Delta_0 - \Delta_0^{\perp}$.

 Note that in Δ_0, the tail $(A_{i_r}, A_{i_r+1}, \ldots)$ is inconsistent. This has to be the case, otherwise every inconsistent set containing A_{i_r} must contain some B earlier in the sequence. This will make $(A_1, A_2, \ldots, A_{i_r-1})$ a less preferable critical set than $\Delta_0^{\perp}$, which is a contradiction.

 We now show that $\Delta_1^{\perp} = \Delta_0^{\perp} - (A_{i_r})$ in (1) and (2) below.

(1) First, we prove that $\Delta_0^{\perp} - (A_{i_r})$ is a critical set in Δ_1. To show this, let $\mathbb{B}$ be an inconsistent subset of Δ_1. It is certainly inconsistent in Δ_0, and hence it intersects $\Delta_0^{\perp}$, and hence it intersects $\Delta_0^{\perp} - (A_{i_r})$. Thus $\Delta_0^{\perp} - (A_{i_r})$ is a critical set.

(2) We now show that $\Delta_0^{\perp} - (A_{i_r})$ is minimal, i.e., it is of lower priority than any other critical set. Let M be a minimally critical set for Δ_1. We want to show $\Delta^{\perp} - (A_{i_r}) \le \mathsf{M}$. To achieve this, we show first that $\mathsf{M} \cup (A_{i_r})$ is a critical set for Δ_0. This will imply that $\Delta_0^{\perp} \le \mathsf{M} \cup (A_{i_r})$. We next show that $\mathsf{M} \le (A_{i_r})$. Together, the first and second items imply that $\Delta_0^{\perp} - (A_{i_r}) \le \mathsf{M}$.

Let $\mathbb{B}$ an inconsistent subset of Δ_0. If A_{i_r} is in $\mathbb{B}$, then it intersects $\mathsf{M} \cup (A_{i_r})$. Otherwise $\mathbb{B}$ is an inconsistent subset of Δ_1 and so intersects M. Thus

$$\Delta_0^{\perp} = (A_1, \ldots, A_{i_r}) \le \mathsf{M} \cup (A_{i_r}).$$

We want to show that

$$(A_{i_r}, \ldots, A_{i_{r-1}}) \le \mathsf{M}.$$

To show this it is sufficient to show that A_{i_r} is the top priority element of $\mathsf{M} \cup (A_{i_r})$. Otherwise let M be the top element of M. We have $A_{i_r} < M$.

We get a contradiction. We observe that the tail $(M, \ldots)$ in Δ_1 is inconsistent. But it is inconsistent in Δ_0 and therefore should intersect $\Delta_0^{\perp}$, which is not possible. Thus, the top element of $\mathsf{M} \cup \{A_{i_r}\}$ is A_{i_r}, and so we can present this set as (M, A_{i_r}).

Summing up, we have shown that $\Delta_0^{\perp} \le (M, A_{i_r})$ and hence $\Delta_0^{\perp} - (A_{i_r}) \le \mathsf{M}$, which proves that $\Delta_0^{\perp} - (A_{i_r})$ is also minimal.

We need to show that the $\star$-computation process applied to the database

$$\Delta_0 = (A_1, \ldots, A_{k+1}, \mathsf{N}, \mathsf{C})$$

yields the set $\Delta_1 - \Delta_0^{\perp}$. We know that the tail $(A_{i_r}, A_{i_r+1}, \ldots)$ is inconsistent and that the tail $(A_{i_r+1}, \ldots)$ is consistent. Thus, the $\star$-process will accept the tail $(A_{i_r+1} \ldots)$ and reject A_{i_r}, and at this point will continue to examine one by one the elements $A_{i_r-1}, A_{i_r-2}, \ldots$.

*By the induction hypothesis, since we proved that the critical set for $\Delta_1 = \Delta_0 -$
(A_{i_r}) is $\Delta_0^{\perp} - (A_{i_r}) = (A_{i_1}, \ldots, A_{i_{r-1}})$, we get that the $\star$-process will exclude exactly
$\Delta_0^{\perp} - (A_{i_r})$. The total result of the process is therefore to exclude $\Delta_0^{\perp}$, which is what
the induction step is supposed to prove.*

This completes the proof of Theorem 6.3.

6.3.2 Comparison with AGM Revision

Let us assume that we are dealing with classical logic and that our wffs are classi-
cal logic formulae with $\Rightarrow$ and $\perp$. $\wedge, \vee, \neg$ are therefore definable. For a successful
comparison we must use our machinery to define a revision process (which we de-
note by $*$) which will be acceptable within the AGM approach but at the same time
remain within our approach too.

We will not do compromise revision because the way it has been presented relies
on labelling and the concept $\vdash_{t,m,n}$, which we do not want to get into for the case of
classical logic. We thus do $*$-revision as in Definition 6.13. For this the only notion
we need is that of a subset of the data that can prove $\perp$, i.e., a notion of a subset
being inconsistent, and any traditional formulation of classical logic can give us that.

Definition 6.16. Let $\sigma = (A_1, A_2, A_3 \ldots)$ be an input stream. Define a sequence of
databases by induction as follows:

$$\Delta_0^* = \varnothing$$

$$\vdots$$

$$\Delta_{n+1}^* = \Delta_n^* * A_{n+1}$$

Compare with Definition 2.16 (page 51) and note that we do not need integrity constraints. This kind of revision can be presented as follows. A database is a sequence
of formulae $\Delta = (A_1, \ldots, A_n)$. An input is a formula C, forming the new sequence
$\Delta_1 = (A_1, \ldots, A_n, C)$. Deduction is as in classical logic, and so the notion of inconsistency is clear. Δ_1 can be considered as an ordinary classical theory $\{A_1, \ldots, A_n, C\}$.
If Δ_1 is inconsistent in classical logic, we need to perform insistent input revision
on Δ_1. We thus introduce labels (just to do our priority calculations),

$$t_1 : A_1, \ldots, t_n : A_n, a : C$$

such that $t_1 < \cdots < t_n < a$, and perform the $*$-revision of Definition 6.13. This will
give us a new theory $\Delta * C$ (if we ignore the labels).

Thus, we have described a process $\Pi_*(\Delta, C)$ for going from Δ to $\Delta * C$.

We now check the AGM postulates for this process. We discussed the AGM
postulates in Section 2.1, but in what follows we will use the formulation of the
postulates for finite belief bases given in Section 2.2 (see also [9]), which we repeat
here for convenience.

(R1) $\psi \circ_a A$ implies A
(R2)   If $\psi \wedge A$ is satisfiable, then $\psi \circ_a A \equiv \psi \wedge A$
(R3)   If A is satisfiable, then $\psi \circ_a A$ is also satisfiable
(R4)   If $\psi_1 \equiv \psi_2$ and $A_1 \equiv A_2$, then $\psi_1 \circ_a A_1 \equiv \psi_2 \circ_a A_2$
(R5) $(\psi \circ_a A) \wedge B$ implies $\psi \circ_a (A \wedge B)$
(R6)   If $(\psi \circ_a A) \wedge B$ is satisfiable, then $\psi \circ_a (A \wedge B)$ implies $(\psi \circ_a A) \wedge B$

We note that there are two main differences between our process and the AGM context:

1. AGM deals with deductively closed theories while we deal with (axiomatic) databases, following [9].
2. Our databases are sequences of formulae, ordered according to priority which we can assume reflects the history of previous updates. This means that certain notions occurring in the AGM context need to be clarified in our context. Among them are what is meant by $\Delta \equiv \Delta'$ (equivalence of two theories) and $\Delta \wedge \varphi$ (conjunction of a theory and a wff).

With this in mind, let us start our comparison by checking the postulates one by one.

(R1) $\psi \circ_a A$ implies A.
   This rule has two parts.
   If A is a consistent input, it means that no rejection is allowed. Indeed since the process assigns to C the highest priority we have, $A \in \Delta * C$.
   If A is inconsistent, our process will reject A. However, had we insisted on leaving A in $\Delta * A$, then it would be inconsistent, and since in classical logic an inconsistent theory can prove anything, we still get $\Delta * A \vdash A$.[17]
   Thus, we can say that Π_* agrees with (R1).

(R2)   If $\psi \wedge A$ is satisfiable, then $\psi \circ_a A \equiv \psi \wedge A$.
   This holds for Π_*.

(R3)   If A is satisfiable, then $\psi \circ_a A$ is also satisfiable.
   Our revision satisfies this principle.

(R4)   If $\psi_1 \equiv \psi_2$ and $A_1 \equiv A_2$, then $\psi_1 \circ_a A_1 \equiv \psi_2 \circ_a A_2$.
   This principle holds, but we need a plausible definition of two theories being equivalent, since our theories are sequences of formulae.[18] We can regard the theories as sets and require that $\bigwedge \Delta \equiv \bigwedge \Delta'$. This, however, is not sufficient, since the revision process depends on the order. If we examine the revision process, we observe that it depends on critical subsets of labels participating

---

[17] Note that in general logics several things can happen. First an inconsistent theory may not prove everything. It makes sense to ask that at least $\Delta * A$ prove A itself. What can happen is that, although A is inconsistent, $\Delta * A$ can still be consistent and still prove the inconsistent part A. This happens in general labelled theories.

[18] For the case of (R4) formulated for epistemic states, Darwiche and Pearl require an identity of states (see Section 2.9.1 and discussion below).

in the inconsistency. Thus, we need to define a notion which will respect the revision process. The only definition we can give is the obvious one.

$$(A_1,\ldots,A_n) \vdash (B_1,\ldots,B_m)$$

if and only if $n = m$ and for all i, $A_i \vdash B_i$. We let $\Delta \equiv \Delta'$ mean $\Delta \vdash \Delta'$ and $\Delta' \vdash \Delta$. To see why we opt for this definition, consider the two databases $\Delta = (a,p,q)$ and $\Delta' = (a,p \wedge q)$ and the update $C = \neg(p \wedge q)$; we have

$$\Delta * C = (a,q,C)$$
$$\Delta' * C = (a,C).$$

We now check $(R5)$ and $(R6)$.

(R5) $(\psi \circ_a A) \wedge B$ implies $\psi \circ_a (A \wedge B)$.
(R6) If $(\psi \circ_a A) \wedge B$ is satisfiable, then $\psi \circ_a (A \wedge B)$ implies $(\psi \circ_a A) \wedge B$.

The above two together say that if φ is consistent with $\Delta * A$, then

$$(\Delta * A) \wedge \varphi \equiv \Delta * (A \wedge \varphi).$$

We need to explain what $(X_1,\ldots,X_n) \wedge \varphi$ means. We take it to mean $(X_1,\ldots, X_{n-1},X_n,\varphi)$, i.e., we add φ as an input to be the highest priority member of Δ. Now assume that Δ is the merge of two sequences $\Delta_a = (A_1,\ldots,A_n)$ and $\Delta_b = (B_1,\ldots,B_m)$. Let $\Delta_1 = (\Delta,A)$ and assume that

$$\Delta * A = (B_1,\ldots,B_m,A).$$

Thus, our consistency maintenance process applied to Δ_1 yields $\Delta * A$. If φ is consistent with $\Delta * A$, we show that the consistency maintenance applied to $\Delta_2 = (\Delta,A,\varphi)$ yields $\Delta_3 = (B_1,\ldots,B_m,A,\varphi)$.
In our proof, we use the fact that Δ_a is a critical set of Δ_1 with lowest priority. Indeed, this was the reason it was thrown out. We claim $(A_1,\ldots,A_n)$ is critical in Δ_3 and is minimal. Let Δ' be a set of wffs leading to inconsistency. If φ is not included in Δ', then Δ' certainly intersects $(A_1,\ldots,A_n)$. If φ is included in Δ' and if Δ' does not intersect $(A_1,\ldots,A_n)$, then φ is not consistent with $\Delta * A$, which is contrary to assumption. Now any other critical set Δ_0 either contains φ, in which case it is of the highest priority, or it does not contain φ, in which case $\Delta_a < \Delta_0$. Thus Δ_a is critical and minimal in Δ_2, and so

$$(\Delta * (A,\varphi)) = (\Delta * A) \wedge \varphi.$$

We have actually proved the following.

$(R^*_{5,6})$ If φ is consistent with $(\Delta * A)$, then

$$(\Delta * A) * \varphi = \Delta * (A,\varphi).$$

Darwiche and Pearl [2] added the following postulates to cover iterated revision (see Section 2.9.1):[19]

(C1) If $\alpha \vdash \beta$ then $(\Delta \circ \beta) \circ \alpha \equiv \Delta \circ \alpha$,
(C2) If $\alpha \vdash \neg\beta$ then $(\Delta \circ \beta) \circ \alpha \vdash \Delta \circ \alpha$,
(C3) $\Delta \circ \alpha \vdash \beta$ implies $(\Delta \circ \beta) \circ \alpha \vdash \beta$,
(C4) If $\Delta \circ \alpha \not\vdash \neg\beta$ then $(\Delta \circ \beta) \circ \alpha \not\vdash \neg\beta$.

Since our process Π_* is a specific algorithmic one, iterating revision is not problematic, and its properties can be figured out. Let us check whether (C1)–(C4) hold for Π_*.

(C1) If $\alpha \vdash \beta$ then $(\Delta * \beta) * \alpha \equiv \Delta * \alpha$.
This property does not hold because we perceive our databases as sequences.
Let
$$\Delta = (c \Rightarrow x \wedge a, x \Rightarrow \bot), \ \beta = c, \ \alpha = c \wedge x.$$
Then
$$\Delta * \beta = (x \Rightarrow \bot, c)$$
$$(\Delta * \beta) * \alpha = (c, c \wedge x)$$
$$\Delta * \alpha = (c \Rightarrow x \wedge a, c \wedge x)$$
which are not the same.

(C2) If $\alpha \vdash \neg\beta$ then $(\Delta * \beta) * \alpha \vdash \Delta * \alpha$.
This does not hold either.[20]
Let
$$\Delta = (a, a \wedge x \Rightarrow \bot), \ \alpha = \neg x \text{ and } \beta = x.$$
Then
$$\Delta * \beta = (a \wedge x \Rightarrow \bot, x)$$
$$(\Delta * \beta) * \alpha = (a \wedge x \Rightarrow \bot, \neg x)$$
$$\Delta * \alpha = (a, a \wedge x \Rightarrow \bot, \neg x).$$

(C3) $\Delta * \alpha \vdash \beta$ implies $(\Delta * \beta) * \alpha \vdash \beta$.
(C4) $\Delta * \alpha \not\vdash \neg\beta$ then $(\Delta * \beta) * \alpha \not\vdash \neg\beta$.
Both (C3) and (C4) hold. In fact we shall prove (C_{3,4}).

---

[19] There is a fine line determining whether Δ is an epistemic state (as in Darwiche and Pearl) or a belief set (as in Katsuno and Mendelzon). Let us not worry about it.
[20] (C2) is controversial. See discussions in Section 2.9.1, page 37, and in the proof of Theorem 4.3, page 121.

($C_{3,4}$) If $\Delta * \alpha$ is consistent with β then $(\Delta * \beta) * \alpha \vdash \beta$.

Assume Δ_α is the sub-database of Δ thrown out by the process Π_*. Thus,

$$\Delta * \alpha = (\Delta - \Delta_\alpha, \alpha).$$

Assume β is consistent with $\Delta * \alpha$. Consider $\Delta * \beta$. Let Δ_β be what is thrown out, that is,

$$\Delta * \beta = (\Delta - \Delta_\beta, \beta).$$

Consider $(\Delta - \Delta_\beta, \beta, \alpha)$. We claim the process Π_* does not throw β out, and so

$$(\Delta * \beta) * \alpha \vdash \beta.$$

Consider the set $\Delta - \Delta_\beta$ as a possible critical set. If every proof of inconsistency with α uses some element from $\Delta - \Delta_\beta$, then the set we throw out will be a subset of $\Delta - \Delta_\beta$ and will not include β.

The other possibility is that there is a proof of inconsistency involving β, α alone. This cannot happen because $\Delta * \alpha$ includes α and is supposed to be consistent with β.

6.4 Controlled Revision

In this section, we describe the main features of a *controlled revision* operation $\otimes$ for a simplified language [6]. Given a database Δ and an input formula A, we want to describe the result of revising Δ by A, in symbols, $\Delta \otimes A$, using this framework. The main idea is that the revision of Δ will take into account not only the input formula A, but also the history of past revisions of Δ. This is of course related to the problem of iterated revision discussed at length in Chapter 4.

We need an adequate labelled representation of our theories which allows us to observe and control the proof and revision processes.

Let $\mathscr{L}$ be a logical language in which A, B, C are propositional wffs. $\mathscr{L}$ also includes the symbol $\perp$ and the logical connectives $\wedge$ and $\rightarrow$. In $\mathscr{L}$, $\perp$ does not necessarily mean *falsity*, but it is an atomic symbol *which we do not want to derive*. We use it to indicate inconsistency conditions in the form $A \rightarrow \perp$ which hold in the database, meaning that A must not be derived.[21]

We start with the basic components and consider the role we want the labels to play later. We define an unlabelled database Δ as a list of formulae:

$$\Delta_0 = (A_1, A_2, \ldots, A_n).$$

We assume that a proof system Π is available for databases in $\mathscr{L}$ and also some notion of inconsistency.[22] Π contains rules of the form:

---

[21] Much in the spirit of the integrity constraints of the previous section.

[22] We use $\Delta \vdash \perp$ to say that Δ is inconsistent.

$$\frac{X_1,\ldots,X_n}{Y}\ (R)$$

The notion of *unlabelled consequence relation* can be defined as follows:

- $\Delta \vdash_0 A$ if $A \in \Delta$
- $\Delta \vdash_k Y$ if for some rule R

$$\frac{X_1,\ldots,X_n}{Y}\ (R)$$

we have that $\Delta \vdash_{m_i} X_i$ ($1 \le i \le n$) and $\max(m_i) = k$.

An input into Δ_0 is a wff B forming the new sequence:

$$\Delta_1 = (A_1, A_2, \ldots, A_n, B)$$

Since Δ_1 can turn out to be inconsistent, we make use of labels to provide the controlled revision of Δ_1. We can think of the revision process as involving a sequence of Δ_i's, where Δ_0 is the initial database, and each Δ_i, $i > 0$, is the database obtained after the addition of the ith input.

Definition 6.17 (Labels). Let $T = \{t_1, t_2, \ldots\}$ be a set of atomic names. A *name* is an element $t_i \in T$ (these names may be real atoms or contain some structure giving information on the wff they name).

A *history* is a sequence $((+m, \pm(m+1), \ldots, \pm(m+k))$, where $m, k \in \mathbb{N}$ and each element of the sequence is intended to refer to a stage of the evolving database.

A *simple labels s* is a pair

$$s = (history_s, name_s)$$

where $history_s$ is the history of s, and $name_s$ is the name of s. A labelled database is a set of labelled formulae $s_i : X_i$, where s_i are simple labels with pairwise different names.

Complex labels can be defined inductively as follows:

- simple labels are complex labels.
- if $s_1, \ldots, s_n$ are complex labels, so is $(R, s_1, \ldots, s_n)$, where R is the name of a rule:

$$\frac{X_1,\ldots,X_n}{Y}\ (R)$$

Obviously, the definition of labels is made to correspond to the rules of the proof theory.

6.4.1 Proof Theory

We now specify when a labelled database Δ proves a formula $s : A$ with a label base β (of simple labels) and k nested rule applications. We use the notation $\Delta \vdash_{k,\beta} s : A$ as follows:

$\Delta \vdash_{0,\beta} s : A$ if $s : A \in \Delta$ and $\beta = \{s\}$.

$\Delta \vdash_{k,\beta} s : A$ if, for some rule

$$\frac{X_1, \ldots, X_n}{A} \ (R)$$

and complex labels $s_1, \ldots, s_n$, we have $\Delta \vdash_{m_i,\beta_i} s_i : X_i$ with $m_i \leq k$ and $\max(m_i) = k$. We put $s = (R, s_1, \ldots, s_n)$ and $\beta = \cup_i \beta_i$.

A simple label is active at stage k if $history_s$ contains $+k$. Assume $\Delta \vdash_{m,\beta} s : A$ for some β and m. We say $s : A$ has an active proof at time k if all labels in β are active at time k.

Definition 6.18 (Inconsistent database). We say that a labelled database Δ is inconsistent at time k if it can actively prove $\bot$ at time k.

Example 6.7. We now explain with an example why we define labels in this way. Consider the language with $\rightarrow$, $\wedge$, $\bot$, and suppose that our rule is modus ponens (MP). Let Δ_0 be the starting database given below.

$$\Delta_0 = \{A_1 \wedge A_2 \rightarrow C, A_1 \wedge A_2 \rightarrow B, A_2, B \rightarrow \bot\}$$

First, for purposes of control, we name the formulae by name labels:

$$\Delta_0 = \{t_1 : A_1 \wedge A_2 \rightarrow C, t_2 : A_1 \wedge A_2 \rightarrow B, t_3 : A_2, t_4 : B \rightarrow \bot\}$$

For each new input, a new name is used. Assume A_1 as input. We put A_1 into Δ_0 with a new name t_5. We then have Δ_0':

$$\Delta_0' = \{t_1 : A_1 \wedge A_2 \rightarrow C, t_2 : A_1 \wedge A_2 \rightarrow B, t_3 : A_2, t_4 : B \rightarrow \bot, t_5 : A_1\}$$

As it happens, Δ_0' is inconsistent. Suppose that our revision algorithm decides to maintain consistency by throwing A_2 out. Then, our revised database Δ_1 at stage 1 is

$$\Delta_1 = \{t_1 : A_1 \wedge A_2 \rightarrow C, t_2 : A_1 \wedge A_2 \rightarrow B, t_4 : B \rightarrow \bot, t_5 : A_1\}$$

However, as we want to record the history of what happens during the revision process, we list all data, annotating what is in, what is out, and when, by using the revision history. Thus, we replace names $t : X$ by names $(+0, t) : X$ for all the data in the initial database. So, in the controlled revision approach, Δ_0 and Δ_1 become, respectively,

$$\Delta_0 = \{((+0), t_1) : A_1 \wedge A_2 \rightarrow C, ((+0), t_2) : A_1 \wedge A_2 \rightarrow B, ((+0), t_3) : A_2,$$
$$((+0), t_4) : B \rightarrow \bot\}$$

$$\Delta_1 = \{((+0, +1), t_1) : A_1 \wedge A_2 \rightarrow C, ((+0, +1), t_2) : A_1 \wedge A_2 \rightarrow B,$$
$$((+0, -1), t_3) : A_2, ((+0, +1), t_4) : B \rightarrow \bot, ((+1), t_5) : A_1\}$$

We call all strings such as $((+0,+1),t_1)$, $((+0,-1),t_3)$, etc., *simple labels*, where the components $(+0,+1)$ and $(+0,-1)$ are called the *history of the label*, and t_1 and t_3 are their names. To avoid confusion, we say that a formula $s : A$ is thrown out (or refused, or rejected) at stage k when $-k$ is in $history_s$.[23]

Remark 6.4. It is possible to apply modus ponens to labelled formulae $(+m,t_i)$: $A \rightarrow B$ and $(-m,t_j) : A$ obtaining

$$s = (MP,(-m,t_j),(+m,t_i)) : B$$

However, recall that s is a *complex label*, and we can tell from it that B is not a valid consequence. It does not have an active proof at "time" m.

It is interesting to see what would happen in the above example if we had used the *compromise revision* policy. As we saw in the previous section, compromise revision allows us to restore consistency by throwing out a formula $s : A$ which causes inconsistency, while at the same time compromising and keeping some of the consequences derived by $s : A$, namely all those formulae which require $s : A$ for their proof, but do not lead to inconsistency. In the last example, whether we choose a non-insistent input policy (i.e., to refuse A_1) or an insistent input policy (by, for instance, deactivating A_2), C would be in $\Delta + A_1$. This is because when A_1 is added to Δ_0, both B and C can be derived by modus ponens. But, B causes inconsistency where C does not. So, in either case, whether rejecting A_1 or A_2, the deduction of B and C would be blocked, but we would still accept C in $\Delta + A_1$.[24]

6.4.2 Policies for Inconsistency

When a database turns out to be inconsistent, we want the controlled revision algorithm to restore its consistency.[25] We have seen that inconsistency arises when the database can prove $\perp$. This happens in case of conflicting input or when a formula allows us to derive $\perp$. To restore consistency we need to adopt some policy to help us decide which formulae to reject. Different policies can be adopted depending on the application area. In this section we want to take into consideration some pure policies and show that it is often desirable to have a combination of different pure options. We will do this by working out some simple examples.

The first policy we want to take into account is a very common principle in belief revision, the so-called *principle of the primacy of the update*, i.e., new information receives the highest priority. We call this policy option the *input priority option*. If we accept this, the record of the history of each formula allows us to impose an

---

[23] Alternatively, we could simply deduce $-k$ from the absence of $+k$ in the history.

[24] Note that in this case C could be proved with labels (t_1,t_3,t_5). We could use this as its name and include it into Δ_1 as $((+1),(t_1,t_3,t_5)) : C$.

[25] We discussed inconsistency management in Chapter 2.13. A further discussion can also be found in [7, 8, 11].

input priority ordering on the formulae of the database. Two formulae entering Δ at the same step have equal priority. Thus, we can compare two labelled conflicting formulae $s_n : A_n$ and $s_i : A_i$ by just comparing their history: we say that $s_n < s_i$ in the case where A_i was more recently added to the database than A_n. Let us analyse the kinds of conflicting inputs that can arise.

Definition 6.19 (Conflicting inputs). Let k be a stage of the evolving database Δ. There are basically three different kinds of conflicting inputs: a *contradictory input* $s_i : A \wedge (A \to \bot)$ enters the database, or a new input *directly conflicts* with some of the inconsistency conditions in Δ, or a new input *indirectly conflicts* with some of the inconsistency conditions in Δ.

An example of direct conflict is input A and database $\Delta = \{A \to \bot\}$, whereas an example of indirect conflict is input A and database $\Delta = \{B, A \wedge B \to \bot\}$.

We now propose a resolution strategy for the inconsistency arising from conflicting inputs in the above cases. We recall that refusing or rejecting a formula $s : A$ at stage k means putting a formula in the database whose *history$_s$* contains $-k$.

In the first case (contradictory input), the most natural policy is to refuse the new input. In the second case (direct conflict), we reject the input A (it is agreed that inconsistency conditions must have priority over any input). In the third case (indirect conflict), it is necessary to distinguish between the non-insistent input policy and the insistent one.

- non-insistent policy: we reject the input A in order to restore consistency.
- insistent input policy: we retain A in Δ and revise it by deactivating some its formulae to form $\Gamma \subseteq \Delta$ such that $\Gamma \cup \{A\} \not\vdash \bot$ (for example, we can make B non-derivable in Δ).

Note that in the insistent case we will usually have several options for restoring consistency. Let $\Gamma_1, \Gamma_2, \Gamma_3, \ldots$ be all of the maximal subsets $\Gamma_i \subseteq \Delta$ such that $\Gamma_i \cup \{A\} \not\vdash \bot$. The controlled revision algorithm will then choose one (or some) of the Γ_i according to certain policy considerations which include:

- the consideration of which parts of Γ_i are active at k and which are inactive;
- the use of some external priority relation π in comparing the Γ_i. The principle of the primacy of the update gives the most recent formula the highest priority. The record of the history for each formula enables us to assign an input priority to wffs in Δ;
- the number of times X was in or out of $\Delta_0, \Delta_1, \ldots$. This is shown by the history label of a formula $X \in \Gamma_i$. This is an important element for evaluating what we call the *persistence priority*: the longer a formula has been in, the more reliable it is. In Example 6.8, we show that the input priority relation gives only inconclusive results, which can be corrected by consideration of the whole history of a formula.

Remark 6.5. It is interesting to note the connection with compromise revision. Let us suppose that at stage k a database Δ is inconsistent because of an input $s : A$. Assume

$\Delta \cup \{A\} \vdash C$, and suppose that (for some reason) we want to retain C. Assume that we are using the insistent input policy. Then, we maintain A and look for a maximal $\Gamma \subseteq \Delta$ such that $\Gamma \cup \{A\}$ is consistent. Let us assume now that Γ does not prove C. We could decide to keep C by defining a $\Gamma' = \{\Gamma\} \cup \{C\}$. Since C is derived from $\Delta \cup \{A\}$, C can have its complex label as name $(+k, complex) : C$. The complex label tells us how C is derived from $\Delta \cup \{A\}$. So a further consideration is whether C is an *earlier compromise*.

Example 6.8. Assume we use modus ponens. Suppose that the initial database is

$$\Delta_0 = \{t_1 : A, t_2 : A \to B\}$$

and the input stream is $(t_3 < t_4 < t_5 < t_6)$:

$$\sigma = \{t_3 : A \wedge C \to \bot, t_4 : C, t_5 : C \to \bot, t_6 : B \to C\}$$

Then, we get

$$\Delta_0 = \{((+0), t_1) : A, ((+0), t_2) : A \to B\}$$

Δ_0 can prove

$$(MP, ((+0), t_2), ((+0), t_1)) : B$$

So, the next database Δ_1 becomes

$$\Delta_1 = \{((+0, +1)), t_1) : A, ((+0, +1), t_2) : A \to B, ((+1), t_3) : A \wedge C \to \bot\}$$

Δ_1 can prove

$$(MP, ((+0, +1), t_2), ((+0, +1), t_1)) : B$$

(Note that B is also a wff from Δ_0. However, the labels are updated since it is now proved in Δ_1.) So, the next database Δ_2 becomes

$$\Delta_2 = \{ ((+0, +1, -2)), t_1) : A, ((+0, +1, +2), t_2) : A \to B,$$
$$((+1, +2), t_3) : A \wedge C \to \bot, ((+2), t_4) : C \}$$

We can still formally prove B:

$$(MP, ((+0, +1, +2), t_2), ((+0, +1, -2), t_1)) : B,$$

but it has no active proof at Δ_2, because we give higher priority to the more recent formula when $t_4 : C$ enters Δ_2 (using the insistent input policy). We reject $t_1 : A$, and then also $(MP, ((+0, +1, +2), t_2), ((+0, +1, -2), t_1)) : B$.[26]

At the fourth stage we have a new input $t_5 : C \to \bot$:

$$\Delta_3 = \{ ((+0, +1, -2, +3)), t_1) : A, ((+0, +1, +2, +3), t_2) : A \to B,$$
$$((+1, +2, +3), t_3) : A \wedge C \to \bot, ((+2, -3), t_4) : C,$$
$$((+3), t_5) : C \to \bot \}$$

---

[26] The compromise revision would maintain B, with label $((+2), (t_2, t_1)) : B$.

Δ_3 can prove

$$(MP,((+0,+1,+2,+3),t_2),((+0,+1,-2,+3),t_1)):B$$

The new input $t_5 : C \rightarrow \perp$ forces us to reject $t_4 : C$. But the record of the history of each formula in the controlled revision allows to reinstate $t_1 : A$ (if we adopt the policy of reinstating as much as possible). Labels show that $t_1 : A$ was rejected because of the conflict with $t_4 : C$ at the previous stage. This sort of intuitive policy is difficult to adopt in the traditional revision approaches, which record no history of the "state" of acceptance of a formula.

To show that the input priority policy is not the most desirable one and that we need to take into account other aspects related to the history of each formula, we assume that t_6: B→C comes into the revised database. In order to restore consistency, we have several options:

Option 1: *insistent input policy*[27]

The new input $t_6 : B \rightarrow C$ leads to $t_4 : C$ by modus ponens. As a consequence $t_6 : C \rightarrow \perp$ would be rejected together with $t_1 : A$ or with $t_3 : A \wedge C \rightarrow \perp$. We can then say we have two options for consistent subsets of Δ_4 (ignore the history component for a moment):

$$\Gamma_1 = \{t_6 : C \rightarrow \perp, t_1 : A\}$$
$$\Gamma_2 = \{t_6 : C \rightarrow \perp, t_3 : A \wedge C \rightarrow \perp\}$$

Comparing Γ_1 and Γ_2, we can state a preference ordering $<$ between the options. $\Gamma_1 < \Gamma_2$ intuitively means that Γ_2 is preferable to Γ_1. If we compare the history of $t_1 : A$ and $t_3 : A \wedge C \rightarrow \perp$, the latter turns out to be more reliable than $t_1 : A$, since it has never been rejected (persistence priority).

On the other hand, in order to block the derivation of $t_4 : C$, we may consider rejecting

$$\Gamma_3 = \{t_2 : A \rightarrow B\}$$

However, $t_2 : A \rightarrow B$ has been in the database since the beginning of the process; so it is not desirable to reject it.

So, how shall we decide between Γ_1 and Γ_3?

Γ_1 contains fewer safe formulae than Γ_3 but, because we also want to retain as many formulae as possible, it could be preferable to reject Γ_3 rather than Γ_1. In such a case, the choice between two options depends on the further requirements of specific applications. In some cases, for example, we can require that data which have been in the database from the beginning cannot be rejected, or that preference be given to a sort of "economic" policy, which allows us to keep as many items of data as possible.

Option 2: *non-insistent input policy.*

---

[27] This is the most natural if we use the input priority policy.

Because we want the history of each formula to be relevant to the revision process, we can reject the new input $t_6 : B \rightarrow C$ rather than $t_1 : A$ or $t_2 : A \rightarrow B$. We can do so even if it has the highest priority, since it is the last input.

We now conclude this section with some discussions.

6.4.3 Conclusions

Controlled revision provides a model for the revision of belief bases, where the revision process keeps control of the full history of updates. We use the history to devise a socialised algorithm on how to obtain $\Delta \otimes A$. We claim that part of the non-monotonicity of some logical theories comes from the history of the status of each formula and from the history of past updates. This can be seen in the following way. Imagine a revision policy allowing for some form of compromise revision and a reinstating priority. Assume that at time n, the current theory is Δ. We must be able to recognise the core part Δ_c of Δ which is composed of all data except the compromise and reinstated wffs. We assume that in case of inconsistency caused by the arrival of new input information, the latter are the first to be rejected. We write $\Delta_c \vdash A$ if A logically follows from Δ_c, and we write $\Delta_c \!\sim\! B$ if $\Delta \vdash B$ (i.e., the $\Delta - \Delta_c$ are the non-monotonic consequences of Δ_c). This is a non-monotonic consequence relation. We can indeed check whether the non-monotonic consequence relation axioms hold.

Assume the input is X and that the updated Δ is Δ', as done previously. The core of Δ' is Δ'_c. If we have an insistent input policy, we get $X \in \Delta'_c$. Clearly, we may have $A \in \Delta$, but $A \notin \Delta'$; hence, $\Delta_c \!\sim\! A$ but $\Delta_c + X \not\!\sim\! A$. However, if $\Delta_c \!\sim\! Y$, then this means that $\Delta \vdash Y$; hence, $\Delta_c + Y$ is consistent. Whereupon $\Delta_c + Y_c = \Delta_c$, and for all Z, $\Delta_c \!\sim\! Z$ if and only if $\Delta_c + Y \!\sim\! Z$, which is *restricted monotonicity*. This is reminiscent of Gärdenfors and Makinson's observation that given a theory K, we can get non-monotonic consequence by $\!\sim\!_K$: $A \!\sim\!_K B$ if and only if $K \circ A \vdash B$ (where $\circ$ is a revision operation) [10].

To achieve this purpose, we still need to investigate which kinds of inputs we can have in non-monotonic theories, from which kinds of observed regularities various generalisations such as non-monotonic rules come, which kinds of pure policies should be used and how we are to combine them. The model we have presented involves numerical values which give a record of the past history. Theories as structured and labelled sets of formulae allow for the definition of an algorithm for controlled revision, in a way that satisfies all these requirements.

Working on controlled revision gives rise to further interesting applications. In particular, such a knowledge revision model suggests relevant aspects for any theory of confirmation and falsification. If Δ is a physical theory, wffs in Δ are experimental results and the logical rules holding in Δ are physical laws, then controlled revision aims to find how to restore the theory in the event of an empirical refutation. Rather than suggesting rational rules deciding reliability among a set of wffs, the purpose of controlled revision is the definition of which consequences we can derive when a structured knowledge system is revised. Controlled revision gives us a tool to annotate the step-by-step history of our theory.

References

1. F. C. C. Dargam. *On Reconciling Conflicting Updates (A Compromise Revision Approach).* PhD thesis, Department of Computing, Imperial College, October 1996.
2. A. Darwiche and J. Pearl. On the logic of iterated belief revision. *Artificial Intelligence,* 89:1–29, 1997.
3. D. M. Gabbay. *Labelled Deductive Systems: Principles and Applications. Basic Principles,* volume 1. Oxford University Press, 1996.
4. D. M. Gabbay. Compromise update and revision: a position paper. In B. Fronhoffer and R. Pareschi, editors, *Dynamic worlds.* Kluwer, 1999.
5. D. M. Gabbay and N. Olivetti. *Goal directed proof theory.* Kluwer, 2000.
6. D. M. Gabbay, G. Pigozzi, and J. Woods. Controlled revision – an algorithmic approach for belief revision. *Journal of Logic and Computation,* 13(1):15–35, 2003.
7. D. M. Gabbay and J. Woods. *Agenda Relevance: A Study in Formal Pragmatics,* volume 1. North-Holland, 2003.
8. D. M. Gabbay and J. Woods. *The Reach of Abduction: Insight and Trial,* volume 2. Elsevier/North-Holland, 2005.
9. H. Katsuno and A. O. Mendelzon. On the difference between updating a knowledge base and revising it. In P. Gärdenfors, editor, *Belief Revision,* pages 183–203. Cambridge University Press, 1992.
10. D. Makinson and P. Gärdenfors. Relations between the logic of theory change and nonmonotonic logic. In Fuhrmann A. and M. Morreau, editors, *The Logic of Theory Change, Workshop, Lecture Notes in Artificial Intelligence, Volume 465,* Konstanz, FRG, October 1989. Springer Verlag.
11. J. Woods. *Paradox and paraconsistency: conflict resolution in the abstract sciences.* Cambridge University Press, 2002.

Chapter 7
Revision by Translation

7.1 Introduction

As we have seen, the traditional AGM theory of belief revision put forward a number of postulates to constrain how the state of beliefs of an agent should change when faced with a new belief that possibly contradicts her previous beliefs. The whole AGM framework was formulated under the assumption that the logic used to represent a belief set was classical. Since classical theories degenerate in the presence of inconsistency, inconsistency plays a major role in the whole process, and this has two major consequences: firstly, a 'proper' revision is only triggered when the new belief is inconsistent with the previous belief set;[1] and secondly, the postulates cannot be applied directly to non-classical logics.

In this chapter, we describe a unifying method for revising theories of non-classical logics. As we have shown in Chapter 2.1, belief revision in classical logic can be seen as an operation $\circ_a$ that, given a theory Δ in classical logic and an input formula ψ, gives a new theory $\Gamma = \Delta \circ_a \psi$ corresponding to the revision of Δ by ψ. The method illustrated in this chapter shows that this machinery can be *exported* to non-classical logics whose semantics is axiomatisable in first-order logic.

The general idea is to define the belief revision operator for the non-classical logics in terms of a standard belief revision operator (for classical logic). Informally, this is done by translating the mechanics of a given object logic L into classical logic, performing the revision process in classical logic and then translating the results back into the object logic. The approach is therefore based on three main components:

1. a sound and complete first-order axiomatisation of the semantics of the object logic L,
2. a domain-dependent notion of *acceptability* for theories of L, and
3. a classical AGM belief revision operation.

---

[1] If the new belief is consistent with the previous belief set, then a revision is equivalent to an expansion.

D. M. Gabbay et al., *Revision, Acceptability and Context*, Cognitive Technologies,
DOI 10.1007/978-3-642-14159-1_7, © Springer-Verlag Berlin Heidelberg 2010

Assume τ to be a translation function from L into classical logic, $\mathscr{A}_L$ to be a sound and complete classical logic axiomatisation of the mechanics of L with respect to its entailment notion, and Acc to be a first-order characterisation of *acceptable L-theories*. A revision operator $*_L$ in the logic L can be defined using the following equation

(7.1) $\Delta *_L \psi = \{\beta \mid \Delta^\tau \circ_a (\psi^\tau \wedge \mathscr{A}_L \wedge Acc) \vdash \beta^\tau\}$

where Δ^τ and ψ^τ are the classical logic translations of Δ and ψ respectively.

The revision of Δ by ψ can therefore be defined in terms of the classical revision of Δ^τ by ψ^τ. The inclusion of the axiomatisation $\mathscr{A}_L$ allows the semantic properties of the object logic L to be preserved during the revision process, so that the revised theory can be mapped back to L. This is why the revision of Δ^τ is defined with respect to ψ^τ and $\mathscr{A}_L$. The formula Acc allows for the consideration of other notions of consistency specific to the object logic or for the representation of some domain-dependent features which differ from classical inconsistency. For non-classical logics that are extensions of classical logic, such as modal and temporal logics, the notion of inconsistency is still classical, so it is identical to the notion of inconsistency in the target classical logic. Thus, if a formula ψ is inconsistent with a theory Δ in the object logic, then its translation ψ^τ would also be inconsistent with the translated theory Δ^τ (in classical logic). Provided ψ is not itself contradictory, the classical revision of Δ^τ by ψ^τ would correspond to a consistent theory in the object logic. For these types of non-classical logics, the revision operator $*_L$ could be more simply defined using the following equation:

(7.2) $\Delta *_L \psi = \{\beta \mid \Delta^\tau \circ_a (\psi^\tau \wedge \mathscr{A}_L) \vdash \beta^\tau\}$

This is the approach adopted and discussed in Section 7.2. However, even in these cases, some domain-dependent notion of acceptability could still be used to further refine the revision process, as is done, for instance, with integrity constraints in database updates (see Section 3.9). The formula Acc would, in this case, be the classical logic definition of domain-dependent constraints, and the revision operator $*_L$ be defined as in (7.1).

In the case of non-classical logics that are not extensions of classical logic, such as *Belnap's four-valued logic*, the notion of consistency differs from that of classical logic. Object theories may not necessarily be semantically inconsistent and yet we expect a revision to be triggered. Let Cn be the closure of a set of formulae under the consequence relation of classical logic and consider the formula $p \wedge \neg p$. This formula is not contradictory in Belnap's logic, in the sense that it has a semantic truth-value in a semantic interpretation, or *set-up*, as Belnap calls it. Under a sound and complete translation τ to classical logic, a theory T containing the formula p^τ would therefore be consistent with $(\neg p)^\tau$, and consequently, the revision of T by $(\neg p)^\tau$ in classical logic would be simply the expansion of T by $(\neg p)^\tau$, i.e., a consistent theory containing $(p \wedge \neg p)^\tau$. In these circumstances, the revision would be equivalent to an expansion. This might not necessarily be what one expects in the object logic. Up to now, this is how belief revision has been defined for paraconsistent logics and the like [16].

What we propose in this chapter is a different approach to revision for non-classical logics. Our view is that a revision process for such logics would benefit from a shift towards the notion of *acceptable belief sets*, by imposing specific restrictions on what an acceptable theory should be in the object logic L, and therefore on what the effect is of revising a theory with respect to the particular notion of acceptability. We assume that such a notion can be provided either by the specific domain of applications or by logical properties. We will illustrate our approach by considering a number of different non-classical logics: the modal logic K in Section 7.2; Łukasiewicz' many-valued logic in Section 7.3, which we generalise for algebraic logics in Section 7.4; and finally, Belnap's four-valued logic in Section 7.5. For each logic, we provide a brief background presentation of the logic; a sound and complete characterisation of the logic in classical logic; and the definition of the belief revision operator with some discussion and illustrative examples.

7.2 Belief Revision for Modal Logic

Modal logic is one of the most well known non-classical logics. It is defined as an extension of classical logic by the addition of operators whose semantics do not reflect the truth-functional property of any classical operator. Although non-classical schools of thought related to this logic started at around the beginning of last century [5, 14, 11], the first model-theoretical approaches to modal logic were introduced only around the 1960s, when Kripke defined a relational semantics for a wide class of modal logics based on *possible worlds* and explicit *accessibility relations* [12, 13].[2] Since then, a wide variety of modal logics have been proposed, and in particular a class of these called *normal modal logics* stands out as being "well-behaved" and intuitively motivated. There is much discussion in the literature about these (see [10] for a survey on modal logics). In the next section we will give a brief description of normal modal logics, limited to the propositional case, so as to introduce the basic model theoretic features of these logics which are captured by the translation function described in Section 7.2.3.

In the next two sections, we provide an introduction to propositional modal logics in general. The reader familiar with these notions can proceed directly to Section 7.2.3, where we present the translation of the modal logic K to classical logic.

7.2.1 An Overview of Propositional Modal Logics

Propositional modal logic extends propositional logic with the two modal operators $\Box$ and $\Diamond$. The language $\mathscr{L}_M$ of the logic is composed of (countably many) propositional letters, p, q, r, p_1, q_1, r_1,...; the logical connectives $\neg$, $\wedge$, $\vee$, $\rightarrow$; and

---

[2] This semantics is also known as a *possible worlds semantics*.

the modal operators $\Box$ and $\Diamond$. The syntax is based on the standard notion of a well-formed formula (wff) [10]. The set of wffs is the smallest set satisfying the following conditions:

(i)   propositional letters are wffs;
(ii) if α is a wff and $\sharp$ is a unary operator (either classical or modal), then $\sharp\alpha$ is a wff;
(iii) if α and β are wffs and $\sharp$ is a *classical* binary operator, then $(\alpha\sharp\beta)$ is a wff.

The operators $\Box$ and $\Diamond$ often express the notions of "it is necessary that" and "it is possible that", respectively, which are inter-definable. Intuitively, saying that a proposition is possible, or possibly true, is equivalent to saying that it is not necessarily false. Thus, $\Diamond\alpha$ is equivalent to $\neg\Box\neg\alpha$. Analogously, saying that a proposition is necessary, or necessarily true, is equivalent to denying that its negation is possible, and hence $\Box\alpha$ can be rewritten as $\neg\Diamond\neg\alpha$. However, for reasons of clarity, we will consider a language containing both operators.

Necessity and possibility are qualifying (i.e., non-functional) attributes of the notion of truth, and as such are often referred to as non-classical operators. In the case of the classical connectives, the truth-value of a formula is a function of the truth-values of the subformulae to which they are applied. For the modal operators, this is not necessarily the case. For example, suppose that α is a contingent truth such as "Hume is a famous philosopher". The truth-value of $\Box\alpha$ cannot be determined only on the basis of the truth-value of α because there might be other "circumstances" (or possible worlds) in which Hume is not or has not been a famous philosopher. The sentence "It is necessary that Hume is a famous philosopher" would therefore be false. On the other hand, it is obvious that sentences of the form "All famous philosophers are philosophers" necessarily hold. Therefore, the interpretation of the modalities $\Box$ and $\Diamond$ depends not only on the truth-value of the formulae they are applied to, but also on a *quantification* over entities called *possible worlds*. These are elements of a mathematical structure, called a *frame*, which can be defined as follows.

Definition 7.1. A *frame* is a pair $\langle W, R \rangle$ where W is a non-empty set and R is a binary relation on W. Members of W are referred to as *possible worlds*, and for any given two worlds $w, w' \in W$, if wRw', then we say that w' is *accessible* from w.

Possible worlds and accessibility relations have been interpreted in different ways in the literature, and are not restricted to logics with the $\Box$ and $\Diamond$ operators only. Different interpretations lead to different (possible worlds) semantics and therefore to different logics. For example, in the case of intuitionistic logic, possible worlds are seen as "pieces of information" which "prove" formulae, and the accessibility relation is seen as the operator of set inclusion. In the case of modal logics, possible worlds are simply considered to be elements of a structure to which the notion of truth is relative. This interpretation, which will also be adopted here, is formally expressed via the definition of a "*valuation* in a frame" given below.

Definition 7.2. Let $\langle W, R \rangle$ be a frame. A *valuation* in $\langle W, R \rangle$ is a function v mapping each propositional letter to a set of possible worlds (a subset of W). That is, for every propositional letter p, $v(p) \subseteq W$ is the set of possible worlds where the proposition p holds.

Intuitively, "$w \in v(p)$" says that p is true at the possible world w. Other equivalent definitions of a valuation are also in common use. For example, the function v is sometimes defined as mapping possible worlds and propositional letters to truth values [10], or alternatively as mapping possible worlds to sets of propositional letters, those holding at the possible world [6]. The above definition has been chosen here because it facilitates a proof of equivalence between the standard possible world semantics and its first-order axiomatisation proposed in Section 7.2.3.

A frame and a valuation function together define a *model*.

Definition 7.3. A *model* is a triple $M = \langle W, R, v \rangle$, where $\langle W, R \rangle$ is a frame and v is a valuation in it. Moreover, w is said to be a possible world of M if $w \in W$.

Models and frames are also referred to as *Kripke models* (or "semantic structures") and *Kripke frames*, respectively. In this chapter these terms will be used interchangeably.

The notion of a model in modal logic is different from the notion of a model in classical logic. The latter is strictly related to the notion of truth — a model is an interpretation which satisfies a given set of formulae — whereas a semantic structure does not necessarily imply the truth of any particular sentence (see [17, 19] for a good introduction to classical logic).[3] In fact, as pointed out before, in modal logic a sentence is true or false only with respect to a particular possible world. A wff α is said to be true at a possible world w of a model M, written $M, w \Vdash \alpha$, if one of the following satisfiability conditions holds.

Definition 7.4. Let $\mathscr{L}_M$ be a propositional modal language, let $M = \langle W, R, v \rangle$ be a model, let w be a possible world of M and let α and β be two wffs of $\mathscr{L}_M$. The satisfiability relation $\Vdash$ is uniquely defined as follows:

1. $M, w \Vdash p$ iff $w \in v(p)$ (for a propositional letter p)
2. $M, w \Vdash \neg \alpha$ iff not $M, w \Vdash \alpha$
3. $M, w \Vdash \alpha \wedge \beta$ iff $M, w \Vdash \alpha$ and $M, w \Vdash \beta$
4. $M, w \Vdash \alpha \vee \beta$ iff $M, w \Vdash \alpha$ or $M, w \Vdash \beta$
5. $M, w \Vdash \alpha \rightarrow \beta$ iff $M, w \Vdash \beta$ or not $M, w \Vdash \alpha$
6. $M, w \Vdash \Box \alpha$ iff, for all $w' \in W$, if wRw' then $M, w' \Vdash \alpha$
7. $M, w \Vdash \Diamond \alpha$ iff there exists a $w' \in W$ such that wRw' and $M, w' \Vdash \alpha$

Note that the definition of satisfiability for classical connectives (the first five clauses of Definition 7.4) reflects the definition of satisfiability used in classical logic. Therefore, in each possible world, the classical fragment of modal logic (i.e., the set of wffs whose main connectives are classical) behaves semantically as classical logic. From this point of view, a model of modal logic can be seen as a "struc-

---

[3] A similar difference is also discussed in Section 7.6.2 between models (or set-ups) of Belnap's four-valued logic and classical logic.

ture" of classical models (one for each possible world) which are interdependent on
each other according to the satisfiability of modal formulae.[4]

The notion of validity in modal logic is also more general than the one in classical
logic. A model is by definition based on a given frame. Different valuation functions
given in the same frame $\langle W,R \rangle$ generate a *class* **C** of models associated with $\langle W,R \rangle$.
Validity can be defined either with respect to a given model or with respect to a
given class **C** of models.

Definition 7.5. Let $M = \langle W,R,v \rangle$ be a model and let α be a wff. α is *valid* in the
model M, in symbols, $M \vDash \alpha$, if for every possible world w of W, $M,w \Vdash \alpha$ (i.e., α
is true at every possible world of the model). Moreover, α is *valid* in a non-empty
class **C** of models generated by $\langle W,R \rangle$, i.e., α is **C**-valid, if for every model $M' \in$ **C**,
$M' \vDash \alpha$ (i.e., α is valid in every model of **C**).

Furthermore, borrowing Fitting's terminology [7], a modal theory can be composed
of a (possibly empty) set of formulae which are true in all the possible worlds of a
model, called *logical* or *global truths*, and a (possibly empty) set of formulae which
are true only at the initial possible world (i.e., a specifically designated world of W,
often denoted by w_0), called *factual* or *local truths*. This distinction is important
when dealing with revision of modal theories.

In Definition 7.5, the class **C** of models is based on a given frame $\langle W,R \rangle$. A wider
collection of models can be obtained by varying the underlying frame structure. In
this case, the notion of validity is usually expressed with respect to the notion of a
(non-empty) collection **F** of frames.

Definition 7.6. Let **F** be a non-empty collection of frames and let α be a wff. α
is *valid* in **F**, i.e., α is **F**-valid, if for each $F \in$ **F**, α is $\mathbf{C}_F$-valid, where $\mathbf{C}_F$ is the
collection of all models based on the frame F.

The notion of **F**-validity is used here to give a formal definition of propositional
modal logics, which will be used throughout this chapter. A *propositional modal
logic* is the set of all **F**-valid wffs for some non-empty collection **F** of frames. Strictly
speaking, this definition only covers *frame logics* (to use Fitting's terminology [7]).
Nevertheless, it identifies a very broad class of systems, including virtually most of
the modal logics that have ever found any application.

The following definition on the other hand provides a purely syntactical chara-
terisation of a particular class of modal logics, called *normal modal logics*, which
we are going to consider in this chapter.

Definition 7.7. A *normal propositional modal logic* **L** can be defined in terms of the
following formulae.

---

[4] This is one of the reasons why modal logic is considered to be an extension of classical logic,
and why the notions of logical inconsistency in the two logics are similar.

- all classical tautologies
- all formulae of the form $\Box(\alpha \to \beta) \to (\Box\alpha \to \Box\beta)$, for any formulae α and β
- the formula β whenever it includes formulae of the form α and $\alpha \to \beta$
- the formula of the form $\Box\alpha$ whenever it includes α
- the formula β whenever it includes a formula α, and β can be obtained by replacing the propositional letters in α uniformly by formulae

Every frame logic is a normal modal logic. For the remainder of this chapter, the term "propositional modal logic" should be understood as meaning "frame logic" or normal propositional modal logic. In subsequent discussions, a particular modal logic will sometimes be (unambiguously) identified by a collection of frames $\mathbf{F}$ for which it is the set of $\mathbf{F}$-valid formulae. Given such a set $\mathbf{F}$, it is possible to define a notion of semantic entailment, $\vDash_{\mathbf{F}}$, between "theories" written in (the modal logic associated with) $\mathbf{F}$ and formulae. In the most general case, modal theories can be defined as a pair $\langle S, U \rangle$, where S is a (possibly empty) set of *global assumptions*, and U is a (possibly empty) set of *local assumptions*. Intuitively, global assumptions are those sentences temporarily assumed to be true in every possible world, whereas local assumptions are sentences temporarily assumed to be true in the actual world. The definition of semantic entailment takes this distinction into account as follows.

Definition 7.8. Let $\mathbf{F}$ be a class of frames, let $\langle S, U \rangle$ be a theory and let α be a modal formula. α is *entailed* from $\langle S, U \rangle$, written $S \vDash_{\mathbf{F}} U \Rightarrow \alpha$, if for every frame $F \in \mathbf{F}$ and for every model M based on F in which all members of S are valid, α is true at every possible world $w \in M$ at which all members of U are true.

Entailed formulae α are in general *local consequences*, except when the given theory is of the form $\langle S, \varnothing \rangle$, for which they are *global consequences*. In practice, the set S is usually empty, in which case a simpler and more conventional notation can be adopted.

Notation 10 *Given a class of frames* $\mathbf{F}$, *a theory* $\langle \varnothing, U \rangle$ *and a modal formula* α, *the expression* $\varnothing \vDash_{\mathbf{F}} U \Rightarrow \alpha$ *will sometimes be written as* $U \vDash_{\mathbf{F}} \alpha$.

Kripke frames can be considered to be essentially classically definable structures, so that certain classes $\mathbf{F}$ of frames can be identified as the sets of models of particular (first or higher order) classical theories, written using the predicate constants R and $=$. In particular, various modal logics whose classes of frames have certain properties, which can be defined in first-order classical logic (e.g., reflexivity, symmetry and transitivity), are very common in the literature. Results in Correspondence Theory [20] have shown a correspondence between such properties and particular modal formulae. For example, it is widely known that the largest collection of frames in which the modal formula $\Box p \to p$ is valid corresponds exactly to the class of frames whose relation R is reflexive, i.e., exactly the set of classical models of the first-order sentence $\forall x R(x,x)$. Table 7.1 gives some examples of modal axiom schemas and the first-order conditions of their associated Kripke frames. Standard notation for the modal logics given by combining zero or more of the first-order conditions of Table 7.1 will be adopted in this chapter. Hence, for instance, $S5$ will stand for the set of formulae valid in all frames which are reflexive, symmetric and transitive, i.e., which are characterised by the axiom schemas $\mathbf{T}$, $\mathbf{4}$ and $\mathbf{B}$.

Modal formulae	First-order conditions
T $\quad \Box\alpha \to \alpha$	$\forall x R(x,x)$
4 $\quad \Box\alpha \to \Box\Box\alpha$	$\forall x,y,z(R(x,y) \wedge R(y,z)) \to R(x,z)$
B $\quad \alpha \to \Box\Diamond\alpha$	$\forall x,y(R(x,y) \to R(y,x))$
D $\quad \Box\alpha \to \Diamond\alpha$	$\forall x\exists y R(x,y)$
5 $\quad \Diamond\alpha \to \Box\Diamond\alpha$	$\forall x,y,z(R(x,y) \wedge R(x,z)) \to R(y,z)$

Table 7.1 Modal formulae and associated first-order conditions

7.2.2 Hilbert Systems for Modal Logics

In this section, a proof-theoretical presentation based on a Hilbert system is given for each standard normal modal logic, together with the standard syntactic definition of the consequence relation. Traditional axiomatisations of modal logics extend standard axiomatic systems for propositional classical logic with specific axiom schemas and inference rules for modal operators. The "smallest" modal logic is the logic K. Axiomatisations of K and its extensions (e.g., T, $S4$, etc..) are given here, all based on Hilbert's axiomatisation of classical propositional logic [9].

Definition 7.9. Let $\mathscr{L}_M$ be a propositional modal language and let α, β and γ be wffs of $\mathscr{L}_M$. The axiomatic system for the modal logic K in the language $\mathscr{L}_M$, written K_{Ax}, is defined as the following set of axiom schemas and rules.

Axioms about $\to$

$\alpha \to (\beta \to \alpha)$ [A1]
$(\alpha \to (\alpha \to \beta)) \to (\alpha \to \beta)$ [A2]
$(\alpha \to (\beta \to \gamma)) \to (\beta \to (\alpha \to \gamma))$ [A3]
$(\beta \to \gamma) \to ((\alpha \to \beta) \to (\alpha \to \gamma))$ [A4]

Axioms about $\wedge$ and $\vee$

$\alpha \wedge \beta \to \alpha$ [A5]
$\alpha \wedge \beta \to \beta$ [A6]
$\alpha \to (\beta \to \alpha \wedge \beta)$ [A7]
$\alpha \to \alpha \vee \beta$ [A8]
$\beta \to \alpha \vee \beta$ [A9]
$((\alpha \to \gamma) \wedge (\beta \to \gamma)) \to ((\alpha \vee \beta) \to \gamma)$ [A10]

Axioms about $\neg$

$(\alpha \to \beta \wedge \neg\beta) \to \neg\alpha$ [A11]
$\neg\neg\alpha \to \alpha$ [A12]

Axioms about $\Box$ and $\Diamond$

$\Box\alpha \rightarrow \neg\Diamond\neg\alpha$ [A13]

$\Box(\alpha \rightarrow \beta) \rightarrow (\Box\alpha \rightarrow \Box\beta)$ [K]

Modus ponens rule

Conclude β from α and $\alpha \rightarrow \beta$ [MP]

Necessitation rule

Conclude $\Box\alpha$ from α [Nec]

The above axiom schemas are global truths — any instantiation holds in each possible world of a given semantic structure. In particular, the set of all instantiations of the axiom schemas [A1]–[A12] together with the rule [MP] gives the first set of wffs described in Definition 7.7 (i.e., all classical tautologies), and the instantiations of [K] correspond to the second set of these formulae.

The distinction between local and global assumptions is also reflected within the syntactic definition of a consequence relation (*derivability relation*). It is important to notice that, in the definition of a derivation given below, the rule [Nec] can only be applied to global assumptions, whereas the rule [MP] can equally be applied to global or local assumptions. This is because, in order to guarantee the soundness of the [Nec] rule, a formula $\Box\alpha$ can only be inferred if α is true at every possible world (i.e., if α is a global assumption).

Definition 7.10. Let K_{Ax} be the axiomatic system for modal logic K, let $\langle S, U \rangle$ be a modal theory and let α be a formula. A K_{Ax} *derivation* of α from $\langle S, U \rangle$ is a sequence of formulae, ending with α, which is composed of two parts. The first (*global*) part consists of formulae which are either instantiations of the axiom schemas, or members of S, or are formulae inferred by previous terms by the application of the two rules [MP] and [Nec]. The second (*local*) part consists of formulae which are either instantiations of axiom schemas, or members of $U \cup S$, or are obtained from previous terms (in either part of the sequence) by the [MP] rule (not by the [Nec] rule).

Definition 7.11. Let K_{Ax} be the axiomatic system for modal logic K, let $\langle S, U \rangle$ be a modal theory and let α be a modal formula. α is *derivable* from $\langle S, U \rangle$ in K_{Ax}, written $S \vdash_{K_{Ax}} U \Rightarrow \alpha$, if there exists a derivation of α from $\langle S, U \rangle$.

Because of the soundness of the axiomatic system K_{Ax}, formulae derived using only global assumptions ($U = \varnothing$) are valid in the class $\mathbf{C}$ of models identified by the set S and, because of the completeness, the closure of the derivability relation generates the whole set of $\mathbf{F}$-valid formulae of the modal logic K. On the other hand, if $U \neq \varnothing$, the derived formulae are local truths — they hold at the possible worlds where the local assumptions hold.

Proofs of soundness and completeness theorems have been described in many places in the literature (see, e.g., [10, 6, 7]). In particular, given the Kripke semantics defined in the previous section and the above notions of derivability relation and semantic entailment, the following equivalence holds for the K_{Ax} axiomatic system, where α is an arbitrary formula and $\langle S, U \rangle$ is an arbitrary theory.

(7.3) $S \vdash_{K_{Ax}} U \Rightarrow \alpha$ iff $S \models_K U \Rightarrow \alpha$

When S is the empty set, the above equivalence can be rewritten in a simpler way as follows:

(7.4) $U \vdash_{K_{Ax}} \alpha$ iff $U \models_K \alpha$

Since this (implicit) approach to modal logic does not allow syntactic reference to possible worlds, the set U is often considered to hold at a particular possible world, called the *actual world* (w_0).

Other modal logics (frame logics) well known in the literature are obtained by extending the above axiomatisation with the associated characteristic axiom schemas. For example, the axiomatic system for T is defined as follows.

Definition 7.12. Let $\mathscr{L}_M$ be a propositional modal language and let K_{Ax} be the axiomatic system for the modal logic K in the language $\mathscr{L}_M$ as defined previously. Let α be a modal formula of $\mathscr{L}_M$. The axiomatic system for T in the language $\mathscr{L}_M$, written T_{Ax}, is $K_{Ax} \cup \{\mathbf{T}\}$, where $\mathbf{T}$ is the axiom schema $\Box \alpha \rightarrow \alpha$.

Any instantiation of the axiom schema $\mathbf{T}$ is a characteristic formula of the class of frames whose accessibility relation satisfies the *reflexivity* condition, i.e., $\forall x R(x,x)$. The addition of this formula to the K_{Ax} system as a global assumption restricts the class $\mathbf{F}$ of frames to those which are reflexive.

Definition 7.12 is just an instance of the more general definition of the axiomatic system for normal modal logic given below.

Definition 7.13. Let $\mathscr{L}_M$ be a propositional modal language, let $\partial \subseteq \{\mathbf{T}, \mathbf{4}, \mathbf{D}, \mathbf{B}, \mathbf{5}\}$ and let K_{Ax} be the axiomatic system for the modal logic K in the language $\mathscr{L}_M$ as defined previously. Let α be a modal formula of $\mathscr{L}_M$. The axiomatic system for $K\partial$ in the language $\mathscr{L}_M$, written $K\partial_{Ax}$, is $K_{Ax} \cup \partial$.

The definition of derivability can be extended appropriately:

Definition 7.14. Let $K\partial_{Ax}$ be the axiomatic system for modal logic $K\partial$, let $\langle S, U \rangle$ be a modal theory and let α be a formula. α is derivable from $\langle S, U \rangle$ in $K\partial_{Ax}$, written $S \vdash_{K\partial_{Ax}} U \Rightarrow \alpha$, if $\Sigma_\partial \cup S \vdash_{K_{Ax}} U \Rightarrow \alpha$, where Σ_∂ is the set of all instantiations of all the axiom schemas in ∂.

Each of these systems is sound and complete (see, for example, [10]) in the following sense.

(7.5) $S \vdash_{K\partial_{Ax}} U \Rightarrow \alpha$ iff $S \models_{K\partial} U \Rightarrow \alpha$

Note that the axiomatic approach to modal logic described above is *uniform* in that the set of inference rules [MP] and [Nec] is common to each of the modal logics $K\partial$ — the difference between one logic and another is captured entirely by the set ∂ of characteristic axiom schemas.

This finishes our introduction to propositional modal logics; we will now concentrate on the modal logic K, which we will use in our definition and analysis of the revision operation.

7.2.3 Translation of the Modal Logic K into Classical Logic

In order to provide a translation, we need a binary predicate R in classical logic to represent the accessibility relation of the logic K and unary predicates $P_1, P_2, P_3, \ldots$ for each propositional symbol p_i of K. We will use the subscript k whenever we wish to emphasize that we mean an operation (relation) in k and differentiate it from its classical logic counterpart (which will not be subscripted).

The idea is to encode the information of satisfiability of modal formulae by worlds into the argument of each unary predicate. In general, for a given world w and formula β the translation method is based on a function τ and can be stated as follows, where $\beta^\tau(w)$ represents $w \Vdash_k \beta$.

$$p_i^\tau(w) = P_i(w)$$
$$(\neg\beta)^\tau(w) = \neg(\beta^\tau(w))$$
$$(\beta \wedge \gamma)^\tau(w) = \beta^\tau(w) \wedge \gamma^\tau(w)$$
$$(\beta \to \gamma)^\tau(w) = \beta^\tau(w) \to \gamma^\tau(w)$$
$$(\Box\beta)^\tau(w) = \forall y(wRy \to \beta^\tau(y))$$

Finally, for a modal theory Δ, we define

$$\Delta^\tau(w) = \{\beta^\tau(w) \mid \beta \in \Delta\}.$$

We have, where w_0 is a completely new constant to Δ and β, and represents the actual world, that

$\Delta \vdash_k \beta$ iff in every Kripke model with actual world w_0, we have $w_0 \Vdash_k \Delta$ implies $w_0 \Vdash_k \beta$ iff in classical logic we have $\Delta^\tau(w_0) \vdash \beta^\tau(w_0)$.

(Correspondence)

(7.6) $\Delta \vdash_k \beta$ iff $T^\tau \cup \Delta^\tau(w_0) \vdash \beta^\tau(w_0)$

The theory T^τ in the case of the logic K is empty (i.e., truth).[5]
If Δ is finite we can let $\delta = \bigwedge \Delta$, and we have

$$\delta \vdash_k \beta \quad \text{iff} \quad \vdash \forall x(\delta^\tau(x) \to \beta^\tau(x))$$

We can define a revision operator $*_k$ for K, as outlined before (we will omit the reference to the actual world w_0 in the rest of this section).

Definition 7.15 (Belief revision in K).

$$\Delta *_k \psi = \{\alpha \mid \Delta^\tau \circ_a (\psi^\tau \wedge T^\tau) \vdash \alpha^\tau\}$$

We can now proceed to check in detail the properties of $*_k$ against the AGM postulates given in Section 2.1:

---

[5] The logic K imposes no properties on R. Had we been translating **S4**, we would have $T^\tau = \{\forall x(xRx) \wedge \forall x \forall y \forall z(xRy \wedge yRz \to xRz)\}$. Our notion also allows for non-normal logics, e.g., if w_0 is the actual world, we can allow reflexivity in w_0 by setting $T^\tau = \{w_0 R w_0\}$.

Properties of $*_k$:

1. $\Delta *_k \psi$ is closed under $\vdash$.
   This can be easily shown.
2. $\Delta *_k \psi \vdash_k \psi$.
   By (K°2), $\psi^\tau \wedge T^\tau \in \Delta^\tau \circ_a (\psi^\tau \wedge T^\tau)$. Since $\Delta^\tau \circ_a (\psi^\tau \wedge T^\tau)$ is closed under $\vdash$, $\Delta^\tau \circ_a (\psi^\tau \wedge T^\tau) \vdash \psi^\tau$, and hence $\psi \in \Delta *_k \psi$, by (K°1), $\Delta *_k \psi \vdash_k \psi$.
3. If ψ is (modally) consistent with Δ, then $\Delta *_k \psi = \mathrm{Cn}_k(\Delta \cup \{\psi\})$.
   We first show that if ψ is modally consistent with Δ, then $\Delta^\tau(k)$ is classically consistent with $\psi^\tau(k) \wedge T^\tau$. This holds because $\Delta \cup \{\psi\}$ has a Kripke model which will give rise to a classical model of the translation. Therefore, $\Theta = \Delta^\tau(k) \circ_a (\psi^\tau(k) \wedge T^\tau)$ is the classical provability closure of $\Delta^\tau(k) \cup \{\psi^\tau(k) \wedge T^\tau\}$. We now have to show that if $\alpha^\tau(k) \in \Theta$, then $\Delta *_k \psi \vdash \alpha$.

Lemma 7.1. *Let Δ be a closed theory. Let Δ^τ be its translation and let $\mathrm{Cn}(\Delta^\tau)$ be its T^τ-closure in classical logic. Let β be such that $\beta^\tau \in \mathrm{Cn}(\Delta^\tau)$. It follows that $\beta \in \Delta$.*

Proof. If $\beta \notin \Delta$, then there exists a Kripke model of $\Delta \cup \{\neg\beta\}$. This gives a classical model of $\Delta^\tau \cup \{T^\tau\} \cup \{\neg\beta^\tau\}$, and so $\beta^\tau \notin \mathrm{Cn}(\Delta^\tau)$.

Lemma 7.2. *Let Δ^τ be a closed classical theory such that $\Delta^\tau \vdash T^\tau$ and let $\Delta = \{\beta \mid \beta^\tau \in \Delta^\tau\}$. Then, if $\Delta \vdash \alpha$, then $\alpha^\tau \in \Delta^\tau$.*

Proof. If $\alpha^\tau \notin \Delta^\tau$, there exists a model of $\Delta^\tau \cup \{\neg\beta^\tau\}$. This can be viewed as a Kripke model of $\Delta \cup \{\neg\beta\}$.

4. $\Delta *_k \psi$ is modally inconsistent only if ψ is modally contradictory.
   If $\Delta *_k \psi$ is inconsistent, then so is $\Delta^\tau \circ_a (\psi^\tau \wedge T^\tau)$, since $\Delta^\tau \circ_a (\psi^\tau \wedge T^\tau)$ is closed under $\vdash$. By (K°5), $\psi^\tau \wedge T^\tau$ is contradictory. But by the correspondence, $\psi^\tau \wedge T^\tau \vdash \bot$ iff $\psi \vdash_k \bot$.
5. If $\psi \equiv_k \varphi$, then $\Delta *_k \psi \equiv \Delta *_k \varphi$.
   By correspondence ((7.6), page 233), and since $\psi \vdash_k \varphi$ and $\varphi \vdash_k \psi$, it follows that $T^\tau \cup \psi^\tau \equiv T^\tau \cup \varphi^\tau$. Therefore, by (K°6), $\Delta \circ_a (T^\tau \cup \psi^\tau) \equiv \Delta \circ_a (T^\tau \cup \varphi^\tau)$, and hence $\Delta *_k \psi \equiv \Delta *_k \varphi$.
6. $\Delta *_k (\psi \wedge \varphi) \subseteq \mathrm{Cn}_k((\Delta *_k \psi) \cup \{\varphi\})$.
   Suppose that $\Delta *_k (\psi \wedge \varphi) \vdash_k \alpha$ for some α. By the definition of $*_k$, $\Delta^\tau \circ_a (\psi^\tau \wedge \varphi^\tau \wedge T^\tau) \vdash \alpha^\tau$. By (K°7), it follows that $\mathrm{Cn}(\Delta^\tau \circ_a (\psi^\tau \wedge T^\tau) \cup \{\varphi^\tau\} \vdash \alpha^\tau$. Notice that for every $\gamma^\tau \in \Delta^\tau \circ_a (\psi^\tau \wedge T^\tau)$, there is a corresponding γ in $\Delta *_k \psi$ (by the definition of $*_k$), and similarly for φ^τ. By correspondence, $\mathrm{Cn}_k((\Delta *_k \psi) \cup \{\varphi\}) \vdash \alpha$.
7. If φ is modally consistent with $\Delta *_k \psi$, then $\mathrm{Cn}((\Delta *_k \psi) \cup \{\varphi\}) \subseteq \Delta *_k (\psi \wedge \varphi)$.
   If φ is modally consistent with $\Delta *_k \psi$, then φ^τ is modally consistent with $\Delta \circ_a (\psi^\tau \wedge T^\tau)$, and then by (K°8), $\mathrm{Cn}(\Delta \circ_a (\psi^\tau \wedge T^\tau) \cup \{\varphi^\tau\}) \subseteq \mathrm{Cn}(\Delta^\tau \circ_a ((\psi \wedge \varphi)^\tau \wedge T^\tau))$. But, $\{\alpha \mid \Delta^\tau \circ_a (\psi^\tau \wedge T^\tau) \vdash \alpha^\tau\} \cup \{\varphi\} \vdash_k \beta$ iff $\Delta^\tau \circ_a (\psi^\tau \wedge T^\tau) \cup \{\varphi^\tau\} \vdash \beta^\tau$.

What we have just proven is that $*_k$ verifies all eight conditions of an AGM operation. Item 3, is actually a proof for postulates $(K°3)$ and $(K°4)$.

The actual process of revision briefly discussed in the example above may be more complex than this. For instance, the object language might have a consistency notion other than that of classical logic or even none at all. We will consider these issues in the next sections. We now proceed to Łukasiewicz' many-valued logics.

7.3 Revising in Łukasiewicz' Finitely Many-Valued Logic Ł_n

7.3.1 Łukasiewicz' Finitely Many-Valued Logic Ł_n

Let $\mathscr{L}_n$ denote the language of Łukasiewicz' finitely many-valued logic $Ł_n$, composed of a set of propositional letters $\mathscr{P}_{Ł_n} = \{p, q, \ldots\}$ and the connectives $\neg$ and $\rightarrow$. We use the special symbols $\top$ and $\bot$ to denote *truth* and *falsity*, respectively. The set of all wffs of $\mathscr{L}_n$, in symbols, $\mathsf{wff}(\mathscr{L}_n)$, is obtained by the standard construction mechanism of formulae. A theory presentation of $Ł_n$ is a (possibly infinite) set of wffs.

$Ł_n$ is characterised by the finite axiomatisation given below.

Definition 7.16 (Axiomatisation of Ł_n). Let α, β and γ be wffs of $\mathscr{L}_n$. The following set of expressions together with the rule of modus ponens provides a proof theory for $Ł_n$. We refer to this set of axioms as $Ax_{Ł_n}$:

1. $\alpha \Rightarrow \alpha$
2. $\alpha \Rightarrow (\beta \Rightarrow \alpha)$
3. $(\alpha \Rightarrow \beta) \Rightarrow ((\beta \Rightarrow \gamma) \Rightarrow (\alpha \Rightarrow \gamma))$
4. $(\alpha \Rightarrow \beta) \Rightarrow ((\gamma \Rightarrow \alpha) \Rightarrow (\gamma \Rightarrow \beta))$
5. $(\alpha \Rightarrow (\beta \Rightarrow \gamma)) \Rightarrow (\beta \Rightarrow (\alpha \Rightarrow \gamma))$
6. $((\alpha \Rightarrow \beta) \Rightarrow \beta) \Rightarrow ((\beta \Rightarrow \alpha) \Rightarrow \alpha)$
7. $((\alpha \Rightarrow \beta) \Rightarrow (\beta \Rightarrow \alpha)) \Rightarrow (\beta \Rightarrow \alpha)$
8. $(\neg \beta \Rightarrow \neg \alpha) \Rightarrow (\alpha \Rightarrow \beta)$
9. $((\alpha^n \Rightarrow \beta) \Rightarrow \alpha) \Rightarrow \alpha$

In the axiomatisation above, $\alpha^1 \Rightarrow \beta \equiv \alpha \Rightarrow \beta$, $\alpha^2 \Rightarrow \beta \equiv \alpha \Rightarrow (\alpha \Rightarrow \beta)$, and so forth.

We now introduce the semantics for the logic $Ł_n$ with the set of n truth-values $\mathscr{T}_{Ł_n} = \{\frac{0}{n-1}, \frac{1}{n-1}, \ldots, \frac{n-1}{n-1}\}$, where $n \in \mathbb{N}$ and $n > 1$. In general, we can single out a set of *designated values* $\mathscr{D} = \{\frac{0}{n-1}, \ldots, \frac{j}{n-1}\}$, $0 \leq j < n - 1$, and a set of *undesignated values* $\mathscr{U} = \{\frac{k}{n-1}, \ldots, \frac{n-1}{n-1}\}$, $k > j$. However, in this chapter, we assume that 0 is the only *designated* value and that 1 is the only *undesignated* value, i.e., $j = 0$ and $k = 1$.

A valuation of $Ł_n$ is a function $h : \mathsf{wff}(\mathscr{L}_n) \longrightarrow \mathscr{T}_{Ł_n}$, constructed from an initial assignment of truth-values to elements of $\mathscr{P}_{Ł_n}$ and extended to complex formulae by means of the truth-table given in Figure 7.1. Note that $\alpha \vee \beta$ can be defined as $((\alpha \to \beta) \to \beta)$ (this gives $s(\alpha \vee \beta) = \min(s(\alpha), s(\beta))$). We also use $\alpha \wedge \beta$ as a shorthand for $\neg((\neg A \to \neg B) \to \neg B)$ (this gives $s(\alpha \wedge \beta) = \max(s(\alpha), s(\beta))$).

$s(\varphi)$	$s(\psi)$	$s(\neg\varphi)$	$s(\varphi \Rightarrow \psi)$	$s(\varphi \wedge \psi)$	$s(\alpha \vee \beta)$
x	y	$1-x$	$\max(0, y-x)$	$\max(x,y)$	$\min(x,y)$

Fig. 7.1 Truth-tables for the connectives in $Ł_n$

Whenever $h(\varphi) < 1$, we say that the valuation h *satisfies* the formula φ, in symbols, $h \Vdash_{Ł_n} \varphi$, or alternatively that the valuation h is a *model* of φ. We use the symbol $\vDash_{Ł_n} \varphi$ to denote the fact that $h(\varphi) = 0$ for all valuations h, i.e., that φ is a tautology in $Ł_n$. Note that for all h, $h(\top) = 0$ and $h(\bot) = 1$.

We want to define what it means for a theory to be 'consistent'. To do this, let us first look at an example. Keep in mind that to us $1 = \bot$ and $0 = \top$.

Consider the formula $x \wedge \neg x$. Its truth-value is $\max(h(x), h(1-x)) > 0$. If $h(x) = 0$ or $h(x) = 1$ we get $h(x \wedge \neg x) = 1$. However, $x \wedge \neg x$ is *consistent* in the sense that for any value $0 < h(x) < 1$ we have the value of $h(x \wedge \neg x) < 1$.

Now consider the formula

$$\neg(x \wedge \neg x)$$

This is not a tautology because its truth-value is

$$1 - h(x \wedge \neg x),$$

and we already showed that for $0 < h(x) < 1$, $h(x \wedge \neg x) < 1$, and hence, for $0 < h(x) < 1$, $h(\neg(x \wedge \neg x)) > 0$. To be a tautology a formula must get 0 for all possible assignments.

Note that $h(\neg\varphi) = 1 - h(\varphi) = \max(0, 1 - h(\varphi)) = h(\varphi \to \bot)$. We take the notion of consistency of $\Delta = \{A_1, \ldots, A_n\}$ to say that Δ does not entail $\bot$ (i.e., that $\bot$ is not a consequence of Δ). But what does "entail" mean? There are two possibilities in the literature for

$$A_1, \ldots, A_n \vDash B.$$

We denote them by $\vDash_{\max}$ and $\vDash_{\text{sum}}$. We start with the latter. We want that $A_1, \ldots, A_n \vDash_{\text{sum}} B$ if and only if $\vDash A_1 \to (A_1 \to \ldots \to (A_n \to B) \ldots)$. In other words, we want the implication $A_1 \to (A_1 \to \ldots \to (A_n \to B) \ldots)$ to be a tautology. For this to happen, we need that for any h, $h(A_1 \to \ldots \to (A_n \to B) \ldots)) = 0$ if and only if $h(A_1) + \ldots + h(A_n) = \sum_{i=1}^{n} h(A_i) \geq h(B)$. In general,

Definition 7.17 ($\vDash_{sum}$). Let Δ be a set of formulae and φ a formula of $\mathscr{L}_n$.

$$\Delta \vDash_{sum} B \text{ if and only if } \sum_{A_i \in \Delta} h(A_i) \geq h(B)$$

The other definition of $A_1, \ldots, A_n \vDash B$ is the "max" definition. We want $A_1, \ldots, A_n$ $\vDash_{max} B$ if and only if $\vDash A_1 \wedge \ldots \wedge A_n \to B$. In semantical terms, this means that $A_1, \ldots, A_n \vDash_{max} B$ if and only if for all h we have $\max_{i=1}^n \{h(A_i)\} \geq h(B)$. More generally, we have:

Definition 7.18 ($\vDash_{max}$). Let Δ be a set of formulae and φ a formula of $\mathscr{L}_n$.

$$\Delta \vDash_{max} B \text{ if and only if } \max_{A_i \in \Delta}\{h(A_i)\} \geq h(B)$$

Remark 7.1. Note that we are not saying that

$$A_1, \ldots, A_n \vDash'_{max} B$$

if every model of $\{A_i\}$ is also a model of B. This would mean that for every h, if $\max h(A_i) < 1$ then $h(B) < 1$.

According to this definition we get

$$\top \vDash'_{max} (A \to \neg A) \to \neg A$$

because for every h, $t = h((A \to \neg A) \to \neg A) < 1$, since $t = max(0, 1 - h(A) - max(0, 1 - h(A) - h(A))) = max(0, 1 - h(A) - max(0, 1 - 2h(A)))$. If $h(A) = 0$, $t = 0 < 1$. For $0 < h(A) < \frac{1}{2}$, $t = h(A) < 1$. For $\frac{1}{2} < h(A) \leq 1$, we have $t = 1 - h(A) < 1$.

We will see that when we translate into classical logic we get this $\vDash'_{max}$ consequence relation.

We prefer the $\vDash_{max}$ definition. Note that the $\vDash_{sum}$ definition satisfies the deduction theorem

$$A_1, \ldots, A_n \vDash_{sum} B \to C \text{ if and only if } A_1, \ldots, A_n, B \vDash_{sum} C.$$

But its weakness from our point of view is that it regards the theory as a multiset of a *sequence*, not as a *set*.

We have, for example, in three-valued logic (with truth-values $\{0, \frac{1}{2}, 1\}$) that $x \wedge \neg x \nvDash_{sum} \bot$, but $x \wedge \neg x, x \wedge \neg x \vDash_{sum} \bot$. This is because

$$x \wedge \neg x \to \bot$$

is not a tautology but

$$(x \wedge \neg x) \to ((x \wedge \neg x) \to \bot)$$

is a tautology.

So, if we look at $\Delta = \{x \wedge \neg x\}$ as a set, then we can certainly take as many copies of its members in a proof as we want. Thus, the consequence relation $\vDash_{sum}$ regards Łukasiewicz' logic as a substructural logic where theories are multisets. Let us hence concentrate on the $\vDash_{max}$ consequence notion.

The reader is warned that $\vDash_{max}$ can have unexpected results. Consider

$$\{A, A \to B\} \overset{?}{\vDash} B.$$

According to $\vDash_{\text{sum}}$ we have to check whether $(A \to B) \to (A \to B)$ is a tautology or alternatively check whether $A \to ((A \to B) \to B)$ is a tautology.

So indeed, $\{A, A \to B\} \vDash_{\text{sum}} B$. How about

$$\{A, A \to B\} \overset{?}{\vDash}_{\text{max}} B$$

We have to check whether $(A \wedge (A \to B)) \to B$ is a tautology. Let $h(A) = \frac{1}{5}, h(B) = \frac{3}{5}$. Hence,

$$h(A \to B) = \frac{2}{5}$$
$$h(A \wedge (A \to B)) = \frac{2}{5}$$

and therefore

$$h((A \wedge (A \to B)) \to B) = \frac{1}{5}.$$

Thus, $\{A, A \to B\} \nvDash_{\text{max}} B$. We do have, however, for any single formula A, that

$$A \vDash_{\text{max}} B \text{ if and only if } A \vDash_{\text{sum}} B.$$

Note that this does not hold for $\vDash'_{\text{max}}$, because as we have shown

$$\top \vDash'_{\text{max}} (A \to \neg A) \to \neg A$$

but not

$$\vDash'_{\text{max}} \top \to ((A \to \neg A) \to \neg A)$$

$\vDash'_{\text{max}}$ takes as tautologies anything that *never* gets $\bot$.

So we take $\vDash_{\text{max}}$ as our consequence notion.

What does it means now for a theory to be $\vDash_{\text{max}}$-consistent? It means that it does not have $\bot$ as a consequence.

Definition 7.19 (Weak consistency). A theory Δ is *weakly consistent* if for some assignment h

$$h(\Delta) = \max\{h(A) | A \in \Delta\} < 1.^6$$

Analogously, we can define a stronger notion of consistency:

Definition 7.20 (Strong consistency). A theory Δ is *strongly consistent* if for some assignment h, $h(\Delta) \in \mathscr{D}$.

The difference becomes clearer when we want to close a theory Δ under the consequence relation. For comparison, for the case of $\vDash_{\text{sum}}$ we define the notion of weak consistency for a multiset Δ by letting

$$h(\Delta) = \sum_{A \in \Delta} h(A)$$

and say that Δ is consistent if and only if there exists an assignment h such that $h(\Delta) < 1$. So, for example, in Ł$_2$, $\{x \wedge \neg x\}$ is consistent while $\{x \wedge \neg x, x \wedge \neg x\}$ is not.

We are now in a position to define the notion of consequence closure of a theory Δ.

Definition 7.21 (Consequence closure for $\models_{max}$). Let Δ be a theory.

$$\mathrm{Cn}_{max}(\Delta) = \{B \mid \text{for some finite } \Delta' \subseteq \Delta, \text{ we have that } \models \wedge_{\varphi_i \in \Delta'} \varphi_i \rightarrow B\}.$$

Lemma 7.3. $\mathrm{Cn}_{max}(\mathrm{Cn}_{max}(\Delta)) = \mathrm{Cn}_{max}(\Delta)$.

Proof. Assume that

1. $\theta_i \subseteq \Delta, i = 1, \ldots, m$
2. $\models \wedge \theta_i \rightarrow B_i, i = 1, \ldots, m$
3. $\models \wedge B_i \rightarrow C$

(1.) and (2.) say that $B_i \in \mathrm{Cn}_{max}(\Delta)$. (3.) says that $C \in \mathrm{Cn}_{max}(\mathrm{Cn}_{max}(\Delta))$. We want to find a $\theta \subseteq \Delta$ such that $\models \wedge \theta \rightarrow C$. This will show that $C \in \mathrm{Cn}_{max}(\Delta)$. Let $\theta = \bigcup_i \theta_i$. If $\not\models \wedge \theta \rightarrow C$, then for $h, h(\theta) < h(C)$. However, from (1.), $\max\{h(\theta_i)\} \geq h(B_i)$ and from (3.) $\max\{h(B_i)\} \geq h(C)$. Let B_j be the max given. Then we have,

$$h(\theta) \geq h(\theta_j) \geq h(B_j) \geq h(C),$$

a contradiction. The other inclusion can be proved in a straightforward way.

Lemma 7.4. $\mathrm{Cn}_{max}(\mathrm{Cn}_{max}(\Delta) \cup \{\varphi\}) = \mathrm{Cn}_{max}(\Delta \cup \{\varphi\})$.

Proof. The proof is similar to the proof of Lemma 7.3, except that in it we need to consider the set $\Delta \cup \{\varphi\}$ instead of Δ.

Remark 7.2. As a matter of interest, how do we define consequence closure for the case of $\models_{sum}$?

We can try to give a similar definition

$$\mathrm{Cn}_{sum}(\Delta) = \{B \mid \text{for some } A_1, \ldots, A_n \text{ in } \Delta, \models A_1 \rightarrow \ldots \rightarrow (A_n \rightarrow B) \ldots)\}$$

But this is not so simple, Δ being a multiset. We let

$$\Delta = \{A\}$$

So $\mathrm{Cn}_{sum}(\Delta) = \{A, A\}$

$$\mathrm{Cn}_{sum}(\mathrm{Cn}_{sum}(\Delta)) = \{A, A, A, A\}$$

etc. We saw that $\{x \wedge \neg x\}$ is consistent while $\{x \wedge \neg x, x \wedge \neg x\}$ is not. See the next lemma for $\models_{max}$.

Lemma 7.5 (for $\models_{max}$).

1. $\Delta \subseteq \mathrm{Cn}_{max}(\Delta)$
2. *If Δ is weakly consistent, so is $\mathrm{Cn}_{max}(\Delta)$.*

Proof.

1. If $A \in \Delta$, then $A \in Cn_{max}(\Delta)$ because $\Delta \models_{max} A \to A$.
2. If $h(\Delta) < 1$ and $\theta \subseteq \Delta$ and $\models \wedge\theta \to B$, then $h(\theta) \geq h(B)$, and since $h(\Delta) \geq h(\theta)$, we get $h(\Delta) \geq h(B)$. But this means that $h(Cn_{max}(\Delta)) = h(\Delta) < 1$.

Lemma 7.6. *Let Δ be a theory and let $B \notin Cn_{max}(\Delta)$ (i.e. $\Delta \not\models_{max} B$). Then for some h,*

$$h(\Delta) < h(B).$$

Proof. If $\Delta \not\models_{max} B$, then for any $\theta \subseteq \Delta, \theta$ finite we have $\not\models_{max} \wedge\theta \to B$. So, for some assignment h_θ, $h_\theta(\theta \to B) > 0$. Therefore, if $\theta = \{A_i\}$

$$\max\{h_\theta(A_i)\} < h_\theta(B).$$

We want an h_Δ such that

$$\max\{h_\Delta(A) | A \in \Delta\} < h_\Delta(B).$$

For each $\theta \subseteq \Delta, \theta$ finite, let $Q_\theta = \{h | h(\theta \to B) > 0\}$. Clearly by our assumptions, Q_θ is not empty. Also $Q_\theta \cap Q_{\theta'} = Q_{\theta \cup \theta'} \neq \emptyset$. Since we have for any h

$$\max\{h(A) | A \in \theta\} < h(B), \text{ and } \max\{h(A) | A \in \theta'\} < h(B)$$
$$\text{if and only if}$$
$$\max\{h(A) | A \in \theta \cup \theta'\} < h(B)$$

Thus, the family Q_θ is a family of non-empty sets closed under intersection. This family can be extended to an ultrafilter $\mathcal{F}$. Thus, $Q_\theta \in \mathcal{F}$ for all $\theta \subseteq \Delta, \theta$ finite.
  Let q be any atom. Consider the sets

$$S_q^x = \{h | h(q) = x\} \text{ for } x \in \{0, \frac{1}{n-1}, \dots, \frac{n-1}{n-1}\}.$$

These sets are disjoint, so only one of them is a large set. Let h_Δ be such that

$$h_\Delta(q) = x \text{ if and only if } S_q^x \in \mathcal{F}.$$

We thus get an assignment to the atoms of the language. We claim

$$\max\{h_\Delta(A) | A \in \Delta\} < h_\Delta(B).$$

Let $S_\varphi^x = \{h | h(\varphi) = x\}$.

Lemma 7.7. *For all φ*

$$S_\varphi^{H_\Delta(\varphi)} \in \mathcal{F}.$$

Proof. By induction on φ. For atomic q this is the definition. Assume this holds for φ_1 and φ_2 and let $h_\Delta(\varphi_1) = x_1$ and $h_\Delta(\varphi_2) = x_2$. So,

$$y = h_\Delta(\varphi_1 \to \varphi_2) = \max(0, h_\Delta(\varphi_2) - h_\Delta(\varphi_1)) = \max(0, x_2 - x_1).$$

So, the set of all h such that $h(\varphi_i = x_i)$ is a large set in $\mathscr{F}$, and hence the intersection is also in $\mathscr{F}$. But this is the set of h that gives $h(\varphi_1) = x_1$ and $h(\varphi_2) = x_2$, and they give $h(\varphi_1 \rightarrow \varphi_2) = y$.

So $S_{\varphi}^y \in \mathscr{F}$.

Assume now that for some $A \in \Delta$

$$h_\Delta(A \rightarrow B) = 0.$$

Then, $S_{A \rightarrow B}^0 \in \mathscr{F}$. But also $S_A \in \mathscr{F}$, being the set of all h such that $h(A \rightarrow B) > 0$. This is impossible because any two sets in $\mathscr{F}$ must have a non-empty intersection.

7.3.2 Translating Łukasiewicz' Many-Valued Logic Ł$_n$ into Classical Logic

We assume that the language of classical logic is formulated with the connectives $\vee$, $\wedge$, $\neg$ and $\rightarrow$ and that its atoms are $\mathscr{P}_n^* = \{p_0^{*,n}, \ldots, p_{\frac{1}{n-1}}^{*,n}, \ldots, p_{\frac{n-1}{n-1}}^{*,n}, q_0^{*,n}, \ldots, q_{\frac{1}{n-1}}^{*,n}, \ldots, q_{\frac{n-1}{n-1}}^{*,n}, \ldots\}$.

A valuation h^* of classical logic gives values to the atoms in $\mathscr{P}_n^*$ in $\{\top, \bot\}$ and is extended to complex formulae in the usual way. We use the symbol $\vDash_{*,n} B^{*,n}$ to denote the fact that the formula $B^{*,n}$ is a tautology in classical logic.

In order to lighten the notation, we will drop the superscript n from now on, since we assume an arbitrary but fixed number of truth-values in Ł$_n$.

Agreement for translation from Ł$_n$ to classical logic

Our translation is done using the following correspondence

$h(p) = \frac{i}{n-1}$ if and only if

1. $h^*(p_{\frac{i}{n-1}}^*) = \top$ and
2. $h^*(p_{\frac{j}{n-1}}^*) = \bot$ for $j \in \{0, \ldots, n-1\} - \{i\}$

In other words, p_x^* is true in a classical logic valuation h^* exactly when the truth value of p in Ł$_n$ is x in some valuation h and the truth-values of all other p_y^*, for $y \neq x$ in h^*, are false.

For that, we need the regulating formulae $\Psi_{p_i}^*$ of classical logic for each $p_i \in \mathscr{P}_{\text{Ł}_n}$:

$$\Psi_{p_i}^* = [\bigvee_{x \in \mathscr{T}_{\text{Ł}_n}} (p_i)_x^*] \wedge \bigwedge_{x,y \in \mathscr{T}_{\text{Ł}_n}, x \neq y} \neg((p_i)_x^* \wedge (p_i)_y^*)$$

The formula $\Psi_{p_i}^*$ is satisfied by a valuation h^* only when exactly one of $p_{\frac{i}{n-1}}^*$ (for $i = 0, \ldots, n-1$) gets value $\top$ (and the others get $\bot$), which hence regulates theories of classical logic containing it to behave as a particular assignment h of Ł$_n$.

Definition 7.22. Let φ be a wff in $\mathcal{L}_n$. We use the term $atoms(\varphi)$ to denote the set of atoms $\{p, q, r, \ldots\}$ appearing in φ. Analogously, we use the term $atoms^*(\varphi)$ to denote the corresponding atoms $\{p_0^*, \ldots, p_{\frac{n-1}{n-1}}^*, q_0^*, \ldots, q_{\frac{n-1}{n-1}}^*, \ldots\}$ in classical logic.

Definition 7.23. Let φ be a wff in $\mathcal{L}_n$. $\tau_n(\varphi) = \wedge_{p_i \in atoms(\varphi)} \Psi_{p_i}^*$.

We now offer a translation $(*)$ of Ł_n into classical logic. We start with the statement of Ł_n, saying that "the value of the wff A in a valuation h is x" (which we denote by $[A]_x$).

Definition 7.24 (The translation function $*$).

1. for $p \in \mathcal{P}_{\text{Ł}_n}$ let $[p]_x^* = p_x^*$
2. $[\neg A]_x^* = [A]_{1-x}^*$
3. $[A \rightarrow B]_x^* = \displaystyle\bigvee_{y, z \in \mathcal{T}_{\text{Ł}_n} \text{ s.t.} x = max(0, z-y)} [A]_y^* \wedge [B]_z^*$
4. $\Delta_x^* = \{\varphi_x^* \mid \varphi \in \Delta\}$

The function $*$ captures in first-order logic the truth-value of a formula of $\mathcal{L}_n$ in a particular assignment h. Later on, we will use this definition in the translation according to a particular entailment semantics (e.g., $\models_{max}$).

Definition 7.25. Let φ be a wff in $\mathcal{L}_n$. $\pi_n(\varphi) = \bigvee_{x \in \mathcal{T}_{\text{Ł}_n}} [\varphi]_x^* \wedge \bigwedge_{x, y \in \mathcal{T}_{\text{Ł}_n}, x \neq y} \neg([\varphi]_x^* \wedge [\varphi]_y^*)$

Lemma 7.8. *Let φ be a wff in $\mathcal{L}_n$; $\tau_n(\varphi)$ be as given in Definition 7.23; and $\pi_n(\varphi)$ be as given in Definition 7.25. It follows that*

$$\models_* \tau_n(\varphi) \rightarrow \pi_n(\varphi)$$

Proof. The proof is done by induction on φ.

1. For φ atomic, i.e., $\varphi = p$ for some $p \in \mathcal{P}_{\text{Ł}_n}$, this holds because $\tau_n(p) = \pi_n(p)$.
2. Assume $\pi_n(\varphi)$ holds. We show that $\neg\pi_n(\varphi)$ also holds. We know that

$$\tau_n \models_* (\bigvee_{x \in \mathcal{T}_{\text{Ł}_n}} [\varphi]_x^*) \wedge \bigwedge_{x, y \in \mathcal{T}_{\text{Ł}_n}, x \neq y} \neg([\varphi]_x^* \wedge [\varphi]_y^*)$$

We need to show that the following holds

$$(\bigvee_{x \in \mathcal{T}_{\text{Ł}_n}} [\neg\varphi]_x^*) \wedge \bigwedge_{x, y \in \mathcal{T}_{\text{Ł}_n}, x \neq y} \neg([\neg\varphi]_x^* \wedge [\neg\varphi]_y^*)$$

But notice that $[\neg\varphi]_u^* = [\varphi]_{1-u}^*$, and since u ranges over $\mathcal{T}_{\text{Ł}_n}$ so does $1-u$. Hence, the first conjunct holds and so does the second one for the same reason.
3. Consider now $\varphi = A \rightarrow B$. We have

$$[\varphi]_x^* = \bigvee_{y, z \in \mathcal{T}_{\text{Ł}_n} \text{ s.t. } x = max(0, z-y)} [A]_y^* \wedge [B]_z^*$$

Let h^* be any classical logic model of τ_n. By the induction hypothesis under τ_n in classical logic, there exists a unique y and a unique z such that $[A]_y^*$ and $[B]_z^*$

hold. This is because $\pi_n(A)$ and $\pi_n(B)$ hold. If we pick $x = max(0, z-y)$, we then have that $[\varphi]^*_x$ holds. Therefore $\bigvee_{x \in \mathscr{T}_{L_n}} [\varphi]^*_x$ holds in any model of τ_n. We now need to show that $\bigwedge_{x_1, x_2 \in \mathscr{T}_{L_n}, x_1 \neq x_2} \neg([A \rightarrow B]^*_{x_1} \wedge [A \rightarrow B]^*_{x_2})$ holds in the model. So, assume that for some x_1 and x_2 we have that $[A \rightarrow B]^*_{x_1}$ and $[A \rightarrow B]^*_{x_2}$ hold in the model. But since by the induction hypothesis there are unique values y and z such that $[A]^*_y$ and $[B]^*_z$ hold, we get that there is a unique $x = max(0, z-y)$ such that $[A \rightarrow B]^*_x$ holds. Therefore, $x = x_1 = x_2$.

What the lemma above says is that any model h^* of a formula $\tau_n(\varphi)$ is also a model of $\pi_n(\varphi)$, and hence we can work with the constraint $\tau_n(\varphi)$ imposed on the atoms of φ only.

We now extend τ_n to a set of formulae Δ in the following way: $\tau_n(\Delta) = \{\tau_n(\varphi) \mid \varphi \in \Delta\}$.

Lemma 7.9. *Let h be a valuation of Ł$_n$ and h^* be defined in classical logic by the correspondence (#) below.*

(#) $\quad h^*(q^*_x) = \top$ *if and only if* $h(q) = x$

It follows that $h^* \models_* \tau_n(\Delta)$ *and* $h^* \models_* [\varphi]^*_{h(\varphi)}$ *for all* $\varphi \in \Delta$.

Proof. *The proof is done by induction on φ using Lemma 7.8.*

Now, since the models of a formula φ were defined as the valuations that assign to it values that are not undesignated, we complete the translation to classical logic in the following way.

Translating into classical logic (case of $\models_{\max}$)

Given a theory Δ, consider $\mathrm{Cn}_{\max}(\Delta)$, the consequence closure of Δ. Its being consistent means that for some $h, h(A) < 1$ for all $A \in \mathrm{Cn}_{\max}(\Delta)$.

Notation 11 *Let φ be a formula of $\mathscr{L}_n$. The term $[\varphi]^*_{<1}$ will abbreviate the formula* $\bigvee_{x<1} [\varphi]^*_x$.

Definition 7.26. Let φ be a wff in $\mathscr{L}_n$. The translation of φ into classical logic, in symbols, φ^τ, is the formula $\tau_n(\varphi) \wedge [\varphi]^*_{<1}$. Similarly, for a set of formulae Δ, we define $\Delta^\tau = \{\varphi^\tau \mid \varphi \in \Delta\}$.

Then $\mathrm{Cn}_{\max}(\Delta)$ is consistent if and only if $\mathrm{Cn}_{\max}(\Delta)^\tau$ is consistent in classical logic.

Lemma 7.10 (Correspondence of consistency). *Let Δ be a set of wffs of $\mathscr{L}_n$, and φ and ψ be formulae of $\mathscr{L}_n$. It follows that*

1. *φ is consistent in Ł$_n$ if and only if φ^τ is consistent in classical logic*
2. *Δ is consistent in Ł$_n$ if and only if Δ^τ is consistent in classical logic*

Proof. The proof of 1 follows from Lemma 7.9 and the proof of 2 given 1 is straight-forward.

Notice that we do not need to define a notion of acceptability for the revision of a theory of $Ł_n$, since inconsistency in $Ł_n$ translates directly into inconsistency into classical logic.

Example 7.1. Let $\varphi = \neg(p \to p)$, which is inconsistent in $Ł_n$, since $h(\neg(p \to p)) = 1$ for all h. We only need to show that the translation will include $[p]_z^*$ and $[p]_y^*$ for some z, y, $z \neq y$, since this contradicts $\tau_n(\varphi)$, which says that the truth-values of propositional variables in φ are uniquely assigned.

Note that each disjunct in $\bigvee_{x<1}[\neg(p \to p)]_x^*$ will include $[p \to p]_{1-x}^* = \bigvee_{z>y}([p]_y^* \wedge [p]_z^*)$. This is because, since $x < 1$, $1 - x > 0$, and hence $1 - x = max(0, z - y) > 0$, and hence $z > y$. Provided there are at least two values in $\mathscr{T}_{Ł_n}$, there is at least one such pair of z and y, and this contradicts $\tau_n(\varphi)$.

7.3.3 Revision in Łukasiewicz' Many-Valued Logic ($Ł_n$)

Revision in $Ł_n$ is defined as a two-stage process. The details are given below.

Definition 7.27 (Revision by translation of $Ł_n$). Let Δ be a set of wff in $\mathscr{L}_n$ and φ be a wff in $\mathscr{L}_n$.

Let the set $\Delta_\varphi^\#$ be defined as

$$\Delta_\varphi^\# = \{\psi \in Cn_{max}(\Delta) \,|\, [\psi]_{<1}^* \in Cn(Cn_{max}(\Delta)_{<1}^*) \circ_a (\tau_n(\Delta) \wedge \varphi^\tau)\}$$

The revision of Δ by φ, in symbols, $\Delta *_{Ł_n} \varphi$, is defined as follows.

$$\Delta *_{Ł_n} \varphi = Cn_{max}(\Delta_\varphi^\# \cup \{\varphi\})$$

Note that, with respect to the general methodology presented in Section 7.1, the axiomatisation $\mathscr{A}_L$ is for this logic embedded into the constraints $\tau_n(\Delta)$ and $\tau_n(\varphi)$, whereas the consistency notion is captured by the constraints $[\alpha]_{<1}^*$ for all formulae α involved in the process.

Furthermore, the following points need to be taken into account.

1. we first take the set of consequences of Δ under $\vDash_{max}$
2. then we need to translate every formula in this set to classical logic (stating that they can have any non-undesignated value)

We now need to work on the revising part. We need to include

1. the constraints on the behaviour of the truth-values for the atoms appearing in Δ (i.e., $\tau_n(\Delta)$), which is included in this part to make sure it is preserved during the revision; and
2. the translation of the revising formula φ itself: φ^τ

Unfortunately, we are not done yet, as the classical logic revision will return many more consequences than the ones that were originally in $\mathrm{Cn}_{\max}(\Delta)$. Some of the new ones are legitimate, since they are the result of the addition of φ to Δ; however, some will in fact be max'-consequences of Δ, for example, $A \vee \neg A$, since the translation of $A \vee \neg A$ gets value less than 1. To single them out, we maintain only those formulae ψ that were originally in $\mathrm{Cn}_{\max}(\Delta)$. This is defined in $\Delta_\varphi^\#$. Note that $\Delta_\varphi^\#$ excludes φ and its consequences in all interesting cases; therefore, we need to add it and close the result under $\mathrm{Cn}_{\max}$.

We could have defined the revision by working with the subsets of $\mathrm{Cn}_{\max}(\Delta)$ that are maximally consistent with φ, but we would have the problem of choosing the right subset of this set. If we want to mimic the behaviour of the $\circ_a$ operation, we let it do its job and weed out the unwanted consequences added by the classical logical consequence closure.

Lemma 7.11. *Let Δ be a theory of Ł$_n$; φ and ψ be formulae of $\mathscr{L}_n$. The following properties hold for $*_{Ł_n}$.*

1. $\Delta *_{Ł_n} \varphi$ *is closed under logical consequence.*
   This comes straight from Definition 7.27.
2. $\Delta *_{Ł_n} \varphi \vDash_{Ł_n} \varphi$.
   Note that according to Definition 7.27, $\varphi \in \Delta *_{Ł_n} \varphi$. Hence, $\max_{A_i \in \Delta *_{Ł_n} \varphi}\{h(A_i)\} \geq h(\varphi)$, and then by Definition 7.18, $\Delta *_{Ł_n} \varphi \vDash_{Ł_n} \varphi$.
3. *If φ is consistent with Δ, then $\Delta *_{Ł_n} \varphi = \mathrm{Cn}_{\max}(\Delta \cup \{\varphi\})$.*
   We already know from Lemma 7.10 that if $\Delta \cup \{\varphi\}$ is consistent, then so is the set $\Delta^\tau \cup \{\varphi^\tau\}$ in classical logic. Consequently, so is the set $\mathrm{Cn}(\mathrm{Cn}_{\max}(\Delta)_{<1}^*) \cup \{(\tau_n(\Delta) \wedge \varphi^\tau)\}$, and hence by (K°3,4), $\mathrm{Cn}(\mathrm{Cn}_{\max}(\Delta)_{<1}^*) * \{(\tau_n(\Delta) \wedge \varphi^\tau)\} = \mathrm{Cn}(\mathrm{Cn}_{\max}(\Delta)_{<1}^*) \cup \{(\tau_n(\Delta) \wedge \varphi^\tau)\}$. Note that by the way we have defined the translation
   $$\{\psi \in \mathrm{Cn}_{\max}(\Delta) \mid [\psi]_{<1}^* \in \mathrm{Cn}(\mathrm{Cn}_{\max}(\Delta)_{<1}^*) \cup \{(\tau_n(\Delta) \wedge \varphi^\tau)\} = \mathrm{Cn}_{\max}(\Delta).$$
   By Lemma 7.4, $\mathrm{Cn}_{\max}(\mathrm{Cn}_{\max}(\Delta) \cup \{\varphi\}) = \mathrm{Cn}_{\max}(\Delta \cup \{\varphi\})$.
4. $\Delta *_{Ł_n} \varphi$ *is inconsistent only if φ is contradictory.*
   By (K°5), Lemma 7.10 and Definition 7.27, $\Delta_\varphi^\#$ is inconsistent only if φ^τ is inconsistent only if φ is contradictory. Therefore, $\Delta *_{Ł_n} \varphi = \mathrm{Cn}_{\max}(\Delta_\varphi^\# \cup \{\varphi\})$ is inconsistent only if φ is contradictory.
5. *If $\varphi \equiv_{Ł_n} \psi$, then $\Delta *_{Ł_n} \varphi \equiv \Delta *_{Ł_n} \psi$.*
   If $\varphi \equiv_{\max} \psi$, then for all h, $h(\varphi) = h(\psi)$. Therefore $\varphi^\tau \equiv \psi^\tau$. By (K°6), $\mathrm{Cn}(\mathrm{Cn}_{\max}(\Delta)_{<1}^*) * \{(\tau_n(\Delta) \wedge \varphi^\tau)\} \equiv \mathrm{Cn}(\mathrm{Cn}_{\max}(\Delta)_{<1}^*) * \{(\tau_n(\Delta) \wedge \psi^\tau)\}$ and hence $\Delta_\varphi^\# = \Delta_\psi^\#$. Since $\varphi \equiv_{Ł_n} \psi$, we have that $\Delta *_{Ł_n} \varphi \equiv \Delta *_{Ł_n} \psi$.
6. $\Delta *_{Ł_n} (\varphi \wedge \psi) \subseteq \mathrm{Cn}_{Ł_n}((\Delta *_{Ł_n} \varphi) \cup \{\psi\})$.
   Suppose that $\alpha \in \Delta *_{Ł_n} (\varphi \wedge \psi)$ for some α. By Definition 7.27, $\alpha \in \mathrm{Cn}_{\max}(\Delta_{\varphi \wedge \psi}^\# \cup \{\varphi \wedge \psi\}$. By (K°7), $\mathrm{Cn}(\mathrm{Cn}_{\max}(\Delta)_{<1}^*) \circ_a (\tau_n(\Delta) \wedge (\varphi \wedge \psi)^\tau) \subseteq \mathrm{Cn}(\mathrm{Cn}_{\max}(\Delta)_{<1}^*) \circ_a (\tau_n(\Delta) \wedge (\varphi)^\tau) \cup \{\psi\})$ $\Delta_0^* \circ_a (\tau_n(\Delta) \wedge \varphi^\tau \wedge \psi^\tau) \vdash \alpha^\tau$. By (K°7), it follows that $\mathrm{Cn}(\Delta_0^* \circ_a (\tau_n(\Delta) \wedge \varphi^\tau \cup \{\psi^\tau\}) \vdash \alpha^\tau$. Notice that for every $\psi^\tau \in \Delta_0^* \circ_a (\tau_n(\Delta) \wedge \varphi^\tau$, there is a corresponding

ψ in $\Delta *_{L_n} \varphi$ (by the definition of $*_{L_n}$), and similarly for ψ^τ. By correspondence, $\mathrm{Cn}_{L_n}((\Delta *_{L_n} \varphi) \cup \{\psi\}) \vdash \alpha$.

7. If ψ is consistent with $\Delta *_{L_n} \varphi$, then $\mathrm{Cn}((\Delta *_{L_n} \varphi) \cup \{\psi\}) \subseteq \Delta *_{L_n} (\varphi \wedge \psi)$.
   If ψ is consistent with $\Delta *_{L_n} \varphi$, then ψ^τ is consistent with $\Delta_0^* \circ_a (\tau_n(\Delta) \wedge \varphi^\tau)$, and then by (K°8), $\mathrm{Cn}(\Delta_0^* \circ_a (\tau_n(\Delta) \wedge \varphi^\tau) \cup \{\psi^\tau\}) \subseteq \mathrm{Cn}(\Delta_0^* \circ_a (\tau_n(\Delta) \wedge (\varphi \wedge \psi)^\tau))$. But, $\{\alpha \mid \Delta_0^* \circ_a (\tau_n(\Delta) \wedge \varphi^\tau) \vdash \alpha^\tau\} \cup \{\psi\} \models_{L_n} \beta$ if and only if $\Delta_0^* \circ_a (\tau_n(\Delta) \wedge \varphi^\tau) \cup \{\psi^\tau\} \vdash \beta^\tau$.

What we have just proven is that $*_{L_n}$ verifies all eight conditions of an AGM operation. Item 3 is actually a proof for postulates (K°3) and (K°4).

7.4 Revising in Algebraic Logics

7.4.1 Translating Algebraic Logic into Classical Logic

We now present a translation method for a class of algebraic logics. This class includes Łukasiewicz' infinitely many-valued logic and classical logic itself.

Let $\mathfrak{L}$ be an algebraic logic defined as follows.

1. $\mathfrak{L}$ has connectives $c_1, \ldots, c_k$, where each c_i is an m_i-ary connective
2. $\mathfrak{L}$ has as truth-values elements of any algebra of the form $\mathfrak{A} = (\mathcal{M}, \mathfrak{D}, f_1, \ldots, f_k)$, where $\mathcal{M}$ is a domain of algebraic elements; $\mathfrak{D} \subseteq \mathcal{M}$ is the set of designated elements and each f_i is an m_i-ary function symbol corresponding to the connectives $c_1, \ldots, c_k$

We assume that the class of models which can serve $\mathfrak{L}$ is defined by some first-order theory Δ. We can assume Δ is finite.

Let $\mathfrak{A}$ be an algebra. A valuation h into $\mathfrak{A}$ assigns an algebraic element $h(q) \in \mathcal{M}$ to every atom q of $\mathfrak{L}$. h is extended to any formula φ of the language by recursively defining

$$h(c_i(A_1, \ldots, A_{m_i})) = f_i(h(A_1), \ldots, h(A_{m_i}))$$

where c_i is the main connective in φ and the A_{m_i}'s are the arguments of c_i.

We say that $\mathfrak{L}_{\mathfrak{A}} \models \varphi$ if and only if for all valuations h into $\mathfrak{A}$ we have that $h(\varphi) \in \mathfrak{D}$. We say that $\mathfrak{L}_\Delta \models \varphi$ if and only if for any model $\mathfrak{A}$ of Δ, we have that $\mathfrak{L}_{\mathfrak{A}} \models \varphi$.

Example 7.2. 1. Classical propositional logic is an algebraic logic for an axiomatic theory of Boolean algebras Δ.
2. Łukasiewicz' infinitely many-valued propositional logic is an algebraic logic for the theory of MV-algebras Δ.
3. Intuitionistic propositional logic is an algebraic logic for the theory of Heyting algebras Δ.

Remark 7.3. Note that an algebra with axioms Δ is written in a language with function symbols $f_1, \ldots, f_n$ and one monadic predicate M. The axioms of Δ may say something about M. We can add to the language an infinite number of monadic predicates $P_1, P_2, \ldots$. Call the new theory Δ^M. If we write no axioms about $\{P_i\}$, then we get that Δ^M is a conservative extension of Δ. Any algebra $\mathfrak{A}$ which is a model of Δ can also be a model of Δ^M, and we define the $\{P_i\}$ arbitrarily, and any model of Δ^M and P_i can be reduced to a model of $\mathfrak{A}$ alone by ignoring the P_i's.

We now define the translation of the algebraic logic $\mathfrak{L}$ into the theory of Δ augmented by P_i. Let h be a valuation giving each atom p_i a variable v_i of the algebraic language. We translate the meta-statement

"The value $h(\varphi)$ of the formula φ in the algebra is x (denoted by $[\varphi]_x$)."

Let us start by associating with each atomic proposition p_i of $\mathfrak{L}$ a monadic predicate P_i of Δ.

1. For atomic p_i we have

$$[p_i]_x = P_i(x)$$

where P_i is a monadic predicate associated with p_i

2. $[c_i(A_1, \ldots, A_{m_i})]_x = \exists y_1, \ldots, y_{m_i}(\bigwedge_{i=1}^{m_i} [A_i]_{y_i} \wedge x = f_i(y_1, \ldots, y_{m_i}))$

For each atom p_i of $\mathfrak{L}$, let Ψ_{p_i} be the following formula in classical logic

$$\Psi_{p_i} = \exists x(P_i(x) \wedge \forall y(P_i(y) \to y = x))$$

For any formula φ of $\mathfrak{L}$ with atoms $atoms(\varphi)$, let

$$\tau(\varphi) = \bigwedge_{p_i \in atoms(\varphi)} \Psi_{p_i}$$

For any formula φ of $\mathfrak{L}$ let Ψ_φ be

$$\Psi_\varphi = \exists x[[\varphi]_x \wedge \forall y([\varphi]_y \to y = x)]$$

Note that this agrees with Ψ_p for atomic p since $[p]_x = P(x)$.
We can now prove by induction on φ the following lemmas.

Lemma 7.12. *In classical logic* $\Delta \vDash \tau(\varphi) \to \Psi_\varphi$

Lemma 7.13. *Let h be a valuation for $\mathfrak{L}$ giving value $h(p) \in \mathcal{M}$ for each atom p. Let $P(h(p))$ hold exactly for $h(p)$ for each atom p. Then we have for any φ that $[\varphi]_{h(\varphi)}$ holds in the algebra.*

Definition 7.28 ($\vDash_{\mathfrak{L}}$). $\Delta \vDash_{\mathfrak{L}} \varphi$ if and only if $\forall \psi \in \Delta \ h(\psi) \in \mathcal{M} \setminus \mathcal{U}$ implies $h(\varphi) \in \mathcal{M} \setminus \mathcal{U}$.

Note that in the case Łukasiewicz' logic this was the definition we did not want (see Remark 7.1). In the case of algebraic logic, we have no choice because we do not have specific knowledge about it. If the algebra have some well-known properties and they are problematic with this definition, then we can use them to define a more appropriate notion of consequence, as we did in the case of Łukasiewicz' logic.

Definition 7.29. A set Γ of wff of $\mathfrak{L}$ is consistent if and only if for some algebra $\mathfrak{A}$ and some valuation h into $\mathfrak{A}$, we have that for every $\varphi \in \Gamma$, $h(\varphi) \in \mathfrak{D}$.

Because we are speaking of a general algebra, we do not have a notion such as max and we have to single out the designated values $\mathfrak{D}$. In case the algebra also has a set of undesignated values $\mathscr{U}$, the notion of consistency amounts to the existence of an assignment that gives a value in $\mathscr{M} \setminus \mathscr{U}$ (i.e., a non undesignated value).

Let Γ be a theory of $\mathfrak{L}$. Let $\Gamma^{\#}$ be a theory of classical logic defined as follows:

$$\Gamma^{\#} = \{\tau(\varphi) \mid \varphi \in \Gamma\} \cup \{\exists y(D(y) \wedge [\varphi]_y) \mid \varphi \in \Gamma\}$$

where $D(y)$ holds if and only if $y \in \mathfrak{D}$.

Lemma 7.14. *Γ is consistent in $\mathfrak{L}$ if and only if $\Delta^M \cup \Gamma^{\#}$ is classically consistent.*

7.4.2 Revision in Algebraic Logics

Definition 7.30. Let $*$ be a revision process in classical logic; Γ be a set of formulae of $\mathfrak{L}$ and φ be a formula of $\mathfrak{L}$. Then we can define a revision process in $\mathfrak{L}$ by $\Gamma * \varphi = \{A \in \Gamma \mid \Gamma^{\#} * (\Delta^M \wedge \tau(\varphi) \wedge \exists y(D(y) \wedge [\varphi]_y)) \vdash [A]_x$ for some $x \in \mathfrak{D}\}$.

Example 7.3 (Classical propositional logic). Consider the theory Γ with the three formulae

(1) $a \rightarrow b$
(2) $a \rightarrow \neg b$
(3) a

Its translation into the theory of Boolean algebra is

(1*) $\exists y(D(y) \wedge \exists x_1, x_2(A(x_1) \wedge B(x_2) \wedge (y = \neg x_1 \vee x_2)))$
(2*) $\exists y(D(y) \wedge \exists x_1, x_2(A(x_1) \wedge B(x_2) \wedge (y = \neg x_1 \vee \neg x_2)))$
(3*) $\exists y(D(y) \wedge A(y))$

where $D(y)$ says that y is designated (i.e., $y = 0$ of the algebra if "0" is "truth") and "=", "$\wedge$", "$\vee$" and "$\neg$" are Boolean algebra operations.

τ says that A and B must hold for unique values, i.e., $\tau = \exists y(A(y) \wedge \forall u(A(u) \rightarrow u = y)) \wedge \exists y(B(y) \wedge \forall u(B(u) \rightarrow u = y))$.

Note that the set of formulae $\{\tau, 1^*, 2^*, 3^*\}$ is consistent if and only if the set of formulae $\{1, 2, 3\}$ is consistent. If we cannot revise τ out, then we must revise $\{1^*, 2^*, 3^*\}$.

Summary of the methodology

In order to provide a revision based on a translation into classical logic we need

1. finite axioms for the algebra and for 0 (or for what it means to be a designated value)
2. some axioms that constrain the uniqueness of the truth-value assignments to propositional atoms
3. finite number of atoms so that the above truth-value axioms are finite

We now turn to Belnap's four-valued logic, which does not have a notion of inconsistency. This will provide a basis for our discussion on *acceptability* of theories.

7.5 Introducing Belnap's Four-Valued Logic

Standard familiar logical systems such as classical logic, modal logic and intuitionistic logic have in common the principle that contradicting information entails any arbitrary sentence. This principle, known as *ex falsum quod libet*, is, however, not always ideal for deduction mechanisms used in practical computer science applications, where information is often derived from possibly inconsistent databases. Alternative systems have been developed, examples of which include the *logic of entailment* (also known as system **E**) and the *relevant implication system* (or system **R**), in which deductions between formulae hold only when there is some "connection" between them (e.g., the formulae share some propositional variable). In [3], Belnap provides a semantic characterisation of first-degree entailment together with a sound and complete axiomatisation, emphasising its connection with the problem of "how a computer should think" [2]. A revised version of the latter can be found in [1].

We provide a translation of Belnap's semantics into a set of first-order logic formulae. Sets of Belnap formulae are translated into a conjunction of atomic predicates. An appropriate classical axiomatisation is defined, which captures the semantic behaviour of Belnap connectives, thus allowing Belnap's notion of entailment to be expressed in terms of classical entailment from the translated theories as done in previous sections in this chapter. This embedding into classical logic has two main advantages. Firstly, it provides the basis for analysing belief revision operations for these types of logics. Secondly, it also allows for a theorem-proving mechanism for four-valued logic using existing theorem provers for classical logic.

7.5.1 Belief Revision in Belnap's Four-Valued Logic

In this section, we describe the approach for defining revision operators for nonclassical logics whose semantics are significantly different from those of classical logic. In this case, the translation mechanism has to mirror the structures upon which the semantics as well as the notion of entailment are based.

The semantic notion of entailment in Belnap's four-valued logic L is based on a lattice with four elements, called the *logical lattice* (**L4**). The translation mechanism needs to reflect the structure of the lattice and express (declaratively) the different truth-value assignments that a formula can assume under given valuations. An axiomatisation expressing the behaviour of the connectives needs also to be defined. Independently of the translation mechanism adopted, such axiomatisation has to be *sound* and *complete* with respect to the semantic notion of entailment of the object logic L. This ensures that, given a translation function τ and a classical logic axiomatisation $\mathscr{A}_L$, for any given theory Δ and formula α in L,

$$\Delta \vdash_L \alpha \text{ iff } \mathscr{A}_L \cup \Delta^\tau \vdash \alpha^\tau$$

where Δ^τ and α^τ are the translations of Δ and α into classical logic, respectively.[7] As before, we will refer to a sound and complete axiomatisation of L in classical logic by the symbol $\mathscr{A}_L$. The method below is only applicable to logics whose semantics are first-order logic axiomatisable.

The second component of our approach is a domain-dependent notion of *acceptability* for a theory in L. As mentioned in Section 7.1, given a revision operator $\circ_a$ for classical logic, we could simply define a revision operator $*_L$ for the logic L in the following way.

(7.7) $\Delta *_L \psi = \{\beta \mid \Delta^\tau \circ_a (\psi^\tau \wedge \mathscr{A}_L) \vdash \beta^\tau\}$

However, if the notion of consistency in the object logic differs from that of classical logic, we will have difficulties, since the AGM revision relies on the notion of (classical) consistency. This can be easily seen in postulate $(K_{3,4}^\circ)$. Revision is only triggered when the new information is inconsistent with the current belief set. In this sense, revision in the translation can only be performed if the translated theory turns out to be *classically* inconsistent. The direct application of our method to logics such as Belnap's four-valued logic, whose notion of inconsistency of a theory is not associated with the non-existence of models of the classical logic translation of that theory, would therefore yield simply to an expansion, since the translation of any Belnap theory is always classically consistent. This is a consequence of the fact that AGM belief revision is completely dependent on the mechanics of classical logic itself.

Our view is that belief revision processes would benefit from a shift towards the more general notion of *acceptable belief sets*. In the particular case of classical logic, it makes sense to require that an acceptable belief set be *at least* consistent, since inconsistency trivialises the notion of consequence in classical logic. However, there is no reason why more specific restrictions could not be imposed, as is the case, for instance, with integrity constraints in database updates. This paves the way for the definition of *relative revision* procedures, where the process is guided by a fixed theory representing a particular notion of acceptable belief sets. For the purpose of this chapter, our 'relative' revision is defined in terms of a notion of acceptability explicitly included in the revision process. Our definition of belief revision for a non-classical logic L is therefore as follows.

---

[7] We use the symbol $\vdash$ without subscript to denote entailment in classical logic, and with subscript to denote entailment on a given object logic.

Definition 7.31 (Belief revision in L). Let $\circ_a$ be a revision operator for classical logic and Acc be a formula expressing a (domain-dependent) notion of acceptability of L-theories. The revision of Δ by ψ, $\Delta *_L \psi$, is defined as

$$\Delta *_L \psi = \{\beta \mid \Delta^\tau \circ_a (\psi^\tau \wedge \mathscr{A}_L \wedge Acc) \vdash \beta^\tau\}$$

This is exactly as before except that the semantic properties of the object logic L as well as the notion of acceptability are included in the revising argument of the procedure, so that we can guarantee that the resulting revised theory is acceptable in the object logic L.

We now introduce Belnap's four-valued logic.

7.6 Belnap's Four-Valued Logic

In database management or query-answering systems, collections of data are prone to include either explicit or hidden inconsistencies. This is due, for instance, to the fact that information may come from different contradicting sources. The use of a classical deductive process without any mechanism for handling inconsistency would not be appropriate in this case, since any arbitrary information is classically derivable from an inconsistent collection of data. Explicit inconsistencies may come from different but equally reliable sources, whereas hidden inconsistencies are identified only by means of deductive reasoning. The motivation for Belnap's approach is to provide a logic less sensitive to inconsistency.

Notation and Terminology

We reserve lower-case letters of the Roman alphabet for atomic symbols in the language $\mathscr{L}_B$ of Belnap's logic. Greek letters will be used in general to refer to wffs of that language (the language of the "object logic"). Larger entities such as structures, sets, theories and languages will often be typeset in calligraphic font, e.g., $\mathscr{A}, \mathscr{B}, \mathscr{C}, \ldots$. In this section and the next, all formulae, sets of formulae, etc., refer to objects of the language of Belnap's logic defined next.

7.6.1 Axiomatising Belnap's Four-Valued Logic

Let the language of Belnap's logic $\mathscr{L}_B$ be composed of a countable set of propositional letters $\{p, q, r, \ldots\}$ and the connectives $\neg$, $\wedge$ and $\vee$. The set of wffs is given by the standard construction of formulae. For the finite case, a Belnap theory can be seen as a single formula given by the conjunction of the formulae in the theory. The formula $\neg p \wedge (\neg q \vee r) \wedge \neg r$ is an example of a possible representation of a finite Belnap theory containing the formulae $\{\neg p, \neg q \vee r, \neg r\}$. Because of the soundness and completeness results of Section 7.6.2, it would not be difficult to extend this logic to deal with infinite theories, and we assume that such an extension exists in some of the proofs done in Section 7.6.5, where the AGM postulates are analysed.

In proof-theoretical terms, Belnap's four-valued logic is characterised by a finite axiomatisation. Given two wffs α and β, the expression $\alpha \rightarrow \beta$ denotes the fact that α *entails* β. In this sense, the symbol $\rightarrow$ can be seen as a derivability relation between formulae, or equally between theories and a formula. The expression $\alpha \leftrightarrow \beta$ denotes that β can be derived from α ($\alpha \rightarrow \beta$) and vice versa, or, semantically, that α and β are equivalent. The axiomatisation given below is known to be sound and complete with respect to the semantics of the logic presented later.

Definition 7.32 (Axiomatisation). Let $\alpha_1, \ldots, \alpha_n, \beta_1, \ldots, \beta_m$ and γ be wffs. A proof theory for Belnap's four-valued logic, denoted by Ax_B, contains the following set of expressions:

1. $\neg\neg\alpha \leftrightarrow \alpha$.
2. $\neg(\alpha \wedge \beta) \leftrightarrow \neg\alpha \vee \neg\beta$.
3. $\neg(\alpha \vee \beta) \leftrightarrow \neg\alpha \wedge \neg\beta$.
4. $\alpha \vee \beta \leftrightarrow \beta \vee \alpha$.
5. $\alpha \vee (\beta \vee \gamma) \leftrightarrow (\alpha \vee \beta) \vee \gamma$.
6. $\alpha \vee (\beta \wedge \gamma) \leftrightarrow (\alpha \vee \beta) \wedge (\alpha \vee \gamma)$.
7. $\alpha \wedge \beta \leftrightarrow \beta \wedge \alpha$.
8. $\alpha \wedge (\beta \wedge \gamma) \leftrightarrow (\alpha \wedge \beta) \wedge \gamma$.
9. $\alpha \wedge (\beta \vee \gamma) \leftrightarrow (\alpha \wedge \beta) \vee (\alpha \wedge \gamma)$.
10. $\alpha_1 \wedge \ldots \wedge \alpha_n \rightarrow \beta_1 \vee \ldots \vee \beta_m$ provided that $\beta_j = \alpha_i$ for some i and j.
11. $\alpha \rightarrow \beta$ and $\beta \rightarrow \gamma$ then $\alpha \rightarrow \gamma$.
12. $\alpha \leftrightarrow \beta$ and $\beta \leftrightarrow \gamma$ then $\alpha \leftrightarrow \gamma$.
13. $\alpha \rightarrow \beta$ if and only if $\neg\beta \rightarrow \neg\alpha$.
14. $(\alpha \vee \beta) \rightarrow \gamma$ if and only if $\alpha \rightarrow \gamma$ and $\beta \rightarrow \gamma$.
15. $\alpha \rightarrow \beta$ if and only if $\beta \leftrightarrow (\alpha \vee \beta)$
16. $\alpha \rightarrow \beta$ if and only if $\alpha \leftrightarrow (\alpha \wedge \beta)$
17. $\alpha \rightarrow (\beta \wedge \gamma)$ if and only if $\alpha \rightarrow \beta$ and $\alpha \rightarrow \gamma$.

The first nine expressions correspond to standard classical properties of negation, disjunction and conjunction (e.g., commutativity, associativity, De Morgan laws). We will sometimes refer to them as the *Belnap axioms*. Expressions 10, 11 and 13 capture respectively the reflexivity, transitivity and contrapositive properties of the derivability relation $\rightarrow$, whereas expressions 14–17 correspond to standard classical rules for introduction and elimination of $\vee$ and $\wedge$, respectively. We will sometimes refer to expressions 11–17 as the *Belnap rules*. Any Belnap expression of the form $\psi \rightarrow \varphi$ can be either an instantiation of one of the axioms 1–10 in Definition 7.32, or obtained using some of the Belnap rules 11–17 together with some axiom instantiations. For any given expression $\psi \rightarrow \varphi$, we therefore define the notion of *length* of the proof as the "least number" of Belnap rule applications needed to show that $\psi \rightarrow \varphi$.

The similarity between the above rules and classical rules shows that four-valued logics are indeed very close to standard classical logic. The basic classical rule, which is missing in Belnap's logic and which makes this logic *paraconsistent* is the rule $(\alpha \land \neg\alpha) \rightarrow \beta$, often referred to as *ex falsum quod libel*. Within a classical framework this rule allows one to derive any arbitrary information from inconsistent assumptions. Belnap's logic does not allow this to be done.

7.6.2 Entailment in Belnap's Four-Valued Logic

The semantics underlying Belnap's logic is four-valued. Let **4** be the set {T, F, Both, None}. The elements of this set are the four different truth-values which an atomic sentence can have within what Belnap calls a given *state of information*. The intuitive meaning of these values is given as follows:

1. p is stated to be true only (T)
2. p is stated to be false only (F)
3. p is stated to be both true and false, for instance, by different sources, or in different points of time (Both), and
4. p's status is unknown. That is, it is neither true, nor false (None).

The four values form a lattice, called the *approximation lattice* and denoted by **A4**, where the ordering relation $\sqsubseteq$ goes "uphill" and respects the monotonicity property, in the sense that information about the truth-value of a formula "grows" from None to Both. **A4** can be seen in Figure 7.2.

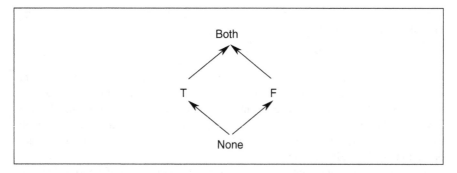

Fig. 7.2 The approximation lattice **A4**

The truth-values of complex formulae are defined based on **A4** and result in the truth-tables shown in Figure 7.3.

The truth-tables also constitute a lattice, called the *logical lattice* and denoted by **L4** (Figure 7.4). In **L4**, logical conjunction is identified with the *meet* operation and logical disjunction with the *join* operation.

The notion of valuation of formulae is expressed in Belnap's logic in terms of *set-ups*. A set-up s is a mapping of the atomic formulae into **4**. Using the truth-tables given in Figure 7.3, each set-up can be extended to a mapping of *all formulae*

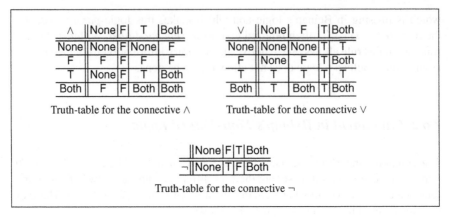

∧	None	F	T	Both
None	None	F	None	F
F	F	F	F	F
T	None	F	T	Both
Both	F	F	Both	Both

Truth-table for the connective ∧

∨	None	F	T	Both
None	None	None	T	T
F	None	F	T	Both
T	T	T	T	T
Both	T	Both	T	Both

Truth-table for the connective ∨

	None	F	T	Both
¬	None	T	F	Both

Truth-table for the connective ¬

Fig. 7.3 Truth-tables for the connectives in Belnap's four-valued logic

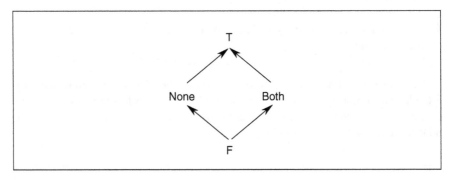

Fig. 7.4 The logical lattice **L4**

into **4**, in the standard inductive way. We call this extended set-up a **4**-*valuation* and denote it with v. Thus, for any formula α and set-up s, the valuation $v(\alpha)$ is always well-defined. This makes Belnap's semantic somewhat different from the classical semantics, because the notion of a model, that is, a valuation that makes a formula true, does not exist. This will have implications for the definition of our revision operation, as we shall see later.

The notion of semantic entailment is then expressed in terms of a partial ordering $\preceq$ associated with the logical lattice **L4**. We will denote the semantic entailment relation with $\Rightarrow$ to distinguish it from the proof-theoretical notion of entailment $\rightarrow$. The two notions are equivalent, as given by the correspondence 7.8, and the symbols $\rightarrow$ and $\Rightarrow$ will be often used interchangeably.

Definition 7.33. Let α and β be wffs. We say that α *entails* β, in symbols, $\alpha \Rightarrow \beta$, if for all **4**-valuations v, $v(\alpha) \preceq v(\beta)$, where $\preceq$ is the partial ordering associated with the lattice **L4**. Analogously, a *non-empty* finite set of formulae Γ *entails* α if the conjunction of all formulae in Γ entails α.

(Correspondence)

(7.8) $\alpha \to \beta$ iff $\alpha \Rightarrow \beta$

Notice that if we restrict our attention to valuations into $\{F, T\}$ only, we get the familiar classic logic notions. We need a parallel to the notion of consistency. This would be *acceptability*, as previously discussed. We say that a theory Δ is *acceptable* if for any wff α, Δ does not prove both α and $\neg\alpha$. This is *our* particular definition for the purposes of this presentation (it is reasonable enough). A consistent (acceptable) theory can tell us that a given formula α is true (T) or false (F) or that its truth-value is unknown (None), but if it says that it is both true and false (Both), then something in the knowledge about α went wrong.

Definition 7.34 (Acceptability of Belnap theories). A theory Δ is *acceptable* if

$$\{\gamma \mid \Delta \to \gamma \text{ and } \Delta \to \neg\gamma\} = \varnothing$$

Note that we do not have that if Δ is not acceptable, then it can prove everything. We now introduce some terminology which will be used throughout the rest of the chapter.

Definition 7.35. Let α be a formula and v a **4**-valuation. We say that α is

- *at least true* under v if $v(\alpha) = T$ or $v(\alpha) = $ Both.
- *at least false* under v if $v(\alpha) = F$ or $v(\alpha) = $ Both.
- *not true* under v if $v(\alpha) = F$ or $v(\alpha) = $ None.
- *not false* under v if $v(\alpha) = T$ or $v(\alpha) = $ None.

Using the above terminology, the notion of semantic entailment between a theory and a formula given in Definition 7.33 can be equivalently expressed as follows.

Definition 7.36. Let Γ be a set of Belnap formulae and α a Belnap formula. Γ entails α if and only if for every **4**-valuation v,

i) if all the formulae in Γ are at least true under v, then α is at least true under v;
ii) if all the formulae in Γ are not false under v, then α is not false under v.

This definition will play an important role in the soundness and completeness proofs of the translation of Belnap theories into first-order logic with respect to the semantics of Belnap's logic.

7.6.3 Generalising Belnap's Notion of Entailment to Infinite Theories

In Belnap's logic the truth-value of a conjunction of formulae is defined inductively from the truth-values of the subformulae. Alternatively, the truth-value can be calculated by taking the meet of the truth-values of the subformulae in **L4**. In that sense, finite sets of formulae and conjunctions behave in the same way. However, the notion of meet is more general, because it can be applied to an infinite set of truth-values.

Notice that belief revision is an operation from belief sets and formulae to belief sets, and a belief set is a set of formulae closed under a consequence relation. When performing the revision in the translation of a Belnap formula to classical logic, we do not have to start with the closure of that formula under Belnap's consequence relation because our axiomatisation already takes care of the missing consequences (in classical logic). However, after we perform the revision in classical logic, we are left with a belief set, as required by $(K^\circ 1)$. This is an *infinite* set of formulae. When we translate back to the language of Belnap's logic, we get an infinite set of formulae. In order to analyse the resulting operation under Belnap's logic's perspective, we need to ensure that the logic's notion of entailment $(\rightarrow)$ behaves well with infinite theories. This is what we show in this section.

Since the evaluation of $\wedge$ and meet in **L4** coincide in Belnap's four-valued logic, this will be our starting point.

Definition 7.37. Let Δ be a (possibly infinite) set of formulae, **S** be the set of all set-ups and s be an arbitrary set-up. We define $val : \mathbf{S} \times \mathscr{P}(\text{wff}_{\mathscr{L}_B}) \longmapsto \mathbf{4}$ as[8]

$$val(s, \Delta) = \sqcap\{s(\varphi) | \varphi \in \Delta\}$$

We now generalise the notion of entailment in Belnap's four-valued logic:

Definition 7.38. Let Δ be a (possibly infinite) set of formulae and φ a formula.

$$\Delta \rightarrow \varphi \text{ iff } \forall s \, [val(s, \Delta) \preceq s(\varphi)]$$

In the finite case, the above definition corresponds to the original notion of entailment in Belnap's logic.

Proposition 7.1. *Let Δ be a finite set of formulae and $\delta = \bigwedge_{\beta_i \in \Delta} \beta_i$. $val(s, \Delta) = s(\delta)$.*

Proof. The proof is by induction on the size of Δ.
Base case: $|\Delta| = 1$. $\Delta = \{\delta'\}$ *for some* δ'. $val(s, \Delta) = \sqcap\{s(\delta')\}$. *By the definition of $\sqcap$,* $val(s, \Delta) = s(\delta') = s(\delta)$.
Inductive Step: *The proposition holds for any Γ such that $|\Gamma| \leq k$. Now, suppose that $|\Delta| = k+1$. $\Delta = \Gamma \cup \{\beta\}$ for some Γ of cardinality k. Let $\gamma = \bigwedge_{\gamma_i \in \Gamma} \gamma_i$. It follows that $val(s, \Delta) = \sqcap\{s(\delta_i) \mid \delta_i \in \Delta\} = val(s, \Gamma) \sqcap s(\beta)$, by the distributivity property of $\sqcap$. By the induction hypothesis, $val(s, \Gamma) = s(\gamma)$. Thus, $val(s, \Delta) = s(\gamma) \sqcap s(\beta) = s(\gamma \wedge \beta) = s(\delta)$, by associativity and distributivity of $\wedge$.*

Corollary 7.1. *Let Δ be a finite set of formulae, φ be a formula and $\delta = \bigwedge_{\beta_i \in \Delta} \beta_i$. $val(s, \Delta) \preceq s(\varphi)$ iff $s(\delta) \preceq s(\varphi)$.*

The extended definition of entailment satisfies the finiteness property, as shown in Theorem 7.2. The proof of this property uses the definitions and theorem that follow.

---

[8] $\mathscr{P}(\text{wff}_{\mathscr{L}_B})$ is the power set of the set of all well-formed formulae in $\mathscr{L}_B$.

Definition 7.39 (Ultra set-up). Let I be a non-empty set, D be an ultrafilter over I and s_i be a set-up for $\mathscr{L}_B$ for each $i \in I$. $S = \Pi_D s_i$ is a function $S : \mathscr{P}_B \longmapsto \mathbf{4}$ defined as follows. For each $p \in \mathscr{P}_B$, $S(p) = u$ iff $\{i \in I \mid s_i(p) = u\} \in D$.

The definition above is extended to complex formulae in the usual way, using the truth-tables given in Figure 7.3. For example, $S(\alpha \wedge \beta) = S(\alpha) \wedge S(\beta)$. It is useful to refer to the particular value of y assigned to formulae by the function S above. The following theorem shows that an ultra set-up as defined above is indeed a **4**-valuation as defined before.

Theorem 7.1 (The fundamental theorem). *For each $\alpha \in \mathscr{L}_B$, $S(\alpha) = u$ iff $\{i \in I \mid s_i(\alpha) = u\} \in D$.*

Proof. The proof is by induction on the complexity of α.
("Only if") The base case follows directly from Definition 7.39.
Assume that the theorem holds for any formula β with at most k connectives. Inductive step: The proof is done by cases on the main connective of α.

($\neg$) α is of the form $\neg\beta$ for some β. Let $S(\neg\beta) = u$ for some u. By the definition of S, $S(\neg\beta) = \neg S(\beta) = \neg u_1$ for some $u_1 = S(\beta)$. Notice that, by the inductive hypothesis, the set $N = \{n \mid s_n(\beta) = u_1\} \in D$. We show that the set $M = \{m \mid s_m(\neg\beta) = u\} = N$, and therefore $M \in D$. Let $k \in M$. Then, $s_k(\neg\beta) = \neg s_k(\beta) = \neg u_2$, for some u_2. By the definition of $\neg$, $\neg u_1 = \neg u_2$ implies that $u_1 = u_2$. Therefore, $k \in N$. Let $k \in N$. Then, $s_k(\beta) = u_1$. By definition of $\neg$, $s_k(\neg\beta) = \neg s_k(\beta) = \neg u_1 = u$. Hence, $k \in M$.

($\wedge$) α is of the form $\beta_1 \wedge \beta_2$ for some β_1 and β_2. Let $S(\alpha) = u$. By definition of S, $u = S(\beta_1) \wedge S(\beta_2)$. Suppose $S(\beta_1) = u_1$ and $S(\beta_2) = u_2$. By inductive hypothesis, $N_1 = \{n \mid s_n(\beta_1) = u_1\} \in D$ and $N_2 = \{n; \mid s_n(\beta_2) = u_2\} \in D$. Since D is a filter, the intersection $N_1 \cap N_2 \in D$. Hence, the set $K = \{k \mid s_k(\beta_1) = u_1$ and $s_k(\beta_2) = u_2\} \in D$. We show that $M = \{m \mid s_m(\beta_1 \wedge \beta_2) = u_1 \wedge u_2\} \in D$. We prove this by showing that $M = K$. Let $m \in M$. Thus, $s_m(\beta_1 \wedge \beta_2) = u_1 \wedge u_2$. By definition of $\wedge$, $s_m(\beta_1 \wedge \beta_2) = s_m(\beta_1) \wedge s_m(\beta_2)$, and therefore $s_m(\beta_1) = u_1$ and $s_m(\beta_2) = u_2$. Then, $s_m \in N_1$ and $s_m \in N_2$, and hence $s_m \in K$. Assume that $k \in K$. By definition of K, $s_k(\beta_1) = u_1$ and $s_k(\beta_2) = u_2$. By definition of $\wedge$, $s_k(\beta_1 \wedge \beta_2) = u_1 \wedge u_2$. Hence, $k \in M$.

($\vee$) The proof is analogous to the previous case.

("If") The base case also follows directly from Definition 7.39.
Assume that the theorem holds for any formula β with at most k connectives. Inductive step: The proof is done by cases on the main connective of α.

($\neg$) α is of the form $\neg\beta$ for some β. Let u be such that the set $N = \{n \mid s_n(\neg\beta) = u\} \in D$. By definition of $\neg$, the set $\{n \mid \neg s_n(\beta) = u\} \in D$. We show that the set $M = \{m \mid s_m(\beta) = \neg u\} \in D$. Suppose that $M \notin D$. By the property of the ultrafilter, the complement set $\{k \mid s_k(\beta) \neq \neg u\} \in D$. By definition of neg, the set $\{k \mid \neg s_k(\beta) \neq \neg\neg u\} \in D$.[9] Therefore, the set $\{k \mid s_k(\neg\beta) \neq u\} \in D$, which is a contradiction since its complement belongs to D.

---

[9] Note that for any $x \in \mathbf{4}$, $\neg\neg x = x$.

($\wedge$) α is of the form $\beta_1 \wedge \beta_2$ for some β_1 and β_2. Let u be such that the set $N = \{n \mid s_n(\beta_1 \wedge \beta_2) = u\} \in D$. Let u_1 and u_2 be such that $M_1 = \{n \mid s_n(\beta_1) = u_1\} \in D$ and $M_2 = \{n \mid s_n(\beta_2) = u_2\} \in D$. By the inductive hypothesis, $S(\beta_1) = u_1$ and the $S(\beta_2) = u_2$, which implies that $S(\alpha) = u_1 \wedge u_2$. Furthermore, since D is a filter, the set $\{n \mid s_n(\beta_1) = u_1$ and $s_n(\beta_2) = u_2\} \in D$. Therefore, the set $\{n \mid s_n(\beta_1 \wedge \beta_2) = u_1 \wedge u_2\} \in D$. Suppose that $u_1 \wedge u_2 \neq u$. Then, by the property of the ultrafilter the complement $\{n \mid s_n(\beta_1 \wedge \beta_2) \neq u_1 \wedge u_2\} \notin D$, and hence $N \notin D$, which is a contradiction. Therefore, $S(\alpha) = u_1 \wedge u_2 = u$.

($\vee$) The proof is analogous to that of the previous case.

Proposition 7.2. Let s be a set-up and Δ an infinite set of formulae. There exists $\Delta_n \subset \Delta$, Δ_n finite, such that for all $\Delta_m \supseteq \Delta_n, s(\Delta_m) = s(\Delta_n)$.

Proof. Suppose that for all Δ_n, there exists $\Delta_m \supseteq \Delta_n$ such that $s(\Delta_m) \neq s(\Delta_n)$. Since $s(\Delta_m) \leq s_m(\Delta_n)$, it follows that $s(\Delta_m) < s(\Delta_n)$. This will lead to an infinite (strict) descending sequence of values in **4**, which is a contradiction, since **4** is finite.

Theorem 7.2 (Finiteness). Let Δ be an infinite theory in Belnap's four-valued logic and φ be a wff. If $\Delta \Rightarrow \varphi$, then there exists $\Delta' \subset \Delta$ s.t. Δ' is finite and $\Delta' \Rightarrow \varphi$.

Proof. By contrapositive. We assume that

(7.9) for all finite $\Delta' \subset \Delta$, $\Delta' \not\Rightarrow \varphi$.

and show that $\Delta \not\Rightarrow \varphi$. By the definition of $\Rightarrow$ and (7.9), we get that $\forall \Delta_i \subset \Delta$; there exists s_i, such that $s_i(\Delta_i) \not\leq s_i(\varphi)$.

  Let $\delta_0, \delta_1, \ldots$ be an enumeration of all formulae in Δ, and I be an index set constructed as follows: $I = \{\Delta_0, \Delta_1, \ldots, \Delta_n, \ldots\}$, where $\Delta_i = \{\delta_0, \ldots, \delta_i\}$. Let D be an ultrafilter over I, defined as $\{\hat{\Delta}_0, \hat{\Delta}_1, \ldots\}$, where $\hat{\Delta}_j = \{\Delta_i \mid i \geq j\}$. Consider the ultraproduct $S = \Pi_D s_i$. By Theorem 7.1, S behaves exactly as a normal set-up, and hence, for any formula α, $S(\alpha) = u_\alpha$ iff $\{m \mid s_m(\alpha) = u_\alpha\} \in D$.

  We show that

(7.10) for all $\Delta' \subset \Delta$, Δ' finite, $S(\Delta') \not\leq S(\varphi)$.

Suppose $\exists \Delta_n \subset \Delta$ s.t. $S(\Delta_n) \leq S(\varphi)$. Let $S(\Delta_n) = u_n$ for some u_n, and $S(\varphi) = f$ for some f. By the definition of S, $N = \{j \mid s_j(\Delta_n) = u_n\} \in D$ and $F = \{k \mid s_k(\varphi) = f\} \in D$. By construction of D, the set $\hat{\Delta}_n = \{i \mid i \geq j\} \in D$, and therefore the set $M = N \cap \hat{\Delta}_n = \{m \mid m \geq j$ and $s_m(\Delta_n) = u_n\} \in D$. Notice that $\Delta_m \supset \Delta_n$ for all $m \in M$, and therefore $s_m(\Delta_m) \leq s_m(\Delta_n)$.

  Consider the set $F \cap M$. Since D is a filter, $F \cap M = \{h \mid s_h(\varphi) = f$ and $s_h(\Delta_n) = u_n\} \in D$. In particular, by the construction of the ultraproduct,

(i) $s_h(\Delta_h) \leq s_h(\Delta_n) = u_n \leq f$, and
(ii) $s_h(\Delta_h) \not\leq s_h(\varphi) = f$

which are in contradiction.

  By Proposition 7.2, there exists $\Delta_n \in I$, such that for all $m \geq n$, $S(\Delta_m) = x$ for a certain $x \in$ **4**. Therefore, $S(\Delta) = x$, and by (7.10), $x \not\leq f$. Hence, we have constructed a set-up S such that $S(\Delta) \not\leq S(\varphi)$, which contradicts the initial hypothesis.

7.6.4 Translating Belnap's Logic into Classical Logic

In this section, we describe our translation approach for Belnap's four-valued logic into first-order logic and show that it is sound and complete with respect to Belnap's semantic notion of entailment. Let $\mathscr{L}$ be a two-sorted first-order logic language composed of the sort $\mathscr{F}$, called *B-formulae*, and the sort $\mathscr{V}$, called *truth-values*.

The set of constants of $\mathscr{F}$ is the set of propositional symbols of $\mathscr{L}_B$, whereas the terms of $\mathscr{F}$ are constructed using three main functions $\neg$, $\wedge$, and $\vee$, which correspond to the connectives in $\mathscr{L}_B$. The set of ground terms of $\mathscr{F}$ is thus equal to the set of wffs in $\mathscr{L}_B$. The sort $\mathscr{V}$ is instead composed of two constant symbols $\{tt, ff\}$, the basic constants from which Belnap's four-valued semantics can be constructed. $\mathscr{L}$ also contains the two-sorted binary predicate *holds*, which takes as first arguments $\mathscr{F}$-terms, and as second arguments $\mathscr{V}$-terms. $\mathscr{F}$ variables will be denoted by x, y, z, etc. First-order formulae are constructed in the usual way.

Ground atomic formulae can be of two types, $holds(\varphi, tt)$ and $holds(\psi, ff)$, for any wffs φ and ψ in $\mathscr{L}_B$. Atomic formulae of the first type mean that "$tt \in v(\varphi)$" for some **4**-valuation v, which is equivalent to saying that, for some **4**-valuation, φ is at least true. Atomic formulae of the second type state that "$ff \in v(\psi)$" for some **4**-valuation v, which is equivalent to saying that, for some **4**-valuation, ψ is at least false. With these two types of atomic formulae it is possible to express Belnap's full four-valued semantics. For example, to say that a formula α has value Both under some **4**-valuation v, we can write $holds(\alpha, tt) \wedge holds(\alpha, ff)$.

The semantical behaviour of the connectives of Belnap's logic is fully captured by the following first-order axiomatisation.

Definition 7.40. Given the two languages $\mathscr{L}_B$ and $\mathscr{L}$, $\mathscr{A}_B$ is the following first-order axiomatisation of Belnap's four-valued semantics:

$$\forall x[holds(x, ff) \leftrightarrow holds(\neg x, tt)] \tag{Ax 1}$$
$$\forall x[holds(x, tt) \leftrightarrow holds(\neg x, ff)] \tag{Ax 2}$$
$$\forall x, y[holds(x \wedge y, tt) \leftrightarrow (holds(x, tt) \wedge holds(y, tt))] \tag{Ax 3}$$
$$\forall x, y[holds(x \wedge y, ff) \leftrightarrow (holds(x, ff) \vee holds(y, ff))] \tag{Ax 4}$$
$$\forall x, y[holds(x \vee y, tt) \leftrightarrow (holds(x, tt) \vee holds(y, tt))] \tag{Ax 5}$$
$$\forall x, y[holds(x \vee y, ff) \leftrightarrow (holds(x, ff) \wedge holds(y, ff))] \tag{Ax 6}$$

The *translation function* τ is a mapping from the set of wffs in $\mathscr{L}_B$ to the set of ground atomic first-order formulae of the form $holds(\varphi, tt)$. For a given formula φ, its first-order logic translation, denoted by $\tau(\varphi)$ (or simply φ^τ), is the atomic formula $holds(\varphi, tt)$. Theories of Belnap's logic are translated into a classical theory whose (first-order logic atomic) formulae are the translation of the formulae included in the theory. In the specific case of finite theories (i.e., finite sets of Belnap's formulae), the translation can equivalently be given by the translation of the conjunction of all the formulae included in the theory.

We are now going to show that the above translation function together with the axiomatisation $\mathscr{A}_B$ is sound and complete with respect to the semantic notion of entailment of **L**.

Theorem 7.3 (Correspondence). *Let ψ and φ be two Belnap formulae.*

$$\psi \to \varphi \text{ iff } \mathscr{A}_B, holds(\psi, \mathsf{tt}) \vdash holds(\varphi, \mathsf{tt}) \text{ and}$$
$$\mathscr{A}_B, \neg holds(\psi, \mathsf{ff}) \vdash \neg holds(\varphi, \mathsf{ff}).$$

The above statement captures, in first-order terms, the notion of entailment given in Definition 7.36 whenever ψ is of the form $\alpha_1 \wedge \ldots \wedge \alpha_n$, with $\{\alpha_1, \ldots, \alpha_n\}$ being a Belnap theory. More specifically, for the first conjunct of the statement, the assumption $holds(\psi, \mathsf{tt})$ is equivalent, by axiom (Ax 3), to $holds(\alpha_1, \mathsf{tt}) \wedge \ldots \wedge holds(\alpha_n, \mathsf{tt})$, which can be read as "all α_i, for each $1 \leq i \leq n$, are at least true". The consequence $holds(\varphi, \mathsf{tt})$ can also be read as φ is at least true. Analogously, for the second conjunct in the statement, the assumption $\neg holds(\psi, \mathsf{ff})$ is equivalent, by axiom (Ax 4), to $\neg holds(\alpha_1, \mathsf{ff}) \wedge \ldots \wedge \neg holds(\alpha_n, \mathsf{ff})$, where each $\neg holds(\alpha_i, \mathsf{ff})$ can be read as "α_i is not false".

The proof of the "if part" of Theorem 7.3 is given by Lemma 7.16, whereas the proof of the "only-if" part is given by Lemma 7.15.

Lemma 7.15 (Completeness). *Let ψ and φ be two formulae of $\mathscr{L}_B$. If $\psi \to \varphi$, then $\mathscr{A}_B, holds(\psi, \mathsf{tt}) \vdash holds(\varphi, \mathsf{tt})$ and $\mathscr{A}_B, \neg holds(\psi, \mathsf{ff}) \vdash \neg holds(\varphi, \mathsf{ff})$.*

Proof. The proof is done by induction on the length n of the derivation $\psi \to \varphi$.
Base case: $n = 0$. Then, $\psi \to \varphi$ can only be an instantiation of one of the axioms 1–10 given in Definition 7.32. The proof is therefore by cases on each of these axioms. Only the most interesting cases are shown here. The remaining ones are proved following the same type of argument.

$\dfrac{\mathscr{A}_B, holds(\alpha_1 \wedge \ldots \wedge \alpha_h, \mathsf{tt})}{}$	(Ax 3)
$\dfrac{holds(\alpha_1, \mathsf{tt}) \wedge \ldots \wedge holds(\alpha_h, \mathsf{tt})}{}$	$(\mathscr{E}\wedge)$
$\dfrac{holds(\alpha_i, \mathsf{tt})}{}$	(equiv. rewriting)
$\dfrac{holds(\beta_j, \mathsf{tt})}{}$	$(\mathscr{I}\vee)$
$\dfrac{holds(\beta_1, \mathsf{tt}) \vee \ldots \vee holds(\beta_k, \mathsf{tt})}{}$	(Ax 5)
$holds(\beta_1 \vee \ldots \vee \beta_k, \mathsf{tt})$	

Fig. 7.5 First-order proof of Belnap axiom 10

Case 1: *$\psi \to \varphi$ is an instantiation of $\alpha_1 \wedge \ldots \wedge \alpha_h \to \beta_1 \vee \ldots \vee \beta_k$ for some h and k such that $\alpha_i = \beta_j$ for some i and j. We show in Figure 7.5 that $\mathscr{A}_B, holds(\alpha_1 \wedge \ldots \wedge \alpha_h, \mathsf{tt}) \vdash holds(\beta_1 \vee \ldots \vee \beta_k, \mathsf{tt})$, and in Figure 7.6 that $\mathscr{A}_B, \neg holds(\alpha_1 \wedge \ldots \wedge \alpha_h, \mathsf{ff}) \vdash \neg holds(\beta_1 \vee \ldots \vee \beta_k, \mathsf{ff})$.*

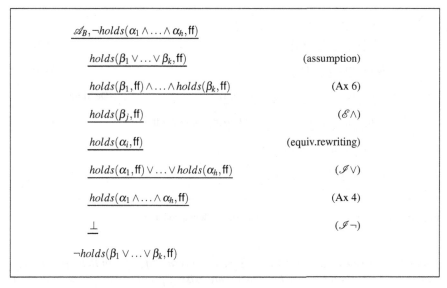

Fig. 7.6 First-order proof of Belnap axiom 10

$$\mathscr{A}_B, \neg holds(\alpha \vee (\beta \wedge \gamma), \mathsf{ff}) \qquad \text{(Ax 6)}$$

$$\neg holds(\alpha, \mathsf{ff}) \vee \neg holds(\beta \wedge \gamma, \mathsf{ff}) \qquad \text{(Ax 4)}$$

$$\neg holds(\alpha, \mathsf{ff}) \vee (\neg holds(\beta, \mathsf{ff}) \wedge \neg holds(\gamma, \mathsf{ff})) \qquad \text{(De Morgan Law)}$$

$$(\neg holds(\alpha, \mathsf{ff}) \vee \neg holds(\beta, \mathsf{ff})) \wedge (\neg holds(\alpha, \mathsf{ff}) \vee \neg holds(\gamma, \mathsf{ff})) \qquad \text{(Ax 6)}$$

$$\neg holds(\alpha \vee \beta, \mathsf{ff}) \wedge \neg holds(\alpha \vee \gamma, \mathsf{ff}) \qquad \text{(Ax 4)}$$

$$\neg holds((\alpha \vee \beta) \wedge (\alpha \vee \gamma), \mathsf{ff})$$

Fig. 7.7 First-order proof of the left-to-right part of Belnap axiom 6

Case 2: $\psi \rightarrow \varphi$ *is an instantiation of* $\alpha \vee (\beta \wedge \gamma) \rightarrow (\alpha \vee \beta) \wedge (\alpha \wedge \gamma)$. *We show in Figure 7.8 that* $\mathscr{A}_B, holds(\alpha \vee (\beta \wedge \gamma), \mathsf{tt}) \rightarrow holds((\alpha \vee \beta) \wedge (\alpha \wedge \gamma), \mathsf{tt})$, *and in Figure 7.7 that* $\mathscr{A}_B, \neg holds(\alpha \vee (\beta \wedge \gamma), \mathsf{ff}) \rightarrow \neg holds((\alpha \vee \beta) \wedge (\alpha \vee \gamma), \mathsf{ff})$. *A similar argument is applied in the case where* $\psi \rightarrow \varphi$ *is an instantiation of* $(\alpha \vee \beta) \wedge (\alpha \wedge \gamma) \rightarrow \alpha \vee (\beta \wedge \gamma)$.

Inductive Step: We assume that there exists a first part of a derivation proving an expression of the form $\alpha \rightarrow \beta$ *with* $n-1$ *applications of Belnap rules, and that the* nth *application of a Belnap rule gives us the expression* $\psi \rightarrow \varphi$. *We reason by cases on each Belnap rule that could have been applied on this* nth *step.*

$$\underline{\mathscr{A}_B, holds(\alpha \vee (\beta \wedge \gamma), \mathsf{tt})} \hspace{4cm} \text{(Ax 5)}$$

$$\underline{holds(\alpha, \mathsf{tt}) \vee holds(\beta \wedge \gamma, \mathsf{tt})} \hspace{3.5cm} \text{(Ax 3)}$$

$$\underline{holds(\alpha, \mathsf{tt}) \vee (holds(\beta, \mathsf{tt}) \wedge holds(\gamma, \mathsf{tt}))} \hspace{2cm} \text{(De Morgan Law)}$$

$$\underline{(holds(\alpha, \mathsf{tt}) \vee holds(\beta, \mathsf{tt})) \wedge (holds(\alpha, \mathsf{tt}) \vee holds(\gamma, \mathsf{tt}))} \hspace{1.5cm} \text{(Ax 5)}$$

$$\underline{holds(\alpha \vee \beta, \mathsf{tt}) \wedge holds(\alpha \vee \gamma, \mathsf{tt})} \hspace{3cm} \text{(Ax 3)}$$

$$holds((\alpha \vee \beta) \wedge (\alpha \vee \gamma), \mathsf{tt})$$

Fig. 7.8 First-order proof of the left-to-right part of Belnap axiom 6

Case 1: *We assume that the last rule application is the "if part" of Belnap rule 13 in Definition 7.32. Therefore, we have that there exists a proof of $\neg\varphi \to \neg\psi$, with $n-1$ rule applications. So, by inductive hypothesis we can say that $\mathscr{A}_B, holds(\neg\varphi, \mathsf{tt}) \vdash holds(\neg\psi, \mathsf{tt})$ and that $\mathscr{A}_B, \neg holds(\neg\varphi, \mathsf{ff}) \vdash \neg holds(\neg\psi, \mathsf{ff})$. We want then to show that*

$$\mathscr{A}_B, holds(\psi, \mathsf{tt}) \vdash holds(\varphi, \mathsf{tt})$$

and that

$$\mathscr{A}_B, \neg holds(\psi, \mathsf{ff}) \vdash \neg holds(\varphi, \mathsf{ff}).$$

From the inductive hypothesis $\mathscr{A}_B, \neg holds(\neg\varphi, \mathsf{ff}) \vdash \neg holds(\neg\psi, \mathsf{ff})$, we get, by the contrapositive of classical logic, that

$$\mathscr{A}_B, holds(\neg\psi, \mathsf{ff}) \vdash holds(\neg\varphi, \mathsf{ff})$$

Hence, using Belnap axiom 2, we get $\mathscr{A}_B, holds(\psi, \mathsf{tt}) \vdash holds(\varphi, \mathsf{tt})$. To show that $\mathscr{A}_B, \neg holds(\psi, \mathsf{ff}) \vdash \neg holds(\varphi, \mathsf{ff})$ we consider the second part of the inductive hypothesis. $\mathscr{A}_B, holds(\neg\varphi, \mathsf{tt}) \vdash holds(\neg\psi, \mathsf{tt})$ gives, by contrapositive of classical logic, that

$$\mathscr{A}_B, \neg holds(\neg\psi, \mathsf{tt}) \vdash \neg holds(\neg\varphi, \mathsf{tt}).$$

Hence, by Belnap axiom 1, $\mathscr{A}_B, \neg holds(\psi, \mathsf{ff}) \vdash \neg holds(\varphi, \mathsf{ff})$. The case for the "only if part" of Belnap rule 13 follows the same argument.

Case 2: *We assume that last rule application is the "if part" of Belnap rule 15 in Definition 7.32. Therefore, we have there exists a proof of $\alpha \to \beta$ with $n-1$ rule applications, where ψ is equal to α and φ is equal to $\alpha \vee \beta$. So, by inductive hypothesis, $\mathscr{A}_B, holds(\alpha, \mathsf{tt}) \vdash holds(\beta, \mathsf{tt})$ and $\mathscr{A}_B, \neg holds(\alpha, \mathsf{ff}) \vdash \neg holds(\beta, \mathsf{ff})$. We want to show that*

1. *$\mathscr{A}_B, holds(\beta, \mathsf{tt}) \vdash holds(\alpha \vee \beta, \mathsf{tt})$ and*
   $\mathscr{A}_B, holds(\alpha \vee \beta, \mathsf{tt}) \vdash holds(\beta, \mathsf{tt})$

2. $\mathscr{A}_B, \neg holds(\beta, \text{ff}) \vdash \neg holds(\alpha \vee \beta, \text{ff})$ and
   $\mathscr{A}_B, \neg holds(\alpha \vee \beta, \text{ff}) \vdash \neg holds(\beta, \text{ff})$.

The first part of (1) is quite straightforward. We show the second part. Assume
$\mathscr{A}_B, holds(\alpha \vee \beta, \text{tt})$. *By axiom (Ax 5) and reflexivity of classical logic,* $\mathscr{A}_B, holds(\alpha \vee$
$\beta, \text{tt}) \vdash \mathscr{A}_B, holds(\alpha, \text{tt}) \vee holds(\beta, \text{tt})$. *By inductive hypothesis,* $\mathscr{A}_B, holds(\alpha, \text{tt}) \vdash$
$holds(\beta, \text{tt})$, *and by reflexivity of classical logic*

$$\mathscr{A}_B, holds(\beta, \text{tt}) \vdash holds(\beta, \text{tt}).$$

Therefore, using classical $\vee$*-introduction rule,*

$$\mathscr{A}_B, holds(\alpha, \text{tt}) \vee holds(\beta, \text{tt}) \vdash holds(\beta, \text{tt}).$$

Hence, $\mathscr{A}_B, holds(\alpha \vee \beta, \text{tt}) \vdash holds(\beta, \text{tt})$. *The proof for (2) follows the same argument.*

All the other cases can be easily proved using appropriate properties and rules of classical logic and, if necessary, the Belnap axioms.

The soundness of the translation to classical logic is based on the idea that for any given **4**-valuation it is always possible to construct a classical interpretation I which satisfies the axioms $\mathscr{A}_B$ and which preserves Belnap's semantic notion of entailment. We first show how such a classical interpretation can be constructed and the properties it has.

Definition 7.41. Let v be a **4**-valuation from the set of wffs in $\mathscr{L}_B$ to the power set $\wp(\{\text{tt}, \text{ff}\})$. A classical interpretation *associated* with v, and denoted by $\mathscr{I}_v$, is a function defined as follows

- $\Phi(\text{tt}) = \text{tt}$ and $\Phi(\text{ff}) = \text{ff}$.

Also, for each ground term α of sort $\mathscr{F}$:

- $\Phi(\alpha) = \alpha$ for each ground term α of sort $\mathscr{F}$.
- $\Phi(holds) = \{\langle \alpha, \text{tt} \rangle \mid \text{tt} \in v(\alpha)\} \cup \{\langle \alpha, \text{ff} \rangle \mid \text{ff} \in v(\alpha))\}$

It is easy to show, by the definition of Φ, that the following properties hold for any formula α in $\mathscr{L}_B$ and **4**-valuation v.

- $v(\alpha) = \text{T}$ if and only if $\Phi \models holds(\alpha, \text{tt}) \wedge \neg holds(\alpha, \text{ff})$
- $v(\alpha) = \text{F}$ if and only if $\Phi \models holds(\alpha, \text{ff}) \wedge \neg holds(\alpha, \text{tt})$
- $v(\alpha) = \text{Both}$ if and only if $\Phi \models holds(\alpha, \text{tt}) \wedge holds(\alpha, \text{ff})$
- $v(\alpha) = \text{None}$ if and only if $\Phi \models \neg holds(\alpha, \text{tt}) \wedge \neg holds(\alpha, \text{ff})$

The following proposition shows that a classical interpretation Φ associated with a given **4**-valuation v is a model of the first-order axioms $\mathscr{A}_B$.

Proposition 7.3. *Let v be a 4-valuation and let Φ be its associated classical interpretation. Then Φ is a model of the classical axiomatisation $\mathscr{A}_B$.*

Proof. The proof is by cases of each axiom of $\mathscr{A}_B$.

Case 1: (Ax 1). *We want to show that $\Phi \models \forall x[holds(x, ff) \leftrightarrow holds(\neg x, tt)]$. We reason by contradiction. We assume that, for some x, $\Phi \models holds(x, ff)$ and $\Phi \not\models holds(\neg x, tt)$. By definition of Φ, $ff \in v(x)$, which implies by the $\neg$ truth table that $tt \in v(\neg x)$. Hence, $\Phi \models holds(\neg x, tt)$, which contradicts the hypothesis. Similarly for the other case, i.e., $\Phi \not\models holds(x, ff)$ and $\Phi \models holds(\neg x, tt)$.*

Case 3: (Ax 3). *We want to show that $\Phi \models \forall x, y[holds(x \wedge y, tt) \leftrightarrow (holds(x, tt) \wedge holds(y, tt))]$. We reason by contradiction. Assume that, for some x, $\Phi \models holds(x \wedge y, tt)$, and $\Phi \not\models holds(x, tt)$ or $\Phi \not\models holds(y, tt)$. By definition of Φ, $tt \in v(x \wedge y)$, which implies by the $\wedge$ truth table that $tt \in v(x)$ and $tt \in v(y)$. Therefore, $\Phi \models holds(x, tt)$ and $\Phi \models holds(y, tt)$, which is in contradiction with the initial hypothesis. The second case, i.e., assume that, for some x, $\Phi \not\models holds(x \wedge y, tt)$, and $\Phi \models holds(x, tt)$ and $\Phi \models holds(y, tt)$, can be proved following the same argument.*

Case 5: (Ax 5). *We want to show that $\Phi \models \forall x, y[holds(x \vee y, tt) \leftrightarrow (holds(x, tt) \vee holds(y, tt))]$. We reason by contradiction. Assume that, for some x, $\Phi \models holds(x \vee y, tt)$, and $\Phi \not\models holds(x, tt)$ and $\Phi \not\models holds(y, tt)$. By definition of Φ, $tt \in v(x \vee y)$, which implies by the $\vee$ truth table that $tt \in v(x)$ or $tt \in v(y)$. Therefore, $\Phi \models holds(x, tt)$ or $\Phi \models holds(y, tt)$, which is in contradiction with the initial hypothesis. The second case, i.e. assume that, for some x, $\Phi \not\models holds(x \vee y, tt)$, and $\Phi \models holds(x, tt)$ or $\Phi \models holds(y, tt)$, can be proved following the same argument.*

Axioms 2, 4 and 6 are proved in a way analogous to that of the proofs of Axioms 1, 3 and 5, respectively.

Lemma 7.16 (Soundness). *Let ψ and φ be two Belnap formulae. If $\mathscr{A}_B, holds(\psi, tt) \vdash holds(\varphi, tt)$ and $\mathscr{A}_B, \neg holds(\psi, ff) \vdash \neg holds(\varphi, ff)$, then $\psi \rightarrow \varphi$.*

*Proof. We prove the contrapositive statement. We assume that $\psi \not\rightarrow \varphi$ and we want to show that either $\mathscr{A}_B, holds(\psi, tt) \not\vdash holds(\varphi, tt)$ or $\mathscr{A}_B, \neg holds(\psi, ff) \not\vdash \neg holds(\varphi, ff)$. The hypothesis $\psi \not\rightarrow \varphi$ implies different possibilities of truth values for ψ and φ according to the ordering relation $\preceq$ over the logical lattice **L4**. We consider these cases individually. $\psi \not\rightarrow \varphi$ implies that for some **4**-valuation v, $v(\psi) \not\preceq v(\varphi)$.*

Case 1: *$v(\psi) = T$ and $v(\varphi) = $ Both. From v, we can construct the associated classical interpretation Φ. By definition, $\Phi \models holds(\psi, tt)$ and $\Phi \models \neg holds(\psi, ff)$. But $\Phi \not\models \neg holds(\varphi, ff)$.*

Case 2: *$v(\psi) = T$ and $v(\varphi) = $ None. Then $tt \notin v(\varphi)$. From v, we can construct the associated classical interpretation Φ. By definition, $\Phi \models holds(\psi, tt)$ and $\Phi \models \neg holds(\psi, ff)$. But $\Phi \not\models holds(\varphi, tt)$.*

Case 3: *$v(\psi) = T$ and $v(\varphi) = F$. Then $tt \notin v(\varphi)$. From v, we can construct the associated classical interpretation Φ. By definition, $\Phi \models holds(\psi, tt)$ and $\Phi \models \neg holds(\psi, ff)$. But $\Phi \not\models holds(\varphi, tt)$.*

Case 4: $v(\psi) = None$ *and* $v(\varphi) = F.$ *Then* $\text{tt} \notin v(\psi)$, $\text{ff} \notin v(\psi)$ *and* $\text{tt} \notin v(\varphi)$. *From v, we can construct the associated classical interpretation* Φ. *By definition,* $\Phi \models \neg holds(\psi, \text{ff})$, *but* $\Phi \not\models \neg holds(\varphi, \text{ff})$.

Case 5: $v(\psi) = Both$ *and* $v(\varphi) = F.$ *Then* $\text{tt} \in v(\psi)$, $\text{ff} \in v(\psi)$ *and* $\text{tt} \notin v(\varphi)$. *From v, we can construct the associated classical interpretation* Φ. *By definition,* $\Phi \models holds(\psi, \text{tt})$, *but* $\Phi \not\models holds(\varphi, \text{tt})$.

7.6.5 Revising in Belnap's Four-Valued Logic

We are now in a position to illustrate our revision approach for non-classical logics with a different notion of consistency than that of classical logic by considering in detail the case of Belnap's four-valued logic. Part of our motivation here is to analyse the role inconsistency plays in the revision process.

We have already mentioned that the theory obtained through a revision operation is always consistent provided that the revising formula itself is not contradictory (see $(K°5)$). More importantly, if the current theory is consistent with the new formula, then no *true* revision is performed, i.e., the revision is equivalent to an expansion. This may cause problems if the notion of consistency of the object language differs significantly from that of classical logic. In such cases, we need to seek alternatives in order to *trigger* the revision process in the translation.

Our view is that one does not need to be limited to the notion of consistency in the object language, as long as some notion of *acceptability* of theories in the object language can be defined via axioms in classical logic.

We want to map the notion of acceptability given in Definition 7.34 to classical logic in such a way that the translation of *unacceptable* Belnap theories results in *inconsistent* classical logic theories, when a true revision can be performed. We also need to ensure that the acceptability notion is included in the revising part, so that, by $(K°2)$, the result of the revision will itself be *acceptable*, as long as the input formula itself is not unacceptable. Our notion of acceptability can be translated to classical logic in the following way:

Definition 7.42. Acceptability axiom for Belnap theories:

$$Acc = \forall \alpha [(holds(\alpha, \text{tt}) \wedge holds(\alpha, \text{ff})) \rightarrow \bot]$$

The coexistence of contradictory (Belnap) information will not be tolerated by the revision process. Propositions will be forced to have *at most* one of the truth-values tt and ff, and thus formulae with truth-value Both with be filtered out. To simplify notation, we use the following convention:

$$holds(\alpha, \text{tt}) = \alpha^+ \quad holds(\neg \alpha, \text{tt}) = \overline{\alpha}^+$$
$$holds(\alpha, \text{ff}) = \alpha^- \quad holds(\neg \alpha, \text{ff}) = \overline{\alpha}^-$$

Furthermore, we use $\neg \alpha^+$ for $\neg holds(\alpha, \text{tt})$, etc.

Belief revision for Belnap's four-valued logic is defined as follows:

Definition 7.43 (Belief revision for Belnap's four-valued logic). Let ψ and φ be two formulae of $\mathscr{L}_B$ and ψ^+ (ψ^-) and φ^+ (φ^-) be their translations to classical logic as described above, respectively. Let $\mathscr{A}_B$ be as in Definition 7.40 and Acc as in Definition 7.42. The revision of ψ by φ, in symbols, $\psi \circ_b \varphi$, is defined as

$$\psi \circ_b \varphi = \{\gamma \mid \psi^+ \circ_a (\varphi^+ \wedge \mathscr{A}_B \wedge Acc) \vdash \gamma^+ \text{ and } \neg\psi^- \circ_a (\neg\varphi^- \wedge \mathscr{A}_B \wedge Acc) \vdash \neg\gamma^-\}.$$

Motivation

Intuitively speaking, the positive *holds* checks the relevant part of one half of the lattice **L4**, i.e., Both and T, whereas the negative *holds* checks the other half, i.e., None and T. F need not be checked, since it is less than or equal any value in **L4**, and therefore cannot affect entailment.

Notice that, without Acc, the revision of ψ by φ is simply $\psi \wedge \varphi$. The correspondence axiom tells us that $\psi \wedge \varphi \rightarrow \gamma$ iff $\mathscr{A}_B \wedge (\psi \wedge \varphi)^+ \vdash \gamma^+$ and $\mathscr{A}_B \wedge \neg(\psi \wedge \varphi)^- \vdash \neg\gamma^-$. Since $\varphi^+ \wedge \mathscr{A}_B$ is consistent with ψ^+, $\psi^+ \circ_a (\varphi^+ \wedge \mathscr{A}_B)$ is just $\psi^+ \wedge \varphi^+ \wedge \mathscr{A}_B$ (the same as for the negative part). The revision then gives us all γ's such that $\psi^+ \wedge \varphi^+ \wedge \mathscr{A}_B \vdash \gamma^+$ and $\neg\psi^- \wedge \neg\varphi^- \wedge \mathscr{A}_B \vdash \neg\gamma^-$. Notice that in the presence of $\mathscr{A}_B$, $\psi^+ \wedge \varphi^+ \iff (\psi \wedge \varphi)^+$ and $\neg\psi^- \wedge \neg\varphi^- \iff \neg(\psi \wedge \varphi)^-$ (from (Ax 3) and (Ax 4), respectively). Therefore, we get all γs such that $\mathscr{A}_B \wedge (\psi \wedge \varphi)^+ \vdash \gamma^+$ and $\mathscr{A}_B \wedge \neg(\psi \wedge \varphi)^- \vdash \neg\gamma^-$, which is $\{\gamma \mid \psi \wedge \varphi \rightarrow \gamma\}$.

AGM postulates under Belnap's perspective

In this section, we analyse properties of the revision operator given in Definition 7.43 with respect to the AGM postulates.

(K°1) $\psi \circ_b \varphi$ is a belief set.

In our terms, this means that the set of Belnap formulae that we receive back from the revision process should be closed under $\rightarrow$. In other words, $\gamma \in \psi \circ_b \varphi$ iff $\psi \circ_b \varphi \rightarrow \gamma$. (only if) if $\gamma \in \psi \circ_b \varphi$, it follows by reflexivity of $\rightarrow$ that $\psi \circ_b \varphi \rightarrow \gamma$. (if) Suppose that $\psi \circ_b \varphi \rightarrow \gamma$; we need to show that $\gamma \in \psi \circ_b \varphi$. By the correspondence theorem, if $\psi \circ_b \varphi \rightarrow \gamma$, then $\{\mathscr{A}_B\} \cup \{\alpha^+ \mid \psi^+ \circ_a (\varphi^+ \wedge \mathscr{A}_B \wedge Acc) \vdash \alpha^+\} \vdash \gamma^+$ and $\{\mathscr{A}_B\} \cup \{\neg\alpha^- \mid \neg\psi^- \circ_a (\neg\varphi^- \wedge \mathscr{A}_B \wedge Acc) \vdash \neg\alpha^-\} \vdash \neg\gamma^-$

Notice that $\{\mathscr{A}_B\} \cup \{\alpha^+ \mid \psi^+ \circ_a (\varphi^+ \wedge \mathscr{A}_B \wedge Acc) \vdash \alpha^+\} \subseteq \psi^+ \circ_a (\varphi^+ \wedge \mathscr{A}_B \wedge Acc)$, since by (K°2), $\mathscr{A}_B \in \psi^+ \circ_a (\varphi^+ \wedge \mathscr{A}_B \wedge Acc)$ and by (K°1), $\psi^+ \circ_a (\varphi^+ \wedge \mathscr{A}_B \wedge Acc)$ is closed under classical logical consequence and hence contains all such α^+. By monotonicity of classical logic, it follows that $\psi^+ \circ_a (\varphi^+ \wedge \mathscr{A}_B \wedge Acc) \vdash \gamma^+$. By a similar argument, we can show that $\neg\psi^- \circ_a (\neg\varphi^- \wedge \mathscr{A}_B \wedge Acc) \vdash \neg\gamma^-$, and hence $\gamma \in \psi \circ_b \varphi$.

(K°2) $\varphi \in \psi \circ_b \varphi$.

Remember that by (K°2), $\varphi^+ \wedge \mathscr{A}_B \wedge Acc \in \psi^+ \circ_a (\varphi^+ \wedge \mathscr{A}_B \wedge Acc)$ and $\neg\varphi^- \wedge \mathscr{A}_B \wedge Acc \in \neg\psi^- \circ_a (\neg\varphi^- \wedge \mathscr{A}_B \wedge Acc)$. By (K°1), $\psi^+ \circ_a (\varphi^+ \wedge \mathscr{A}_B \wedge Acc) \vdash \varphi^+ \wedge$

$\mathscr{A}_B \wedge Acc$, and hence $\psi^+ \circ_a(\varphi^+ \wedge \mathscr{A}_B \wedge Acc) \vdash \varphi^+$. Similarly, $\neg\psi^- \circ_a(\neg\varphi^- \wedge \mathscr{A}_B \wedge Acc) \vdash \neg\varphi^-$. By Definition 7.43, $\varphi \in \psi \circ_b \varphi$.

We argued in Section 2.1, page 17, that for non-classical logics, the two postulates $(K^\circ 3)$ and $(K^\circ 4)$ are equivalent to the following postulate $(K^\circ_{3,4})$:

$(K^\circ_{3,4})$ If A is consistent with K, then $K \circ_a A = \mathrm{Cn}_b(K \cup \{A\})$. In this case, being "consistent" means *acceptable*. In other words, acceptability plays no role in the revision process.

$(K^\circ 5)$ $\psi \circ_b \varphi = \psi_\perp$ only if φ is contradictory.

Similarly, this should have the interpretation "$\psi \circ_b \varphi$ is unacceptable, only if φ is (itself) unacceptable". This can be shown if we remember that we artificially forced the translation of unacceptable Belnap theories to be classically inconsistent. This means, for instance, that if φ is not itself unacceptable, then $\psi^+ \circ_a(\varphi^+ \wedge \mathscr{A}_B \wedge Acc)$ is classically consistent.

Suppose $\psi \circ_b \varphi$ is unacceptable; we must show that φ is unacceptable. From the assumption, it follows that

(7.11) $\psi \circ_b \varphi \to \gamma$ and $\psi \circ_b \varphi \to \neg\gamma$

for some γ in $\mathscr{L}_B$. By the correspondence theorem and (7.11),

$$\{\mathscr{A}_B\} \cup \{\alpha^+ \mid \psi^+ \circ_a(\varphi^+ \wedge \mathscr{A}_B \wedge Acc) \vdash \alpha^+\} \vdash \gamma^+.$$

Notice that $\{\mathscr{A}_B\} \cup \{\alpha^+ \mid \psi^+ \circ_a(\varphi^+ \wedge \mathscr{A}_B \wedge Acc) \vdash \alpha^+\} \subseteq \psi^+ \circ_a(\varphi^+ \wedge \mathscr{A}_B \wedge Acc)$ since by $(K^\circ 2)$, $\mathscr{A}_B \in \psi^+ \circ_a(\varphi^+ \wedge \mathscr{A}_B \wedge Acc)$, and by $(K^\circ 1)$, $\psi^+ \circ_a(\varphi^+ \wedge \mathscr{A}_B \wedge Acc)$ is closed under classical logical consequence and hence contains all such α^+. Also notice that by the correspondence theorem and (7.11), $\{\mathscr{A}_B\} \cup \{\alpha^+ \mid \psi^+ \circ_a(\varphi^+ \wedge \mathscr{A}_B \wedge Acc) \vdash \alpha^+\} \vdash \overline{\gamma}^+$. For the same reason, $\{\mathscr{A}_B\} \cup \{\alpha^+ \mid \psi^+ \circ_a(\varphi^+ \wedge \mathscr{A}_B \wedge Acc) \vdash \alpha^+\} \subseteq \psi^+ \circ_a(\varphi^+ \wedge \mathscr{A}_B \wedge Acc)$, and therefore $\psi^+ \circ_a(\varphi^+ \wedge \mathscr{A}_B \wedge Acc) \vdash \gamma^+ \wedge \overline{\gamma}^+ = holds(\gamma, \mathrm{tt}) \wedge holds(\neg\gamma, \mathrm{tt})$.

Now, $\mathscr{A}_B \wedge holds(\neg\gamma, \mathrm{tt}) \vdash holds(\gamma, \mathrm{ff})$. By $(K^\circ 1)$, $\psi^+ \circ_a(\varphi^+ \wedge \mathscr{A}_B \wedge Acc) \vdash holds(\gamma, \mathrm{tt}) \wedge holds(\gamma, \mathrm{ff})$. $Acc \in \psi^+ \circ_a(\varphi^+ \wedge \mathscr{A}_B \wedge Acc)$. Therefore, $\psi^+ \circ_a(\varphi^+ \wedge \mathscr{A}_B \wedge Acc) \vdash \perp$. By $(K^\circ 5)$, $(\varphi^+ \wedge \mathscr{A}_B \wedge Acc)$ must be contradictory. $\mathscr{A}_B$ and Acc do not introduce any inconsistencies, so it must be the case that φ is itself unacceptable.

$(K^\circ 6)$ If $\varphi \equiv_b \gamma$, then $\psi \circ_b \varphi \equiv_b \psi \circ_b \gamma$.

In Belnap's logic, $\varphi \equiv_b \gamma$ means $\varphi \to \gamma$ and $\gamma \to \varphi$. By the correspondence, $\mathscr{A}_B \vdash holds(\varphi, \mathrm{tt}) \leftrightarrow holds(\gamma, \mathrm{tt})$, and also $\mathscr{A}_B \vdash \neg holds(\varphi, \mathrm{ff}) \leftrightarrow \neg holds(\gamma, \mathrm{ff})$. We show the positive part only. The negative part is similar. It is easy to see that $\vdash (\mathscr{A}_B \wedge \varphi^+) \leftrightarrow (\mathscr{A}_B \wedge \gamma^+)$. By $(K^\circ 6)$, $\psi^+ \circ_a(\varphi^+ \wedge \mathscr{A}_B \wedge Acc) \equiv \psi^+ \circ_a(\gamma^+ \wedge \mathscr{A}_B \wedge Acc)$. The same happens with the negative part, and therefore, by the definition of revision in Belnap's logic, $\psi \circ_b \varphi = \psi \circ_b \gamma$, and hence $\psi \circ_b \varphi \equiv_b \psi \circ_b \gamma$.

We argued in Section 2.1, page 18, that the two postulates $(K^\circ 7)$ and $(K^\circ 8)$ are equivalent to $(K^\circ_{7,8})$ below:

$(K_{7,8}^{\circ})$ $Cn_b(\psi\circ_b\varphi\cup\{\gamma\}) = \psi\circ_b(\varphi\wedge\gamma)$, when γ is consistent with $\psi\circ_b\varphi$.

In this case, being "consistent" means being *acceptable*. Acceptability plays therefore no role in the revision process above, and hence $\psi\circ_b\varphi\cup\{\gamma\}$ is *acceptable*. In first-order logic terms, this means that the acceptability axiom is never used in the derivation of translated Belnap formulae. We sketch the proof as follows. Let us look first at the formulae in the set $\psi\circ_b\varphi\cup\{\gamma\}$. These are the formulae in the set $\{\alpha \mid \psi^+\circ_a(\varphi^+\wedge\mathscr{A}_B\wedge Acc) \vdash \alpha^+$ and $\neg\psi^-\circ_a(\neg\varphi^-\wedge\mathscr{A}_B\wedge Acc) \vdash \neg\alpha^-\}\cup\{\gamma\}$. On the other hand, the formulae in the set $\psi\circ_b(\varphi\wedge\gamma)$ are the same formulae in the set $\{\beta \mid \psi^+\circ_a((\varphi\wedge\gamma)^+\wedge\mathscr{A}_B\wedge Acc)\vdash\beta^+$ and $\neg\psi^-\circ_a(\neg(\varphi\wedge\psi)^-\wedge\mathscr{A}_B\wedge Acc)\vdash\neg\beta^-\}$. Now, by the assumption and $(K_{7,8}^{\circ})$ for $\circ_a$, we have that $Cn(\psi^+\circ_a(\varphi^+\wedge\mathscr{A}_B\wedge Acc)\cup\{\gamma^+\}) = \psi^+\circ_a((\varphi\wedge\gamma)^+\wedge\mathscr{A}_B\wedge Acc)$. Notice that $\mathscr{A}_B \in \psi^+\circ_a(\varphi^+\wedge\mathscr{A}_B\wedge Acc)\cup\{\gamma^+\}$. It is easy to show that $\psi^+\circ_a(\varphi^+\wedge\mathscr{A}_B\wedge Acc)\cup\{\gamma^+\}\vdash\beta^+$ and $\neg\psi^-\circ_a(\neg\varphi^-\wedge\mathscr{A}_B\wedge Acc)\cup\{\neg\gamma^-\}\vdash\neg\beta^-$ iff $\beta\in Cn_b(\{\alpha\mid\psi^+\circ_a(\varphi^+\wedge\mathscr{A}_B\wedge Acc)\vdash\alpha^+$ and $\neg\psi^-\circ_a(\neg\varphi^-\wedge\mathscr{A}_B\wedge Acc)\vdash\neg\alpha^-\}\cup\{\gamma\})$. Similarly, $\psi^+\circ_a((\varphi\wedge\gamma)^+\wedge\mathscr{A}_B\wedge Acc)\vdash\beta^+$ and $\neg\psi^-\circ_a(\neg(\varphi\wedge\gamma)^-\wedge\mathscr{A}_B\wedge Acc)\vdash\neg\beta^-$ iff $\beta\in Cn_b(\{\alpha\mid\psi^+\circ_a((\varphi\wedge\gamma)^+\wedge\mathscr{A}_B\wedge Acc)\vdash\alpha^+$ and $\neg\psi^-\circ_a(\neg(\varphi\wedge\gamma)^-\wedge\mathscr{A}_B\wedge Acc)\vdash\neg\alpha^-\})$.

7.7 Conclusions and Discussions

In this chapter, we presented a way of exporting an AGM revision process defined for classical logic to some non-classical logics. We have illustrated our methodology by considering three types of logics. We started with the case of propositional modal logic, whose notion of consistency is similar to that of classical logic; then we considered Łukasiewicz' many-valued logics, whose notion of consistency is somewhat different but is still defined; and finally we investigated Belnap's four-valued logic, which does not have a notion of consistency.

We have also outlined a general methodology for algebraic logics and shown that our approach can be used for any non-classical logic whose semantics is first-order logic axiomatisable.

We have shown that if the object logic has a notion of consistency that can be mapped into consistency in classical logic, then our approach can be used in a more or less straightforward way. This is because AGM revision is deeply connected with the notion of consistency in classical logic. Translations into classical logic of theories of object logics where the semantics is significantly different (e.g., paraconsistent logics) will always be consistent, and hence revisions will amount to simple expansions.[10] However, the fact that these logics do not trivialise in the face of "inconsistency" does not mean that every belief set in these logics is "rational", so a more general notion to replace the role of consistency in classical logic needs to be defined. We have called this notion "acceptability", and in our setting the only requirement is that it can be expressed in classical logic. We do not claim to provide

---

[10] This is in agreement with [18, page 6] and [15, page 219], which noted that some of the sphere semantics based on some paraconsistent logics show that revisions and expansions are equivalent.

an analysis of what this notion should be in various non-classical scenarios. Our aim in this chapter was to provide a quick way to export a revision machinery in classical logic to these logics. For the case of Belnap's four-valued logic we deemed acceptable those theories which do not prove a proposition and its negation. When applied in this context, our revision approach *filters out* all contradictions, leaving only non-controversial information. This is much in the spirit of the idea of "locally restoring consistency", proposed by Restall and Slaney in [16], except that in our case the "vocabulary", whose beliefs are left untouched, is restricted to the atoms for which contradictory beliefs are not held. As Restall and Slaney suggest, it is also possible to restore consistency gradually instead, by defining successive notions of acceptability which concentrate on particular sets of atoms at each time (also in the spirit of [8]).

There are considerable benefits for adopting our approach. Various translation mechanisms have been developed for many non-classical logics, which allow the mimicking of the non-classical logical reasoning within the context of classical logic. Existing results in the literature have already shown the benefits that such translation mechanisms can bring, e.g., to give an object logic semantics [4]; to compare it with other logics; to get decidability/undecidability results; to make use of automated deduction of classical logic; etc. Moreover, revision theory for classical logic is very well developed. As we have seen in this book, there are various possibilities and further fine-tuning involved, and using translation mechanisms into classical logic will not only open a wealth of distinctions for the source logic, but may also enrich classical logic revision itself with new ideas and problems arising from non-classical logics. Acceptability is an example.

We make some further comments on revision by translation as part of the general methodology, called *logic by translation*, in Chapter 9.

We now turn to the problem of contraction and how to bring this notion to the object level. This is the topic of the next chapter.

References

1. A. R. Anderson, Nuel D. Belnap, and J. M. Dunn. *Entailment*, volume 2, chapter 12, "Applications and Discussion", §81 "A useful four-valued logic: How a computer should think", pages 506–541. Princeton University Press, 1992.
2. N. Belnap. How a computer should think. In G. Ryle, editor, *Contemporary Aspects of Philosophy*, pages 30–56. Oriel Press, 1977.
3. N. Belnap. A useful four-valued logic. In J. M. Dunn and G. Epstein, editors, *Modern Uses of Multiple-valued Logic*, pages 8–37. D. Reidel, 1977.
4. K. Broda, A. Russo, and D. M. Gabbay. *Discovering World with Fuzzy Logic: Perspectives and Approaches to the Formalisation of Human-Consistent Logical Systems*, chapter A Unified Compilation Style Labelled Deductive Systems for Modal, Substructural and Fuzzy Logic, pages 495–547. Springer Verlag, 2000.
5. R. Bull and K. Segerberg. Basic modal logic. In D. Gabbay and F. Guenthner, editors, *Handbook of Philosophical Logic*, volume 2, pages 1–88. Reidel Publishing Company, 1984.
6. B. F. Chellas. *Modal Logic, an Introduction*. Cambridge University Press, New York and London, 1980.

7. M. Fitting. Basic modal logic. In D. M. Gabbay, C. J. Hogger, and J. A. Robinson, editors, *Handbook of Logic in Artificial Intelligence and Logic Programming*, volume 1 — Logical Foundations. Oxford Science Publications, 1993.

8. A. Fuhrmann. Theory contraction through base contraction. *Journal of Philosophical Logic*, 20(2):175–203, May 1991. DOI 10.1007/BF00284974.

9. D. Hilbert. The foundation of mathematics. In J. Van Heijennort, editor, *From Frege to Godel: A Source Book in Mathematical Logic, 1873-1931*, pages 464–479. Harvard University Press, Cambridge, Massachussetts, 1968.

10. G. Hughes and M. Cresswell. *An Introduction to Modal Logics*. Methuen, London, 1968.

11. E. Jónsson and A. Tarski. Boolean algebras with operators, part I. *American Journal of Mathematics*, 73:891–939, 1951.

12. S. A. Kripke. A completeness theorem in modal logic. *Journal of Symbolic Logic*, 24:1–4, 1959.

13. S. A. Kripke. Semantic analysis of modal logics I, normal propositional calculi. *Zeitschrift für mathematische Logik und Glundlagen der Mathematik*, 9:67–96, 1963.

14. E. J. Lemmon. *The "Lemmon Notes": An Introduction to Modal Logic*. Basil Blackwell, Oxford, 1977. Written in collaboration with Dana Scott; edited by Krister Segerberg. American Philosophical Quarterly Monograph Series, Monograph No. 11.

15. G. Priest. Paraconsistent belief revision. *Theoria*, 67:214–228, 2001.

16. G. Restall and J. Slaney. Realistic belief revision. In Michel De Glas and Zdzislaw Pawlak, editors, *WOCFAI 95: Proceedings of the Second World Conference on the Fundamentals of Artificial Intelligence*, pages 67–378. Angkor, July 1995.

17. D. Scott. Notes on the formalization of logic. Study aids monographs, no. 3, University of Oxford, Subfaculty of Philosophy, 1981. Compiled by Dana Scott with the aid of David Bostock, Graeme Forbes, Daniel Isaacson and Gören Sundholm.

18. K. Tanaka. What does paraconsistency do? The case of belief revision. *The Logica Yearbook*, pages 188–197, 1997.

19. A. Tarski. *Introduction to Logic and to the Methodology of Deductive Sciences*. Oxford University Press, 1994. Fourth Edition.

20. J. van Benthem. Correspondence theory. In D. Gabbay and F. Guenthner, editors, *Handbook of Philosophical Logic*, volume 2, pages 167–247. D. Reidel, 1984.

Chapter 8
Object-Level Deletion

8.1 Introduction

We have seen that the interesting cases for belief revision involve the removal of information from the existing belief set. Therefore, the investigation of techniques for deletion plays an important role in the process.

In general, there are several areas in applied logic where deletion of information is involved in one way or another:

1. belief contraction (see Section 3.7.1)
2. actions triggered by statements of the form 'If *condition*, then *remove A*', which are extensively used in database systems
3. resource considerations in relevance and linear logics, where addition or removal of resource can affect provability
4. free logic and the like, where existence and non-existence of individuals affects quantification

All of these areas have certain logical difficulties relating to the *removal* of elements. In this chapter, we explain the difficulties and offer a comprehensive logical model from a novel point of view: we look at ways of defining deletion at the *object level*.

We start by discussing object and meta-leval operations in general.

8.2 Object-Level × Meta-Level Operations

Let L be a logic in a language $\mathscr{L}$ and let $\vdash$ be its consequence relation. We assume for simplicity that theories Δ in this logic are sets or multisets of wffs (as opposed to more complex data structures) and that $\vdash$ is a relation of the form $\Delta \vdash A$ between theories Δ and wffs A, satisfying the usual properties of consequence.

Consider a meta-level operation $\mathbf{M}$ in L of the form $\mathbf{M}(\Delta, B) = \Delta'$, taking a theory Δ and a wff B and yielding a new theory Δ'. We say that this operation is of type

D. M. Gabbay et al., *Revision, Acceptability and Context*, Cognitive Technologies,
DOI 10.1007/978-3-642-14159-1_8, © Springer-Verlag Berlin Heidelberg 2010

$(t,f) \mapsto t$ (i.e., (theory, formula) $\mapsto$ theory). Similarly, we can have other operations $\mathbf{M}_1, \mathbf{M}_2, \ldots$ of all kinds of types. An operation of type $(t,f) \mapsto t$ can be anything ranging from something like very simple addition such as

- $\mathbf{M}_a(\Delta, B) = \Delta \cup \{B\}$

to the more complex deletion operator[1]

- $\mathbf{M}_d(\Delta, B) = \begin{cases} \Delta - B, & \text{if } B \in \Delta \\ \Delta & \text{if } B \notin \Delta \end{cases}$

and even further to the really sophisticated revision operator:

- $\mathbf{M}_r(\Delta, B) =$ the result of applying the revision procedure obtained by the Levi Identity, where the contraction mechanism is Grosof's contraction, described on page 276.

Definition 8.1. Given a set of operations $\mathbf{M}_1, \ldots, \mathbf{M}_n$ of types $\tau_1, \ldots, \tau_n$, respectively, we can define the family $\mathscr{F}$ of operations *generated* by them by induction as follows:

1. $\mathbf{M}_i$ are in $\mathscr{F}$
2. If $\mathbf{M}$ is in $\mathscr{F}$ of type $(t_1, \ldots, t_m) \mapsto r$ and $\mathbf{N}_j$, $j = 1, \ldots, m$, are in $\mathscr{F}$ of types $(r_1^j, \ldots, r_{k(j)}^j) \mapsto t_j$ and we assume $\{r_1^1, \ldots, r_{k(m)}^m\}$ contains only the m' distinct types $\{r_1, \ldots, r_{m'}\}$, then $\mathbf{N} = \mathbf{M}(\mathbf{N}_1, \ldots, \mathbf{N}_m)$ is also in $\mathscr{F}$ and is of type $(r_1, \ldots, r_{m'}) \mapsto r$.

Given an operation $\mathbf{N}$ and operations $\mathbf{N}_1, \ldots, \mathbf{N}_m$, it is natural to ask whether $\mathbf{N}$ is definable (i.e., can be generated) from $\mathbf{N}_1, \ldots, \mathbf{N}_m$. This is important for applications, where $\mathbf{N}_i$ are well understood, and so $\mathbf{N}$ can also be better understood, being generated from $\mathbf{N}_i$.

Of special interest are the so-called *object-level* operations, defined as follows:

Definition 8.2 (Object-level operations).

1. $\mathbf{M}_a(\Delta, B)$ is an object-level operation.[2]
2. If $\sharp(B_1, \ldots, B_k)$ is a k-place connective of the language, then $\mathbf{M}_\sharp(B_1, \ldots, B_k) = \sharp(B_1, \ldots, B_k)$ is an object-level operation of type $(\underbrace{f \ldots f}_{k \text{ times}}) \mapsto f$.
3. Any $\mathbf{N}$ generated by the operations in (1) and (2) above is an object-level operation.

Why are we interested in object-level operations? The reason is simple. If we know that $\mathbf{N}$ is equivalent or is definable as an object-level operation, then its behaviour can be well understood logically because $\vdash$ is available for the object-level formulae and theories of the language. In many cases $\vdash$ is machine-implemented!

Let us then formulate the general problem facing us.

---

[1] There are several versions of this operator. The most well known is *contraction*. $\mathbf{M}_c(\Delta, B) = \Delta'$ such that $\Delta' \nvdash B$ in case $\Delta \vdash B$, and $\Delta' = \Delta$ if $\Delta \nvdash B$.

[2] If $\wedge$ is in the language and Δ is finite, then $\mathbf{M}_a(\Delta, B)$ is $(\bigwedge \Delta) \wedge B$. Otherwise, we consider $\mathbf{M}_a$ as an object-level operation anyway, because it is so simple and fundamental.

Problem 8.1 (Object-level realisation of meta-level operations). Given a meta-level operation $\mathbf{M}$ for a logic L in a language $\mathcal{L}$, find a conservative extension L' of L in a language $\mathcal{L}' \supseteq \mathcal{L}$ and an extension $\mathbf{M}'$ of $\mathbf{M}$ to $\mathcal{L}'$ such that $\mathbf{M}'$ is object-level-definable in L'.

One can always tackle this problem by brute force. Let $\mathbf{M}$ be an operation for the logic L in language $\mathcal{L}$. We can always add a suitable new connective $\sharp_{\mathbf{M}}$ and form a richer language $\mathcal{L}'$ and write suitable additional axioms for $\sharp_{\mathbf{M}}$ to obtain a correct and (hopefully conservative) extension L' of L which can characterise $\sharp_{\mathbf{M}}$ as $\mathbf{M}$. In fact, if successful, this extension will be the minimal extension of L in which $\mathbf{M}$ is object-level-definable. Although it sounds easy to add suitable connectives to the language $\mathcal{L}$ with suitable axioms, there is a lot to prove and a lot to adjust. It may be conceptually a brute-force method, but technically it can be very demanding and not always successful. See, for example, the body of literature concerning the conditional $A > B$ compared with non-monotonic consequence $A \mathrel{\vert\!\sim} B$ (in the meta-level).[3]

Another example in classical logic is the AGM revision operation. We can add a binary connective "∘" to the language with a view that a revision operator $\mathbf{M}_\circ(\Delta, B)$ be represented as $(\bigwedge \Delta) \circ B$. The AGM axioms can be written for "∘", but we need semantics, completeness, proof theory, etc. This is not a simple task. In general, it is an art to do such a minimal extension properly and successfully. In fact, as far as we know, this has never been fully done for revision. There is some work of Katsuno and Mendelzon for the one-level connective "∘" (without nested iterations) [13].

We refer to this process as bringing the meta-level $\mathbf{M}$ of L into the object level of L'. If L' is well understood, then we will have found a way of 'controlling' $\mathbf{M}$ in the logic L'.

Of course, the best scenario is to find an independently motivated extension L' with meaningful connectives in which $\mathbf{M}$ is defined in the object level. L' need not be a minimal extension of L.

Let us consider the special operation of deletion, $\mathbf{M}_d(\Delta, A) = \Delta'$. To delete A from Δ, we simply take it out if it is there. It may be that $A \notin \Delta$ but $\Delta \vdash A$, in which case we want to make sure also that $\Delta' \nvdash A$.

This chapter is concerned with doing such deletions in the object level. First, note that the operation $\mathbf{M}_d(\Delta, A)$ really depends on A more than it depends on Δ. We can expect A to be taken out more or less in the same manner from any Δ. To this end, we introduce a connective $\bigcirc$ and call $\bigcirc(A)$ the anti-formula of A, which takes A out of any Δ, i.e., $\{A, \bigcirc(A)\} \equiv \varnothing$. For more details, see Section 8.5 and, of course, the rest of the chapter.

Let us mention now a methodological problem. The way deletion is done in the object level differs from logic to logic. The big division is between, say, linear logic, a resource-bounded logic (use A exactly once), and intuitionistic logic, a resource-unbounded logic (use A as many times as you need). Deletion is done differently in those logics. It can be presented nicely and smoothly in a Gentzen formulation of

---

[3] See Section 2.3 for a discussion on conditionals.

linear logic, and needs to be done completely differently and in a much more complicated way for intuitionistic logic, using a goal-directed formulation with negation as failure.

However, if we use several different proof formulations for linear logic, namely Gentzen as well as a goal directed formulation with negation as failure, then both methods of object-level deletion can be realised in linear logic itself, and the methods can be vividly compared.

Furthermore, armed with our deletion capabilities in linear logic, we can make use of labelled deductive systems (LDSs) to provide a general deletion framework for many logics (see [7] for an introduction to LDSs). We can use linear logic as labels and uniformly perform object-level deletion (by manipulating the labels) in any logic which has a labelled formulation. The strategy is involved and requires that initially we give, for the sake of a more general theory of deletion, several proof presentations of linear logic, some of which are needed only later in the chapter.

8.3 The Need for Object-Level Deletion

Having explained the idea of bringing a meta-level operation **M** into the object level, we note that the present section attempts to bring the operation of deletion from the meta-level into the object level. The rest of this section is to motivate the need to do so. Why is it essential for us to extend logic to allow us to do deletion in the object level? Our motivation comes from several areas mainly associated with belief revision and consistency maintenance, especially the theory of contraction. Thus, in this section we are going to say a few words about how deletion plays an important role in revision and why we can have much better systems if deletion could be done in the object level. Let us start with a little background on AGM revision and contraction.

We have seen that revisions and contractions are closely related. In fact, one operation can be defined in terms of the other using the so called Levi and Harper identities (see page 19 and [12, pp. 69–70]).

Contractions have also been extensively used in database systems in the form of deletions triggered by preconditions. Both the belief contraction and the database approaches have their limitations. The former cannot handle tautologies, and the latter has no formal semantics for deletion. We shall see that our approach to object-level deletion overcomes some of these limitations.

Belief contraction formalised

Given a logic L, e.g., classical logic, a theory Δ and a wff A, it is sometimes desirable to contract Δ to a theory $\Delta' \subseteq \Delta$ such that $\Delta' \nvdash_L A$.

If $-$ is a contraction operation, Δ is a theory representing the belief set of an agent and A is a wff, then $\Delta-A$ represents the new belief set after the contraction of Δ by A. We expect $-$ to satisfy some standard requirements, the most well known of which are the AGM postulates for contraction presented on page 78. We recall the postulates below, but this time we follow Hansson's terminology [16, pp. 65–70], which is more appropriate for the investigation in this chapter.

AGM postulates for contraction

success:
If $\nvdash A$, then $\Delta-A \nvdash A$

inclusion:
$\Delta-A \subseteq \Delta$

vacuity:
If $\Delta \nvdash A$, then $\Delta-A = \Delta$

relevance:
If $\Delta \vdash B$ and $\Delta-A \nvdash B$, then for some Δ', $\Delta-A \subseteq \Delta' \subset \Delta$, we have that $\Delta' \nvdash A$, but $\Delta' \cup \{B\} \vdash A$.

core retainment:
If $\Delta \vdash B$ and $\Delta-A \nvdash B$, then there exists a $\Delta' \subseteq \Delta$, such that $\Delta' \nvdash A$, but $\Delta' \cup \{B\} \vdash A$.

closure:
If Δ is logically closed, then so is $\Delta-A$, for any formula A.

relative closure:
If $\Delta-A \vdash B$ and $B \in \Delta$, then $B \in \Delta-A$.

extensionality:
If $A \equiv B$, then $\Delta-A \equiv \Delta-B$

uniformity:
If for all $\Delta' \subset \Delta$

$\Delta' \vdash A$ if and only if $\Delta' \vdash B$

then

$\Delta-A \equiv \Delta-B.$

These postulates, as well as the AGM postulates for revision, were formulated for classical logic. The contraction postulates make formal sense for any monotonic logic (they use consequence only), unlike the revision postulates (see Chapter 7). However, even though the contraction postulates make formal sense, they may not be intuitively correct for some of the currently used applied non-classical logics.

Let us examine this claim more carefully. We choose a contraction algorithm originally due to Grosof [15]; see also [9].

Grosof's contraction

Let $A_1, A_2, A_3, \ldots$ be a universal enumeration of all wffs of the language. Let Δ be any theory in the language and $\vdash\!\!\!\sim$ be a consequence relation. Δ is deductively *closed* if whenever $\Delta\vdash\!\!\!\sim A$, we have $A \in \Delta$. This notion is good for non-monotonic consequence as well because such a consequence is usually required to satisfy Gabbay's restricted monotonicity rule

$$\frac{\Delta\vdash\!\!\!\sim A; \Delta\vdash\!\!\!\sim B}{\Delta + A \vdash\!\!\!\sim B}\ .$$

Thus, Δ can be represented as $\{A_{f(1)}, A_{f(2)}, \ldots\}$ with f an index function such that $f(i) < f(j)$ for $i < j$, picking up the formulae in Δ. Suppose $\Delta\vdash\!\!\!\sim A$ and we want a $\Delta' \subseteq \Delta$ such that $\Delta' \not\vdash\!\!\!\sim A$. Define Δ'_n, $n = 1, 2, \ldots$, as follows.

$$\Delta'_0 = \varnothing$$

$$\Delta'_{n+1} = \Delta'_n + A_{f(n+1)} \text{ if } \Delta'_n + A_{f(n+1)} \not\vdash\!\!\!\sim A$$

$$\Delta'_{n+1} = \Delta'_n \text{ otherwise.}$$

Let $\Delta' = \bigcup_n \Delta'_n$.

Note that we need monotonicity to have the algorithm work properly. We need the property that

$$\Delta'_n \vdash\!\!\!\sim X \text{ implies } \Delta'_{n+1} \vdash\!\!\!\sim X.$$

One can verify that for monotonic logic, Δ' is closed (we need the fact that $\Delta'\vdash\!\!\!\sim X$ implies $\Delta\vdash\!\!\!\sim X$) and all the other AGM contraction postulates hold.

In the non-monotonic case we need to rethink what we want as rationality postulates. Suppose Δ is a consistent theory and we receive an input formula A. If $\Delta \cup \{A\}\vdash\!\!\!\sim \bot$, i.e., it is inconsistent, we can restore consistency not only by contracting some B from $\Delta \cup \{A\}$, but also by expanding it, i.e., by adding some B such that $\Delta \cup \{A, B\} \not\vdash\!\!\!\sim \bot$. In fact, we might prefer to restore consistency by adding information rather than by deleting information.

A crucial, and widely accepted, feature of belief contraction is the fact that tautologies are never contracted. The reason for this is that the theory of belief contraction relies on the mechanics of the underlying logical formalism.

However, there are strong arguments in favour of a new theory without this restriction.

Argument 1: conditional contraction and the deduction theorem

Conditional contraction occurs in many computer systems, in the form of rules such as

"If condition, then remove A".

In such systems, whenever `condition` is satisfied, the contraction of `A` is performed. Rules of this kind are called *triggers* in database management systems. For example, consider the following SQL[4] statement:

```
CREATE TRIGGER update_employee
AFTER DELETE employee
REFERENCING OLD ROW AS old_emp_row
BEGIN
    DELETE FROM dependent
    WHERE empl_num = old_emp_row.empl_num;
END;
```

The statement above specifies a *conditional* contraction. Whenever a row is deleted in the table `employee`, rows in the table `dependent` with the same employee number must also be deleted. It really means, when `condition` follows from the database Δ, then delete some records [2].

We note that a database with a conditional commitment to deletion of incoming information is different from a database without the commitment in the object level. By having this sort of condition specified at the meta-level, it becomes difficult to analyse and identify possible inconsistencies in the rules of the system. Furthermore, some of these operations might *cascade*, i.e., cause other deletions to be performed.

There is a need to formalise an object-level marker in Δ, not a meta-level one. The need stems from logical reasons, e.g., the relation with deduction, as well as from practical ones. In addition to the uniform-level treatment of the conditions, the same reasoning engine used to provide information from the database can also be used to perform the trigger operations. We thus propose to write $C \Rightarrow \bigcirc(A)$ in the object level to express the conditional deletion "If C, then remove A".[5]

Notice that $\bigcirc(A)$ must be used only once, for repeated use of $\bigcirc$ will fail the deduction theorem, as can be seen below:

$$\{\bigcirc(A)\} \cup \{A\} \equiv \varnothing \vdash A \Rightarrow A.$$

But by the deduction theorem (that is, if we do want to have one)

---

[4] For an overview of SQL, see [5, 14].

[5] Furthermore, the availability of $\bigcirc(A)$ and the fact that $\{A, \bigcirc(A)\} \equiv \varnothing$ allow us to extend the deduction theorem

$$\Delta, A \vdash B \text{ if and only if } \Delta \vdash A \Rightarrow B,$$

to a generalised form

$$\Delta \vdash B \text{ if and only if } \Delta \cup \{\bigcirc(A)\} \vdash A \Rightarrow B$$

To get the old deduction theorem, let $\Delta' = \Delta \cup \{A\}$; then,

$$\Delta' \vdash B \quad \text{if and only if } \Delta' \cup \{\bigcirc(A)\} \vdash A \Rightarrow B$$
$$\text{if and only if } \Delta \cup \{A\} \cup \{\bigcirc(A)\} \vdash A \Rightarrow B$$
$$\text{if and only if } \Delta \vdash A \Rightarrow B$$

$$\{\bigcirc(A)\} \cup \{A\} \vdash A \Rightarrow A$$

if and only if

$$\{\bigcirc(A)\} \cup \{A\} \cup \{A\} \vdash A$$

if and only if

$$\varnothing \vdash A$$

Notice that we do not advocate the contraction of tautologies in general. The example above shows the contraction of a particular *instance* of a tautology. This point is explored in more detail later.

The considerations above are also connected with resource logics. In relevance logic we have $\Delta = \{A, B, B \Rightarrow C\} \nvdash C$ because A is not used; but we can have a deduction theorem in the form $\Delta \vdash \bigcirc(A) \Rightarrow B$.

Argument 2: action theory

In data updates we have instructions of the form

"Ensure that A does not follow from Δ at any time".

For example, in wanting to keep a certain space free, a logical robot can be given instructions of this sort. In other critical systems, one may need to ascertain that certain properties will not hold at any time. This differs from the previous examples in that *there is no specific preconditions associated with the contraction*, and it involves actions.

Argument 3: iterated revision

In some contexts, it is necessary to trigger the execution of actions following a specific *evolution* of the system. The *timing* of the execution of these actions can be purely *temporal*, as in the requirement to trigger the action within a given number of units of time, or *logical*, i.e., when a given sequence of states occurs at a given time. In the latter case, the system must identify the correct situation and then perform the corresponding action accordingly.

In a sense, this is related to the problem of iterated revisions [3, 6, 18, 4, 11, 21], with the difference that the actual stream of inputs also plays a crucial role in the sequence of *future* revisions.

Argument 4: free logic and logics with non-existent elements

Free logics allow for variables to range over elements which may not exist in the domain. Consider a situation where an element does not exist (e.g., an heir to the throne) but which also has a 'contract' to be 'removed' if it were to come into existence. History teaches us that such cases are abundant. Another example of this kind (pointed out by Michael Gabbay) is the antibodies in an immune system. They are in the system to destroy certain elements when they show up. We need a logic for this. A domain with antibody $(\alpha x)\varphi(x)$ set to 'eliminate any x such that $\varphi(x)$' is not the same as a domain without the antibody. Furthermore, the antibody, by its nature, is best defined using formulae $\varphi(x)$, which allows us to distinguish between $(ix)\varphi(x)$ and $(ix)\psi(x)$ even though they may be extensionally the same. The antibodies they generate (namely $(\alpha x)\varphi(x)$ and $(\alpha x)\psi(x)$) are not the same.[6,7]

8.4 Strategy of the Technique

We have motivated the need for object-level deletion in the previous section. It is now time to explain our strategy for the technique, namely to explain the basic idea of object-level deletion and to give an overview of the contents of subsequent sections.

The basic idea is to augment an object language $\mathcal{L}$ with an unary operator $\bigcirc(\ )$ with the following intuitive meaning:

For any formula A, $\bigcirc(A)$ is its corresponding *anti-formula*. The sole objective of $\bigcirc(A)$ is to annihilate A should it be included in a given theory.

Thus, we define $\mathbf{M}_d(\Delta, A) = \Delta \cup \{\bigcirc(A)\}$. Notice that $\mathbf{M}_d$ depends essentially on A, as $\bigcirc(A)$ does the job of deletion.

The simplest case is when A does not follow from a database Δ and one tries to expand Δ by A. If $\bigcirc(A)$ is in Δ, the expansion will be immediately followed by a contraction by A. Thus, if $A \notin \Delta, \mathbf{M}_d(\Delta, A) = \Delta \cup \{\bigcirc(A)\} \neq \Delta$.

For any formula A and theory Δ such that $\Delta \nvdash A$, $\mathbf{M}_d(\Delta, A)$ is a theory with a marker ready to delete A, we have that

$$\Delta \cup \{\bigcirc(A)\} \cup \{A\} \equiv \Delta$$

In addition, we have a general deduction theorem, namely for any formula B

$$\Delta \vdash B \text{ if and only if } \Delta \cup \{\bigcirc(A)\} \vdash A \Rightarrow B$$

The mechanism involved in anti-formulae and its intuitive procedural nature is quite clear:

---

[6] We can create antibodies using anti-formulae only: Let a be an element and $P(x)$ a unary predicate; then, $\bigcirc(P(a)) \wedge \bigcirc(\sim P(a))$ does not allow a to have the property P, nor does it allow a to have the property $\sim P$. Are we forced into a multi-valued logic? What happens if we allow P to range over all formulae? Can an element exist without any properties at all?

[7] The question of existence of elements will not be dealt with in this chapter. It needs to be studied in a more general philosophical context. See, for example, Woods [22].

'$\bigcirc(A)$' is a 'device' which takes out 'A' from the databases if 'A' is there, or $\bigcirc(A)$ lies in the database waiting to take A out if A is not there.

This intuitive concept is independent of any logic. Our problem, for a given logic L, is to find an internal logical device (possibly dependent on L) which can do the same job of deletion. In other words, we want to define '$\bigcirc(A)$' in the object language of L. We should not expect that the same logical device would work for several different logics, or indeed that for a fixed logic L only one such device is available.

A little reflection (done in detail in the next section) shows that it might be easier to find such logical devices in substructural implicational logics. The implication is of course essential since contraction involves consequence and the area of substructural logics involves resource controls which may be exploited.

It turns out that indeed substructural logics allow us to define $\bigcirc(A)$, but that there is a difference in how it is done between logics like linear logic, where there is a resource limitation, and logics like relevant and intuitionistic implication, where there is not. The way to implement $\bigcirc(A)$ is not uniform across the landscape of these logics.

This chapter will present several logical devices for anti-formulae.

To explain the basic idea, think of the basic situation of

$$\Delta, A \vdash B.$$

Consider $\Delta \vdash B$ and assume $A \in \Delta$. In resource limited logics, A contributes to (is used by) the proof of B. So, in order to to 'delete' A we can 'divert' its 'use' to something else, say by adding $A \Rightarrow x$ to the database.

If A is used to get x, then it is no longer available to get B and is therefore effectively deleted and we have an effective contraction of B. Of course, we get x instead of B. In general, this is not desirable. It turns out that in linear logic and weaker logics one can take x to be the unit of the logic (we denote it by $\mathbf{e}$) which amounts to 'nothing'.[8] Thus, we divert A to prove $\mathbf{e}$ by adding $A \Rightarrow \mathbf{e}$.[9]

---

[8] This will be explained in the next section. In Girard's linear logic, $\mathbf{e}$ is denoted by $\mathbf{1}$. Girard's notation for other connectives is as follows:

$A \multimap B$ for our $A \Rightarrow B$
$A^{\perp}$ for negation of A
$A \otimes B$ for multiplication (fusion)
$\top$ for truth
$\mathbf{0}$ for bottom (falsity)

$\mathbf{e}$ (or $\mathbf{1}$) corresponds to the empty database. In intuitionistic logic the empty database is taken to be truth $\top$ (top).

Thus, in linear logic $\nvdash \top \Rightarrow \mathbf{1}$, but in intuitionistic logic $\vdash \top = \mathbf{1}$. In linear logic $\mathbf{1}^{\perp} = \mathbf{0}$.

[9] One can more easily see the role of anti-formula $\bigcirc(A)$ in linear logic through its semantical interpretation. Linear logic is complete for semantical evaluation in commutative semigroups with unity. The basic truth condition for $A \Rightarrow B$ is

● $t \vDash A \Rightarrow B$ if and only if $\forall s(s \vDash A \Rightarrow t \cdot s \vDash B)$.

If the semigroup is a group, we let

$t \vDash \bigcirc(A)$ if and only if $t^{-1} \vDash A$.

This strategy does not work for relevant and intuitionistic logic. In intuitionistic logic, for example, A can be used as many times as necessary and so cannot be diverted. Moreover, in intuitionistic logic, **e** becomes *truth*, $\top$, and is not exactly 'nothing'.

We thus need a different approach to deletion in the cases of relevant and intuitionistic logics. We have two options:

1. to give intuitionistic logic a suitable labelled formulation and execute deletion there, or
2. to use the device of negation as failure $\neg$ for N-Prolog (N-Prolog has intuitionistic implication computationally read in a goal-directed way). This allows us to perform deletion.[10]

The negation as failure device can be used in resource logic as well, provided we give these logics a sound and complete goal-directed formulation and define negation as failure for these logics. It is good to do that for the sake of comparison.

Thus, to present our results properly we need a Gentzen formulation for linear logic to do deletion via $\bigcirc(A) = A \Rightarrow \mathbf{e}$, and a goal-directed and a labelled formulation for intuitionistic logic to do deletion there. Since the two logics are distinct and the methods are distinct, it is good for the sake of comparison to give linear logic both a Gentzen and a goal-directed formulation and do both deletions in the same system. Thus, we need to start with a goal directed formulation for substructural logics.

For the sake of expository completeness,[11] we also give a Hilbert formulation for these logics.

Section 8.5 presents substructural implications through a Hilbert formulation, goal-directed formulation and a semantic characterisation. Section 8.6 discusses the addition of anti-formulae to concatenation and linear logic. Section 8.7 discusses failure in resource logics. The rest of the chapter deals with resource-unbounded logics.

8.5 Substructural Logics

We begin to explore the logical nature of anti-formulae by trying to add the anti-formula operators to a variety of implicational substructural logics. For this purpose

---

The details are worked out in the next section.

[10] Ordinary Prolog can perform deletion in the object language. Let $\bigwedge a_i \Rightarrow b$ be a clause. Let n be a new atom. Then $\neg n \wedge \bigwedge a_i \Rightarrow b$ is effectively the same clause, which can be 'deleted' by adding n. Note that this kind of deletion is 'physical' deletion and not 'logical' deletion. Thus, for example, assume that $\Delta \vdash B$ in a resource logic and assume that we want to delete B. We can logically do that by adding $B \Rightarrow \mathbf{e}$, which will divert B to nothing. However, we cannot delete B physically (unless $B \in \Delta$); we can only physically delete some of the premises in Δ which are needed to prove B.

[11] The literature on substructural logics is abundant but has no standard notation or standard semantics or standard proof theory. If we just give references, the reader is likely to be lost. So we need to do our own presentation in this chapter.

we need to introduce substructural logics. This is the job of the present section. We give Hilbert and Gentzen formulations in Section 8.5.1, goal-directed formulation in Section 8.5.2 and semantics in Section 8.5.3. All of these results are, in principle, already known [1, 7, 8, 9], but we need to fix our approach and make life easy for our reader, and formulate our logics in a way compatible with the new results of this chapter.

8.5.1 Hilbert and Gentzen Formulations

Definition 8.3 (Hilbert formulation). Consider a propositional language with atoms $\{q_1, q_2, \dots, \}$, implication $\Rightarrow$ and a propositional constant **e**. The following list of axioms and rules can be used to define a Hilbert system formulation for several logics.

For $\Delta = (A_1, \dots, A_n)$, let $\Delta \Rightarrow B$ mean $A_1 \Rightarrow (A_2 \Rightarrow \dots \Rightarrow (A_n \Rightarrow B)\dots)$. Let $\varnothing \Rightarrow B$ mean B.

Axioms for $\Rightarrow$

1. $A \Rightarrow A$
2. $(A \Rightarrow B) \Rightarrow ((C \Rightarrow A) \Rightarrow (C \Rightarrow B))$
3. $(A \Rightarrow (B \Rightarrow C)) \Rightarrow (B \Rightarrow (A \Rightarrow C))$
4. $(A \Rightarrow (B \Rightarrow C) \Rightarrow ((A \Rightarrow B) \Rightarrow (A \Rightarrow C))$
5. $A \Rightarrow (B \Rightarrow A)$

Rules

6. $$\dfrac{\vdash A \Rightarrow B}{\vdash (B \Rightarrow C) \Rightarrow (A \Rightarrow C)}$$

7. $$\dfrac{\vdash A;\ \vdash A \Rightarrow B}{\vdash B}$$

8. $$\dfrac{\vdash A \Rightarrow B}{\vdash (B \Rightarrow C) \Rightarrow (A \Rightarrow C)}$$

9. $$\dfrac{\vdash A}{\vdash (A \Rightarrow B) \Rightarrow B}$$

10. $$\dfrac{\vdash A \Rightarrow B}{\vdash (B \Rightarrow C) \Rightarrow (A \Rightarrow C)}$$

11. $\vdash$ **e**

12. $$\dfrac{\vdash A \Rightarrow B}{\vdash (B \Rightarrow C) \Rightarrow (A \Rightarrow C)}$$

13. **upward e-rule**:

$$\frac{\vdash \Gamma \Rightarrow \mathbf{e}; \vdash \Delta \Rightarrow (\Theta \Rightarrow B)}{\vdash \Delta \Rightarrow (\Gamma \Rightarrow (\Theta \Rightarrow B))}$$

14. **downward e-rule**:

$$\frac{\vdash \Gamma \Rightarrow \mathbf{e}; \vdash \Delta \Rightarrow (\Gamma \Rightarrow (\Theta \Rightarrow B))}{\vdash \Delta \Rightarrow (\Theta \Rightarrow B))}$$

The reader will recognise that (4), (5) and (7) are sufficient to define intuitionistic logic. However, this list allows us to define weaker systems:

Concatenation logic (**CL**)	(1)–(2), (6)–(7)
Strong concatenation logic (**SCL**)	(1)–(2), (6)–(8)
Linear logic (**LL**)	(1)–(3), (6)–(7), (9)
Relevance logic (**R**)	(1)–(4), (6)–(7)

Rule (8) is provable from axiom (3). However, it yields a genuine extension of concatenation logic.

If we have $\mathbf{e}$ in the language, then we add (9)–(11). Rule (10) makes $\mathbf{e}$ a *worthless* piece of information and, if we add rule (11), then $\mathbf{e}$ becomes the *empty* piece of information.

See [7, 1, 20] and the section below.

Definition 8.4. Let L be one of the logics named in Definition 8.3. We define the notion $\vdash_L A$ as follows:

1. $\vdash_L A$ if and only if there exists a sequence of wffs $A_0, A_1, \ldots, A_n = A$ such that each element in the sequence is either a substitution instance of an axiom or is obtained from one or two previous elements of the sequence using a rule (i.e., (6), (7), (8), (10) or (11)).
2. Let $(A_1, \ldots, A_n)$ be a sequence of wffs. We write $(A_1, \ldots, A_n) \vdash_L B$ to mean $\vdash_L A_1 \Rightarrow (\ldots \Rightarrow (A_n \Rightarrow B) \ldots)$.
3. Obviously the deduction theorem holds by definition.

The above is the traditional definition of $\vdash_L$.

Let us prove the cut theorem as an example which will be useful later

Lemma 8.1. *Let L be a logic stronger than concatenation logic, then (1) and (2) below imply (3) below:*

1. $\vdash_L (A_1 \Rightarrow \ldots \Rightarrow (A_n \Rightarrow (A \Rightarrow B)) \ldots)$
2. $\vdash_L D_1 \Rightarrow (\ldots \Rightarrow (D_m \Rightarrow A) \ldots)$
3. $\vdash_L A_1 \Rightarrow \ldots \Rightarrow (A_n \Rightarrow (D_1 \Rightarrow \ldots \Rightarrow (D_m \Rightarrow B) \ldots) \ldots)$

Proof. By induction on m and n.

Case $m = 0$, n arbitrary
This case needs to be considered only for extensions L containing axiom (8) of Definition 8.3. We can assume $n \geq 1$, since the case $m = n = 0$ is modus ponens. We have

1. $\vdash_L A_1 \Rightarrow (A_2 \Rightarrow \dots \Rightarrow (A_n \Rightarrow (A \Rightarrow B)\dots))$
2. $\vdash_L A$

We need to show

3. $\vdash_L A_1 \Rightarrow (A_2 \Rightarrow \dots \Rightarrow (A_n \Rightarrow B)\dots)$

From (2) we get

$\vdash_L (A \Rightarrow B) \Rightarrow B$

and from axiom (2)

$\vdash_L (A_n \Rightarrow (A \Rightarrow B)) \Rightarrow (A_n \Rightarrow B);$

by repeated use of axiom (2) we get

$\vdash_L (A_1 \Rightarrow \dots \Rightarrow (A_n \Rightarrow (A \Rightarrow B)\dots) \Rightarrow (A_1 \Rightarrow \dots \Rightarrow (A_n \Rightarrow B)\dots))$

and we therefore get

$\vdash_L A_1 \Rightarrow \dots \Rightarrow (A_n \Rightarrow B)\dots).$

Case $m = n = 1$
We have to show that (1) and (2) imply (3):

1. $\vdash_L A_1 \Rightarrow (A \Rightarrow B)$
2. $\vdash_L (D_1 \Rightarrow A)$
3. $\vdash_L A_1 \Rightarrow (D_1 \Rightarrow B)$

From rule (6), we get using (2) that

4. $\vdash_L (A \Rightarrow B) \Rightarrow (D_1 \Rightarrow B)$

and using axiom (2) we get

5. $(A_1 \Rightarrow (A \Rightarrow B)) \Rightarrow (A_1 \Rightarrow (D_1 \Rightarrow B))$

We get (3) by modus ponens of (1) and (5).

Case $m = 1$, n **arbitrary**
From $\vdash_L D_1 \Rightarrow A$ *we get* $\vdash_L (A \Rightarrow B) \Rightarrow (D_1 \Rightarrow B)$ *and by induction on n we prove:*

$\vdash_L (A_1 \Rightarrow \dots \Rightarrow (A_n \Rightarrow (A \Rightarrow B)\dots) \Rightarrow$
$(A_1 \Rightarrow \dots \Rightarrow A_n \Rightarrow (D_1 \Rightarrow B)\dots)$

For n = 1 this follows from axiom (2). Assume the above for n and get it for n+1 by another application of axiom (2).

Case $m + 1$, n **arbitrary**
We have

$$\vdash_L (A \Rightarrow B) \Rightarrow ((D_{m+1} \Rightarrow A) \Rightarrow (D_{m+1} \Rightarrow B));$$

hence,

$$\vdash_L A_1 \Rightarrow \ldots \Rightarrow (A_n \Rightarrow (A \Rightarrow B)) \ldots)$$
$$\Rightarrow ((A_1 \Rightarrow \ldots \Rightarrow (A_n \Rightarrow ((D_{m+1} \Rightarrow A) \Rightarrow (D_{m+1} \Rightarrow B)) \ldots)$$

and therefore

$$\vdash_L A_1 \Rightarrow \ldots \Rightarrow (A_n \Rightarrow (D_{m+1} \Rightarrow A) \Rightarrow (D_{m+1} \Rightarrow B) \ldots);$$

on the other hand, we have

$$\vdash_L D_1 \Rightarrow \ldots (D_m \Rightarrow (D_{m+1} \Rightarrow A) \ldots);$$

hence, by the induction hypothesis we get

$$\vdash_L A_1 \Rightarrow \ldots \Rightarrow (A_n \Rightarrow (D_1 \Rightarrow \ldots (D_m \Rightarrow (D_{m+1} \Rightarrow B) \ldots)$$

This completes the proof of Lemma 8.1.

Theorem 8.1 (Cut rule for concatenation logic).

$$(A_1, \ldots, A_n, B, C_1, \ldots, C_m) \vdash X$$

and

$$(B_1, \ldots, B_k) \vdash B$$

imply

$$(A_1, \ldots, A_n, B_1, \ldots, B_k, C_1, \ldots, C_m) \vdash X$$

Proof. Follows from Lemma 8.1, because by Definition 8.4 we have:

$$\vdash A_1 \Rightarrow \ldots \Rightarrow (A_n \Rightarrow (B \Rightarrow (C_1 \Rightarrow \ldots \Rightarrow (C_m \Rightarrow X) \ldots) \ldots)$$

and

$$\vdash B_1 (\Rightarrow \ldots \Rightarrow (B_k \Rightarrow B) \ldots)$$

Lemma 8.2. *Concatenation logic with* **e** *equals strong concatenation logic.*

Proof. We have to show that rule (8) of Definition 8.3 can be proved. Here is the proof:

1. $\vdash B$, *assumption*
2. $\vdash \mathbf{e} \Rightarrow B$, *from rule (10)*
3. $\vdash (B \Rightarrow C) \Rightarrow (\mathbf{e} \Rightarrow C)$, *from rule (6)*
4. $\vdash (B \Rightarrow C) \Rightarrow C$, *from rule (11)*

Remark 8.1. **e** *is not truth* $\top$. We do not have $\vdash \top \Rightarrow \mathbf{e}$. Only in stronger logics like intuitionistic logic do we have $\top = \mathbf{e}$. See [20, page 32]. We shall see that semantically **e** names the unit in the semigroup semantics. It stands for the empty theory.

The next definition gives Gentzen rules for our logics. Our logics will be defined as a family of valid sequents of the form $\Delta \vdash A$, where Δ is a database of wffs and A is a wff. The nature of Δ depends on the logic at hand. Some sequents are taken as axioms while others are generated by rules. The following are the details:

Definition 8.5 (Gentzen formulation).

1. The databases of Δ can be

   a. lists of wffs, for the case of concatenation logic and strong concatenation logic.
   b. multisets of wffs for the case of linear logic.
   c. sets of wffs for the case of relevant and intuitionistic logic.
   d. Let Δ_1, Δ_2 be two databases. We define the operation $\Delta_1 + \Delta_2$, which yields another database, as follows:
      - $\Delta_1 + \Delta_2 = \Delta_1 * \Delta_2$ for concatenation logic, where $*$ is concatenation of sequences.
      - $\Delta_1 + \Delta_2 = \Delta_1 \cup \Delta_2$ for linear logic, where $\cup$ is multiset union, or for relevance and intuitionistic logics, where $\cup$ is set union.
   e. Let A be a wff. We write A also for the database containing A alone.
   f. Let $\Delta = A_1 + \ldots + A_n$ and $B = B_1 \Rightarrow (\ldots \Rightarrow (B_n \Rightarrow q) \ldots)$. Write $\Delta \Rightarrow B$ for $A_1 \Rightarrow (\ldots \Rightarrow (A_n \Rightarrow B) \ldots)$.

2. We take as axioms all sequents of the form $A \vdash A$ for concatenation, linear and relevant logics, and all sequents of the form $\Delta + A \vdash A$, for intuitionistic logic.
3. The closure rules are the same for all our logics; they are the following:

   - **Deduction rule**
     $(A_1, \ldots, A_n) \vdash A \Rightarrow B$ if and only if $(A_1, \ldots, A_n, A) \vdash B$
   - **Cut rule**
     $(A_1, \ldots, A_n, B, C_1, \ldots, C_m) \vdash X$
     and
     $(B_1, \ldots, B_k) \vdash B$
     imply
     $(A_1, \ldots, A_n, B_1, \ldots, B_k, C_1, \ldots, C_m) \vdash X$

4. When **e** is present in the language we have three additional rules:

   - $\varnothing \vdash \mathbf{e}$
   - **upward e-rule**
     $\Gamma \vdash \mathbf{e}$ and $\Delta + \Theta \vdash A$ imply $\Delta + \Gamma + \Theta \vdash A$
   - **downward e-rule**
     $\Gamma \vdash \mathbf{e}$ and $\Delta + \Gamma + \Theta \vdash A$ imply $\Delta + \Theta \vdash A$

   Together the above two rules give the following combined **e**-rule:

   - Assume $\Gamma \vdash \mathbf{e}$; then, $\Delta + \Gamma + \Theta \vdash A$ if and only if $\Delta + \Theta \vdash A$.

5. The respective logics are defined as the smallest family of sequents containing all the axioms and closed under the rules.

It is clear that the previous definition is not algorithmic. Given a particular Δ and A, we do not have an inductive algorithm which allows us to check whether $\Delta \vdash A$ holds or not. The goal-directed approach provides us with a very successful algorithm for computing whether the query A succeeds from a database Δ (we use $\Delta \vdash^? A$ to denote the query A from database Δ). We shall present it later. Meanwhile, let us consider some examples involving the e-rules in concatenation logic.

Example 8.1.

1. We show $(A \Rightarrow \mathbf{e}) \Rightarrow \mathbf{e} \vdash A$.
   Since $A \Rightarrow \mathbf{e} \vdash A \Rightarrow \mathbf{e}$, we get $(A \Rightarrow \mathbf{e}) + A \vdash \mathbf{e}$, and hence by the downward e-rule we get that for any X, if $((A \Rightarrow \mathbf{e}) \Rightarrow \mathbf{e}) + (A \Rightarrow \mathbf{e}) + A \vdash X$, then $(A \Rightarrow \mathbf{e}) \Rightarrow \mathbf{e} \vdash X$.
   However, since we have that $((A \Rightarrow \mathbf{e}) \Rightarrow \mathbf{e}) + (A \Rightarrow \mathbf{e}) \vdash \mathbf{e}$, we get by the upward e-rule that for all X, if $A \vdash X$, then $((A \Rightarrow \mathbf{e}) \Rightarrow \mathbf{e}) + (A \Rightarrow \mathbf{e}) + A \vdash X$.
   Letting $X = A$ we get our result.
2. We show $A \vdash (A \Rightarrow \mathbf{e}) \Rightarrow \mathbf{e}$.
   This is the same as $A + (A \Rightarrow \mathbf{e}) \vdash \mathbf{e}$, (namely to get $\mathbf{e}$ we can do modus ponens to the left).
   Since $((A \Rightarrow \mathbf{e}) \Rightarrow \mathbf{e}) + (A \Rightarrow \mathbf{e}) \vdash \mathbf{e}$, we have that the above holds if and only if

   $$((A \Rightarrow \mathbf{e}) \Rightarrow \mathbf{e}) + (A \Rightarrow \mathbf{e}) + A + (A \Rightarrow \mathbf{e}) \vdash \mathbf{e}$$

   holds. But

   $$(A \Rightarrow \mathbf{e}) + A \vdash \mathbf{e}.$$

   Hence, we continue: the above holds if and only if $((A \Rightarrow \mathbf{e}) \Rightarrow \mathbf{e}) + (A \Rightarrow \mathbf{e}) \vdash \mathbf{e}$, which does hold.
3. We now show that $(A \Rightarrow \mathbf{e}) + ((A \Rightarrow B) \Rightarrow \mathbf{e}) + B \vdash \mathbf{e}$.
   The following is the proof.
   From (2) above we have

   $$B + (B \Rightarrow \mathbf{e}) \vdash \mathbf{e}$$

   By Cut, since $(A \Rightarrow B) + A \vdash B$, we get

   $$(A \Rightarrow B) + A + (B \Rightarrow \mathbf{e}) \vdash \mathbf{e}.$$

   Hence, (3) holds if and only if the following holds:

   $$(A \Rightarrow \mathbf{e}) + ((A \Rightarrow B) \Rightarrow \mathbf{e}) + (A \Rightarrow B) + A + (B \Rightarrow \mathbf{e}) + B \vdash \mathbf{e};$$

   but the latter does indeed hold.

Lemma 8.3. *The Hilbert and Gentzen formulations (Definitions 8.3 and 8.5, respectively) define the same logics.*

Proof. First, we show that all axioms of Definition 8.3 can be derived in the Gentzen system.

1. Since $A \Rightarrow B \vdash A \Rightarrow B$ we get $A \Rightarrow B + A \vdash B$.

2. *To show axiom (2) of Definition 8.3 we use the cut rule as follows: Let $X = A \Rightarrow$*
   $B, Y_1 = C \Rightarrow A, Y_2 = C, U = A, V = B$; then,

$$\vdash X \Rightarrow (U \Rightarrow V)$$

is

$$\vdash (A \Rightarrow B) \Rightarrow (A \Rightarrow B)$$

and

$$\vdash Y_1 \Rightarrow (Y_2 \Rightarrow U)$$

is

$$\vdash (C \Rightarrow A) \Rightarrow (C \Rightarrow A);$$

by the rule we get

$$\vdash X \Rightarrow (Y_1 \Rightarrow (Y_2 \Rightarrow V)),$$

which is

$$\vdash (A \Rightarrow B) \Rightarrow ((C \Rightarrow A) \Rightarrow (C \Rightarrow B)).$$

3. *Axiom (3) of Definition 8.3 follows from the deduction rule for the multiset case.*
4. *Axiom (4) follows from the deduction rule for sets $A \Rightarrow (B \Rightarrow C) + A + B \vdash C$. By*
   Cut, since $A \Rightarrow B$, $A \vdash B$, we get $A \Rightarrow (B \Rightarrow C) + A + A \Rightarrow B \vdash C$.
5. *Axiom (5) for intuitionistic logic holds since $A + B \vdash A$ is a Gentzen axiom.*
6–8. *follow from the cut rule.*
9–11. *follow from the Gentzen **e**-rules.*

To show the second direction, that the Hilbert system gives rise to the Gentzen system, we use the deduction theorem and the cut theorem available for the Hilbert system.

8.5.2 Goal-Directed Proof Theory

This section introduces goal-directed computation (Prolog-like) for substructural logics. The goal-directed methodology runs across the landscape of logics (see [10] for details), and gives a formulation of these logics with a strong cut property. The goal-directed approach is especially suitable for introducing meta-predicates into the language. Such predicates follow the computation procedure and inductively define various concepts and objects related to the logic, such as interpolation formulae, abduction sets, negation as failure and relevance. In our case, we can define deletion inductively as a meta-predicate on the computation. Definition 8.6 below gives a goal-directed computation for several logics, all in one go, which may make it look complex, but it is actually very simple.

The goal-directed computation is best appreciated as an algorithmic refinement of a Gentzen formulation of substructural logics.

The basic intuition for $\Delta \vdash q$ in our logics is that we have the situation whereby $\Delta = (A_1 \Rightarrow \ldots \Rightarrow (A_n \Rightarrow q)\ldots) + \Delta_1 + \ldots + \Delta_n$, and for $i = 1, \ldots, n, \Delta_i \vdash A_i$.

In other words, the leftmost element in the database, $A = (A_1 \Rightarrow (\ldots \Rightarrow (A_n \Rightarrow q)\ldots)$, is the main implication (the *ticket*) and the rest of the data can be grouped into smaller databases proving the minor premises of the main implication (i.e., $A_1, \ldots, A_n$) in the correct order. In linear logic there is no order, but we can still use the same notation $\Delta = A + \Delta_1 + \ldots + \Delta_n$.

In concatenation logic, $\Delta_1, \ldots, \Delta_n$ must all be non-empty, while in strong concatenation logic and linear logic Δ_i may be empty.[12] Note that A is 'used' only once, and the proof proceeds with the smaller, simpler problems $\Delta_i \vdash A_i$. We take as axioms in these logics the expressions $q \vdash q$, q atomic, and use the deduction theorem $\Delta \vdash A \Rightarrow B$ if and only if $\Delta, A \vdash B$ to simplify the goals.

Example 8.2. A simple example will illustrate the above. Consider

$$\Delta_0 = (b \Rightarrow (a_2 \Rightarrow q)) + (a_1 \Rightarrow b) + a_1 + a_2.$$

The computation of q from this database succeeds because the leftmost wff is $b \Rightarrow (a_2 \Rightarrow q)$. It can give us q with the partition of the rest of the data into $\Delta_1 = (a_1 \Rightarrow b) + a_1)$, which proves b, and $\Delta_2 = a_2$, which proves a_2.

To be in full control of our derivation we also keep track of how many steps and what wffs we use in the computation. We count as a step any time we use the leftmost wff and partition the rest of the database accordingly. The leftmost formula is said to have been used in that step. The following is a proper description of the computation.

1. $(b \Rightarrow (a_2 \Rightarrow q)) + (a_1 \Rightarrow b) + a_1 + a_2 \vdash^? q$ succeeds because we can *use* $b \Rightarrow (a_2 \Rightarrow q)$ in one step and partition the rest of the data into two subcomputations as follows:
2.

   2.1. $(a_1 \Rightarrow b) + a_2 \vdash^? b$
   2.2. $a_2 \vdash^? a_2$

Computation (2.1) succeeds in another step using $a_1 \Rightarrow b$ because the computation

3. $a_1 \vdash^? a_1$

succeeds immediately.

To get to (3) we used wffs $(b \Rightarrow (a_1 \Rightarrow q))$ and $(a_1 \Rightarrow b)$ in two steps, and computation (3) itself uses a_1 in one more step, bringing to three the total number of steps on this branch of the computation. As for the other branch, computation (2.2) succeeds immediately using a_2.

Thus, the total computation succeeds in a maximum of three nested steps using all of the database.

To refer to the above computation we use a meta-predicate

$$\text{success}(\Delta_0, q) = 1, \text{ in } k \text{ steps,}$$

---

[12] Thus, for example, we have in these logics that $(p \Rightarrow p) \Rightarrow q + \varnothing \vdash q$.

which is defined as follows:

1. success$(\Delta_0, q) = 1$ in three steps since we can *use* the leftmost element of Δ_0, namely $(b \Rightarrow (a_2 \Rightarrow q))$, and the rest of Δ_0 can be partitioned into Δ_1, Δ_2 such that we have:
2.

    2.1. success$(\Delta_1, b) = 1$ in two steps.
    2.2. success$(\Delta_2, a_2) = 1$ in one step and $3 = 1 + \text{Max}(2, 1)$.

Definition 8.6 below defines this success $= 1$ predicate. In fact, Definition 8.6 takes the opportunity to define *Failure* as well (success $= 0$). This is easy to do since the notion of *Failure* is clear, namely $\Delta \vdash^? q$ immediately fails if the leftmost wff in Δ is *not* of the form $A_1 \Rightarrow (\ldots \Rightarrow (A_n \Rightarrow q) \ldots)$ (and therefore nothing is being used).

We may as well define the notion of success$(\Gamma, q) = 0$ in k steps. We use induction based on immediate failure (namely failure in one step using nothing).

The two definitions of success $= 1$ and success $= 0$ do not interact inductively and so are independent of one another. We just define them side by side.

The reader should be warned that the concept of which formulae are used in the computation as defined in Definition 8.6 is adequate to tell us exactly what is used to succeed, but is too simple-minded to tell us what is used in the case of failure.

Failure will be amply discussed and defined in the section dealing with negation as failure.

If $\mathbf{e}$ is in the language then the definition becomes slightly more complex. $\mathbf{e}$ denotes the worthless information or, more strongly, the empty database, $\mathbf{e} = \varnothing$, depending on the axioms adopted for $\mathbf{e}$. So, first we have to allow that $\varnothing \vdash \mathbf{e}$ and also the rule $\Delta + \mathbf{e} + \Theta \vdash A$ if $\Delta + \Theta \vdash A$. This makes $\mathbf{e}$ worthless. If we also add the converse, that $\Delta + \Theta \vdash A$ if $\Delta + \mathbf{e} + \Theta \vdash A$, this forces $\mathbf{e}$ to be $\varnothing$.

Furthermore, if we want to have cut, we must also accept that if $\Delta + \Theta \vdash q$, then $\Delta + \Delta_e + \Theta \vdash q$, provided $\Delta_e \vdash \mathbf{e}$. Thus, if $A + \Delta_1 + \ldots + \Delta_n \vdash q$ holds then also

$$\Delta_e + \Delta + \Theta_1 + \Delta_1 + \Theta_2 + \ldots + \Theta_n + \Delta_n + \Theta_{n+1} \vdash q$$

must hold, provided that

$$\Delta_e \vdash \mathbf{e}, \Theta_1 \vdash \mathbf{e}, \ldots, \Theta_{n+1} \vdash \mathbf{e}.^{13}$$

This complicates the inductive definition because we have to allow for the Θ_is and Δ_e in the inductive clause.

Let us present the (Gentzen-like) rules from a computational point of view:

1. $q \vdash q$
2. $\varnothing \vdash \mathbf{e}$
3. $\mathbf{e} + \ldots + \mathbf{e} \vdash \mathbf{e}$

---

[13] Compare with the upward $\mathbf{e}$-rule in the semantics for the logic in Section 8.5.3:

    $t \models A$ and $s \models \mathbf{e}$ imply $t \circ s \models A$ and $s \circ t \models A$.

4. $\Delta \vdash A \Rightarrow B$ if and only if $\Delta + A \vdash B$
5. $\Delta_e + A_1 \Rightarrow (\ldots \Rightarrow (A_n \Rightarrow q)\ldots) + \Theta_1 + \Delta_1 + \ldots + \Theta_n + \Delta_n + \Theta_{n+1} \vdash q$ if $\Delta_e \vdash$
   $\mathbf{e}, \Theta_i \vdash \mathbf{e}, i = 1, \ldots, n+1$ and $\Delta_j \vdash A_j, j = 1\ldots, n$.

The above rules (1)–(5) are reduction rules, in the sense that they always reduce a complex problem $\Delta \vdash A$ to simpler ones $\Delta' \vdash A'$, with smaller Δ' and smaller A'.

However, we are missing the upward e-rule, and this one actually *complicates* the problem

6. $\Delta_1 + \Delta_2 \vdash A$ if $\Delta_1 + \Theta + \Delta_2 \vdash A$ and $\Theta \vdash \mathbf{e}$.

The definitions below define a predicate $\text{success}(\Delta, A) = 1$ by simplifying Δ, i.e., it corresponds to rules (1)–(5) above. It does not allow for rule (6). This is so that we can keep track of the complexity of the computation. We can also define $\text{success}(\Delta, A) = 0$, which means-clear cut *failure*. Together, they give decidability.

Of course $\Delta \vdash A$ can be recovered from $\text{success}(\Delta, A) = 1$ by using clause (6). So, we define $\text{success}^*(\Delta, A) = 1$ as follows:

- $\text{success}^*(A_1 + \ldots + A_n, A) = 1$ if and only if for some $\Theta_0, \ldots, \Theta_n$ such that $\text{success}(\Theta_i, \mathbf{e}) = 1$, $i = 0, \ldots, n$, we have $\text{success}(\Theta_0 + A_1 + \Theta_1 + \ldots + A_n + \Theta_n, A) = 1$.

We let $\Delta \vdash A$ be $\text{success}^*(\Delta, A) = 1$.

Note that to keep complexity under check we must be able to estimate the complexity of Θ_i. This is possible to do. In fact, if the original problem is $E_1 + \ldots + E_r \vdash^? q$ where E_i are formulae, then we can expect success from

$$\Theta_0 + E_1 + \Theta_1 + \ldots + E_n + \Theta_n \vdash q$$

where Θ_i are built up from subformulae appearing in some $E_j, j = 1, \ldots n$. This claim, of course, needs to be proved properly.

Obviously, the goal-directed proof theory should define the same systems as the ones presented as Hilbert systems under the same names in Definition 8.3. The equivalence can be obtained from the completeness for the same semantical interpretation below. Recall the opening discussion of this section.

The definition below also characterises *failure in k steps* (success = 0). We need this to introduce negation as failure '$\neg$' into substructural logics by letting: $\text{success}(\Delta, \neg A) = 1$ if and only if $\text{success}(\Delta, A) = 0$.

However, the simultaneous inductive definition of both $\text{success}(\Delta, A) = 1$ and $\text{success}(\Delta, A) = 0$ makes the definition slightly complex. In fact, it becomes even more complex because we are counting steps (success in k steps) as well as identifying the resources used in each step. Now to the details.

Definition 8.6 (Success in a goal-directed computation). Let Δ be a database and A a wff. We define the meta-predicate $\text{success}(\Delta, A) = x$, where $x = 0, 1$, in k steps, by induction, as follows:

1. $\text{success}(\Delta, q) = 1$ if q is atomic and $\mathbf{e} + \cdots + \mathbf{e} + q + \mathbf{e} + \ldots \mathbf{e} = \Delta$, or $q = \mathbf{e}$ and $\Delta = \varnothing$. This is the case of one step, *immediate* success. The wff used in this step is q.

$\text{success}(\Delta,q) = 0$ if q is atomic and there is no formula of the form $A_1 \Rightarrow (\dots \Rightarrow (A_n \Rightarrow q)\dots)$ in Δ, and if $q = \mathbf{e}$ we also require that $\Delta \neq \varnothing$. This is the case of one step, *immediate* failure. No wff is used.

2. $\text{success}(\Delta, A \Rightarrow B) = x$ in k steps if and only if $\text{success}(\Delta + A, B) = x$ in k steps. No wff is used.

3. $\text{success}(\Delta,q) = 1$ (respectively, 0) in $k+1$ steps if for some (respectively, all) wffs A in Δ such that (a) and (b) below hold we have that (c) holds for the case of the language without $\mathbf{e}$ and (c$'$) holds for the case of the language with $\mathbf{e}$, where:

   a. $\Delta = \Delta_e + A + \Delta'$
   b. $A = A_1 \Rightarrow (\dots (A_n \Rightarrow q)\dots)$
   c. For the case of language without $\mathbf{e}$:
      $\Delta_e = \varnothing$ and for some (respectively, for any) partition $\delta = (\Delta'_1,\dots,\Delta'_n)$ of Δ' such that $\Delta'_1 \neq \varnothing, \dots, \Delta'_n \neq \varnothing$ and such that $\Delta' = \Delta'_1 + \dots + \Delta'_n$ we have that for all (respectively, some) $1 \leq j \leq n$ the following holds:
      $\text{success}(\Delta'_j, A_j) = 1$ (respectively, $\text{success}(\Delta'_j, A_j) = 0$) in k_j^{δ} steps, and $\text{Max}_j(k_j^{\delta}) = k$.

   c$'$. For the case of language with $\mathbf{e}$:
      $\text{success}(\Delta_e, \mathbf{e}) = 1$ (respectively, $\text{success}(\Delta_e, \mathbf{e}) = 0$) in k_0 steps and (respectively, or) for some (respectively, any) partition $\delta = (\Delta'_1, \dots, \Delta'_r), n \leq r$ and some (respectively, any) $1 \leq m_1 < m_2 < \dots < m_n \leq r$ we have $\Delta' = \Delta'_1 + \dots + \Delta'_r$, and for all (respectively, some) $1 \leq j \leq r$ we have $\text{success}(\Delta_j, x_j) = 1$ (respectively, $\text{success}(\Delta_j, x_j) = 0$) in k_j^{δ} steps, and the following hold.
      a. If $j = m_j$ then $x_j = A_i, 1 \leq i \leq n$; otherwise $x_j = \mathbf{e}$;
      b. $\max_j^{\delta}(k_j) = k$.

   In the case of success $= 1$, by virtue of the choice of wff A in (a) we say that the wff A is used in this step. In case of failure for all choices of A we say that all of these A's are used.

4. Note that clause (3) above works equally for concatenation and linear logics with the respective meaning of $+$.

5. Note that the condition $\Delta'_i \neq 0$ in clause (3.c) makes $\text{success}((A \Rightarrow A) \Rightarrow B, B) = 0$. If we relinquish this condition then rule (8) of Definition 8.3 becomes valid. Therefore, the success predicate does not have this condition for the case of linear logic and strong concatenation logic.

6. Let $\text{success}^*(\Delta, A)$ be defined in terms of success as follows: $\text{success}^*(A_1 + \dots + A_n, A) = 1$ if and only if for some $\Theta_0, \dots, \Theta_n$ such that $\text{success}(\Theta_i, \mathbf{e}) = 1$, $i = 0, \dots, n$, we have $\text{success}(\Theta_0 + A_1 + \Theta_1 + \dots + A_n + \Theta_n, A) = 1$.

Example 8.3. Let us illustrate the machinery of failure by considering the problem of

$$\Delta = (b \Rightarrow (a_2 \Rightarrow q)) + (a_1 \Rightarrow b) + a_1 + a_2 + y \vdash^? q.$$

with a_1, a_2, q, b, y all distinct atoms.

We will try to succeed, but in fact we are going to fail. We use the multiset Θ to accumulate the wffs used in the computation. We cannot say we have immediate failure because the left clause has q as its head. We therefore proceed and use this clause and put into Θ the formula $b \Rightarrow (a_2 \Rightarrow q)$.

We need to find a partition δ of $\Delta' = (a_1 \Rightarrow b) + a_1 + a_2 + y$ of the form

$$\delta = (\Delta_1^\delta, \Delta_2^\delta)$$

such that

$$\Delta' = \Delta_1^\delta + \Delta_2^\delta, \ \Delta_i^\delta \neq \varnothing$$

and

$$\Delta_i^\delta \vdash a_i, \ i = 1, 2.$$

Failure means that for all such partitions δ, either $\Delta_1^\delta \vdash^? a_1$ fails or $\Delta_2^\delta \vdash^? a_2$ fails or both fail.

Let us enumerate our possible partitions for the case of concatenation logic (for linear logic there will be more partitions):

$$\Delta_1^1 = (a_1 \Rightarrow b) \qquad\qquad \Delta_2^1 = a_1 + a_2 + y$$

$$\Delta_1^2 = (a_1 \Rightarrow b) + a_1 \qquad \Delta_2^2 = a_2 + y$$

$$\Delta_1^3 = (a_1 \Rightarrow b) + a_1 + a_2 \qquad \Delta_2^3 = y.$$

We can easily see that we have the following

1. *For partition δ_1:*

   $\Delta_1^1 \vdash a_1$ fails in two steps and uses $a_1 \Rightarrow b$ (one step to use $a_1 \Rightarrow b$ and the next step to fail).
   $\Delta_2^1 \vdash^? a_2$ fails in one step using nothing.

2. *For partition δ_2:*

   $\Delta_1^2 \vdash^? a_1$ succeeds in two steps using $(a_1 \Rightarrow b)$ and a_1.
   $\Delta_2^2 \vdash^? a_2$ fails in two steps using a_2.

3. *For partition δ_3:*

   $\Delta_1^3 \vdash^? a_1$ fails in three steps using $(a_1 \Rightarrow b) + a_1$
   $\Delta_2^3 \vdash^? a_2$ fails in one step using nothing.

To show that $\Delta \vdash^? q$ fails we must show that after using $b \Rightarrow (a_2 \Rightarrow q)$ each partition fails.

We show this by selecting for each $i = 1, 2, 3$ a value $f(i)$, $1 \leq f(i) \leq 2$ such that $\Delta_{f(i)}^i \vdash^? a_{f(i)}$ fails.

For each selection f, a possibly different overall sequence of formulae is used. The maximal nested number of steps leading to failure will also depend on the choice of f.

Table 8.1

Choice	steps	Θ is all the sequences in this column
$\Delta_1^1, \Delta_2^2, \Delta_1^3$	4	$(b \Rightarrow (a_2 \Rightarrow q)), (a_1 \Rightarrow b), a_2, (a_1 \Rightarrow b), a_1$
$\Delta_2^1, \Delta_2^2, \Delta_1^3$	4	$(b \Rightarrow (a_2 \Rightarrow q)), (a_1 \Rightarrow b), a_1$
$\Delta_2^1, \Delta_2^2, \Delta_2^3$	3	$(b \Rightarrow (a_2 \Rightarrow q)), a_2$
$\Delta_1^1, \Delta_2^2, \Delta_2^3$	3	$(b \Rightarrow (a_2 \Rightarrow q)), a_2$

Table 8.1 below shows our options for f and the maximal nested number of steps and the sequences of wffs used in the overall failure of $\Delta \vdash^? q$:

It is clear from Table 8.1 that to show that $\Delta \vdash^? q$ fails we need at least three steps, in which case we use the resources of $b \Rightarrow (a_2 \Rightarrow q)$ and a_2.

If we want to maximise the (wasteful) use of resources, we choose the first choice $(\Delta_1^1, \Delta_2^2, \Delta_1^3)$ and fail in four steps. We use all wffs except y, including $(a_1 \Rightarrow b)$ which is used twice.

Theorem 8.2 (Cut theorem for concatenation and linear implications). *Let $\Delta = \Delta_0 + C + \Theta_0$. We require that C appear in Δ, but Δ_0 and/or Θ_0 may be empty. Then (1) and (2) imply (3).*

1. $\text{success}(\Delta, q) = 1$ *in m steps.*
2. $\text{success}(\Gamma, C) = 1$ *in n steps.*
3. $\text{success}((\Delta_0 + \Gamma + \Theta_0), q) = 1$ *in at most $n + m - 1$ steps.*

Proof.

i. *To prepare the ground for our induction, we begin with (1). The computation of (1) has to go through a formula D in the database. Write D as $D = D_1 \Rightarrow (\dots \Rightarrow (D_k \Rightarrow q)\dots)$ and write the database as*

$$\Delta_0 + C + \Theta_0 = \Gamma_1 + \dots + \Gamma_t + D + \Gamma_1' + \dots + \Gamma_r', k \leq r.$$

We have that $\text{success}(\Gamma_j, \mathbf{e}) = 1$, $1 \leq j \leq t$, in at most $m - 1$ steps, and for each $1 \leq j \leq r$, $\text{success}(\Gamma_j', X_j) = 1$ in at most $m - 1$ steps, where X_j is either one of $(D_1, \dots, D_k)$ or $\mathbf{e}$, and the appropriate conditions of item 3 of Definition 8.6 hold. There are two possibilities for D. Either $D = C$ or $D \neq C$. Our proof will distinguish these two subcases. We now continue with the proof and refer to the above as the situation described in (i).

ii. *Case $m = 1$, C arbitrary In this case, we must have $\Delta = \mathbf{e} + \dots + \mathbf{e} + q + \mathbf{e} + \dots + \mathbf{e}$ and (3) holds.*

iii. *Case C is an atom p, m arbitrary This case is proved by induction on m.*

   a. *Case $m = 1$ follows from (ii).*

b. *In case m, we have from (1) that q unifies with a formula D, as described above in (i).*

Subcase $D = C$.
In this subcase the database has the form $\Sigma\Theta_j^0 + q + \Sigma\Theta_j^1$ with success$(\Theta_j^i, \mathbf{e})$ = 1 in less than m steps. The cut, (3), then holds for $\Sigma\Theta_j^0 + \Gamma + \Sigma\Theta_j^1$ by continuing the computation through Γ in view of (2).

Subcase $D \neq C$.
In this subcase we get that $C \in \Gamma_s'$ for some $1 \leq s \leq r$ or $C \in \Gamma_s$ for some $1 \leq s \leq t$, and for each $1 \leq j \leq r$ we have success$(\Gamma_j', X_j) = 1$, and success$(\Gamma_j, \mathbf{e}) = 1$, $1 \leq j \leq t$, in at most $m-1$ steps. Assume $C \in \Gamma_s'$, without loss of generality. $C \in \Gamma_s'$ means that $\Gamma_s' = \Delta_s' + C + \Theta_s'$. By the induction hypothesis we have that success$(\Delta_s' + \Gamma + \Theta_s', X_s) = 1$ in at most $n+m-2$ steps. Hence, we have success$(\Gamma_1 + \ldots + \Gamma_t + D + \Gamma_1' + \ldots + \Gamma_{s-1}' + \Delta_s' + \Gamma + \Theta_s' + \Gamma_{s+1}' + \ldots + \Gamma_r', q) = 1$, which is (3), in at most $n+m-1$ steps.

iv. *m arbitrary and C arbitrary*
Assume by induction that the theorem holds for any pair m', C', provided that either $m' < m$ or C' is a subformula of C. We now prove the theorem for arbitrary m and C. We refer to the situation described in (i) and distinguish two subcases.

Subcase $C \neq D$
This subcase proceeds as in subcase $C \neq D$ of (iii), subcase (b).

Subcase $C = D$
In this subcase we have for each $1 \leq j \leq r$

(*) success$(\Gamma_j', X_j) = 1$ and success$(\Gamma_j, \mathbf{e}) = 1$ *in at most $m-1$ steps.*
We take a closer look at (2), which is success$(\Gamma, C) = 1$ in n steps. Since $C = D$, we get that (2) means:
success$(\Gamma + D_1 + \ldots + D_k, q) = 1$ *in n steps.*
We can now use the induction hypothesis for subformulae of C and arbitrary m repeatedly for (2) and (*) and get:
success$(\Gamma_1 + \ldots + \Gamma_t + \Gamma + \Gamma_1' + \ldots + \Gamma_r', q) = 1$ *at most $n+m-1$ steps, which is (3), as needed.*
Note that the cut is done in parallel, and that is why we got $n+m-1$ steps at the most.

Remark 8.2. Note that if we define $\Delta_1 + \Delta_2 \vdash A$ if and only if for some Θ, success$(\Theta, \mathbf{e}) = 1$ and success$(\Delta_1 + \Theta + \Delta_2, A) = 1$, then cut will still hold for $\vdash$.

The above considerations define the goal-directed proof theory for concatenation and linear implications. Since our considerations have to do with deletions, it is important to address the problem of anti-formulae and provable equivalence, i.e., that $\vdash A \equiv B$ implies $\vdash \bigcirc(A) \equiv \bigcirc(B)$ (see Analysis 8.6.4, Section 8.6.1, below).

The next two lemmas solve this problem for the language without $\mathbf{e}$. In concatenation logic A is provably equivalent to B if and only if $A = B$, and so we have no problem there. In strong concatenation logic and linear logic, we have theorems like $\vdash ((p \Rightarrow p) \Rightarrow q) \Rightarrow q$, but not the converse, $\nvdash q \Rightarrow ((p \Rightarrow p) \Rightarrow q)$. So we need not worry about the effect of 'redundant' theorems. However, in linear logic we are allowed to permute the antecedents $((A \Rightarrow (B \Rightarrow C)$ is logically equivalent to $B \Rightarrow (A \Rightarrow C))$. If we 'ignore' these permutations, then again we can say that A is equivalent to B in linear logic if and only if A 'equals' B.

Lemma 8.4 (Equivalence in concatenation logic without e). *Let $A \equiv B$ mean that* $success(A,B) = success(B,A) = 1$. *Then we have that $A \equiv B$ implies $A = B$.*

Proof. By induction on the structure of B and A.

Case $B = q$ atomic
$success(A_1 \Rightarrow \dots (A_n \Rightarrow q) \dots), q) = 1$ *implies $A = q$.*

Case $A = (A_1 \Rightarrow (\dots \Rightarrow (A_n = p) \dots)), B = (B_1 \Rightarrow (\dots \Rightarrow (B_m \Rightarrow q) \dots)))$
For $success(A,B)$ *to hold we must have $p = q$ and $n \leq m$. By symmetry, $m = n$. We therefore have that* $success(A_i, B_i) = 1$, $i = 1, \dots, m$, *and by symmetry also* $success(B_i, A_i) = 1$, $i = 1, \dots, n$. *By the induction hypothesis, $A_i = B_i$ and hence $A = B$.*

Lemma 8.5 (Equivalence in linear logic without e).

1. *Define* $perm(A)$, *the set of permutations of the wff A by induction as follows:*

$$perm(q) = \{q\}$$
$$perm(A_1 \Rightarrow (\dots \Rightarrow (A_n \Rightarrow q) \dots)) =$$
$$\{B_{\sigma(1)} \Rightarrow (\dots \Rightarrow (B_{\sigma(n)} \Rightarrow q) \dots) | B_i \in perm(A_i)$$
$$\text{and } (\sigma(1), \dots, \sigma(n)) \text{ is a permutation of } (1, \dots, n)\}.$$

   Note that $perm(A)$ *is finite.*

2. *The following holds:*
   $A \equiv B$ *if and only if $A \in perm(B)$.*

Proof. By induction on the structure of A and B.

Case $B = q$ atomic
In this case we must have $A = B = q$.

Case $A = (A_1 \Rightarrow (\dots \Rightarrow (A_n \Rightarrow p) \dots))$ and $B = (B_1 \Rightarrow (\dots \Rightarrow (B_m \Rightarrow q) \dots))$
In this case we must have $m = n$ and $p = q$. We must also have, since $success(A,B) = 1$, *that for some permutation* $\sigma, \sigma = (\sigma(1), \dots, \sigma(n))$ *of* $(1, \dots, n)$ *that* $success(A_i, B_{\sigma(i)}) = 1$ *for $i = 1, \dots, n$.*
   Similarly, by symmetry there exists a permutation $\eta = (\eta(1), \dots, \eta(n))$ *such that* $success(B_i, A_{\eta(i)}) = 1$ *for $i = 1, \dots, n$.*
   To prove the theorem, we must show that there exists a permutation ε such that for each i we have $success(A_i, B_{\varepsilon(i)}) = success(B_{\varepsilon(i)}, A_i) = 1$.
   We are actually going to show that $\varepsilon = \sigma$ will do.
   Choose an arbitrary i. We have
   $success(A_i, B_{\sigma(i)}) = 1$.
   We show that $success(B_{\sigma(i)}, A_i) = 1$ *also holds. We ask, what is the value of $\eta(\sigma(i))$? If $\eta(\sigma(i)) = i$ we are finished. Otherwise $\eta(\sigma(i)) \neq i$. We have*

success$(B_{\sigma(i)}, A_{\eta(\sigma(i))}) = 1$. *Consider* $B_{\sigma\eta\sigma(i)}$. *We have* success$(A_{\eta\sigma(i)}, B_{\sigma\eta\sigma(i)}) = 1$.

What is $A_{\eta\sigma\eta\sigma(i)}$? *It cannot be* $A_{\eta\sigma(i)}$ *because* η *is one-to-one. So it is either* A_i, *in which case we are finished because we have* success$(B_{\sigma\eta\sigma(i)}, A_{\eta\sigma\eta\sigma(i)}) = 1$, *and we can use Cut (transitivity); or it is a new element.*

If we proceed in this way we get that $A_{(\eta\sigma)^k(i)}$ *is either* A_i, *in which case we are finished, or a new element different from all* $A_{(\eta\sigma)^j(i)}, 1 \leq j \leq k$. *Since our set is finite, sooner or later we get* A_i.

We now have an ε *which makes* $A_i, B_{\varepsilon(i)}$ *provably equivalent. By the induction hypothesis they are* perms *of each other, and hence A is a* perm *of B as well.*

The preceding theorem shows that we can write the formulae of the logic in a slightly different way and get no provable ambiguity.

Definition 8.7. Define wffs of linear logic in a slightly different way. Call them n-wffs (normal form wffs).

1. An atom q is an n-wff.
2. If $A_1, \ldots, A_n$ are n-wffs then the multiset $\{A_1, \ldots, A_n\}$ is a database.
3. If Δ is a database and q an atom then $\Delta \Rightarrow q$ is an n-wff.

Note that the goal-directed computation works for databases and n-wffs because we use multisets in the definition anyway.

We actually proved the following.

Lemma 8.6. *For every wff A there exists a unique n-wff* $\mathbf{n}(A)$ *which is equivalent to it, and*

$$\mathrm{perm}(A) = \{B \mid B \equiv \mathbf{n}(A)\}.$$

8.5.3 Semantics

We now introduce several semantical interpretations for our logics. These will be used to introduce anti-formulae in Section 8.6. Our language contains the connective $\Rightarrow$ and the constant **e**.

We begin by explaining the nature of the semantics involved and the related questions we consider. We choose for our logics algebraic semantics of the form $(S, \circ, \leq, e)$ (in Definitions 8.10–8.11 below), where $(S, \circ, e)$ is a (non-commutative but) associative semigroup with a left unit e. Think of the elements $t \in S$ as pieces of information and think of the semantic relation $t \vDash A$ as saying that *the information t supports the formula A*. The operation $t \circ s$ is *fusion* of information. The basic truth definition for $\Rightarrow$ is

- $t \vDash A \Rightarrow B$ if and only if $\forall s(s \vDash A \rightarrow t \circ s \vDash B)$.

Different logics will have slight variations on this clause.

e represents the empty information, and thus in the semigroup we have e as a unit:

- $e \circ x = x \circ e = x$

If the language contains a constant **e** we have several options for interpreting it. The weakest option is to interpret **e** as *worthless* information. This corresponds to the upward semantic property, where $\Pi_{i=1}^{n} t_i$ (abbreviated Πt_i) means $t_1 \circ t_2 \circ \ldots \circ t_n$.

- $\Pi(t_i \circ s_i) \vDash A$ if $s_i \vDash$ **e** and $\Pi t_i \vDash A$

This semantic property corresponds to the upward **e**-rule.

We can ask for a stronger condition on **e**, corresponding to the downward **e**-rule, namely that **e** represent the *empty* information.

- $\Pi t_i \vDash A$ if $s_i \vDash$ **e** and $\Pi(t_i \circ s_i) \vDash A$

The ordering $\leq$ represents an increase in information. We therefore expect

- $t \leq s$ and $t \vDash A \rightarrow s \vDash A$
- $t \leq t'$ and $s \leq s' \rightarrow t \circ s \leq t' \circ s'$.

Note that the last condition implies the upward **e**-rule. If $e \leq s$ then $t = t \circ e \leq t \circ s$. Hence, $t \vDash A \rightarrow t \circ s \vDash A$.

The above semantics corresponds to concatenation logic. If the semigroup is commutative, we get semantics for linear logic.

The canonical model for the logic is built up from all formulae and databases of the language.

Thus, in the canonical model we have that t, s are databases and

$t \leq s$ means $s \vdash t^{14}$
$t \vDash A$ means $t \vdash A$

and we further have

$t \vDash A$ if and only if $t_A \leq A$, where $t_A = A = \min\{x | x \vDash A\}$.

$\Rightarrow$ corresponds to a *residuation* operation in the semigroup, which we denote by $\twoheadrightarrow$, satisfying:

- $u \leq t \circ s$ if and only if $s \twoheadrightarrow u \leq t$

The above is the deduction theorem

- $t \circ s \vdash u$ if and only if $t \vdash s \Rightarrow u$.

---

[14] As defined in Definition 8.11, item 2.

Definition 8.8 (Semigroups).

1. We know from algebra the notion of a partially ordered *semigroup with a left identity*. This is a system $(S, \leq, \circ, e)$ with a partial order $\leq$, with an associative binary multiplication $(x, y) \mapsto x \circ y$ and a left unity e satisfying $e \circ x = x$. We require the following monotonicity condition of $\circ$ (relative to $\leq$) to hold:

$$x \leq y \text{ and } x' \leq y' \to x \circ x' \leq y \circ y'.$$

2. The semigroup is commutative if $x \circ y = y \circ x$ holds for all x, y.
3. A semigroup is free if it is freely generated from a set of atomic generators. Let $\mathscr{A} = \{e, a_1, a_2, \ldots\}$ be a set of atomic generators with e intended as the (left or left and right) identity. The elements of the free semigroup are all words of the form $a_1 \circ a_2 \circ \ldots \circ a_n$, with n arbitrary and $a_i \in \mathscr{A}$. This makes the word a sequence $(a_1, \ldots, a_n)$. If we impose commutativity then this word is essentially the multiset $\{a_1, \ldots, a_n\}$.
4. A semigroup may satisfy the left inverse axiom: $\forall x \exists y (y \circ x = e)$.
   The left inverse may not be unique, nor may we have that the double inverse of an element is itself, i.e., we may not have that $z \circ y = e \wedge y \circ x = e \to x = z$. However, if the semigroup is commutative then there are unique left and right inverses and we get a commutative group. This holds because

   $$z \circ y \circ x = (z \circ y) \circ x = e \circ x = x$$
   $$z \circ y \circ x = z \circ (y \circ x) = z \circ e = z$$

   Hence $z = x$.
5. The monotonicity of $\circ$ implies the (algebraic) upward **e**-rule:

   - $e \leq s_1$ and $e \leq s_2$ imply for any t and y

     $$t \leq y \to t \leq s_1 \circ y \circ s_2.$$

   A semigroup may also satisfy the (algebraic) downward **e**-rule.

   - $e \leq s_1$ and $e \leq s_2$ imply for any t and y

     $$t \leq s_1 \circ y \circ s_2 \to t \leq s.$$

   Both rules can be written as

   - $e \leq s_1$ and $e \leq s_2$ imply for any t, y

     $$t \leq y \text{ if and only if } t \leq s_1 \circ y \circ s_2.$$

6. A semigroup is left-residuated if and only if there exists a binary operation $\twoheadrightarrow$ satisfying for all u, t, s and all x, x', y, y'

   - $u \leq t \circ s$ if and only if $s \twoheadrightarrow u \leq t$.
   - $x' \leq x$ and $y \leq y' \to x \twoheadrightarrow y \leq x' \twoheadrightarrow y'$

7. See [17] for an algebraic background and [7] for more on concatenation and linear implications.

Lemma 8.7. *In a left-residuated semigroup with a left and right identity satisfying the downward **e**-rule we have that for any t, $(t \twoheadrightarrow e)$ is a unique left inverse of t.*

Proof. 1. *The presence of the downward **e**-rule means that for every y, x and every s_i such that $e \leq s_i$*

$$x \leq y \text{ if and only if } x \leq s_1 \circ y \circ s_2.$$

2. *From (1), for $x = t$ and $s = ((t \twoheadrightarrow e) \twoheadrightarrow e) \circ (t \twoheadrightarrow e)$ we get $t \leq t$ if and only if $t \leq (t \twoheadrightarrow e) \twoheadrightarrow e) \circ (t \twoheadrightarrow e) \circ t$ if and only if $t \leq (t \twoheadrightarrow e) \twoheadrightarrow e$.*
Similarly, for $x = (t \twoheadrightarrow e) \twoheadrightarrow e$ and $s = (t \twoheadrightarrow e) \circ t$ we get $(t \twoheadrightarrow e) \twoheadrightarrow e \leq t$.
Thus, we get that $((t \twoheadrightarrow e) \twoheadrightarrow e) = t$.
The latter implies that also $t \circ (t \twoheadrightarrow e) = e$.
3. *We now show that if $y \circ t = e$ then $y = t \twoheadrightarrow e$.*
Consider $= y \circ t \circ (t \twoheadrightarrow e)$; we have $z = (t \twoheadrightarrow e)$ since $y \circ t = e$ and also $z = y$ since $t \circ (t \twoheadrightarrow e) = e$.

Definition 8.9 (Partially ordered semigroups and semantics).

1. Let $(S, \circ, \leq, e)$ be a semigroup with left and right identity e and with a partial ordering $\leq$, satisfying the downward **e**-rule.
2. Let h be an assignment giving for each atomic q a subset $h(q) \subseteq S$ satisfying the conditions for all atomic q and **e**:

   - $e \in h(\mathbf{e})$
   - $t \in h(q)$ and $t \leq s \rightarrow s \in h(q)$.

   Consider the model $\mathbf{m} = (S, \circ, \leq, e, h)$ with satisfaction defined by

   - $t \vDash \mathbf{e}$ if and only if $e \leq t$
   - $t \vDash q$ if and only if $t \in h(q)$
   - $t \vDash A \Rightarrow B$ if and only if $\forall s (s \vDash A \text{ imply } t \circ s \vDash B)$ (in the case of concatenation logic we also require that $s \neq e \lor t = e$)

3. We say this model is *sharp* if and only if for all atomic A there exists a t_A such that for all y, $y \vDash A$ if and only if $t_A \leq y$.
4. Let $\mathbf{m} \vDash A$ if and only if $e \vDash A$.

Lemma 8.8. *Let $(S, \circ, \leq, e, h)$ be a left-residuated sharp model. The following holds:*

1. *For any wff A there exists a $t_A \in S$ such that for all y*

   $$y \vDash A \text{ if and only if } t_A \leq y.$$

2. *$t \vDash A$ and $s \vDash \mathbf{e}$ imply $t \circ s \vDash A$ and $s \circ t \vDash A$.*

Proof. By induction on A.
Case A atomic.
For atomic A conditions (1) and (2) hold by the assumptions on S.

Case $A \Rightarrow B$.
Assume (1) and (2) hold for A and B; we show they hold for $A \Rightarrow B$.

We show (1):

$t \vDash A \Rightarrow B$ *if and only if* $\forall s(s \vDash A \rightarrow t \circ s \vDash B)$
if and only if $\forall s(t_A \leq s \rightarrow t_B \leq t \circ s)$
if and only if $\forall s(t_A \leq s \rightarrow s \twoheadrightarrow t_B \leq t)$ *if and only if* $t_A \twoheadrightarrow t_B \leq t$.

We show (2):

Assume $t \vDash A \Rightarrow B$ *and* $s \vDash \mathbf{e}$. *We show* $t \circ s \vDash A \Rightarrow B$. *We know that* $\forall x(x \vDash A \rightarrow t \circ x \vDash B)$. *By the induction hypothesis* $x \vDash A \rightarrow s \circ x \vDash A$, *and hence* $t \circ s \circ x \vDash B$. *Hence,* $t \circ s \vDash A \Rightarrow B$.

Similarly, since $(t \circ x \vDash B \Rightarrow s \circ t \circ x \vDash B)$, *we get* $s \circ t \vDash A \Rightarrow B$.

Note that (2) is proved without assuming the semigroup is residuated.

Let us now proceed with our definitions and completeness proofs.

Definition 8.10 (Free semantics for concatenation and linear $\Rightarrow$ and e).

1. Let T be a set of atomic elements. Let S^* (respectively, $S^\#$ for linear logic) be the set of all finite sequences (respectively, multisets) of elements from T, including the empty sequence (respectively, multiset) $\varnothing$.
   Define $+$ on this set by[15]

   $t + s = t * s$ (respectively, $t \cup s$),

   where $*$ is concatenation of sequences and $\cup$ is multiset union.

2. Let h be an assignment giving for each atomic q a subset $h(q) \subseteq S$ (where S is either S^* or $S^\#$, depending on the logic). We require that $\varnothing \in h(\mathbf{e})$ and the following condition (#) holds:

   (#) For all $t, s, t \in h(q) \wedge s \in h(\mathbf{e}) \rightarrow t + s \in h(q)$ and $s + t \in h(q)$.

   This is the upward **e**-rule. Note that if we further require $h(\mathbf{e}) = \{\varnothing\}$, we get what we call the *strict free model*, satisfying also the downward **e**-rule.

3. A structure $\mathbf{m} = (S, +, \varnothing, h)$ is called a free model.

4. Define satisfaction $t \vDash A$ for $t \in S$ and a wff A as follows ($\vDash$ is $\vDash^*$ for concatenation logic without **e**, or $\vDash^\#$ for linear logic or logic with **e**, respectively, depending on the logic).

   - $t \vDash \mathbf{e}$ if and only if $t \in h(\mathbf{e})$.
   - $t \vDash q$ if and only if $t \in h(q)$, q atomic.
   - $\varnothing \vDash^* A \Rightarrow B$ if and only if $\forall s(s \vDash A \rightarrow t + s \vDash B)$.
   - $t \vDash^* A \Rightarrow B$ for $t \neq \varnothing$ if and only if $\forall s(s \vDash A \wedge s \neq \varnothing \rightarrow t + s \vDash B)$.[16]

---

[15] We use the symbol '+' for combining databases and for combining information in the free model. We use the symbol '∘' for a general semigroup operation. Thus '+' and '∘' are actually doing the same job. Similarly for '∅' and '*e*'.

[16] If we allow $t \neq \varnothing$ and $s = \varnothing$ in the definition of $\vDash^*$ $(A \Rightarrow B)$ then the rule

$$\frac{\vdash A}{\vdash (A \Rightarrow B) \Rightarrow B}$$

becomes valid. In linear logic it is valid because $\vdash A \Rightarrow ((A \Rightarrow B) \Rightarrow B)$.
  See [7, Section 2.4].

- $t \vDash^{\#} A \Rightarrow B$ if and only if $\forall s$ $(s \vDash^{\#} A \rightarrow t + s \vDash^{\#} B)$.

5. We say $\mathbf{m} \vDash A$ if and only if $\varnothing \vDash A$.
6. We say $\vDash A$ if and only if $\forall \mathbf{m}(\mathbf{m} \vDash A)$.
7. We say $\mathbf{m}$ is a realistic model if and only if for any wff A there exists a $t \neq \varnothing$ such that $t \vDash A$.
8. Note that in this semantics $\varnothing$ is the actual world and we are using a non-normal possible world semantics.
9. If we allow $\top$ and $\bot$ in the language then we let $h(\top) = S$ and $h(\bot) = \varnothing$.[17]

Lemma 8.9. *In a free model we have*

(#) $t \vDash A$ and $s \vDash \mathbf{e}$ imply $t + s \vDash A$ and $s + t \vDash A$.

Proof. By induction on A.

1. *For atomic A this is property (#) of h.*
2. *Assume $t \vDash A$ and $s \vDash \mathbf{e}$. Then, $t \vDash A \Rightarrow B$ if and only if for all $x, x \vDash A \rightarrow t + x \vDash B$. By the induction hypothesis, $s + t + x \vDash B$ and $s + x \vDash A$; hence, by definition, $s + t \vDash A \Rightarrow B$ and $t + s \vDash A \Rightarrow B$.*

The reader can verify that for the Hilbert systems under the same name of Definition 8.3, we have $\vdash A$ implies $\vDash A$. If our model is strict, i.e., it also satisfies the downward **e**-rule, then we get soundness for success*:

Lemma 8.10 (Soundness for success). *Let $\Delta = \Delta_e + A_0 + \ldots + A_n$.*
   If success$(\Delta_e + A_0 + \ldots + A_n, q) = 1$ *in m steps then* $\vDash \Delta_e \Rightarrow (A_0 \Rightarrow \ldots \Rightarrow (A_n \Rightarrow q)\ldots)$.

Proof. By induction on m

1. *If $m = 1$, then if $\Delta = (\mathbf{e} + \ldots + \mathbf{e} + q + \mathbf{e} + \ldots \mathbf{e})$, then it is clear that $\vDash \Delta \Rightarrow q$, by Lemma 8.9.*
   If $\Delta = \varnothing$ and $q = \mathbf{e}$ then clearly $\vDash \mathbf{e}$.
2. *Let $A_0 = (D_1 \Rightarrow (\ldots \Rightarrow (D_k \Rightarrow q)\ldots))$. Assume* success$(\Delta_e, \mathbf{e}) = 1$ *and* success$(A_0 + \Delta_1 + \ldots + \Delta_r, q) = 1$ *where $k \leq r$ and $\Delta_{j+1} = A_{n_j+1} + \ldots + A_{n_{j+1}}$ and $1 \leq n_1 \leq n_2 \leq \ldots \leq n_r$ and $n_r = n$ and the appropriate conditions of item 3 of Definition 8.6 hold.*
   This means that success$(\Delta_j, X_j) = 1, j = 1, \ldots, r$. *By the induction hypothesis we have that in any $\mathbf{m}$*

   $\mathbf{m} \vDash \Delta_e \Rightarrow \mathbf{e}$ and $\mathbf{m} \vDash \Delta_j \Rightarrow X_j$.

Note that X_j is either $\mathbf{e}$ or one of $(D_1, \ldots, D_k)$ and the order of the D_i is preserved. We want to show that for any $\mathbf{m}$, $\mathbf{m} \vDash \Delta_e \Rightarrow (A_0 \Rightarrow (A_1 \Rightarrow \ldots \Rightarrow (A_n \Rightarrow q)\ldots))$. The latter holds if for all $t_0, t_1, \ldots, t_n$, such that (in concatenation logic) the appropriate conditions are satisfied, and $t_i \vDash A_i$ for $i = 0, \ldots, n$, we have $t_0 + t_1 + \ldots + t_n \vDash q$.

---

[17] Do not confuse this with the condition for $h(\mathbf{e})$, namely that $\varnothing \in h(\mathbf{e})$. We can have, for example, $h(\mathbf{e}) = \{\varnothing\}$.

Since $\mathbf{m} \vDash \Delta_j \Rightarrow X_j$, *we get that* $s_j = t_{n_j+1} + \ldots + t_{n_{j+1}} \vDash X_j$ *for* $j = 1, \ldots, r-1$.
Since $t_0 \vDash A_0$ *we get that* $t_0 + s_1 \ldots + s_r \vDash q$.

Definition 8.11 (Free canonical model for success).[18]

1. Let S be the set of all theories of the language. Any $t \in S$ has the form $t = \varnothing$ or $t = A_1 + \ldots + A_n$, where $+$ has the meaning of the respective logic. S is *generated* from the wffs using $+$. To create a strict model, we need to identify any $\Delta + \mathbf{e} + \Theta$ with $\Delta + \Theta$. In particular, we identify $\mathbf{e}$ with $\varnothing$. This can be done properly only for the success* predicate, not for the success predicate. If Δ_1 and Δ_2 are identified, then for any A, $\mathrm{success}(\Delta_1, A) = 1$ in k steps if and only if $\mathrm{success}(\Delta_2, A) = 1$ in k steps. This follows from Definition 8.6.
We shall continue our definition with the success predicate.

2. Define $\leq$ on S as follows:

   - $A \leq B$ if and only if $\mathrm{success}(B, A) = 1$
   - $t = (A_1, \ldots, A_n) \leq s$ if and only if for some $s_1, \ldots, s_n$ we have $s = s_1 + \ldots + s_n$ and $\mathrm{success}(s_i, A_i) = 1$ for $1 \leq i \leq n$.

3. Let h be defined by $h(q) = \{t \in S | \mathrm{success}(t, q) = 1\}$

4. Note that from the cut theorem the following holds in this model.

   a. $\leq$ is a partial ordering
   b. $t \in h(q)$ and $t \leq s$ imply $s \in h(q)$
   c. $h(q)$ has a first element t_q and we have

   $$h(q) = \{t | t_q \leq t\}.$$

   t_q is a generator (the wff q).
   d. $t \leq s$ and $t' \leq s'$ imply $t + t' \leq s + s'$
   e. $t \in h(q)$ and $s \in h(\mathbf{e}) \to t + s \in h(q)$ and $s + t \in h(q)$.
   f. There exists a residuation operation $\twoheadrightarrow$ in the algebra for generators such that for any generator u, and any t, s we have $u \leq t + s$ if and only if $s \twoheadrightarrow u \leq t$. This follows from the deduction theorem, with $s \twoheadrightarrow u$ being the generator $s \Rightarrow u$.
   We also have $x' \leq x$ and $y \leq y' \to x \twoheadrightarrow y \leq x' \twoheadrightarrow y'$.
   g. Each element t has a left-inverse $t \twoheadrightarrow \varnothing$ (i.e., the left inverse of Δ is $\Delta \Rightarrow \mathbf{e}$).

Lemma 8.11 (Completeness). *If* $\mathrm{success}(\Delta, q) = 0$ *then for some free realistic model* $\mathbf{m}, \mathbf{m} \nVDash \Delta \Rightarrow q$.

Proof. Consider the canonical free model of the language. In this model we have $h(q) = \{\Delta | \mathrm{success}(\Delta, q) = 1\}$. *We now prove for all A and Δ the following holds.*

(*) $\Delta \vDash A$ *if and only if* $\mathrm{success}(\Delta, A) = 1$.

---

[18] We can define the same canonical model using the Hilbert system of Definition 2.1. Replace 'success$((A_1, \ldots, A_n), B) = 1$' by '$(A_1, \ldots, A_n) \vdash B$'.
   The crucial step is that the same cut theorem holds for both the 'success' and the '$\vdash$' formulations.

The proof is by induction on A using the cut theorem.

1. Case atomic q
   Follows by definition.
2. Case $A \Rightarrow B$
   Assume $\Delta \vDash A \Rightarrow B$. Then for all Δ' such that $\Delta' \vDash A$ we have that $\Delta + \Delta' \vDash B$. Let Δ' be A. Then $\Delta + A \vDash B$. By the induction hypothesis success$(\Delta + A, B) = 1$; hence, success$(\Delta, A \Rightarrow B) = 1$. Assume success$(\Delta, A \Rightarrow B) = 1$. We need to show $\Delta \vDash A \Rightarrow B$. By the induction hypothesis we must show that whenever success$(\Gamma, A) = 1$, success$(\Delta + \Gamma, B) = 1$. Since success$(\Delta + A, B) = 1$ we can use Cut and get the result.

Note that this canonical model is realistic.

Remark 8.3. Note that in the canonical model we have not used the partial order. Nevertheless, one can prove that the following holds.

Let $h(A) = \{t \in S \mid t \vDash A\}$. Then $h(A)$ has a first element t_A and $h(A) = \{x \mid t_A \leq x\}$, which is a generator (the wff A).

Lemma 8.12 (Soundness and completeness). *(strong) Concatenation logic with **e**, defined by axioms (1)–(2) and (6)–(10) of Definition 8.3, is sound and complete for semigroup semantics. The addition of the downward **e**-rule to the logic requires the downward **e**-rule to hold in the semigroup.*

Proof. We need to show the following:
If success$(A_0 + \ldots + A_n, q) = 1$, *then for any* **m**,

$$\mathbf{m} \vDash A_0 \Rightarrow (\ldots \Rightarrow (A_n \Rightarrow q) \ldots)$$

See the proof of Lemma 8.10.

Completeness follows because the canonical model of Definition 8.11 satisfies all the conditions of the semantics. In fact, the canonical model is sharp.

Remark 8.4. The semantics for linear logic is that of commutative semigroups with ordering $\leq$. The semantic satisfaction condition for $\Rightarrow$ is

$$t \vDash A \Rightarrow B \text{ if and only if } \forall s(s \vDash A \Rightarrow t \circ s \vDash B).$$

8.6 Introducing Anti-formulae in Concatenation and Linear Logic

To add anti-formulae to our language we need to add a connective $\bigcirc(A)$ to the language, with suitable axioms, which is invariant under provable equivalence and which has the desired meaning.

The best way to determine whether $\bigcirc$ does have the desired meaning is to give it either a semantical interpretation or a good (goal-directed) proof theory. We first intuitively explore our possibilities and options for $\bigcirc$ in Section 8.6.1, and try to give some answers in Section 8.6.2. Comparison of $\bigcirc$ with negation $\neg$ is carried out in Section 8.6.3.

8.6.1 Analysis

Definition 8.12 (Anti-formulae). We now add to the implicational language of Definition 8.3 the unary anti-formula connective $\bigcirc(X)$.

Let $A^{[n]} \Rightarrow B$ be $A \Rightarrow (\ldots \Rightarrow (A \Rightarrow B)\ldots)$ with n copies of A.

Let $C^{[1,\ldots,n]} \Rightarrow B$ be $C_1 \Rightarrow (\ldots \Rightarrow (C_n \Rightarrow B)\ldots)$.

Consider the following axioms:

The axiom $\alpha \equiv \beta$ abbreviates two axioms, $\alpha \Rightarrow \beta$ and $\beta \Rightarrow \alpha$.

1. $(\bigcirc(A) \Rightarrow (A \Rightarrow B)) \equiv B$
2. $(\bigcirc(A) \Rightarrow (C^{[1,\ldots,n]} \Rightarrow (A \Rightarrow B)\ldots) \equiv (C^{[1,\ldots,n]} \Rightarrow B)$
3k. $(\bigcirc(A) \Rightarrow (A^{[k]} \Rightarrow B)) \equiv B$
4k. $(\bigcirc(A) \Rightarrow (C_1)^{[1,\ldots,n_1]} \Rightarrow (A \Rightarrow (C_2)^{[1,\ldots,n_2]} \Rightarrow \ldots (A \Rightarrow (C_k)^{[1,\ldots,n_k]}) \Rightarrow B)\ldots) \equiv ((C_1)^{[1,\ldots,n_1]} \Rightarrow \ldots \Rightarrow ((C_k)^{[1,\ldots,n_k]} \Rightarrow B)\ldots)$

and

1*. $(A \Rightarrow (\bigcirc(A) \Rightarrow B)) \equiv B$

Similarly (2*), (3*k), (4*k) are obtained from the unstarred versions by swapping the occurrences of 'A' and '$\bigcirc(A)$'.

To understand the meaning of these axioms, think of concatenation logic. This logic is the same as the right-hand implicational part of the Lambek calculus. Its data structures are sequences of formulae of the form $(A_1,\ldots,A_n)$. It is the smallest logic such that $A \vdash A$ holds and the deduction theorem

$$(A_1,\ldots A_n,A) \vdash B \text{ if and only if } (A_1\ldots A_n) \vdash A \Rightarrow B$$

also holds.

It satisfies cut:

$$(A_1,\ldots,A_n) \vdash B \text{ and } (C_1,\ldots,C_k,B,D_1,\ldots,D_m) \vdash E$$

imply

$$(C_1,\ldots,C_k,A_1,\ldots,A_n,D_1,\ldots,D_m) \vdash E.$$

Axiom (1) says that if $\bigcirc(A)$ and A appear next to each other in this order in the database list, they annihilate each other. Thus, $(A_1,\ldots A_n,\bigcirc(A),A,B_1,\ldots,B_k) \vdash E$ if and only if $(A_1,\ldots,A_n,B_1,\ldots,B_k) \vdash E$.

Axiom (2) allows for annihilation at a distance.

Both axioms allow for annihilating one copy only from the right-hand side.

Axioms (3k) and (4k) allow for annihilation of k copies exactly, from the right hand side.

If we want annihilation from the left, we should adopt axiom (1*).

1*. $(A \Rightarrow (\bigcirc(A) \Rightarrow B)) \Rightarrow B$.

and similarly the other starred axioms.

Analysis 8.6.1 (Anti-formulae and the deduction theorem) *Consider concatenation logic with axiom (1) of anti-formulae (Definition 8.12). We try to explore its properties and problems.*

We can formulate a deduction theorem (left-sided)

DTL: $(A_1,\ldots,A_n) \vdash B$ *if and only if* $(A_1,\ldots,A_n,\bigcirc(A)) \vdash A \Rightarrow B$

Notice that in order for this deduction theorem to reduce to the familiar one, we need also (1*) (annihilation to the left).

$$A \Rightarrow B \vdash A \Rightarrow B$$

if and only if, by the familiar deduction theorem,

$$((A \Rightarrow B), A) \vdash B$$

if and only if, by the anti-formula deduction theorem,

$$(A \Rightarrow B, A, \bigcirc(A)) \vdash A \Rightarrow B.$$

We thus need that

$$(A \Rightarrow B, A, \bigcirc(A)) \equiv (A \Rightarrow B).$$

Since A, B are arbitrary we should also expect $(A, \bigcirc(A)) = \varnothing$ *to hold.*

We may ask whether we could start with axiom (1*) only, and formulate the deduction theorem as right-sided.

DTR: $(A_1,\ldots,A_n) \vdash B$ *if and only if* $(A_1,\ldots,A_n,A) \vdash \bigcirc(A) \Rightarrow B$

Is this compatible with the traditional deduction theorem without the need of axiom (1)?

We continue.

$$(A_1,\ldots,A_n,A) \vdash \bigcirc(A) \Rightarrow B$$

if and only if

$$(A_1,\ldots,A_n) \vdash A \Rightarrow (\bigcirc(A) \Rightarrow B)$$

if and only if (by (1*))

$$(A_1,\ldots,A_n) \vdash B$$

Can this deduction theorem get us into trouble? Let us check:

$$(A_1,\ldots,A_n,A) \vdash B$$

if and only if

$$(A_1,\ldots,A_n) \vdash A \Rightarrow B$$

if and only if

$$(A_1,\ldots,A_n,\bigcirc(A)) \vdash A \Rightarrow (A \Rightarrow B).$$

In this logic, $A \Rightarrow (A \Rightarrow B)$ is not the same as $A \Rightarrow B$. So it looks like we are safe. Of course, we still need to show consistency of, say, concatenation logic and axiom

(1) for an anti-formula and the deduction theorem, either by providing a semantics or by means of an algorithmic proof.

It is clear, however, that in any logic where $A \Rightarrow (A \Rightarrow B) \vdash A \Rightarrow B$, such as relevance or intuitionistic logic, we can continue and show that

$$(A_1, \ldots, A_n, \bigcirc(A)) \vdash A \Rightarrow B$$

and hence

$$(A_1, \ldots, A_n) \vdash B.$$

Thus, we have it in such logics that $(A_1, \ldots, A_n, A) \vdash B$ implies $(A_1, \ldots, A_n) \vdash B$.

This is a bad outcome, needless to say. So for intuitionistic logic and relevance logics we cannot have both the axiom $(\bigcirc(A) \Rightarrow (A \Rightarrow B)) \Rightarrow B$ for anti-formulae and the deduction theorem. If we hope for both of these rules we need to retain the idea of our data structures as multisets or lists.

Analysis 8.6.2 (Anti-formulae and negation) *We must also deal with negation in this system. It seems that negation will have to be paraconsistent. Otherwise we could have $\{A, \neg A\} \vdash \bigcirc(A), \{A, \neg A\} \vdash \bigcirc(\neg A), \{A, \neg A\} \vdash X$, and hence $\varnothing = \{A, \neg A, \bigcirc(A), \bigcirc(\neg A)\} \vdash X$ for arbitrary X.*

Analysis 8.6.3 (Anti-formulae and resource considerations) *Consider the database list $(\odot(A), \bigcirc(A), A)$, where $\odot(A)$ abbreviates $\bigcirc^2(A)$. Given our current understanding of concatenation logic, we can annihilate the first two and get that it is equivalent to (A), or the last two and get that it is equivalent to $(\odot(A))$. This would yield that A is provably equivalent to $\odot(A)$. We may not be happy with that, since $\odot(A)$ is supposed to cancel $\bigcirc(A)$ not to be A.*

However, it would also imply annihilation to the right, since $(A, \bigcirc(A))$ is equivalent to $(\odot(A), \bigcirc(A))$.

We can exploit the fact that our database is a list and annihilate left to right, scanning the list. Thus $(\odot(A), \bigcirc(A), A)$ is equivalent to A, but $(\bigcirc(A), \odot(A), A)$ cannot be reduced, and $(\bigcirc(A), A, \odot(A))$ is equivalent to $\odot(A)$.

This will not work for linear logic, in which data structures are multisets and no order is available.[19]

We have further problems in intuitionistic logic, where $A \Rightarrow B$ and $A^{[n]} \Rightarrow B$ are equivalent. It makes no sense to talk about how many copies $\bigcirc(A)$ can annihilate and then disappear. Suppose we say $\bigcirc(A)$ can annihilate k copies of A. This would give

$$\{\bigcirc(A), A\} \equiv \{\bigcirc(A), A, A^k\} \equiv \{A\}.$$

It is better to say $\bigcirc(A)$ can annihilate any number of copies A, i.e.,

$$\{\bigcirc(A), A^k\} \equiv \{\bigcirc(A)\}.$$

In other words, once $\bigcirc(A) \in \Delta$, it stays there forever (unless it is itself taken out by $\odot(A)$) preventing any copies of A getting into Δ. To take $\bigcirc(A)$ out we use $\odot(A)$.

---

[19] We shall see that it is reasonable to have $\odot(A) \equiv A$ in linear logic, and thus $\{\odot(A), \bigcirc(A), A\} \equiv A$.

This approach will work across all logics, including concatenation logic. We can also ensure that $\odot(A)$ is neither the same as A, nor is related to it. We have to be careful in how we understand the database $\Delta = \{A, \bigcirc(A), \odot(A)\}$ because, as we have already discussed, it does seem to give $\odot(A) = A$. We must consider a proof theory from Δ that says $\bigcirc(A)$ annihilates A provided it cannot be annihilated itself. Such proof procedures are known from the area of defeasible logics, but they are non-monotonic in nature, i.e., $\Delta = (A) \vdash A$ but $\Delta + \bigcirc(A) \nvdash A$.

Another point to consider in resource logic is the question of whether $\bigcirc(A)$ is a resource to be used in proofs or just a marker. Consider the database $\{\bigcirc(A), A \Rightarrow B, (A \Rightarrow B) \Rightarrow B\}$. Does it prove B? In linear logic all data has to be used. Is $\bigcirc(A)$ a data item to be used, or just anti-data?

Analysis 8.6.4 (Anti-formulae and provable equivalence) *Another question to consider is whether $\bigcirc(X)$ is invariant under provable equivalence; i.e., whether it is a proper connective or not. We shall examine this question later in the chapter. This is a general problem of deletion in logic.*

In concatenation logic one can show that $A \vdash B$ and $B \vdash A$ imply $A = B$ (i.e., B is identical with A), and so the problem does not arise. We can indeed have that $X_1 \vdash X_2$ and $X_2 \vdash X_1$ imply $\bigcirc(X_1) \vdash \bigcirc(X_2)$ and $\bigcirc(X_2) \vdash \bigcirc(X_1)$. Similar provisions can be made for linear logic.

Let us explore what other rules we want satisfied. First, we expect

$$(\bigcirc(A) \Rightarrow (A \Rightarrow B)) \equiv B.$$

This rule is essentially the same as the rewrite rules

$$\frac{\Delta + \bigcirc(A) + A + \Theta}{\Delta + \Theta}$$

and

$$\frac{\Delta + \Theta}{\Delta + \bigcirc(A) + A + \Theta}$$

which mean that the same wffs succeed from each of these databases.[20]

Consider our proof theory from a forward point of view.

Suppose we have that q succeeds from

$$A \Rightarrow (B \Rightarrow q) + \Delta.$$

The only way to achieve that is that $\Delta = \Delta_1 + \Delta_2$ and A succeeds from Δ_1 and B succeeds from Δ_2.

---

[20] Note that rule (8) of Definition 8.3 becomes derivable as follows:

$\vdash B$	assumption
$\vdash \bigcirc A \Rightarrow (A \Rightarrow B)$	from the assumption
$\vdash (B \Rightarrow C) \Rightarrow (\bigcirc A \Rightarrow (A \Rightarrow C))$	using rule (6)

which gives

$$\vdash (B \Rightarrow C) \Rightarrow C.$$

Therefore, annihilating q requires the annihilation of its proof, namely,

$$\bigcirc(\Delta_2) + \bigcirc(\Delta_1) + \bigcirc(A \Rightarrow (B \Rightarrow q))$$

($\bigcirc$ operates in the inverse order on $+$ because we annihilate left to right).
This suggests the following three additional properties

$$\bigcirc(A) + \bigcirc(B) \equiv \bigcirc(B + A)$$
$$\bigcirc(A) + \bigcirc(A \Rightarrow B) \Rightarrow \bigcirc(B)$$

and

$$\frac{A \vdash B}{\bigcirc(A) \vdash \bigcirc(B)} ;$$

in particular,

$$\frac{\vdash B}{\vdash \bigcirc(B)} .$$

Therefore, $\bigcirc(A)$ should be compared with a necessity operator $\Box A$, not with negation connective $\neg A$, which has the rule

$$\frac{A \vdash B}{\neg B \vdash \neg A} .$$

Let us make some conclusions and observations from our preliminary analysis.

Observation 8.6.1 (Resource logics are more suited for the anti-formula concept) *Our analysis 8.6.1 of the deduction theorem and axioms (1), (1*) show that concatenation logic with the list data structure can hopefully coherently accommodate what we want better than can the stronger logics. We saw we can make use of the available structure of the database.*

Observation 8.6.2 (Non-monotonic defeasibility underlying the anti-formula concept) *The reader may be surprised that we are stressing this point. Of course deletion is non-monotonic; we start with $A \vdash A$, we delete A and we get $\varnothing \nvdash A$. Since we are doing deletion of A by addition of $\bigcirc(A)$, we may expect to get a non-monotonic logic. True, we agree with the reader that this is obvious. What was not obvious, however, is what we found in analysis 8.6.3, namely, that to do the deletion sequences correctly (i.e., to do proper proof theory from data involving many $\bigcirc(X_i)$ of various degrees), we need a proper defeasible proof theory. This may involve structures and labels (LDSs); see [7].*

Observation 8.6.3 (Relation to contraction) *We started in Section 8.3 by pointing out that AGM contraction does not handle tautologies. We proposed the idea of anti-formulae and the preceding two observations show that we may need some structured defeasible logic and proof theory to do coherent justice to the anti-formula concept. So, suppose we succeed in formulating some very simple logic with $\Rightarrow, \bigcirc( )$ and some axioms. This logic is non-monotonic. How do we relate the two operations $\Delta + \bigcirc(X)$ and $\Delta - X$ (i.e., anti-formula addition and the meta-level operation of contraction)? We do not have AGM postulates for contraction for logics other than classical logic! To do the job properly we must provide the following:*

1. *propose a new theory of contraction and revision for non-monotonic logics and compare our proposal with the spirit of the AGM postulates*
2. *define in the meta-level the operation $\Delta - X$ for our logic (ignoring that anti-formulae $\bigcirc(X)$ are available) and then compare $\Delta - X$ with $\Delta + \bigcirc(X)$*

So our point is that in defining any system with $\bigcirc(X)$ we would probably need to supply ourselves with an independently plausible revision process.

Note that revision of non-classical logics can done indirectly via a translation mechanism as discussed in Chapter 7.

At this point the reader will agree that we need some sort of a model for a language with anti-formulae. Either a semantic model or a computational model, so that we can see at least one coherent use of this concept. Such a model will help us with our abstract considerations.

8.6.2 Introducing Anti-formulae into Logics with $\Rightarrow$ and e

We now have both semantics and proof theory for concatenation logic, strong concatenation logic and linear logic with $\Rightarrow$ and **e**. We are in a position to examine several options for introducing the operator $\bigcirc$ into the language.

The semigroup semantics will help us give meaning to $\bigcirc(A)$. There are two ways of introducing $\bigcirc(A)$ in our logic:

1. Using **e**, defining

   - $\bigcirc(A) = A \Rightarrow \mathbf{e}$

2. Using the semigroup semantics, by assuming that the semigroup is a group, (namely that every t has an inverse t^{-1}), and defining

   - $t \vDash \bigcirc(A)$ if and only if $t^{-1} \vDash A$

   The two options become the same in a residuated semigroup where $t \twoheadrightarrow e$ is the inverse of t.

   When we look at $\bigcirc(A)$ as a modal operator, we can also check under what conditions the familiar modality laws hold, namely

- $\vdash \bigcirc(A) \Rightarrow (\bigcirc(A \Rightarrow B) \Rightarrow \bigcirc(B))$

- $\dfrac{\vdash A}{\vdash \bigcirc(A)}$

or we may consider a weaker rule

- $\vdash \bigcirc(A) \Rightarrow (\bigcirc(A \Rightarrow \bigcirc(B))) \Rightarrow B$

and of course conditions corresponding to the axiom

- $\vdash \odot(A) \Rightarrow A$

Looking at $\bigcirc$ as a modality is conceptually important because $\bigcirc(A)$ means *Delete*(A) and we get deletion as a modality! We shall see that if the semigroup is a group with residuation, then $\bigcirc$ is a modality.

Definition 8.13 (Semantical definition for $\bigcirc$). Let $(S, \circ, \leq, e, h)$ be a sharp (but not necessarily residuated) semigroup model satisfying the downward e-rule, as defined in Definitions 8.8 and 8.9 for the language with $\Rightarrow$ only.

Assume every element has a left inverse and that e is a left and right unit.

1. Consider the following semantic condition for $\bigcirc$:

   • $t \vDash \bigcirc(A)$ if and only if $\forall y(y \vDash A \rightarrow e \leq t \circ y)$

2. Note that if the semigroup is a group, then $\forall t \exists! y(x \circ y = e)$. Let t^{-1} be the inverse of t; then, the semantic condition becomes

   • $t \vDash \bigcirc(A)$ if and only if $t^{-1} \vDash A$

3. Further, note that if the semigroup is residuated, then we can let t^{-1} be $(t \twoheadrightarrow e)$.

Lemma 8.13. *In the residuated sharp model of Definition 8.9, we have the following:*

1. For every A there exists a t_A such that for all t, $t \vDash A$ if and only if $t_A \leq t$
2. $t \vDash A$ and $e \leq s \rightarrow t \circ s \vDash A$ and $s \circ t \vDash A$

Proof. First we prove (1): Since the model is sharp, this holds for atomic A. Assume by induction that t_A and t_B exist. Let $t_{A \Rightarrow B} = t_A \twoheadrightarrow t_B$ and $t_{\bigcirc(A)} = t_A \twoheadrightarrow e$.
We have

• $t_A \twoheadrightarrow t_B \leq t$ *if and only if* $t_B \leq t \circ t_A$
• $t_{\bigcirc(A)} \leq t$ *if and only if* $e \leq t \circ t_A$

Therefore,

$$t \vDash A \Rightarrow B \text{ if and only if } \forall x(t_A \leq x \rightarrow t_B \leq t \circ x)$$
$$\text{if and only if } \forall x(t_A \leq x \rightarrow x \twoheadrightarrow t_B \leq t)$$
$$\text{if and only if } t_A \twoheadrightarrow t_B \leq t$$

$$t \vDash \bigcirc(A) \text{ if and only if } \forall x(t_A \leq x \rightarrow e \leq t \circ x)$$
$$\text{if and only if } t_{\bigcirc(A)} \leq t$$

Second, the proof of (2) is by induction as done in Lemma 8.8.

Lemma 8.14. *In the model of Definition 8.13 the following hold:*

1. $t \vDash A \wedge t \leq s \rightarrow s \vDash A$
2. If $\mathbf{e}$ is available in the language, then

$$t \vDash \bigcirc(A) \text{ if and only if } t \vDash A \Rightarrow \mathbf{e}$$

3. $t \vDash B$ if and only if $t \vDash \bigcirc(A) \Rightarrow (A \Rightarrow B)$

4. $t \vDash \bigcirc(A)$ and $s \vDash \bigcirc(A \Rightarrow \bigcirc(B))$ imply $t \circ s \vDash B$.

5. If the residuated semigroup is a group, then $t \vDash \bigcirc(A)$ and $s \vDash \bigcirc(A \Rightarrow B)$ imply $t \circ s \vDash \bigcirc(B)$

6. if $e \vDash A$ then $e \vDash \bigcirc(A)$.

Proof. (1) and (2) can be verified directly.

To prove (3), first assume $t \vDash B$. Let $s_1 \vDash \bigcirc(A)$ and $s_2 \vDash A$. We need to show that $t \circ s_1 \circ s_2 \vDash B$. But since $s_1 \vDash \bigcirc(A)$, we have $e \leq s_1 \circ s_2$, and hence $t \leq t \circ e \leq t \circ s_1 \circ s_2$, and hence $t \circ s_1 \circ s_2 \vDash B$.

Now assume $t \vDash \bigcirc(A) \Rightarrow (A \Rightarrow B)$. We need to show that $t \vDash B$. Since the model is sharp, there exists a t_A such that $t_A \vDash A$ and $\forall y (y \vDash A \rightarrow t_A \leq y)$. Let x be a left inverse of t_A (i.e., $x \circ t_A = e$). We show that $x \vDash \bigcirc(A)$. Let $y \vDash A$; then $t_A \leq y$, and therefore $e = x \circ t_A \leq x \circ y$. This shows that $x \vDash \bigcirc(A)$. Therefore, since $t \vDash \bigcirc(A) \Rightarrow (A \Rightarrow B)$, we must have $t \circ x \circ t_A \vDash B$. But $t = t \circ e = t \circ x \circ t_A$, and so $t \vDash B$.

To show (4), assume $t \vDash \bigcirc(A)$ and $s \vDash \bigcirc(A \Rightarrow \bigcirc(B))$. We need to show $t \circ s \vDash B$. Let $x \vDash A, u \vDash A \Rightarrow \bigcirc(B), y \vDash B$. We have $e \leq t \circ x, e \leq s \circ u, e \leq u \circ x \circ y$.

We therefore have, by (2), $x \twoheadrightarrow e \leq t$ and $u \twoheadrightarrow e \leq s$, and therefore $(x \twoheadrightarrow e) \circ (u \twoheadrightarrow e) \leq t \circ s$. Since $e \leq u \circ x \circ y$, we have by item 2 of Lemma 8.14 that for all X

$$(x \twoheadrightarrow e) \circ (u \twoheadrightarrow e) \vDash X \text{ if and only if } (x \twoheadrightarrow e) \circ (u \twoheadrightarrow e) \circ u \circ x \circ y \vDash X;$$

but $y \leq (x \twoheadrightarrow e) \circ (u \twoheadrightarrow e) \circ u \circ x \circ y$ and hence $t \circ s \vDash B$.

To show (5), we can observe that when the residuated semigroup is a group, there exists a unique inverse t^{-1} of any t, and $t^{-1} = t \twoheadrightarrow e$. We have

- $t \vDash \bigcirc(A)$ if and only if $t^{-1} \vDash A$

and therefore we have that $\circledcirc(A) \equiv A$ holds and (5) can be obtained from (4).

One can give a more direct proof in this case.

Since $t \vDash \bigcirc(A)$, we have $t^{-1} \vDash A$. Since $\vDash s \vDash \bigcirc(A \Rightarrow B)$, we have $s^{-1} \vDash A \Rightarrow B$. Hence, $(t \circ s^{-1} = s^{-1} \circ t^{-1}) \vDash B$, and hence $t \circ s \vDash \bigcirc(B)$.

To show (6), note that if $e \vDash A$ and $t \vDash A$, then $e \leq t$ since the model is sharp, and hence $e \vDash \bigcirc(A)$.

Remark 8.5. We need our semigroup model to satisfy the downward **e**-rule and be residuated and sharp. In such a model, $\bigcirc(A)$ can be taken as $A \Rightarrow \mathbf{e}$ if **e** is available, and otherwise as a modality, as we saw in Lemma 8.14. Fortunately, the free canonical model of Definition 8.11 satisfies all of these conditions, and we have completeness of our logics for such models.

We therefore have the following options for $\bigcirc$.

1. We can start with the language with $\Rightarrow$ only. Using the canonical model of Definition 8.11, we prove completeness for sharp residuated models. We can now exploit these models to define semantics for the language with $\Rightarrow, \bigcirc$ as in Definition 8.11; Lemma 8.14 will show that the following axioms are valid in this semantics:

    a. $\vDash (\bigcirc(A) \Rightarrow (A \Rightarrow B)) \equiv B$
    b. $\vDash A$ implies $\vDash \bigcirc(A)$

c. $\vDash A \Rightarrow B$ implies $\vDash \bigcirc(A) \Rightarrow \bigcirc(B)$

d. $\vDash \bigcirc(A) \Rightarrow (\bigcirc(A \Rightarrow B) \Rightarrow \bigcirc(B))$

Taking this approach we would need a direct completeness theorem for the language with $\Rightarrow, \bigcirc$ and the axioms above for the sharp residuated semigroup with downward **e**-rule semantics. We have already noted that axioms (b)–(d) characterise $\bigcirc$ as a modality added to $\Rightarrow$. Looking at $\bigcirc$ in this way we can expect semantics with models of the form $(S, \circ, \leq, R, e, h)$, where $\circ$ serves $\Rightarrow$ and R is a binary relation. Satisfaction is defined by

$$t \vDash \bigcirc(A) \text{ if and only if } \forall s(tRs \rightarrow s \vDash A).$$

In fact, we have tRs if and only if $s = t^{-1} = (t \twoheadrightarrow e)$.

2. We can use our completeness theorem for the language with $\Rightarrow,$ **e** for sharp residuated semantics and *define* $\bigcirc(A)$ as $A \Rightarrow$ **e**.

Actually, the two approaches are the same, because we have $t_{\bigcirc(A)} = t_A \twoheadrightarrow e$ in the model.

Example 8.4. We need the residuation to have $\vDash B \Rightarrow (\bigcirc(A) \Rightarrow (A \Rightarrow B))$, which is very basic to our consideration.

1. Consider the following free model without residuation and a language with $\Rightarrow$ and $\bigcirc$. Consider a set $\mathscr{A}^0$ of atoms of the form $\{a_1, a_2, a_3, \ldots\}$ and for each $n \geq 1$ a set $\mathscr{A}^{-n}$ of atoms of the form $\{a_1^{-n}, a_2^{-n}, \ldots\}$. The idea is that if a represents a wff A, then a^{-1} represents $\bigcirc(A)$. Let

   - $T = \bigcup_{n \geq 0} \mathscr{A}^{-n}$ (for concatenation logic)
   - $T = \mathscr{A} \cup \mathscr{A}^{-1}$ (for linear logic).

   Let S be the set of all finite sequences of elements of T, including $\varnothing$.
   Consider the following context-free reduction rule on elements of S:

   $$\rho : \frac{t + a^{-(n+1)} + a^{-n} + s}{t + s},$$

   where $a^0 = a$ and where in linear logic or strong concatenation logic, with success* predicate, $a^{-2} = a$.
   Let $\bar{t}$ denote the maximal irreducible reduct of t and $\bar{S} = \{\bar{t} \mid t \in S\}$.
   Consider a model $\mathbf{m} = (\bar{S}, +, \varnothing, h)$, where $h(\varnothing) = \{\varnothing\}$, and $h(q) \in \mathscr{A}^0$ for q atomic.

2. For $t \in S$ define $\bigcirc(t)$ as follows:

   - $\bigcirc(a^{-n}) = a^{-n-1}, n \geq 0$ (in concatenation logic with success predicate)
   - $\bigcirc(a) = a^{-1}$ and $\bigcirc(a^{-1}) = a$ (in linear logic or in concatenation logic with success* predicate)
   - $\bigcirc(t + s) = \bigcirc(s) + \bigcirc(t)$
   - $\bigcirc(\varnothing) = \varnothing$

3. Define $\vDash$ by

- $t \vDash q$ if and only if $\bar{t} \in h(q)$
- $t \vDash A \Rightarrow B$ is defined as before
- $t \vDash \bigcirc(A)$ if and only if $\bigcirc(t) \vDash A$

Note that we have that if $t \vDash q$ and $s \vDash \varnothing$, then $t + s \vDash q$ and $s + t \vDash q$.

4. $\mathbf{m}$ is said to be sharp if for any A there is a $t \neq \varnothing$ such that $t \vDash A$.

The following holds.

Let $\mathbf{m}$ be a sharp model as in Definition 8.9. Then

1. $\varnothing \vDash (\bigcirc(A) \Rightarrow (A \Rightarrow B)) \Rightarrow B$.
2. $\varnothing \vDash \bigcirc(A) \Rightarrow (\bigcirc(A \Rightarrow B) \Rightarrow \bigcirc(B))$
3. $$\dfrac{\vDash A}{\vDash \bigcirc(A)}$$

Here is the proof:

1. We need to show that for any $t \neq \varnothing$ (respectively, for linear logic for any t), (1) implies (2) below

   a. $t \vDash \bigcirc(A) \Rightarrow (A \Rightarrow B)$
   b. $t \vDash B$

   Assume (1); then, for any t_1, t_2 such that $t_1 \vDash \bigcirc(A)$ and $t_2 \vDash A$ we have $t + t_1 + t_2 \vDash B$. Since the model is realistic, there exists a t_2 such that $t_2 \vDash A$. Therefore, by definition, $\bigcirc(t_2) \vDash \bigcirc(A)$. Let $t_1 = \bigcirc(t_2)$. Hence, from (1) we get that $t + \bigcirc(t_2) + t_2 \vDash B$. But $t + \bigcirc(t_2) + t_2$ reduces to t, and hence $t \vDash B$.

2. We need to show that for any t_1, t_2

   $$t_1 \vDash \bigcirc(A) \text{ and } t_2 \vDash \bigcirc(A \Rightarrow B) \text{ imply } (t_1 + t_2) \vDash \bigcirc(B).$$

   From our assumptions we get $\bigcirc(t_1) \vDash A$ and $\bigcirc(t_2) \vDash A \Rightarrow B$, and hence $\bigcirc(t_2) + \bigcirc(t_1) \vDash B$, but $\bigcirc(t_1 + t_2) = \bigcirc(t_2) + \bigcirc(t_1)$ and $(t_1 + t_2) \vDash \bigcirc(B)$ if and only if $\bigcirc(t_1 + t_2) \vDash B$; hence, we have $(t_1 + t_2) \vDash \bigcirc(B)$.

3. This rule can be immediately verified.

This semantics looks good so far, except for the following:

Does $\varnothing \vDash B \Rightarrow (\bigcirc(A) = (A \Rightarrow B))$?

Let us check.

Assume $t \vDash B$ and $s_1 \vDash \bigcirc(A)$ and $s_2 \vDash A$. We need to show that $t + s_1 + s_2 \vDash B$. We seem to be stuck here! The obvious statement to hope for is that $s_1 + s_2$ reduces using ρ to $\varnothing$, but it is not clear how to show that. It holds for atomic A in view of the condition on h, but it does not propagate through implication. We need to use the fact that $s_1 \vDash \bigcirc(A)$ if and only if $\bigcirc(s_1) \vDash A$. But how can we use this fact?

We need a more careful construction of the models for $\bigcirc$. We need residuation.[21]

---

[21] In the strict canonical model we will have that $t + s_1 + s_2$ and t are equivalent databases. But then of course the canonical model is also residuated.

8.6.3 Anti-formulae and Negation

This section compares $\bigcirc(A)$ with negation $\neg A$.[22] We perform the comparison in linear logic (**LL**). We will see that they are not the same. Consider the language with $\Rightarrow, \mathbf{e}$ and the axioms and rules (1)–(3), (6)–(12). This gives us a logic complete for semigroup models of the form $(S, \circ, \leq, e, h)$, where the semigroup is a commutative group with residuation $\twoheadrightarrow$ and $\bigcirc(A)$ is defined as $A \Rightarrow \mathbf{e}$, and the inverse of t is $t \twoheadrightarrow e$. We add negation $\neg A$ into this system and have a single system with both $\bigcirc(A)$ and $\neg A$. Note that $\bigcirc(A)$ may collapse to $\neg A$ in stronger systems.

Let us proceed with the definitions.

Definition 8.14. Let $\mathbf{LL}(\neg)$ be the extension of **LL** with a unary connective $\neg$ and the following Hilbert axioms (numbering continuing from Definition 8.3).

15. $\neg\neg A \Leftrightarrow A$
16. $(\neg(A \Rightarrow \neg B) \Rightarrow C) \Leftrightarrow ((A \Rightarrow (B \Rightarrow C)))$
17. $(A \Rightarrow B) \Rightarrow (\neg B \Rightarrow \neg A)$.

Remark 8.6. In $\mathbf{LL}(\neg), \neg(A \Rightarrow \neg B)$ can act as fusion $A \otimes B$ (see Footnote 8).

We can generate negation internally within **LL** as follows.

We choose an arbitrary atom $\bot$ in the language of implicational **LL** and define for any wff $A, \neg A = A \Rightarrow \bot$. Consider the fragment $\mathbf{LL}^\bot$ of all wffs built up from atomic sentences of the form $(q \Rightarrow \bot) \Rightarrow \bot$. In this fragment, we can identify $\neg X$ as $X \Rightarrow \bot$ and we still have $\bigcirc(X)$ as $X \Rightarrow \mathbf{e}$. The following sequence of lemmas establishes these claims.

Lemma 8.15. *Let $\bot$ be an arbitrary atom in $\mathbf{LL}$; then the following holds:*

1. $\vdash_{\mathbf{LL}} ((A \Rightarrow \bot) \Rightarrow \bot) \Leftrightarrow (((((A \Rightarrow \bot) \Rightarrow \bot) \Rightarrow \bot) \Rightarrow \bot)$
2. *Let $\mathbf{LL}^\bot$ be the fragment of $\mathbf{LL}$ built up using $\Rightarrow$ inductively as follows:*

   a. $\bot$ *is a wff of $\mathbf{LL}^\bot$. If q is any atom then $(q \Rightarrow \bot) \Rightarrow \bot$ is a wff of $\mathbf{LL}^\bot$*
   b. *If A and B are wffs of $\mathbf{LL}^\bot$ so is $A \Rightarrow B$.*
   Then, for any A of $\mathbf{LL}^\bot$ we have
   $$\vdash_{\mathbf{LL}} A \Leftrightarrow ((A \Rightarrow \bot) \Rightarrow \bot)$$

   c. *Let A, B and C be formulae of $\mathbf{LL}^\bot$ then*
   $$\vdash_{\mathbf{LL}} (((A \Rightarrow (B \Rightarrow \bot)) \Rightarrow \bot) \Rightarrow C) \Leftrightarrow (A \Rightarrow (B \Rightarrow C)).$$

Proof. 1. First, observe that
$$\vdash_{\mathbf{LL}} A \Rightarrow ((A \Rightarrow \bot) \Rightarrow \bot),$$

---

[22] We are using $\neg A$ for negation of A. The symbol '$\neg$' is used for negation as failure in the paragraphs preceding Definition 8.6 and in Sections 8.7 and 8.8. Such multiple use is compatible with the general literature. If we use both negations in the same logic at the same time (and it is consistently possible to do so in many cases), we shall use $\neg_f$ and $\neg_\bot$ to distinguish between them.

because

$$\vdash_{\mathbf{LL}} (A \Rightarrow \perp) \Rightarrow (A \Rightarrow \perp).$$

Second, observe that since

$$\vdash_{\mathbf{LL}} (A \Rightarrow B) \Rightarrow [(B \Rightarrow C) \Rightarrow (A \Rightarrow C)]$$

we get for $C = \perp$ that

$$\vdash (A \Rightarrow B) \Rightarrow [(B \Rightarrow \perp) \Rightarrow (A \Rightarrow \perp)].$$

Hence, by using our first and second observations, since

$$\vdash_{\mathbf{LL}} ((A \Rightarrow \perp) \Rightarrow (((A \Rightarrow \perp) \Rightarrow \perp) \Rightarrow \perp,$$

we get that

$$\vdash (((((A \Rightarrow \perp) \Rightarrow \perp) \Rightarrow \perp) \Rightarrow \perp) \Rightarrow ((A \Rightarrow \perp) \Rightarrow \perp),$$

which proves (1).

2. *Let A be a wff of* $\mathbf{LL}^{\perp}$. *We show*

$$\vdash_{\mathbf{LL}} ((A \Rightarrow \perp) \Rightarrow \perp) \Rightarrow A.$$

We prove this by induction on the structure of A. For A of the form $(q \Rightarrow \perp) \Rightarrow \perp$, *this is proved in (1).*
Assume

$$\vdash A \Leftrightarrow ((A \Rightarrow \perp) \Rightarrow \perp)$$
$$\vdash B \Leftrightarrow ((A \Rightarrow \perp) \Rightarrow \perp);$$

we shall show

  a. $\vdash (((A \Rightarrow B) \Rightarrow \perp) \Rightarrow \perp) \Rightarrow (A \Rightarrow B)$;
    we can show instead
  (a') $\vdash (((A \Rightarrow B) \Rightarrow \perp) \Rightarrow \perp) \Rightarrow (A \Rightarrow ((B \Rightarrow \perp) \Rightarrow \perp))$;
    we have

$$\vdash (A \Rightarrow B) \Rightarrow ((B \Rightarrow \perp) \Rightarrow (A \Rightarrow \perp))$$

  hence,
  b. $\vdash A \Rightarrow ((B \Rightarrow \perp) \Rightarrow ((A \Rightarrow B) \Rightarrow \perp))$;
    since

$$\vdash (p \Rightarrow (q \Rightarrow r)) \Rightarrow ((r \Rightarrow s) \Rightarrow (p \Rightarrow (q \Rightarrow s))),$$

  we get for $p = A, q = B \Rightarrow \perp, r = (A \Rightarrow B) \Rightarrow \perp$ *and* $s = \perp$ *the formula*

$$\vdash (b) \Rightarrow (a'),$$

  and by modus ponens we get $\vdash (a')$.

3. *Since* $\vdash A \Rightarrow (B \Rightarrow ((A \Rightarrow (B \Rightarrow \bot)) \Rightarrow \bot))$, *we get*

$$\vdash (((A \Rightarrow (B \Rightarrow \bot)) \Rightarrow \bot) \Rightarrow C) \Rightarrow (A \Rightarrow (B \Rightarrow C)).$$

For the other direction, in order to show

$$\vdash (A \Rightarrow (B \Rightarrow C)) \Rightarrow (((A \Rightarrow (B \Rightarrow \bot)) \Rightarrow \bot) \Rightarrow C),$$

we show instead that

$$\vdash (A \Rightarrow (B \Rightarrow C)) \Rightarrow ((A \Rightarrow (B \Rightarrow \bot)) \Rightarrow \bot) \Rightarrow ((C \Rightarrow \bot) \Rightarrow \bot)))$$

using the fact that

$$\vdash ((C \Rightarrow \bot) \Rightarrow \bot) \Rightarrow C.$$

The above follows from

$$\vdash (A \Rightarrow (B \Rightarrow C)) \Rightarrow ((C \Rightarrow \bot) \Rightarrow (A \Rightarrow (B \Rightarrow \bot))),$$

which is indeed provable.

Lemma 8.16. *Let $\bot$ be an arbitrary atom. Let $\tau^{\bot}$ be a translation from $\mathbf{LL}(\neg)$ of Definition 3.14 into $\mathbf{LL}$ defined as follows:*

1. *$\tau^{\bot}(q) = def\, (q \Rightarrow \bot) \Rightarrow \bot$ for atomic q.*
2. *$\tau^{\bot}(A \Rightarrow B) = \tau^{\bot}(A) \Rightarrow \tau^{\bot}(B)$.*
3. *$\tau^{\bot}(\neg A) = \tau^{\bot}(A) \Rightarrow \bot$.*

Then, the following holds:

$$\mathbf{LL}(\neg) \vdash A \text{ if and only if } \mathbf{LL} \vdash \tau^{\bot}(A).$$

Proof. 1. Assume $\mathbf{LL}(\neg) \vdash A$. Consider $\tau^{\bot}(A)$. This formula is in the fragment $\mathbf{LL}^{\bot}$ of $\mathbf{LL}$ as defined in Lemma 8.15. By that same lemma, the $\tau^{\bot}$ translations of the axioms of $\mathbf{LL}(\neg)$ are theorems of $\mathbf{LL}$. The translation of modus ponens itself and the translation of $(A \Rightarrow B) \Rightarrow (\neg B \Rightarrow \neg A)$ is a theorem of $\mathbf{LL}$. Therefore, any $\mathbf{LL}(\neg)$ proof of A will be translated into an $\mathbf{LL}$ proof of $\tau^{\bot}(A)$, and hence $\mathbf{LL} \vdash \tau^{\bot}(A)$.

2. *Assume that $\mathbf{LL}(\neg) \not\vdash A$. We will show that $\mathbf{LL} \not\vdash \tau^{\bot}(A)$ by constructing a counter-model. We begin with $\mathbf{LL}(\neg)$. We can consider $\mathbf{LL}(\neg)$ as a version of $\mathbf{LL}$ without $\neg$ by viewing any wff of the form $\neg B$ as atomic. Thus, we pretend that $\neg$ is a symbol generating new atoms. We construct the canonical $\mathbf{LL}$ structure (S, h) of this language as in Definition 8.11, amended by Footnote 18. In this canonical structure, the elements are all multisets of $\mathbf{LL}(\neg)$ formulae $\{A_1, \ldots, A_n\}$. For atomic q (and also for negated $\neg B$, which we consider as atomic), we have:*

$$\{A_1, \ldots, A_n\} \models q \text{ if and only if } \vdash_{\mathbf{LL}(\neg)} A_1 \Rightarrow \ldots \Rightarrow (A_n \Rightarrow q) \ldots)$$

and

$$\{A_1, \ldots, A_n\} \models \neg B = 1 \text{ if and only if } \vdash_{\mathbf{LL}(\neg)} A_1 \Rightarrow \ldots \Rightarrow (A_n \Rightarrow \neg B) \ldots).$$

We can prove by induction on $\rightarrow$ that for any wff C built up from these 'atoms' we have:

$$\{A_1,\dots,A_n\} \vDash C \text{ if and only if } \vdash_{\mathbf{LL}(\neg)} A_1 \Rightarrow (A_2 \Rightarrow \dots \Rightarrow (A_n \Rightarrow C)\dots).$$

What we do not have in this structure is an inductive condition for the value of
$t \vDash \neg B$. *Our next step is to obtain such an inductive clause.*

The language $\mathbf{LL}(\neg)$ *has real atoms* $\{q_1, q_2, \dots\}$. *We pretended that any negated formula of the form* $\neg B$ *is also an 'atom' and got the canonical structure* (S, h) *for the language with 'atoms'* $\{q_i\}$ *and* $\{\neg B\}$. *We now want to create a new atom* $\bot$ *and reduce* $\neg B$ *to* $B \Rightarrow \bot$.

We begin by taking a new atomic letter $\bot$ *and defining a new assignment* h' *on the atoms* $\{q_i\} \cup \{\bot\}$. h' *is defined using the following clauses:*

- $\{A_1,\dots,A_n\} \vDash' q$ *if and only if* $\{A_1,\dots,A_n\} \vDash q$ *for atomic* $q \neq \bot$.
- $\{A_1,\dots,A_n\} \vDash' \bot$ *if and only if* $\vdash_{\mathbf{LL}(\neg)} A_1 \Rightarrow \dots \Rightarrow (A_{n-1} \Rightarrow \neg A_n)\dots).$

Notice that in $\mathbf{LL}(\neg)$ *the second condition is equivalent to the following:*

$$\vdash_{\mathbf{LL}(\neg)} A_1 \Rightarrow \dots A_{i-1} \Rightarrow (A_{i-1} \Rightarrow \dots \Rightarrow (A_n \Rightarrow \neg A_i)\dots).$$

We now have a structure for the language $\mathbf{LL}^\bot$, *i.e.,* $\mathbf{LL}$ *with* $\bot$. *Consider a formula* A *of the language* $\mathbf{LL}(\neg)$. *It gets a truth value* $\{A_1,\dots,A_n\} \vDash A$ *at the point* $\{A_1,\dots,A_n\}$ *under* h *by considering as 'atoms' in it any real atom* q_i *and any subformula of the form* $\neg B$. *In parallel we can consider* $\{A_1,\dots,A_m\} \vDash' \tau^\bot(A)$. *This function also gives a value because* $\tau^\bot(A)$ *is a formula built up from real atoms* q_i *and* $\bot$, *and* h' *is an assignment for this language. How are these two values related?*

(*) *and* (**) *of Claim 8.16 below give us the connection.*

Claim. *For any* A *we have:*

(*) $\{A_1,\dots,A_n\} \vDash A$ *if and only if* $\{A_1,\dots,A_n\} \vDash' \tau^\bot(A)$.

(**) *For any* B *of* $\mathbf{LL}(\neg)$ *we have:*

$$\{A_1,\dots,A_n\} \vDash \neg B \text{ if and only if } \{A_1,\dots,A_n\} \vDash' \tau^\bot(B) \Rightarrow \bot.$$

Proof.
Case of atomic $q \neq \bot$
First note that for q *atomic,* $\tau^\bot(q) \Rightarrow \bot$ *is* $((q \Rightarrow \bot) \Rightarrow \bot) \Rightarrow \bot$, *which is equivalent to* $q \Rightarrow \bot$ *in* $\mathbf{LL}$. *Thus, to prove* (**) *in the atomic case it is sufficient to show that* $t \vDash \neg q$ *if and only if* $t \vDash' q \Rightarrow \bot$. *Using that we prove* (*), *namely that* $t \vDash q$ *if and only if* $t \vDash' (q \Rightarrow \bot) \Rightarrow \bot$.

1. *First, we prove* (**).
   Note that:
   a. $\{A_1,\dots,A_n\} \vDash \neg q$ *if and only if by definition* $\vdash_{\mathbf{LL}(\neg)} A_1 \Rightarrow \dots \Rightarrow (A_n \Rightarrow \neg q)\dots).$
   On the other hand we also have

b. $\{A_1,\ldots,A_n\} \vDash q \Rightarrow \bot$ *if and only if for any* $\{B_1,\ldots,B_m\}$, *if* $\{B_1,\ldots,B_m\} \vDash' q$, *then* $\{A_1,\ldots,A_n,B_1,\ldots,B_m\} \vDash' \bot$.
The above holds if and only if whenever

$$\vdash_{\mathbf{LL}(\neg)} B_1 \Rightarrow (\ldots \Rightarrow (B_m \Rightarrow q)\ldots),$$

then

$$\vdash_{\mathbf{LL}(\neg)} A_1 \Rightarrow (\ldots \Rightarrow A_n \Rightarrow (B_1 \Rightarrow \ldots \Rightarrow (B_{m-1} \Rightarrow \neg B_n))\ldots).$$

Assume (a) and show (b):
If $\vdash_{\mathbf{LL}(\neg)} B_1 \Rightarrow (\ldots \Rightarrow (B_m \Rightarrow q)\ldots)$, *then* $\vdash_{\mathbf{LL}(\neg)} B_1 \Rightarrow (\ldots \Rightarrow (\neg q \Rightarrow \neg B_m)\ldots)$, *or equivalently* $\vdash_{\mathbf{LL}(\neg)} \neg q \Rightarrow (B_1 \Rightarrow \ldots \Rightarrow (B_{m-1} \Rightarrow \neg B_m)\ldots)$, *and hence from (a) we get*

$$\vdash A_1 \Rightarrow (\ldots A_n \Rightarrow (B_1 \Rightarrow \ldots (B_{m-1} \Rightarrow \neg B_m))\ldots).$$

Assume (b) and show (a). From (b) we get by taking $m = 1$ and $B_m = q$ that
$\vdash_{\mathbf{L}(\neg)} A_1 \Rightarrow (\ldots \Rightarrow (A_n \Rightarrow \neg q)\ldots)$, *which is (a).*

2. *We now prove (*).*
Assume that $\{A_1,\ldots,A_n\} \vDash q$. *Then* $\vdash_{\mathbf{LL}(\neg)} A_1 \Rightarrow (\ldots \Rightarrow (A_n \Rightarrow q)\ldots)$.
To show $\{A_1,\ldots,A_n\} \vDash' \tau^\perp(q)$, *observe that since* $\tau^\perp(q)$ *is* $(q \Rightarrow \bot) \Rightarrow \bot$, *we need to show that* $\{A_1,\ldots,A_n\} \vDash' (q \Rightarrow \bot) \Rightarrow \bot$. *Let* $\{B_1,\ldots,B_m\}$ *be such that* $\{B_1,\ldots,B_m\} \vDash' q \Rightarrow \bot$. *We want to show* $\{A_1,\ldots,A_n,B_1,\ldots,B_m\} \vDash' q \Rightarrow \bot$.
By (**), which we have already proved for atomic q, we deduce that

$$\vdash_{\mathbf{LL}(\neg)} B_1 \Rightarrow (\ldots(B_m \Rightarrow \neg q)\ldots);$$

hence,

$$\vdash_{\mathbf{LL}(\neg)} q \Rightarrow (B_1 \Rightarrow \ldots \Rightarrow (B_{m-1} \Rightarrow \neg B_m)\ldots);$$

hence,

$$\vdash_{\mathbf{LL}(\neg)} A_1 \Rightarrow \ldots \Rightarrow (A_n \Rightarrow \ldots \Rightarrow (B_{m-1} \Rightarrow \neg B_m)\ldots);$$

hence, by definition,

$$\{A_1,\ldots,A_n,B_1,\ldots,B_m\} \vDash' \bot.$$

For the other direction, assume $\{A_1,\ldots,A_n\} \vDash' (q \Rightarrow \bot) \Rightarrow \bot$. *We show that* $\vdash_{\mathbf{LL}(\neg)} A_1 \Rightarrow \ldots \Rightarrow (A_n \Rightarrow q)\ldots)$.
From (**) we get that $\{\neg q\} \vDash' q \Rightarrow \bot$, *and hence*

$$\{A_1,\ldots,A_n,\neg q\} \vDash' \bot;$$

and hence

$$\vdash_{\mathbf{LL}(\neg)} A_1 \Rightarrow \ldots \Rightarrow (A_n \Rightarrow q)\ldots);$$

and hence

$$\{A_1, \ldots A_n\} \vdash q.$$

This concludes the proof of both (*) and (**) for the case of atomic q. Note that we also got the following:

(***) $t \vDash' q$ if and only if $t \vDash' (q \Rightarrow \bot) \Rightarrow \bot$ for q atomic.

The non-atomic case
We first prove (**):
Assume

$$\{A_1, \ldots, A_n\} \vdash \neg B.$$

Then,

$$\vdash_{\mathbf{LL}(\neg)} A_1 \Rightarrow \ldots \Rightarrow (A_n \Rightarrow \neg B)\ldots).$$

We show

$$\{A_1, \ldots, A_n\} \vDash' \tau^{\perp}(B) \Rightarrow \bot.$$

Assume

$$\{B_1, \ldots, B_m\} \vDash' \tau^{\perp}(B).$$

Then by the induction hypothesis, from (*) we get

$$\vdash_{\mathbf{LL}(\neg)} B_1 \Rightarrow \ldots \Rightarrow (B_m \Rightarrow B)$$

or

$$\vdash_{\mathbf{LL}(\neg)} \neg B \Rightarrow (B_1 \Rightarrow \ldots (B_{m-1} \Rightarrow \neg B_m)\ldots).$$

Therefore,

$$\vdash_{\mathbf{LL}(\neg)} A_1 \Rightarrow \ldots \Rightarrow (A_n \Rightarrow B_1 \Rightarrow (B_{m-1} \Rightarrow \neg B_m)\ldots).$$

and so, by definition,

$$\{A_1, \ldots, A_n, B_1, \ldots, B_m\} \vDash' \bot.$$

For the other direction, assume

$$\{A_1, \ldots, A_n\} \vDash' \tau^{\perp}(B) \Rightarrow \bot;$$

we show

$$\{A_1, \ldots, A_n\} \vDash \neg B.$$

By the induction hypothesis, $\{B\} \vDash' \tau^{\perp}(B)$, and so $\{A_1, \ldots, A_n, B\} \vDash' \bot$, and so, by definition,

$$\vdash_{\mathbf{LL}(\neg)} A_1 \Rightarrow \ldots \Rightarrow (A_n \Rightarrow \neg B)\ldots);$$

hence,

$$\{A_1, \ldots, A_n\} \vDash \neg B.$$

It is now possible to prove (*) for the non-atomic case. For the case $A = \neg B$ note that $\tau^\perp(\neg B)$ is $\tau^\perp(B) \Rightarrow \perp$. For B atomic, the result follows from (***), and for the other B the result follows from (**). The case of $B = C \Rightarrow D$ is also immediate because $\tau^\perp$ commutes with $\Rightarrow$, and both $\vDash$ and $\vDash'$ follow the same truth table for $\Rightarrow$.

We have now concluded the proofs of (*) and (**) of Claim 8.16, and we can resume the main line of the proof of our lemma.

Let A be such that $\mathbf{LL}(\neg) \nvdash A$. Consider the structure (S, h). We have $\varnothing \nvdash A$. Consider the structure (S, h'). We have $\varnothing \nvDash' \tau^\perp(A)$. It therefore follows that $\mathbf{LL} \nvdash \tau^\perp(A)$.

This concludes the proof of Lemma 8.16.

8.7 The Notion of Failure in Resource Logics

We have already mentioned in Section 8.2 that the device of deleting a wff A from a database Δ by diverting it as a resource to prove nothing (adding $A \Rightarrow \mathbf{e}$ and proving $\mathbf{e}$) works in resource logics only. This device works in systems where the number of times A can be used is limited. In relevance and intuitionistic logics, where there is no limit on how many times A may be used, or in resource logics with the modality '!' (where A! allows for A to be used many times), we need to employ another device, that of *negation as failure*, to successfully execute deletion.

It is the task of this section to show how this can be done and to introduce the notion of failure. See, however, Footnote 10.

The use of negation as failure (we use '$\neg$' for such negation in this section) as a device for deletion works for limited resource logics as well as for intuitionistic logic. Thus, for a logic such as linear logic, there are two ways to delete a wff A, one by adding $A \Rightarrow \mathbf{e}$ to the data and one by using negation as failure.

The following example compares the two approaches:

Let $\Delta = \{A\}$. We have $\Delta \vdash A$. We want to delete A from Δ by *addition*.

To delete A from Δ, we add $A \Rightarrow \mathbf{e}$. Thus, we let $\Delta' = \Delta + A \Rightarrow \mathbf{e}$.

We have $\Delta \nvdash A$ and $\Delta' \vdash \mathbf{e}$.

To use negation as failure we *name* A by the new propositional constant n_A and present the database as $\Delta_0 = \{\neg n_A \Rightarrow A\}$.

We rely on the goal-directed computation and compute as follows:

$\{\neg n_A \Rightarrow A\} \vdash^? A$ succeeds

$\qquad$ if $\varnothing \vdash^? \neg n_A$ succeeds

$\qquad$ if $\varnothing \vdash^? n_A$ $\quad$ fails

$\qquad$ if *success*.

To delete $\neg n_A \Rightarrow A$ from the database Δ_0, we simply add n_A, and get $\Delta'_0 = \{n_A, \neg n_A \Rightarrow A\}$. We have

$\{n_A, \neg n_A \Rightarrow A\} \vdash^? A$ succeeds

$\qquad$ if $\{n_A\} \vdash^? \neg n_A$ succeeds

$\qquad$ if $\{n_A\} \vdash^? n_A$ $\quad$ fails

$\qquad$ if *failure* $\qquad$ (because $\{n_A\} \vdash^? n_A$ actually succeeds).

The notion of failure in a resource logic is problematic. We need to define the notion of what resources are being used in the course of demonstrating failure (see Example 8.3).

This notion is problematic for several reasons. Let us perform an analysis of the notion for the case of linear logic in a goal-directed computation:

Remark 8.7 (Analysis of failure in linear logic).

1. Linear logic without negation as failure requires each resource to be used exactly once. In the presence of failure, we may need to demonstrate that each candidate avenue for success ends up in failure. This means that in the course of showing failure, a formula can be used more than once, provided the instances of use are in parallel trials for success.
2. The computation may split into two parallel computations both of which have to succeed. Therefore, to demonstrate failure it is sufficient to show that at least one of them fails. It may be the case that both can be shown to fail. Which option do we choose to show the overall failure? The failure of one option may use more resources than the other!
3. How does the use of resources relate to the deduction theorem?
   Consider the problem

   $$A \vdash^? A \Rightarrow ((A \Rightarrow B) \Rightarrow B);$$

   by the deduction theorem this problem is equivalent to :

   $$A, A, A \Rightarrow B \vdash^? B.$$

   This problem can fail by using both $A, A \Rightarrow B$ of the original goal, in which case the original database (namely the first A) is *not* used, or by using A from the original database, in which case the second A is not used, but we can say that the original database was fully used in demonstrating failure!

   Do we want to make such distinctions?
4. Consider the case of immediate failure from a database Δ. What resources are used in such a step?

The above considerations immediately lead us to consider the logical notion of $(\Delta \mid \Theta) \vdash_L A$, meaning A can be proved from Δ (using an assumed algorithm of the logic L) by mean of resources Θ. Thus, the usual consequence $\Delta \vdash_{LL} A$ in linear logic becomes $(\Delta \mid \Delta) \vdash_{LL} A$ in our new notation.

The new notion includes the old notion as a special case but allows for more flexibility on two fronts.

1. The notion of resource (language of Θ) need not be in terms of (the language of) Δ.
2. We can deal more easily with the notion of what resources are used during failure. In fact, the *resource cost set*

$$C_{\Delta,A} = \{(\Theta \mid \Delta) \mid \Theta \vdash_L A\}$$

is available for further logical considerations.

There is no compelling reason in the case of linear logic to stick to $(\Delta \mid \Delta) \vdash A$, as opposed to $(\Delta \mid \Theta) \vdash A$, with $\Theta \subseteq \Delta$. Both notions make the resource use quite clear. However, with Θ explicitly brought into the front line we can be more specific and more sensitive as to how and what resources are used, by putting (a new) logic and structure into Θ.

Example 8.5 (How to use resources to control proofs).

1. Consider the following problem in linear logic:

$$\Delta = \{q, q, q \Rightarrow a, q \Rightarrow a\} \vdash^? a$$

This computation fails.
To demonstrate failure, we need to go to the two possible subcomputations (using each copy of $q \Rightarrow a$) and then ask $?q$, and try each q in the database in turn. Thus, to demonstrate failure we need to use the resources

$$\Theta = \{2q, 2q, 1(q \Rightarrow a), 1(q \Rightarrow a)\}$$

where nB means B needs to be used n times. We also allow for $n = 0$.
We wrote '$2q, 2q$' in Θ rather than '$4q$' because we have two copies of q in Δ, and we used each twice. However, in linear logic we need not make such distinctions.
2. Consider the problem

$$\Delta = \{q, q, r\} \vdash^? q.$$

Here, q fails using the resources $\Theta = \{q, q\}$. Each q has to be used, but fails because Δ contains more.
By the deduction theorem this problem becomes the previous problem in (1). The resources used to demonstrate the failure of this problem therefore reside in the antecedent. Thus, in general the resources used to show failure of $\Delta \vdash^? A$ may be also drawn from within A and may exceed Δ.

We are now ready for our first sequence of definitions.

Definition 8.15 (Linear logic with failure). Consider a language with $\Rightarrow$ (linear implication) and $\neg$ (negation as failure).

1. We define the notions of a *data wff*, a *goal wff* and a *database* as follows.

   a. for atom q, q is a data wff and q and $\neg q$ are goal wffs.
   b. if Δ is a multiset of goal wffs (respectively, of data wffs) and q is an atom, then $\Delta \Rightarrow q$ is a data wff (respectively, $\Delta \Rightarrow q$ and $\Delta \Rightarrow \neg q$ are goal wffs), Δ is the *body* and $q, \neg q$ are the *heads*.
   c. A *database* is a multiset of data wffs.[23]
   d. Let Δ be a database and let $\alpha \in \Delta$. Let $k \geq 0$ be a number. A k partition of Δ for α is any set of pairwise disjoint databases $\Delta_1, \ldots, \Delta_k$ such that $\{\alpha\} \cup \Delta_1 \cup \ldots \cup \Delta_k = \Delta$.

2. We define the notion of $\text{success}(\Delta \mid \Theta, A) = x, x \in \{0, 1\}$ for this language, where Δ is the database, Θ are the resources used and A is the goal.

   a. *Case $A = q$, q atomic*
      (immediate success)

      $$\text{success}(\Delta | \{q\}, q) = 1 \text{ if } \Delta = \{q\}.$$

   b. *Case $A = \neg q, q$ atomic*
      (immediate success)

      $$\text{success}(\Delta | \Theta, \neg q) = 1$$

      if there is no formula in Δ with head q and $\Theta = \varnothing$, or if $q \in \Delta, \{q\} \neq \Delta$ and all the formulae in Δ with head q are of the form q (i.e., $\Gamma \Rightarrow q$ with $\Gamma = \varnothing$) and $\Theta = $ multiset of all q such that $q \in \Delta$.[24]
   c. For q atomic

      $$\text{success}(\Delta | \Theta, q) = x \text{ if and only if } \text{success}(\Delta | \Theta, \neg q) = 1 - x.$$

   d. $\text{success}(\Delta | \Theta, \Gamma \Rightarrow q) = x$ if and only if $\text{success}((\Delta \cup \Gamma) | \Theta, q) = x$.
   e. $\text{success}(\Delta | \Theta, q) = 1$ if for some $\{\alpha_1, \ldots, \alpha_k\} \Rightarrow q \in \Delta$ there exists a partition $\Delta = (\Delta_1, \ldots, \Delta_k)$ such that
      i. $\Delta_1, \ldots, \Delta_k$ are all pairwise disjoint.
      ii. $\Delta = \Delta_1 \cup \ldots \cup \Delta_k \cup \{\{\alpha_1, \ldots, \alpha_n\} \Rightarrow q\}$.
      iii. For some $\Theta_1, \ldots, \Theta_k$ we have that for $1 \leq i \leq k$
         $\text{success}(\Delta_i | \Theta_i, \alpha_i) = 1$.
      iv. $\Theta = \bigcup_{i=1}^k \Theta_i$.
   f. $\text{success}(\Delta | \Theta, \neg q) = 1$ if and only if we have the following situation:
      i. $\Gamma_i \Rightarrow q, i = 1, \ldots, k, \Gamma_i = \{\alpha_1^i, \ldots, \alpha_{m(i)}^i\}$ are all the formulae with head q in Δ

---

[23] We do not want to have something like $\neg q$ in the database. We do not know what it means. It is OK as a goal, it means that the computation with $\vdash^? q$ fails. Therefore, we needed to define data wff and goal wff recursively, to avoid $\neg q$ positioned in such a way in a goal as to force us to add it to the data. Thus $\neg q \Rightarrow a$ is a data wff but not a goal wff.

[24] See Example 8.5, item 3.

ii. For each $1 \leq i \leq k$, let $\delta_1^i, \ldots, \delta_{n(i)}^i$ be all possible $m(i)$ partitions of Δ for
$\Gamma_i \Rightarrow q$.

iii. For each such partition δ_j^i, there exists an index $1 \leq f(\delta_j^i) \leq m(i)$ and
resource $\Theta_{f(\delta_j^i)}^{\delta_j^i}$ such that $\text{success}(\Delta | \Theta_{f(\delta_j^i)}^{\delta_j^i}, \alpha_{f(\delta_j^i)}^i) = 0$

iv. We have $\Theta = \bigcup_{\delta_j^i, f(\delta_j^i)} \Theta_{f(\delta_j^i)}^{\delta_j^i}$.

3. Note that the meta-predicate $\text{success}(\Delta | \Theta, A) = x$ can hold for several Θs for the same fixed Δ and A. There may be several computations, some more costly than others.

Remark 8.8 (Two negations).

1. Let $\neg_f$ denote negation as failure and let $\mathbf{LL}(\neg_f)$ be the logic defined by $\Delta \vdash_{\mathbf{LL}(\neg_f)} A$ if and only if $\text{success}(\Delta | \Delta, A) = 1$.
2. Let $\neg_\perp$ be ordinary negation as defined in Section 8.6.3. Consider the logic $\mathbf{LL}(\neg_\perp)$ as defined there. Since $\mathbf{LL}(\neg_\perp)$ can be identified as a sublanguage of $\mathbf{LL}$ (by fixing an arbitrary atom $\perp$ and using the $\tau^\perp$ translation), it can also be identified as part of $\mathbf{LL}(\neg_f)$, through the same translation. Alternatively, adding $\neg_f$ to $\mathbf{LL}$ automatically adds $\neg_f$ to $\mathbf{LL}(\neg_\perp)$.

We can thus see immediately that we can have a system $\mathbf{LL}(\neg_\perp, \neg_f)$ with both negations.

8.8 Deletion in Resource-Unbounded Logics

In the previous sections, we put forward a solution to the problem of object-level deletion by using the idea of diverting a formula B towards proving nothing. To recap this idea briefly, consider the case of linear logic. In this logic we have $\Delta \vdash B$ iff each element of Δ is correctly used in the proof of B *exactly once*. Linear logic contains a constant $\mathbf{e}$ which is a multiplicative unit (Girard calls it **1**). $\mathbf{e}$ is basically equivalent to any theorem of the logic (it becomes $\top$ in stronger logics) such that essentially $X \Rightarrow (\mathbf{e} \Rightarrow Y)$ is equivalent to $X \Rightarrow Y$ for all X and Y. If we let $\bigcirc(B) = B \Rightarrow \mathbf{e}$, then to delete B we simply add to the data $B \Rightarrow \mathbf{e}$. B is now diverted to proving $\mathbf{e}$, which is nothing. In other words, B is deleted. So going back to our example Δ, we can add $B' \Rightarrow \mathbf{e}$ for object-level physical deletion or $B \Rightarrow \mathbf{e}$ for object-level logical deletion. $B' \Rightarrow \mathbf{e}$ will delete B' (same effect as physical deletion) and $B \Rightarrow \mathbf{e}$ will delete/divert B the minute it is derived (logical deletion). This idea works provided there is a resource bound on the number of times a formula can be used. If there is no such bound, as in intuitionistic logic, other (object-level) means for deleting are to be found. This is what we do in the remaining of this chapter.

There are two main ways we shall consider. We illustrate by examples.

Example 8.6. Let Δ be

1. A
2. $(B \Rightarrow A) \Rightarrow (A \Rightarrow (A \Rightarrow C))$

Clearly, $\Delta \vdash C$ in intuitionistic logic.

We want to delete A.

The first method is to use negation as failure in a goal-directed formulation of the logic; see Section 8.10 below. Let n_1, n_2 be new propositional constants naming (1) and (2), and let $\neg$ be negation as failure. Let Δ^* be

$1^* \ \neg n_1 \rightarrow (1)$
$2^* \ \neg n_2 \rightarrow (2)$

Δ^* is equivalent to Δ as long as n_1, n_2 are not in Δ^*. We refer to n_1, n_2 as names of (1) and (2) because we are using them to write $(1^*), (2^*)$ respectively. To delete (1^*) we add n_1. To delete (2^*) we add n_2.

To use $\neg$ for deletion we need to use names systematically.

Example 8.7. Consider the database Δ of the previous example and turn the logic into a labelled deductive system (LDS) allowing each wff to name (i.e., to be a label acting as a name for) itself. Our database $\Delta^{\sharp}$ becomes

$1^{\sharp} \ (1){:}(1)$
$2^{\sharp} \ (2){:}(2)$

We propagate labels by *resource accumulation*. That is, we use the following rule (see next section):

$$\frac{t : A; s : A \Rightarrow B}{st : B}$$

Let us see how we prove C:

$3^{\sharp}$ (1): $B \Rightarrow A$ from subcomputation $(3.1^{\sharp})$–$(3.2^{\sharp})$:

$3.1^{\sharp} \ x : B$	assumption
x	arbitrary label
$3.2^{\sharp}$ (1) : A from $(1^{\sharp})$	

Exit (1): $B \Rightarrow A$

Now by modus ponens, using $(1^{\sharp})$ twice and $(2^{\sharp}), (3^{\sharp})$ once, we get
$4^{\sharp}$ (2)(1)(1)(1) : C

We get a proof of C with a label indicating exactly which wffs of $\Delta^{\sharp}$ were used in the proof and how many times they were used.

It is a logical option in the LDS context to put conditions on the kinds of labels allowed in acceptable proofs. In fact, we have to put such conditions if we want the deduction theorem to hold (see Example 8.8 below). In the above special LDS formulation of our logic, suppose we have shown that

$\Gamma \vdash t : C$

where t itself is a database in, say, linear logic or any resource logic L where the databases are multisets. Suppose we stipulate that the proof of $t : C$ from Γ is accepted provided $t \vdash_L C$.

Thus, $\Delta \vdash_\sharp C$ iff $\Delta^\sharp \vdash t : C$ and $t \vdash_L C$.

If L is a resource logic, and we want to logically delete $t : C$, then we can delete from t instead of from Δ, and we know how to do that.

In our example, change the label of $A : A$ (i.e., of item (1) of Δ) into $\{A, \bigcirc(A)\} : A$. If we now proceed with the same proof as before, we will end up with $t \cup \{\bigcirc(A)\} \nvdash_L C$.

Of course, we have to make sure that deletion from t is done in the LDS object-level and is not just physical meta-level deletion.

We will consider both options in the remaining of this chapter.

8.9 Logical Deletion in LDS

This section will use an LDS formulation for intuitionistic $\Rightarrow$ and show how to effect logical deletion using the labels.

First, let us recall our problem in the case of intuitionistic $\Rightarrow$.

Suppose we have $A \vdash A$. Here, $\Delta = \{A\}$, and we have $\Delta \vdash A$.

This holds in any logic L. Say we want to delete A from Δ. In linear logic, we can do it easily, as we have seen in Section 8.6. Add $\bigcirc(A)$ to delete A. Thus, let $\Delta - A = \Delta \cup \{\bigcirc(A)\} = \{A, \bigcirc(A)\}$, which is equivalent to $\varnothing$. In fact, we have seen that $\bigcirc(A)$ can be defined as $\bigcirc(A) = (A \Rightarrow \mathbf{e})$. In intuitionistic logic we cannot do that because even if databases are taken as multisets, we still have

$$\{A\} \equiv \{A, A\}.$$

Hence, we would expect

$$\varnothing \equiv \{A, \bigcirc(A)\} \equiv \{A, \bigcirc(A), A\} \equiv \{A\},$$

so we cannot just use $\bigcirc(A)$ in the same way.

Our proposed solution to this problem is done in two steps:

Step 1: Give an equivalent formulation of intuitionistic logic as a labelled deductive system (LDS).

Step 2: Define object-level deletion in the LDS formulation.

The following is a series of definitions setting the scene for the LDS mechanisms for deletion.

To fix our notation, let $\mathbf{I}$ be the logic of intuitionistic $\Rightarrow$ and let $\mathbf{LL_e}$ be linear logic for $\Rightarrow$ and $\mathbf{e}$, defined using the following axioms and rules from Definiton 8.3.

Definition 8.16 (Axioms and rules for LL$_e$).

1. $A \Rightarrow A$

2. $(A \Rightarrow B) \Rightarrow ((C \Rightarrow A) \Rightarrow (C \Rightarrow B))$
3. $(A \Rightarrow (B \Rightarrow C)) \Rightarrow ((A \Rightarrow B) \Rightarrow (A \Rightarrow C))$

6. $$\dfrac{\vdash A \Rightarrow B}{\vdash (B \Rightarrow C) \Rightarrow (A \Rightarrow C)}$$

7. $$\dfrac{\vdash A; \vdash A \Rightarrow B}{\vdash B}$$

9. $$\dfrac{\vdash A}{\vdash (A \Rightarrow B) \Rightarrow B}$$

11. $\vdash \mathbf{e}$

For a multiset $\Gamma = \{A_1, \ldots, A_n\}$ of wffs, let $\Gamma \Rightarrow A$ be $A_1 \Rightarrow (\ldots \Rightarrow (A_n \Rightarrow A) \ldots)$. By axiom (2), this is independent of the order. Using this notation we have the following axiom.

18. $\vdash \Gamma \Rightarrow \mathbf{e}$ implies that $\vdash \Delta \Rightarrow B$ iff $\vdash \Delta \cup \Gamma \Rightarrow B$.

One can prove that $\mathbf{e}$ is equivalent to any B such that $\vdash B$. Thus $\mathbf{e}$ is a constant standing for any theorem.

We now define the kind of LDS we need.

Definition 8.17 (Resource LDS for $\Rightarrow$). Let $\mathcal{L}$ be a language with atomic propositions $\{q_1, q_2, \ldots\}$ and a binary $\Rightarrow$. Let $\mathcal{A}$ be a set of atomic labels. Let α be a function giving for each label variable x and a formula X a new label $\alpha(x, X)$. Let f be a binary function from multisets of labels to multisets of labels. Let $\gamma(x)$ be a label containing a variable x. Let $Exit(x, \gamma(x))$ be a partial function giving a label δ not containing x when defined. Let φ be a binary predicate on multisets of labels.
Define the following concepts:

1. A declarative unit has the form $t : A$ where t is a multiset of atomic labels and A is a wff.
2. A database Δ is a set of declarative units, together with a notion $\Delta + (t : A)$ of input of declarative units $t : A$ into Δ.
3. The $\Rightarrow E$ rule has the form:
$$\dfrac{t : A \Rightarrow B; s : A; \varphi(t, s)}{f(t, s) : B}$$
4. The $\Rightarrow I$ rule has the form:
   To show $t : A \Rightarrow B$, assume $\alpha(x, A) : A$, and further assume $\forall y \varphi(y, \alpha(x, A))$, where x is a new variable for atomic label, and then show $\gamma(x) : B$, where $Exit(x, \gamma(x)) = t$.

Example 8.8. The following example explains the various components of Definition 8.17. Consider the implication $\Rightarrow$ of intuitionistic logic. This can be presented using the two natural deduction rules:

$\Rightarrow E$: $\dfrac{A, A \Rightarrow B}{B}$

and

$\Rightarrow I$:   To show $A \Rightarrow B$, assume A and show B.

Thus, to show

$$A \Rightarrow (A \Rightarrow B) \vdash A \Rightarrow B$$

in intuitionistic logic, we assume A and then use A twice in modus ponens with $A \Rightarrow (A \Rightarrow B)$ to get B.

Similarly, to show $A \vdash B \Rightarrow A$, we assume B and then show A, even without using B because we already have A.

Linear implication $\Rightarrow$ requires that all assumptions be used exactly once each. Thus, $A \Rightarrow (A \Rightarrow B) \nvdash A \Rightarrow B$ because A needs to be used twice, and $A \nvdash B \Rightarrow A$ because B is not used.

A general resource implication may have all kinds of conditions on the proofs. The best way to express them is to label the assumptions (label all the data, and whenever you use the $\Rightarrow I$ rule, use a new label to label the new assumption) and propagate the labels. The functions and predicates α, φ, f and Exit help us control and express what we want.

Definition 8.18 (Consequence). Let Δ be an *LDS* theory as in Definition 8.17 and let $t : A$ be a declarative unit. We define the consequence $\Delta \vdash_C t : A$ subject to a condition $C(t, \Delta)$ as follows.

First, define $\vdash_{m,n}$ for m, n non-negative integers. m counts the total number of uses of the $\Rightarrow E$ rule in the proof and n counts the maximal number of nested uses of $\Rightarrow I$ in the proof.

1. $\Delta \vdash_{0,0} t : A$ if $t : A \in \Delta$.
2. If $\Delta \vdash_{m_1, n_1} t : A$ and $\Delta \vdash_{m_2, n_2} s : A \Rightarrow B$ and $\varphi(s, t)$ hold, then $\Delta \vdash_{m,n} f(s, t) : B$, where

   $$n = \max(n_1, n_2) \text{ and}$$
   $$m = m_1 + m_2 + 1$$

   Note that $\varphi(s, t)$ may be used to control the order in which the assumptions are used. For example, suppose we have a data item of the form $x : A \Rightarrow A$ and suppose we also have just proved $t : A$. We can use φ to force an immediate $\Rightarrow E$ step with $x : A \Rightarrow A$ and get $f(x, t) : A$. This has the effect of 'sticking' the label x into t the 'moment' A is proved (with label t). See Example 8.15
3. $\Delta \vdash_{m,n+1} t : A \Rightarrow B$ if for some new variable x we have $\Delta + \{\alpha(x, A) : A\} \vdash_{m,n} \gamma(x) : B$ and $Exit(x, \gamma(x))$ is defined and is equal to t.
4. Let $\Delta \vdash_C t : A$ hold if for some m, n, $\Delta \vdash_{m,n} t : A$ and condition $C(t, \Delta)$ holds.

Example 8.9. We now explain the role of the condition C appearing in Definition 8.18.

Consider again

330 8 Object-Level Deletion

$$A \Rightarrow (A \Rightarrow B) \vdash^? A \Rightarrow B.$$

Using labels, we get

$$t : A \Rightarrow (A \Rightarrow B) \vdash^? t : A \Rightarrow B.$$

We assume $x : A$ with arbitrary x and prove $\gamma(x) = txx : B$. The label $\gamma(x) = txx$ tells us that A was used twice in the proof of B. The function $Exit(x, \gamma(x))$ wants to exit with label t. This is allowed if x appears exactly once and then we exit with $\gamma(x) - x$. So, Exit is used to control the resource conditions.

Now consider the equivalent proof problem (if we want the deduction theorem to hold) of

$$t_1 : A \Rightarrow (A \Rightarrow B), t_2 : A \vdash^? B.$$

In this case we can prove $t_1 t_2 t_2 : B$. There is no use of Exit, and so how do we block this proof? We need another predicate C for such a case. C will really be defined using iterations of the Exit condition.

Example 8.10. We show how to get linear $\Rightarrow$ as an LDS of this form. Let $\mathscr{A}$ be a set of atomic labels. A database has the form $\{t_1 : A_1, \ldots, t_n : A_n\}$ where all t_i are pairwise disjoint, and we regard 't' as a unit multiset $\{t\}$. Let $\alpha(x, A)$ be x and let $f(t, s) = t \cup s$, where t and s are multisets. Let $\varphi(x, y) = \top$. Let $Exit(x, \gamma(x))$ be defined if x occurs in $\gamma(x)$ exactly once, and in this case $Exit(x, \gamma(x)) = \gamma(x) - x$ (i.e., take x out of $\gamma(x)$).

Let $C(t, \{t_1 : A_1, \ldots, t_n : A_n\})$ be the condition $t = \{t_1, \ldots, t_n\}$.

We obviously have that $\Delta \vdash_C t : A$ if and only if A is proved from Δ using each assumption exactly once!

Definition 8.19 (LL_e : I-logic). We define an LDS version of intuitionistic $\Rightarrow$ where the labels come from linear logic with anti-formulae (i.e., $\Rightarrow$ and $\mathbf{e}$ logic), as defined previously in this chapter.

1. A label is any multiset of $\Rightarrow, \mathbf{e}$ formulae.
2. A declarative unit is a labelled $\Rightarrow$ formula.
3. The $\Rightarrow E$ rule has the form

$$\frac{t : A; \ s : A \Rightarrow B}{t \cup s : B}$$

where $\cup$ is the multiset union.
4. The $\Rightarrow I$ rule has the form:
   To show $\Delta \vdash t : A \Rightarrow B$, assume $\{x\} : A$ for x new atomic label and show $\gamma(x) : B$. The exit condition is $\gamma(x/A) \vdash_{LL_e} B$ and $t = \gamma(x) \cup \{\bigcirc(x)\}(x/A)$, where x/A is the result of substituting A for x.[25]
5. Let a database Δ be a multiset of labelled formulae of the form $\{\Theta_1 : A_1, \ldots, \Theta_n : A_n\}$, where A_i are formulae with $\Rightarrow$ and Θ_i are multisets of wffs with $\Rightarrow$ and $\mathbf{e}$.

---

[25] To explain the definition of t, assume A was used in the proof of B k times, $k \geq 0$. For $k = 0, t = \gamma \cup \{\bigcirc(A)\}$, and otherwise t has in it the number of copies of A required to facilitate the proof of B. Thus, we would expect $t \vdash_{LL_e} A \Rightarrow B$.

6. Define $\Delta \vdash_{m,n} \Theta : B$ as follows:

  6.1. $\Delta \vdash_{0,0} \Theta : B$ if $\Theta : B \in \Delta$.

  6.2. If $\Delta \vdash_{m_1,n_1} t : A$ and $\Delta \vdash_{m_2,n_2} s : A \Rightarrow B$, then $\Delta \vdash_{m,n} s \cup t : B$, where $n = \max(n_1, n_2)$ and $m = m_1 + m_2 + 1$.

  6.3. $\Delta \vdash_{m,n+1} t : A \Rightarrow B$ if $\Delta \cup \{\{x\} : A\} \vdash_{m,n} \gamma : B$ and $\gamma(x/A) \vdash_{\mathbf{LL_e}} B$, and $t = \gamma \cup \{\bigcirc(A)\}$ if x is not in γ and $t = \gamma(A) \cup \{\bigcirc(A)\}$ otherwise.

  6.4. $\Delta \vdash_C t : A$ if for some m, n, $\Delta \vdash_{m,n} t : A$ and $C(\Delta, t : A)$ hold.

7. Let $C(\Delta, t : A)$ be $t \vdash_{\mathbf{LL_e}} A$.

Example 8.11.

(1) In intuitionistic logic we have

$$A \Rightarrow (A \Rightarrow B) \vdash_{\mathbf{I}} A \Rightarrow B$$

The derivation is as follows:

1. $A \Rightarrow (A \Rightarrow B)$ data
2. Show $A \Rightarrow B$ from box subcomputation

> 2.1 A assumption
> 2.2 $A \Rightarrow B$, using $\Rightarrow E$, (1) and (2.1)
> 2.3 B, using $\Rightarrow E$ (2.2) and (2.1)

Exit $A \Rightarrow B$

(2) The same proof can be done in $\mathbf{LL_e} : \mathbf{I}$ logic as follows:

  1^*. $\{A \Rightarrow (A \Rightarrow B)\} : A \Rightarrow (A \Rightarrow B)$ data

  2^*. Show $\{\bigcirc(A), A, A, A \Rightarrow (A \Rightarrow B)\} : A \Rightarrow B$ from box subcomputation

> 2.1^* $\{x\} : A$ assumption
> 2.2^* $\{x, A \Rightarrow (A \Rightarrow B)\} : A \Rightarrow B$, using $\Rightarrow E$, (1^*) and (2.1^*)
> 2.3^* $\gamma(x) = \{x, x, A \Rightarrow (A \Rightarrow B)\} : B$, using $\Rightarrow E$ (2.2^*) and (2.1^*)
> 2.4^* The exit condition $\gamma(A) \vdash_{\mathbf{LL_e}} B$ holds.

Exit with $\{\bigcirc(A), A, A, (A \Rightarrow (A \Rightarrow B))\} : B$

  3^*. The proof of (2^*) is acceptable because in linear logic with $\Rightarrow$ and $\mathbf{e}$ (where $\bigcirc(X)$ is $X \Rightarrow \mathbf{e}$), we have $\{\bigcirc(A), A, A, A \Rightarrow (A \Rightarrow B)\} \vdash A \Rightarrow B$.

Example 8.12.

(1) Let us look at the proof of $A \vdash_{\mathbf{I}} B \Rightarrow A$.

1. A assumption
2. $B \Rightarrow A$, from box subcomputation

> 2.1 B assumption
> 2.2 A, from (1)

Exit $B \Rightarrow A$

(2) Let us do the same in $\mathbf{LL_e} : \mathbf{I}$

1^*. $\{A\} : A$ assumption
2^*. Show $\{\bigcirc(B), A\} : B \Rightarrow A$, from box subcomputation

2.1^* $\{x\} : B$ assumption
2.2^* $\{A\} : A$ from (1^*)
2.3^* The exit condition holds

Exit $\{A, \bigcirc(B)\} : B \Rightarrow A$

We have defined the $\mathbf{LL_e} : \mathbf{I}$ logic and have given some examples of proofs in this logic. We need to show now that it is equivalent to intuitionistic logic $\mathbf{I}$. This will complete Step 1 of our strategy.

For the next theorem it is convenient to consider the databases for intuitionistic logic as multisets of wffs. This allows us to compare provability in $\mathbf{I}$ to that of $\mathbf{LL_e}$ and $\mathbf{LL_e} : \mathbf{I}$.

Let Δ be a multiset $\Delta = \{A_1, \ldots, A_n\}$, let Δ' be $\{\{A_1\} : A_1, \ldots, \{A_n\} : A_n\}$. Δ' is a labelled database of $\mathbf{LL_e} : \mathbf{I}$.

We can now state the following theorem.

Theorem 8.3. *Let $\Delta = \{A_1, \ldots, A_n\}$ be a multiset. Let $\Delta' = \{\{A_1\} : A_1, \ldots, \{A_n\} : A_n\}$. Then we have for any B that (1) and (2) below are equivalent:*

1. $\Delta \vdash_{m,n} B$ in $\mathbf{I}$.
2. For some t, we have $\Delta' \vdash_{m,n} t : B$ in $\mathbf{LL_e} : I$ with $t \vdash_{L_e} B$.

Proof. Any proof in $\mathbf{LL_e} : \mathbf{I}$ is a valid proof in $\mathbf{I}$ if we ignore the labels. Thus, one direction of our theorem holds. We show the other direction by induction on the index (m, n) of the proof of $\Delta \vdash_{m,n} B$.

Case $(0, 0)$
This means that for some i, $B = A_i$. Then, $\{A_i\} : A_i \in \Delta'$, and since $\{A_i\} \vdash_{\mathbf{LL_e}} A$ we get $\Delta' \vdash_{\mathbf{LL_e}:I} \{A_i\} : A_i$.

Case (m, n), $\Rightarrow E$ rule:
This means that for some k_1, k_2 such that $1 + k_1 + k_2 = m$ and for some n_1, n_2 such that $max(n_1, n_2) = n$ and for some A we have $\Delta \vdash_{k_1, n_1} A$ and $\Delta \vdash_{k_2, n_2} A \Rightarrow B$ in $\mathbf{I}$.

By the induction hypothesis, we have t_1, t_2 such that $\Delta' \vdash_{k_1, n_1} t_1 : A$ and $\Delta' \vdash_{k_1, n_2} t_2 : A \Rightarrow B$ in $\mathbf{LL_e} : \mathbf{I}$, with $t_1 \vdash_{\mathbf{LL_e}} A$ and $t_2 \vdash_{\mathbf{LL_e}} A \Rightarrow B$. Hence, $\Delta' \vdash_{m,n} t_1 \cup t_2 : B$ and $t_1 \cup t_2 \vdash_{\mathbf{LL_e}} B$.

Case $(m, n+1)$, $\Rightarrow I$ rule:
This is the case where we used the $\Rightarrow I$ rule. This means that B has the form $B = (B_1 \Rightarrow B_2)$, and that we assumed B_1, and from $\Delta \cup \{B_1\}$ we proved B_2 with index (m, n). By the induction hypothesis for the database $\Delta' \cup \{x : B_1\}$ (for the substitution $x = B_1$), we have $\Delta \vdash_{m,n} \gamma(B_1) : B_2$ and $\gamma(B_1) \vdash_{\mathbf{LL_e}} B_2$.

From the deduction theorem for $\mathbf{LL_e}$[26] we have $\gamma \vdash_{\mathbf{LL_e}} B_2$ if and only if $\gamma \cup \{\bigcirc(B_1)\} \vdash_{\mathbf{LL_e}} B_1 \Rightarrow B_2$.

---

[26] The deduction theorem for $\mathbf{LL_e}$ says that for any γ, X and B (no matter whether X is in γ or not), we have $\gamma \vdash B$ if and only if $\gamma \cup \{\bigcirc(X)\} \vdash X \Rightarrow B$. This gives the usual deduction theorem as a

By the rules $\mathbf{LL_e} : \mathbf{I}$ *we can exit with* $\gamma(B_1) \cup \{\bigcirc(B_1)\}$, *and hence* $\Delta' \vdash_{m,n+1}$
$\gamma \cup \{\bigcirc(B_1)\} : B$ *with* $\gamma \cup \{\bigcirc(B_1)\} \vdash_{\mathbf{LL_e}} B$.
This completes the proof of the theorem.

We now have the machinery to do deletion. We are ready for Step 2 of our strat-
egy: namely, we work in $\mathbf{LL_e} : \mathbf{I}$ instead of $\mathbf{I}$ and do deletion there. Theorem 8.3
allows us to do that. The question is how to execute deletion. Assume $\{A\} : A \in \Delta$
needs to be deleted; one's first attempt is simply to add $\bigcirc(A)$ to the label of A,
obtaining $\{\bigcirc(A),A\} : A$ and thus deleting A.

The following example illustrates our point.

Example 8.13. Let us see how to delete A in the $\mathbf{LL_e} : \mathbf{I}$ version of the proof of
Example 8.11. To delete A add $\{\bigcirc(A)\} : A$.

If we do that, the database becomes

1**. $\bigcirc(A) : A, \{A \Rightarrow (A \Rightarrow B)\} : A \Rightarrow (A \Rightarrow B)$.

The box proof of $A \Rightarrow B$ becomes

2.1**. $\{\bigcirc(A),A\} : A$ assumption

(we are inputting into the database $\{A\} : A$. Since $\{\bigcirc(A)\} : A$ is already there,
the overall label is the multiset union, i.e., $\{\bigcirc(A),A\} : A$.

If we continue the proof we get

2.2**. $\{\bigcirc(A),A,A \Rightarrow (A \Rightarrow B)\} : A \Rightarrow B$

2.3**. $\{\bigcirc(A),A,A,A \Rightarrow (A \Rightarrow B)\} : B$

2.4**. If the exit condition is satisfied, we exit with $\{\bigcirc(A),\bigcirc(A),A,A,A \Rightarrow (A \Rightarrow B)\}$:
$A \Rightarrow B$.

Line 2.4** does not work because in linear logic the label $\{\bigcirc(A),\bigcirc(A),A,A,A \Rightarrow$
$(A \Rightarrow B)\}$ is equivalent to $\{A \Rightarrow (A \Rightarrow B)\}$ and it does not prove $A \Rightarrow B$.

The problem with the previous example is that it is not an object-level deletion.
Even in *LDS*, changing a label in a database is meta-level. We can add $\{\bigcirc(A)\} : A$
to Δ, but unless we have a rule for aggregating labels, it will not help. We still have
$\{\{\bigcirc(A)\} : A, \{A\} : A\} \vdash \{A\} : A$.

Somehow we want to put something in the database of the form $x : X$ (this is a
logical move) and force it to interact with $\{A\} : A$, and thus delete it. The answer is
to put $\{\bigcirc(A)\} : A \Rightarrow A$ in the database. If we use modus ponens,

$$\frac{\{\bigcirc(A)\} : A \Rightarrow A, \{A\} : A}{\{\bigcirc(A),A\} : A}$$

Can we force these two to interact? The answer is yes if we change the logic
slightly. Recall that the difference between linear logic and intuitionistic logic is

---

special case because $\gamma \cup \{X\} \vdash B$ if and only if $\gamma \cup \{X,\bigcirc(X)\} \vdash X \Rightarrow B$ if and only if $\gamma \vdash X \Rightarrow B$,
because $\{\bigcirc(X),X\} \equiv \mathbf{e}$ and $\gamma \cup \{\mathbf{e}\} \equiv \gamma$.

that linear logic wants each assumption to be used exactly once while intuitionistic logic does not care. We can have a compromise between the two. A database has the form $\Delta_1 \cup \Delta_2$. The elements of the multiset Δ_1 have all to be used exactly once, but we do not care about the elements of Δ_2. Therefore, we can put $\{\bigcirc(A)\} : A \Rightarrow A$ into Δ_1. It has to be used, and when used it will add $\{\bigcirc(A)\}$ to the label of A. This of course allows us to do logical deletion as well. We do not care if A is in the database or not. This solution might have some technical problems. For instance, suppose $\Delta \nvdash A$ from Δ. If we delete A, i.e., add $\{\bigcirc(A) : A\}$ to Δ, then it *cannot* be used and the new database cannot prove anything. Put differently, we *do not* have the meta-level rule for vacuous deletion:

- If $\Delta \nvdash A$ then **Delete**$(\Delta, A) = \Delta$; see Example 8.29.

Note that we have the same problem in linear logic itself. In the previous section, we saw that to delete A from Δ we add $\bigcirc(A) = A \Rightarrow \mathbf{e}$. But if $\Delta \nvdash A$, then we are stuck with $\bigcirc(A)$ in the database. This is a topic for further investigation, but let us look at some examples.

Example 8.14 (Logical deletion).

(1) In intuitionistic logic we have that the database

  1. $C \Rightarrow A$
  2. C
  3. $D \Rightarrow A$
  4. D
  5. $A \Rightarrow B$

proves B. The same holds in $\mathbf{LL_e : I}$ logic. The proofs will be the same except that in $\mathbf{LL_e : I}$ logic the multiset label will record what assumptions have been used and how many times they were used. Thus, using (1), (2) and (5), we can prove B. In $\mathbf{LL_e : I}$ logic we prove $\{(1),(2),(5)\} : B$, and of course $\{(1),(2),(5)\} \vdash B$ in linear logic.

In order to delete D in $\mathbf{LL_e : I}$ logic, we add $\{\bigcirc(D)\} : D \Rightarrow D$, and force modus ponens with $\{D\} : D$; so the label of D becomes $\{\bigcirc(D), D\} : D$. This will not affect the above proof of B from (1), (2), (5).

If we also delete C in a similar way, the label of C will become $\{\bigcirc(C), C\} : C$ and the above proof will end up with a label $\{\bigcirc(C), C, C \Rightarrow A, A \Rightarrow B\}$.

In linear logic with $\Rightarrow$ and $\mathbf{e}$, this database does not prove B, and hence the $\mathbf{LL_e : I}$ proof of B is blocked.

Let us now delete A. This means we add to the database $\{\bigcirc(A)\} : A \Rightarrow A$. However, since A is not in the database, we really want to do *logical deletion*: the minute A is proved, it must be deleted. So we should have the following sequence:

Step 1: From $C \Rightarrow A$ and C get A
Step 2: Delete A

Let us see what the labels do:

Step 1*: From $\{C\} : C$ and $\{C \Rightarrow A\} : C \Rightarrow A$ get $\{C, C \Rightarrow A\} : A$.

Step 2*: Since $\{\bigcirc(A)\} : A \Rightarrow A$ is in the database, if we force modus ponens at this point, then the current label of A becomes $\{\bigcirc(A), C, C \Rightarrow A\}$. This label does not prove A in linear logic.

The problem is that using (3) and (4) we can get another copy of A and thus rescue the proof, and we must remember that $\{\bigcirc(A)\} : A \Rightarrow A$ has already been spent, i.e., one copy of A has already been deleted!

We can make the problem more severe. Why not use (1) and (2) again to get another copy of A? In intuitionistic logic we can use the data as many times as we want. Hence we can get A with the label $\{C, C \Rightarrow A, C, C \Rightarrow A\}$. Adding $\bigcirc(A)$ will leave us with one copy of A!

Obviously our thinking of our resource management is not clear-cut enough.

Let us look more closely at the problem mentioned in Example 8.14. $\mathbf{LL_e}$ proof theory works as follows:

To have $\Delta \vdash A$, we must be able to decompose Δ into (possibly empty) subsets Δ_i, Γ_j such that $\Delta = \bigcup_i \Delta_i \cup \bigcup_j \Gamma_j$ such that $\Delta_i \vdash A_i$, $\Gamma_j \vdash \mathbf{e}$ and $\Theta = \{A_i\} \vdash B$.

Note that we know how to delete A_1 from Θ if it is written in Θ explicitly, but how do we logically delete A_1 from Δ? The way we do it in $\mathbf{LL_e}$ is that we add $\bigcirc(A_1)$ to Δ. When A_1 is proved, $\bigcirc(A_1)$ will cancel it. However, in $\mathbf{LL_e} : \mathbf{I}$, Δ is accumulated dynamically during the proof, so how and where are we going to get $\bigcirc(A_1)$ as a label?

The solution is simple. We add the item of data $\{\bigcirc(A_1)\} : A_1 \Rightarrow A_1$.

As soon as A_1 is proved with a label $t : A_1$, if we perform modus ponens with $\{\bigcirc(A_1)\} : A_1 \Rightarrow A_1$, then this will add $\bigcirc(A_1)$ to the label t.

Our problem is now how to force the proof procedure to use this new clause as soon as A_1 is proved. Here, we use φ. It is best explained by example:

Example 8.15.

(1) $A_1 : A_1$
(2) $A_2 : A_2$
(3) $(A_1 \Rightarrow B) : A_1 \Rightarrow B$
(4) $(A_2 \Rightarrow B) : A_2 \Rightarrow B$

This proves B. How do we logically delete B? We add

(5) $\bigcirc(B) : B \Rightarrow B$

Let $\varphi(s, t)$ be $(t \nvdash B \vee s \vdash \bigcirc(B))$.

Now we can do modus ponens with (1), (3) or (2), (4) because B is not provable from the label. But once B is provable, the only modus ponens we can do (because of φ) is with $\bigcirc(B) : B \Rightarrow B$, which will delete B from the label and we can continue our modus ponens.

There is still a problem with this proposed solution. To delete B we need to change φ and this changing operation is also meta-level.

Another option for logical deletion is to compute in the meta-level what physical assumptions we need to physically delete in order to affect the logical deletion, and we know how to do that! But this is not as satisfactory as the proof-theoretical method.

8.10 Introducing N-Prolog with Negation as Failure

We can give meaning to anti-formulae in intuitionistic logic by translating them into N-Prolog with negation as failure. N-Prolog is intuitionistic implication augmented by negation as failure $\neg$. In the N-Prolog system we can perform deletion by addition. This N-Prolog deletion will satisfy that, if $\Delta \not\vdash A$, then the result of deleting A from Δ yields Δ. This section will introduce N-Prolog. The definitions are as follows.

Definition 8.20. Consider a propositional language with $\Rightarrow, \perp$ and $\neg$. Define the notions of *literal*, *data clause* and *goal clause* as follows.

1. An atom q or $\perp$ or $\neg q$ or $\neg\perp$ are literals.[27] q and $\perp$ are *positive* and $\neg q$ and $\neg\perp$ are *negative*.
2. A positive literal is a data clause and a literal is a goal clause.
3. If $A_1,\ldots,A_n$ are goal clauses, then $A_1 \Rightarrow (\ldots \Rightarrow (A_n \Rightarrow q)\ldots)$ is a data clause, where q is a positive literal. We say q is the *head* of the clause.
4. If $A_1,\ldots,A_n$ are data clauses and q is a literal, then $A_1 \Rightarrow (\ldots \Rightarrow (A_n \Rightarrow q)\ldots)$ is a goal clause, with head q.

Definition 8.21 (Success for N-Prolog).

1. *Immediate success case*

   a. $Success(\Delta,q) = 1$ if $q \in \Delta$ for q a positive literal.
   b. $Success(\Delta,\neg q) = 1$ if q is not the head of any clause in Δ, for q a positive literal.

2. *Implication Case*

   $Success(\Delta, B \Rightarrow C) = x$ if $Success(\Delta \cup \{B\}, C) = x$.
3. *Immediate failure case*

   a. $Success(\Delta,q) = 0$ if q is not the head of any clause in Δ, for q a positive literal.
   b. $Success(\Delta,\neg q) = 0$ if $q \in \Delta$, q a positive literal.

4. *Cut reduction case*

   $Success(\Delta,q) = 1$ (respectively, $Success(\Delta,q) = 0$), for q a positive literal, if for some (respectively, all) clauses of the form $A_1 \Rightarrow (\ldots \Rightarrow (A_n \Rightarrow q')\ldots)$ in Δ with $q' = q$ or $q' = \perp$ we have that for all (respectively, some) $1 \leq i \leq n$, we have $Success(\Delta,A_i) = 1$ (respectively, $Success(\Delta,A_i) = 0$).

---

[27] $\neg\perp$ is actually $\top$.

5. *Negation as failure case*

$Success(\Delta, \neg q) = x$ if and only if $Success(\Delta, q) = 1 - x$.

6. *Consequence*

We have $\Delta \vdash A$ if and only if $Success(\Delta, A) = 1$.

The above (1)–(6) define $\{\Rightarrow, \bot, \neg\}$ as N-Prolog.

Note that for the language without $\neg$, with $\Rightarrow$, $\bot$ only, we have completeness: $\Delta \vdash G$ in intuitionistic logic if and only if $success(\Delta, G) = 1$.

If we do not allow for embedded implications and do not allow for $\bot$, then we get the usual Prolog clauses with negation as failure, written in the form $q_1 \Rightarrow (\ldots \Rightarrow (q_n \Rightarrow q)\ldots)$, where q_i, $1 \leq i \leq n$, are literals and q is a positive literal.

Remark 8.9. We saw that the language of N-Prolog is obtained from that of intuitionistic implication (with $\bot$) by adding the negation as failure connective $\neg$. The meaning of $\neg A$ in the goal-directed computation of the previous Definition 8.21 is that A fails, i.e.,

$Success(\Delta, \neg A) = x$ if and only if $Success(\Delta, A) = 1 - x$.

Because of the deduction theorem (the implication case 2 of Definition 8.21) we have that

$\neg(A_1 \Rightarrow \ldots (A_n \Rightarrow q)\ldots)$

is equivalent to

$A_1 \Rightarrow (\ldots \Rightarrow (A_n \Rightarrow \neg q)\ldots)$

and so it is sufficient to allow for the $\neg$ connective to apply to atoms only.

We must take care that $\neg q$ never occur as a head of a clause in databases, but occur only in goals. This is because we do not have a meaning for $\neg q$ as an element of a database. We can of course try to give it some (integrity constraint?) meaning, but that is another story.[28]

Hence, we can accept a clause such as

$a \Rightarrow \neg q$

as a goal clause but not as a data clause.

However,

$(a \Rightarrow \neg q) \Rightarrow r$

is acceptable as a data clause. Similarly, we cannot accept $\neg q \Rightarrow a$ as a goal clause or $(\neg q \Rightarrow r) \Rightarrow r$ as a data clause, since either case would force us to put $\neg q$ in the database. This explains the rationale of Definition 8.20.

N-Prolog is a pretty powerful system. It allows us to delete through addition and to perform many meta-level operations in the object level. Let us illustrate its properties through some examples and then give general definitions.

---

[28] We shall see later that it may be convenient to allow goals of the form $\neg q \Rightarrow a$ provided we say what it means to 'add $\neg q$ to the data'. We may interpret this as 'Delete all clauses with head q' from the database, and keep deleting such clauses as long as $\neg q$ is in the database.

Example 8.16 (Properties of negation as failure). In ordinary Prolog, the database Δ does not change. Thus, given a clause in Δ with negation $\neg a$ in it, the meaning of $\neg a$ is 'a fails from Δ', where Δ is the program.

In N-Prolog, the program Δ changes throughout the computation, and hence the meaning of $\neg a$ is dynamic; it means 'a fails from the current database'. Consider Δ with

1. $\neg a \Rightarrow q$
2. $(b \Rightarrow q) \Rightarrow q$

A query is represented as $?q$. If we use (1) first, $\neg a$ means a failure from (1) and (2). If we use (2) first, we ask for $b \Rightarrow q$, and therefore we add

3. b

to the database and ask $?q$, and then using (1) we get that $\neg a$ means 'failure from (1), (2) and (3)'.

N-Prolog with negation as failure does not satisfy Cut. We have, for example, that

$$\neg n \Rightarrow x \vdash x$$

and that

$$\neg n \Rightarrow x, x \vdash n \Rightarrow x$$

but

$$\neg n \Rightarrow x \nvdash n \Rightarrow x$$

These features make it more difficult to give semantics for $\neg$. Nevertheless, semantics for N-Prolog with negation as failure was given by Olivetti and Terracini in a very long paper [19].

The goal-directed process allows us to define the deletion. Assume we have $\Delta \vdash A$ and are seeking a suitable $\Delta' \subset \Delta$ such that $\Delta' \nvdash A$. We look at $success(\Delta, A) = 1$. We follow the computation until we get to steps of immediate success (clause (1) in Definition 8.21). At that step some q is indeed in the then-current theory Δ_i. We spoil the computation by taking q out of Δ_i.

The following example explains our options.

Example 8.17. Let Δ_0 be $\{q \Rightarrow a, r_0 \Rightarrow (r_1 \Rightarrow a), q, r_0, r_1\}$. We have $\Delta_0 \vdash a$. We are looking for $\Delta_0' \subset \Delta$ such that $\Delta_0' \nvdash a$. We follow the computation. There are two ways a can be proved: either from q or from $\{r_0, r_1\}$. So, to spoil the success we need to take out either $\{q, r_0\}$ or $\{q, r_1\}$. Let $Abduce^-(\Delta, A)$, a meta-predicate to be defined below, give us all the options for sets to *delete*, to take out to spoil $\Delta \vdash A$ (if $\Delta \nvdash A$, the result is $\varnothing$). Then, in our case $Abduce^-(\Delta_0, a) = \{\{q, r_1\}, \{q, r_0\}\} = $ Delete$(\{q, r_1\})$ or Delete$(\{q, r_0\})$.

Notice that this process removes only atoms. Thus, $\Delta_0^i = \{q \Rightarrow a, r_0 \Rightarrow (r_1 \Rightarrow a), r_{1-i}\}$ for $i = 0, 1$ and $\Delta_0^i \nvdash a$.

We could have removed $q \Rightarrow a$ and $r_0 \Rightarrow (r_1 \Rightarrow a)$ and got a Δ' such that $\Delta' \nvdash a$, but our *deletion* process does not do that.[29]

Example 8.18. This example shows the need for anti-formulae $\bigcirc(A)$, which in our context we also write as $Delete(A)$.[30]

We have

$$success(\Delta, A \Rightarrow B) = success(\Delta \cup \{A\}, B).$$

Therefore, we want something like

$$Abduce^-(\Delta, A \Rightarrow B) = A \Rightarrow Abduce^-(\Delta \cup \{A\}, B)$$

So, $Abduce^-(\varnothing, q \Rightarrow q)$ should equal $q \Rightarrow Abduce^-(\{q\}, q)$, but $Abduce^-(\{q\}, q) = Delete(q)$. Thus, the theory we need is $q \Rightarrow Delete(q)$. Whereupon

$$q \Rightarrow Delete(q) \nvdash q \Rightarrow q.$$

The following is a formal definition of $Abduce^-$ using the operator $Delete$. The problem is that we do not have a logic for $Delete$. This is what we are looking for.

Definition 8.22 (Abduce$^-$ for intuitionistic logic). $Abduce^-(\Delta, Q)$ is a family of sets of pseudo formulae of the form $A_1 \Rightarrow (\ldots \Rightarrow (A_n \Rightarrow Delete(q))\ldots)$, where $Delete$ is a meta-predicate and q is atomic.

1. $Abduce^-(\Delta, Q) = \{\varnothing\}$ if $\Delta ? Q = 0$
2. $Abduce^-(\Delta, q) = \{Delete(q)\}$ if $q \in \Delta$, q is atomic and is the only clause in Δ with head q
3. $Abduce^-(\Delta, A_1 \Rightarrow (A_2 \Rightarrow \ldots (A_n \Rightarrow q)\ldots)) = \{A_1 \Rightarrow (A_2 \Rightarrow \ldots (A_n \Rightarrow X)\ldots) | X \in Abduce^-(\Delta \cup \{A_1, \ldots, A_n\}, q)\}$, where $A_1 \Rightarrow (\ldots \Rightarrow (A_n \Rightarrow X)\ldots) = \{A_1 \Rightarrow (\ldots \Rightarrow (A_n \Rightarrow y)\ldots) | y \in X\}$

For clause (4) below, we need to assume that

$$B^j = (B_1^j \Rightarrow \ldots \Rightarrow (B_{n(j)}^j \Rightarrow q)\ldots), j = 1, \ldots, m,$$

lists all clauses of heads q in Δ.

We also need the notion of a choice function $\mathbf{c}$. For each $1 \le j \le m, \mathbf{c}(j)$ is a theory $\Gamma = \mathbf{c}(j)$ such that for some $1 \le i \le n(j)$, $\Gamma \in Abduce^-(\Delta, B^j)$.

4. $Abduce^-(\Delta, q) = \{\Gamma_{\mathbf{c}} \mid \mathbf{c}$ is a choice function as explained above, and $\Gamma_{\mathbf{c}} = \bigcup_{j=1}^m \Gamma_{\mathbf{c}(j)}\}$.

---

[29] This is a serious commitment, which may not be intuitive in some applications. Consider a political party's commitment to disclose (D) all cash gifts (G) to the party's chairperson. This can be formalised as $G \Rightarrow D$. Suppose we want to delete this. Using our method, to achieve $G \Rightarrow D \nvdash G \Rightarrow D$, we consider the equivalent problem of $G, G \Rightarrow D \nvdash D$, and delete G. This means a policy of denying all gifts rather than changing the rule.

[30] We thus change notation and write $Delete(A)$ for $\bigcirc(A)$. It is easier to use for complex expressions.

The explanation for clause (4) is the following: for each clause B^j as above, we want to choose an $1 \le i \le n(j)$ such that $\Delta ? B_i^j = 0$. To ensure that we look to $Abduce^-(\Delta, B_i^j)$.

Our choice functions are functions $\mathbf{c}$ choosing for each $j = 1, \dots, m$ and $1 \le i \le j$, a theory $\mathbf{c}(j) \in Abduce^-(\Delta, B_i^j)$.

Let $\Gamma_{\mathbf{c}} = \bigcup_{j=1}^m \Gamma_{\mathbf{c}(j)}$.

Note that Definition 8.22 gives a connection between $\bigcirc(X)$ (or $Delete(X)$) and contraction in intuitionistic logic.

$Abduce^-(\Delta, A)$ gives us formulae with $Delete(X)$ in them. Add these to Δ and in the suitable logical extension, which we are still trying to formulate, the addition does the job of deletion.

Example 8.19 (Deletion by addition).

1. Consider the database Δ of the preceding example and suppose that we want to delete clause (1). How do we do it? We want to do it by addition! Let n_1, n_2 be two new atoms. Consider the database Δ^* with

   (1*) $\neg n_1 \Rightarrow (\neg a \Rightarrow q)$
   (2*) $\neg n_2 \Rightarrow ((b \Rightarrow q) \Rightarrow q)$

   Clearly, since n_1, n_2 are new atoms which are not heads of any clause in Δ^*, we have for any z

   • $Success(\Delta, z) = Success(\Delta^*, z)$.

   Now we can effectively delete (1*) from Δ^* by adding n_1, and delete (2*) from Δ^* by adding n_2.

2. We can also make sure we can delete, for example, all clauses in the database with head q. To achieve this, let f be a unary function giving for each atom q of the language a new atom $f(q)$ (thus, we also have $ff(q), f^3(q), \dots$). Let Δ be a database and let $B = A_1 \Rightarrow (\dots \Rightarrow (A_n \Rightarrow q) \dots)$ be any clause with head q. Rewrite Δ to $\Delta^\sharp$ by replacing each B above by $\neg f(q) \Rightarrow B = \neg f(q) \Rightarrow (A_1 \Rightarrow \dots \Rightarrow (A_n \Rightarrow q) \dots)$.
   Clearly, by adding $f(q)$ to $\Delta^\sharp$ we delete all clauses with head q.

   Let us now do this naming in a systematic way.
   We first show how to do this operationally. Start with a language $\mathscr{L}_0$. Let $n_1^1, n_2^1, \dots$ be an infinite sequence of new names not in $\mathscr{L}_0$. Form $\mathscr{L}_1$ using these names. Get new names $n_1^2, n_2^2, \dots$ and form $\mathscr{L}_2$, and go on to form $\mathscr{L}_k$, $k = 1, 2 \dots$. We can now assume every wff φ has a unique name n_φ.
   Starting with a database Δ of the form $\Delta = \{A_1, \dots, A_k\}$, replace it with the database $\Delta' = \{\neg n_1 \Rightarrow A_1, \dots, \neg n_k \rightarrow A_k\}$, where n_i is the name of A_i.
   Make a note, for future use, of which name names which items in the database. Whenever we add a formula B to the database, add it with a new name, i.e., add $\neg n_r \Rightarrow B$, where n_r is the unique name of B. This operational rule is also applied to deletion. Thus, to delete B, we add n_r. However, since n_r is to be added, we follow

our procedure and actually add $\neg n_s \Rightarrow n_r$, where n_s is the unique name of n_r. The best way to do this is to record the steps in the computation and use the step as an index. Now, to add B back after it has been deleted, we can delete the deletion of B, i.e., we add $\neg m_2 \Rightarrow n_s$, where m_2 is the unique name of n_s.

So, comparing with our $\lambda X \bigcirc(X)$ notation, we have the following correspondence:

- wff B : $\neg n_r \Rightarrow B$
- wff $\bigcirc(B)$: $\neg n_s \Rightarrow n_r$
- wff $\bigcirc(\bigcirc(B))$: $\neg m_2 \Rightarrow n_s$

etc.

Example 8.20. Let us revisit Example 8.15, using this method.

1. $\neg n_1 \Rightarrow A_1$
2. $\neg n_2 \Rightarrow A_2$
3. $\neg n_3 \Rightarrow (A_1 \Rightarrow B)$
4. $\neg n_4 \Rightarrow (A_2 \Rightarrow B)$

This proves B. How do we logically delete B? In the *N*-Prolog method we cannot do that. We can only calculate what items of data the proof of B depends on and delete them. So we need to add, for example,

$\qquad \neg n_5 \Rightarrow n_1$

and

$\qquad \neg n_6 \Rightarrow n_2.$

Remark 8.10. Note that the *N*-Prolog approach does satisfy that, if $A \notin \Delta$, then deleting A from Δ yields Δ. To achieve this we need to systematically give names to wffs.

What we cannot do is delete wffs B that can be proved from Δ but are not physically in Δ. To delete such a B we need to find which sets of assumptions from Δ can be used to prove B and then delete from Δ enough assumptions to destroy all possible proofs. Here, we need the assistance of the meta-predicate $Abduce^-$. It will identify such assumptions. This will be addressed in Section 8.11. Note that we might need to do conditional deletion, i.e., introduce expressions of the form $q \Rightarrow \mathbf{Delete}(r)$.

Actually we can use a device to delete such a B. Let r_B be a special name for B; different from B's standard name. Add $B \Rightarrow r_B$ to the database and try to prove r_B. This will succeed only if B can be proved. So, if we ask for r_B whenever we want B, then we can delete r_B by deleting $B \Rightarrow r_B$ (see Section 8.13 and Remark 8.31).

Definition 8.23 (*N*-Prolog sublanguage allowing systematic deletion).

1. Let $Q_i = \{q_j^i \mid j = 1, 2, 3, \ldots\}$, $i = 1, 2, 3 \ldots$ be pairwise disjoint sets of atoms. Let f be a function symbol creating new atoms. Let $\mathscr{L}_0$ be the *N*-Prolog language with $\Rightarrow, \perp$ and $\neg$ based on the atoms $Q_0 = \{q_1, q_2, \ldots\}$, and let $\mathscr{L}_n$ be the language based on the atoms in $\bigcup_{i=0}^{n}(Q_i \cup \bigcup_{m=1}^{\infty}\{f^m(x) \mid x \in Q_i\})$.
   Assume that for atoms $x \in \bigcup_n Q_n, f^m(x), m = 1, 2, \ldots$ are all pairwise different.

2. For each wff A of $\mathscr{L}_m$, let $\mathbf{n}(m+1,A)$ be a unique atom from Q_{m+1} associated with A, acting as its name. Thus, for $A \neq B$ we have $\mathbf{n}(m+1,A) \neq \mathbf{n}(m+1,B)$.

3. Let A be a wff of $\mathscr{L}_m$. Let $A_d^{[m+1]}$ and $A_g^{[m+1]}$ be the wffs of $\mathscr{L}_{m+1}$, the result of naming all subformulae of A for data or for goal, respectively. We define these wffs by structural induction based on Definition 8.20 as follows:

- $q_d^{[m+1]} = \neg f(q) \Rightarrow (\neg \mathbf{n}(m+1,q) \Rightarrow q)^{31}$

  $q_g^{[m+1]} = q$

  for q atomic or $\perp$ or of the form $f^m(x)$, x atomic

- $(\neg q)_d^{[m+1]} = 1 = f(q)^{32}$

  $\neg q_g^{[m+1]} = \neg q$

  for q atomic or $\perp$ or of the form $f^m(x)$, x atomic

- If $B = (A_1 \Rightarrow \ldots \Rightarrow (A_n \Rightarrow q) \ldots)$ is a data clause, then A_i are goal clauses, and we let
  $$B_d^{[m+1]} = \neg f(q) \Rightarrow \neg \mathbf{n}(m+1,B) \Rightarrow (A_{1,g}^{[m+1]} \Rightarrow \ldots \Rightarrow (A_{n,g}^{[m+1]} \Rightarrow q) \ldots))$$

- If $B = (A_1 \Rightarrow \ldots \Rightarrow (A_n \Rightarrow q) \ldots)$ is a goal clause, then A_i are data clauses, and we let
  $$B_g^{[m+1]} = A_{1,d}^{[m+1]} \Rightarrow (\ldots \Rightarrow (A_{n,d}^{[m+1]} \Rightarrow q) \ldots).$$

Lemma 8.17. *Let Δ be a database of wffs in $\mathscr{L}_m$ and let $\Delta_d^{[m+1]} = \{A_d^{[m+1]} | A \in \Delta\}$. Then for any z, $\mathrm{Success}(\Delta,z) = \mathrm{Success}(\Delta_d^{[m+1]}, z_g^{[m+1]})$.*

Proof. Proved by induction on the computation, and follows from the fact that none of the new names are heads in $\Delta_d^{[m+1]}$.
We follow the inductive steps of Definition 8.21.

1. Immediate success/failure case

  a. $\mathrm{Success}(\Delta,q) = 1$ *if* $q \in \Delta$. *But* $q \in \Delta$ *if and only if* $\neg f(q) \Rightarrow (\neg \mathbf{n}(m+1,q) \Rightarrow q)$ *is in* $\Delta_d^{[m+1]}$. *Hence,* $\mathrm{Success}(\Delta_d^{[m+1]},q) = 1$, *since* $\mathbf{n}(m+1,q)$ *is not a head in* $\Delta_d^{[m+1]}$.

  b. $\mathrm{Success}(\Delta,q) = 0$ *if* q *is not a head in* Δ. *But then,* q *is not a head in* $\Delta_d^{[m+1]}$, *and hence* $\mathrm{Success}(\Delta_d^{[m+1]},q) = 0$.

---

[31] $\neg f(q)$ is the negation as failure of the 'name' of the clause head 'q'. It is put in so that we can delete all clauses with head q in one action by adding '$f(q)$'. $\mathbf{n}(m+1,q)$ is the name of this particular atomic clause. We put in $\neg \mathbf{n}(m+1,q)$ so that we can delete this particular clause by adding its name. Thus, any clause $A \Rightarrow q$ becomes $\neg f(q) \wedge \neg \mathbf{n}(m+1,A) \wedge A \Rightarrow q$ or, if written with $\Rightarrow$ alone, becomes $\neg f(q) \Rightarrow ((\neg \mathbf{n}(m+1,A) \Rightarrow (A \Rightarrow q))$.

[32] The significance of this definition becomes apparent in light of Example 8.16

c. If $Success(\Delta_d^{[m+1]}, q)$ is 1 using one step (not counting the $?\neg f(q)$ and $?\neg \mathbf{n}$ kinds of steps), then $\neg f(q) \Rightarrow (\neg \mathbf{n}(m+1, q) \Rightarrow q)$ must be in $\Delta_d^{[m+1]}$, and hence $q \in \Delta$. Hence, $Success(\Delta, q) = 1$ in one step.

d. Clearly, if $Success(\Delta_d^{[m+1]}, q)$ is 0 in one step, then q is not a head in Δ, and $Success(\Delta, q) = 0$.

2. Implication case
$Success(\Delta, A_1 \Rightarrow \ldots \Rightarrow (A_n \Rightarrow q)\ldots) = Success(\Delta \cup \{A_i\}, q) =$ (by induction)
$success(\Delta_d^{[m+1]} \cup \{A_{i,d}^{[m+1]}\}, q) = Success(\Delta_d^{[m+1]}, A_1 \Rightarrow \ldots A_n \Rightarrow q)\ldots)_g^{[m+1]}).$

3. Cut rule case
$Success(\Delta, q) = 1$ (respectively, 0) if and only if for all (respectively, some) $A = (A_1 \Rightarrow \ldots \Rightarrow (A_n \Rightarrow q)\ldots))$ in Δ we have that for all (respectively, some) $Success(\Delta, A_i) = 1$ (respectively, 0) if and only if (by induction) for all (respectively, some) $A_d^{[m+1]} \in \Delta_d^{[m+1]}$ we have that for all (respectively, some) $A_{i,g}^{[m+1]}$, $Success(\Delta_d^{[m+1]}, A_{i,g}^{[m+1]}) = 1$ (respectively, 0). Note that $\neg f(q)$ and $\neg \mathbf{n}(m+1, A)$ succeed from $\Delta_d^{[m+1]}$, and hence can be disregarded. We continue if and only if $Success(\Delta_d^{[m+1]}, q) = 1$ (respectively, 0).

Lemma 8.18.

1. Let Δ be a database of $\mathcal{L}_m$ and let $A \in \Delta$ with head x. Then $(\Delta - \{A\})_d^{[m+1]}$ is N-Prolog equivalent to $\Delta_d^{[m+1]} \cup \{\mathbf{n}(m+1, A)\}$. In other words, for any q, $Success(\Delta - \{A\}, q) = Success((\Delta - \{A\})_d^{[m+1]}, q) = Success(\Delta_d^{[m+1]} \cup \{\mathbf{n}(m+1, A)\}, q)$.

2. Let $A_i \in \Delta$ list all clauses in Δ with head q; then $(\Delta - \{A_i\})_d^{[m+1]}$ is N-Prolog equivalent to $\Delta_d^{[m+1]} \cup \{f(q)\}$.

Proof. The proof is clear since $A_d^{[m+1]}$ has the form $\neg f(x) \Rightarrow (\neg \mathbf{n}(m+1, A) \Rightarrow A')$.

The last lemma gives deletion by addition. Let us see how it works.

Example 8.21. Consider

$$p \vdash p$$

We want to make p not provable. Obviously, we need to delete p.

The above is equivalent (after inserting all the appropriate names) to $\neg f(p) \Rightarrow (\neg \mathbf{n}(p) \Rightarrow p) \vdash p$.

Hence, we delete p by adding $\mathbf{n}(p)$. We get the database

$$\{\neg f(p) \Rightarrow (\neg \mathbf{n}(p) \Rightarrow p), \mathbf{n}(p)\}$$

and this database is equivalent to $\varnothing$.

8.11 Exploring Deletion via Addition

We saw in Remark 8.10 that we need the *Abduce⁻* meta-predicate to enable us to make a logical deletion by deleting from the data enough assumptions to destroy all possible proofs. This section studies this meta-predicate.

The aim of this section is to check whether, within the framework of *N*-Prolog with negation as failure and our naming methodology, we can give meaning to the deletion meta-predicate *Abduce⁻* of Definition 8.22, i.e., effectively add to the database expressions which mean $A \Rightarrow Delete(X)$. Here, $Delete(X)$ is our $\bigcirc(X)$.

Let us see what we can do so far. Consider again the problem of stopping by deletion the fact that $p \vdash p$. Obviously, we should delete p and get $\varnothing \nvdash p$. The problem of $p \vdash p$ is equivalent to the problem of $\varnothing \vdash p \Rightarrow p$. So what do we delete from $\varnothing$ to stop $p \Rightarrow p$ from being provable? Does it make sense to want a tautology not to be provable? Well, let us examine the equivalent problem, using Lemma 8.17. The problem becomes $\neg f(p) \Rightarrow (\neg \mathbf{n}(p) \Rightarrow p) \vdash p$, which is equivalent to $\varnothing \vdash (\neg f(p) \Rightarrow (\neg \mathbf{n}(p) \Rightarrow p)) \Rightarrow p$. To delete p, we add $\mathbf{n}(p)$. Thus, $\mathbf{n}(p) \nvdash (\neg f(p) \Rightarrow (\neg \mathbf{n}(p) \Rightarrow p)) \Rightarrow p$.

In fact, $\mathbf{n}(p)$ is the anti-formula for $\neg f(p) \Rightarrow (\neg \mathbf{n}(p) \Rightarrow p)$, and $\mathbf{n}(p)$ deletes it. There are still some points to check in the next example. In the previous example, we performed the abduction in the language of $\varnothing \vdash p \Rightarrow p$. We discovered we need to add $p \Rightarrow Delete(p)$; then we moved to the translation of the problem above in the language with names, namely to $\varnothing \vdash (\neg f(p) \Rightarrow (\neg \mathbf{n}(p) \Rightarrow p)) \Rightarrow p$, and added the translation of $p \Rightarrow Delete(p)$, namely $(\neg f(p) \Rightarrow (\mathbf{n}(p) \Rightarrow p)) \Rightarrow \mathbf{n}(p)$.

The question is, what will we find if we apply the abduction process directly in the translation language?

Example 8.22. Let us apply our abduction process of Definition 8.22 to the database and query

$$\varnothing \vdash p \Rightarrow p.$$

We consider the equivalent problem of

$$\varnothing \vdash (\neg f(p) \Rightarrow (\neg \mathbf{n}(p) \Rightarrow p)) \Rightarrow p.$$

We have it that

$$Abduce^-(\varnothing, (\neg f(p) \Rightarrow (\neg \mathbf{n}(p) \Rightarrow p)) \Rightarrow p)$$

is equal to

$$(\neg f(p) \Rightarrow (\neg \mathbf{n}(p) \Rightarrow p)) \Rightarrow Abduce^-(\neg f(p) \Rightarrow (\neg \mathbf{n}(p) \Rightarrow p), p).$$

We continue:

$$Abduce^-(\neg f(p) \Rightarrow (\neg \mathbf{n}(p) \Rightarrow p), p)$$

is equal to

$$Abduce^-(\neg f(p) \Rightarrow (\neg \mathbf{n}(p) \Rightarrow p), \neg f(p)) \cup$$
$$Abduce^-(\neg f(p) \Rightarrow (\neg \mathbf{n}(p) \Rightarrow p), \neg \mathbf{n}(p))$$

and this is equal to[33]

$$Abduce^+(\neg f(p) \Rightarrow (\neg \mathbf{n}(p) \Rightarrow p), f(p)) \cup$$
$$Abduce^+(\neg f(p) \Rightarrow (\neg \mathbf{n}(p) \Rightarrow p), \mathbf{n}(p))$$

which is equal to

$$\{\{\mathbf{n}(p)\}, \{f(p)\}\}$$

Thus, the abduced formulae are either

$$(\neg f(\mathbf{n}(p)) \Rightarrow (\neg f(p) \Rightarrow (\neg \mathbf{n}(p) \Rightarrow p)) \Rightarrow \mathbf{n}(p))$$

or

$$\neg f f(p) \Rightarrow ((\neg f(p) \Rightarrow (\neg \mathbf{n}(p) \Rightarrow p)) \Rightarrow f(p)).$$

We can agree to abduce only on names of the form $\mathbf{n}(A)$, A a wff, because that was the original intention. In fact, we abduce only on names of the form $\mathbf{n}(q)$, q atomic, because our original abduction process either added or deleted atoms.

The clause $f(p)$ is intended to delete when necessary (i.e., when $\neg p$ is supposed to be added into the database) all clauses with head p. Thus, it does not participate in the abduction. Its purpose is different.

The above example shows we may have a problem. The clause abduced in the example is a goal clause, not a data clause. If we put it in the database and ask for $?\mathbf{n}(p)$, we need to ask for $\neg \mathbf{n}(p) \Rightarrow p$, and so we need to put $\neg \mathbf{n}(p)$ in the database. We thus get the new database and query $\Delta = \{\neg \mathbf{n}(p), \neg f(\mathbf{n}(p)) \Rightarrow (\neg f(p) \Rightarrow (\neg \mathbf{n}(p) \Rightarrow p)) \Rightarrow \mathbf{n}(p))\}?p$.

We have not said what putting $\neg \mathbf{n}(p)$ in a database means, i.e., N-Prolog with negation as failure does not tell us what it means to put a literal $\neg q$ into a database. In fact, the language makes the distinctions of data clauses and goal clauses in order that the problem of putting a $\neg q$ into databases will never arise! However, we have already made provisions in the translation of Definition 8.23 that the translation of $\neg q_d^{[m+1]}$ is $f(q)$; thus, to add $\neg \mathbf{n}(p)$ means to add $f(\mathbf{n}(p))$. This indeed will kill any clause with head $\mathbf{n}(p)$.

We seem to have two options for solving our abduction problem:

Option 1. Use a *modified N-Prolog.*

This option will allow for inserting literal $\neg q$ into databases and allow also for clauses of the form $\neg q \Rightarrow A$ to be goal clauses provided A is a goal clause. We need to say what it means to have $\neg q$ in a database Δ. Let us agree that we view $\neg q$ as an *integrity constraint, cancelling* all clauses in Δ with head q.[34]

---

[33] $Abduce^+(\Delta, q)$ is what is needed to add to Δ to make q succeed. An inductive definition for $Abduce^+$ can be given, similar to $Abduce^-$. But in our case it is clear what needs to be added.

[34] Adding $f(q)$ will continue to delete forever any clause with head q.

Thus, if Δ contains $\neg q$, then no clause of the form $A_1 \Rightarrow (\dots \Rightarrow (A_n \Rightarrow q)\dots)$ can be used in any computation in Δ (more specifically, items (1a), (3b) and (4) of Definition 8.21 must be qualified by the phrase 'and $\neg q$ is not in Δ' and items (1b), (3b) and (4) must be qualified by the phrase 'or $\neg q$ is in Δ').

The reader may note that N-Prolog actually knows how to do deletions, and so really that this modification can be implemented within N-Prolog itself, through the translation of Definition 8.23.

Option 2. Change the definition of *Abduce*$^-$.

We eliminate the clause in the *Abduce*$^-$ definition (Definition 8.22) which puts us in this undesirable situation, namely item 3 of Definition 8.22

(*) $Abduce^-(\Delta, A_1 \Rightarrow \dots (A_n \Rightarrow q)\dots) =$
$$A_1 \Rightarrow (\dots (A_n \Rightarrow Abduce^-(\Delta \cup \{A_i\}, q))\dots) \text{ replacing it with the}$$
rule

(**) $Abduce^-(\Delta, A_1 \Rightarrow \dots (A_n \Rightarrow q)\dots) = Abduce^-(\Delta \cup \{A_i\}, q)$

(**) will mean that we add $\mathbf{n}(p)$ to our database.

Our initial position may be that we are reluctant to adopt Option 1, even though N-Prolog with negation as failure is a well-known system with good semantics. We want to explore other options first. Unfortunately, Option 2 is unacceptable because it would give unintuitive results, as the next example shows:

Example 8.23. Consider the database Γ containing:

1. $p \Rightarrow (r \Rightarrow q)$
2. $r \Rightarrow a$
3. r

This database can prove a and it can also prove $p \Rightarrow q$.

Suppose we want to make sure, using *Abduce*$^-$, that $p \Rightarrow q$ does not follow. Then (*) gives us

$$Abduce^-(\Gamma, p \Rightarrow q) = p \Rightarrow Abduce^-(\Gamma \cup \{p\}, q),$$

which gives us two possibilities for abduction, which we will loosely write as $p \Rightarrow Delete(p)$ and $p \Rightarrow Delete(r)$.

If we use (**) we get the two options $Delete(p)$ and $Delete(r)$.

Let us choose the option of deleting r in some way.

Using (*) means that our database is primed to delete r as soon as p is introduced into it. But as long as p has not been introduced into Γ, our database does have r in it and can therefore prove a.

Using (**), on the other hand, deletes r immediately. So even if p never arrives, a cannot be proved.

This seems counterintuitive. $A \Rightarrow B$ has the interpretation that whenever A holds B must be true. Thus, $p \Rightarrow Delete(r)$ may mean 'in case of emergency relax budgetary restrictions on spending'. We do not want to delete r now — only when p happens!

So it looks as if we are stuck without any new options. What shall we do? Shall we now adopt Option 1?

Let us check one more angle. We tried to use (**) in $Abduce^-(\Gamma, p \Rightarrow q)$ and got counterintuitive results. Let us ask, does the problem arise in the context of the naming scheme we introduced? In other words, if we use (**) in $Abduce^-(\Gamma_d^{[m+1]}, (p \Rightarrow q)_g^{[m+1]})$, do we still get a problem?

Example 8.24. Let us see what happens to our database when we use names.
Our database becomes (call it Γ_d for short):[35]

(1*) $\neg n_1 \Rightarrow (r \Rightarrow (p \Rightarrow q))$
(2*) $\neg n_2 \Rightarrow (r \Rightarrow a)$
(3*) $\neg n_3 \Rightarrow r$

Our goal becomes $(\neg n_4 \Rightarrow p) \Rightarrow q$.
We want the goal to fail.
If we use (*) we get that we have two possibilities for deletion via addition: we either add

(4*) $(\neg n_4 \Rightarrow p) \Rightarrow n_4$

corresponding to $p \Rightarrow Delete(p)$, or we add

(5*) $(\neg n_4 \Rightarrow p) \Rightarrow n_3$

corresponding to $p \Rightarrow Delete(r)$.

If we use (**) we get that we need to either add n_4 (corresponding to $Delete(p)$) or add n_3 (corresponding to $Delete(r)$).

We seem to have the same problem as before.

So we are still in a search for a third option.

It seems that we were either operating in the language $\mathscr{L}$ of Γ, in which case $Abduce^-(\Gamma, p \Rightarrow q)$ gave us $p \Rightarrow Delete(r)$, which is not part of the Γ language, or we were operating in the language of N-Prolog, into which we translated Γ (to Γ_d) and $p \Rightarrow q$ to $(p \Rightarrow q)_g$ and applied $Abduce^-(\Gamma_d, (p \Rightarrow q)_g)$ and got a new kind of difficulty. What we have not yet considered is the following:

Option 3. Mixed option

This option is a compromise on languages. We first execute the abduction in the language of Γ and get the abduced set (i.e., $p \Rightarrow Delete(r)$ and $p \Rightarrow Delete(p)$ in our example), and then *translate* the abduced set into N-Prolog and add it to Γ_d. This way the abduction for Γ_d is done in the original language (of Γ) and then translated, and is not directly executed in the translation (i.e., in N-Prolog).

Will Option 3 solve our difficulties? Our experience so far, in Example 8.24 and the discussion preceding, is encouraging.

Let us check.

---

[35] We omit to add, for the sake of simplicity, the names $\neg f(q), \neg f(a)$ and $\neg f(r)$ in the respective clauses.

Example 8.25. The translation of Γ is Γ_d below (again we omit the use of the f function).

$(1^*)\ \neg n_1 \Rightarrow (r \Rightarrow (p \Rightarrow q))$
$(2^*)\ \neg n_2 \Rightarrow (r \Rightarrow a)$
$(3^*)\ \neg n_3 \Rightarrow r.$

If we do the *Abduce$^-$*$(\Gamma, p \Rightarrow q)$ we get, as we have seen before, two possibilities for abduction, $p \Rightarrow Delete(r)$ and $p \Rightarrow Delete(p)$. Let us examine what happens with each choice in turn.

1. Case of $p \Rightarrow Delete(r)$:
   In this case r is in the database, so it has a name n_3. So, let us agree to

   • Translate '*Delete*(X)' as the *name of X*, '$\mathbf{n}(X)$'.

   So we add to Γ_d the clause

$(6^*)\ p \Rightarrow n_3.$

   Let us see now whether $\Gamma_d + (6^*) \vdash p \Rightarrow q?$
   The answer is no because $\Gamma_d + (6^*) + p \nvdash q$, because r is no longer provable. In fact, even if we ask as a goal the translation of $p \Rightarrow q$, namely $(\neg n_4 \Rightarrow p) \Rightarrow q$, we still get that $\Gamma_d + (6^*) + (\neg n_4 \Rightarrow p) \nvdash q$ because p is still provable, and hence r is thrown out.

2. Case of $p \Rightarrow Delete(p)$
   The first problem in this case is that p does not have a name. The answer is that we have given clauses their names in a systematic way, so p does indeed have a name; it is $\mathbf{n}(p) = n_4$, and so we can add

$(7^*)\ p \Rightarrow n_4$

   to Γ_d in this case.
   To check whether

$$\Gamma_d + (7^*) \vdash ?p \Rightarrow q$$

   we have to be careful and require that the computation be done in *N*-Prolog with names. We know this choice works for case (1): so we must ask not for $p \Rightarrow q$, but for its translation, i.e., $(p \Rightarrow q)_g = (\neg n_4 \Rightarrow p) \Rightarrow q$.
   This gives

$$\Gamma_d + (7^*) + \neg n_4 \Rightarrow p \vdash ?q$$

   and of course we loop. We have the two clauses

$$p \Rightarrow n_4$$
$$\neg n_4 \Rightarrow p$$

   and we need to ask $?p$, hoping it would fail, but it actually loops. This is no cause for alarm. These two clauses are actually clauses of ordinary Prolog with negation as failure, and a lot is known about looping in ordinary Prolog. We just want a device which will fail p. The trouble is that this is a genuine loop. If p fails, then n_4 must succeed from the second clause, and therefore p must succeed from the first clause. Any technical device which may work for this example may not work to our satisfaction in more complex examples.

Example 8.26 (Problems with loops). Continuing the previous example, we know, however, that we are dealing with a specific task of finding a way of executing deletion by addition and that we are not concerned with the general problem of resolving nasty loops in ordinary Prolog. We may therefore utilise any specific features of our problem towards the success of our task. We note first that N-Prolog is based on intuitionistic logic, which is complete for a goal-directed computation with diminishing resource, where whenever a clause is used, it is immediately deleted. See [10, Section 3.1]. The policy of diminishing resource eliminates loops. Can this help us?

Let us look at our loop again. The database is

$$p \Rightarrow n_4$$
$$\neg n_4 \Rightarrow p.$$

If we ask for $?p = 1$ we get

$$\{p \Rightarrow n_4, \neg n_4 \Rightarrow p\}?p = 1$$

if

$$\{p \Rightarrow n_4\}?\neg n_4 = 1$$

if

$$\{p \Rightarrow n_4\}?n_4 = 0$$

if

$$\varnothing?n_4 = 0$$

if

Success.

Now ask for $?n_4 = 1$.

$$\{p \Rightarrow n_4, \neg n_4 \Rightarrow p\}?n_4 = 1$$

if

$$\{\neg n_4 \Rightarrow p\}?p = 1$$

if

$$\varnothing?\neg n_4 = 1$$

if

$$\varnothing?n_4 = 0$$

if

Success.

We get that both n_4 and p succeed. This is nonsense. The diminishing resource policy does not work in the presence of negation as failure.

However, we still may be able to save the situation. We recall that anti-formulae are to be used only once. This means that the data item $p \Rightarrow n_4$, which represents the black hole, should be used only once, while the data item $\neg n_4 \Rightarrow p$, which represents p is a genuine data item, can be used as many times as needed.

Let us reconsider our loop with this in mind:

$$\{p \Rightarrow n, \neg n_4 \Rightarrow p\}?p = 1$$

if

$$\{p \Rightarrow n_4, \neg n_4 \Rightarrow p\}?\neg n_4 = 1$$

if

$$\{p \Rightarrow n_4, \neg n_4 \Rightarrow p\}?n_4 = 0$$

if

$$\{\neg n_4 \Rightarrow p\}?p = 0$$

if

$$\varnothing?\neg n_4 = 0$$

if

$$\varnothing?n_4 = 1$$

if

failure.

So p fails. This is good.

How about $?n_4 = 1$. This should succeed.

$$\{\Rightarrow n_4, \neg n_4 \Rightarrow p\}?n_4 = 1$$

if

$$\{\neg n_4 \Rightarrow p\}?p = 1$$

if

$$\varnothing?\neg n_4 = 1$$

if

$$\varnothing?n_4 = 0$$

if

success.

It looks as if we have made it. n_4 succeeds and p fails.[36]

We have one more item to check. We need to check Example 8.25, where we chose the possibility of $p \Rightarrow Delete(r)$ and added

(6^*) $p \Rightarrow n_3$;

does it still work with (6^*) being a once-only clause? The answer is yes. We use (6^*) only once in this example.

It is time now to move to the next section and give a formal definition of how we are to deal with $Abduce^-$ of Definition 8.22.

But before we do that, why not go back to Option 1, and see how it fares with our example?

Example 8.27. According to Option 1 we have the following database after $Abduce^-(\varnothing, (\neg f(p) \Rightarrow (\neg \mathbf{n}(p) \Rightarrow p)) \Rightarrow p)$ of Example 8.24 has been executed and the result of the abduction added to $\varnothing$:

$$\Delta^* = \{(\neg f(\mathbf{n}(p) \Rightarrow (\neg \mathbf{n}(p) \Rightarrow p))) \Rightarrow \mathbf{n}(p)\}.$$

Let us ask whether $?(\neg f(p) \Rightarrow (\neg \mathbf{n}(p) \Rightarrow p)) \Rightarrow p = 1$ from this database. We get the above reducing to

$$\{\neg f(\mathbf{n}(p)) \Rightarrow (\neg \mathbf{n}(p) \Rightarrow p)) \Rightarrow \mathbf{n}(p), \neg f(p) \Rightarrow (\neg \mathbf{n}(p) \Rightarrow p)\}?p = 1$$

which (since $?\neg f(p) = 1$) reduces to

$$\{\neg f(\mathbf{n}(p)) \Rightarrow (\neg \mathbf{n}(p) \Rightarrow p)) \Rightarrow \mathbf{n}(p), \neg f(p) \Rightarrow (\neg \mathbf{n}(p) \Rightarrow p)\}?\mathbf{n}(p) = 0$$

which (since $?\neg f(\mathbf{n}(p)) = 1$) reduces to

$$\{\neg f(\mathbf{n}(p)) \Rightarrow ((\neg \mathbf{n}(p) \Rightarrow p)) \Rightarrow \mathbf{n}(p), \neg f(p) \Rightarrow (\neg \mathbf{n}(p) \Rightarrow p), f(\mathbf{n}(p))\}?p = 0.$$

The presence of $f(\mathbf{n}(p))$ cancels all clauses with head $\mathbf{n}(p)$, and so our problem reduces to[37]

$$\{\neg f(p) \Rightarrow (\neg \mathbf{n}(p) \Rightarrow p)\}?p = 0$$

which reduces to

$$\{\neg f(p) \Rightarrow (\neg \mathbf{n}(p) \Rightarrow p)\}?\mathbf{n}(p) = 1$$

which fails, as required.

---

[36] Think of our database classically: $(\neg n_4 \Rightarrow p) \wedge (p \Rightarrow n_4)$ is equivalent to $(\neg p \Rightarrow n_4) \wedge (p \Rightarrow n_4)$, which is equivalent to n_4. It is not surprising therefore that n_4 succeeds and p fails.

[37] Notice that the minute $(\neg \mathbf{n}(p) \Rightarrow \neg p) \Rightarrow \mathbf{n}(p)$ was used, $\neg \mathbf{n}(p)$ was supposed to be added to the database, and thus $f(\mathbf{n}(p))$ was added and thus cancelled the use of the clauses, *making it a use-once clause only*. This is fully compatible with our view! To add $\neg \mathbf{n}(p)$, we added $f(\mathbf{n}(p))$ as required in item 3 of Definition 8.19.

Let us now check whether $?\mathbf{n}(p) = 1$ succeeds.

$$\{\neg f(\mathbf{n}(p)) \Rightarrow ((\neg\mathbf{n}(p) \Rightarrow p)) \Rightarrow \mathbf{n}(p), \neg f(p) \Rightarrow (\neg\mathbf{n}(p) \Rightarrow p)\}?\mathbf{n}(p) = 1$$

reduces (since $?\neg f(\mathbf{n}(p)) = 1$ at this stage) to

$$\{\neg f(\mathbf{n}(p)) \Rightarrow ((\neg\mathbf{n}(p) \Rightarrow p)) \Rightarrow \mathbf{n}(p), \neg f(p) \Rightarrow (\neg\mathbf{n}(p) \Rightarrow p), f(\mathbf{n}(p))\}?p = 1$$

and this reduces to

$$\{\neg f(p) \Rightarrow (\neg\mathbf{n}(p) \Rightarrow p)\}?p = 1$$

which reduces to

$$\{\neg f(p) \Rightarrow (\neg\mathbf{n}(p) \Rightarrow p)\}?\mathbf{n}(p) = 0$$

which succeeds.

So all is well.

Let us also check Example 8.23 according to Option 1.

Example 8.28. Our database is (we omit the use of f):

(1*) $\neg n_1 = \neg(r \Rightarrow (p \Rightarrow q))$
(2*) $\neg n_2 \Rightarrow (r \Rightarrow a)$
(3*) $\neg n_3 \Rightarrow r$.

The goal to fail is

$$(\neg n_4 \Rightarrow p) \Rightarrow q.$$

The two possible abduced sentences are

(4*) $(\neg n_4 \Rightarrow p) \Rightarrow n_4$

corresponding to $p \Rightarrow Delete(p)$ and

(5*) $(\neg n_4 \Rightarrow p) \Rightarrow n_3$

corresponding to $p \Rightarrow Delete(r)$.

Let us check if the job gets done.[38]

First we check

$$\{(1^*) - (3^*), (4^*)\}?(\neg n_4 \Rightarrow p) \Rightarrow q = 1$$

This reduces to

$$\{(1^*) - (3^*), (4^*), \neg n_4 \Rightarrow p\}?q = 1$$

From (1*), and using (3*), this reduces to

---

[38] Notice again that any clause of the form $(\neg x \Rightarrow q) \Rightarrow x$ is a use-once-only clause. The minute it is used with $?x$, it immediately adds $\neg x$ to the database and continues with $?q$, thus immediately cancelling itself.

In fact, any clause of the form $x \Rightarrow q$ can be made a once-only clause by 'equivalently' replacing it by $(\neg x \Rightarrow q) \Rightarrow x$ (provided no other clauses $A \Rightarrow x$ exist).

$$\{(1^*) - (3^*), (4^*), \neg n_4 \Rightarrow p\}?p = 1$$

which reduces to

$$\{(1^*) - (3^*), (4^*), \neg n_4 \Rightarrow p\}?n_4 = 0$$

which reduces to (from (4^*))

$$\{(1^*) - (3^*), (4^*), \neg n_4 \Rightarrow p, \neg n_4\}?p = 0$$

which reduces to (by using $\neg n_4 \Rightarrow p$ and simplifying, since $\neg n_4$ cancels (4^*))

$$\{(1^*) - (3^*), \neg n_4 \Rightarrow p\}?n_4 = 1$$

which fails.

8.12 A Formal System for Deletion via Addition

We begin with a methodological remark. The discussion in the previous section gave us hope that $Abduce^-$ can be given respectable meaning and semantics by translating it into N-Prolog with negation as failure. The task of this section is to show how it can be done formally. We basically need to give meaning to expressions like $p \Rightarrow Delete(q)$.

The methodological point we want to make is that once we succeed in our task, we no longer need to actually work in N-Prolog. We can extend our language of intuitionistic $\Rightarrow$ and $\bot$ with a $Delete(X)$ predicate or $\bigcirc(X)$, and work out the local rules via the translation into N-Prolog. This should be our final aim.

First, let us examine whether some intuitive properties for anti-formulae discussed in Section 8.3 hold for the N-Prolog translation.

1. *Annihilation*
   This rule says that

   $$\Delta + X + \bigcirc(X) = \Delta$$

   If $*$ is the translation into N-Prolog, then we need to check whether

   $$\Delta^* + \neg \mathbf{n}(X) \Rightarrow X + \mathbf{n}(X) = \Delta^*$$

   where $\Gamma_1 = \Gamma_2$ means $\Gamma_1?Y = \Gamma_2?Y$ for every Y, i.e., Γ_1, Γ_2 give the same answers. This is clearly true.

2. *Black-hole deduction theorem*
   The deduction theorem says

   $$\Delta \vdash A \text{ if and only if } \Delta + \bigcirc(X) \vdash X \Rightarrow A$$

   where

   $$\Delta, A, X$$

   are arbitrary. Translated, it becomes

$$\Delta_d \vdash A_g \text{ if and only if } \Delta_d + \mathbf{n}(X) \vdash (\neg\mathbf{n}(X) \Rightarrow X) \Rightarrow A_g.$$

We have already noticed that we need the *once-only* rule, because without it we could have the wrong results. Consider

$$X \Rightarrow A \vdash X \Rightarrow A;$$

hence, by the black-hole deduction theorem for X we get

$$X \Rightarrow A + \bigcirc(X) \vdash X \Rightarrow (X \Rightarrow A);$$

hence,

$$X \Rightarrow A + \bigcirc(X) + X + X \vdash A;$$

hence,

$$X \Rightarrow A \vdash A.$$

Let us see what happens in the translation.
Let

$$n_1 = \mathbf{n}(X \Rightarrow A)$$
$$n_2 = \mathbf{n}(X)$$

The translation of $X \Rightarrow A \vdash X \Rightarrow A$ becomes $(X \Rightarrow A)_d \vdash (X \Rightarrow A)_g$, namely

$$\neg n_1 \Rightarrow (X \Rightarrow A) \vdash (\neg n_2 \Rightarrow X) \Rightarrow A;$$

hence, by the black-hole deduction theorem for X

$$\neg n_1 \Rightarrow (X \Rightarrow A) + n_2 \vdash (\neg n_2 \Rightarrow X) \Rightarrow (\neg n_2 \Rightarrow X) \Rightarrow A$$

which is equivalent to

$$\neg n_1 \Rightarrow (X \Rightarrow A) + n_2 + (\neg n_2 \Rightarrow X) + (\neg n_2 \Rightarrow X) \vdash A.$$

It is clear that we need a once-only use of n_2; otherwise we get $\neg n_1 \Rightarrow (X \Rightarrow A) \vdash A$.

Consider now a database with $\{X, \bigcirc(X), \odot(X)\}$. What would be its translation? The obvious choice is to take $\{\neg\mathbf{n}(X) \Rightarrow X, \neg\mathbf{n}(\mathbf{n}(X) \Rightarrow \mathbf{n}(X)), \mathbf{n}(\mathbf{n}(X))\}$.

We may think, however, that we are not being consistent in naming. We usually name 'X' by '$\mathbf{n}(X)$' and put '$\neg\mathbf{n}(X) \Rightarrow X$' in the database as the translation of 'X'. But if '$\mathbf{n}(X)$' is also named by '$\mathbf{n}(\mathbf{n}(X))$', then if we put '$\neg\mathbf{n}(\mathbf{n}(X) \Rightarrow \mathbf{n}(X))$' in the database as the translation of '$\mathbf{n}(X)$', then, to be consistent, '$\neg\mathbf{n}(X) \Rightarrow X$' should be translated as $\neg(\neg\mathbf{n}(\mathbf{n}(X) \Rightarrow \mathbf{n}(X))) \Rightarrow X$, which is equivalent to $(\neg\mathbf{n}(\mathbf{n}(X) \Rightarrow \neg\mathbf{n}(X)) \Rightarrow X$.

We therefore might consider the translation:

$$(X)_d = (\neg\mathbf{n}(\mathbf{n}(x) \Rightarrow \neg\mathbf{n}(X))) \Rightarrow X$$
$$\bigcirc(X) = \neg\mathbf{n}(\mathbf{n}(X)) \Rightarrow \mathbf{n}(X)$$

and

$$\odot(X) = \mathbf{n}(\mathbf{n}(X))$$

We shall see that this translation does not give the correct results. Let us check what can be proved from the database containing all three. We have

$$\Delta = \{X, \bigcirc(X), \odot(X)\}_d =$$
$$\{(\neg \mathbf{n}(\mathbf{n}(X)) \Rightarrow \neg \mathbf{n}(X)) \Rightarrow X, \neg \mathbf{n}(\mathbf{n}(X)) \Rightarrow \mathbf{n}(X), \mathbf{n}(\mathbf{n}(X))\}$$

We ask

$$\Delta?X = 1$$

if

$$\Delta \cup \{\neg \mathbf{n}(\mathbf{n}(X))\}?\neg \mathbf{n}(X) = 1$$

if

$$\Delta \cup \{\neg \mathbf{n}(\mathbf{n}(X))\}?\mathbf{n}(X) = 0$$

if

$$\Delta \cup \{\neg \mathbf{n}(\mathbf{n}(X)\}?\mathbf{n}(\mathbf{n}(X)) = 1$$

if

fail.

Similarly,

$$\Delta?\mathbf{n}(X) = 0$$

succeeds, and

$$\Delta?\mathbf{n}(\mathbf{n}(X)) = 1$$

succeeds.

Since the name of X fails, $?X$ must succeed; but this is not the case!

We should have translated $(X)_d$ as $\neg \mathbf{n}(X) \Rightarrow X$, and the database $\{X, \bigcirc(X), \odot(X)\}_d$ should be $\{\neg \mathbf{n}(X) \Rightarrow X, \neg \mathbf{n}(\mathbf{n}(X)) \Rightarrow \mathbf{n}(X), \mathbf{n}(\mathbf{n}(X))\}$.

This database does give the right answers.

Notice that $X \neq \odot(X)$ in this translation. In fact, $\{\odot(X), \bigcirc(X)\} = \varnothing$, and annihilation is done in order from higher anti-formulae to lower ones.

8.13 Concluding Remarks

We saw that we can execute deletion in the object level by adding to the language the anti-formula operator $\bigcirc(A)$ and defining $\mathbf{M}_d(\Delta, A) = \Delta \cup \{\bigcirc(A)\}$. If $\Delta \vdash A$, then $\bigcirc(A)$ destroys A, because in the logic we have that $\{A, \bigcirc(A)\}$ is equivalent to $\varnothing$.

The problem arises when $\Delta \nvdash A$. We would expect that $\mathbf{M}_d(\Delta, A) = \Delta$ in this case. However, $\Delta' = \Delta \cup \{\bigcirc(A)\}$ is *not* equivalent to Δ. This is because $\bigcirc(A)$ sits in Δ' waiting for A to come, in order to delete it the moment it arrives. This aspect of the logic allows us to have a general deduction theorem

$$\Delta \vdash X \text{ iff } \Delta \cup \{\bigcirc(A)\} \vdash A \Rightarrow X.$$

In linear logic, it is important not to delete A from Δ when $\Delta \nvdash A$. The reason is simple. If we add $\bigcirc(A)$ to Δ, then Δ cannot prove anything anymore because this $\bigcirc(A)$ will have to be used in the proof. Thus, for example, we have $B \vdash B$ but $B, \bigcirc(A) \nvdash B$.

The reader might ask why we do not improve on linear logic and have two kinds of assumptions, those which need to be used and those which need not necessarily be used, so the data can be presented as

A　　use exactly once
A!　　use as many times as needed
A↓　　use at most once but possibly not at all

This would not solve the problem, because $\bigcirc(A)↓$ is *not* context-sensitive. We want $\bigcirc(A)↓$ to be activated when $\Delta \vdash A$, and be inactive when $\Delta \nvdash A$.

So we want to have $\bigcirc(A)↓, B \vdash B$, because we need not use $\bigcirc(A)↓$, but $\bigcirc(A)↓, B, B \Rightarrow A \nvdash A$ because A is destroyed by $\bigcirc(A)↓$, which has to be used in this context.

We will now discuss some open issues. We want to address the problem of what happens when we want to delete A from Δ in the case where $\Delta \nvdash A$. We also want to see how to improve the N-Prolog model and be able to logically delete formulae A from Δ in case $A \notin \Delta$ but $\Delta \vdash A$.

The following examples illustrate what can happen.

Example 8.29 (Vacuous deletion). Suppose $\Delta \nvdash A$. We want to execute the operation of deletion of A from Δ, which we denote as $\Delta' = \mathbf{Delete}(\Delta, A)$. What do we get in this case? Shall we expect that $\Delta' = \Delta$? Using the methods given in the beginning of this chapter, we have $\mathbf{Delete}(\Delta, A) = \Delta \cup \{A \Rightarrow \mathbf{e}\}$, and so, for example, $\mathbf{Delete}(\{B\}, A) = \{B, A \Rightarrow \mathbf{e}\} = \Delta'$. Now $\Delta' \nvdash B$ because $A \Rightarrow \mathbf{e}$ cannot be used. This may be undesirable! We might try to solve the problem by allowing the system to ignore $A \Rightarrow \mathbf{e}$; no need to use it. We get some form of variation of linear logic, but this is not satisfactory because using or not using $A \Rightarrow \mathbf{e}$ should be context-independent of whether A is among the data or not.

Example 8.30 (Conditional deletion). Consider the following database:

1. B
2. $A \Rightarrow (B \Rightarrow C)$

This database proves $A \Rightarrow C$. Suppose we want to delete A. We can add

3. $(A \Rightarrow \mathbf{e})$

Since A is not in the database, nor provable from it, we would expect to be able to still prove $A \Rightarrow C$. How do we prove $A \Rightarrow C$? We need to assume A and prove C; so let us do so. We get

1. B

2. $A \Rightarrow (B \Rightarrow C)$
3. $A \Rightarrow \mathbf{e}$
4. A

From this database C cannot be proved because A is deleted.
To avoid this we must indicate that

3. $A \Rightarrow \mathbf{e}$

is not accessible. This gives a proof theory similar to that of strict implication, where $A, A \Rightarrow B \nvdash B$ when A is atomic, to be used when A is assumed. So we must use box proof theory as follows:

1. B data
2. $A \Rightarrow (B \Rightarrow C)$ data
3. $A \Rightarrow \mathbf{e}$ local deletion
4. $A \Rightarrow C$ from Box

> 3.1 A assumption
> 3.2 $B \Rightarrow C$, from (2) and (3.1)
> 3.3 C, from (3.2) and (1).
>
> Note that (3) is not accessible and so 3.1 cannot be deleted.

Example 8.31. As an example of logical deletion in *N*-Prolog, let us reconsider Example 8.20. The data in this example proves B, but we have no means to perform logical deletion. We now show how to do it in *N*-Prolog.

With each wff X associate three names:

1. n_X, a name for deleting X if it is among the data. This means we put X in as $\neg n_X \Rightarrow X$.
2. r_X and q_X, two names to use when X is a goal (to be proved). We agree to prove $\gamma(X) = ((\neg q_X \wedge X \Rightarrow r_X) \Rightarrow r_X)$ instead of proving X.

Let us see what happens in this case. To show $\gamma(X)$, we add to the data

$$\neg q_X \wedge X \Rightarrow r_X$$

and ask for r_X.

The only way for r_X to succeed is by q_X failing and X succeeding. If q_X and r_X are new names, then r_X succeeds iff X succeeds and q_X was not added deliberately to stop X from succeeding.

So, in our example, we ask for $\gamma(B)$ whenever we want to prove B. To delete B logically, we add q_B.

The above is just an idea and needs to be investigated. Suppose we also have in our database a clause $B \Rightarrow Y$. Adding q_B deletes B for the purpose of asking B, because we need to ask $\gamma(B)$. But if we ask for Y (i.e., ask for $\gamma(Y)$), the query will succeed because we can still get B, and by using $B \Rightarrow Y$ we can get Y.

References

1. A. Anderson and N. D. Belnap. *Entailment: The Logic of Relevance and Necessity*. Princeton University Press, Princeton, NJ, 1975.
2. T. Connolly and C. Begg. *Database Systems: A Practical Approach to Design, Implementation and Management*. Addison-Wesley, 4th edition, 2004.
3. A. Darwiche and J. Pearl. On the logic of iterated belief revision. In Ronald Fagin, editor, *Proceedings of the 5th International Conference on Principles of Knowledge Representation and Reasoning*, pages 5–23. Morgan Kaufmann, Pacific Grove, CA, March 1994.
4. A. Darwiche and J. Pearl. On the logic of iterated belief revision. *Artificial Intelligence*, 89:1–29, 1997.
5. C. J. Date and H. Darwen. *A Guide to the SQL Standard: A User's Guide to the Standard Database Language*. Addison-Wesley Longman, Inc., 4th edition edition, 1997.
6. M. Freund and D. Lehmann. Belief revision and rational inference. Technical Report TR 94-16, The Leibniz Center for Research in Computer Science, Institute of Computer Science, Hebrew University, July 1994.
7. D. M. Gabbay. *Labelled Deductive Systems: Principles and Applications. Basic Principles*, volume 1. Oxford University Press, 1996.
8. D. M. Gabbay. *Elementary Logics: A Procedural Perspective*. Prentice-Hall, 1998.
9. D. M. Gabbay. Compromise update and revision: a position paper. In B. Fronhoffer and R. Pareschi, editors, *Dynamic worlds*. Kluwer, 1999.
10. D. M. Gabbay and N. Olivetti. *Goal directed proof theory*. Kluwer, 2000.
11. D. M. Gabbay and O. Rodrigues. Structured belief bases: a practical approach to prioritised base revision. In D. M. Gabbay, Rudolf Kruse, Andreas Nonnengart, and Hans Jürgen Ohlbach, editors, *Proceedings of First Internation Joint Conference on Qualitative and Quantitative Practical Reasoning*, pages 267–281. Springer-Verlag, June 1997.
12. P. Gärdenfors. *Knowledge in Flux: Modeling the Dynamics of Epistemic States*. A Bradford Book — The MIT Press, Cambridge, Massachusetts, and London, England, 1988.
13. G. Grahne, Alberto O. Mendelzon, and R. Reiter. On the semantics of belief revision systems. In *Proceedings of the International Conference on Theoretical Aspects of Reasoning about Knowledge*, pages 132–142. Morgan Kaufmann, 1992.
14. J. R. Groff and P. N. Weinberg. *SQL: The Complete Reference*. osborne/McGraw-Hill, 1999.
15. B. N. Grosof. *Updating and structure in non-monotonic theories*. PhD thesis, Stanford University, 1992.
16. S. O. Hansson. *A Textbook of Belief Dynamics: Theory Change and Database Updating*. Kluwer Academic Publishers, The Netherlands, 1999.
17. A. G. Kurosh. *General Algebra*. Chelsea Publishing Company, 1963.
18. D. Lehmann. Belief revision, revised. In *Proceedings of the 14th International Joint Conference of Artificial Intelligence (IJCAI-95)*, pages 1534–1540, 1995.
19. N. Olivetti and L. Terracini. N-Prolog and equivalence of logic programs. *Journal of Logic, Language and Information*, 1:253–340, 1992.
20. G. Restall. *An Introduction to Substructural Logics*. Routledge, New York, New York, 2000.
21. O. Rodrigues. *A methodology for iterated information change*. PhD thesis, Department of Computing, Imperial College, 1998.
22. J. Woods. *The logic of fiction: philosophical soundings of deviant logic*. Mouton, The Hague and Paris, 1974.

Chapter 9
Conclusions and Discussions

In this book we provided a comprehensive set of methodologies to tackle the problem of *belief revision*. The methodologies determine *acceptability* criteria for the result of the revision operation based on the *context* in which the operation takes place. In what follows, we summarise the main points raised in the book and we end with some discussions in Section 9.2.

9.1 Concluding Remarks

1. The methodologies of prioritised databases (Section 4.4), controlled revision (Section 6.4), compromise revision (Section 6.3) and structured clusters (Chapter 5) are instances of a more general methodology, not necessarily connected only with revision, that we call *damage control*.

   Let us elaborate on this.

   Given a theory T, we move to a revised theory T'. Say $T' = T \circ A$ is the result of revising T by the input A. For the purpose of this discussion, assume that T' is $T \cup \{A\} - B$, where $B \subseteq T$ is what we remove from T to guarantee consistency. Now, T is embedded in a bigger environment. We consider two such *context* environments.

   a. What T can prove, e.g., $T \vdash X$
   b. That T may have been revised before, i.e., it is part of an iterated revision process.

   The damage control problem is how to minimise the effect of the revision $T' = T \circ A$ on the environment in which T resides; for example,

   a. If $T \vdash X$ and $T' \nvdash X$, can we add X to T'? This depends on the revision algorithm used. For example, suppose our theory T is

D. M. Gabbay et al., *Revision, Acceptability and Context*, Cognitive Technologies,
DOI 10.1007/978-3-642-14159-1_9, © Springer-Verlag Berlin Heidelberg 2010

$$T = \neg A \wedge B \to X$$
$$\neg A$$
$$B$$
$$A \wedge B \to Y$$

and we receive input A. Our revision mechanism may give us the revised T' as follows, where we replace $\neg A$ by A.

$$T' = \neg A \wedge B \to X$$
$$A \wedge B \to Y$$
$$B$$
$$A$$

Now $T' \not\vdash X$, but $T' + X$ is consistent. Can we leave X in T'? We called this approach *compromise revision* (see Section 6.3) and showed some scenarios in which it is appropriate.

Now suppose we get another input $\neg Y$. What should be our $T'' = T' \circ Y$?

We have some choices of revision, including to take either A out or B out. We know that $\neg A$ was in, and was pushed out in a previous stage. Obviously, a better choice is to let

$$T_1'' = \neg A \wedge B \to X$$
$$\neg A$$
$$B$$
$$A \wedge B \to Y$$
$$\neg Y$$

rather than one of the two simple

$$T_2'' = \neg A \wedge B \to X \qquad\qquad T_3'' = \neg A \wedge B \to X$$
$$A \wedge B \to Y \qquad\qquad\qquad A \wedge B \to Y$$
$$B \qquad\qquad\qquad\qquad\qquad A$$
$$\neg Y \qquad\qquad\qquad\qquad\qquad \neg Y$$

which we would do if we were not able to remember past revisions.

Thus, the general methodology is as follows. Given an algorithm $\mathscr{A}$ for moving from state $\mathbf{S}$ to $\mathbf{S}'$ in some environment, make sure $\mathscr{A}$ works together with a damage control algorithm $\mathscr{D}$ which limits the effect on the environment.

2. *Logic by translation*

   In Chapter 7, we offered the reader the idea of *revision by translation*. To revise a theory Δ in a logic L, we translate Δ and L into classical logic, translate the details of the inconsistency and revise in classical logic to get a solution. We then translate the solution back into the original logic L.

This is one case of the methodology which we call *logic by translation*. Besides the methodology of revision by translation given in this book, we outline here two more examples.

The first is *interpolation by translation*. Let L be a logic and assume $A \vdash_L B$. Interpolation says that there exists a sentence I in the common language of A and B such that $A \vdash_L I \vdash_L B$. Assume we have a sound and complete translation of the logic L into classical logic and τ translates formulae from L into classical logic. We would have in classical logic that

$$\tau(A) \cup \tau(L) \vdash \tau(B) \text{ iff } A \vdash_L B$$

where $\tau(L)$ contains axioms in classical logic describing the behaviour of L.

Therefore, in classical logic there exists an interpolant π. We get

$$\tau(A) \cup \tau(L) \vdash \pi \vdash \tau(B).$$

All we need to do is to find an I in the logic L such that $\tau(I) = \pi$; then we would have

$$A \vdash_L I \vdash_L B.$$

Two possibilities

a. For some A and B no I can be found. In this case, probably L has no interpolation, but we can guess how to strengthen L into $L^* \supseteq L$ to get interpolation.
b. We can always find such an I, in which case we have interpolation in L.[1]

See [6] for details.

Our next example is finding semantical conditions for axioms of modal logic. We use logic by translation and abduction in classical logic to find the conditions. Let us illustrate the idea.

Modal logic semantics uses a binary relation R. This can be expressed in classical logic as a theory $\mathbf{T}(R)$ of R. The modal axioms can be translated into $\mathbf{T}(R)$ by

$$t \vDash \Box A \text{ iff } \forall y(tRy \rightarrow y \vDash A).$$

Let $\varphi(t,A)$ be a wff of classical logic saying $t \vDash A$. If we want to adopt A, i.e., make it an axiom, we have to translate it as

$$\forall t \varphi(t,A).$$

To find the condition on R ($\mathbf{C}(R)$) corresponding to the axiom A, we look for a formula $\mathbf{C}(R)$ involving R only, such that in classical logic

$$\mathbf{T}(R) \cup \mathbf{C}(R) \vdash \forall t \varphi(t,A).$$

Finding $\mathbf{C}(R)$ is a process of abduction in classical logic. For example, for the axiom $\Box A \rightarrow A$, we get $\mathbf{C}(R) \equiv \forall x(xRx)$.

---

[1] In the literature, this is called *repairing the interpolation theorem*, and there are many articles for individual logics L. See, for instance, [2, 4].

3. *Deletion — anti-formulae*
   Chapter 8 deals with anti-formulae and deletions, which is also part of a general methodology.

   As we have seen, revision can be described in terms of contractions, i.e., *deletion*. Deletion is a meta-level process, since we remove something out of the system. Deletion is not only meta-level; it is an almost physical act. Given a theory $T = \{A_1,\ldots,A_n\}$, we can physically in the meta-level delete A_1 (take it out) and end up with $T_1 = \{A_2,\ldots,A_n\}$. But suppose $T \vdash B$; how do we 'delete' B? We can define some revision process in the meta-level that will pass to some maximal $T_B \subsetneq T,$[2] such that $T_B \not\vdash B$. The question is, can we delete from within the system in the object level itself?

   Thus, the general methodological question, which is more fundamental than revision, is, how can we delete in the object level?

   There are two ways of doing it.

   a. *Hierarchical method*
      Let T be a system. We know deletion is meta-level in T; so let $\mathbf{D}_1(T) = \mathbf{D}(T) \supseteq T$ be a meta-system capable of describing deletion in T. So, for example, $\mathbf{D}_1(T)$ can describe how T proves any B, and describe a revision process of how to pass from a $T \vdash B$ to a $T_B \not\vdash B$. $\mathbf{D}_1(T)$ cannot describe deletion in $\mathbf{D}_1(T)$ itself, but it can describe deletion in T.

      Define by induction

      $$\mathbf{D}_{n+1}(T) = \mathbf{D}(\mathbf{D}_n(T))$$

      Then, $\mathbf{D}_{n+1}(T)$ can describe deletion in $\mathbf{D}_n(T), \mathbf{D}_{n-1}(T),\ldots,\mathbf{D}_1(T)$, and T. Let $\mathbf{D}_\infty(T) = \bigcup_n \mathbf{D}_n(T)$. Then $\mathbf{D}_\infty(T)$ can describe deletion in itself. Because if we let φ be any wff to be considered for deletion, if $\varphi \in \mathbf{D}_\infty(T)$, then $\varphi \in \mathbf{D}_n(T)$ for some n. Hence, $\mathbf{D}_{n+1}(T) \subseteq \mathbf{D}_\infty(T)$ can talk about the deletion of φ.

   b. The second method of deletion in the object level works for resource logics. If $T \vdash B$, then T uses some resources R_B to prove B. Add to T some 'diversion' $\varnothing$ to prove using these resources, so that by using them to prove $\varnothing$, it will no longer be possible to prove B. Thus, essentially what we do is to add a new 'resource' axiom $R_B \to \varnothing$ so that T will prove $\varnothing$ using R_B, and then cannot continue to prove B because R_B has been spent.

      It is a technical matter how to force the system to use R_B to prove $\varnothing$, rather than ignore $\varnothing$ and use R_B to prove B.

      Once we know how to do this for resource logics, we can extend it to any logic.

      The idea of anti-formula flows from the concept of *wasted resources*. Let us write $R_B \to \varnothing$ as $\mathscr{B}$. Then, in any system where $\mathscr{B}$ is present, B cannot be

---

[2] Much in the spirit of the subsets that *fail to imply a sentence* — see Definition 4.1, page 109.

proved, because the minute R_B is available to prove B, it will be diverted to prove nothing $\varnothing$.

We get $\mathscr{B} + B = \varnothing$, or $R_B \to \varnothing + B \vdash \varnothing$.

In the hierarchical case, $\mathscr{B}$ is simply the wff **Delete**(B). So if $B \in \mathbf{D}_n(T)$, then $\mathscr{B} \in \mathbf{D}_{n+1}(T)$.

4. *Revision in context*

   Most revision processes are purely logical. They do not pay attention to the meanings of the symbols of the participating theory T.

   In real life, revisions rely on meaning very heavily. If I say 'Harry came to the party yesterday' and you say 'but Harry was at a conference yesterday', I can revise the theory by saying 'I mean Harry Junior, not Harry Senior', or 'I mean the conference dinner which really was a party'.

   We can do that because our mental states are non-monotonic. They give some data and leave the rest to be added by common sense. Let us write $\Delta \approx B$ to mean B follows from Δ by common-sense knowledge of the world. Note that we use $\approx$ to distinguish it not only from the classical monotonic consequence relation $\vdash$, but also from the formal non-monotonic consequence relation $\vdash\hspace{-0.6em}\sim$. As usual, $\vdash$ is the classical derivability relation.

   $\vdash\hspace{-0.6em}\sim$ is purely formal non-monotonic logic. It does not *interpret* its symbols, but only yields consequences. The commonsense $\approx$ consequence

   a. interprets the symbols of L
   b. proceeds to derive consequences using common sense.

   Now suppose $\Delta \approx B$, and we get as an input $\neg B$; how do we revise Δ? We have a number of options:

   a. we can reinterpret the symbols
   b. we can move from Δ to $\Delta \cup \{\neg B\}$ and let common sense derive the new consequences
   c. we can take retract something from Δ to have $\Delta' \subsetneq \Delta$, and consider $\Delta' \cup \{\neg B\}$

   The key unexplored component here is the reinterpretation of the symbols, because attaching the right meaning to them is a very common cause of apparent inconsistency.

   This needs to be studied further.

5. *Algorithmic revision in context* This is a combination of 1. and 4. The parallel is how common sense revises in context. It means what kind of algorithms move from $\{X \mid \Delta \approx X\}$ to $\{X \mid \Delta' \approx X\}$, where Δ' is the revised version of Δ, in a way that limits the 'damage' or the 'change'. You can call it damage control in a commonsense context.

   This is a new area of research which is partly philosophical and partly psychological/experimental. It is possible to study how humans do it.

Example 9.1.
A woman says:

> John is the man standing near the door wearing a blue tie.

We look at the door; there are two men there. One wearing a green tie and one wearing a red tie. Do you choose the man with the green tie? The one with the red tie? Neither?

If you choose neither and receive the information that the woman is colour-blind, which one would you choose now?

9.2 Discussions

1. *Declarative revision*
   Declarative revision does not cover how to revise/adapt procedures which involve actions. Actions have declarative models describing what they do. Consider the three-state model below.

   $$s_0 \xrightarrow{a_1} s_1$$
   $$s_0 \xrightarrow{a_2} s_2$$

   In order to describe this model we need something like the following:

   $Result(s_0, a_1, s_1)$ applying action a in state s_0 results in state s_1
   $Result(s_0, a_2, s_2)$ applying action b in state s_0 results in state s_2
   $State(t, s)$ the system is in state s at time t
   A collection of time points $0, 1, 2, \ldots$
   $Time(j)$ the current time is j
   $Take(t, a)$ action a was taken at time t
   Axioms   to describe general properties, such as the following: the system cannot be at two different states at the same time, and other obvious properties

   Now consider the theory $\Delta = \{State(0, s_0), Take(0, a_1)\}$ and the input $State(1, s_2)$. This is obviously *inconsistent*. A revision procedure will remove either $State(0, s_0)$ or $Take(0, a_1)$.

   We want to *replace* $Take(0, a_1)$ with $Take(0, a_2)$. The reason for this is that we want to *prove* the input from a sequence of actions.

   So, as a revision problem, we have languages L_1, L_2 describing actions and states, respectively; a collection of system properties $\mathscr{A}_S$ and a theory $\Delta = \Delta_{L_1} \cup \Delta_{L_2} \cup \mathscr{A}_S$ to be revised by an input φ in the language L_2 (i.e., the input is a *goal state*).

   The problem then becomes how to revise Δ_{L_1} to obtain a theory $\Delta_{L_1}^{\star}$, such that

$$\Delta_{L_1}^{\star} \cup \Delta_{L_2} \cup \mathscr{A}_S \vdash \varphi.$$

2. *Relative revision*

Another aspect of revision is revision relative to a theory. Given a theory Δ which is generally consistent, Δ may be inconsistent relative to a fixed theory Θ; that is, $\Delta \cup \Theta$ is inconsistent. We want to revise Δ so as to find another theory $\Delta' \subseteq \Delta$, such that $\Delta' \cup \Theta$ is consistent. If Θ is finite, this amounts to the usual belief revision of Δ relative to the input $\varphi = \bigwedge \Theta$. If Θ is infinite, then we have an altogether different scenario. One can apply the same algorithm for maintaining consistency that is used for the finite case. For example, we can enumerate the sentences of Δ as $\delta_1, \delta_2, \dots$ and inductively define

$$\Delta_0 = \Theta \quad (\Theta \text{ is consistent})$$
$$\Delta_{n+1} = \begin{cases} \Delta_n \cup \{\delta_n\}, & \text{if this is consistent; or} \\ \Delta_n, & \text{otherwise} \end{cases}$$

We then let the revised theory be $\Delta^* = \mathrm{Cn}(\cup_n \Delta_n)$.

Δ^* depends only on the arbitrary enumeration of Δ. It takes no account of the meaning of Δ.

Other methods of revision may use Θ to an advantage. For example, model-theoretical methods which look at the models of Δ and models of Θ and use some distance consideration to extract models of $\Delta' \cup \Theta$, for $\Delta' \subset \Delta$, may give a more significant role to the models of Θ, and thus implicitly make use of what Θ says. In fact, some concepts may be meaningful only relative to Θ, and then such concepts can be used in the revision.

3. *Revision of non-monotonic theories*

Non-monotonic theories adjust themselves automatically to input because $\Delta \cup \alpha$ does not necessarily prove what Δ proves. Thus, we need to ask, how can a non-monotonic theory be "inconsistent"? A better notion is that of unacceptability, as discussed in Chapter 7. Thus, we say that Δ is not acceptable if the set $\{\alpha \mid \Delta \vdash \alpha\}$ is not acceptable.

Now suppose a theory Δ is acceptable, but $\Gamma = \Delta \cup \{\alpha\}$ is not. We can revise Γ by either removing some formulae from it or by *adding* formulae to it.

The simplest example of this idea is a logic program with *negation by failure*. Consider the program P below

C1: $(\neg a \wedge b) \Rightarrow c$
C2: b

and assume that a program containing c is unacceptable. We can revise P by either removing C1 and/or C2 or by adding a.

This means we need different algorithms for revision of non-monotonic theories.

There is a well-known connection between AGM and non-monotonic logics [12]. Let K be a fixed theory and let $\circ_a$ be an AGM revision operation. We have that, for a fixed K,

$$\alpha \mathrel{|\!\sim}_K \beta \text{ iff } K \circ_a \alpha \vdash \beta$$

Now,

$$\Delta \mathrel{|\!\sim}_K \beta \text{ iff } K \circ_a \Delta \vdash \beta$$

However, the original AGM formulation is not defined for revisions of *theories*, such as Δ above.

4. *Revision of quantified theories*
   This has applications in two main paradigms, which we present next.

   a. *Revision by non-monotonic explanation*
      The idea behind *revision by non-monotonic explanation* is based on common-sense procedures used in day-to-day conflict resolution:
      - the procedures involve querying (obtaining more information)
      - solving conflicts by analysing the context in which observations are made and seeing if a change in circumstances can make these (conflicting) observations compatible
      - the classical example is that of colours that *appear* to be different in different lighting scenarios, e.g., a dark blue colour may appear to be black under incandescent lighting.
      - the main point is the identification of the commonsense rules used to solve conflicts
      - this will involve the analyses of case studies, possibly taken from real-life situations

      Traditional AGM belief revision and its variations deal with the problem of maintaining consistency of a theory during the process of information change with respect to the underlying logic of the theory. In other words, given an inconsistent theory Δ, consistency is maintained without taking into consideration the meaning of Δ, and generally involves the removal of formulae from Δ by some algorithm whose considerations involve the consequence notion only. We may give preference to some elements of Δ according to how much participation they display towards the inconsistency, but no consideration is paid to what the statements actually say. So, for example, given the theory Δ with the formulae
      i. a
      ii. $a \Rightarrow b$
      iii. $a \Rightarrow \neg b$
      iv. $a \Rightarrow c$
      v. $a \Rightarrow \neg c$
      we might realise that the simplest way of maintaining consistency is to delete a rather than, say, delete $a \Rightarrow \neg b$ and $a \Rightarrow \neg c$.

      However, if we know the meaning of a, b and c, we might opt for keeping a in Δ.

The idea of using "meaning" in consistency considerations came from our paper on the connections between belief revision and voting [7]. This idea is most effective and useful in the context of predicate logic revision.

Existing research deals mainly with the propositional cases. Most real-life examples are predicate examples. When we say "predicate" we do not necessarily mean the use of quantifiers. We mean the use of predicates. So, for example,

i. $P(a) \Rightarrow Q(b)$
ii. $P(a) \Rightarrow \neg Q(b)$
iii. $P(a)$

is in predicate language but is technically propositional. It involves no quantifiers.

Traditional propositional AGM revision will take something out, maybe $P(a)$, but the fact that P is a property may allow us to use additional mechanisms. Consider the following:

i. John is wearing a dark blue suit
ii. John is wearing a black suit
iii. $\forall x (Blue(x) \wedge Black(x) \Rightarrow \perp)$
iv. $\forall x (DarkBlue(x) \Rightarrow Blue(x))$

We can say observation ii was made in the evening under artificial light and everyone knows that dark blue looks black under these circumstances. So, Δ is indeed consistent, and furthermore we can infer that John was wearing a dark blue suit.

To do this formally, we need a meta-level system to reason about Δ. This system, call it $\mathcal{M}$, can reason about context and consistency of Δ. If it knows the context of how the data came to be in Δ, it can resolve the inconsistency by reinterpreting the predicates. We call this process *revision by non-monotonic explanation*.

This sort of "explaining away" inconsistency is done extensively in politics and law. If we have a conflicting statement by a politician or apparently conflicting laws, a smooth politician or an experienced barrister may impose his own explanation on them by adding some plausible context to each of them.

The task of belief revision by non-monotonic explanation is to set up the commonsense norms for the meta-theory $\mathcal{M}$ which controls the explanation.

b. *Quantifier restriction*
Another useful device which is indeed a good commonsense method for resolving some inconsistency is the restriction of the range of quantifiers. Consider the Barber paradox:

"The Barber shaves all those who do not shave themselves."

The paradox can be translated to first-order logic in the following way.

$$\exists x \forall y (Shaves(x,y) \iff \neg Shaves(y,y))$$

The question arises: who shaves the Barber?

We instantiate x with the Barber. If he does not shave himself, i.e.,

$\neg Shaves(Barber, Barber)$,

then the above formula will require $Shaves(Barber, Barber)$ (since he will shave all those who do not shave themselves, including himself), which is a contradiction. On the other hand, if the Barber shaves himself, i.e,

$Shaves(Barber, Barber)$,

the double implication will also require that $\neg Shaves(Barber, Barber)$, which is again a contradiction.

The inconsistency can be resolved by restricting the range of the quantifier, namely the Barber shaves all those (other than himself) who do not shave themselves.

Suppose the domain of the language is D, and let $d \in D$ be the element to which the existential variable x is mapped. In this particular example, the range of the universal quantifier should have been restricted to $D\backslash\{d\}$. We can annotate this by introducing a new predicate symbol R and defining the extension of R in the interpretation as $D\backslash\{d\}$. Therefore, we can then rewrite the original formula as

$$\exists x \forall y [R(y) \Rightarrow (Shaves(x,y) \iff \neg Shaves(y,y))]$$

The complication is that the definition of R has to be done dynamically, since we can only state it when we know the particular value assigned to existential variable. When this value is known in advance, as happens in the case of ground instances, the methodology is easier to apply.

Consider now the famous birds and penguins example. Our Δ is the theory containing

i. $\forall x[bird(x) \Rightarrow fly(x)]$
ii. $\forall x[penguin(x) \Rightarrow \neg fly(x)]$
iii. $\forall x[penguin(x) \Rightarrow bird(x)]$

Our Θ is the theory containing

i. $bird(tweety)$

Thus, we have that $\Delta \cup \Theta$ is inconsistent. It is obvious that in the general rule $\forall x[bird(x) \Rightarrow fly(x)]$, the range of the universal quantifier should have been restricted to those elements of the domain which do not have the property of being penguins. So, in this case we can make the definition of R explicitly a priori, $\forall x[R(x) \iff \neg Penguin(x)]$, and we have i rewritten as

i'. $\forall x[R(x) \Rightarrow (bird(x) \Rightarrow fly(x))]$

We then get a new theory $\Delta^R = \Delta \setminus \{i.\} \cup \{i'.\}$, the axiom on R, namely, $\Phi_R = \{\forall x [R(x) \iff \neg Penguin(x)]\}$, and the original Θ, and we have that $\Delta^R \cup \Phi_R \cup \Theta$ is consistent.

The quantifier restriction method is simple to state. Given Θ, a consistent theory, and Δ, also a consistent theory, assume that $\Delta \cup \Theta$ is not consistent. Let $R(x)$ be a unary predicate and let Δ^R be Δ with all or some quantifiers restricted to R. Then, some axioms on R, Φ_R may be reasonable, and may be such that $\Theta \cup \Phi_R \cup \Delta$ is consistent.

In practice, we suspect several Rs may be used for different parts of Δ. We may even assume $R(x)$ is defined using the symbols of Δ, i.e., we use some formula $\varphi(x)$ in the language of Δ or Θ.

5. *Connections between revision and social choice theory*
Connections between the above areas can be systematically analysed by applying general principles/ideas to a particular problem and seeing how they interact. We recognise the following scenarios:[3]

a. *Voting.* There are several conflicting demands/preferences, and we are looking for a collective compromise.
b. *Belief revision.* We are facing an inconsistent or unacceptable logical theory, and we are looking for a way out.
c. *Belief merging* [9, 10, 8, 11] We are trying to aggregate knowledge bases which together are possibly inconsistent.
d. *Fibring/combining systems* [5]. We are facing a problem which has two different aspects to it. We know how to handle each aspect on its own and we want to combine/fibre our solutions together and apply the combination to the problem as a whole. For example, an application may involve both obligations and time. We know logics of obligations and permissions and we know temporal logics. How do we put them together?

Our best bet in bringing the above areas together is to look at a problem which can be equally considered by each one of them, and compare how they would deal with it. In this way we can learn from each point of view and export ideas to the others.

For the case of belief revision, belief merging and voting, our strategy for investigation can be outlined as follows.

Step 1. Start with an example of theory revision of a theory T by an input formula τ.
Step 2. See this as a *voting problem*, i.e., consider τ as the formula expressing the voting rules, and the voters as a classical logic theory T. If the voters' preferences are incompatible, the revision of T by τ will seek a compromise consistent with the voting rules. This, in the case of a maxichoice

---

[3] See [7] for a more comprehensive analysis.

revision function, will be obtained from a maximal subset of T consistent with τ. We compare the a priori philosophical demands of revision theory and voting and find that while revision theory may pick a dictator, voting does not want one.

Step 3. Now that we have a connection between voters and the voting rules (by seeing them as logical structures), we can apply the same reasoning for the case of belief merging. In this case, we see voters as individual belief bases and the voting rules as integrity constraints. We also find that this approach is not entirely satisfactory.

Step 4. We continue by analysing how the way of thinking in one view can enrich the way of thinking in the other views.

Essentially, this problem involves reasoning about orders, and there are two natural moves one can make with logic theories involving orders. One has to do with the way we interpret the order itself, whereas the other has to do with the kind of logic we use to represent and manipulate it. We note that

a. Logical theories need not be complete or associated with any particular *strict* linear order.
b. Theories can assume numerical fuzzy values (i.e., values need not be restricted to just *true* or *false*, but can be taken from a range of points inbetween).

From the voting point of view, (a.) means the voters may be uncertain about how all outcomes compare with each other, but may be clear about how some of them do, i.e., a voter may not have a particular preference between outcomes x and y, but may prefer z to either. In addition, voters may give conditional preferences (for example: if a voter prefers a to b, then she might also expect to prefer c to d).

As for (b.), numerical values do appear in *range voting* in a natural way.

A number of authors have investigated ways of combining preference relations [1, 13]. The difference in this way of seeing the problem is that we bring the mechanism for representing preferences to the object level itself, and hence can analyse it from an entirely logical perspective. We outline these ideas next.

Consider the language of predicate logic with binary relation $<$; the constants a, b, c and the equality symbol $=$. Assume the axioms $\forall x (x = a \lor x = b \lor x = c)$ and $a \neq b \neq c$ (this means $\neg (a = b) \land \neg (b = c) \land \neg (a = c)$). Let T be $Cn(\{a < b, b < c, c < a\})$ and consider an input τ to T saying that $<$ is a strict linear order of the three elements a, b, c.

It can be clearly seen that both $a < c$ and $c < a$ will follow from $T + \tau$ (because of transitivity), and this contradicts asymmetry; hence, $T + \tau$ is not consistent. If we want to analyse what aspects of T are compatible with a strict linear order of a, b, c, we can consider the revision of T by τ. This would replace $T + \tau$ with a new consistent theory $T \circ \tau$ containing τ, by making minimal changes in T. As we saw in Section 2.1, the AGM postulates constrain how the new theory $T \circ \tau$ is related to τ and to T. The new theory $T \circ \tau$ is closed under logical consequence, i.e., if $T \circ \tau \vdash A$, then $A \in T \circ \tau$, but the AGM framework does not give an algorithm for how to find any such $T \circ \tau$. One algorithm which can do the job is given below.

Starting with $T_\perp \neg \tau^4 = \{T_1, T_2, T_3, ...\}$, $T \circ \tau$ can be constructed from any $T_i \in T_\perp \neg \tau$, say $\mathrm{Cn}(T_1 \cup \{\tau\})$ (this would give a maxichoice revision of T by τ). We can find such $T_i \cup \{\tau\}$ by listing all sentences which T proves as the list $A_1, ..., A_n, ...$ and defining a sequence $S_0 \subseteq S_1 \subseteq S_2, ...$ as follows. Let $S_0 = \{\tau\}$, and for $n \geq 0$, define S_{n+1} in the following way:

$$S_{n+1} = \begin{cases} S_n \cup \{A_{n+1}\}, & \text{if this set is consistent} \\ S_n, & \text{otherwise} \end{cases}$$

Finally, let $S = \bigcup_{i \in \mathbb{N}} S_i$.

If we want to look at what we retain from our original T, we see that $S - \{\tau\} \subseteq T$ is a maximal subtheory of T consistent with τ, i.e., $S - \{\tau\} = T_i$ for some i. Which T_i we get depends on the way we present T as a sequence.

Let us now see what happens if we apply these procedures to our concrete example. τ says that $\{a, b, c\}$ is strictly linearly ordered. T says that $a < b$ and $b < c$ and $c < a$. T is not consistent with τ. The maximal subtheories of T consistent with τ include:

$T_1 = \mathrm{Cn}(\{a < b, b < c\})$
$T_2 = \mathrm{Cn}(\{b < c, c < a\})$
$T_3 = \mathrm{Cn}(\{a < b, c < a\})$

When τ is added to these, we get the three options for revision below:

$V_1 = \mathrm{Cn}(\{a < b, b < c, \tau\}$
$V_2 = \mathrm{Cn}(\{b < c, c < a, \tau\}$
$V_3 = \mathrm{Cn}(\{c < a, a < b, \tau\}$

Note that this logical revision philosophy/approach is entirely compatible with AGM revision and hence uses three basic assumptions:

a. We must replace the inconsistent $T + \tau$ by a single consistent theory $T \circ \tau$.
b. This replacement contains τ and as much of T as possible. Certainly we do not want anything not in T to be admitted to $T \circ \tau$, even if it is consistent with it.
c. We are dealing with two-valued logic. In other words, preferences have to be represented as yes/no statements (as opposed to numerical, probabilistic or fuzzy values).

From the revision point of view, our voting example consists of three candidate options, a, b and c, and several voters who express their total preferences regarding these options. When put together, these preferences result in the theory T. So, for example, we could have had the following preferences:

---

[4] This is defined on page 109.

Voter 1 — $a < b, b < c$
Voter 2 — $b < c, c < a$
Voter 3 — $c < a, a < b$

Since we need to make a group decision here, we require a compromise functional H based on the preferences of Voter 1, Voter 2 and Voter 3, motivated by some general principles, such that:

H(Voter 1, Voter 2, Voter 3) = Some compromise preference, (i.e., technically some new voter).

We have some reasonable conditions on H, for instance, fairness conditions for a voting system (see [3]). One such condition is the *non-dictatorship requirement*. In practice, this means that we do not want H to be a projection. Another condition is the principle of independence of irrelevant alternatives (IIA), i.e., the group decision on how two distinct elements x and y relate ($x < y$ or $y < x$) depends only on how the different voters voted on their relationship. Note that whereas the principle of non-dictatorship is a purely meta-level one on the function H and does not make use of the contents of the theories T_i, IIA relates to the properties of the order predicate of T_i.

Let us now look at our revision example from the voting point of view. The consistent theories T_1, T_2, and T_3 can stand for voters. The sentence τ is a statement of the layout of the voting system. It specifies the alternatives $\{a,b,c\}$ and says that the combination of the voters preferences is strictly linearly ordered. We immediately observe that the theory T can be obtained back from the voters as the result of a majority vote.

$a < b$ is voted by V_1, V_3
$b < c$ is voted by V_1, V_2
$c < a$ is voted by V_2, V_3

We now have a voting interpretation of our revision theory situation. What does maxichoice logical revision do in this situation? It simply chooses a linear order that is compatible with a majority voting. This is not always the case. We can construct a consistent theory T from a number of voters $V_1, V_2, \ldots$ that is incompatible with the voting rules τ, but whose subsequent revision by τ will not necessarily pick a dictator even if the revision turns out to be maxichoice. This is illustrated below.

Let $V_1 = \{a < b, b < c, a < c\}$ and $V_2 = \{c < b, b < a, c < a\}$ and τ be the voting rules as before. Now take $T = V_1 \cup V_2 = \{a < b, b < c, a < c, c < b, b < a, c < a\}$. T is consistent, since it does not know about the properties of linear orders. If we now enforce these, i.e., revise T by τ, a maxichoice revision would look at $T_\perp \neg \tau$ (see page 109). One of the sets in $T_\perp \neg \tau$ is, for instance, $\{a < c, c < b, a < b\}$, which together with τ would result in a strict linear order which does not correspond to either V_1 or V_2. In the voting example, this may be a desirable outcome.

Let us return to the expectations of voting theory from the point of view of revision theory. Voting theory expects some compromise vote satisfying certain conditions. Belief revision tries to find some compromise between all the $T_i \subseteq T$ that are consistent with τ. It will seek some compromise theory S_{comp} which will be acceptable to all. This is left mostly for the selection function S shown on page 109 (see Definition 4.2).

Maxichoice revision operations look at all T_is and sets $T \circ \tau$ as $T_i + \tau$ for some T_i. In general, this T_i is not constrained at all to containing consequences of all of the voters. Full meet revisions will be too restrictive and comprise only the consequences of the voting system τ (since $S(T_\perp \neg \tau) = \varnothing$). On the other hand, partial meet revisions would be based on the particular subsets T_i selected by S, which again could leave the wishes of some voters out — an unfair prospect. Therefore, an acceptable S_{comp} from the voting point of view would have to rely on some meta-level principle in the case of AGM revision functions. What can we then expect of the relationship between S_{comp} and AGM? In summary,

a. If we stick with AGM, certain conditions of the voting system (τ) can be enforced, but we cannot ensure a fair outcome unless we also adopt some meta-level principles.
b. However, the AGM postulates may hold for a desirable S_{comp} even though they do not incorporate themselves any fairness principles from the voting point of view.

Let us now show what result we obtain when we apply a majoritarian model-based merging operator to the same example. As before, we want to restrict the set of all possible outcomes to the set of linear preference orderings satisfying transitivity, totality and asymmetry. That is, we make our integrity contraints $IC = \tau$. This results in the six possible preference orderings K_1—K_6 illustrated in the following table. In order to simplify the presentation, we consider only three propositions, $a < b$, $b < c$ and $a < c$. These are sufficient to represent all possible linear orders with the three elements a, b and c (note that $(a < b) = 0$ iff $(b < a) = 1$). We use $x < y < z$ as a shorthand for $Cn(\{x < y, y < z, \tau\})$.

	$a < b$	$b < c$	$a < c$	order
K_1	0	0	0	$c < b < a$
K_2	0	1	0	$b < c < a$
K_3	0	1	1	$b < a < c$
K_4	1	0	0	$c < a < b$
K_5	1	0	1	$a < c < b$
K_6	1	1	1	$a < b < c$

Each voter V_i of our example is satisfied exactly by one of these models:

$V_1 = \{(1,1,1)\}$ (K_6)
$V_2 = \{(0,1,0)\}$ (K_2)
$V_3 = \{(1,0,0)\}$ (K_4)

When we calculate the distances between each V_i and the possible social outcomes, we obtain the following result:

	$d(.,V_1)$	$d(.,V_2)$	$d(.,V_3)$	$D^d(.,\underline{V})$
K_1	3	1	1	5
K_2	2	0	2	4
K_3	1	1	3	5
K_4	2	2	0	4
K_5	1	3	1	5
K_6	0	2	2	4

There are three social orderings with minimal distance to the profile $\underline{V} = \{V_1, V_2, V_3\}$. These are K_2, K_4 and K_6, which coincide respectively with V_2 V_3 and V_1, respectively. The result of the belief merging operator is a tie: $\Delta_{IC}(\underline{V}) = \{V_1 \vee V_2 \vee V_3\}$ .This means that, although belief merging (with the help of the IC) avoids the paradoxical result, this is done at the price of indecision, i.e., there is no procedure to decide which V_i should be taken to represent the collective preference — this effectively means no election.

The investigation of these connections is ongoing; see [7] for more details.

References

1. H. Andreka, M. D. Ryan, and P.-Y. Schobbens. Operators and laws for combining preference relations. *Journal of Logic and Computation*, 12:13–53, 2002.
2. C. Areces, P. Blackburn, and M. Marx. Repairing the interpolation theorem in quantified modal logic. *Annals of Pure and Applied Logic*, 124, 2003. DOI:10.1016/S0168-0072(03)00059-9.
3. K. Arrow. *Social choice and individual values*. Cowles Foundation Monograph Series, second edition, 1963.
4. W. Carnielli, J. Rasga, and C. Sernadas. Preservation of interpolation features by fibring. *Journal of Logic and Computation*, 18(1):123–151, 2008. 10.1093/logcom/exm061.
5. D. M. Gabbay. *Fibring Logics*, volume 38 of *Oxford Logic Guides*. Oxford Univesity Press, 1998.
6. D. M. Gabbay and L. Maksimova. *Interpolation and Definability. Modal and Intuitionistic Logics.*, volume 1. Oxford Science Publications, 2005.
7. D. M. Gabbay, G. Pigozzi, and O. Rodrigues. Belief revision, belief merging and voting. In G. Bonanno, W. van der Hoek, and M. Wooldridge, editors, *Proceedings of the Seventh Conference on Logic and the Foundations of Games and Decision Theory (LOFT06)*, pages 71–78. University of Liverpool, 2006.
8. S. Konieczny, J. Lang, and P. Marquis. Da^2 merging operators. *Artificial Intelligence*, 157:49–79, 2004.
9. S. Konieczny and R. Pino-Pérez. *Proceedings of KR'98*, chapter On the logic of merging, pages 488–498. Morgan Kaufmann, 1998.
10. S. Konieczny and R. Pino-Pérez. Merging information under constraints: a logical framework. *Journal of Logic and Computation*, 12(5):773–808, 2002.

11. S. Konieczny and R. Pino-Pérez. Propositional belief base merging or how to merge beliefs/goals coming from several sources and some links with social choice theory. *European Journal of Operational Research*, 160(3):785–802, 2005.
12. D. Makinson and P. Gärdenfors. Relations between the logic of theory change and nonmonotonic logic. In Fuhrmann A. and M. Morreau, editors, *The Logic of Theory Change, Workshop, Lecture Notes in Artificial Intelligence, Volume 465*, Konstanz, FRG, October 1989. Springer Verlag.
13. F. Rossi, M. S. Pini, K. B. Venable, and T. Walsh. Aggregating preferences cannot be fair. In *Proceedings of the 10th Conference on Theoretical Aspects of Rationality and Knowledge*. ACM Digital Library, June 2005.

List of Symbols

Symbols

D 57
G 86
G^i 86
$K_\perp$ 15
$K_\perp \varphi$ 109
S 109
$[\cdot]$ 40
\$ 23
Mod 38, 113
(C1)–(C4) 39
(R*1)–(R*6) 38
(I1)–(I7) 40
(R1)–(R6) 20, 211
(U1)–(U8) 32
$\Vdash$ 9
$\Vdash_\$$ 23
$\odot$ 99
$-$ 78
$\diamond$ 32
bel 38
mod 9
$\circledcirc_r$ 101
$\circledcirc$ 62
χ 58, 61
C 90
$\circ_d$ 86
diff 63
dist 59
$\frown_\ominus$ 83
$\equiv$ 10
$\perp$ 82
inf 9
level 124
$\Box\!\!\rightarrow$ 22
$\mathbb{N}$ 8
$\mathbb{R}$ 8
mcs 144
min 10, 21

mps 158
$\Downarrow$ 129
$⁎$ 129
$\circ_r$ 69
paths$(\mathscr{M}_K)$ 140
paths$^\top(\mathscr{M}_K)$ 143
$\preceq$ 153, 154
ψ_p^+ 86
ψ_p^- 86
σ 140
$\sqsubseteq$ 128
$\sqsubseteq_I$ 64
sup 9
$\frown_⁎$ 68
$\frown_\circ$ 89
$\top$ 82
$\twoheadrightarrow$ 298
$\diamond_r$ 92
val 126
var 66, 87
ε 112
$\vdash$ 9
ξ_{diff} 97
d 55
$dist$ 67
$dist_{\mathscr{I}}$ 66
g 86
res 87
$\mathscr{I}$ 9
$\mathscr{P}$ 9
ff 9
(CR1)–(CR4) 40
La 143
tt 9
$-$ 15
$+$ 15
$\circ_a^{\mathrm{IC}}$ 133
$\mathbf{L}$ 9
$\oplus$ 82

D. M. Gabbay et al., *Revision, Acceptability and Context*, Cognitive Technologies, 377
DOI 10.1007/978-3-642-14159-1, © Springer-Verlag Berlin Heidelberg 2010

Subject Index

Symbols

A

B

C